Governance and
American Politics

Governance and American Politics

CLASSIC AND CURRENT PERSPECTIVES

James P. Pfiffner

George Mason University

HARCOURT BRACE COLLEGE PUBLISHERS

FORT WORTH PHILADELPHIA SAN DIEGO NEW YORK ORLANDO AUSTIN SAN ANTONIO
TORONTO MONTREAL LONDON SYDNEY TOKYO

Publisher	TED BUCHHOLZ
Acquisitions Editor	DAVID TATOM
Developmental Editor	FRITZ SCHANZ
Project Editor	JOHN HAAKENSON
Production Manager	SERENA MANNING
Art Director	PEGGY YOUNG

Cover Image: © 1993 Steven Gottlieb/ FPG International Corp.

ISBN: 0–15–501000–X

Library of Congress Catalog Card Number: 94–075059

Address for Editorial Correspondence: Harcourt Brace College Publishers, 301 Commerce Street, Suite 3700, Fort Worth, TX 76102.

Address for Orders: Harcourt Brace & Company, 6277 Sea Harbor Drive, Orlando, FL 32887–6777. 1–800–782–4479, or 1–800–433–0001 (in Florida).

(Copyright Acknowledgments begin on page 658 which constitutes a continuation of this copyright page.)

Printed in the United States of America

4 5 6 7 8 9 0 1 2 3   016   9 8 7 6 5 4 3 2 1

FOR DEB H. PFIFFNER

and our children
Megan Cyr (1982)
Katherine Courtney (1985)
Morgan Meehan (1987)

Preface

The purpose of this edited volume of readings is to provide students and teachers with a collection of first-rate analyses of the American system of governance by scholars, journalists, and participants in the process. These readings raise issues of enduring concern and seek to place recent events into a broad historical and developmental context as we approach the twenty-first century. The theme of this volume—governance—emphasizes the challenge of holding together a modern industrialized nation characterized by diverse interests. The institutions and processes of governance include, but are broader than, the institutions of government: the presidency, executive branch departments and agencies, Congress, and the courts.

Governance also refers to the broader societal arrangements through which we govern ourselves and includes the relationships between government and society at large. For example, the public and private sectors of the economy must cooperate for the system of governance to work. Throughout our history, we have sought to balance the needs and interests of government and society with the rights of individuals. Non-governmental actors, such as the media, political parties, and organized groups have always played important roles in our political system.

This volume of readings is divided into four broad sections: The Constitutional Basis of the American Political System, The National Government: Separate Institutions Sharing Power, Political Behavior and the Policy Process, and Public Policy. A concluding section, Alternative Futures, provides different perspectives on the future of American governance and of international challenges. The 58 articles in the book are arranged in 16 sections, each focused on a subset of issues in American government. These sections correspond to the major subdivisions in most introductory textbooks on American Government and can be easily adapted to whatever approach individual teachers prefer in organizing an introductory course on American politics and government. This reader can be used with a standard introductory American Government textbook or with a selection of short, supplemental textbooks.

Each section provides several readings on different aspects of the topic. For instance, in sections on the constitutional basis and on the institutions, there is an article on origins often reaching back to the Constitution and the *Federalist* Papers. Then, in all of the sections, there are readings providing a historical and developmental perspective, which explain how the U.S. system has arrived at current arrangements. Last, all sections contain current analytical articles that draw upon the best research in political science and upon the insights of journalists capturing the human dimension of politics. Many of the readings in the table of contents are cross-referenced to other essays in this volume to show which are relevant to and which might be read with any given section.

To make the topics as accessible as possible, each section of three to six articles is preceded by an overview essay that introduces the major issues relating to governance and provides historical, political, and social context for the topic. Also, these introductions briefly discuss the readings, that is, their overall concerns, their themes, and how they relate to one another. These short introductions are followed by a list of Key Terms to reinforce important definitions. Each individual selection is also preceded by a one- or two-paragraph headnote that identifies the author and briefly discusses the individual reading. The selection is followed by several questions, Points to Ponder, that are intended to provoke reflection and discussion about the selection and its relation to other readings in the book. The Key Terms and Points to Ponder can be adapted easily to serve as identification or essay questions on course examinations.

The selections were chosen for their accessibility and for their different and often conflicting perspectives, all of which will encourage students to make their own judgments about American politics. For instance, Charles Beard and Martin Diamond disagree about the motives of the Framers of the Constitution. Robert Bork and Laurence Tribe have contrasting perspectives on judicial activism. Herbert Hill and Thomas Sowell present different approaches to affirmative action. Each article can stand on its own as a coherent analysis of the topic, for the articles are well developed. The only short selections are those from the *Federalist* Papers.

Also, the readings were chosen to represent the best of what political scientists, historians, journalists, and governmental leaders have to say about American governance. Selections from the *Federalist* Papers by James Madison and Alexander Hamilton introduce the sections on governmental institutions. There are classic scholarly articles on the American Constitution by Charles Beard, John Roche, Martin Diamond, and Samuel Huntington. Some selections have become standard and are written by well-known political scientists, such as Richard Neustadt, Nelson Polsby, V. O. Key, Morris Fiorina, and Richard Fenno. There are recent articles by established scholars, such as Hugh Heclo, James Sundquist, Francis Rourke, and James Q. Wilson. Some selections are quite provocative and are written by some of our best contemporary journalists, such as Kevin Phillips, E. J. Dionne, Brooks Jackson, and Hedrick Smith. In addition, there are reflections by participants in the political process, such as David Gergen, and Ruth Bader Ginsburg.

This textbook also contains several topics that are not usually included in American Government readers. I have included a section on corruption and abuse of power; this will provide a perspective to students who are bombarded by media allegations of wrongdoing in public office. In selecting readings for this section, I have chosen those that distinguish between real corruption, which is illegal, and practices that are ethically questionable but, nevertheless, are legal and widely accepted in our system of governance. Several selections analyze the inherent ambiguity of campaign finance and constituent service by members of Congress. I have also tried to explain clearly why abuse of power, for example, in Watergate or Iran-Contra, is damaging to our polity. The purpose of this section is not to invite student cynicism; rather it is to acknowledge that our political system does, indeed, have faults and to distinguish between mere "headline" scandal and serious threats to our polity. The section is also based on the premise that the best preventative of future abuse is the awareness and vigilance of citizens.

The Alternative Futures section, which closes this volume, is also unique. As we approach the twenty-first century, the world has been undergoing historical changes, from the disintegration of the Soviet Union, to the resurgence of religious fundamentalist movements throughout the world, to the amazing new technologies that are transforming the world. The United States must respond to these historic changes in order to shape its future. However, if we are to consciously prepare for the future by making the best choices in the present, we must have some idea of what the future might hold. The purpose of the concluding section, then, is to provide alternative visions as articulated by several of the most perceptive scholars today. Their visions and prescriptions do not agree, but the purpose here is not and cannot be to offer definitive solutions. Rather, it is to expose students to the complexity and to the challenge of such ideas. With this in mind, perhaps students can arrive at their own best judgments as to what the important issues and questions are.

I would like to thank the following friends and colleagues for their help and advice in the preparation of this volume: Paul Baker, Tim Conlan, Bob Dudley, Hugh Heclo, Barbara Knight, Jane Long, Priscilla Regan, John Sacco, Dennis F. Thompson, Toni Travis, and Louise White. I would like to thank David Tatom, Acquisitions Editor, for initiating and steering the project, Fritz Schanz, Developmental Editor, for his careful editorial suggestions, Carolyn Crabtree for her careful and professional copyediting, and John Haakenson, Project Editor, for overseeing editorial and production processes. Several teachers of American Government went through my initial and revised table of contents and made many useful suggestions, and I would like to acknowledge their help: Susan Banducci, Oregon State University; Tom Bellows, University of Texas; Barbara Brown, Southern Illinois University; Ernest Greco, University of Massachusetts; Stephanie Lee, Florida State University; Linda Norman, California State University–San Bernandino; Edward Platt, Indiana University at Pennsylvania; Delbert Ringquist, Central Michigan University; and Lawrence Weil, Rhode Island College. Finally, I want to thank my family for their love and patience as I was working on this project.

Contents

PART I

Constitutional Basis of the American Political System

Chapter 1

CONSTITUTIONAL ORIGINS
AND AMERICAN VALUES

When the delegates from the five states that met in Annapolis in 1786 convinced the Continental Congress to support a convention in Philadelphia to revise the Articles of Confederation, few people had any inkling that they were about to embark upon a historic journey. Most delegates were convinced that the Articles of Confederation were not sufficient to accommodate the growing new nation and favored some sort of reform. But a few of the Framers had the vision to seize the unprecedented opportunity to create a new form of government. Throughout the long, hot summer of 1787 in Philadelphia the Framers struggled in the debates over political principle and the pragmatic realities of political power. Finally, in September they had agreed upon a constitution for the United States that was to endure for centuries, and they set out to convince their fellow citizens to ratify their plan. The system of government they designed struck an enduring balance between stability and change, democracy and limited government, and central power and local control.

Governing Under the Articles of Confederation

When the delegates from the states met in Philadelphia in May of 1787 the newly established nation was facing difficulties. The central government under the Articles of Confederation could not cope with domestic, economic, and foreign challenges to the newly independent states. The Continental Congress consisted of one house with each state having between three and five delegates who could cast one vote per state. There was no independent executive to act separately from the legislature. The powers of the central government were restricted to those that were clearly national, including conducting war, making treaties, regulating money, and running a postal service.

The greatest constraint on the power of the central government was the sovereignty of the thirteen states, which were unwilling to cede too much authority to the central government and which were continually fighting with each other over economic issues. Political factions in the states used state regulations to discriminate against economic goods from other states. Tariffs were used to give economic advantage to home state merchants. The central government under the Articles had no authority to stop this restraint of trade by the state governments.

Revolutionary War debts had piled up and were coming due, but the central government could only make assessments against the states; it could not force the states to pay their share. Foreign nations had designs on the territory of the new nation and Britain was threatening to negotiate a resolution of the Revolutionary War separately with the different states.

When the delegates from five states met in Annapolis to attempt to deal with trade issues, they decided to recommend a broader convention to deal with the underlying issues of sovereignty. And so 55 delegates convened in May 1787 to consider the more basic issues underlying the problems produced by the Articles of Confederation. What they achieved amounted to a radical revision of their system of governance.

The Framers came to Philadelphia well aware of the deficiencies of the Articles of Confederation and the economic and political challenges facing the confederation of states. Their vision, or at least the vision of the victorious Federalists, was to "form a more perfect union" and create a government capable of dealing with the problems facing them.

The broad question was one of governance, not merely government design. Just as important as the structure of government institutions was the relationship of the government to the rest of society. How extensive would be its powers and what would be the realms of privacy or individual rights upon which the government could not impinge? How would power be divided between the state governments and the central government? Thus the Framers were designing a *system of governance* as well as the institutions of government when they met in 1787.

The Constitution

The primary problem facing the Framers was how to give the new central government enough power to govern the nation, but, at the same time, build in safeguards so that a concentration of power would not lead to tyranny. A legislative branch had to be designed with enough power to enact national policy yet not be easily swayed by demagogic appeals that might lead to oppressive laws. An executive position had to be created that had the power to administer the government effectively, yet would not abuse its power. A judiciary had to be formed that could settle important legal issues in the best interests of the people, yet be insulated from immediate political pressure. Finally, the power of the central government had to be sufficient to deal with issues common to all the states, yet not deprive the individual states of their own legitimate powers.

American Political Values

The political values of the colonists were formed by a rejection of what they saw as the defects of many of the European governments and forged in their own struggle against British rule. Foremost among these American values was a belief in individual liberty and a corresponding fear of centralized power. Americans also rejected the class-based social structures of European societies and held to a strong egalitarian ethic reflected in the democratic dimensions of the Constitution. Among their political values was the conviction drawn from the French political philosopher Montesquieu that governmental powers should be separated into legislative, executive, and judicial branches.

The challenge to a group of people with these values was how to design a government that would protect individual freedom from the potential abuse of majority tyranny and at the same time be strong enough to govern a growing nation. Any realistic system of governance necessarily entails a certain degree of power delegated to the government. Equal treatment under the law might be enforced, but inequalities among different people in the society would emerge as the economy developed. Thus the challenge facing the Framers of the Constitution was how to achieve the right balance between basic American values that were antigovernment in nature and a viable system of governance with enough authority to survive divisive political battles.

The Legislative Branch

One major sticking point was the composition of the legislature. The states with small populations were afraid that legislative representation based on population (the "Virginia Plan") would allow the large states to dominate the new government. The larger states wanted to ensure that their interests could not be outvoted by the smaller states if each state had only one vote, as in the "New Jersey Plan."

The Great Compromise (or "Connecticut Plan") to solve this central problem was proposed by Roger Sherman of Connecticut. There would be two bodies in the legislature, one apportioned according to population to accommodate the more populous states, the other house composed equally with two senators representing each state. Great Britain and most of the states had bicameral legislatures, so the idea of a divided legislature was familiar to the colonists. The lower chamber, the House of Representatives, would serve the democratic function of representing the constituents in congressional districts. With elections every two years, members would be directly answerable to the people.

The Senate, in contrast, would be a more aristocratic body. Its members would be selected by state legislatures and would presumably be composed of men of character. The six-year overlapping terms would provide a certain amount of insulation from the passions of the moment that might sway the House. George Washington referred to the Senate as the saucer that cools the legislative tea. Thus the Framers' ambivalence toward democracy was embodied in the very structure of the Congress.

The Executive Branch

The colonists' experience with King George III of England was reflected in the Declaration of Independence: "The history of the present King of Great Britain is a history of repeated injuries and usurpations, all having in direct object the establishment of an absolute Tyranny over these States." In addition, the colonial governors were often seen as petty tyrants by the colonists. So one might expect that the Framers of the Constitution would be suspicious of executive power and thus create a government dominated by the representatives of the people in the legislatures.

This did not happen. The Framers created a government with an independent executive precisely because of the experience of the states after 1776. The lack of an independent executive under the Articles of Confederation was partly to blame for inability of the Continental Congress to act expeditiously. In addition, the experience of the separate states under legislatively dominated state governments was not entirely satisfactory. The state legislatures sometimes abused their authority and did not respect minority rights. James Madison came to feel that legislative power was abused, and in *Federalist* No. 48 he stated: "The Legislative department is everywhere extending the sphere of its activity, and drawing all power into its impetuous vortex."

To remain independent, the executive could not be chosen by the legislature, which was one of the most likely options considered by the Framers. On the other hand, an executive chosen directly by the people might easily lead to demagoguery and tyranny. So the Framers settled on selection of the president by an electoral college that would be chosen in a manner decided upon by the state legislatures. The presidency was also made more powerful by the provision for reelection, though limited to four-year terms. Although it seems natural to us that a chief executive be only one person, the Framers considered the possibility of giving the executive power to more than one person, but that option clearly would have diluted the power of the office.

The Judicial Branch

Under the Articles of Confederation there was no federal judiciary. With a new Constitution and a law-making legislature, there had to be a central adjudicatory institution to decide controversies arising under the laws. Thus Article III of the Constitution established the Supreme Court and provided that Congress could establish other courts in the judicial system.

In order for the interpretation of the laws to be insulated from direct political pressure, judges would have tenure for life during good behavior and could be removed only by impeachment. The judiciary would not be completely free of politics, however, because judges were to be appointed by the president and confirmed by the Senate. Although Alexander Hamilton argued in *Federalist* No. 78 that the Supreme Court would have the power to decide whether acts of Congress were compatible with the Constitution, the power of judicial review was not asserted by the Court until 1803 and then exercised only occasionally in the early decades of the Republic.

Checks and Balances

The Framers' fear of tyranny led them to build into the Constitution a number of checks on the concentration of power. The most important guard against tyranny was the allocation of powers among the three branches. And the legislature itself was divided into two houses with different terms of office, different constituencies, and different means of selection. Other checks included the presidential veto and the right of the Senate to consent to presidential appointments and treaties. The two main governmental powers of the purse and the sword were split. The president was commander in chief of the armed forces, but Congress had to declare war. The president would spend money through the executive branch agencies, but Congress would have to appropriate that money. These constitutional checks and balances would later be supplemented by political checks and balances, such as political parties.

Federalism

The other main guard against concentrated power was federalism. Although the states were ceding important powers to the national government, they were guaranteed a republican form of government, and their constitutional status could not be altered under the new Constitution. But more important, the rights of the states would be jealously guarded by their senators and representatives in the Congress. Although the national government might become more powerful than the governments of the states, it could not ignore their interests or wishes.

An Enduring Structure

Aside from its creation in Philadelphia in 1787, the most striking aspect of the U.S. Constitution is its endurance. The governmental framework and essential features are still in operation after more than two centuries, making it the oldest written constitution still in use. The survival of the nation and the Constitution was made possible by the political, social, geographical, and economic circumstances of the United States. But an important key to the endurance of the Constitution is its articulation of general principles within a flexible framework.

The flexibility of the Constitution comes not so much from its provisions for amendment, which have been exercised fewer than thirty times over two centuries despite hundreds of proposals for change. Rather, the flexibility comes from the ability of the general governmental framework to accommodate tremendous changes throughout our history. The Framers did not provide in the Constitution for political parties, primary elections, the president's cabinet, or a large executive branch bureaucracy. Yet these institutions have become important elements of our system of governance. The Framers could not have imagined the technological changes brought about by modern means of communications and travel. Nor could they have expected the growth in geographical size and population of the country or the effects of a civil and several world wars. Yet the constitutional framework they established has endured and provided the means for the nation to govern itself during these changes over the past two hundred years.

The Readings

The readings in this section explore a range of perspectives on the significance of the Constitution. For most of the nineteenth century the framing of the Constitution was seen as a heroic moment in human history, in accord with Hamilton's argument in *Federalist* No. 1. But in the twentieth century alternative explanations of the founding were raised by scholars. These newer interpretations, as reflected in the readings, view the Framers as a self-protective elite, as practical politicians, or as sophisticated protectors of minority rights. The readings conclude with a contrast between the ideals of American political culture and the reality of American political history.

In the first selection, Alexander Hamilton in *Federalist* No. 1 presents the initial arguments of a series of articles that would advocate the adoption of the new Constitution by the state conventions. In his essay Hamilton presents the question of ratification as a monumental departure in human history and a grand experiment in self-government.

The new nation was created by a revolt against British authority, but its new Constitution did not amount to a revolution in societal values or economic relationships as had happened in the French or Russian revolutions. In explaining the limits on democracy, some scholars, such as Charles Beard in the second selection, argue that the main motivation of the Framers was to protect the propertied class from any governmental action that might threaten the rights of that elite class. He argues that the Constitution was a conspiracy of the landed to protect their own class interests.

Developed in the early twentieth century, Beard's thesis was iconoclastic. Until that time most American analyses of the making of the Constitution presented the Framers as wise Platonic guardians who created a perfectly balanced framework that would ensure justice to all and prevent tyranny. Thus

Beard's thesis that the Framers were merely self-serving in their constitutional design was a radical reinterpretation of the origins of the document.

Other analyses, such as that by John Roche, have emphasized the very practical political problems faced by the Framers. While they wanted to form a stronger central government and create an independent executive, they also had to sell their product to the "folks back home." Ratification by the states was by no means certain, and the Framers were very sensitive to their constituencies in making the compromises that went into drafting the Constitution.

In limiting the ability of any one branch or a majority of the people to dominate the new government, the Framers intended to protect minority rights. They wanted to guard against a possible tyranny of the majority. Thus, according to Martin Diamond, the Framers were true democrats and not grasping plutocrats as Beard had posited. The protection of minority rights would ensure that political opposition to the government in power would be protected as legitimate and that those in power could be replaced by those in opposition. This analysis by Diamond also contrasts with the political expediency theory of Roche. Diamond tries to restore to the Framers some of their luster by arguing that their design was a self-conscious and well-constructed balance between majority rule and minority rights.

Part of the reason for the endurance of the Constitution is its ability to accommodate the often conflicting ideals of Americans. Samuel Huntington contrasts the conflicts between Americans' ideals and our institutions and argues that there is often a gap between the two (the IvI gap). For instance, the ideal of equity can easily come into conflict with our value of individualism. A constitution of limited government will at times limit the powers of the majority and thus of democracy. In his article Huntington analyzes how these conflicting ideals have been accommodated within our constitutional structure.

This flexibility exists in part because the Constitution provided the framework for dealing with basic questions but did not provide final answers to fundamental issues. The separation of powers endures, but the balance between the president and Congress has always been in flux, the pendulum at times bringing presidential domination, at times congressional prevalence, and often deadlock between the two. The role of the judiciary has always been in question, and the Supreme Court has at times been the bulwark of the status quo and at other times the leader of the popular branches in political change. The national government has come to play important roles in most areas of public policy, but state and local governments have always been closer to the people and provided most of the public services. At the end of the twentieth century the states are experiencing a resurgence of their roles and an increased capacity to carry out their duties.

All the important questions thus remain at issue. What is the right balance between the states and the national government? What is the appropriate balance between the president and Congress? What role do the courts play in a democracy? How can large, executive branch bureaucracies be held account-able to the people? How do we ensure free elections?

These questions have been raised throughout the history of the country. We have no final answers, but our answer to the broader question of governance is that the Constitution must provide a governing framework and a political process through which these questions can be answered anew for each generation. That is the enduring value of the Constitution.

KEY TERMS

American political values: primary values, including individual liberty, lim-ited government, democracy, and equality

limited government: the idea that government should not have unlimited power over its citizens, but should be limited in the scope of its powers

Federalist **Papers:** a series of 85 articles written in 1787 and 1788 defending the Constitution and urging its adoption by the states

economic interpretation of the Constitution: the argument that the Constitution was designed to protect the economic interests of the elite who framed it

reform caucus: a group of leaders attempting to make marginal improve-ments rather than instigate revolutionary change

1

FEDERALIST NO. 1
Alexander Hamilton

Federalist No. 1 is the first of 85 Federalist *papers written by Alexander Hamilton, James Madison, or John Jay (who, due to ill health, wrote only five). The essays of 1500 to 2000 words appeared as a series of articles in New York newspapers between October 1787 and April 1788 under the pseudonym "Publius." The purpose of the essays was to convince the citizens of the states, and particularly the delegates to the states' constitutional conventions, that they ought to ratify the newly formulated Constitution.*

In the first Federalist, *Hamilton sets the stage by making a general argument that the enterprise envisioned by the writers of the Constitution was a grand departure for human history as well as for the 13 states. He anticipates potential arguments against ratification and urges his fellow citizens to make the right decision and support the new Constitution.*

According to Hamilton the stakes are high. The citizens of the states are to settle no less a question than "whether societies of men are really capable or not of establishing good government from reflection and choice, or whether they are forever destined to depend for their political constitutions on accident and force." Thus Hamilton illustrates the Framers' faith in reason and the conviction that the framework devised in 1787 could alter the course of history.

To the People of the State of New York:

After an unequivocal experience of the inefficiency of the subsisting federal government, you are called upon to deliberate on a new Constitution for the United States of America. The subject speaks its own importance; comprehending in its consequences nothing less than the existence of the UNION, the safety and welfare of the parts of which it is composed, the fate of an empire in many respects the most interesting in the world. It has been frequently remarked that it seems to have been reserved to the people of this country, by their conduct and example, to decide the important question, whether societies of men are really capable or not of establishing good government from reflection and choice, or whether they are forever destined to depend for their political constitutions on accident and force. If there be any truth in the remark, the crisis at which we are arrived may with propriety be regarded as the era in which that decision is to be made; and a wrong election of the part we shall act may, in this view, deserve to be considered as the general misfortune of mankind.

This idea will add the inducements of philanthropy to those of patriotism, to heighten the solicitude which all considerate and good men must feel for the event. Happy will it be if our choice should be directed by a judicious estimate of our true interests, unperplexed and unbiased by considerations not connected with the public good. But this is a thing more ardently to be wished than seriously to be expected. The plan offered to our deliberations affects too many particular interests, innovates upon too many local institutions, not to involve in its discussion a variety of objects foreign to its merits, and of views, passions and prejudices little favorable to the discovery of truth.

Among the most formidable of the obstacles which the new Constitution will have to encounter may readily be distinguished the obvious interest of a certain class of men in every State to resist all changes which may hazard a diminution of the power, emolument, and consequence of the offices they hold under the State establishments; and the perverted ambition of another class of men, who will either hope to aggrandize themselves by the confusions of their country, or will flatter themselves with fairer prospects of elevation from the subdivision of the empire into several partial confederacies than from its union under one government.

It is not, however, my design to dwell upon observations of this nature. I am well aware that it would be disingenuous to resolve indiscriminately the opposition of any set of men (merely because their situations might subject them to suspicion) into interested or ambitious views. Candor will oblige us to admit that even such men may be actuated by upright intentions; and it cannot be doubted that much of the opposition which has made its appearance, or may hereafter make its appearance, will spring from sources, blameless at least, if not respectable—the honest errors of minds led astray by preconceived jealousies and fears. So numerous indeed and so powerful are the causes which serve to give a false bias to the judgment, that we, upon many occasions, see wise and good men on the wrong as well as on the right side of questions of the first magnitude to society. This circumstance, if duly attended to, would furnish a lesson of moderation to those who are ever so much persuaded of their being in the right in any controversy. And a further reason for caution, in this respect, might be drawn from the reflection that we are not always sure that those who advocate the truth are influenced by purer principles than their antagonists. Ambition, avarice, personal animosity, party opposition, and many other motives not more laudable than these, are apt to operate as well upon those who support as those who oppose the right side of a question. Were there not even these inducements to moderation, nothing could be more ill-judged than that intolerant spirit which has, at all times, characterized political parties. For in politics, as in religion, it is equally absurd to aim at making proselytes by fire and sword. Heresies in either can rarely be cured by persecution.

And yet, however just these sentiments will be allowed to be we have already sufficient indications that it will happen in this as in all former cases of great national discussion. A torrent of angry and malignant passions will be let loose. To judge from the conduct of the opposite parties, we shall be led to conclude that they will mutually hope to evince the justness of their opinions, and to increase the number of their converts by the loudness of their declamations and the bitterness of their invectives. An enlightened zeal for the energy and efficiency of government will be stigmatized as the offspring of a temper fond of despotic power and hostile to the principles of liberty. An over-scrupulous jealousy of danger to the rights of the people, which is more commonly the fault of the head than of the heart, will be represented as a mere pretense and artifice, the stale bait for popularity at the expense of the public good. It will be forgotten, on the one hand, that jealousy is the usual concomitant of love, and that the noble enthusiasm of liberty is apt to be infected with a spirit of narrow and illiberal distrust. On the other hand, it will be equally forgotten that the vigor of government is essential to the security of liberty; that, in the contemplation of a sound and well-informed judgment, their interest can never be separated; and that a dangerous ambition more often lurks behind the specious mask of zeal for the rights of the people than under the forbidding appearance of zeal for the firmness and efficiency of government. History will teach us that the former has been found a much more certain road to the introduction of despotism than the latter, and that of those men who have overturned the liberties of republics, the greatest number have begun their career by paying an obsequious court to the people; commencing demagogues, and ending tyrants.

In the course of the preceding observations, I have had an eye, my fellow-citizens, to putting you upon your guard against all attempts, from whatever quarter, to influence your decision, in a matter of the utmost moment to your welfare, by any impressions other than those which may result from the evidence of truth. You will, no doubt, at the same time, have collected from the general scope of them, that they proceed from a source not unfriendly to the new Constitution. Yes, my countrymen, I own to you that, after having given it an attentive consideration, I am clearly of opinion it is your interest to adopt it. I am convinced that this is the safest course for your liberty, your dignity, and your happiness. I affect not reserves which I do not feel. I will not amuse you with an appearance of deliberation when I have decided. I frankly acknowledge to you my convictions, and I will freely lay before you the reasons on which they are founded. The consciousness of good intentions disdains ambiguity. I shall not, however, multiply professions on this head. My motives must remain in the depository of my own breast. My arguments will be open to all, and may be judged of by all. They shall at least be offered in a spirit which will not disgrace the cause of truth.

I propose, in a series of papers, to discuss the following interesting particulars:— *The utility of the UNION to your political prosperity* — *The insufficiency of the present Confederation to preserve that Union* — *The necessity of a government at least equally energetic with the one proposed, to the attainment of this object* — *The conformity of the proposed Constitution to the true principles of republican government* — *Its analogy to your own State constitution* — and lastly, *The additional security which its adoption will afford to the preservation of that species of government, to liberty and to property.*

In the progress of this discussion I shall endeavor to give a satisfactory answer to all the objections which shall have made their appearance, that may seem to have any claim to your attention.

It may perhaps be thought superfluous to offer arguments to prove the utility of the UNION, a point, no doubt, deeply engraved in the hearts of the great body of the people in every State, and one which, it may be imagined, has no adversaries. But the fact is, that we already hear it whispered in the private circles of those who oppose the new Constitution, that the thirteen States are of too great extent for any general system, and that we must of necessity resort to separate confederacies of distinct portions of the whole.*

---

* The same idea, tracing the arguments to their consequences, is held out in several of the late publications against the new Constitution.–PUBLIUS.

This doctrine will, in all probability, be gradually propagated, till it has votaries enough to countenance an open avowal of it. For nothing can be more evident, to those who are able to take an enlarged view of the subject, than the alternative of an adoption of the new Constitution or a dismemberment of the Union. It will therefore be of use to begin by examining the advantages of that Union, the certain evils, and the probable dangers, to which every State will be exposed from its dissolution. This shall accordingly constitute the subject of my next address.

Publius.

POINTS TO PONDER

1. What was Hamilton's purpose in this essay?
2. Who was Hamilton trying to convince?
3. Contrast Hamilton's argument with the arguments presented in the essays by Beard, Roche, and Diamond. Which of the three visions of the framing of the Constitution is closest to that of Hamilton? In what way?

2

"THE CONSTITUTION AS AN ECONOMIC DOCUMENT"
Charles A. Beard

Much of the analysis of the Constitution in the nineteenth century was based on the ideas embodied in the document and on the sources of those ideas in the Framers' thoughts and in the political thinkers they had studied. Historian Charles A. Beard (1874–1948), however, presents a basic challenge to this approach by arguing that it is equally, if not more important, to examine the economic interests of those who framed the document and the economic consequences of the ratification of the Constitution—that is, qui bono? *(who benefits?).*

In his book An Economic Interpretation of the Constitution of the United States *(first published in 1913), Beard argues that, if one looks beyond the "superficial" aspects of the Constitution to its "true inwardness," it becomes clear that the document was written by self-conscious representatives of the propertied class for their own benefit. The main argument presented in this selection is that the limits to majority rule in the Constitution assured the propertied class that a majority of the less privileged could not easily use the government to challenge the economic position of the elite or severely limit the rights of property.*

Although Beard's evidence and analysis have been challenged by other scholars, his work represents an important approach to understanding politics. In Beard's analysis, economic self-interest determined the motivations of the Framers, and the result was a system in which the privileged could continue to prevail.

It is difficult for the superficial student of the Constitution, who has read only the commentaries of the legists, to conceive of that instrument as an economic document. It places no property qualifications on voters or officers; it gives no outward recognition of any economic groups in society; it mentions no special privileges to be conferred upon any class. It betrays no feeling, such as vibrates through the French constitution of 1791; its language is cold, formal, and severe.

The true inwardness of the Constitution is not revealed by an examination of its provisions as simple propositions of law; but by a long and careful study of the voluminous correspondence of the period, contemporary newspapers and pamphlets, the records of the debates in the Convention at Philadelphia and in the several state conventions, and particularly, *The Federalist*, which was widely circulated during the struggle over ratification. The correspondence shows the exact character of the evils which the Constitution was intended to remedy; the records of the proceedings in the Philadelphia Convention reveal the successive steps in the building of the framework of the government under the pressure of economic interests; the pamphlets and newspapers disclose the ideas of the contestants over the ratification; and *The Federalist* presents the political science of the new system as conceived by three of the profoundest thinkers of the period, Hamilton, Madison, and Jay.

Doubtless, the most illuminating of these sources on the economic character of the Constitution are the records of the debates in the Convention, which have come down to us in fragmentary form; and a thorough treatment of material forces reflected in the several clauses of the instrument of government created by the grave assembly at Philadelphia would require a rewriting of the history of the proceedings in the light of the great interests represented there. But an entire volume would scarcely suffice to present the results of such a survey, and an undertaking of this character is accordingly impossible here.

The Federalist, on the other hand, presents in a relatively brief and systematic form an economic interpretation of the Constitution by the men best fitted, through an intimate knowledge of the ideals of the framers, to expound the political science of the new government. This wonderful piece of argumentation by Hamilton, Madison, and Jay is in fact the finest study in the economic interpretation of politics which exists in any language; and whoever would understand the Constitution as an economic document need hardly go beyond it. It is true that the tone of the writers is somewhat modified on account of the fact that they are appealing to the voters to ratify the

Constitution, but at the same time they are, by the force of circumstances, compelled to convince large economic groups that safety and strength lie in the adoption of the new system.

Indeed, every fundamental appeal in it is to some material and substantial interest. Sometimes it is to the people at large in the name of protection against invading armies and European coalitions. Sometimes it is to the commercial classes whose business is represented as prostrate before the follies of the Confederation. Now it is to creditors seeking relief against paper money and the assaults of the agrarians in general; now it is to the holders of federal securities which are depreciating toward the vanishing point. But above all, it is to the owners of personalty anxious to find a foil against the attacks of levelling democracy, that the authors of *The Federalist* address their most cogent arguments in favor of ratification. It is true there is much discussion of the details of the new frame-work of government, to which even some friends of reform took exceptions; but Madison and Hamilton both knew that these were incidental matters when compared with the sound basis upon which the superstructure rested.

In reading the pages of this remarkable work as a study in political economy, it is important to bear in mind that the system, which the authors are describing, consisted of two fundamental parts—one positive, the other negative:

I. A government endowed with certain positive powers, but so constructed as to break the force of majority rule and prevent invasions of the property rights of minorities.

II. Restrictions on the state legislatures which had been so vigorous in their attacks on capital.

Under some circumstances, action is the immediate interest of the dominant party; and whenever it desires to make an economic gain through governmental functioning, it must have, of course, a system endowed with the requisite powers.

Examples of this are to be found in protective tariffs, in ship subsidies, in railway land grants, in river and harbor improvements, and so on through the catalogue of so-called "paternalistic" legislation. Of course it may be shown that the "general good" is the ostensible object of any particular act; but the general good is a passive force, and unless we know who are the several individuals that benefit in its name, it has no meaning. When it is so analyzed, immediate and remote beneficiaries are discovered; and the former are usually found to have been the dynamic element in securing the legislation. Take for example, the economic interests of the advocates who appear in tariff hearings at Washington.

On the obverse side, dominant interests quite as often benefit from the prevention of governmental action as from positive assistance. They are able to take care of themselves if let alone within the circle of protection created by the law. Indeed, most owners of property have as much to fear from positive governmental action as from their inability to secure advantageous legislation. Particularly is this true where the field of private property is already extended to cover practically every form of tangible and intangible wealth. This was clearly set forth by Hamilton: "It may perhaps be said that the power of preventing bad laws includes that of preventing good ones. . . . But this objection will have little weight with those who can properly estimate the mischiefs of that inconstancy and mutability in the laws which form the greatest blemish in the character and genius of our governments. They will consider every institution calculated to restrain the excess of law-making, and to keep things in the same state in which they happen to be at any given period, as more likely to do good than harm. . . . The injury which may possibly be done by defeating a few good laws will be amply compensated by the advantage of preventing a number of bad ones."

The Underlying Political Science of the Constitution

Before taking up the economic implications of the structure of the federal government, it is important to ascertain what, in the opinion of *The Federalist*, is the basis of all government. The most philosophical examination of the foundations of political science is made by Madison in the tenth number. Here he lays down, in no uncertain language, the principle that the first and elemental concern of every government is economic.

1. "The first object of government," he declares, is the protection of "the diversity in the faculties of men, from which the rights of property originate." The chief business of government, from which, perforce, its essential nature must be derived, consists in the control and adjustment of conflicting economic interests. After enumerating the various forms of propertied interests which spring up inevitably in modern society, he adds: "The regulation of these various and interfering interests forms the principal task of modern legislation, and involves the spirit of party and faction in the ordinary operations of the government."

2. What are the chief causes of these conflicting political forces with which the government must concern itself? Madison answers. Of course fanciful and frivolous distinctions have sometimes been the cause of violent conflicts; "but the most common and durable source of factions has been the various and unequal distribution of property. Those who hold and those who are without property have ever formed distinct interests in society. Those who are creditors, and those who are debtors, fall under a like discrimination. A landed interest, a manufacturing interest, a mercantile interest, a moneyed interest, with many lesser interests grow up of necessity in civilized nations, and divide them into different classes actuated by different sentiments and views."

3. The theories of government which men entertain are emotional reactions to their property interests. "From the protection of different and unequal faculties of acquiring property, the possession of different degrees and kinds of

property immediately results; *and from the influence of these on the sentiments and views of the respective proprietors, ensues a division of society into different interests and parties.*" Legislatures reflect these interests. "What," he asks, "are the different classes of legislators but advocates and parties to the causes which they determine." There is no help for it. "The causes of faction cannot be removed," and "we well know that neither moral nor religious motives can be relied on as an adequate control."

4. Unequal distribution of property is inevitable, and from it contending factions will rise in the state. The government will reflect them, for they will have their separate principles and "sentiments"; but the supreme danger will arise from the fusion of certain interests into an overbearing majority, which Madison, in another place, prophesied would be the landless proletariat,—an overbearing majority which will make its "rights" paramount, and sacrifice the "rights" of the minority. "To secure the public good," he declares, "and private rights against the danger of such a faction and at the same time preserve the spirit and the form of popular government is then the great object to which our inquiries are directed."

5. How is this to be done? Since the contending classes cannot be eliminated and their interests are bound to be reflected in politics, the only way out lies in making it difficult for enough contending interests to fuse into a majority, and in balancing one over against another. The machinery for doing this is created by the new Constitution and by the Union. (*a*) Public views are to be refined and enlarged "by passing them through the medium of a chosen body of citizens." (*b*) The very size of the Union will enable the inclusion of more interests so that the danger of an overbearing majority is not so great. "The smaller the society, the fewer probably will be the distinct parties and interests composing it; the fewer the distinct parties and interests, the more frequently will a majority be found of the same party. . . . Extend the sphere, and you take in a greater variety of parties and interests; you make it less probable that a majority of the whole will have a common motive to invade the rights of other citizens; or if such a common motive exists, it will be more difficult for all who feel it to discover their strength and to act in unison with each other."

Q. E. D., "in the extent and proper structure of the Union, therefore, we behold a republican remedy for the diseases most incident to republican government."

I. The Structure of Government or the Balance of Powers

The fundamental theory of political economy thus stated by Madison was the basis of the original American conception of the balance of powers which is formulated at length in four numbers of *The Federalist* and consists of the following elements:

1. No mere parchment separation of departments of government will be effective. "The legislative department is everywhere extending the sphere of

its activity, and drawing all power into its impetuous vortex. The founders of our republic . . . seem never for a moment to have turned their eyes from the danger to liberty from the overgrown and all-grasping prerogative of an hereditary magistrate, supported and fortified by an hereditary branch of the legislative authority. They seem never to have recollected the danger from legislative usurpations, which, by assembling all power in the same hands, must lead to the same tyranny as is threatened by executive usurpations."

2. Some sure mode of checking usurpations in the government must be provided, other than frequent appeals to the people. "There appear to be insuperable objections against the proposed recurrence to the people as a provision in all cases for keeping the several departments of power within their constitutional limits." In a contest between the legislature and the other branches of the government, the former would doubtless be victorious on account of the ability of the legislators to plead their cause with the people.

3. What then can be depended upon to keep the government in close rein? "The only answer that can be given is, that as all these exterior provisions are found to be inadequate, the defect must be supplied by so contriving the interior structure of the government as that its several constituent parts may, by their mutual relations, be the means of keeping each other in their proper places. . . . It is of great importance in a republic not only to guard the society against the oppression of its rulers, but to guard one part of the society against the injustice of the other part. Different interests necessarily exist in different classes of citizens. If a majority be united by a common interest, the rights of the minority will be insecure." There are two ways of obviating this danger: one is by establishing a monarch independent of popular will, and the other is by reflecting these contending interests (so far as their representatives may be enfranchised) in the very structure of the government itself so that a majority cannot dominate the minority—which minority is of course composed of those who possess property that may be attacked. "Society itself will be broken into so many parts, interests, and classes of citizens, that the rights of individuals, or of the minority, will be in little danger from interested combinations of the majority."

4. The structure of the government as devised at Philadelphia reflects these several interests and makes improbable any danger to the minority from the majority. "The House of Representatives being to be elected immediately by the people, the Senate by the State legislatures, the President by electors chosen for that purpose by the people, there would be little probability of a common interest to cement these different branches in a predilection for any particular class of electors."

5. All of these diverse interests appear in the amending process but they are further reinforced against majorities. An amendment must receive a two-thirds vote in each of the two houses so constituted and the approval of three-fourths of the states.

6. The economic corollary of this system is as follows: Property interests may, through their superior weight in power and intelligence, secure advantageous legislation whenever necessary, and they may at the same time obtain immunity from control by parliamentary majorities.

If we examine carefully the delicate instrument by which the framers sought to check certain kinds of positive action that might be advocated to the detriment of established and acquired rights, we cannot help marvelling at their skill. Their leading idea was to break up the attacking forces at the starting point: the source of political authority for the several branches of the government. This disintegration of positive action at the source was further facilitated by the differentiation in the terms given to the respective departments of the government. And the crowning counterweight to "an interested and over-bearing majority," as Madison phrased it, was secured in the peculiar position assigned to the judiciary, and the use of the sanctity and mystery of the law as a foil to democratic attacks.

It will be seen on examination that no two of the leading branches of the government are derived from the same source. The House of Representatives springs from the mass of the people whom the states may see fit to enfranchise. The Senate is elected by the legislatures of the states, which were, in 1787, almost uniformly based on property qualifications, sometimes with a differentiation between the sources of the upper and lower houses. The President is to be chosen by electors selected as the legislatures of the states may determine—at all events by an authority one degree removed from the voters at large. The judiciary is to be chosen by the President and the Senate, both removed from direct popular control and holding for longer terms than the House.

A sharp differentiation is made in the terms of the several authorities, so that a complete renewal of the government at one stroke is impossible. The House of Representatives is chosen for two years; the Senators for six, but not at one election, for one-third go out every two years. The President is chosen for four years. The judges of the Supreme Court hold for life. Thus "popular distempers," as eighteenth century publicists called them, are not only restrained from working their havoc through direct elections, but they are further checked by the requirement that they must last six years in order to make their effects felt in the political department of the government, providing they can break through the barriers imposed by the indirect election of the Senate and the President. Finally, there is the check of judicial control that can be overcome only through the manipulation of the appointing power which requires time, or through the operation of a cumbersome amending system.

The keystone of the whole structure is, in fact, the system provided for judicial control—the most unique contribution to the science of government which has been made by American political genius. It is claimed by some recent writers that it was not the intention of the framers of the Constitution to confer upon the Supreme Court the power of passing upon the constitutionality of statutes enacted by Congress; but in view of the evidence on the other side, it is incumbent upon those who make this assertion to bring forward positive evidence to the effect that judicial control was not a part of the Philadelphia programme. Certainly, the authors of *The Federalist* entertained no doubts on the point, and they conceived it to be such an excellent principle that they were careful to explain it to the electors to whom they addressed their arguments.

After elaborating fully the principle of judicial control over legislation under the Constitution, Hamilton enumerates the advantages to be derived from it. Speaking on the point of tenure during good behavior, he says: "In a monarchy it is an excellent barrier to the despotism of the prince; in a republic it is no less an excellent barrier to the encroachments and oppressions of the representative body. . . . If, then, the courts of justice are to be considered as the bulwarks of a limited Constitution against legislative encroachments, this consideration will afford a strong argument for the permanent tenure of judicial offices, since nothing will contribute so much as this to that independent spirit in the judges which must be essential to the faithful performance of so arduous a duty. . . . But it is not with a view to infractions of the Constitution only that the independence of the judges may be an essential safeguard against the effects of occasional ill humors in the society. These sometimes extend no farther than to the injury of private rights of particular classes of citizens, by unjust and partial laws. Here also the firmness of the judicial magistracy is of vast importance in mitigating the severity and confining the operation of such laws. It not only serves to moderate the immediate mischiefs of those which may have been passed, but it operates as a check upon the legislative body in passing them; who, perceiving that obstacles to the success of iniquitous intention are to be expected from the scruples of the courts, are in a manner compelled, by the very motives of injustice they meditate, to qualify their attempts. This is a circumstance calculated to have more influence upon the character of our governments than but few may be aware of."

Nevertheless, it may be asked why, if the protection of property rights lay at the basis of the new system, there is in the Constitution no provision for property qualifications for voters or for elected officials and representatives. This is, indeed, peculiar when it is recalled that the constitutional history of England is in a large part a record of conflict over the weight in the government to be enjoyed by definite economic groups, and over the removal of the property qualifications early imposed on members of the House of Commons and on the voters at large. But the explanation of the absence of property qualifications from the Constitution is not difficult.

The members of the Convention were, in general, not opposed to property qualifications as such, either for officers or voters. "Several propositions," says Mr. S. H. Miller, "were made in the federal Convention in regard to property qualifications. A motion was carried instructing the committee to fix upon such qualifications for members of Congress. The committee could not agree upon the amount and reported in favor of leaving the matter to the legislature. Charles Pinckney objected to this plan as giving too much power to the first legislature. . . . Ellsworth objected to a property qualification on account of the difficulty of fixing the amount. If it was made high enough for the South, it would not be applicable to the Eastern States. Franklin was the only speaker who opposed the proposition to require property on principle, saying that 'some of the greatest rogues he was ever acquainted with were the richest rogues.' A resolution was also carried to require a property qualification for the Presidency. Hence it was evident that the lack of all property requirements for office in the United States Constitution was not owing to any opposition of the convention to such qualifications per se."

Propositions to establish property restrictions were defeated, not because they were believed to be inherently opposed to the genius of American government, but for economic reasons—strange as it may seem. These economic reasons were clearly set forth by Madison in the debate over landed qualifications for legislators in July, when he showed, first, that slight property qualifications would not keep out the small farmers whose paper money schemes had been so disastrous to personalty; and, secondly, that landed property qualifications would exclude from Congress the representatives of "those classes of citizens who were not landholders," *i.e.* the personalty interests. This was true, he thought, because the mercantile and manufacturing classes would hardly be willing to turn their personalty into sufficient quantities of landed property to make them eligible for a seat in Congress.

The other members also knew that they had most to fear from the very electors who would be enfranchised under a slight freehold restriction, for the paper money party was everywhere bottomed on the small farming class. As Gorham remarked, the elections at Philadelphia, New York, and Boston, "where the merchants and mechanics vote, are at least as good as those made by freeholders only." The fact emerges, therefore, that the personalty interests reflected in the Convention could, in truth, see no safeguard at all in a freehold qualification against the assaults on vested personalty rights which had been made by the agrarians in every state. And it was obviously impossible to establish a personalty test, had they so desired, for there would have been no chance of securing a ratification of the Constitution at the hands of legislatures chosen by freeholders, or at the hands of conventions selected by them.

A very neat example of this antagonism between realty and personalty in the Convention came out on July 26, when Mason made, and Charles Pinckney supported, a motion imposing landed qualifications on members of Congress and excluding from that body "persons having unsettled accounts with or being indebted to the United States." In bringing up this motion Mason "observed that persons of the latter descriptions had frequently got into the state legislatures in order to promote laws that might shelter their delinquencies; and that this evil had crept into Congress if report was to be regarded."

Gouverneur Morris was on his feet in an instant. If qualifications were to be imposed, they should be laid on electors, not elected persons. The disqualification would fall upon creditors of the United States, for there were but few who owed the government anything. He knew that under this rule very few members of the Convention could get into the new government which they were establishing. "As to persons having unsettled accounts, he believed them to be pretty many. He thought, however, that such a discrimination would be both odious and useless and in many instances unjust and cruel. The delay of settlement had been more the fault of the public than of individuals. What will be done with those patriotic Citizens who have lent money or services or property to their country, without having been yet able to obtain a liquidation of their claims? Are they to be excluded?" On thinking it over, Morris added to his remarks on the subject, saying, "It was a precept of great antiquity as well as of high authority that we should not be righteous overmuch. He thought we ought to be equally on our guard against being wise overmuch. . . . The parliamentary qualifications quoted by Colonel Mason had been disregarded in practice; and was but a scheme of the landed against the monied interest."

Gerry thought that the inconvenience of excluding some worthy creditors and debtors was of less importance than the advantages offered by the resolution, but, after some reflection, he added that "if property be one object of government, provisions for securing it cannot be improper." King safely remarked that there might be a great danger in imposing a landed qualification, because "it would exclude the monied interest, whose aids may be essential in particular emergencies to the public safety."

Madison had no confidence in the effectiveness of the landed qualification and moved to strike it out, adding, "Landed possessions were no certain evidence of real wealth. Many enjoyed them to a great extent who were more in debt than they were worth. The unjust laws of the states had proceeded more from this class of men than any others. It had often happened that men who had acquired landed property on credit got into the Legislatures with a view of promoting an unjust protection against their Creditors. In the next place, if a small quantity of land should be made the standard, it would be no security; if a large one, it would exclude the proper representatives of those classes of Citizens who were not landholders." For these and other reasons he opposed the landed qualifications and suggested that property qualifications on the voters would be better.

The motion to strike out the "landed" qualification for legislators was carried by a vote of ten to one; the proposition to strike out the disqualification of persons having unsettled accounts with the United States was carried by a vote of nine to two. Finally the proposition to exclude persons who were indebted to the United States was likewise defeated by a vote of nine to two, after Pinckney had called attention to the fact that "it would exclude persons who had purchased confiscated property or should purchase Western territory of the public and might be some obstacle to the sale of the latter."

Indeed, there was little risk to personalty in thus allowing the Constitution to go to the states for approval without any property qualifications on voters other than those which the state might see fit to impose. Only one branch of new government, the House of Representatives, was required to be elected by popular vote; and, in case of popular choice of presidential electors might be established, a safeguard was secured by the indirect process. Two controlling bodies, the Senate and Supreme Court, were removed altogether from the possibility of popular election except by constitutional amendment. Finally, the conservative members of the Convention were doubly fortified in the fact that nearly all of the state constitutions then in force provided real or personal property qualifications for voters anyway, and radical democratic changes did not seem perilously near.

* * * *

Conclusions

The movement for the Constitution of the United States was originated and carried through principally by four groups of personalty interests which had been adversely affected under the Articles of Confederation: money, public securities, manufactures, and trade and shipping.

The first firm steps toward the formation of the Constitution were taken by a small and active group of men immediately interested through their personal possessions in the outcome of their labors.

No popular vote was taken directly or indirectly on the proposition to call the Convention which drafted the Constitution.

A large propertyless mass was, under the prevailing suffrage qualifications, excluded at the outset from participation (through representatives) in the work of framing the Constitution.

The members of the Philadelphia Convention which drafted the Constitution were, with a few exceptions, immediately, directly, and personally interested in, and derived economic advantages from, the establishment of the new system.

The Constitution was essentially an economic document based upon the concept that the fundamental private rights of property are anterior to government and morally beyond the reach of popular majorities.

The major portion of the members of the Convention are on record as recognizing the claim of property to a special and defensive position in the Constitution.

In the ratification of the Constitution, about three-fourths of the adult males failed to vote on the question, having abstained from the elections at which delegates to the state conventions were chosen, either on account of their indifference or their disfranchisement by property qualifications.

The Constitution was ratified by a vote of probably not more than one-sixth of adult males.

It is questionable whether a majority of the voters participating in the elections for the state conventions in New York, Massachusetts, New Hampshire, Virginia, and South Carolina, actually approved the ratification of the Constitution.

The leaders who supported the Constitution in the ratifying conventions represented the same economic groups as the members of the Philadelphia Convention; and in a large number of instances they were also directly and personally interested in the outcome of their efforts.

In the ratification, it became manifest that the line of cleavage for and against the Constitution was between substantial personalty interests on the one hand and the small farming and debtor interests on the other.

The Constitution was not created by "the whole people" as the jurists have said; neither was it created by "the states" as Southern nullifiers long contended; but it was the work of a consolidated group whose interests knew no state boundaries and were truly national in their scope.

POINTS TO PONDER

1. What is the main evidence Beard presents in coming to his conclusions about the Framers' intentions?
2. What features of the Constitution make it biased in favor of property owners, according to Beard?
3. Were the Framers a more elite group than other cohorts of governing officials throughout the history of the United States?

3

"THE FOUNDING FATHERS: A REFORM CAUCUS IN ACTION"
John P. Roche

To political scientist John P. Roche of Brandeis University, the framing of the Constitution was not a plot for the protection of self-interest by a propertied elite, as Beard thought. But neither was it an exercise in architectonic political theory in which government structures were deduced from fundamental principles. Rather it was the result of the pulling and hauling of politics in which the Federalists, who favored the new central government, kept firmly in mind that they had to win approval of their plan by "the folks back home" in their respective states.

In the following article published in the American Political Science Review *in 1961, Roche notes that the Federalists saw the need for a strong central government that would act directly on* the people. *It would be much more than a confederation of states. But in pursuing this radical proposal they acted as a "nationalist reform caucus." In Roche's judgment the Constitution is "a patch-work sewn together under the pressure of both time and events by a group of extremely talented democratic politicians." Thus the elite was democratic, not economic, and the result was a political hodgepodge, not a coherent theoretical edifice.*

Over the last century and a half, the work of the Constitutional Convention and the motives of the Founding Fathers have been analyzed under a number of different ideological auspices. To one generation of historians, the hand of God was moving in the assembly; under a later dispensation, the dialectic (at various levels of philosophical sophistication) replaced the Deity: "relationships of production" moved into the niche previously reserved for Love of Country. Thus in counterpoint to the Zeitgeist, the Framers have undergone miraculous metamorphoses: at one time acclaimed as liberals and bold social engineers, today they appear in the guise of sound Burkean conservatives, men who in our time would subscribe to *Fortune*, look to Walter Lippmann for political theory, and chuckle patronizingly at the antics of Barry Goldwater. The implicit assumption is that if James Madison were among us, he would be President of the Ford Foundation, while Alexander Hamilton would chair the Committee for Economic Development.

The "Fathers" have thus been admitted to our best circles; the revolutionary ferocity which confiscated all Tory property in reach and populated New Brunswick with outlaws has been converted by the "Miltown School" of American historians into a benign dedication to "consensus" and "prescriptive rights." The Daughters of the American Revolution have, through the ministrations of Professors Boorstin, Hartz, and Rossiter, at last found ancestors worthy of their descendants. It is not my purpose here to argue that the "Fathers" were, in fact, radical revolutionaries; that proposition has been brilliantly demonstrated by Robert R. Palmer in his *Age of the Democratic Revolution*. My concern is with the further position that not only were they revolutionaries, but also they were democrats. Indeed, in my view, there is one fundamental truth about the Founding Fathers that *every* generation of Zeitgeisters has done its best to obscure: They were first and foremost superb democratic politicians. I suspect that in a contemporary setting, James Madison would be Speaker of the House of Representatives and Hamilton would be the *eminence grise* dominating (*pace* Theodore Sorenson or Sherman

Adams) the Executive Office of the President. They were, with their colleagues, *political men*—not metaphysicians, disembodied conservatives or Agents of History—and as recent research into the nature of American politics in the 1780s confirms, they were committed (perhaps willy-nilly) to working within the democratic framework, within a universe of public approval. Charles Beard *and* the filiopietists to the contrary notwithstanding, the Philadelphia Convention was not a College of Cardinals or a council of Platonic guardians working within a manipulative, predemocratic framework; it was a *nationalist* reform caucus which had to operate with great delicacy and skill in a political cosmos full of enemies to achieve the one definitive goal—popular approbation.

Perhaps the time has come, to borrow Walton Hamilton's fine phrase, to raise the Framers from immortality to mortality, to give them credit for their magnificent demonstration of the art of democratic politics. The point must be reemphasized; they *made* history and did it within the limits of consensus. There was nothing inevitable about the future in 1787; the *Zeitgeist*, that fine Hegelian technique of begging causal questions, could only be discerned in retrospect. What they did was to hammer out a pragmatic compromise which would both bolster the "National interest" and be acceptable to the people. What inspiration they got came from their collective experience as professional politicians in a democratic society. As John Dickinson put it to his fellow delegates on August 13, "Experience must be our guide. Reason may mislead us."

In this context, let us examine the problems they confronted and the solutions they evolved. The Convention has been described picturesquely as a counter-revolutionary junta and the Constitution as a *coup d'etat*, but this has been accomplished by withdrawing the whole history of the movement for constitutional reform from its true context. No doubt the goals of the constitutional elite were "subversive" to the existing political order, but it is overlooked that their subversion could only have succeeded if the people of the United States endorsed it by regularized procedures. Indubitably they were "plotting" to establish a much stronger central government than existed under the Articles, but only in the sense in which one could argue equally well that John F. Kennedy was, from 1956 to 1960, "plotting" to become President. In short, on the fundamental *procedural* level, the Constitutionalists had to work according to the prevailing rules of the game. Whether they liked it or not is a topic for spiritualists—and is irrelevant: one may be quite certain that had Washington agreed to play the De Gaulle (as the Cincinnati once urged), Hamilton would willingly have held his horse, but such fertile speculation in no way alters the actual context in which events took place.

I

When the Constitutionalists went forth to subvert the Confederation, they utilized the mechanisms of political legitimacy. And the roadblocks which confronted them were formidable. At the same time, they were endowed with certain potent political assets. The history of the United States from 1786 to 1790 was largely one of a masterful employment of political expertise by the Constitutionalists as against bumbling, erratic behavior by the opponents of reform. Effectively, the Constitutionalists had to induce the states, by democratic techniques of coercion, to emasculate themselves. To be specific, if New York had refused to join the new Union, the project was doomed; yet before New York was safely in, the reluctant state legislature had *sua sponte* to take the following steps: (1) agree to send delegates to the Philadelphia Convention; (2) provide maintenance for these delegates (these were distinct stages: New Hampshire was early in naming delegates, but did not provide for their maintenance until July); (3) set up the special *ad hoc* convention to decide on ratification; and (4) concede to the decision of the *ad hoc* convention that New York should participate. New York admittedly was a tricky state, with a strong interest in a *status quo* which permitted her to exploit New Jersey and Connecticut, but the same legal hurdles existed in every state. And at the risk of becoming boring, it must be reiterated that the *only* weapon in the Constitutionalist arsenal was an effective mobilization of public opinion.

The group which undertook this struggle was an interesting amalgam of a few dedicated nationalists with the self-interested spokesmen of various parochial bailiwicks. The Georgians, for example, wanted a strong central authority to provide military protection for their huge, underpopulated state against the Creek Confederacy; Jerseymen and Connecticuters wanted to escape from economic bondage to New York; the Virginians hoped to establish a system which would give that great state its rightful place in the councils of the republic. The dominant figures in the politics of these states therefore cooperated in the call for the Convention. In other states, the thrust towards national reform was taken up by opposition groups who added the "national interest" to their weapons system; in Pennsylvania, for instance, the group fighting to revise the Constitution of 1776 came out four-square behind the Constitutionalists, and in New York, Hamilton and the Schuyler *ambiance* took the same tack against George Clinton. There was, of course, a large element of personality in the affair: there is reason to suspect that Patrick Henry's opposition to the Convention and the Constitution was founded on his conviction that Jefferson was behind both, and a close study of local politics elsewhere would surely reveal that others supported the Constitution for the simple (and politically quite sufficient) reason that the "wrong" people were against it.

To say this is not to suggest that the Constitution rested on a foundation of impure or base motives. It is rather to argue that in politics there are no immaculate conceptions, and that in the drive for a stronger general government, motives of all sorts played a part. Few men in the history of mankind have espoused a view of the "common good" or "public interest" that militated against their private status; even Plato with all his reverence for disembodied reason managed to put philosophers on top of the pile. Thus it is not surprising that a number of diversified private interests joined to push the nationalist public interest; what would have been surprising was the absence of such a pragmatic united front. And the fact remains that, however motivated, these men did demonstrate a willingness to compromise their parochial interests in behalf of an ideal which took shape before their eyes and under their ministrations.

As Stanley Elkins and Eric McKitrick have suggested in a perceptive essay, what distinguished the leaders of the Constitutionalist caucus from their enemies was a "Continental" approach to political, economic and military issues. To the extent that they shared an institutional base of operations, it was the Continental Congress (thirty-nine of the delegates to the Federal Convention had served in Congress), and this was hardly a locale which inspired respect for the state governments. Robert de Jouvenal observed French politics half a century ago and noted that a revolutionary Deputy had more in common with a non-revolutionary Deputy than he had with a revolutionary non-Deputy; similarly one can surmise that membership in the Congress under the Articles of Confederation worked to establish a continental frame of reference, that a Congressman from Pennsylvania and one from South Carolina would share a universe of discourse which provided them with a conceptual common denominator *vis á vis* their respective state legislatures. This was particularly true with respect to external affairs: the average state legislator was probably about as concerned with foreign policy then as he is today, but Congressmen were constantly forced to take the broad view of American prestige, were compelled to listen to the reports of Secretary John Jay and to the dispatches and pleas from their frustrated envoys in Britain, France and Spain. From considerations such as these, a "Continental" ideology developed which seems to have demanded a revision of our domestic institutions primarily on the ground that only by invigorating our general government could we assume our rightful place in the international arena. Indeed, an argument with great force—particularly since Washington was its incarnation—urged that our very survival in the Hobbesian jungle of world politics depended upon a reordering and strengthening of our national sovereignty.

Note that I am not endorsing the "Critical Period" thesis; on the contrary, Merrill Jensen seems to me quite sound in his view that for most Americans, engaged as they were in self-sustaining agriculture, the "Critical Period" was not particularly critical. In fact, the great achievement of the Constitutionalists was their ultimate success in convincing the elected representatives of a majority of the white male population that change was imperative. A small group of political leaders with a Continental vision and essentially a consciousness of the United States' *international* impotence, provided the matrix of the movement. To their standard other leaders rallied with their own parallel ambitions. Their great assets were (1) the presence in their caucus of the one authentic American "father figure," George Washington, whose prestige was enormous;

(2) the energy and talent of their leadership (in which one must include the towering intellectuals of the time, John Adams and Thomas Jefferson, despite their absence abroad), and their communications "network," which was far superior to anything on the opposition side; (3) the preemptive skill which made "their" issue The Issue and kept the locally oriented opposition permanently on the defensive; and (4) the subjective consideration that these men were spokesmen of a new and compelling credo: *American* nationalism, that ill-defined but nonetheless potent sense of collective purpose that emerged from the American Revolution.

Despite great institutional handicaps, the Constitutionalists managed in the mid-1780s to mount an offensive which gained momentum as years went by. Their greatest problem was lethargy, and paradoxically, the number of barriers in their path may have proved an advantage in the long run. Beginning with the initial battle to get the Constitutional Convention called and delegates appointed, they could never relax, never let up the pressure. In practical terms, this meant that the local "organizations" created by the Constitutionalists were perpetually in movement building up their cadres for the next fight. (The word organization has to be used with great caution: a political organization in the United States—as in contemporary England—generally consisted of a magnate and his following, or a coalition of magnates. This did not necessarily mean that it was "undemocratic" or "aristocratic," in the Aristotelian sense of the word: while a few magnates such as the Livingstons could draft their followings, most exercised their leadership without coercion on the basis of popular endorsement. The absence of organized opposition did not imply the impossibility of competition any more than low public participation in elections necessarily indicated an undemocratic suffrage.)

The Constitutionalists got the jump on the "opposition" (a collective noun: opposition*s* would be more correct) at the outset with the demand for a Convention. Their opponents were caught in an old political trap: they were not being asked to approve any specific program of reform, but only to endorse a meeting to discuss and recommend needed reforms. If they took a hard line at the first stage, they were put in the position of glorifying the *status quo* and of denying the need for *any* changes. Moreover the Constitutionalists could go to the people with a persuasive argument for "fair play"—"How can you condemn reform before you know precisely what is involved?" Since the state legislatures obviously would have the final say on any proposals that might emerge from the Convention, the Constitutionalists were merely reasonable men asking for a chance. Besides, since they did not make any concrete proposals at that stage, they were in a position to capitalize on every sort of generalized discontent with the Confederation.

Perhaps because of their poor intelligence system, perhaps because of overconfidence generated by the failure of all previous efforts to alter the Articles, the opposition awoke too late to the dangers that confronted them in 1787.

Not only did the Constitutionalists manage to get every state but Rhode Island (where politics were enlivened by a party system reminiscent of the "Blues" and the "Greens" in the Byzantine Empire) to appoint delegates to Philadelphia, but when the results were in, it appeared that they dominated the delegations. Given the apathy of the opposition, this was a natural phenomenon: in an ideologically nonpolarized political atmosphere those who get appointed to a special committee are likely to be the men who supported the movement for its creation. Even George Clinton, who seems to have been the first opposition leader to awake to the possibility of trouble, could not prevent the New York legislature from appointing Alexander Hamilton—though he did have the foresight to send two of his henchmen to dominate the delegation. Incidentally, much has been made of the fact that the delegates to Philadelphia were not elected by the people; some have adduced this fact as evidence of the "undemocratic" character of the gathering. But put in the context of the time, this argument is wholly specious: the central government under the Articles was considered a creature of the component states and in all the states but Rhode Island, Connecticut and New Hampshire, members of the national Congress were chosen by the state legislatures. This was not a consequence of elitism or fear of the mob; it was a logical extension of states'-rights doctrine to guarantee that the national institution did not end-run the state legislatures and make direct contact with the people.

II

With delegations safely named, the focus shifted to Philadelphia. While waiting for a quorum to assemble, James Madison got busy and drafted the so-called Randolph or Virginia Plan with the aid of the Virginia delegation. This was a political master-stroke. Its consequence was that once business got underway, the framework of discussion was established on Madison's terms. There was no interminable argument over agenda; instead the delegates took the Virginia Resolutions—"just for purposes of discussion"—as their point of departure. And along with Madison's proposals, many of which were buried in the course of the summer, went his major premise: a new start on a Constitution rather than piecemeal amendment. This was not necessarily revolutionary—a little exegesis could demonstrate that a new Constitution might be formulated as "amendments" to the Articles of Confederation—but Madison's proposal that this "lump sum" amendment go into effect after approval by nine states (the Articles required unanimous state approval for any amendment) was thoroughly subversive.

Standard treatments of the Convention divide the delegates into "nationalists" and "states'-righters" with various improvised shadings ("moderate nationalists," etc.), but these are *a posteriori* categories which obfuscate more than they clarify. What is striking to one who analyzes the Convention as a case-study in democratic politics is the lack of clear-cut ideological divisions in the Convention. Indeed, I submit that the evidence—Madison's *Notes*, the correspondence of the delegates, and debates on ratification—indicates that this was a remarkably homogeneous body on the ideological level. Yates and Lansing, Clinton's two chaperones for Hamilton, left in disgust on July 10. (Is there anything more tedious than sitting through endless disputes on matters one deems fundamentally misconceived? It takes an iron will to spend a hot summer as an ideological *agent provocateur*.) Luther Martin, Maryland's bibulous narcissist, left on September 4 in a huff when he discovered that others did not share his self-esteem; others went home for personal reasons. But the hard core of delegates accepted a grinding regimen throughout the attrition of a Philadelphia summer precisely because they shared the Constitutionalist goal.

Basic differences of opinion emerged, of course, but these were not ideological; they were *structural*. If the so-called "states'-rights" group had not accepted the fundamental purposes of the Convention, they could simply have pulled out and by doing so have aborted the whole enterprise. Instead of bolting, they returned day after day to argue and to compromise. An interesting symbol of this basic homogeneity was the initial agreement on secrecy: these professional politicians did not want to become prisoners of publicity; they wanted to retain that freedom of maneuver which is only possible when men are not forced to take public stands in the preliminary stages of negotiation. There was no legal means of binding the tongues of the delegates: at any stage in the game a delegate with basic principled objections to the emerging project could have taken the stump (as Luther Martin did after his exit) and denounced the convention to the skies. Yet Madison did not even inform Thomas Jefferson in Paris of the course of the deliberations and available correspondence indicates that the delegates generally observed the injunction. Secrecy is certainly uncharacteristic of any assembly marked by strong ideological polarization. This was noted at the time: the *New York Daily Advertiser*, August 14, 1787, commented that the " . . . profound secrecy hitherto observed by the Convention [we consider] a happy omen, as it demonstrates that the spirit of party on any great and essential point cannot have arisen to any height."

Commentators on the Constitution who have read *The Federalist* in lieu of reading the actual debates have credited the Fathers with the invention of a sublime concept called "Federalism." Unfortunately *The Federalist* is probative evidence for only one proposition: that Hamilton and Madison were inspired propagandists with a genius for retrospective symmetry. Federalism, as the theory is generally defined, was an improvisation which was later promoted into a political theory. Experts on "federalism" should take to heart the advice of David Hume, who warned in his *Of the Rise and Progress of the Arts and Sciences* that " . . . there is no subject in which we must proceed with more caution than in [history], lest we assign causes which never existed and reduce what is merely contingent to stable and universal principles." In any event, the final balance in the Constitution between the states and the nation must have come as a great disappointment to Madison, while Hamilton's unitary views are too well known to need elucidation.

It is indeed astonishing how those who have glibly designated James Madison the "father" of Federalism have overlooked the solid body of fact which indicates that he shared Hamilton's quest for a unitary central government. To be specific, they have avoided examining the clear import of the Madison-Virginia Plan, and have disregarded Madison's dogged inch-by-inch retreat from the bastions of centralization. The Virginia Plan envisioned a unitary national government effectively freed from and dominant over the states. The lower house of the national legislature was to be elected directly by the people of the states with membership proportional to population. The upper house was to be selected by the lower and the two chambers would elect the executive and choose the judges. The national government would be thus cut completely loose from the states.

The structure of the general government was freed from state control in a truly radical fashion, but the scope of the authority of the national sovereign as Madison initially formulated it was breathtaking—it was a formulation worthy of the Sage of Malmesbury himself. The national legislature was to be empowered to disallow the acts of state legislatures, and the central government was vested, in addition to the powers of the nation under the Articles of Confederation, with plenary authority wherever " . . . the separate States are incompetent or in which the harmony of the United States may be interrupted by the exercise of individual legislation." Finally, just to lock the door against state intrusion, the national Congress was to be given the power to use military force on recalcitrant states. This was Madison's "model" of an ideal national government, though it later received little publicity in *The Federalist*.

The interesting thing was the reaction of the Convention to this militant program for a strong autonomous central government. Some delegates were startled, some obviously leery of so comprehensive a project of reform, but nobody set off any fireworks and nobody walked out. Moreover, in the two weeks that followed, the Virginia Plan received substantial endorsement *en principe*; the initial temper of the gathering can be deduced from the approval "without debate or dissent," on May 31, of the Sixth Resolution which granted Congress the authority to disallow state legislation " . . . contravening *in its opinion* the Articles of Union." Indeed, an amendment was included to bar states from contravening national treaties.

The Virginia Plan may therefore be considered, in ideological terms, as the delegates' Utopia, but as the discussions continued and became more specific, many of those present began to have second thoughts. After all, they were not residents of Utopia or guardians in Plato's Republic who could simply impose a philosophical ideal on subordinate strata of the population. They were practical politicians in a democratic society, and no matter what their private dreams might be, they had to take home an acceptable package and defend it—and their own political futures—against predictable attack. On June 14 the breaking point between dream and reality took place. Apparently realizing that under the Virginia Plan, Massachusetts, Virginia and Pennsylvania could virtually dominate the national government—and probably appreciating that to sell this program to "the folks back home" would be impossible—the delegates from the small states dug in their heels and demanded time for a consideration of alternatives. One gets a graphic sense of the inner politics from John Dickinson's reproach to Madison: "You see the consequences of pushing things too far. Some of the members from the small States wish for two branches in the General Legislature and are friends to a good National Government; but we would sooner submit to a foreign power than . . . be deprived of an equality of suffrage in both branches of the Legislature, and thereby be thrown under the domination of the large States."

The bare outline of the *Journal* entry for Tuesday, June 14, is suggestive to anyone with extensive experience in deliberative bodies. "It was moved by Mr. Patterson [*sic*, Paterson's name was one of those consistently misspelled by Madison and everybody else] seconded by Mr. Randolph that the further consideration of the report from the Committee of the whole House [endorsing the Virginia Plan] be postponed til tomorrow and before the question of postponement was taken. It was moved by Mr. Randolph seconded by Mr. Patterson that the House adjourn." The House adjourned by obvious prearrangement of the two principals: since the preceding Saturday when Brearley and Paterson of New Jersey had announced their fundamental discontent with the representational features of the Virginia Plan, the informal pressure had certainly been building up to slow down the steamroller. Doubtless there were extended arguments at the Indian Queen between Madison and Paterson, the latter insisting that events were moving rapidly towards a probably disastrous conclusion, towards a political suicide pact. Now the process of accommodation was put into action smoothly—and wisely, given the character and strength of the doubters. Madison had the votes, but this was one of those situations where the enforcement of mechanical majoritarianism could easily have destroyed the objectives of the majority: the Constitutionalists were in quest of a qualitative as well as a quantitative consensus. This was hardly from deference to local Quaker custom; it was a political imperative if they were to attain ratification.

III

According to the standard script, at this point the "states'-rights" group intervened in force behind the New Jersey Plan, which has been characteristically portrayed as a reversion to the *status quo* under the Articles of Confederation with but minor modifications. A careful examination of the evidence indicates that only in a marginal sense is this an accurate description. It is true that the New Jersey Plan put the states back into the institutional picture, but one could argue that to do so was a recognition of political reality rather than an affirmation of states'-rights. A serious case can be made that the advocates of the New Jersey Plan, far from being ideological addicts of states'-rights, intended to substitute for the Virginia Plan a system which would both retain strong national power and have a chance of adoption in the states. The leading spokesman for this project asserted quite clearly that his views were based more on counsels of expediency than on principle; said Paterson on June 16: "I came here not to speak my own sentiments, but the sentiments of those who sent me. Our object is not such a Governmt. as may be best in itself, but such a one as our Constituents have authorized us to prepare, and as they will approve." This is Madison's version; in Yates' transcription, there is a crucial sentence following the remarks above: "I believe that a little practical virtue is to be preferred to the finest theoretical principles, which cannot be carried into effect." In his preliminary speech on June 9, Paterson had stated " . . . to the public mind we must accommodate ourselves," and in his notes for this and his later effort as well, the emphasis is the same. The *structure* of government under the Articles should be retained:

> 2. Because it accords with the Sentiments of the People
> [Proof:] 1. Coms. [Commissions from state legislatures defining the jurisdiction of the delegates]
>   2. News-papers—Political Barometer. Jersey never would have sent Delegates under the first [Virginia] Plan—
> Not here to sport Opinions of my own. Wt. [What] can be done. A little practicable Virtue preferrable to Theory.

This was a defense of political acumen, not of states'-rights. In fact, Paterson's notes of his speech can easily be construed as an argument for attaining the substantive objectives of the Virginia Plan by a sound political route, *i.e.*, pouring the new wine in the old bottles. With a shrewd eye, Paterson queried:

> Will the Operation and Force of the [central] Govt. depend upon the mode of Representn.—No—it will depend upon the Quantum of Power lodged in the leg. ex. and judy. Departments—Give [the existing] Congress the same Powers that you intend to give the two Branches, [under the Virginia Plan] and I apprehend they will act with as much Propriety and more Energy . . .

In other words, the advocates of the New Jersey Plan concentrated their fire on what they held to be *political liabilities* of the Virginia Plan—which were matters of institutional structure—rather than on the proposed scope of national authority. Indeed, the Supremacy Clause of the Constitution first saw the light of day in Paterson's Sixth Resolution; the New Jersey Plan contemplated the use of military force to secure compliance with national law; and finally Paterson made clear his view that under either the Virginia or the New Jersey systems, the general government would " . . . act on individuals and not on states." From the states'-rights viewpoint, this was heresy: the fundament of that doctrine was the proposition that any central government had as its constituents the states, not the people, and could only reach the people through the agency of the state government.

Paterson then reopened the agenda of the Convention, but he did so within a distinctly nationalist framework. Paterson's position was one of favoring a strong central government in principle, but opposing one which in fact *put the big states in the saddle*. (The Virginia Plan, for all its abstract merits, did very well by Virginia.) As evidence for this speculation, there is a curious and intriguing proposal among Paterson's preliminary drafts of the New Jersey Plan:

> Whereas it is necessary in Order to form the People of the U. S. of America in to a Nation, that the States should be consolidated, by which means all the Citizens thereof will become equally intitled to and will equally participate in the same Privileges and Rights . . . it is therefore resolved, that all the Lands contained within the Limits of each state individually, and the U. S. generally be considered as constituting one Body or Mass, and be divided into thirteen or more integral parts.
>
> Resolved, That such Divisions or integral Parts shall be styled Districts.

This makes it sound as though Paterson was prepared to accept a strong unified central government along the lines of the Virginia Plan if the existing states were eliminated. He may have gotten the idea from his New Jersey colleague Judge David Brearley, who on June 9 had commented that the only remedy to the dilemma over representation was " . . . that a map of the U. S. be spread out, that all the existing boundaries be erased, and that a new partition of the whole be made into 13 equal parts." According to Yates, Brearley added at this point, " . . . then a government on the present [Virginia Plan] system will be just."

This proposition was never pushed—it was patently unrealistic—but one can appreciate its purpose: it would have separated the men from the boys in the large-state delegations. How attached would the Virginians have been to their reform principles if Virginia were to disappear as a component geographical unit (the largest) for representational purposes? Up to this point, the Virginians had been in the happy position of supporting high ideals with that inner confidence born of knowledge that the "public interest" they endorsed would nourish their private interest. Worse, they had shown little willingness to compromise. Now the delegates from the small states announced that they were unprepared to be offered up as sacrificial victims to a "national interest" which reflected Virginia's parochial ambition. Caustic Charles Pinckney was not far off when he remarked sardonically that " . . . the whole [conflict] comes to this": "Give N. Jersey an equal vote, and she will dismiss her scruples, and concur in the Natil. system." What he rather unfairly did not add was that the Jersey delegates were not free agents who could adhere to their private convictions; they had to take back, sponsor and risk their reputations on the reforms approved by the Convention—and in New Jersey, not in Virginia.

* * * *

It would be tedious to continue a blow-by-blow analysis of the work of the delegates; the critical fight was over representation of the states and once the Connecticut Compromise was adopted on July 17, the Convention was over the hump. Madison, James Wilson, and Gouverneur Morris of New York (who was there representing Pennsylvania!) fought the compromise all the way in a last-ditch effort to get a unitary state with parliamentary supremacy. But their allies deserted them and they demonstrated after their defeat the essentially opportunist character of their objections—using "opportunist" here in a non-pejorative sense, to indicate a willingness to swallow their objections and get on with the business. Moreover, once the compromise had carried (by five states to four, with one state divided), its advocates threw themselves vigorously into the job of strengthening the general government's substantive powers—as might have been predicted, indeed, from Paterson's early statements. It nourishes an increased respect for Madison's devotion to the art of politics, to realize that this dogged fighter could sit down six months later and prepare essays for *The Federalist* in contradiction to his basic convictions about the true course the Convention should have taken.

* * * *

To conclude, the Constitution was neither a victory for abstract theory nor a great practical success. Well over half a million men had to die on the battlefields of the Civil War before certain constitutional principles could be defined—a baleful consideration which is somehow overlooked in our customary tributes to the farsighted genius of the Framers and to the supposed American talent for "constitutionalism." The Constitution was, however, a vivid demonstration of effective democratic political action, and of the forging of a national elite which literally persuaded its countrymen to hoist themselves by their own boot straps. American pro-consuls would be wise not to translate the Constitution into Japanese, or Swahili, or treat it as a work of semi-Divine origin; but when students of comparative politics examine the process of nation-building in countries newly freed from colonial rule, they may find the American experience instructive as a classic example of the potentialities of a democratic elite.

POINTS TO PONDER

1. Why does Roche characterize the Constitutional Convention as a "reform caucus"?

2. According to Roche, what was the main challenge facing the Framers?
3. How does Roche's analysis of the Framers' motivations and actions contrast with the explanations of Beard and Diamond?

4

"DEMOCRACY AND *THE FEDERALIST*: A RECONSIDERATION OF THE FRAMERS' INTENT"*

Martin Diamond

Martin Diamond, a political scientist at Claremont Men's College, argues in this article published in 1959 in The American Political Science Review *that the Constitution is not purposely antidemocratic, as Beard and others have argued. Nor is it merely the result of pragmatic political compromise as Roche argued. Diamond posits rather that the Constitution was a new form of popular government designed to protect minority rights. Although designing a popular government responsive to the people, the Framers were self-consciously aware of the dangers of democracy about which political philosophers had written since the time of the Greeks.*

There is a difference between procedural democracy, which would assure majority rule, and substantive democracy, which would assure just outcomes. Thus the problem arises: Might a majority of the citizens deprive a minority of democratic rights and basic justice? Diamond argues that to prevent the dangers of a majority riding roughshod over a political minority, the Constitution built in protections against sweeping actions on the part of majorities: the judiciary, the Senate, separation of powers, checks and balances. Rather than protecting a propertied elite, the Framers were guarding against the abuse of democracy evident in political history.

Thus, argues Diamond, when modern critics paint the Framers as antidemocratic, they miss one of the main intentions of the Constitution. Judged by the standards of their time, the Framers were not self-serving elitists, but "wise partisans of democracy."

It has been a common teaching among modern historians of the guiding ideas in the foundation of our government that the Constitution of the United States embodied a reaction against the democratic principles espoused in the Declaration of Independence. This view has largely been accepted by political scientists and has therefore had important consequences for the way American political development has been studied. I shall present here a contrary view of the political theory of the Framers and examine some of its consequences.

* An earlier version of this was written at the request of the Fund for the Republic; the Fund's generous assistance is here gratefully acknowledged.

What is the relevance of the political thought of the Founding Fathers to an understanding of contemporary problems of liberty and justice? Four possible ways of looking at the Founding Fathers immediately suggest themselves. First, it may be that they possessed wisdom, a set of political principles still inherently adequate, and needing only to be supplemented by skill in their proper contemporary application. Second, it may be that, while the Founding Fathers' principles are still sound, they are applicable only to a part of our problems, but not to that part which is peculiarly modern; and thus new principles are needed to be joined together with the old ones. Third, it may be that the Founding Fathers have simply become [outdated]; they dealt with bygone problems and their principles were relevant only to those old problems. Fourth, they may have been wrong or radically inadequate even for their own time.

Each of these four possible conclusions requires the same foundation: an understanding of the political thought of the Founding Fathers. To decide whether to apply their wisdom, or to add to their wisdom, or to reject it as irrelevant or as unwise, it is absolutely necessary to understand what they said, why they said it, and what they meant by it. At the same time, however, to understand their claim to wisdom is to evaluate it: to know wherein they were wise and wherein they were not, or wherein (and why) their wisdom is unavailing for our problems. Moreover, even if it turns out that our modern problems require wholly new principles for their solution, an excellent way to discover those new principles would be to see what it is about modernity that has outmoded the principles of the Founding Fathers. For example, it is possible that modern developments are themselves partly the outcome of the particular attempt to solve the problem of freedom and justice upon which this country was founded. That is, our modern difficulties may testify to fundamental errors in the thought of the Founding Fathers; and, in the process of discerning those errors, we may discover what better principles would be.

The solution of our contemporary problems requires very great wisdom indeed. And in that fact lies the greatest justification for studying anew the political thought of the Founding Fathers. For that thought remains the finest American thought on political matters. In studying them we may raise ourselves to their level. In achieving their level we may free ourselves from limitations that, ironically, they tend to impose upon us, *i.e.*, insofar as we tend to be creatures of the society they founded. And in so freeing ourselves we may be enabled, if it is necessary, to go beyond their wisdom. The Founding Fathers still loom so large in our life that the contemporary political problem of liberty and justice for Americans could be stated as the need to choose whether to apply their wisdom, amend their wisdom, or reject it. Only an understanding of them will tell us how to choose.

For the reflections on the Fathers which follow, I employ chiefly *The Federalist* as the clue to the political theory upon which rested the founding of the American Republic. That this would be inadequate for a systematic study of the Founding Fathers goes without saying. But it is the one book, "to which," as Jefferson wrote in 1825, "appeal is habitually made by all, and rarely declined or denied by any as evidence of the general opinion of those who framed and of those who accepted the Constitution of the United States, on questions as to its genuine meaning." As such it is the indispensable starting point for systematic study.

I

Our major political problems today are problems of democracy; and, as much as anything else, the *Federalist* papers are a teaching about democracy. The conclusion of one of the most important of these papers states what is also the most important theme in the entire work: the necessity for "a republican remedy for the diseases most incident to republican government." The theme is clearly repeated in a passage where Thomas Jefferson is praised for displaying equally "a fervent attachment to republican government and an enlightened view of the dangerous propensities against which it ought to be guarded." *The Federalist*, thus, stresses its commitment to republican or popular government, but, of course, insists that this must be an enlightened commitment.

But *The Federalist* and the Founding Fathers generally have not been taken at their word. Predominantly, they are understood as being only quasi- or even anti-democrats. Modern American historical writing, at least until very recently, has generally seen the Constitution as some sort of apostasy from, or reaction to, the radically democratic implications of the Declaration of Independence—a reaction that was undone by the great "democratic breakthroughs" of Jeffersonianism, Jacksonianism, etc. This view, I believe, involves a false understanding of the crucial political issues involved in the founding of the American Republic. Further, it is based implicitly upon a questionable modern approach to democracy and has tended to have the effect, moreover, of relegating the political teaching of the Founding Fathers to the pre-democratic past and thus of making it of no vital concern to moderns. The Founding Fathers themselves repeatedly stressed that their Constitution was wholly consistent with the true principles of republican or popular government. The prevailing modern opinion, in varying degrees and in different ways, rejects that claim. It thus becomes important to understand what was the relation of the Founding Fathers to popular government or democracy.

I have deliberately used interchangeably their terms, "popular government" and "democracy." The Founding Fathers, of course, did not use the terms entirely synonymously and the idea that they were less than "democrats" has been fortified by the fact that they sometimes defined "democracy" invidiously in comparison with "republic." But this fact does not really justify the opinion. For their basic view was that *popular government was the genus, and democracy and republic were two species* of that genus of government. What distinguished popular government from other genera of government was that in it, political authority is "derived from the great body of the society, not from . . . [any] favoured class of it." With respect to this decisive question, of where political authority is lodged, democracy and republic—as *The Federalist* uses the terms—differ not in the least. Republics, equally with democracies, may claim to be wholly a form of popular government. This is neither to deny the difference between the two, nor to depreciate the importance *The Federalist* attached to the difference; but in *The Federalist's* view, the difference does not relate to the essential principle of popular government. Democracy means in *The Federalist* that form of popular government where the citizens "assemble and administer the government in person." Republics differ in that the people rule through representatives and, of course, in the consequences of that difference. The crucial point is that republics and democracies are equally forms of popular government, but that the one form is vastly preferable to the other because of the substantive consequences of the difference in form. Those historians who consider the Founding Fathers as less than "democrats," miss or reject the Founders' central contention that, while being perfectly faithful to the *principle* of popular government, they had solved the *problem* of popular government.

In what way is the Constitution ordinarily thought to be less democratic than the Declaration? The argument is usually that the former is characterized by fear of the people, by preoccupation with minority interests and rights, and by measures therefore taken against the power of majorities. The Declaration, it is true, does not display these features, but this is no proof of a fundamental difference of principle between the two. Is it not obviously possible that the difference is due only to a difference in the tasks to which the two documents were addressed? And is it not further possible that the democratic principles of the Declaration are not only compatible with the prophylactic measures of the Constitution, but actually imply them?

The Declaration of Independence formulates two criteria for judging whether any government is good, or indeed legitimate. Good government must rest, procedurally, upon the consent of the governed. Good government, substantively, must do only certain things, *e.g.*, secure certain rights. This may be stated another way by borrowing a phrase from Locke, appropriate enough when discussing the Declaration. That "the people shall be judge" is of the essence of democracy, is its peculiar form or method of proceeding. That the people shall judge rightly is the substantive problem of democracy. But whether the procedure will bring about the substance is problematic. Between the Declaration's two criteria, then, a tension exists: consent can be given or obtained for governmental actions which are not right—at least as the men of 1776 saw the right. (To give an obvious example from their point of view: the people may freely but wrongly vote away the protection due to property.) Thus the Declaration clearly contained, although it did not resolve, a fundamental problem. Solving the problem was not its task; that was the task for the framers of the Constitution. But the man who wrote the Declaration of

Independence and the leading men who supported it were perfectly aware of the difficulty, and of the necessity for a "republican remedy."

What the text of the Declaration, taken alone, tells of its meaning may easily be substantiated by the testimony of its author and supporters. Consider only that Jefferson, with no known change of heart at all, said of *The Federalist* that it was "the best commentary on the principles of government which was ever written." Jefferson, it must be remembered, came firmly to recommend the adoption of the Constitution, his criticisms of it having come down only to a proposal for rotation in the Presidency and for the subsequent adoption of a bill of rights. I do not, of course, deny the peculiar character of "Jeffersonianism" nor the importance to many things of its proper understanding. I only state here that it is certain that Jefferson, unlike later historians, did not view the Constitution as a retrogression from democracy. Or further, consider that John Adams, now celebrated as America's great conservative, was so enthusiastic about Jefferson's draft of the Declaration as to wish on his own account that hardly a word be changed. And this same Adams, also without any change of heart and without complaint, accepted the Constitution as embodying many of his own views on government.

The idea that the Constitution was a falling back from the fuller democracy of the Declaration thus rests in part upon a false reading of the Declaration as free from the concerns regarding democracy that the framers of the Constitution felt. Perhaps only those would so read it who take for granted a perfect, self-subsisting harmony between consent (equality) and the proper aim of government (justice), or between consent and individual rights (liberty). This assumption was utterly foreign to the leading men of the Declaration.

II

The Declaration has wrongly been converted into, as it were, a super-democratic document; has the Constitution wrongly been converted in the modern view into an insufficiently democratic document? The only basis for depreciating the democratic character of the Constitution lies in its framers' apprehensive diagnosis of the "diseases," "defects" or "evil propensities" of democracy, and in their remedies. But if what the Founders considered to be defects *are* genuine defects, and if the remedies, without violating the principles of popular government, *are* genuine remedies, then it would be unreasonable to call the Founders anti- or quasi-democrats. Rather, they would be the wise partisans of democracy; a man is not a better democrat but only a foolish democrat if he ignores real defects inherent in popular government. Thus, the question becomes: are there natural defects to democracy and, if there are, what are the best remedies?

In part, the Founding Fathers answered this question by employing a traditional mode of political analysis. They believed there were several basic possible regimes, each having several possible forms. Of these possible regimes they believed the best, or at least the best for America, to be popular government, but only if purged of its defects. At any rate, an unpurged popular government they believed to be indefensible. They believed there were several forms of popular government, crucial among these direct democracy and republican— or representative—government (the latter perhaps divisible into two distinct forms, large and small republics). Their constitution and their defense of it constitute an argument for that form of popular government (large republic) in which the "evil propensities" would be weakest or most susceptible of remedy.

The whole of the thought of the Founding Fathers is intelligible and, especially, the evaluation of their claim to be wise partisans of popular government is possible, only if the words *"disease," "defect,"* and *"evil propensity"* are allowed their full force. Unlike modern "value-free" social scientists, the Founding Fathers believed that true knowledge of the good and bad in human conduct was possible, and that they themselves possessed sufficient knowledge to discern the really grave defects of popular government and their proper remedies. The modern relativistic or positivistic theories, implicitly employed by most commentators on the Founding Fathers, deny the possibility of such true knowledge and therefore deny that the Founding Fathers *could* have been actuated by knowledge of the good rather than by passion or interest. (I deliberately employ the language of *Federalist* No. 10. Madison defined faction, in part, as a group "united and actuated by . . . passion, or . . . interest." That is, factions are groups *not*—as presumably the authors of *The Federalist* were—actuated by reason.) How this modern view of the value problem supports the conception of the Constitution as less democratic than the Declaration is clear. The Founding Fathers did in fact seek to prejudice the outcome of democracy; they sought to alter, by certain restraints, the likelihood that the majority would decide certain political issues in bad ways. These restraints the Founders justified as mitigating the natural defects of democracy. But, say the moderns, there are no "bad" political decisions, wrong-in-themselves, from reaching which the majority ought to be restrained. Therefore, ultimately, nothing other than the specific interests of the Founders can explain their zeal in restraining democracy. And inasmuch as the restraints were typically placed on the many in the interest of the propertied, the departure of the Constitution is "anti-democratic" or "thermidorean." In short, according to this view, there cannot be what the Founders claimed to possess, "an *enlightened* view of the dangerous propensities against which [popular government] . . . ought to be guarded," the substantive goodness or badness of such propensities being a matter of opinion or taste on which reason can shed no light.

What are some of the arrangements which have been considered signs of "undemocratic" features of the Constitution? The process by which the Constitution may be amended is often cited in evidence. Everyone is familiar with the arithmetic which shows that a remarkably small minority could prevent passage of a constitutional amendment supported by an overwhelming majority of the people. That is, bare majorities in the thirteen least populous states could prevent passage of an amendment desired by overwhelming majorities in the thirty-six most populous states. But let us, for a reason to be made clear in a moment, turn that arithmetic around. Bare majorities in the thirty-seven least populous states can pass amendments against the opposition of overwhelming majorities in the twelve most populous states. And this would mean in actual votes today (and would have meant for the thirteen original states) constitutional amendment by a minority against the opposition of a majority of citizens. My point is simply that, while the amending procedure does involve qualified majorities, the qualification is not of the kind that requires an especially large numerical majority for action.

I suggest that the real aim and practical effect of the complicated amending procedure was not at all to give power to minorities, but to ensure that passage of an amendment would require a *nationally* distributed majority, though one that legally could consist of a bare numerical majority. It was only adventitious that the procedure has the theoretical possibility of a minority blocking (or passing) an amendment. The aim of requiring nationally distributed majorities was, I think, to ensure that no amendment could be passed simply with the support of the few states or sections sufficiently numerous to provide a bare majority. No doubt it was also believed that it would be difficult for such a national majority to form or become effective save for the decent purposes that could command national agreement, and this difficulty was surely deemed a great virtue of the amending process. This is what I think *The Federalist* really means when it praises the amending process and says that "it guards equally against that extreme facility, which would render the Constitution too mutable; and that extreme difficulty, which might perpetuate its discovered faults." All I wish to emphasize here is that the actual method adopted, with respect to the numerical size of majorities, is meant to leave all legal power in the hands of ordinary majorities so long as they are national majorities. The departure from simple majoritarianism is, at least, not in an oligarchic or aristocratic direction. In this crucial respect, the amending procedure does conform strictly to the principles of republican (popular) government.

Consider next the suffrage question. It has long been assumed as proof of an anti-democratic element in the Constitution that the Founding Fathers depended for the working of their Constitution upon a substantially limited franchise. Just as the Constitution allegedly was ratified by a highly qualified electorate, so too, it is held, was the new government to be based upon a suffrage subject to substantial property qualifications. This view has only recently been seriously challenged, especially by Robert E. Brown, whose detailed researches convince him that the property qualifications in nearly all the original states were probably so small as to exclude never more than twenty-five per cent, and in most cases as little as only five to ten per cent, of the adult white male population. That is, the property qualifications were not designed to exclude the mass of the poor but only the small proportion which lacked a concrete—however small—stake in society, *i.e.*, primarily the transients or "idlers."

The Constitution, of course, left the suffrage question to the decision of the individual states. What is the implication of that fact for deciding what sort of suffrage the Framers had in mind? The immediately popular branch of the national legislature was to be elected by voters who "shall have the qualifications requisite for electors of the most numerous branch of the State Legislature." The mode of election to the electoral college for the Presidency and to the Senate is also left to "be prescribed in each State by the legislature thereof." At a minimum, it may be stated that the Framers did not themselves attempt to reduce, or prevent the expansion of, the suffrage; that question was left wholly to the states—and these were, ironically, the very hotbeds of post-revolutionary democracy from the rule of which it is familiarly alleged that the Founders sought to escape.

In general, the conclusion seems inescapable that the states had a far broader suffrage than is ordinarily thought, and nothing in the actions of the Framers suggests any expectation or prospect of the reduction of the suffrage. Again, as in the question of the amending process, I suggest that the Constitution represented no departure whatsoever from the democratic standards of the Revolutionary period, or from any democratic standards then generally recognized.

What of the Senate? The organization of the Senate, its term of office and its staggered mode of replacement, its election by state legislatures rather than directly by the people, among other things, have been used to demonstrate the undemocratic character of the Senate as intended by the Framers. Was this not a device to represent property and not people, and was it not intended therefore to be a non-popular element in the government? I suggest, on the contrary, that the really important thing is that the Framers thought they had found a way to protect property *without* representing it. That the Founders intended the Senate to be one of the crucial devices for remedying the defects of democracy is certainly true. But *The Federalist* argues that the Senate, as actually proposed in the Constitution, was calculated to be such a device as would operate only in a way that "will consist . . . with the genuine principles of republican government." I believe that the claim is just.

Rather than viewing the Senate from the perspective of modern experience and opinions, consider how radically democratic the Senate appears when viewed from a pre-modern perspective. The model of a divided legislature that the Founders had most in mind was probably the English Parliament. There the House of Lords was thought to provide some of the beneficial checks upon the popular Commons which it was hoped the Senate would supply in the American Constitution. But the American Senate was to possess none of the qualities which permitted the House of Lords to fulfill its role; *i.e.,* its hereditary basis, or membership upon election by the Crown, or any of its other aristocratic characteristics. Yet the Founding Fathers knew that the advantages of having both a Senate and a House would "be in proportion to the dissimilarity in the genius of the two bodies." What is remarkable is that, in seeking to secure this dissimilarity, they did not in any respect go beyond the limits permitted by the "genuine principles of republican government."

Not only is this dramatically demonstrated in comparison with the English House of Lords, but also in comparison with all earlier theory regarding the division of the legislative power. The aim of such a division in earlier thought is to secure a balance between the aristocratic and democratic elements of a polity. This is connected with the pre-modern preference for a *mixed* republic, which was rejected by the Founders in favor of a *democratic* republic. And the traditional way to secure this balance or mixture was to give one house or office to the suffrages of the few and one to the suffrages of the many. Nothing of the kind is involved in the American Senate. Indeed, on this issue, so often cited as evidence of the Founders' undemocratic predilections, the very opposite is the case. The Senate is a constitutional device which *par excellence* reveals the strategy of the Founders. They wanted something like the advantages earlier thinkers had seen in a mixed legislative power, but they thought this was possible (and perhaps preferable) without any introduction whatsoever of aristocratic power into their system. What pre-modern thought had seen in an aristocratic senate—wisdom, nobility, manners, religion, etc.— the Founding Fathers converted into stability, enlightened self-interest, a "temperate and respectable body of citizens." The qualities of a senate having thus been altered (involving perhaps comparable changes in the notion of the ends of government), it became possible to secure these advantages through a Senate based wholly upon popular principles. Or so I would characterize a Senate whose membership required no property qualification and which was appointed (or elected in the manner prescribed) by State legislatures which, in their own turn, were elected annually or biennially by a nearly universal manhood suffrage.

The great claim of *The Federalist* is that the Constitution represents the fulfillment of a truly novel experiment, of "a revolution which has no parallel in the annals of society," and which is decisive for the happiness of "the whole human race." And the novelty, I argue, consisted in solving the problems of popular government by means which yet maintain the government "wholly popular." In defending that claim against the idea of the Constitution as a retreat from democracy I have dealt thus far only with the easier task: the demonstration that the constitutional devices and arrangements do not derogate from the legal power of majorities to rule. What remains is to examine the claim that the Constitution did in fact remedy the natural defects of democracy. Before any effort is made in this direction, it may be useful to summarize some of the implications and possible utility of the analysis thus far.

Above all, the merit of the suggestions I have made, if they are accurate in describing the intention and action of the Founders, is that it makes the Founders available to us for the study of modern problems. I have tried to restore to them their *bona fides* as partisans of democracy. This done, we may take seriously the question whether they were, as they claimed to be, wise partisans of democracy or popular government. If they were partisans of democracy and if the regime they created was decisively democratic, then they speak to us not merely about bygone problems, not from a viewpoint—in this regard—radically different from our own, but as men addressing themselves to problems identical in principle with our own. They are a source from within our own heritage which teaches us the way to put the question to democracy, a way which is rejected by certain prevailing modern ideas. But we cannot avail ourselves of their assistance if we consider American history to be a succession of democratizations which overcame the Founding Fathers' intentions. On that view it is easy to regard them as simply outmoded. If I am right regarding the extent of democracy in their thought and regime, then they are not outmoded by modern events but rather are tested by them. American history, on this view, is not primarily the replacement of a pre-democratic regime by a democratic regime, but is rather a continuing testimony to how the Founding Fathers' democratic regime has worked out in modern circumstances. The whole of our national experience thus becomes a way of judging the Founders' principles, of judging democracy itself, or of pondering the flaws of democracy and the means to its improvement.

POINTS TO PONDER

1. In a democracy the majority rules. What limits to majority rule did the Framers build into the Constitution?
2. According to Diamond, how could the Framers be viewed as democrats —that is, in favor of rule by the people—despite the limits to majority rule?
3. How does Diamond's view of the Framers differ from that of Charles Beard? How does it differ from John Roche's?

5

"THE GAP: THE AMERICAN CREED VERSUS POLITICAL AUTHORITY"
Samuel Huntington

The political values of Americans vary widely, but scholar Samuel Huntington argues that there exists a central "American Creed," and that it can be summarized as an "antipower ethic." The creed embraces the values of equality, liberty, individualism, constitutionalism, and democracy. The problem is that these values are often mutually exclusive and each of them presents tensions with governmental power.

In the following selection from his book American Politics: The Promise of Disharmony *(1981), Samuel Huntington shows how the separate values of the American creed undercut the legitimacy of governmental authority. He emphasizes the hostility of American political thought to the legitimacy of a powerful central government or "the state" in European thought and tradition.*

Huntington concludes by showing how American political values inevitably lead to a contradiction between our political ideals and our governmental institutions (the IvI gap). Awareness of this gap between our ideals and the reality of American politics helps us understand the origins of political conflict among Americans who espouse similar values. According to Huntington, the gap promises disharmony but also the potential for progress.

Consensus and Instability

Studies of American politics often point to the widespread consensus on the basic elements of the American Creed as evidence of the stability of the American political system. The assumption is that consensus on values translates into support for institutions. It is, indeed, frequently assumed that the stability of a democracy is particularly dependent upon the existence of a broad agreement on democratic values; democracy cannot work if a substantial portion of the public is basically opposed to it and supports authoritarian movements to the left, right, or center. Deeply felt class divisions over the proper sources of political authority, church-state relations, or the role of the state in the economy clearly can give rise to major instabilities in a democratic political system. When people think about instability, they typically have in mind this cleavage-based instability, and they tend to believe that anything that moderates the polarization, develops cross-cutting cleavages, or furnishes a basis for consensus will also contribute to greater political stability. And in a deeply polarized society, such measures may well enhance stability.

From this analysis, however, it is often implied that because dissension means instability, consensus therefore enhances stability. If people agree on democratic values, the successful functioning of democratic institutions is more or less assured. In fact, this is not necessarily the case. Just as there is an instability that follows from an excess of cleavage, so also there is an instability that follows from an excess of consensus. In comparison with Europe, the United States has had relatively little class warfare and ideological conflict. But it has had its own forms of political instability, which have in large part been rooted in the content of the American political consensus.

Whether or not a consensus on political values contributes to political stability depends on the nature of those values and the relation between them and the political institutions and practices in the society. If the prevailing political values legitimize and sanctify those institutions and practices, they enhance political stability. It is, however, quite conceivable that the core ideals and values of the consensus may provide a basis for challenging the legitimacy of the dominant political institutions and practices. This is precisely the case in the United States, and it is a phenomenon that is characteristic of politics in the United States as of that of no other major society.

The widespread consensus on liberal-democratic values provides the basis for challenging the legitimacy of American political practices and the authority of American political institutions. The consensus constitutes an external standard for judging institutions, and often for judging them harshly. Political institutions and practices never measure up to the ideals and values of the Creed, and hence can be seen as illegitimate. The extent to which this challenge manifests itself overtly depends on the way in which people perceive those institutions and practices. At times, people can look at politics as it is practiced in the United States and be blind to any divergence of this practice from the ideals of the American Creed. At other times, people may also perceive a vast gap between politics as it is in practice and politics as it should be according to the norms of the American Creed. Intense awareness of this gap becomes a driving force for reformation of the political system. These efforts to bring political reality into accord with political principle are the major source of political change in America.

Cleavage in the United States thus does not take the form of idea versus idea, as in Europe, but rather of idea versus fact. The conflict is between two groups who believe in the same political principles: those who find it in their interest to change existing institutions immediately so as to make them comply with those principles, and those who accept the validity of the principles but who perceive existing institutions as being in accord with the principles insofar as this is feasible. Other societies may be more divided than the United States along class lines and over conflicting Weltanschauungs, but it is the peculiar fate of Americans that the beliefs that unite them as a nation should also divide them as a people. The same Creed that is the source of national identity is also the source of political instability. Conflict is the child of consensus, and the most passionate and traumatic controversies among Americans derive from the liberal-democratic values on which they so overwhelmingly agree.

The Antipower Ethic

The basic ideas of the American Creed—equality, liberty, individualism, constitutionalism, democracy—clearly do not constitute a systematic ideology, and they do not necessarily have any logical consistency. At some point, liberty and equality may clash, individualism may run counter to constitutionalism, and democracy or majority rule may infringe on both. Precisely because it is not an intellectualized ideology, the American Creed can live with such inconsistencies.

Logically inconsistent as they seem to philosophers, these ideas do have a single common thrust and import for the relations between society and government: all the varying elements in the American Creed unite in imposing limits on power and on the institutions of government. The essence of constitutionalism is the restraint of governmental power through fundamental law. The essence of liberalism is freedom from governmental control—the vindication of liberty against power, as Bernard Bailyn summed up the argument for the American Revolution. The essence of individualism is the right of each person to act in accordance with his own conscience and to control his own destiny free of external restraint, except insofar as such restraint is necessary to ensure comparable rights to others. The essence of egalitarianism is rejection of the idea that one person has the right to exercise power over another. The essence of democracy is popular control over government, directly or through representatives, and the responsiveness of governmental officials to public opinion. In sum, the distinctive aspect of the American Creed is its antigovernment character. Opposition to power, and suspicion of government as the most dangerous embodiment of power, are the central themes of American political thought.

When major inequalities in wealth emerged in the latter part of the nineteenth century, Americans developed a "gospel of wealth" to legitimate them. Great wealth was the reward for great effort, great merit, great risks. They continued to believe that gospel well into the twentieth century. In contrast, Americans have never developed a justification for major inequalities of power. Thus, while Americans may have a gospel of wealth, they have never had—and, in the nature of things, cannot have—a gospel of power. Instead, they have a pervasive antipower ethic.

"If there is one message I have gotten from the Pentagon Papers," Daniel Ellsberg told a cheering crowd of MIT students in the fall of 1971, "it is to distrust authority, distrust the President, distrust the men in power, because power does corrupt, even in America." If there were any who did not get the message from the Pentagon Papers, they almost surely did shortly thereafter from the Watergate tapes. It is an old message, a refrain continually repeated through more than two hundred years of American history. The "first Americans," Charles Hendel argued, "still regarded authority with a jealous eye, wary and fearful of it in any guise. This general attitude became an ingrained habit of American character" and flowered into "an uncritical general philosophy unfavorable to authority in any form. . . . The free, responsible, self-governing individual is thought of as self-sufficient."

During the Revolutionary years, this attitude manifested itself in the contraposition of liberty and power. In Europe, as James Madison said, power granted charters to liberty; in America, liberty granted charters to power. The Jacksonians gave renewed emphasis to the dichotomy: the issue, John C. Calhoun said in 1826, was "between power and liberty." More explicitly, government itself, even democratic government, was a threat to liberty. "It is under the word *government*," declared the leading Jacksonian journal, "that the subtle danger lurks. Understood as a central consolidated power, managing and directing the various general interests of the society, all government is evil, and the parent of evil."

The opposition to power and government remained characteristic of the American outlook in the twentieth century. "For as long as polls have been taken, when Americans have been asked about their attitudes toward government *in the abstract*, the attitudes expressed have been preponderantly negative." Compared to other peoples, Americans have relatively high trust in each other, but a much lower trust in government. The American tradition involves "high amounts of community and regime trust together with limited amounts of authority trust. . . . The lack of trust mentioned by Dickens, and especially by Bryce, relates to the political authorities and not to the regime and community levels."

* * * *

Americans have tended to interpret those two potentially conflicting values of the American Creed—equality and social mobility—in such as way as to be compatible with opposition to authority. In a variety of ways, Cora Du Bois has pointed out, the "American hostility to figures in authority" has operated "to play down status differences" and to produce an informality and familiarity in manners or, in Bryce's term, "equality of estimation." Success is valued, but some forms of success, particularly those that do not involve hierarchical authority relationships, are valued considerably more than others. "Upward mobility is valued as successful activity, but when it reaches a point where it outstrips the premise of equality and the focal value of conformity it borders on *hubris*. . . . It is the boss, the politician, the teacher, the 'big shots' who are disvalued figures to the extent that their superordinate position implies authority. It is the movie star and the baseball hero who are valued figures since their pre-eminence connotes no authority but at the same time dramatizes the meteoric rise to fame and popularity through hard work and youthful striving." Winning the race against others is good; exercising power over others is bad. Americans may praise famous men but they do not celebrate powerful ones. Similarly, the man who does achieve, the "self-made man" (itself an American term), "likes to boast of his achievement, to exaggerate the obscurity of his origin, and to point out the 'Horatio Alger' quality of his career." In Europe, on the other hand, the upwardly mobile person more "often prefers to forget his origins if they are in a lower class."

Antipathy to power produces ambivalence toward wealth. "Equality" in American thinking has rarely been interpreted as economic equality in terms of wealth and income, but rather as equality of opportunity. Major social innovations such as free, universal, compulsory public education have been justified in large part by this value. Economic inequalities are legitimate insofar as they are the result of talent, work, achievement. Great wealth also becomes legitimate when it is used for socially beneficent purposes. The American tradition of philanthropy, unique in the world, is the tribute that illiberal concentrations of wealth pay to the norms of a liberal society. More generally, money becomes evil not when it is used to buy goods but when it is used to buy power. Large accumulations of wealth are acceptable until they are transformed into monopolies and trusts, which exercise economic power by dominating the marketplace. The American antitrust mania, unique among industrialized societies, focuses precisely on the point at which wealth becomes power. Similarly, economic inequalities become evil when they are translated into political inequalities. As a result, considerable effort has been invested over the years to exposing and regulating lobbying and political contributions. This outlook also manifests itself in the ambivalent American attitude toward "bigness." In objects it is good; in organizations—which involve the structuring of power—it is bad. Big buildings, big automobiles, big wealth in the sense of individual wealth, have historically been viewed favorably. Big business, big labor, and, most particularly, big government have been viewed unfavorably.

The IvI Gap

In his classic study of race relations in the United States, Gunnar Myrdal brilliantly pinpointed "an American dilemma" that existed between the deep beliefs in the concepts of liberty, equality, and individualism of the American Creed and the actual treatment of black people in American society. He probed, however, only one manifestation (albeit the most dramatic one) of the widespread gap between American political ideals and institutions—referred to here as "the IvI gap." What he termed "an" American dilemma is really "the" American dilemma, the central agony of American politics.

American liberal and democratic ideas form a standing and powerful indictment of almost all political institutions, including American ones. No government can exist without some measure of hierarchy, inequality, arbitrary power, secrecy, deception, and established patterns of superordination and subordination. The American Creed, however, challenges the legitimacy of all these characteristics of government. Its ideas run counter to the nature of government in general. They run counter to the nature of highly bureaucratized and centralized modern government. They run counter to both the original and inherited nature of American government.

Therein lies the dilemma. In the United States, government is legitimate to the extent to which it reflects the basic principles of the American Creed. Government can never, however, reflect those principles perfectly, and it is therefore illegitimate to the extent to which people take seriously the principles of the American Creed. If people try to make government more legitimate by bringing political practice more into accord with political principle, they will weaken government rather than strengthen it. Because of the inherently antigovernment character of the American Creed, government that is strong is illegitimate, government that is legitimate is weak.

In practice, in comparison with European societies, government has always been weak in America. This weakness originally was the product of the fact that no need existed in the United States to centralize power and establish a strong government in order to overthrow feudalism. In this sense, as Tocqueville pointed out, Americans "arrived at a state of democracy without having to endure a democratic revolution and . . . are born equal instead of becoming so." The absence of feudalism thus eliminated a major negative impetus to strong government. The presence in its place of a pervasive consensus on liberal and democratic values furnished an additional, positive incentive to limit government. In the absence of a consensus, strong government would have been necessary; as Hartz pointed out, it is only because the images that the framers of the Constitution had of American society were erroneous that the system of divided and checked government that they created was able to last. The fact of consensus thus made possible weak political institutions. The content of the consensus reinforced the weakness of those institutions.

Strong government has historically emerged in response to the need either to destroy a traditional society or to fight against foreign enemies. In the seventeenth-century era of state-building in Europe, absolute monarchs engaged in both activities simultaneously and unremittingly. From the start, the United States was spared the need to do the first, and shortly after its birth it was spared the need to do the second in any serious way until well into the twentieth century. The United States was able to maintain national independence and national security without having to create a strong apparatus. When this situation seemed to change in the 1940s and 1950s, many of the instrumentalities of a strong state machinery were created. This development took place, however, only because Americans at that time were relatively unconcerned about realizing their political values in their domestic political practice, however much they might have been concerned about protecting those institutions from foreign threats. In the 1960s, when Americans became concerned about the gap between their political ideals and their political institutions, they began to eviscerate the political and governmental institutions that had been developed to deal with foreign enemies.

* * * *

The continued existence of the United States means that Americans will continue to suffer from cognitive dissonance. They will continue to attempt to come to terms with that dissonance through some combination of moralism, cynicism, complacency, and hypocrisy. The greatest danger to the IvI gap would come when any substantial portion of the American population carried to an extreme any one of these responses. An excess of moralism, hypocrisy, cynicism, or complacency could do in the American system. A totally complacent toleration of the IvI gap could lead to the corruption and decay of American liberal-democratic institutions. Uncritical hypocrisy, blind to the existence of the gap and fervent in its commitment to American principles, could lead to imperialistic expansion, ending in either military or political disaster abroad or the undermining of democracy at home. Cynical acceptance of the gap could lead to a gradual abandonment of American ideals and their replacement either by a Thrasymachusian might-makes-right morality or by some other set of political beliefs. Finally, intense moralism could lead Americans to destroy the freest institutions on earth because they believed they deserved something better.

To maintain their ideals and institutions, Americans have no recourse but to temper and balance their responses to the IvI gap. The threats to the future of the American condition can be reduced to the extent that Americans:

—continue to believe in their liberal, democratic, and individualistic ideals and also recognize the extent to which their institutions and behavior fall short of these ideals;

—feel guilty about the existence of the gap but take comfort from the fact that American political institutions are more liberal and democratic than those of any other human society past or present;

—attempt to reduce the gap between institutions and ideals but accept the fact that the imperfections of human nature mean the gap can never be eliminated;

—believe in the universal validity of American ideals but also understand their limited applicability to other societies; and

—support the maintenance of American power necessary to protect and promote liberal ideals and institutions in the world arena, but recognize the dangers such power could pose to liberal ideals and institutions at home.

Critics say that America is a lie because its reality falls so far short of its ideals. They are wrong. America is not a lie; it is a disappointment. But it can be a disappointment only because it is also a hope.

POINTS TO PONDER

1. According to Huntington, what are the main values of Americans?
2. How do these values come into conflict in the Constitution?
3. How do these values come into conflict in contemporary times?
4. Is this tension (or contradiction) between our basic values and the reality of our political institutions, which often do not measure up to our ideals, good or bad for the polity?

Chapter 2

❦

FEDERALISM

Contemporary governments in the world can be divided between those that are unitary and those that are federal in structure. In a unitary state all local subdivisions are legally dependent upon the central government. In a federal system local governments have a certain amount of authority independent of the central government (for example, revenue-raising authority or administrative control). In the United States that independence is guaranteed by the constitutional status of the states. Local governments are creatures of state governments.

The tension between the federal government and the states has continued to be a major factor in American politics. As the articles in this section make clear, the federal government has won its major policy battles with the states over the past two centuries. But state governments continue to be dynamic and important components of our federal system of governance.

Federal and State Powers Under the Articles of Confederation

When the Framers met in Philadelphia in 1787 one of their major tasks was to deal with the problems caused by the lack of power of the central government under the Articles of Confederation. Under the Articles the states were sovereign and could not be compelled to contribute money to the central government. In exercising their sovereign powers, states levied tariffs against goods from neighboring states and in other ways discriminated in commerce in favor of local merchants at the expense of out-of-state purveyors of goods and services. In addition, the national government did not have the full power to finance and maintain an army and navy or the authority and unity to deal effectively with foreign nations.

Thus the Framers knew they had to create a more powerful central government, but in doing so they had to persuade the states to cede part of their sovereignty to the new national government. This was not an easy task, and the states had to be convinced that their independence would not be completely subsumed under a new national government. The basic governance issue of the division of power between the formerly sovereign states and the new national government was crucial. Settling this issue to the satisfaction of the states was a condition for ratification of the Constitution.

The Framers proposed that the new government would not be a unitary government, as were European states, in which the constituent governments were completely dependent on the central government for their existence, financing, and operation. Nor would it be a confederation of sovereign states as existed at the time of the constitutional convention. It would be, rather, a mixed system of shared sovereignty in which both levels of government (national and state) would act directly on citizens. In addition, elected officials at both levels (House of Representatives, governors, state legislators) would be directly elected by citizens.

To assure the states that their sovereignty would not be eliminated, the Constitution enumerated the powers of the central government in Article I, and provided in the Tenth Amendment that all powers not delegated were reserved to the states or the people. It guaranteed each state a republican form of government, two senators, and at least one representative. In addition, it was understood that most direct functions of government, including the administration of voting, would be controlled and carried out by the states and their subunits (cities, counties, and so on).

Movement Toward Increased Centralization

Despite the formal guarantees of state sovereignty and the reassurance of the Framers, the social and economic development of the United States as well as laws and Supreme Court decisions have led to a national government that can assert national priorities and reach into virtually every area of public policy. In a landmark case, *McCulloch v. Maryland* (1819), the Supreme Court established national supremacy by ruling that the national government had the authority to create a bank and that states did not have the power to tax it. In his opinion Chief Justice John Marshall argued that even though the power to charter a bank was not enumerated in the Constitution, the national government had the "implied" power because of the "necessary and proper" clause of the Constitution. The decision also confirmed the constitutional principle that national laws would be superior to the laws of the states.

Industrialization

Given the developments of the twentieth century and the demands of a modern industrial economy, it is not surprising that the United States has become more centralized. Two world wars and the Great Depression led to the national government playing a much more active role in the economy. Technological transformations in travel, communications, and industry have led to an integration of our society much greater than the Framers ever dreamed.

The growth of large corporations with considerable economic power and branches in many states spurred the creation of independent regulatory agencies at the national level. Individual states are clearly not capable of regulating industries, such as radio and television broadcast networks, that need uniform national standards.

In the mid-twentieth century the interstate highway system was developed, primarily with federal money and according to national standards. The leverage of federal highway funds was used in the 1980s to enforce a uniform minimum drinking age of 21 throughout the fifty states.

With increased industrialization came the significant costs of pollution. The polluting consequences of large-scale industrial activity could not be contained within state boundaries. Responding to political pressure, Congress moved to limit the consequences of pollution with the Clean Air Act of 1970 and the Water Pollution Control Act of 1972.

Although pollution control laws were federal, state and local governments would implement them by building water pollution abatement plants with federal funds and enforcing air pollution standards at the local level. There has been considerable conflict between states and the federal government over the financing and enforcement of these pollution laws.

Federal Programs

The second half of the twentieth century brought a plethora of federal programs (over five hundred) to help state and local governments. At its peak in 1978, federal financing of these programs reached 20 percent of state and local expenditures. Liberals in the Democratic party sought to assure that the disadvantaged were afforded a better chance to achieve the American dream. The laws of the Great Society and the War on Poverty established federal programs in health, education, welfare, and housing that were intended to bring the benefits of an affluent society to all its citizens.

The significance and scope of these expanding programs were indicated by the creation of new cabinet departments to administer them. The Department of Housing and Urban Development was created in 1965 to administer federal aid for housing for the poor and the financing of programs for home ownership. The Department of Health, Education, and Welfare (1953) was split in 1980 into the Department of Health and Human Services and the Department of Education. The Department of Transportation (1966) promoted and regulated the air, water, and land transportation industries throughout the country. Departmental status for these policy areas indicated an increasing federal presence in what used to be primarily local government functions.

Legislation and Supreme Court Rulings

Liberal Democrats sought to use the power of the federal government to mitigate the evils of racism and segregation. Buttressed by Supreme Court decisions, federal policies and programs invaded many areas traditionally controlled by state and local governments and defeated the argument of states' rights used by their opponents. The seminal Supreme Court case in the area of civil rights was *Brown v. Board of Education* (1954), which declared that racially segregated schools were inherently unequal and commanded the integration of the nation's schools. The *Brown* decision and subsequent Court rulings along with laws have had a major impact on federalism in the United States.

Although school systems are locally financed and administered, they are now held to federal standards for racial integration. Legislation, such as the Civil Rights Act of 1964 and the Equal Employment Opportunity Act of 1972, further expanded the role of the federal government in racial integration. President Eisenhower in 1957 and President Kennedy in 1962 sent federal troops to enforce federal policy on the integration of schools.

Supreme Court rulings have also had a major impact on law enforcement at the local level. Through the application of the Bill of Rights to the states through the Fourteenth Amendment, the right to legal representation in criminal cases was established in *Gideon v. Wainright* (1963). The right to be warned of one's constitutional right to remain silent under police interrogation was established in *Miranda v. Arizona* (1966).

Mapp v. Ohio (1961) applied to the states the federal rule that evidence improperly obtained could not be used in criminal trials. These federal standards of criminal procedure produced a revolution in local law enforcement throughout the United States.

The Politics of Federalism

The Republican party in general has provided a counterweight to the centralizing policy preferences of the Democrats in the mid-twentieth century. Republican arguments have been that state governments are closer to the people and to local conditions and that central government programs tend to be too bureaucratized and wasteful. Thus President Eisenhower pulled back from some of the active social policies of the New Deal, and President Nixon pursued a "New Federalism" that would return programs and resources to the states.

One argument for increasing federal aid was that the national (or federal) government was better equipped in terms of resources (money) and trained personnel than were most states and thus had the capacity to provide programs that some states lacked. But by the peak of federal activism (in terms of programs and financial aid to state and local governments) in the 1970s, the states had made great progress in their capacity to govern themselves and administer complex social programs. Most state legislators earned professional salaries, met throughout the year, and were served by professional staffs. Most governors served four-year terms, could succeed themselves, and could appoint most state executive branch officials. Most states levied both an income tax and a state sales tax to support programs and a professional civil service to carry them out. Thus most states had the capacity to pursue their public policy goals.

But when President Reagan sought sweeping changes in existing federal fiscal relationships by "swapping" state and federal programs to more clearly divide national and state functions and "devolve" many federal programs to the state level, his hopes were dashed on the realities of contemporary fiscal federalism. States found that the demand by their citizens for active governmental programs in most areas of economic and social policy precluded their easy abolishment, and the temptation of federal money to carry out the popular programs was too great to resist.

Thus, despite the improved capacity of state and local governments and the vague desire to "straighten out" the separate jurisdictions of the state and federal governments, the political reality of the late twentieth century is that the balance of public policy control will remain with the federal government. Certainly the administration of such traditionally local functions as education, police and fire protection, local business regulation, and public roads will be carried out primarily by state and local governments. But no significant area of public policy will remain untouched by the national government in Washington.

The Readings

From the arguments over ratification of the Constitution onward there has been tension between the jurisdiction of the federal government on the one hand and that of state and local governments on the other. The following readings trace this tension from the ratification debates to the practical intermingling of functions among all three levels of government. But when there is a conflict between national and local priorities in important areas, such as civil liberties or the rights of the accused, national priorities most often prevail.

In *Federalist* No. 39, James Madison argued that the new Constitution would create a mixed system rather than a completely national government or a confederation of sovereign states. He pointed out that the national government would be supreme in a number of ways, but that the new government would be dependent on the states in its creation (ratification of the Constitution), in the selection of Senators by state legislatures, and in the selection of the president through the electoral college.

At one level our federal system can be understood as "dual," with the national government acting in its sphere and the state governments controlling local policy-making (for example, in education, health, and welfare). But, as pointed out by Morton Grodzins in his article, there has always been an "inseparable mingling of policy making among the levels of government—federal, state, and local." Despite sincere intentions to straighten out the system by cleanly dividing and separating the functions of the national

and state governments, none of the many proposals has ever been implemented. Instead, Grodzins argues, the United States has both suffered and benefited
from "decentralization by mild chaos."

Political factors have also contributed to the emergence of the national
government as supreme. As scholar James Sundquist lays out in his article in
this section, the independence of state government has been broken down by
the Civil War Amendments (Thirteenth, Fourteenth, and Fifteenth) to the
Constitution and the laws and regulations designed to assure the civil rights of
African Americans. The reach of national laws has been extended to all areas
of commerce, from antitrust to child labor to the hiring and firing of workers.
Fiscal federalism has been brought to bear on virtually all areas of local public
policy through the provision of federal money and the requirements that enforce compliance with national priorities.

KEY TERMS

direct democracy: a government actually conducted by the citizens, possible
only in a very small polity, not large nation-states

republic: a government conducted by elected representatives of the people
rather than by citizens directly

federalism: a system of governance in which constituent governments retain
some powers and rights not exercised by the central government

Tenth Amendment: final item in the Bill of Rights that provides that all
powers not delegated to the national government by the Constitution nor prohibited to the states are reserved to the states or to the people

6

FEDERALIST NO. 39
James Madison

In Federalist No. 39 *James Madison defines a republic as a government that derives its
powers from the people and whose officeholders are limited in their terms. The Republic
of the United States was to have a mixed national and federal form. It would be federal
in that conventions in the states would have to ratify the Constitution, the Senate would
represent individual states, and the president would be selected by electors chosen by
states. The House of Representatives, on the other hand, would be elected directly by the
people and would thus be a national rather than a federal institution. The jurisdiction of
the central government, while being limited, would extend throughout the country to
reach citizens as individuals and thus be national. Madison was trying to assure his*

fellow citizens that the new Constitution would not create a central government that would usurp all the powers of the states.

To the People of the State of New York:

The last paper having concluded the observations which were meant to introduce a candid survey of the plan of government reported by the convention, we now proceed to the execution of that part of our undertaking.

The first question that offers itself is, whether the general form and aspect of the government be strictly republican. It is evident that no other form would be reconcilable with the genius of the people of America; with the fundamental principles of the Revolution; or with that honorable determination which animates every votary of freedom, to rest all our political experiments on the capacity of mankind for self-government. If the plan of the convention, therefore, be found to depart from the republican character, its advocates must abandon it as no longer defensible.

What, then, are the distinctive characters of the republican form? Were an answer to this question to be sought, not by recurring to principles, but in the application of the term by political writers, to the constitutions of different States, no satisfactory one would ever be found. Holland, in which no particle of the supreme authority is derived from the people, has passed almost universally under the denomination of a republic. The same title has been bestowed on Venice, where absolute power over the great body of the people is exercised, in the most absolute manner, by a small body of hereditary nobles. Poland, which is a mixture of aristocracy and of monarchy in their worst forms, has been dignified with the same appellation. The government of England, which has one republican branch only, combined with an hereditary aristocracy and monarchy, has, with equal impropriety, been frequently placed on the list of republics. These examples, which are nearly as dissimilar to each other as to a genuine republic, show the extreme inaccuracy with which the term has been used in political disquisitions.

If we resort for a criterion to the different principles on which different forms of government are established, we may define a republic to be, or at least may bestow that name on, a government which derives all its powers directly or indirectly from the great body of the people, and is administered by persons holding their offices during pleasure, for a limited period, or during good behavior. It is *essential* to such a government that it be derived from the great body of the society, not from an inconsiderable proportion, or a favored class of it: otherwise a handful of tyrannical nobles, exercising their oppressions by a delegation of their powers, might aspire to the rank of republicans, and claim for their government that the persons administering it be appointed, either directly or indirectly, by the people; and that they hold their appointments by either of the tenures just specified; otherwise every government in the United

States, as well as every other popular government that has been or can be well organized or well executed, would be degraded from the republican character. According to the Constitution of every State in the Union, some one or other of the officers of government are appointed indirectly only by the people. According to most of them, the chief magistrate himself is so appointed. And according to one, this mode of appointment is extended to one of the co-ordinate branches of the legislature. According to all the constitutions, also, the tenure of the highest offices is extended to a definite period, and in many instances, both within the legislative and executive departments, to a period of years. According to the provisions of most of the constitutions, again, as well as according to the most respectable and received opinions on the subject, the members of the judiciary department are to retain their offices by the firm tenure of good behavior.

On comparing the Constitution planned by the convention with the standard here fixed, we perceive at once that it is, in the most rigid sense, conformable to it. The House of Representatives, like that of one branch at least of all the State legislatures, is elected immediately by the great body of the people. The Senate, like the present Congress, and the Senate of Maryland, derives its appointment indirectly from the people. The President is indirectly derived from the choice of the people, according to the example in most of the States. Even the judges, with all other officers of the Union, will, as in the several States, be the choice, though a remote choice, of the people themselves. The duration of the appointments is equally conformable to the republican standard, and to the model of State constitutions. The House of Representatives is periodically elective, as in all the States; and for the period of two years, as in the State of South Carolina. The Senate is elective, for the period of six years; which is but one year more than the period of the Senate of Maryland, and but two more than that of the Senates of New York and Virginia. The President is to continue in office for the period of four years; as in New York and Delaware the chief magistrate is elected for three years, and in South Carolina for two years. In the other States the election is annual. In several of the States, however, no constitutional provision is made for the impeachment of the chief magistrate. And in Delaware and Virginia he is not impeachable till out of office. The President of the United States is impeachable at any time during his continuance in office. The tenure by which the judges are to hold their places is, as it unquestionably ought to be, that of good behavior. The tenure of the ministerial offices generally will be a subject of legal regulation, conformably to the reason of the case and the example of the State constitutions.

Could any further proof be required of the republican complexion of this system, the most decisive one might be found in its absolute prohibition of titles of nobility, both under the federal and the State governments; and in its express guarantee of the republican form to each of the latter.

"But it was not sufficient," say the adversaries of the proposed Constitution, "for the convention to adhere to the republican form. They ought, with equal care, to have preserved the *federal* form, which regards the Union as a *Confederacy* of sovereign states; instead of which, they have framed a *national* government, which regards the Union as a *consolidation* of the States." And it is asked by what authority this bold and radical innovation was undertaken? The handle which has been made of this objection requires that it should be examined with some precision.

Without inquiring into the accuracy of the distinction on which the objection is founded, it will be necessary to a just estimate of its force, first, to ascertain the real character of the government in question; secondly, to inquire how far the convention were authorized to propose such a government; and thirdly, how far the duty they owed their country could supply any defect of regular authority.

First. — In order to ascertain the real character of the government, it may be considered in relation to the foundation on which it is to be established; to the sources from which its ordinary powers are to be drawn; to the operation of those powers; to the extent of them; and to the authority by which future changes in the government are to be introduced.

On examining the first relation, it appears, on one hand, that the Constitution is to be founded on the assent and ratification of the people of America, given by deputies elected for the special purpose; but, on the other, that this assent and ratification is to be given by the people, not as individuals composing one entire nation, but as composing the distinct and independent States to which they respectively belong. It is to be the assent and ratification of the several States, derived from the supreme authority in each State, — the authority of the people themselves. The act, therefore, establishing the Constitution, will not be a *national*, but a *federal* act.

That it will be a federal and not a national act, as these terms are understood by the objectors; the act of the people, as forming so many independent States, not as forming one aggregate nation, is obvious from this single consideration, that it is to result neither from the decision of a *majority* of the people of the Union, nor from that of a *majority* of the States. It must result from the *unanimous* assent of the several States that are parties to it, differing no otherwise from their ordinary assent than in its being expressed, not by the legislative authority, but by that of the people themselves. Were the people regarded in this transaction as forming one nation, the will of the majority of the whole people of the United States would bind the minority, in the same manner as the majority in each State must bind the minority; and the will of the majority must be determined either by a comparison of the individual votes, or by considering the will of the majority of the States as evidence of the will of a majority of the people of the United States. Neither of these rules has been adopted. Each State, in ratifying the Constitution, is considered as a sovereign body, independent of all others, and only to be bound by its own voluntary act. In this relation, then, the new Constitution will, if established, be a *federal*, and not a *national*, constitution.

The next relation is to the sources from which the ordinary powers of government are to be derived. The House of Representatives will derive its powers from the people of America; and the people will be represented in the same proportion, and on the same principle, as they are in the legislature of a particular State. So far the government is *national*, not *federal*. The Senate, on the other hand, will derive its powers from the States, as political and coequal societies; and these will be represented on the principle of equality in the Senate, as they now are in the existing Congress. So far the government is *federal*, not *national*. The executive power will be derived from a very compound source. The immediate election of the President is to be made by the States in their political characters. The votes allotted to them are in a compound ratio, which considers them partly as distinct and coequal societies, partly as unequal members of the same society. The eventual election, again, is to be made by that branch of the legislature which consists of the national representatives; but in this particular act they are to be thrown into the form of individual delegations, from so many distinct and coequal bodies politic. From this aspect of the government, it appears to be of a mixed character, presenting at least as many *federal* as *national* features.

The difference between a federal and national government, as it relates to the *operation of the government*, is supposed to consist in this, that in the former the powers operate on the political bodies composing the Confederacy, in their political capacities; in the latter, on the individual citizens composing the nation, in their individual capacities. On trying the Constitution by this criterion, it falls under the *national*, not the *federal* character; though perhaps not so completely as has been understood. In several cases, and particularly in the trial of controversies to which States may be parties, they must be viewed and proceeded against in their collective and political capacities only. So far the national countenance of the government on this side seems to be disfigured by a few federal features. But this blemish is perhaps unavoidable in any plan; and the operation of the government on the people, in their individual capacities, in its ordinary and most essential proceeding, may, on the whole, designate it, in this relation, a *national* government.

But if the government be national with regard to the *operation* of its powers, it changes its aspect again when we contemplate it in relation to the *extent* of its powers. The idea of a national government involves in it, not only an authority over the individual citizens, but an indefinite supremacy over all persons and things, so far as they are objects of lawful government. Among a people consolidated into one nation, this supremacy is completely vested in the national legislature. Among communities united for particular purposes, it is vested partly in the general and partly in the municipal legislatures. In the former case, all local authorities are subordinate to the supreme; and may be controlled, directed, or abolished by it at pleasure. In the latter, the local or municipal authorities form distinct and independent portions of the supremacy, no more subject, within their respective spheres, to the general authority than the general authority is subject to them within its own sphere. In this relation, then, the proposed government cannot be deemed a *national* one; since its jurisdiction extends to certain enumerated objects only, and leaves to the several States a residuary and inviolable sovereignty over all other objects. It is true that in controversies relating to the boundary between the two jurisdictions, the tribunal which is ultimately to decide, is to be established under the general government. But this does not change the principle of the case. The decision is to be impartially made, according to the rules of the Constitution; and all the usual and most effectual precautions are taken to secure this impartiality. Some such tribunal is clearly essential to prevent an appeal to the sword and a dissolution of the compact; and that it ought to be established under the general rather than under the local governments, or, to speak more properly, that it could be safely established under the first alone, is a position not likely to be combated.

If we try the Constitution by its last relation to the authority by which amendments are to be made, we find it neither wholly *national nor wholly federal.* Were it wholly national, the supreme and ultimate authority would reside in the *majority* of the people of the Union; and this authority would be competent at all times, like that of a majority of every national society, to alter, or abolish its established government. Were it wholly federal, on the other hand, the concurrence of each State in the Union would be essential to every alteration that would be binding on all. The mode provided by the plan of the convention is not founded on either of these principles. In requiring more than a majority, and particularly in computing the proportion by *States,* not by *citizens,* it departs from the *national* and advances towards the *federal* character; in rendering the concurrence of less than the whole number of States sufficient, it loses again the *federal* and partakes of the *national* character.

The proposed Constitution, therefore, is, in strictness, neither a national nor a federal Constitution, but a composition of both. In its foundation it is federal, not national; in the source from which the ordinary powers of the government are drawn, it is partly federal and partly national; in the operation of these powers, it is national, not federal; in the extent of them, again, it is federal, not national; and, finally, in the authoritative mode of introducing amendments, it is neither wholly federal nor wholly national.

Publius.

POINTS TO PONDER

1. According to Madison, in what ways was the ratification of the Constitution a *federal* act and in what ways was it a *national* act?
2. Distinguish between a unitary and a federal government.
3. In the light of two hundred years of experience with American federalism, evaluate Madison's assurances to the states.

7

"THE FEDERAL SYSTEM"
Morton Grodzins

Morton Grodzins, who was a political scientist at the University of Chicago, here argues that the simple idea of dual federalism, with national jurisdiction being cleanly divided from state government jurisdiction, is not merely out of date, it never existed. This argument was provocative when it was written in 1960, well before the great burst of fiscal federalism in the Great Society legislation of Lyndon Johnson. According to Grodzins in this excerpt from Goals for Americans, *the principle of American federalism has always been that the national government has access to greater fiscal resources (tax revenues) and thus finances a number of programs that are administered at the state and local levels. The lack of strong national political parties leads to a system that is open to political influence and thus very responsive to state and local pressures on national policy-making. We should not be surprised, then, that many national programs provide direct benefits and participation in their administration for state and local governments.*

Federalism is a device for dividing decisions and functions of government. As the constitutional fathers well understood, the federal structure is a means, not an end. The pages that follow are therefore not concerned with an exposition of American federalism as a formal, legal set of relationships. The focus, rather, is on the purpose of federalism, that is to say, on the distribution of power between central and peripheral units of government.

The Sharing of Functions

The American form of government is often, but erroneously, symbolized by a three-layer cake. A far more accurate image is the rainbow or marble cake, characterized by an inseparable mingling of differently colored ingredients, the colors appearing in vertical and diagonal strands and unexpected whirls. As colors are mixed in the marble cake, so functions are mixed in the American federal system. Consider the health officer, styled "sanitarian," of a rural county in a border state. He embodies the whole idea of the marble cake of government.

The sanitarian is appointed by the state under merit standards established by the federal government. His base salary comes jointly from state and federal funds, the county provides him with an office and office amenities and pays a portion of his expenses, and the largest city in the county also contributes to his salary and office by virtue of his appointment as a city plumbing inspector. It is impossible from moment to moment to tell under which governmental hat the sanitarian operates. His work of inspecting the purity of food is carried out under federal standards; but he is enforcing state laws when inspecting commodities that have not been in interstate commerce; and somewhat perversely he also acts under state authority when inspecting milk coming into the county from producing areas across the state border. He is a federal officer when impounding impure drugs shipped from a neighboring state; a federal-state officer when distributing typhoid immunization serum; a state officer when enforcing standards of industrial hygiene; a state-local officer when inspecting the city's water supply; and (to complete the circle) a local officer when insisting that the city butchers adopt more hygienic methods of handling their garbage. But he cannot and does not think of himself as acting in these separate capacities. All business in the county that concerns public health and sanitation he considers his business. Paid largely from federal funds, he does not find it strange to attend meetings of the city council to give expert advice on matters ranging from rotten apples to rabies control. He is even deputized as a member of both the city and county police forces.

The sanitarian is an extreme case, but he accurately represents an important aspect of the whole range of governmental activities in the United States. Functions are not neatly parceled out among the many governments. They are shared functions. It is difficult to find any governmental activity which does not involve all three of the so-called "levels" of the federal system. In the most local of local functions—law enforcement or education, for example—the federal and state governments play important roles. In what, *a priori*, may be considered the purest central government activities—the conduct of foreign affairs, for example—the state and local governments have considerable responsibilities, directly and indirectly.

The federal grant programs are only the most obvious example of shared functions. They also most clearly exhibit how sharing serves to disperse governmental powers. The grants utilize the greater wealth-gathering abilities of the central government and establish nation-wide standards, yet they are "in aid" of functions carried out under state law, with considerable state and local discretion. The national supervision of such programs is largely a process of mutual accommodation. Leading state and local officials, acting through their professional organizations, are in considerable part responsible for the very standards that national officers try to persuade all state and local officers to accept.

Even in the absence of joint financing, federal-state-local collaboration is the characteristic mode of action. Federal expertise is available to aid in the building of a local jail (which may later be used to house federal prisoners), to improve a local water purification system, to step up building inspections, to provide standards for state and local personnel in protecting housewives against dishonest butchers' scales, to prevent gas explosions, or to produce a land use plan. States and localities, on the other hand, take important formal responsibilities in the development of national programs for atomic energy, civil defense, the regulation of commerce, and the protection of purity in foods and drugs; local political weight is always a factor in the operation of even a post office or a military establishment. From abattoirs and accounting through zoning and zoo administration, any governmental activity is almost certain to involve the influence, if not the formal administration, of all three planes of the federal system.

Attempts to Unwind the Federal System

Within the past dozen years there have been four major attempts to reform or reorganize the federal system: the first (1947–49) and second (1953–55) Hoover Commissions on Executive Organization; the Kestnbaum Commission on Intergovernmental Relations (1953–55); and the Joint Federal-State Action Committee (1957–59). All four of these groups have aimed to minimize federal activities. None of them has recognized the sharing of functions as the characteristic way American governments do things. Even when making recommendations for joint action, these official commissions take the view (as expressed in the Kestnbaum report) that "the main tradition of American federalism [is] the tradition of separateness." All four have, in varying degrees, worked to separate functions and tax sources.

The history of the Joint Federal-State Action Committee is especially instructive. The committee was established at the suggestion of President Eisenhower, who charged it, first of all, "to designate functions which the States are ready and willing to assume and finance that are now performed or financed wholly or in part by the Federal Government." He also gave the committee the task of recommending "Federal and State revenue adjustments required to enable the States to assume such functions."*

The committee subsequently established seemed most favorably situated to accomplish the task of functional separation. It was composed of distinguished and able men, including among its personnel three leading members of the President's cabinet, the director of the Bureau of the Budget, and ten state governors. It had the full support of the President at every point, and it worked hard and conscientiously. Excellent staff studies were supplied by the Bureau of the Budget, the White House, the Treasury Department, and, from the state side, the Council of State Governments. It had available to it a large mass of research data, including the sixteen recently completed volumes of the Kestnbaum Commission. There existed no disagreements on party lines within the committee and, of course, no constitutional impediments to its mission. The President, his cabinet members, and all the governors (with one possible

---

* The President's third suggestion was that the committee "identify functions and responsibilities likely to require state or federal attention in the future and . . . recommend the level of state effort, or federal effort, or both, that will be needed to assure effective action." The committee initially devoted little attention to this problem. Upon discovering the difficulty of making separatist recommendations, i.e., for turning over federal functions and taxes to the states, it developed a series of proposals looking to greater effectiveness in intergovernmental collaboration. The committee was succeeded by a legislatively-based, 26-member Advisory Commission on Intergovernmental Relations, established September 29, 1959.

exception) on the committee completely agreed on the desirability of decen-tralization-via-separation-of-functions-and-taxes. They were unanimous in wanting to justify the committee's name and to produce action, not just another report.

The committee worked for more than two years. It found exactly two programs to recommend for transfer from federal to state hands. One was the federal grant program for vocational education (including practical-nurse training and aid to fishery trades); the other was federal grants for municipal waste treatment plants. The programs together cost the federal government less than $80 million in 1957, slightly more than two per cent of the total federal grants for that year. To allow the states to pay for these programs, the committee recommended that they be allowed a credit against the federal tax on local telephone calls. Calculations showed that this offset device, plus an equalizing factor, would give every state at least 40 per cent more from the tax than it received from the federal government in vocational education and sewage disposal grants. Some states were "equalized" to receive twice as much.

The recommendations were modest enough, and the generous financing feature seemed calculated to gain state support. The President recommended to Congress that all points of the program be legislated. None of them was, none has been since, and none is likely to be.

A Point of History

The American federal system has never been a system of separated governmental activities. There has never been a time when it was possible to put neat labels on discrete "federal," "state," and "local" functions. Even before the Constitution, a statute of 1785, reinforced by the Northwest Ordinance of 1787, gave grants-in-land to the states for public schools. Thus the national government was a prime force in making possible what is now taken to be the most local function of all, primary and secondary education. More important, the nation, before it was fully organized, established by this action a first principle of American federalism: the national government would use its superior resources to initiate and support national programs, principally administered by the states and localities.

The essential unity of state and federal financial systems was again recognized in the earliest constitutional days with the assumption by the federal government of the Revolutionary War debts of the states. Other points of federal-state collaboration during the Federalist period concerned the militia, law enforcement, court practices, the administration of elections, public health measures, pilot laws, and many other matters.

The nineteenth century is widely believed to have been the preeminent period of duality in the American system. Lord Bryce at the end of the century described (in *The American Commonwealth*) the federal and state governments as "distinct and separate in their action." The system, he said, was "like a great factory wherein two sets of machinery are at work, their revolving wheels apparently intermixed, their bands crossing one another, yet each set doing its own work without touching or hampering the other." Great works may contain gross errors. Bryce was wrong. The nineteenth century, like the early days of the republic, was a period principally characterized by intergovernmental collaboration.

Decisions of the Supreme Court are often cited as evidence of nineteenth century duality. In the early part of the century the Court, heavily weighted with Federalists, was intent upon enlarging the sphere of national authority; in the later years (and to the 1930's) its actions were in the direction of paring down national powers and indeed all governmental authority. Decisions referred to "areas of exclusive competence" exercised by the federal government and the states; to their powers being "separate and distinct;" and to neither being able "to intrude within the jurisdiction of the other."

Judicial rhetoric is not always consistent with judicial action, and the Court did not always adhere to separatist doctrine. Indeed, its rhetoric sometimes indicated a positive view of cooperation. In any case, the Court was rarely, if ever, directly confronted with the issue of cooperation *vs.* separation as such. Rather it was concerned with defining permissible areas of action for the central government and the states; or with saying with respect to a point at issue whether any government could take action. The Marshall Court contributed to intergovernmental cooperation by the very act of permitting federal operations where they had not existed before. Furthermore, even Marshall was willing to allow interstate commerce to be affected by the states in their use of the police power. Later courts also upheld state laws that had an impact on interstate commerce, just as they approved the expansion of the national commerce power, as in statutes providing for the control of telegraphic communication or prohibiting the interstate transportation of lotteries, impure foods and drugs, and prostitutes. Similar room for cooperation was found outside the commerce field, notably in the Court's refusal to interfere with federal grants in land or cash to the states. Although research to clinch the point has not been completed, it is probably true that the Supreme Court from 1800 to 1936 allowed far more federal-state collaboration than it blocked.

Political behavior and administrative action of the nineteenth century provide positive evidence that, throughout the entire era of so-called dual federalism, the many governments in the American federal system continued the close administrative and fiscal collaboration of the earlier period. Governmental activities were not extensive. But relative to what governments did, intergovernmental cooperation during the last century was comparable with that existing today.

Occasional presidential vetoes (from Madison to Buchanan) of cash and land grants are evidence of constitutional and ideological apprehensions about the extensive expansion of federal activities which produced widespread intergovernmental collaboration. In perspective, however, the vetoes are a more important evidence of the continuous search, not least by state officials, for ways and means to involve the central government in a wide variety of joint programs. The search was successful.

Grants-in-land and grants-in-services from the national government were of first importance in virtually all the principal functions undertaken by the states and their local subsidiaries. Land grants were made to the states for, among other purposes, elementary schools, colleges, and special educational institutions; roads, canals, rivers, harbors, and railroads; reclamation of desert and swamp lands; and veterans' welfare. In fact whatever was at the focus of state attention became the recipient of national grants. (Then, as today, national grants established state emphasis as well as followed it.) If Connecticut wished to establish a program for the care and education of the deaf and dumb, federal money in the form of a land grant was found to aid that program. If higher education relating to agriculture became a pressing need, Congress could dip into the public domain and make appropriate grants to states. If the need for swamp drainage and flood control appeared, the federal government could supply both grants-in-land and, from the Army's Corps of Engineers, the services of the only trained engineers then available.

Aid also went in the other direction. The federal government, theoretically in exclusive control of the Indian population, relied continuously (and not always wisely) on the experience and resources of state and local governments. State militias were an all-important ingredient in the nation's armed forces. State governments became unofficial but real partners in federal programs for homesteading, reclamation, tree culture, law enforcement, inland waterways, the nation's internal communications system (including highway and railroad routes), and veterans' aid of various sorts. Administrative contacts were voluminous, and the whole process of interaction was lubricated, then as today, by constituent-conscious members of Congress.

The essential continuity of the collaborative system is best demonstrated by the history of the grants. The land grant tended to become a cash grant based on the calculated disposable value of the land, and the cash grant tended to become an annual grant based upon the national government's superior tax powers. In 1887, only three years before the frontier was officially closed, thus signaling the end of the disposable public domain, Congress enacted the first continuing cash grants.

A long, extensive, and continuous experience is therefore the foundation of the present system of shared functions characteristic of the American federal system, what we have called the marble cake of government. It is a misjudgment of our history and our present situation to believe that a neat separation of governmental functions could take place without drastic alterations in our society and system of government.

POINTS TO PONDER

1. What does Grodzins mean in using the layer cake and the marble cake metaphors?

2. When was the layer cake metaphor an accurate representation of the relationship of state and local governments to the national government?
3. Why have attempts to "unwind the federal system" failed in the past? Is
it likely they will succeed in the future?

8

"AMERICAN FEDERALISM:
EVOLUTION, STATUS, AND PROSPECTS"
James Sundquist

*In the following paper presented in 1986, James Sundquist traces the political struggle
over the past two centuries between those who have advocated a more powerful central
government in the United States and those who have wanted a more limited central government—those whose rallying cry has been "states' rights." In Sundquist's view, although the states' rights advocates have often had a rhetorical edge in appealing to
Americans' distrust of centralized power, the advocates of centralization have won the war.*

*Sundquist, a political scientist at the Brookings Institution, attributes the national-
ization of public policy to technology, world wars, and economic disasters. At the policy
level, however, a driving force has been the national governmental guarantee of equal
rights and due process of law to all citizens, especially African Americans, through the
judicial interpretation of the Fourteenth Amendment. The regulation of the economy has
been another force undermining the independence of the states. Finally, Sundquist looks
at the impact of fiscal federalism—that is, the provision of money by the federal government to state and local governments to carry out national purposes. Sundquist concludes
that, although the balance of national versus state and local power runs in cycles, the
overall tide of national domination is irreversible.*

In our two centuries of national life under the Constitution, the nature of the
federal system that the Founding Fathers created has lain always in the realm of
controversy. Sometimes the controversy has bubbled up and exploded in a
constitutional crisis, as in the Great Depression of the 1930s, and once in a
civil war, in the 1860s. Yet even in more tranquil times, the balance of power
and responsibility between the federal government, on the one hand, and state
and local governments, on the other, has been unceasingly the subject of legal
debate and political struggle.

On one side of the struggle have been the centralizers, the advocates of
strong national government. Their case has been a pragmatic one—the
national government has more power, and more resources, to get things
done, whether the object be to carry out major public works, or regulate the

economy, or ensure the protection of the rights of minorities, or enhance the general welfare by pouring money into education and health and welfare and a limitless range of other domestic governmental activities. On the other side have been those who opposed these national undertakings, on whatever grounds—whether for reasons of policy or on strictly constitutional concerns—and who have defended the status quo by pleading what used to be called "states' rights" but is now termed "state responsibilities," by calling forth traditional values of local self-reliance and citing the language of the Constitution and the intent of the Framers, and by warning that the aggrandizement of the far-off government in Washington can only mean the loss of liberty and freedom of individuals and their communities throughout America.

On balance, of course, the centralizers have won. The immediate and tangible benefits have outweighed the theoretical and conjectural losses. Power and responsibility have flowed to Washington, throughout the whole two centuries and especially in the past half century, and that fact sets the tone of the current controversy. The question of the federal balance is not in crisis stage today, but it is surely bubbling. President Reagan was elected, and reelected, on a pledge to reverse the trend of history and disperse power out of Washington, back to the states and localities. In 1982, he proposed what he called his New Federalism—a major swap of responsibilities between the federal and state governments. That failed, but the idea is still very much alive. A distinguished bipartisan Committee on Federalism and National Purpose, headed by a governor (Charles S. Robb of Virginia) and a former governor (Senator Daniel J. Evans of Washington), declared a few months ago that the federal system needs "a thorough overhaul" and proposed its own exchange of responsibilities. The official Advisory Commission on Intergovernmental Relations has weighed in with a plan for the federal government to give up a range of programs along with certain excise taxes to pay for them. The National Governors Association has still another plan. Pending agreement on any such wholesale reordering of the federal-state balance—which does not seem likely soon—the Reagan Administration and the Congress have been proceeding piecemeal, drastically reducing the federal role in assisting state and local governments—so much so that the president of the National League of Cities foresees the end of "the federal system as we know it" and the National Governors Association protests "attempts to shift current federal costs back to states and localities under the guise of federalism."

* * * *

The Constitutional Design

Alexander Hamilton stood almost alone at the Constitutional Convention of 1787 in favoring the abolition of the states. "Two sovereignties can not coexist within the same limits," contended Hamilton, and great economy could be attained by placing all responsibility in the new national government. He did not actually propose so drastic a step, however; the "shock" to "public opinion," he acknowledged, would be too great. The reaction of his fellow delegates when Hamilton spoke bore out that judgment; they were sufficiently shocked that Hamilton was constrained to explain himself at the next session. He meant merely that the states should be abolished "as states," but should remain as "subordinate jurisdictions" because of the vast expanse of the country to be governed. But the subordination should be clear; the national government should have unlimited authority.

Hamilton had the support of George Read of Delaware, who agreed that the states "must be done away." But that was all. The leader of Read's own Delaware delegation, John Dickinson, spoke the consensus of the Framers when he observed that a "combination" of the State Governments with the National Government was "as politic as it was unavoidable." The delegates to the convention were, after all, *delegates*, not wholly independent spirits. They had been chosen, and in some cases instructed, by their state legislatures. They were assigned only to propose revisions of the Articles of Confederation, which existed, and would therefore continue, as a league of the thirteen fledgling states. In the convention, they voted as state delegations—each with one vote—rather than as individuals. When their handiwork was finished, it had to be approved, in some manner, by the states, and the delegates could hardly return to their sponsors and patrons and say, in effect, "We decided to wipe you out."

Yet, if the Confederation had not palpably failed, the delegates would never have been sent to Philadelphia. And everyone knew what caused the failure: the nation was the subordinate jurisdiction. The Continental Congress was wholly dependent on the states, possessing not even an independent taxing power. A national government resting not on the states but on the people had, therefore, to be conceived and to achieve that purpose, the conclave at Philadelphia had to become a "runaway convention." The Virginia plan, which became the initial basis of discussion, was couched as a series of amendments to the Articles of Confederation, but that was not its spirit. In that plan, the national government would not merely be freed from dependence on the states but would be supreme over them. The first branch of the national legislature—what became the House of Representatives—would be elected directly by the people. The legislature would not only have unrestricted lawmaking authority in the areas of responsibility assigned to it but would also be empowered to veto any state legislation "and to call forth the force of the Union against any member of the Union failing to fulfill its duty under the articles thereof." The Union would guarantee that each state maintained a republican form of government. State officials would have to take an oath to support the "Articles of Union" and, thereby, the national government those articles created. Ratification of the articles would not be by the state governments but by popular conventions held in each state.

Accepting the goals of a strong and unfettered national government, on the one hand, and a continued role for the states, on the other, the delegates struggled for the rest of the summer to define the balance. More delegates feared that the new national government would be too weak than that it would be too powerful; John Wilson of Pennsylvania was echoed by many when he foresaw no probability that the states would be "devoured" by the Union. "In all confederated systems ancient and modern the reverse had happened," said Wilson, "the Generality being destroyed gradually by the usurpations of the parts composing it." Delegates from the small states worried at first about being devoured, and some rallied behind the New Jersey alternative to the Virginia plan, but they were outnumbered and defeated, and once the Grand Compromise was reached that gave each state equal representation in the Senate, their anxieties faded and they were caught up with the Virginians and Pennsylvanians in the nationalistic fervor.

All the essentials for national supremacy were then written into the Constitution. The Constitution, and laws and treaties made under its authority, were declared "the supreme law of the land," superior to state constitutions and laws. While the provision in the Virginia plan that the Congress have a veto power over state laws was rejected as too burdensome and offensive—and unnecessary as well because both the state and federal judiciaries would enforce the Constitution and hence protect the national government against state usurpation—from the Virginia scheme were retained the national guarantee of republican government, the oath by state officials to support the national government, and the ratification of the Constitution by popular conventions. The significance of the ratification process was reaffirmed by the first seven and last twelve words of the preamble: "We, the people of the United States . . . do ordain and establish this Constitution for the United States of America." The Articles of Confederation was a compact among states; to ordain and establish the Constitution, the state governments—except for organizing the conventions—did not even play a part. Finally, a series of specific prohibitions on state action—on such matters as entering into treaties, making war, coining money, and levying tariffs—was adopted as Section 10 of Article I.

So the supremacy of the national government was solidly established and reinforced. How, then, would the Constitution ensure the preservation of a vital role for the states—that nicely-balanced state-national combination that every delegate sought, even the few who, like Hamilton, might have preferred otherwise but had to go along out of respect for political necessity? For the first two months of the Convention, the delegates shied away from trying to precisely define, or limit, the legislative powers of the Congress. The Virginia plan said only that the new Congress would inherit the legislative powers of the Continental Congress, as enumerated in the Articles of Confederation, but beyond that would "legislate in all cases to which the separate States are incompetent, or in which the harmony of the United States may be interrupted by the exercise of individual Legislation." To this was added the power "to legislate in all Cases for the general Interests of the Union." All this language would have left the Congress free to decide for itself on what matters the states were incompetent and what legislation would further the general interests of the Union.

The only safeguard would have been self-restraint on the part of the Congress. Clearly, that was no satisfactory answer—not for a Convention whose delegates were obsessed with the threat of tyranny and imbued with the concept of checks and balances. In the first discussion of the subject, James Madison confessed he had come to Philadelphia with "a strong bias in favor of an enumeration and definition" of the powers of the legislature but also "doubts concerning its practicability," and his doubts had become stronger. But sentiment grew that an effort should be made, and the Committee of Detail undertook the task. It picked up the enumeration from the Articles of Confederation, added a few more items, then topped the list with a catch-all power "to make all laws that shall be necessary and proper for carrying into execution the foregoing powers, and all other powers vested, by this Constitution, in the Government of the United States. . . ." Subsequent committees added to the enumeration. Among the words picked up from the Articles of Confederation and accepted without dissent or even discussion were those of the marvelously ambiguous "general welfare" clause: "The Congress shall have Power to lay and collect Taxes . . . to pay the Debts and provide for the common Defence and general Welfare of the United States. . . ."

Meanwhile, the delegates created what they thought was a potent structural device for defending the states against a Congress whose laws would be supreme. That was the United States Senate. In the first debate on the composition of the Congress, Charles Pinckney of South Carolina suggested that if the new House of Representatives were to be popularly elected, the other house—the Senate—should "shew the sovereignty" of the states, and Richard Dobbs Spaight of North Carolina moved that the Senators be appointed by the state legislatures. The motion was withdrawn that day, but was eventually adopted. Just as each branch of government, through the checks and balances of the constitutional structure, was provided the means of self-defense, so must the states have that capacity, argued George Mason of Virginia, "and the only mode left of giving it to them, was by allowing them to appoint the second branch of the national legislature." As the Convention wore on, the Senate came to be seen as the one great bulwark of states' rights. When the Senate acted, in the view of the delegates, it would be the states themselves acting collectively. The members of that body would not be plenipotentiaries but ambassadors. "No law or resolution can now be passed," wrote Madison in *The Federalist*, "without the concurrence, first, of a majority of the people, and then of a majority of the States."

Even so, the nationalists had to defend their Constitution against a powerful attack from those who contended that the rights and powers of the states, as well as the liberties of individual citizens, would be at the mercy of an all-powerful central government. The solution that saved the Constitution was agreement by its supporters to write into their document a Bill of Rights. The first nine amendments, adopted by the First Congress, concerned the rights of individuals, the tenth the rights of the states. That Tenth Amendment read: "The powers not delegated to the United States by the Constitution, nor prohibited by it to the States, are reserved to the States respectively, or to the people." Thus was it finally settled that the national government was one of limited and enumerated powers.

But the doubts expressed by Madison have haunted the nation for two centuries. Was it ever practicable to try to enumerate and limit the power of the national government? Who would enforce the limitation? One school of thought was that the Congress itself, its members bound by oath to support the Constitution, should be relied on to live within its enumerated powers—particularly since the Senate, as a body made up of state ambassadors, could be counted on to check any invasion of state powers. But the larger body of opinion, even in 1787, expected the judiciary to invalidate unconstitutional laws, and in 1803 John Marshall made it official. In *Madison* v. *Marbury*, the Court for the first time voided a law on grounds of unconstitutionality; the country accepted that assumption of judicial power, and since then the Court has been the final referee, whenever it chose to assume the role, in conflicts between federal and state power—between the two sovereignties that Hamilton protested could not coexist in the same territory but that the original Constitution, augmented by the Tenth Amendment, proclaimed must do so.

Two centuries later, Hamilton is the clear winner of that argument. The Tenth Amendment has become a dead letter. Only once in the last fifty years has the Supreme Court found a law of Congress to be an unconstitutional invasion of state power and state rights, and event[ually] that one decision was reversed. By now, scarcely a single function of government, even those activities most characteristically local, had escaped the reach of federal legislation, and the federal judiciary itself has extended a long arm as well into realms where the states once had exclusive jurisdiction. The national government has attained what Hamilton sought, but what the overwhelming majority of his Convention colleagues expressly disavowed—unlimited authority.

Let us review how and why that has come about.

Two Centuries of Nationalization

Underlying all the other causes of the nationalization of the United States is, of course, technology. With the telegraph and the telephone, communication overcame distance, and every American could be in touch with every other American in whatever corner of the country. The railroad, then the automobile, and finally the airplane placed every American community within a few hours' distance of every other community—including the national capital in Washington—and stimulated intermingling and the sense of national community. The telegraph, the motion picture, the radio, and finally television most effectively of all, brought the same body of information within reach of every American and subjected everyone to unifying cultural influences. And these inventions—along with others, such as refrigeration and food preservatives—nationalized the economy as well. As the nation was knit together, so was the world, and the importance of the national center, which perforce must manage relationships—especially economic relationships—between Americans and other inhabitants of the globe, was enhanced. Crises that were national in scale and demanded a commensurate response contributed to the nationalization of the country, too—notably the slavery controversy, the Great Depression, and the post–World War II civil rights turmoil, each in its own way. All these forces and events wrought changes in the institutions of the government, both in composition and in conduct, expanded the people's concept as to what their national government should do, and even produced nationalizing amendments to the Constitution itself.

* * * *

Nationalization of Rights and Liberties

The Civil War left another great constitutional legacy—the Fourteenth Amendment. That amendment, along with the Thirteenth (outlawing slavery) and the Fifteenth (guaranteeing the right to vote), were aimed directly at establishing the equal rights of the newly-freed former slaves, but all were written in broad language. The Fourteenth Amendment declared that all persons born or naturalized in the United States, and subject to its jurisdiction, were citizens of the United States as well as of their respective states. It then prohibited, in only fifty-two words, state legislation that would "abridge the privileges or immunities" of citizens of the United States, or deprive them of "life, liberty, or property, without due process of law," or deny them "equal protection of the laws."

Only six years after the amendment was approved by the Congress, and four years after its ratification by the states, the Supreme Court split five-to-four in deciding what it meant. If nine justices who lived through the period of that amendment's framing could not agree on what the Framers—who were themselves still very much alive—intended, one may wonder parenthetically about the feasibility of Mr. Meese's concept of a Jurisprudence of Original Intention. In any event, a majority of five justices in 1873 concentrated on the language of the fifty-two words and found logic by which to construe them narrowly. But four justices in the minority read what they sensed to be the spirit of the Amendment and interpreted it expansively.

The question was whether the right to do business free of monopolistic restraint was one of the "privileges and immunities" guaranteed to "citizens of the United States" by the Fourteenth Amendment. The majority said no. If the complainants were citizens of the United States, they were also citizens of their respective states. Traditionally, protection against monopoly had been a liberty belonging to the citizens of the states. Were the Court to nationalize all the rights of the citizens of the states, wrote Justice Miller for the majority, it "would constitute this Court a perpetual censor upon all legislation of the States, on the civil rights of their own citizens. . . ." That would be "so great a departure from the structure and spirit of our institutions" as to "radically change the whole theory of the relations of the State and Federal governments

to each other." It would "fetter and degrade the State governments by sub-
jecting them to the control of Congress, in the exercise of powers heretofore
universally conceded to them of the most ordinary and fundamental character. . . ." This, said the Court, was not intended.

The dissenters read quite a different intent. The amendment, said Justice
Field for the minority, was adopted "to place the common rights of American
citizens under the protection of the National Government." A citizen of a particular state was only a citizen of the United States who happened to be resid-
ing in that state, and the "fundamental rights, privileges, and immunities
which belong to him as a free man and a free citizen, now belong to him as a
citizen of the United States, and are not dependent upon his citizenship of any
State." And what were those fundamental rights, privileges, and immunities?
Justice Field did not attempt a full enumeration, but contended that the right
to do business was among them. In a separate opinion, Justice Bradley argued
that the "mischief to be remedied [by the Amendment] was not merely slavery
and its . . . consequences, but that spirit of insubordination and disloyalty to
the National Government. . . . The Amendment was an attempt to give voice
to the strong National yearning for that time . . . in which American citizenship should be a sure guaranty of safety, and in which every citizen of the
United States might stand erect on every portion of its soil, in the full enjoy-
ment of every right and privilege belonging to a free man. . . ."

Since the Fourteenth Amendment gave the Supreme Court an inescapable
duty to void state legislation that violated the privileges and immunities, due
process of law, and equal protection clauses, the Court could scarcely have
avoided becoming the "perpetual censor" of the states that Justice Miller
feared. A censor may approve or disapprove, but it cannot avoid deciding.
And with only a few ambiguous words as guides, the Court could also hardly
fail to interpret them in terms of the "strong yearnings" of the nation—not
just those of 1866–68, with which Justice Bradley felt confidently in tune,
but those of each generation of justices' own time. At any rate, the Court has
done just that, and the prediction that the whole theory of federalism could
be radically changed—uttered so fearfully by the *Slaughterhouse* majority but
anticipated so hopefully by the minority—has been fulfilled.

For a time, the principal censorship was exercised by the Court to protect
corporations from state regulation under the due process clause, treating corporations as "persons." But that era passed, and beginning with the Gitlow
case in 1925 the impact of the Court has been to extend the various provisions of the Bill of Rights, one by one, to the states. Over the six decades
since then, the guarantees of freedom of speech, press, assembly, and religion;
of immunity from unreasonable search and seizure, self-incrimination, and
cruel and unusual punishment; the rights of accused persons to counsel, and
to a speedy and public trial by jury, and to other procedural protections have
been incorporated into the Fourteenth Amendment.

Beyond that, the Court has steadily expanded the interpretation of various
clauses in the Bill of Rights, discerning "penumbrae" that surround the

written words. Freedom of assembly has become freedom of association, in- volving much more than merely the right to meet. The freedom of religion clause, which refers only to laws that might "establish" a religion or prohibit the "free exercise" thereof, has been read to require "a wall of separation be- tween church and state." The words "right of privacy" do not appear in the Constitution, but in striking down Connecticut's anticontraceptive law, the court was able to construct such a right from provisions of the First, Third, Fourth, and Fifth Amendments. Justice Douglas, speaking for the majority in that case, also cited the Ninth Amendment, which declares that "The enu- meration in the Constitution of certain rights shall not be construed to deny or disparage others retained by the people." Thus the Fourteenth Amend- ment, in guaranteeing to citizens of the United States their privileges and immunities and in assuring them the protections of due process, has com- pelled the justices to search for those other rights to which the Ninth Amendment has reference. And the majority and concurring opinions in the *Griswold* case expressed the freedom that justices feel to look beyond consti- tutional and statutory changes to tradition and philosophy for answers. Thus, Justice Douglas found privacy to be a right "older than the Bill of Rights," and essential to sustaining the "sacred" institution of marriage. Justice Gold- berg, with Chief Justice Warren and Justice Brennan concurring, found that the Fourteenth Amendment protects "those personal rights that are funda- mental." Justice Harlan found the test to be whether a law violates "basic val- ues 'implicit in the concept of ordered liberty'." That was the Warren Court, but in 1973 the Burger Court, with only two dissents, extended the right of privacy doctrine to strike down antiabortion laws, in the celebrated case of *Roe* v. *Wade.*

Meanwhile, under the equal protection clause, the federal judiciary has thrust itself forcefully into regulating the conduct of state and local gov- ernments. In 1954, the Warren Court reached its decision in the school in- tegration cases that revolutionized "with all deliberate speed" the social structure of an entire region of the country. And in 1962, it began moni- toring the apportionment of state legislatures, city councils, and boards of county commissioners to assure the application of the "one man, one vote" principle. Federal judges have found themselves deeply involved in the administration of local school systems, not only to enforce desegregation by elaborate busing schemes but also to ensure the equitable distribution of resources among schools, and the intervention has extended to other areas of state and municipal administration, such as recreation programs, where discrimination could be shown to exist.

When the Congress and the executive branch have acted to enforce the guarantees of the post–Civil War amendments "by appropriate legislation"— as each of the three amendments invites them to do—the Supreme Court has, of course, upheld them. It has had no difficulty sustaining the civil rights laws of the 1960s and most actions taken under them, extending even to the federal takeover of the voter registration machinery in southern states.

Future Supreme Courts, Congresses and presidents might move in the direction of showing greater deference to state and local legislators, administrators, and judges and intervening less in their affairs, but the essential point is that this is for the national government itself to decide, through its instrumentalities—the federal judiciary, the Congress and the president. In the entire realm of civil rights and liberties, the reach of the national government is limited only by that government's self-restraint.

Nationalization of Economic Regulation

For a full century and a half, the Supreme Court struggled to give meaning to the Tenth Amendment in the field of economic affairs by drawing a line between federal and state responsibilities. Then it gave up. In this field, too, the states had to surrender to national supremacy.

John Marshall announced the principle in 1819, in *McCulloch* v. *Maryland*:

> In America, the powers of sovereignty are divided between the government of the Union, and those of the states. They are each sovereign, with respect to the objects committed to it, and neither sovereign with respect to the objects committed to the other.

This doctrine, which has been called "dual federalism," was reiterated and refined over the ensuing decades. In 1859, Marshall's successor, Chief Justice Taney, expressed it this way:

> And the powers of the General Government, and of the State, although both exist and are exercised within the same territorial limits, are yet separate and distinct sovereignties, acting separately and independently of each other, within their respective spheres.

During the first hundred years, the Court was concerned primarily with protecting interstate commerce from burdensome state regulation, rather than the other way around. But steam locomotion and other technological developments were bringing about the integration of the country's economy at a rapid and accelerating pace, symbolized by the growth of giant railroads and the formation of great trusts, and that aroused the demand for national regulation of monopolies, symbolized in turn by the Interstate Commerce Act of 1887 and the Sherman Anti-Trust Act of 1890. The cry for reform spread to the conditions under which workers labored, particularly women and children workers.

The Supreme Court then was urgently confronted with the question of where to draw the line between the two sovereigns. The logic was inescapable. If the general government and the states were to act separately and independently within their respective spheres, those spheres had to be demarked, and the Court would have to be the referee. For half a century, it tried valiantly to fill that role.

When the Congress acted under the clause empowering it "to regulate commerce with foreign nations and among the several states," the principle seemed clear enough; commerce was plainly the movement of goods, and commerce became interstate only when a boundary was crossed. That excluded manufacture, as the Court decided in an early anti-trust case. The American Sugar Refining Company had achieved a nearly complete monopoly of the manufacture of its product but, held the Court, "it does not follow that an attempt to monopolize, or the actual monopoly of, the manufacture was an attempt . . . to monopolize commerce, even though, in order to dispose of the product, the instrumentality of commerce was necessarily invoked." Regulation of manufacture was not a commercial power but a police power, and to preserve the police power for the states was essential to the "preservation of the autonomy of the States as required by our dual form of government." Only one justice dissented from that reasoning. But, while manufacture was not commerce, marketing could be. In another anti-trust case a decade later, the Court upheld a prohibition against collusive bidding at livestock markets on the ground that the markets were part of a "current of commerce among the States."

The Congress could legislate morality if interstate movement were involved, and acts prohibiting the interstate shipment of lottery tickets, liquor, impure foods, stolen cars, and so-called "white slaves" were upheld. But when the Congress tried to ban from interstate commerce the products of child labor, the Court drew the line. That, too, was a regulation of manufacture, not of transportation, and the police power, the majority reminded the Congress, was not among the national government's enumerated powers. A four-justice minority found the distinction unconvincing; if the government could prohibit the movement of "strong drink" across state lines, it should likewise be permitted to prohibit commerce in "the product of ruined lives." The Congress tried again, using its tax rather than its commerce power, but the Court would not be circumvented. The "prohibitory and regulatory effect and purpose" of the tax on the profits of employers of child labor, said the justices, was "palpable." This time only one justice dissented.

When the Great Depression struck, the Court sought stubbornly—or courageously, depending on the point of view—to defend the federal-state boundary line that it had been drawing, slowly and tortuously, over half a century. Franklin Roosevelt and the Congress conceived one emergency measure after another, but the Court judged them all by the same standards it had been applying, and many of the central efforts of the New Deal went the way of the child labor laws and the case against the sugar trust. The National Industrial Recovery Act was voided because it sought to regulate the wages and hours of workers in poultry slaughterhouses, which had only an indirect effect on interstate commerce, and if federal authority extended that far "the authority of the State over its domestic concerns would exist only by sufferance of the federal government." The first Agricultural Adjustment Act was invalidated because it was "a statutory plan to regulate and control agricultural production, a matter beyond the powers delegated to the federal government." The Bituminous Coal Conservation Act of 1935 fell because it sought to regulate wages and prices in coal production, but the coal had not yet entered the flow of commerce, and the evils that the law sought to remedy "are all local evils."

Justice Cardozo, speaking for a three-justice minority in the coal case, pointed out that the Court had forbidden the states to regulate the prices of goods moving in interstate commerce. If the national government were also forbidden to control prices, they would be "withdrawn altogether from government supervision," said Cardozo. "If such a vacuum were permitted, many a public evil would be left without a remedy." Citing the Court's holdings that the federal government could regulate economic activities that had a "direct" effect on interstate commerce, as distinct from only an indirect effect, he felt that the prices of coal came within the definition. "But," he protested, "a great principle of constitutional law is not susceptible of comprehensive statement in an adjective."

But that was the last time the Supreme Court has seen economic problems as "local evils." By the next year, 1937, Justice Cardozo was writing for the majority. A newly constituted five-justice bloc—Chief Justice Hughes and Justice Roberts having joined the three earlier dissenters—upheld the National Labor Relations Act and the Social Security Act. The minority protested that the Court was reversing well-established principles that had been reiterated as recently as the major cases of 1935 and 1936. In his social security case dissent, Justice McReynolds wrote that the judiciary theretofore had left the states "really free to exercise governmental powers, not delegated or prohibited, without interference by the Federal Government through threats of punitive measures or offers of seductive favors. Unfortunately, the decision just announced opens the way for practical annihilation of this theory; and no cloud of words or ostentatious parade of irrelevant statistics should be permitted to obscure that fact. . . . Forever, so far as we can see, the States are expected to function under federal direction concerning an internal matter." . . . In regulating the private economy, the authority of the Congress to go as far as it may wish is no longer subject to any challenge.

Nationalization of Policy and Program Decisions through Grants-in-Aid

At the very time that the Supreme Court was most resolutely shutting the door on expansion of federal power under the commerce clause, it removed altogether the gate that might have prevented federal aggrandizement through a means no less potent—the grant-in-aid.

During the century when the Court reiterated the doctrine of dual federalism—the concept of separate, distinct, and independent sovereignties in "their respective spheres"—the state sphere would presumably be defined to include those functions that the states then performed, insofar as the activities were not assigned to the federal government in its enumerated powers, or in the "implied powers" necessary to make the enumerated powers meaningful. From the outset, there was considerable overlapping; both levels of government were engaged in road building, for example, because construction of "postroads" was among the enumerated powers. States chartered banks, but so did the federal government, and the Supreme Court found that its power to do so was implied by its enumerated responsibilities for fiscal management. The federal government could justify dredging rivers and harbors, and building and operating canals, under both its national security and its interstate commerce powers. But vast areas of public responsibility were clearly in the sphere of the states, under even the broadest concept of dual federalism—education, police and fire protection, care of the poor and the sick, municipal water supply and sanitation, museums, libraries, and so on. Yet even here, the national government found ways to intervene on an ad hoc, case-by-case basis, whenever causes that were both worthy and politically powerful presented themselves.

The initial device for that purpose was the original form of grant-in-aid—the conditional grant to the states of public lands. As early as 1818, a land grant helped to finance a model school in Hartford for the education of the deaf and mute. Roads, canals, and then railroad projects were wholly or partially financed by land grants. In the new states and territories, land grants were earmarked for support of the common schools. In 1862, the first act was passed giving a land grant to every state for a specific purpose—establishment of colleges of agriculture and mechanical arts. Many of the projects involved intimate and cooperative relations between federal and state administrators in what Daniel J. Elazar, the historian of nineteenth-century federalism, calls "a broadly institutionalized system of collaboration" that was never dual federalism in the strict sense at all, but what he calls "cooperative federalism" from the beginning.

There were, of course, strict constructions in those days—mainly in the majority Democratic party. They drew a line at direct appropriations from the national treasury advocated by the opposition Whigs for what they judged to be state responsibilities. When Congress voted direct appropriations for local navigation projects or other internal improvements, Democratic presidents Madison, Monroe, Jackson, Tyler, Polk, Pierce, and Buchanan all found it their duty to protect the Constitutional federal system as they understood it by vetoing the spending measures. Yet enough strict-constructionists who rejected monetary appropriations accepted land grants to make the cooperative system possible; to them, "land grants could be rationalized as gifts by the federal government in its capacity as property owner rather than grants made in its governmental capacity."

After the Civil War, the Republicans were the dominant party; their presidents generally embraced the Constitutional philosophy of their Whig predecessors, and the Democratic party reversed its stand as well. That made it unanimous; river and harbor projects, however local in character, became a federal responsibility, to be followed in this century by irrigation and hydroelectric power projects. But, in addition to undertaking its own public works, the federal government found a way to extend its reach in a regularized and continuous way into any and all areas of state responsibility that struck the fancy of Congresses and presidents, through the acceptance and development of cash grants-in-aid to state and local governments. Cash was a resource of far richer potential than land—at a time when the country was running out of desirable and undeveloped public domain—and by permitting annual appropriations rather than one-time grants it vastly expanded the possible range and volume of federal assistance.

The first grant-in-aid was enacted in 1879 to provide teaching materials for the blind. Care of the handicapped, as well as education in general, were clearly state responsibilities, but the constitutionality of federal assistance was not challenged. Who could be against helping blind people? A few years later came aid for state agricultural experiment stations at the land-grant colleges; this must have seemed like a logical and incremental step, since the federal government had initiated the land-grant colleges and had as much interest in making them effective as in establishing them in the first place. Then came aid for homes for Civil War veterans. Again, who could be against taking care of destitute soldiers who had risked their lives in battle?

But such innocent measures set the precedent. From that time forward, any interest group disappointed in the amount of funds it could extract from state and local legislatures for a favored program had a court of appeal. It could turn to Washington, find friendly members of Congress to introduce the authorizing legislation, and if its political power—reinforced by log-rolling—were sufficient, get federal money to augment state funds. It could even turn the whole process around, and use the federal money to coerce the states into making appropriations, by making the federal grant condition on state matching in some specified proportion. By reading the history of the expansion of grants-in-aid, one can measure the relative influence of interest groups. In a rural nation, as might be expected, the farmers initially were able to mount the strongest lobby. Along with the agriculture experiment stations came the establishment of land-grant colleges, with their heavy emphasis on agricultural research and training, a cooperative forestry program, the cooperative extension service, vocational education with its emphasis on vocational agriculture, and the federal-aid highway program "to get the farmers out of the mud."

Not until four decades after the invention of grants-in-aid did the constitutional question reach the Supreme Court. And there it died, for in this instance the Court concluded that it could not assume its accustomed role as the great arbiter of the federal system. Neither the state of Massachusetts nor an individual taxpayer, challenging the constitutionality of a maternal and child health grant-in-aid program, had standing to sue because neither was injured. In a unanimous opinion written by Justice Sutherland, the Court held that the powers of the state "are not invaded, since the statute imposes no obligation but simply extends an option which the State is free to accept or reject. . . . If the Congress enacted it with the ulterior purpose of tempting them to yield, that purpose may be effectively frustrated by the simple expedient of not yielding." As for the taxpayer, her interest was "comparatively minute and indeterminable; and the effect upon future taxation . . . so remote, fluctuating and uncertain, that no basis is afforded for an appeal to the preventive powers of a court of equity." Moreover, to give any taxpayer the right to a judicial test of the constitutionality of every federal expenditure would place an intolerable burden on the legal system. The whole issue of grants-in-aid, said Sutherland, was for political rather than judicial determination.

With this carte blanche from the judiciary, political forces in the next couple of decades brought about an explosion of grants-in-aid and, with it, a recasting of the federal system. In the Great Depression, the federal government took on the major responsibility for financing public welfare, entered the field of housing, introduced a series of grants for health services, and on a temporary basis subsidized public works of all kinds. In the 1940s came aid for hospital and airport construction, urban renewal, the school lunch program, and several more types of health grants. The 1950s saw the interstate highway system, aid for federally-impacted education systems, the National Defense Education Act, aid for sewage plants and libraries, and medical assistance for the aged. Then, in the 1960s, the floodgates collapsed entirely. Federal aid poured forth for the remaining activities of state and local government, including those that had been held most sacrosanct by the theorists of federalism—elementary and secondary education and law enforcement. Not only did the Great Society introduce half a hundred new categorical grants, but in its public works and public employment programs, its community action program under the Economic Opportunity Act, and its model cities program, it authorized funds for any municipal purpose whatsoever. The federal government had now invaded not just some but *all* of the activities of government that had been traditionally state and local.

Some like to characterize this entire trend as usurpation, with states and cities depicted as the victims of federal aggression. But if the states and local governments were victimized, they were not only willing but in most cases eager. Justice Sutherland was surely unrealistic in suggesting that it would be "simple" for states and local governments to reject proffered federal aid; the inducement of money is too powerful, and when it has been distributed by formulae it has rarely been resisted—no matter what conditions Congress may attach. But beyond that, the states and cities have been the initiators of many of the grant programs, and those that have been developed in Washington have seldom been opposed by the organizations of state and local governments. The cities, in particular, have been powerful lobbies for increased federal assistance of whatever kind. The United States Conference of Mayors came into being, indeed, for the express purpose of prying billions of dollars out of the federal treasury to meet local employment and welfare needs during the Great Depression, and it has stayed in being to support aid for airports, hospitals, urban renewal, and other local functions. The organized mayors were the prime force behind creation of the Department of Housing and Urban Development, to serve as a point of leadership for devising and carrying out a constructive national approach to urban problems.

With the assumption of partial financial responsibility by Washington came the assumption of ultimate policy responsibility as well, for as the well-worn adage has it, "he who pays the piper calls the tune." The Supreme Court put it more elegantly in 1942: "The United States may regulate that which it subsidizes." Up to a point, one may argue, the federal government has a positive duty to set standards and conditions for the programs it assists, to assure that its money is spent wisely and effectively. Yet the temptation to go beyond rules necessary just to protect the federal investment, to use grants as a vehicle for unrelated policy intervention has proved irresistible—as witness the establishment of a national 55-mile-per-hour speed limit, and most recently, a minimum drinking age of twenty-one (a measure supported by the ostensibly anti-federal Reagan administration!) by authorizing the withholding of federal highway funds from states that refused to conform their laws to the national will.

Not the money but the "strings attached" are the source of annoyance to state and local officials and strain in the federal system. Organizations representing state and local governments have waged a steady, if selective, warfare against federal control—as distinct from federal aid—and they have won a share of the battles. But state and local officialdom is by no means unanimous; professional administrators and technical specialists, including heads of departments, often support federal conditions as the way of forcing acceptance of policies that, on their own, they could not persuade their elected superiors and lawmakers to adopt. Within these professional networks, systems of consultation have been regularized, whereby proposed federal policies and regulations are reviewed, debated, and usually agreed upon. So the relationships that have emerged since the concepts of dual federalism were buried by events that have quite properly been called "cooperative federalism."

* * * *

In any case, we can anticipate that the scope of the federal role in American society will continue to be at the center of the partisan debate in the future as in the past. The federal-state balance will constantly shift, depending on who wins elections, which party is in power, the ideology of particular presidents, senators and congressmen, and the cyclical shifts in the mood of the country as it responds to changing circumstances and historical events.

And that is as it should be. Today's federalism reflects what two centuries of experience has taught the nation: that a flexible federal system that is constantly reshaped by the interplay of political forces is far preferable to one that is frozen in a fixed Constitutional mold.

POINTS TO PONDER

1. According to Sundquist, who has won the battle over states' rights? How and why?

2. How has the Supreme Court's interpretation of the Fourteenth Amendment affected state and local governments?
3. What is the likelihood that the federal system can be sorted out into distinct jurisdictions? Why?

PART II

The National Government: Separate Institutions Sharing Power

Chapter 3

✦✦

CONGRESS: THE FIRST BRANCH

In establishing Congress in Article I of the Constitution, the Framers signaled their expectation that most policy-making by the national government would originate in Congress. The Framers gave Congress "All legislative Powers herein granted . . ." and the authority "To make all Laws which shall be necessary and proper. . . ."

In fulfilling its constitutional obligations over the past two centuries Congress has developed from a small, personal group of leaders in the nineteenth century to the large, institutionalized policy-making body it is at the end of the twentieth century. Its role in national policy-making has expanded along with the role of the national government in American life. Throughout our history, but particularly since the mid-twentieth century, Congress has vied with the president over national leadership. Presidential power has waxed since the 1930s, but after the "imperial presidencies" of Lyndon Johnson and Richard Nixon, Congress reasserted its role in national policy-making. It is likely that, as the Framers intended, the balance between the two branches will continue to shift around a central equilibrium.

Establishing Congress

The Framers gave the new national legislature much broader powers than the Continental Congress possessed. Although the Framers saw a legislature as a guardian of the people against the potential usurpation of a strong executive or monarch, their experience under the Articles of Confederation also made them sensitive to the dangers of legislative abuse.

The grand compromise that was struck by the Framers—with House representation based on population and the Senate comprising two members from each state, regardless of population—served to limit the power of Congress. The necessity of passing each bill in exactly the same form in each chamber before it goes to the president for signing has always been a significant inhibition to the easy passage of laws. The issue of governance thus becomes more problematical, with national policy-making inhibited by this major division within the legislature. The condition that in contemporary times we call gridlock is enhanced by the Framers' decision to have a bicameral legislature.

Organization and Power Within Congress

The differing nature of the two houses, particularly their differences in size and constituency, has led to important differences in their structures and operations. The modern House, with many more members than the Senate, has of necessity been more hierarchical. The need to organize debate and impose some order on 435 representatives has led to strictly limited debate and tight procedures for decision making.

Within this broad generalization, power in the House has shifted over the years. At the turn of the century the House leadership, particularly the Speaker, held almost dictatorial power. In mid-century, power had devolved to the standing committee chairs who acted as jealous barons guarding their own policy fiefdoms. With the reforms of the 1970s, power was dispersed and devolved to the subcommittee level. But as a reaction to this fragmentation the power of the leadership has been built up again in the 1990s, though not to a concentration comparable to the centralization that existed at the beginning of the century.

Committees in the House can afford to be more specialized than those in the Senate because of the larger number of representatives. There are 22 standing committees in the House to which proposed bills are referred. The bills are then referred to subcommittees that hold hearings, deliberate, and then report out their recommendations to the full committee. The full committee reports the bill to the full House for final debate, possible amendments, and vote. An indication of the fragmentation and decentralization of power in the House is the number of subcommittees, which increased from 69 in 1951 to 135 in 1992.

The smaller Senate has traditionally been the more deliberative body, with individual senators engaging in long debates over the broad issues of American politics. The Senate, in contrast to the House, operates by "unanimous consent," and the objection of one senator or a small group willing to mount a filibuster can bring legislative business to a halt. The tradition of individual deliberation and debate has been so strong that it has become institutionalized in Rule XXII, which allows individual senators the right to hold the floor as long as they wish, allowing a small group of senators through a filibuster to prevent the rest of the body from considering a controversial piece of legislation.

Because there are fewer senators than House members, senators belong to more committees, have larger staffs, and are less specialized. The Senate has 16 standing committees and 87 subcommittees. Since the middle of the twentieth century, the Senate has evolved from an exclusive club of powerful insiders to a forum of political leaders. Television has allowed individual senators to present themselves to the public as generalist political leaders and potential presidential candidates.

It is often remarked that the U.S. Congress is the most powerful independent legislative body in the world. The primary reason for this is that Congress is clearly independent of the executive branch and shares constitutional powers, in contrast with parliamentary systems in which the prime minister as well as other cabinet ministers are members of the legislature. The power of Congress is also a result of the elaborate committee systems with significant staff resources in the two houses. In the nineteenth century Woodrow Wilson observed that Congress debating on the floor was Congress on display, while Congress in committee deliberations was Congress at work. Another reason for the relative power and independence of Congress is the large professional staff system that supports it, including personal staff, committee staff, and large institutions such as the Legislative Research Service, the General Accounting Office, the Congressional Budget Office, and the Office of Technology Assessment.

Party Discipline

In contrast with most parliamentary systems, the U.S. Congress has little party discipline. Membership in most European legislatures is controlled by the political party, and the party places candidates on the ballot at election time. In the United States, however, individuals nominate themselves to run for Congress under a party label. If a potential candidate meets the filing requirements and wants to run for office as a Democrat or Republican, there is little the party can do to prevent this from happening.

One major consequence of this is that there is little party discipline in Congress. Although most of the time most members vote with their party, there is no way to force party discipline, and in significant cases a number of members will defect on important votes. It is an unwritten rule that members' own political interests in their state or district are more important than voting with the party in Congress. In fact, even in key votes, presidents cannot count on support from members of their own party more than two thirds of the time. But they can count on substantial opposition from the other party most of the time.

The Effectiveness of Congress

The result of the constitutional separation of powers and independent sources of selection of members in states and districts is that Congress is not a highly efficient and predictable legislative machine. It does, however, accomplish one major function intended by the Framers—it *represents* well the diversity of interests throughout the nation. There are few significant political interests that cannot find some voice in Congress.

Congress also performs well another important function intended by the Framers: that of *deliberation*. Whether it is individual senators talking for hours about the issue of the day or the House and Senate bickering for weeks in conference committee over the final language in law, few important pieces of legislation get through Congress without serious deliberation.

These positive characteristics of representation and deliberation, however, inhibit another expectation we have of Congress: that it decide and *legislate*. In the give and take of congressional debate and the pulling and hauling of political interests, many proposed laws on important issues are watered down by compromise or killed in the legislative process. Presidents are often frustrated when their agenda items are changed or stopped in Congress. In the 1960s liberal scholar James McGregor Burns called this the "deadlock of democracy" when a conservative Congress frustrated John Kennedy and other proponents of civil rights legislation.

Citizens of different political persuasions are frustrated when major outstanding issues of public concern—such as the national debt or foreign policy issues—are avoided rather than addressed outright and concerted action taken. In the 1980s and 1990s this age-old problem of American governance was often referred to as gridlock, and promises to cure gridlock were staples of the 1992 presidential campaign. These frustrations along with occasional scandals and Americans' historical distrust of governmental power have resulted in a popular disdain for Congress as an institution, despite a very high victory rate for members who seek reelection.

Congress also suffers a disadvantage in contrast with the presidency and the Supreme Court in that its policy deliberations are relatively more open to public scrutiny. It is easier to see compromises being made and bargains being struck in the legislative process than in the Supreme Court chambers or the policy staff offices of the executive branch. Like watching a sausage maker, you can see what goes into the machine, not merely the dressed-up product. It should not be surprising, then, that the American public does not hold Congress in high esteem and that proposals to give more power to the president and limit legislative terms are popular. Thus the effectiveness of Congress in performing the functions of representation and deliberation undercuts citizens' perceptions of its effectiveness because they can more easily see the bargaining and compromising that go into passage of legislation.

The Readings

The selections in this section take up some of the major institutional issues facing the Congress at the end of the twentieth century, including the conflict between its representational functions and legislative responsibilities and its current (and perennial) unpopularity. The political circumstances that allow large-scale legislative change occur only occasionally in the United States, but the incentives for members to take care of their own districts and states are constant. These tendencies have led to criticisms of Congress and calls for limits on legislative terms and grants of more power to the president. The readings put these developments into perspective and explain the important role of Congress in the American system of governance.

The differing sizes of the two houses of Congress lead to different operating procedures and customs, but the differing terms of office also lead to different characteristics. The differences are discussed in the *Federalist* Papers, particularly in *Federalist* Nos. 57 and 62 by James Madison, excerpted in this section. Madison argues that those elected to the House will be esteemed by the voters for their virtue, and that their good behavior will be assured by the need to run for reelection every two years. In contemporary times this responsiveness is evident in members' frequent trips back to their districts, casework for their constituents, and efforts to secure federal projects in their districts.

In explaining the longer terms for senators, Madison argues that larger assemblies tend "to yield to the impulse of sudden and violent passions." Thus the Senate would act as a check on the larger House to guard against "improper" acts of legislation. George Washington referred to the Senate as the saucer that cools the legislative tea, because it would subject legislation passed impulsively by the House to cool deliberation. The Senate has been at times more liberal and at other times more conservative than the House, but it has also developed into the "upper" house. In contemporary times each senator is one of one hundred and thus enjoys greater visibility than House members who are only one of 435. In addition the Senate term of six years (with overlapping terms) makes it more insulated from the passions of the moment than the biennially elected House.

Although the division of the legislature into two houses and the separation of powers lead to a political system that is difficult to change suddenly, there have been periods of active change. In his selection, Nelson Polsby singles out three recent periods of legislative activity: the New Deal (1933–1937), the World War II period (1939–1946), and the Great Society period (1964–1968). These periods of activism have been interspersed with periods of relative stalemate. Polsby argues that it takes a crisis or concerted political leadership to induce the American political system to make sudden changes.

Polsby also traces the development of the Senate from a relatively closed club of insiders to a more open body in which individual senators much more actively pursue their own public policy goals and presidential ambitions. In the House Polsby observes that the electoral changes in the South that led to the election of more Republican members ironically also led to the liberalization of the House. Because it no longer had to deal with as many southern conservative Democrats, the Democratic caucus has become more responsive to liberal interests. Finally, Polsby describes how the Congress as an institution has provided itself with many more staff resources to counter the advantages enjoyed by the executive branch in analytic resources. These changes since the 1970s have contributed to Congress's new willingness to assert itself in the implementation of public policy.

As the role of the national government has grown since the New Deal there are many more opportunities for members of Congress to take credit with their constituents for what the government provides to their districts. Morris Fiorina argues that the symbiosis between members of Congress and federal bureaucrats has corrupted the system. Although providing government goods and services to constituents is not illegal, it leads to a neglect of the common good and an emphasis on "pork barrel" spending in which special interests gain at the expense of the public interest. Fiorina argues that the incentive to take a stand on general public policy issues will inevitably disappoint some constituents, but pork barrel and casework (helping individual constituents) will only make friends.

Thus Fiorina argues that there is every incentive for Congress to increase the size of government because that will result in more casework and credit-taking by members of Congress. Although Fiorina's analysis of the dynamics and consequences of a large national government is very insightful, it is also one-dimensional in that it sees members of Congress as acting only in their own self-interest and being unable to vote for what they think is the best public policy for the country. Given this set of incentives, it is hard to explain how programs would ever be cut or taxes increased. Thus there must be some other, more public-spirited motives that also influence members' votes.

On election day 1990, 76 percent of the voters responding to an exit poll disapproved of the way that Congress was doing its job, yet in that same election about 95 percent of the representatives who sought reelection were returned to office. The gap between citizens' evaluation of their own representative in Congress and their evaluation of Congress as an institution has been a consistent pattern in recent decades.

In an article written in 1972, Richard Fenno offers several explanations of this paradox. He points out that we use different criteria to judge our own members than we use to judge the institution. We want our own representatives to not stray too far from our own policy views, and we expect them to pay close attention to the district's interests. But we expect the Congress as a whole to deal with the nation's problems. The former is more easily accomplished than the latter, and members put more energy into it because pleasing constituents is the key to survival in Congress. We also judge Congress by a changing set of standards. Even in 1992 when there were 110 new members elected to Congress due to retirements and primary defeats, 93 percent of House members who ran in the general election won.

Certainly the advantages of incumbency—name recognition, subsidized postage, media coverage, PAC contributions, and so on—are important factors in reelection. Challengers are at a disadvantage in most of these areas and are usually less experienced in electoral politics. Because of the high reelection rates and despite the regular turnover of House seats (due to incumbents choosing not to run again), political pressure to impose limits on congressional terms has increased in the 1990s.

In 1992, 14 states voted in favor of term limits, usually setting a limit of 12 years: two Senate terms or six House terms. Nelson Polsby in a second selection argues that term limits, even if they are constitutional, are not a good idea. Most members of Congress, he argues, are hard working and are re-elected because they pay close attention to their constituents. If the voters' options to return these representatives to Congress were limited, Polsby argues that the power of those whose tenure in Washington is more permanent would gain relatively more power. That is, lobbyists, executive branch bureaucrats, and congressional staffers, none of whom has to stand for election, would have more leverage than they do now. In addition, there is no guarantee that the members elected to replace experienced representatives at the end of their cycle would act any differently or produce better public policy. They would, however, be less experienced.

Polsby also takes issue with those who favor giving the president the authority to exercise an item veto, that is, the ability to veto *part* of a bill rather than taking all or nothing. This would shift a significant amount of power from Congress to the president, which, argues Polsby, would be unwise.

In addition to these selections, other chapters in this volume take up issues of congressional campaign financing, lobbying, and the treatment of Congress by the media.

KEY TERMS

bicameral legislature: a governing body composed of two separate chambers, as in the Congress and most of the states of the Union

bill: a proposed law in Congress

committee system: a division of labor in which the work of the Congress is apportioned to specialized standing committees before measures are reported to the floor for a vote

filibuster: a practice in which any senator can hold the floor for as long as desired. This unlimited debate can be used to prevent votes on bills that would probably pass if brought to the floor.

item veto: the authority of a chief executive to reject only part of a bill, a power possessed by governors of most states. As the Constitution now stands, a president can veto only a full bill.

party discipline: the practice in which members of the majority party vote with their leadership in all important legislative matters, a condition that does *not* characterize American political parties in Congress.

term limits: laws that specify the number of terms a state's members of Congress may serve. The question of whether these laws are constitutional has not yet been settled.

9

FEDERALIST NOS. 57, 62
James Madison

In Federalist *No. 57 Madison defends the institution of the House of Representatives against the charges of those who were criticizing the proposed Constitution. He argues that the popularly elected representatives will be highly esteemed in their communities and that they will remain attentive to the wishes of their constituents through frequent elections.*

In Federalist *No. 62 Madison defends the proposed Senate as being composed of people of greater maturity and stability of character than representatives. Because of this and of the longer terms in office, the Senate will provide a "salutary check on government" that will guard against the danger of too rapid changes in public policy in response to elections to the House.*

No. 57

To the People of the State of New York:

The *third* charge against the House of Representatives is, that it will be taken from that class of citizens which will have least sympathy with the mass of the people, and be mostly likely to aim at an ambitious sacrifice of the many to the aggrandizement of the few.

Of all the objections which have been framed against the federal Constitution, this is perhaps the most extraordinary. Whilst the objection itself is leveled against a pretended oligarchy, the principle of it strikes at the very root of republican government.

The aim of every political constitution is, or ought to be, first to obtain for rulers men who possess most wisdom to discern, and most virtue to pursue, the common good of the society; and in the next place, to take the most effectual precautions for keeping them virtuous whilst they continue to hold their public trust. The elective mode of obtaining rulers is the characteristic policy of republican government. The means relied on in this form of government for preventing their degeneracy are numerous and various. The most effectual one is such a limitation of the term of appointments as will maintain a proper responsibility to the people.

Let me now ask what circumstance there is in the constitution of the House of Representatives that violates the principles of republican government, or favors the elevation of the few on the ruins of the many? Let me ask whether every circumstance is not, on the contrary, strictly conformable to these principles, and scrupulously impartial to the rights and pretensions of every class and description of citizens?

Who are to be the electors of the federal representatives? Not the rich, more than the poor; not the learned, more than the ignorant; not the haughty heirs of distinguished names, more than the humble sons of obscurity and unpropitious fortune. The electors are to be the great body of the people of the United States. They are to be the same who exercise the right in every State of electing the corresponding branch of the legislature of the State.

Who are to be the objects of popular choice? Every citizen whose merit may recommend him to the esteem and confidence of his country. No qualification of wealth, of birth, of religious faith, or of civil profession is permitted to fetter the judgment or disappoint the inclination of the people.

If we consider the situation of the men on whom the free suffrages of their fellow-citizens may confer the representative trust, we shall find it involving every security which can be devised or desired for their fidelity to their constituents.

In the first place, as they will have been distinguished by the preference of their fellow-citizens, we are to presume that in general they will be somewhat distinguished also by those qualifications which entitle them to it, and which promise a sincere and scrupulous regard to the nature of their engagements.

In the second place, they will enter into the public service under circumstances which cannot fail to produce a temporary affection at least to their constituents. There is in every breast a sensibility to marks of honor, of favor, of esteem, and of confidence, which, apart from all considerations of interest, is some pledge for grateful and benevolent returns. Ingratitude is a common topic of declamation against human nature; and it must be confessed that instances of it are but too frequent and flagrant, both in public and in private life. But the universal and extreme indignation which it inspires is itself a proof of the energy and prevalence of the contrary sentiment.

In the third place, those ties which bind the representative to his constituents are strengthened by motives of a more selfish nature. His pride and vanity attach him to a form of government which favors his pretensions and give him a share in its honors and distinctions. Whatever hopes or projects might be entertained by a few aspiring characters, it must generally happen that a great proportion of the men deriving their advancement from their influence with the people, would have more to hope from a preservation of the favor, than from innovations in the government subversive of the authority of the people.

All these securities, however, would be found very insufficient without the restraint of frequent elections. Hence, in the fourth place, the House of Representatives is so constituted as to support in the members an habitual recollection to their dependence on the people. Before the sentiments impressed on their minds by the mode of their elevation can be effaced by the exercise of power, they will be compelled to anticipate the moment when their power is to cease, when their exercise of it is to be reviewed, and when they must descend to the level from which they were raised: there for ever to remain unless a faithful discharge of their trust shall have established their true title to a renewal of it.

I will add, as a fifth circumstance in the situation of the House of Representatives, restraining them from oppressive measures, that they can make no law which will not have its full operation on themselves and their friends, as well as on the great mass of the society. This has always been deemed one of the strongest bonds by which human policy can connect the rulers and the people together. It creates between them that communion of interests and sympathy of sentiments of which few governments have furnished examples; but without which every government degenerates into tyranny. If it be asked what is to restrain the House of Representatives from making legal discriminations in favor of themselves and a particular class of the society? I answer: the genius of the whole system; the nature of just and constitutional laws; and above all, the vigilant, and manly spirit which actuates the people of America — a spirit which nourishes freedom, and in return is nourished by it.

If this spirit shall ever be so far debased as to tolerate a law not obligatory on the legislature, as well as on the people, the people will be prepared to tolerate anything but liberty.

Such will be the relation between the House of Representatives and their constituents. Duty, gratitude, interest, ambition itself, are the chords by which they will be bound to fidelity and sympathy with the great mass of the people. It is possible that these may all be insufficient to control the caprice and wickedness of man. But are they not all that government will admit, and that human prudence can devise? Are they not the genuine and the characteristic means by which republican government provides for the liberty and happiness of the people? Are they not the identical means on which every State government in the Union relies for the attainment of these important ends? What then are we to understand by the objection which this paper has combated? What are we to say to the men who profess the most flaming zeal for republican government, yet boldly impeach the fundamental principle of it; who pretend to be champions for the right and the capacity of the people to choose their own rulers, yet maintain that they will prefer those only who will immediately and infallibly betray the trust committed to them?

No. 62*

To the People of the State of New York:

Having examined the constitution of the House of Representatives, and answered such of the objections against it as seemed to merit notice, I enter next on the examination of the Senate.

---

* Authorship of Nos. 62 and 63 has been disputed. An analysis of the contents has shown Madison to be the more likely author, but he probably wrote after consultation with Hamilton who had undertaken to write two further papers (65 and 66) on the Senate.

The heads into which this member of the government may be considered are: I. The qualification of senators; II. The appointment of them by the State legislatures; III. The equality of representation in the Senate; IV. The number of senators, and the term for which they are to be elected; V. The powers vested in the Senate.

I. The qualifications proposed for senators, as distinguished from those of representatives, consist in a more advanced age and a longer period of citizenship. A senator must be thirty years of age at least; as a representative must be twenty-five. And the former must have been a citizen nine years; as seven years are required for the latter. The propriety of these distinctions is explained by the nature of the senatorial trust, which, requiring greater extent of information and stability of character, requires at the same time that the senator should have reached a period of life most likely to supply these advantages; and which, participating immediately in transactions with foreign nations, ought to be exercised by none who are not thoroughly weaned from the prepossessions and habits incident to foreign birth and education. The term of nine years appears to be a prudent mediocrity between a total exclusion of adopted citizens, whose merits and talents may claim a share in the public confidence, and an indiscriminate and hasty admission of them, which might create a channel for foreign influence on the national councils.

II. It is equally unnecessary to dilate on the appointment of senators by the State legislatures. Among the various modes which might have been devised for constituting this branch of the government, that which has been proposed by the convention is probably the most congenial with the public opinion. It is recommended by the double advantage of favoring a select appointment, and of giving to the State governments such an agency in the formation of the federal government as must secure the authority of the former, and may form a convenient link between the two systems.

III. The equality of representation in the Senate is another point, which, being evidently the result of compromise between the opposite pretensions of the large and the small States, does not call for much discussion. If indeed it be right, that among a people thoroughly incorporated into one nation, every district ought to have a *proportional* share in the government, and that among independent and sovereign States, bound together by a simple league, the parties, however unequal in size, ought to have an *equal* share in the common councils, it does not appear to be without some reason that in a compound republic, partaking both of the national and federal character, the government ought to be founded on a mixture of the principles of proportional and equal representation. But it is superfluous to try, by the standard of theory, a part of the Constitution which is allowed on all hands to be the result, not of theory, but "of a spirit of amity, and that mutual deference and concession which the peculiarity of our political situation rendered indispensable." A common government, with powers equal to its objects, is called for by the voice, and still more loudly by the political situation, of America. A government founded on principles more consonant to the wishes of the larger States is not likely to be obtained from the smaller States. The only option, then, for the former, lies between the proposed government and a government still more objectionable. Under this alternative, the advice of prudence must be to embrace the lesser evil; and, instead of indulging a fruitless anticipation of the possible mischiefs which may ensue, to contemplate rather the advantageous consequences which may qualify the sacrifice.

In this spirit it may be remarked, that the equal vote allowed to each State is at once a constitutional recognition of the portion of sovereignty remaining in the individual States, and an instrument for preserving the residuary sovereignty. So far the equality ought to be no less acceptable to the large than to the small States; since they are not less solicitous to guard, by every possible expedient, against an improper consolidation of the States into one simple republic.

Another advantage accruing from this ingredient in the constitution of the Senate is the additional impediment it must prove against improper acts of legislation. No law or resolution can now be passed without the concurrence, first, of a majority of the people, and then, of a majority of the States. It must be acknowledged that this complicated check on legislation may in some instances be injurious as well as beneficial; and that the peculiar defense which it involves in favor of the smaller States would be more rational, if any interests common to them, and distinct from those of the other States, would otherwise be exposed to peculiar danger. But as the larger States will always be able, by their power over the supplies, to defeat unreasonable exertions of this prerogative of the lesser States, and as the facility and excess of law-making seem to be the diseases to which our governments are most liable, it is not impossible that this part of the Constitution may be more convenient in practice than it appears to many in contemplation.

IV. The number of senators, and the duration of their appointment, come next to be considered. In order to form an accurate judgment on both these points, it will be proper to inquire into the purposes which are to be answered by a senate; and in order to ascertain these, it will be necessary to review the inconveniences which a republic must suffer from the want of such an institution.

First. It is a misfortune incident to republican government, though in a less degree than to other governments, that those who administer it may forget their obligations to their constituents, and prove unfaithful to their important trust. In this point of view, a senate, a second branch of the legislative assembly, distinct from, and dividing the power with, a first, must be in all cases a salutary check on the government. It doubles the security to the people, by requiring the concurrence of two distinct bodies in schemes of usurpation or perfidy, where the ambition or corruption of one would otherwise be sufficient. This is a precaution founded on such clear principles, and now so well understood in the United States, that it would be more than superfluous to enlarge on it. I will barely remark, that as the improbability of sinister combinations will be in proportion to the dissimilarity in the genius of the two bodies, it must be politic to distinguish them from each other by every circumstance which will consist with a due harmony in all proper measures, and with the genuine principles of republican government.

Secondly. The necessity of a senate is not less indicated by the propensity of all single and numerous assemblies to yield to the impulse of sudden and violent passions, and to be seduced by factious leaders into intemperate and pernicious resolutions. Examples on this subject might be cited without number; and from proceedings within the United States, as well as from the history of other nations. But a position that will not be contradicted need not be proved. All that need be remarked is, that a body which is to correct this infirmity ought itself to be free from it, and consequently ought to be less numerous. It ought, moreover, to possess great firmness, and consequently ought to hold its authority by a tenure of considerable duration.

Thirdly. Another defect to be supplied by a senate lies in a want of due acquaintance with the objects and principles of legislation. It is not possible that an assembly of men called for the most part from pursuits of a private nature, continued in appointment for a short time, and led by no permanent motive to devote the intervals of public occupation to a study of the laws, the affairs, and the comprehensive interests of their country, should, if left wholly to themselves, escape a variety of important errors in the exercise of their legislative trust. It may be affirmed, on the best grounds, that no small share of the present embarrassments of America is to be charged on the blunders of our governments; and that these have proceeded from the heads rather than the hearts of most of the authors of them. What indeed are all the repealing, explaining, and amending laws, which fill and disgrace our voluminous codes, but so many monuments of deficient wisdom; so many impeachments exhibited by each succeeding against each preceding session; so many admonitions to the people of the value of those aids which may be expected from a well-constituted senate?

A good government implies two things: first, fidelity to the object of government, which is the happiness of the people; secondly, a knowledge of the means by which that object can be best attained. Some governments are deficient in both these qualities; most governments are deficient in the first. I scruple not to assert that in American governments too little attention has been paid to the last. The federal Constitution avoids this error; and that merits particular notice, it provides for the last in a mode which increases the security for the first.

Fourthly. The mutability in the public councils arising from a rapid succession of new members, however qualified they may be, points out, in the strongest manner, the necessity of some stable institution in the government. Every new election in the States is found to change one half of the representatives. From this change of men must proceed a change of opinions; and from a change of opinions, a change of measures. But a continual change even of good measures is inconsistent with every rule of prudence and every prospect of success. The remark is verified in private life, and becomes more just, as well as more important, in national transactions.

POINTS TO PONDER

1. According to Madison, what will ensure that representatives remain faithful to their duties to their constituents?
2. What does Madison say are the most important functions of the Senate?
3. Why are the terms of office of the two bodies different?

10

"POLITICAL CHANGE AND THE CHARACTER OF THE CONTEMPORARY CONGRESS"
Nelson W. Polsby

University of California–Berkeley political scientist Nelson Polsby traces the alternating cycles of active congressional innovation in lawmaking and periods of relative stalemate in postwar American politics. In this article published in Anthony King's The New American Political System *(1990), Polsby describes the contrasting institutional cultures of the two houses of Congress and their changes over the years. He traces the tremendous growth in staff resources that Congress gave itself to counter the rise of the imperial presidency in the 1970s. Finally, Polsby outlines the sources of significant change in the twentieth-century Congress.*

The purpose of this chapter is to describe the main characteristics of the contemporary Congress, especially as they have emerged from slightly less contemporary features of the political landscape. In a world of change, Americans have been able to rely upon great stability in their political institutions. They have been deprived of the stimulus of occupying armies, or the refreshment of an internal revolution, or some other constitutional upheaval leading to a wholly new and different political order. Such upheavals have frequently emerged in the modern world over the past half-century, transforming the governments under which large chunks of the world's population exist. Nevertheless I shall argue that meaningful change has come to the American political system within living memory, and even to that seemingly rock-solid fortress of continuity and stasis, the U.S. Congress.

Continuity and Change—An Overview

As we look at the past half-century of Congress as a historical whole, it is possible to discern an alternating and somewhat overlapping pattern of activity and retrenchment, of focus and stalemate in congressional affairs. Three times during the fifty-year period, Congress has gone through episodes of high productivity and strong coordination; and through three somewhat longer episodes, Congress has more or less ridden at anchor in the political system at large. Neither one mode nor the other is exclusively "natural" to Congress. Although the legitimacy of congressional behavior in either mode is frequently the subject of hot dispute, both roles are historically characteristic of Congress, and both fully express the powers of Congress as contemplated in the overall constitutional design. The design confides to Congress two complementary assignments: to represent the American people in at least some approximation of their variety and diversity and to provide a forum for the taking of significant policy initiatives. When there are great variation and disparity in the opinions of Americans about public policy, this fact is bound to be recognized in pulling and hauling on Capitol Hill; when there are unanimity and resolution, Congress moves its business with dispatch.

I will be brief and schematic in identifying episodes of concentrated congressional activity over the past fifty years. In these historical moments, Congress initiates or ratifies sizable expansions of federal activity, focuses its energies effectively, and undertakes policy innovation. The first of these moments was the enactment of the New Deal (1933–1936) in which the political innovations of Franklin Roosevelt's first 100 days occurred, including the revision of banking laws, the formation of the Securities and Exchange Commission, the establishment of a social security system, and the passage of the Wagner Act, among other events. The second moment was the creation of wartime agencies in Washington (1939–1946), which greatly increased the administrative capacities of central government and broke through congressional resistance to governmental economic forecasting and planning and to an administratively augmented presidency. This episode included, among others, the Budget Act of 1939; the establishment of the Office of War Mobilization and (later) Reconversion; the Employment Act of 1946, which created, among other things, a Council of Economic Advisers; the consolidation of civilian control of the armed services into a Defense Department; and the establishment of the Central Intelligence Agency, the Atomic Energy Commission, and the National Science Foundation. The third moment was the New Frontier–Great Society (1963–1969). This period saw the completion of the New Deal: the enactment of Medicare and civil rights laws and the creation or enhancement of federal bureaucracies (such as the Department of Housing and Urban Development) dedicated to less-advantaged clientele.

Interspersed with these episodes of innovation have been episodes of stalemate and retrenchment. We remember, for example, the thwarting of the later New Deal (1937–1941), in which President Roosevelt attempted, and failed, to pack the Supreme Court after the Court found many early New Deal measures unconstitutional. Roosevelt then attempted, and failed, to defeat conservative Democratic members of Congress in the 1938 election, and Congress no longer produced a cornucopia of new legislation. In time, "Doctor New Deal" gave way to "Doctor Win-the-War." Then, from roughly 1950, when the Truman administration began to be bogged down in loyalty-security issues, and all through the Eisenhower administration, when the threat of a presidential veto prevented all but the most consensual of congressional initiatives, on into most of the Kennedy presidency, in which the dominance of conservative committee chairmen in Congress narrowed the president's agenda (1950–1963), Congress and the presidency existed in a sort of equilibrium described by one liberal commentator as a "deadlock of democracy." Since 1968, there has been a period of consolidation in reaction to the most recent set of policy innovations, and during most of this time Congress has been in Democratic while the presidency has been in Republican hands. During most of these three periods, political innovation has been resisted or at a stalemate, and little or no consensus has existed favoring new departures in governmental policy. Private authority has been preferred to the authority of central government.

That periods of stalemate should last, on average, about twice as long as periods of innovation ought not greatly to surprise even the most casual student of human nature. In important respects, the U.S. population resembles the population that attempted to build the Tower of Babel. The point of that Biblical fable is perfectly straightforward: to undertake great public works, it helps if everyone speaks the same language. Finding that language in the expression of common goals and organizing concerted strategies toward those goals are not trivial tasks when formal power and autonomy are dispersed and it is necessary to mobilize the consent of majorities several times over—first in subcommittees, then in committees, and then on the floor of each of two legislative chambers. The most prevalent alternative form of coordination—dictatorship—is scarcely relevant to the politics of a free and self-governing people. Far more relevant is the simple fact . . . that it takes time to gather up the consensus necessary to move a bicameral representative body that exists independently within a constitutional separation of powers.

Crises of various sorts—notably, a depression, a war, and a presidential assassination—have done a great deal to press Congress toward bouts of innovative activity. In contrast, reforms of congressional procedures have played little or no role in galvanizing forward motion on the policy front. The era's most comprehensive overhaul of procedures, the reform of the committee system in 1946, came at the start of a long period of stalemate. Other important institutional changes included Lyndon Johnson's redesign of the seniority rules for assigning Democratic senators to committees, which occurred during the Eisenhower lull, the 1961 packing of the House Rules Committee, and various reorganizations and reforms of the House in the mid-1970s. All these changes were significant in creating institutionalized settings for a more successful and better coordinated deployment of the resources of the majority party in Congress, but none was sufficient in and of itself to create an avalanche of new and innovative public policies. Avalanches require the cooperation of the president. Even so, the most important facts about the capacity of Congress to respond—to presidential leadership or to leadership within Congress itself—are encoded in Congress's own organizational structure and in the ways in which the changing composition of Congress makes an impact upon congressional organization.

The Contemporary Senate

The chief changes that have overtaken the U.S. Senate in the past half-century can be compactly described. It has become a more national and outward-looking and a less state-oriented and inward-looking institution. Now, as a matter of course, senators interest themselves in constituencies beyond those mobilized exclusively in their home states and seek to influence national policy on the assumption that it is politically useful to them to achieve national recognition and national resonance in their work. This sea change in the expectations of senators and in the way they do their work, and therefore in the role of the Senate in the political system, I believe has been driven, in large part, by a fundamental change in the career prospects of U.S. senators that occurred in the early 1950s as the result of the arrival on the scene of national television.

We are fortunate in having a superb baseline from which to measure the transformation of the Senate. In 1957 William S. White, congressional correspondent of the *New York Times*, published a book, *Citadel*, which admirably captures the spirit of the place—the prevailing institutional ideology, in effect—as it had been handed down and as he experienced it. What he described was a rather stuffy and comfortable club, complete with leather chairs, snoozing members, obsequious attendants, cigar smoke, and bourbon and run more or less exclusively for the benefit of a small number of elderly and important men. Internal norms of "clubability" were what mattered, White explained. Ideology did not matter, although it seemed to be coincidentally the case that the most significant people in the place, the old bulls who constituted the "inner club," as White called it, just so happened to be themselves conservative, mostly southern, and ill-disposed toward much of the New Deal, though not the part, presumably, that sent resources to southern farmers, or invented tax breaks for the oil industry. And they tended to be against the advance of civil rights, sometimes immoderately so, even though the institution was alleged to prize moderation. White made the claim that the more progressive senators tended to give offense primarily because of their lack of deference to the collegial norms of the place and not because of the substance of their views. One could not do well in the Senate by seeking publicity, he argued, or by running for "other" offices—presumably the presidency.

White argued that in its essence the Senate of those days was fulfilling its historic constitutional purpose of "cooling the legislative tea" by providing a calm, skeptical, and carefully deliberative counterweight to an allegedly more impulsive House of Representatives and a demonstrably more innovative and demanding presidency. What he described, however, was in large measure the very successful pursuit of parochial interest, sometimes clothed in statesmanship, sometimes not. The southerners who ran the place, insofar as they actually did so, attended with great care to the local prejudices of the small and lily-white electorates that sent them to Washington. No doubt they were obliged to do so to stay in the Senate, but nevertheless this was a clear prerequisite that allowed the more able among them to adopt an interest in broader concerns, such as foreign or military affairs or health care.

There were some questions about the descriptive accuracy of White's portrait by the time it reached print. On the whole, it was accepted by a great many of those journalists and biographers who wrote about the Senate during the 1960s and even thereafter. It is common to find in magazine profiles of senators of that era, for example, some attempt to assess whether the subject was "in" or "outside" the "inner club," and one writer once went so far as to publish what he advertised as a guess at a comprehensive listing of the club's members. This suggests that White captured something about the Senate that had high credibility among observers.

By the time *Citadel* was published, however, two forces were transforming the Senate radically. One was television, as I have mentioned, and the other was Lyndon Johnson. Television, it appears, happened very suddenly indeed to the U.S. Senate. In March 1951, a senator who had not much weight in the institution, Estes Kefauver of Tennessee, became an overnight media star as the result of the daytime broadcast of hearings of his committee's investigation of organized crime. Kefauver went on to run in the 1952 presidential primary elections—very successfully—and more or less on the strength of his lucky burst of publicity, he became a factor in the presidential nominating politics of the Democratic party for the rest of his life.

From the 1950s onward, senators in wholesale lots, if they could manage it, began to maneuver themselves toward active roles in presidential nominating politics. Some of them simply used the Senate as a publicity springboard from which they could launch themselves. Kefauver and, more successfully, John Kennedy pursued that strategy. Others, following the early lead of Arthur Vandenberg and Robert A. Taft and, notably, Hubert Humphrey sought to use their position in the Senate to pursue national policy goals in a way that would commend themselves to the party leaders who in those days controlled the presidential nominating process. In short, they began to invent the Senate as an arena within which, and not merely from which, one could launch a presidential bid.

Lyndon Johnson's ambitions led him to the latter strategy. Under the patronage of elders of the old inner club, he became the Democratic leader of the Senate mid-way through his first term as senator. He managed the business of his party in the Senate in part with an eye toward national office—refusing, for example, to join the southerners who put him into the leadership in overtly opposing civil rights initiatives.

Johnson's leadership of the Senate also greatly changed the institution itself. Decisions by consensus of senior members were replaced by the accretion of powers, large and small, in Johnson's own hands. Ralph Huitt, Joseph Clark, and others have left us a picture of a body that was being explicitly managed by an assiduous, indeed a compulsively driven, leader anxious to make a record and advance his career by coordinating as many different things as he could reach within the institution.

By the time Johnson ascended to the vice presidency in 1961, the old citadel had largely disappeared. Senators were in no mood to continue the highly centralized pattern of leadership that Johnson had imposed on the institution. It was a great virtue that Mike Mansfield, Johnson's successor, vastly preferred a lighter touch on the reins. But the Senate did not return to the collegial pattern of the old inner club. In the meantime the goals of senators had shifted perceptibly. A senator was in the White House—the first one originally elected to the presidency since Warren G. Harding. He had beaten a former member of the Senate in the general election as well as several in the prenomination period to get there. And a senator was vice president. At least ten senators—Russell, Kerr, Lodge, Johnson, Kefauver, Kennedy, Taft, Vandenberg, Symington, and Humphrey—had been serious contenders for the presidency over the past couple of nomination cycles.

In the 1930s and 1940s, it was unusual for senators to run for president, to cultivate national constituencies in the pursuit of policy initiatives, or to go out of their way to court publicity. Now all these activities are usual. Indeed, for a senator not to do so nowadays may even occasion comment. These changes in the way individual senators conduct their jobs—facilitated by an enormous increase in staff, space, and equipment—have also wrought changes in the Senate's role as a corporate entity in the political system. As it has become a less collegial and reactive body, it has become more enterprising and innovative with respect to public policy. The Senate is now a place in which public policy ideas are tried out, floated, deliberated, and sometimes parked as they await the proper constellation of forces leading to eventual enactment. The careers of senators, and of the staffs of senators, depend far more on engagement with the new and far less upon the preservation of the old than was true forty or fifty years ago.

The Contemporary House of Representatives

As recently as twenty years ago, an observer might have said that, of all of the institutions of American government, the House of Representatives had been least touched by change since the creation of most of the institutions of modern America in the early years of the twentieth century. Not since 1919 had an ongoing committee assignment in the House violated the criterion of seniority. New committee assignments were doled out by committees on committees of each party, much influenced by the leaders of key state delegations. Committee chairmen—those most senior in committee service in the House majority party—dominated the policy-making process within their respective domains, sometimes collaborating with ranking minority members, sometimes not. The Republican conference—the assembly of all Republican members—was considerably more influential than its counterpart body, the House Democratic caucus, in expressing a party mainstream ideological position. This was understandable in light of the fact that Republicans in the House were, on the whole, far more ideologically united. For the most part, both the conference and the caucus were moribund, meeting to do serious business only once in every two years, to nominate and elect party leaders and to ratify the work of their respective committees on committees. For the rest of the time, party leaders—the Speaker, majority and minority leaders, and party whips—had custody of all the routines and schedules that are at the heart of the management of a complex legislative body, but they were constrained to exercise their power more or less in the fashion of tugboats urging a gigantic ocean liner along a course it intends to pursue anyway.

In recent years, however, change has finally come to the House of Representatives. Its main outlines are these: committee chairmen, once beyond reach, have been deposed and threatened with removal on several occasions since 1950, mainly for being out of step with mainstream sentiment among the Democratic members of the caucus; committees on committees have been reconstituted to give party leaders much more power, including the power unilaterally to appoint members to the key scheduling committee, the Rules Committee; and uniform rules of committee conduct have been written so as to spread power downward and outward to subcommittees and their chairmen. As subcommittees have gained autonomy and party leaders have gained responsibilities, power has slipped away from the chairmen of full committees, who have been the major losers in the transformations that have taken place.

The main engine of change has been the House Democratic caucus. Because the House has been firmly in the hands of a Democratic majority since 1954, what has happened to the Democrats is of paramount concern in following developments in the House. From 1937 until quite recently, the divisions within the caucus were sufficient to neutralize any attempts to use the caucus to coordinate the majority party. Southern Democrats—about 100 strong during most of the period, and virtually all of them from safe seats—made up almost half the Democratic members of the House—sometimes a little less, depending on Democratic electoral fortunes in the rest of the country. And about two-thirds of the southern Democrats were Dixiecrats, which meant that they were opposed to Democrats from the rest of the country on most issues of public policy and were perfectly willing to make coalitions with House Republicans to stop liberal legislation. So the actual ideological division in the House as a whole was frequently closely balanced when conservatives were not slightly in the lead. This made of the House the graveyard of many liberal proposals during the Truman and Kennedy presidencies.

From time to time, House members closer to the mainstream of the national party would become restive. A small uprising of the peasants took place after the 1958 election, for example, when a flood of newly elected liberal Democrats descended on the House. As Speaker Rayburn saw all too clearly, this was bound to have no legislative consequences over the short run, since liberal initiatives could not in any event survive an Eisenhower veto. In their impatience a few young leaders of the party in the House—notably Eugene McCarthy, Lee Metcalf, and Frank Thompson—organized what in time became a programmatically oriented substitute for the caucus, the Democratic Study Group. This group soon embraced most ideologically mainstream Democratic members. It took more than a few years for the House Democratic leadership to become comfortable with the study group, which at its most effective acted as the sort of communications system and rallying-point that the official Democratic whip system could not provide, because of its obligation to serve all Democratic members, whatever their ideological stripe.

By the 1970s, the caucus had absorbed many of these functions of the study group and had revived as an instrument of House leadership after a fifty-year period of quiescence. What had happened was this: slightly more than a score of Dixiecrats had disappeared from the House, and they had been replaced by Republicans. It is not altogether intuitively obvious that a gain of about twenty-five Republican seats in the House would be a proximate cause of the liberalization of the House, but this, more or less, is what happened. It was, to be sure, not the new Republican members themselves, most of whom were ferociously conservative, who were the instruments of change but rather the drastic change in the make-up of the Democratic caucus that did the job, enabling the caucus to take initiatives that only a few years earlier would have torn it apart.

Indirectly, of course, these changes were the product of the nationalization of the South, of demographic changes that made the South more like the rest of the country, and of the party realignments that made it possible for southern Republicans to run for House seats and win. Promiscuous and ill-founded claims of party realignment at the national level have given the whole idea of realignment a bad name among careful analysts. If there has been a party realignment anywhere in America these past fifty years, however, it has occurred in the South, and it has led to liberalization in the House of Representatives.

Congressional-Presidential Relations and the Growth of Congressional Staff

The president is the most interested observer of Congress and its most devoted lobbyist. Congress, despite its full complement of internal institutional imperatives, must nevertheless somehow coordinate its activities with the president. Hence, significant changes in the presidency over the past fifty years have had a great impact on Congress. Of these, two have had the greatest importance. The growth of a systematic congressional liaison service—a staff of full-time professionals in the White House that deals exclusively with Congress—is the less significant of the two. More important has been the capture of the presidency of executive agencies—notably the Bureau of the Budget, now the Office of Management and Budget (OMB)—that once provided more or less neutrally competent ad hoc service to the legislative branch.

Starting with the Johnson administration, and accelerating with the Nixon presidency, a great many of the underlying facts and numbers on which legislation depends, and which used to be supplied routinely to Congress by the executive branch, became subject to presidential political influence. Mistrust of the presidency, known in Johnson's day as a "credibility gap," began to develop on Capitol Hill along a broad front, and not only with respect to the Vietnam War. Soon, Congress felt the need for access to its own information and completely changed its pattern of staffing.

The sheer numbers are staggering. Two entirely new congressional agencies were created: the Office of Technology Assessment in 1974 and the Congressional Budget Office (CBO) in 1975. The CBO in particular had an almost immediate impact. Staffed by nearly 200 economists and other professionals, the CBO's budget estimates quickly developed a reputation for realism that overshadowed the increasingly partisan and massaged numbers of the OMB. Very soon it became a commonplace of Washington practice to conduct bipartisan or nonpartisan discussions of live economic issues using Congressional Budget Office, not Office of Management and Budget, numbers.

Between 1960 and 1980, the staff of the Congressional Research Service of the Library of Congress was increased fourfold; and the numbers of employees assigned to the House and the Senate, to individual members and to committees, jumped comparably. By 1985, roughly 25,000 staff members worked for Congress. This includes only the Congressional Research Service component of the Library of Congress, and only the one-third of the General Accounting Office employees who work directly for Congress. In 1957, 2,441 staff were employed by House members and 1,115 by Senate members; by 1985, those numbers had turned into 7,528 and 4,097, respectively. In 1960, 440 staff were employed by House standing committees, and 470 by Senate standing committees; in 1985, those numbers had become 2,009 and 1,080, respectively. The growth in a couple of short decades has been remarkable. The growth in another measure is even more remarkable: in the forty years from 1946 to 1986, while the consumer price index rose 450.8 percent legislative branch appropriations rose 2,859.3 percent.

An inspection of the year-to-year figures shows double digits in the growth of congressional appropriations after Lyndon Johnson's 1964 landslide, continuing right through the Nixon era. There is no adequate way to quantify the attitudes of mistrust that appear to have caused these figures to lift off the planet earth when and as they did, but it is possible to speculate about the causes of the creation of a legislative bureaucracy after so many years in which the legislative branch found it possible to live comfortably with a comparatively thin roster of professional staff. Loss of comity with the executive branch, driven by the development of a greatly augmented presidential branch of government, is by far the most plausible explanation.

Under the old dispensation, what congressional staff were professional at was looking after the political needs of members, mixed in, in exceptional cases like the House Appropriations Committee, with some attention to oversight of the executive. On the whole, service on the staff of Congress did not require much interest in or competence at public policy analysis, much less political innovation. Expertise came with long years on the job rather than as the result of professional training. Today, while the numbers of professionals employed by Congress has burgeoned, their average age has shrunk, and they now come to Capitol Hill with professional credentials. Many more of them—not just in absolute numbers, but as a proportion of the whole—focus on policy and on promoting their employers' interests through the advocacy or adoption of public policy positions. This is most noticeable in the Senate, where senators are stretched so thin by the multiple responsibilities of committee work that it is largely impossible for them to keep track of everything personally. Their staff members do it for them, and in the process not infrequently engage in sophisticated forms of political entrepreneurship on their principal's behalf. Sometimes it is a part of a staff member's duties not only to seize and promote a policy position or to make or adopt an issue in behalf of one's principal, but also to engage the interest and approval of the principal as well.

Staff members with these extraordinary opportunities to affect public policy tend not to devote their lives to congressional service as so many of their predecessors did, but to job hop around the policy subcommunity on which they are making a mark. So not only are congressional staff different today in their sheer numbers, but also they are different in the ways in which they define their jobs, different in their training, and different in their career expectations. Collectively, they resemble their counterparts in the political entourages of the presidential appointees who run the federal agencies of downtown Washington far more than they do preceding generations of staff members on Capitol Hill. They have brought increased capability to Congress to deal substantively with policy, and they have done much to provide a link between Congress and the increasingly specialized and professionalized worlds of policy makers, policy advisers, and lawyers and foundation, university, and think tank personnel who make up the various policy subcommunities of Washington and throughout the United States. There was a time when Congress, and congressional staff, stood aloof from the communications networks maintained by these policy subcommunities. This is no longer true.

POINTS TO PONDER

1. What are the main functions of Congress?
2. According to Polsby, under what circumstances will Congress move slowly and when will it work with dispatch?

3. How has the Senate changed in the past half-century? What have been the driving forces of these changes?
4. Why is the House less conservative than it was at midcentury?
5. How would James Madison react to the contemporary Congress? What would surprise him and what would he expect to see?

11

"THE RISE OF
THE WASHINGTON ESTABLISHMENT"
Morris P. Fiorina

In the following excerpt from his book Congress: Keystone of the Washington Establishment *(1989), Harvard political scientist Morris Fiorina argues that the combination of Congress members' motivation for reelection and the growth of the federal government have resulted in a symbiotic relationship between bureaucrats and members of Congress. Each derives professional rewards from continuing to increase the size of the federal establishment—larger budgets and greater jurisdiction for bureaucrats, reelection for members of Congress. Fiorina's perspective is one-dimensional in that he sees individuals as primarily motivated by narrow self-interest, with no systemic forces in favor of the common good. On the other hand, his analysis is powerful because self-interest is undoubtedly an important, if not primary, motivator, and the assumption of this motivation seems to explain much congressional activity in dealing with the executive branch.*

Dramatis Personae

I assume that most people most of the time act in their own self-interest. This is not to say that human beings seek only to amass tangible wealth but rather to say that human beings seek to achieve their own ends—tangible and intangible—rather than the ends of their fellow men. I do not condemn such behavior nor do I condone it (although I rather sympathize with Thoreau's comment that "if I knew for a certainty that a man was coming to my house with the conscious design of doing me good, I should run for my life"). I only claim that political and economic theories which presume self-interested behavior will prove to be more widely applicable than those which build on more altruistic assumptions.

What does the axiom imply when used in the specific context of this book, a context peopled by congressmen, bureaucrats, and voters? I assume that the primary goal of the typical congressman is reelection. Over and above the $57,000 salary plus "perks" and outside money, the office of congressman carries with it prestige, excitement, and power. It is a seat in the cockpit of government. But in order to retain the status, excitement, and power (not to mention more tangible things) of office, the congressman must win reelection every two years. Even those congressmen genuinely concerned with good public policy must achieve reelection in order to continue their work. Whether narrowly self-serving or more publicly oriented, the individual congressman finds reelection to be at least a necessary condition for the achievement of his goals.

Moreover, there is a kind of natural selection process at work in the electoral arena. On average, those congressmen who are not primarily interested in reelection will not achieve reelection as often as those who are interested. We, the people, help to weed out congressmen whose primary motivation is not reelection. We admire politicians who courageously adopt the aloof role of the disinterested statesman, but we vote for those politicians who follow our wishes and do us favors.

What about the bureaucrats? A specification of their goals is somewhat more controversial—those who speak of appointed officials as public servants obviously take a more benign view than those who speak of them as bureaucrats. The literature provides ample justification for asserting that most bureaucrats wish to protect and nurture their agencies. The typical bureaucrat can be expected to seek to expand his agency in terms of personal, budget, and mission. One's status in Washington (again, not to mention more tangible things) is roughly proportional to the importance of the operation one oversees. And the sheer size of the operation is taken to be a measure of importance. As with congressmen, the specified goals apply even to those bureaucrats who genuinely believe in their agency's mission. If they believe in the efficacy of their programs, they naturally wish to expand them and add new ones. All of this requires more money and more people. The genuinely committed bureaucrat is just as likely to seek to expand his agency as the proverbial empire-builder.

And what of the third element in the equation, us? What do we, the voters who support the Washington system, strive for? Each of us wishes to receive a maximum of benefits from government for the minimum cost. This goal suggests maximum government efficiency, on the one hand, but it also suggests mutual exploitation on the other. Each of us favors an arrangement in which our fellow citizens pay for our benefits.

With these brief descriptions of the cast of characters in hand, let us proceed.

Tammany Hall Goes to Washington

What should we expect from a legislative body composed of individuals whose first priority is their continued tenure in office? We should expect, first, that the normal activities of its members are those calculated to enhance their chances of reelection. And we should expect, second, that the members would devise and maintain institutional arrangements which facilitate their electoral activities. . . .

For most of the twentieth century, congressmen have engaged in a mix of three kinds of activities: lawmaking, pork barreling, and casework. Congress is first and foremost a lawmaking body, at least according to constitutional theory. In every postwar session Congress "considers" thousands of bills and resolutions, many hundreds of which are brought to a record vote (over 500 in each chamber in the 93d Congress). Naturally the critical consideration in taking a position for the record is the maximization of approval in the home district. If the district is unaffected by and unconcerned with the matter at hand, the congressman may then take into account the general welfare of the country. (This sounds cynical, but remember that "profiles in courage" are sufficiently rare that their occurrence inspires books and articles.) Abetted by political scientists of the pluralist school, politicians have propounded an ideology which maintains that the good of the country on any given issue is simply what is best for a majority of congressional districts. This ideology provides a philosophical justification for what congressmen do while acting in their own self-interest.

A second activity favored by congressmen consists of efforts to bring home the bacon to their districts. Many popular articles have been written about the pork barrel, a term originally applied to rivers and harbors legislation but now generalized to cover all manner of federal largesse. Congressmen consider new dams, federal buildings, sewage treatment plants, urban renewal projects, etc. as sweet plums to be plucked. Federal projects are highly visible, their economic impact is easily detected by constituents, and sometimes they even produce something of value to the district. The average constituent may have some trouble translating his congressman's vote on some civil rights issue into a change in his personal welfare. But the workers hired and supplies purchased in connection with a big federal project provide benefits that are widely appreciated. The historical importance congressmen attach to the pork barrel is reflected in the rules of the House. That body accords certain classes of legislation "privileged" status: they may come directly to the floor without passing through the Rules Committee, a traditional graveyard for legislation. What kinds of legislation are privileged? Taxing and spending bills, for one: the government's power to raise and spend money must be kept relatively unfettered. But in addition, the omnibus rivers and harbors bills of the Public Works Committee and public lands bills from the Interior Committee share privileged status. The House will allow a civil rights or defense procurement or environmental bill to languish in the Rules Committee, but it takes special precautions to insure that nothing slows down the approval of dams and irrigation projects.

A third major activity takes up perhaps as much time as the other two combined. Traditionally, constituents appeal to their congressman for myriad favors and services. Sometimes only information is needed, but often constituents request that their congressman intervene in the internal workings of federal agencies to affect a decision in a favorable way, to reverse an adverse decision, or simply to speed up the glacial bureaucratic process. On the basis of extensive personal interviews with congressmen, Charles Clapp writes:

Denied a favorable ruling by the bureaucracy on a matter of direct concern to him, puzzled or irked by delays in obtaining a decision, confused by the administrative maze through which he is directed to proceed, or ignorant of whom to write, a constituent may turn to his congressman for help. These letters offer great potential for political benefit to the congressman since they affect the constituent personally. If the legislator can be of assistance, he may gain a firm ally; if he is indifferent, he may even lose votes.

Actually congressmen are in an almost unique position in our system, a position shared only with high-level members of the executive branch. Congressmen possess the power to expedite and influence bureaucratic decisions. This capability flows directly from congressional control over what bureaucrats value most: higher budgets and new program authorizations. In a very real sense each congressman is a monopoly supplier of bureaucratic unsticking services for his district.

Every year the federal budget passes through the appropriations committees of Congress. Generally these committees make perfunctory cuts. But on occasion they vent displeasure on an agency and leave it bleeding all over the Capitol. The most extreme case of which I am aware came when the House committee took away the entire budget of the Division of Labor Standards in 1947 (some of the budget was restored elsewhere in the appropriations process). Deep and serious cuts are made occasionally, and the threat of such cuts keeps most agencies attentive to congressional wishes. Professors Richard Fenno and Aaron Wildavsky have provided extensive documentary and interview evidence of the great respect (and even terror) federal bureaucrats show for the House Appropriations Committee. Moreover, the bureaucracy must keep coming back to Congress to have its old programs reauthorized and new ones added. Again, most such decisions are perfunctory, but exceptions are sufficiently frequent that bureaucrats do not forget the basis of their agencies' existence. For example, the Law Enforcement Assistance Administration (LEAA) and the Food Stamps Program had no easy time of it this last Congress (94th). The bureaucracy needs congressional approval in order to survive, let alone expand. Thus, when a congressman calls about some minor bureaucratic decision or regulation, the bureaucracy considers his accommodation a small price to pay for the goodwill its cooperation will produce, particularly if he has any connection to the substantive committee or the appropriations subcommittee to which it reports.

From the standpoint of capturing voters, the congressman's lawmaking activities differ in two important respects from his pork-barrel and casework activities. First, programmatic actions are inherently controversial. Unless his district is homogeneous, a congressman will find his district divided on many major issues. Thus when he casts a vote, introduces a piece of nontrivial legislation, or makes a speech with policy content he will displease some elements of his district. Some constituents may applaud the congressman's civil rights record, but others believe integration is going too fast. Some support foreign aid, while others believe it's money poured down a rathole. Some advocate economic equality, others stew over welfare cheaters. On such policy matters the congressman can expect to make friends as well as enemies. Presumably he will behave so as to maximize the excess of the former over the latter, but nevertheless a policy stand will generally make some enemies.

In contrast, the pork barrel and casework are relatively less controversial. New federal projects bring jobs, shiny new facilities, and general economic prosperity, or so people believe. Snipping ribbons at the dedication of a new post office or dam is a much more pleasant pursuit than disposing of a constitutional amendment on abortion. Republicans and Democrats, conservatives and liberals, all generally prefer a richer district to a poorer one. Of course, in recent years the river damming and stream-bed straightening activities of the Army Corps of Engineers have aroused some opposition among environmentalists. Congressmen happily reacted by absorbing the opposition and adding environmentalism to the pork barrel: water treatment plants are currently a hot congressional item.

Casework is even less controversial. Some poor, aggrieved constituent becomes enmeshed in the tentacles of an evil bureaucracy and calls upon Congressman St. George to do battle with the dragon. Again Clapp writes:

> A person who has a reasonable complaint or query is regarded as providing an opportunity rather than as adding an extra burden to an already busy office. The party affiliation of the individual even when known to be different from that of the congressman does not normally act as a deterrent to action. Some legislators have built their reputations and their majorities on a program of service to all constituents irrespective of party. Regularly, voters affiliated with the opposition in other contests lend strong support to the lawmaker whose intervention has helped them in their struggle with the bureaucracy.

Even following the revelation of sexual improprieties, Wayne Hays won his Ohio Democratic primary by a two-to-one margin. According to a *Los Angeles Times* feature story, Hays's constituency base was built on a foundation of personal service to constituents:

> They receive help in speeding up bureaucratic action on various kinds of federal assistance—black lung benefits to disabled miners and their families, Social Security payments, veterans' benefits and passports.
>
> Some constituents still tell with pleasure of how Hays stormed clear to the seventh floor of the State Department and into secretary of State Dean Rusk's office to demand, successfully, the quick issuance of a passport to an Ohioan.

Practicing politicians will tell you that word of mouth is still the most effective mode of communication. News of favors to constituents gets around and no doubt is embellished in the process.

In sum, when considering the benefits of his programmatic activities, the congressman must tote up gains and losses to arrive at a net profit. Pork barreling and casework, however, are basically pure profit.

A second way in which programmatic activities differ from casework and the pork barrel is the difficulty of assigning responsibility to the former as compared with the latter. No congressman can seriously claim that he is responsible for the 1964 Civil Rights Act, the ABM, or the 1972 Revenue Sharing Act. Most constituents do have some vague notion that their congressman is only one of hundreds and their senator one of an even hundred. Even committee chairmen have a difficult time claiming credit for a piece of major legislation, let alone a rank-and-file congressman. Ah, but casework, and the pork barrel. In dealing with the bureaucracy, the congressman is not merely one vote of 435. Rather, he is a nonpartisan power, someone whose phone calls snap an office to attention. He is not kept on hold. The constituent who receives aid believes that his congressman and his congressman alone got results. Similarly, congressmen find it easy to claim credit for federal projects awarded their districts. The congressman may have instigated the proposal for the project in the first place, issued regular progress reports, and ultimately announced the award through his office. Maybe he can't claim credit for the 1965 Voting Rights Act, but he can take credit for Littletown's spanking new sewage treatment plant.

Overall then, programmatic activities are dangerous (controversial), on the one hand, and programmatic accomplishments are difficult to claim credit for, on the other. While less exciting, casework and pork barreling are both safe and profitable. For a reelection-oriented congressman the choice is obvious.

The key to the rise of the Washington establishment (and the vanishing marginals) is the following observation: *the growth of an activist federal government has stimulated a change in the mix of congressional activities.* Specifically, a lesser proportion of congressional effort is now going into programmatic activities and a greater proportion into pork-barrel and casework activities. As a result, today's congressmen make relatively fewer enemies and relatively more friends among the people of their districts.

To elaborate, a basic fact of life in twentieth-century America is the growth of the federal role and its attendant bureaucracy. Bureaucracy is the characteristic mode of delivering public goods and services. Ceteris paribus, the more the government attempts to do for people, the more extensive a bureaucracy it creates. As the scope of government expands, more and more citizens find themselves in direct contact with the federal government. Consider the rise in such contacts upon passage of the Social Security Act, work relief projects and other New Deal programs. Consider the millions of additional citizens touched by the veterans' programs of the postwar period. Consider the untold numbers whom the Great Society and its aftermath brought face to face with the federal government. In 1930 the federal bureaucracy was small and rather distant from the everyday concerns of Americans. By 1975 it was neither small nor distant.

As the years have passed, more and more citizens and groups have found themselves dealing with the federal bureaucracy. They may be seeking positive actions—eligibility for various benefits and awards of government grants. Or they may be seeking relief from the costs imposed by bureaucratic regulations—on working conditions, racial and sexual quotas, market restrictions, and numerous other subjects. While not malevolent, bureaucracies make mistakes, both of commission and omission, and normal attempts at redress often meet with unresponsiveness and inflexibility and sometimes seeming incorrigibility. Whatever the problem, the citizen's congressman is a source of succor. The greater the scope of government activity, the greater the demand for his services.

Private monopolists can regulate the demand for their product by raising or lowering the price. Congressmen have no such (legal) option. When the demand for their services rises, they have no real choice except to meet that demand—to supply more bureaucratic unsticking services—so long as they would rather be elected than unelected. This vulnerability to escalating constituency demands is largely academic, though. I seriously doubt that congressmen resist their gradual transformation from national legislators to errand boy–ombudsmen. As we have noted, casework is all profit. Congressmen have buried proposals to relieve the casework burden by establishing a national ombudsman or Congressman Reuss's proposed Administrative Counsel of the Congress. One of the congressmen interviewed by Clapp stated:

> Before I came to Washington I used to think that it might be nice if the individual states had administrative arms here that would take care of necessary liaison between citizens and the national government. But a congressman running for reelection is interested in building fences by providing personal services. The system is set to reelect incumbents regardless of party, and incumbents wouldn't dream of giving any of this service function away to any subagency. As an elected member I feel the same way.

In fact, it is probable that at least some congressmen deliberately stimulate the demand for their bureaucratic fixit services. . . . Recall that the new Republican in district A travels about his district saying:

> I'm your man in Washington. What are your problems? How can I help you?

And in district B, did the demand for the congressman's services rise so much between 1962 and 1964 that a "regiment" of constituency staff became necessary? Or, having access to the regiment, did the new Democrat stimulate the demand to which he would apply his regiment?

In addition to greatly increased casework, let us not forget that the growth of the federal role has also greatly expanded the federal pork barrel. The creative pork barreler need not limit himself to dams and post offices—rather old-fashioned interests. Today, creative congressmen can cadge LEAA money for the local police, urban renewal and housing money for local politicians, educational program grants for the local education bureaucracy. And there are sewage treatment plants, worker training and retraining programs, health services, and programs for the elderly. The pork barrel is full to overflowing. The conscientious congressman can stimulate applications for federal assistance (the sheer number of programs makes it difficult for local officials to stay current with the possibilities), put in a good word during consideration, and announce favorable decisions amid great fanfare.

In sum, everyday decisions by large and growing federal bureaucracy bestow significant tangible benefits and impose significant tangible costs. Congressmen can affect these decisions. Ergo, the more decisions the bureaucracy has the opportunity to make, the more opportunities there are for the congressman to build up credits.

The nature of the Washington system is now quite clear. Congressmen (typically the majority Democrats) earn electoral credits by establishing various federal programs (the minority Republicans typically earn credits by fighting the good fight). The legislation is drafted in very general terms, so some agency, existing or newly established, must translate a vague policy mandate into a functioning program, a process that necessitates the promulgation of numerous rules and regulations and, incidentally, the trampling of numerous toes. At the next stage, aggrieved and/or hopeful constituents petition their congressman to intervene in the complex (or at least obscure) decision processes of the bureaucracy. The cycle closes when the congressman lends a sympathetic ear, piously denounces the evils of bureaucracy, intervenes in the latter's decisions, and rides a grateful electorate to ever more impressive electoral showings. Congressmen take credit coming and going. They are the alpha and the omega.

The popular frustration with the permanent government in Washington is partly justified, but to a considerable degree it is misplaced resentment. *Congress is the linchpin of the Washington establishment.* The bureaucracy serves as a convenient lightning rod for public frustration and a convenient whipping boy for congressmen. But so long as the bureaucracy accommodates congressmen, the latter will oblige with ever larger budgets and grants of authority. Congress does not just react to big government—it creates it. All of Washington prospers. More and more bureaucrats promulgate more and more regulations and dispense more and more money. Fewer and fewer congressmen suffer electoral defeat. Elements of the electorate benefit from government programs, and all of the electorate is eligible for ombudsman services. But the general, long-term welfare of the United States is no more than an incidental by-product of the system.

POINTS TO PONDER

1. What is the relationship between congressional incentives and the growth of the federal bureaucracy?
2. According to Fiorina, what primarily motivates members of Congress? What are the consequences of their votes based on these motives?
3. What would the Framers say about Fiorina's analysis?

12

~~~~

"IF, AS RALPH NADER SAYS, CONGRESS IS 'THE BROKEN BRANCH,' HOW COME WE LOVE OUR CONGRESSMEN SO MUCH?"

Richard F. Fenno, Jr.

University of Rochester political scientist Richard Fenno, Jr., is one of the foremost scholars of Congress in the twentieth century. His analyses of the internal workings of congressional committees and the relationship of members of Congress with their home constituencies have illuminated our understanding of congressional structure and motivation. In the following article originally presented in 1972, he offers an explanation of why public opinion polls show that Congress as an institution is held in low esteem, yet individual members are popular and continue to be reelected. Ironically, candidates for Congress often "run for Congress by running against Congress" as an institution. Fenno's explanation has to do with the attention members pay to pleasing their home constituencies and the effect of that concern on the performance of committees in Congress.

Off and on during the past two years, I accompanied ten members of the House of Representatives as they traveled around in their home districts. In every one of those districts I heard a common theme, one that I had not expected. Invariably, the representative I was with—young or old, liberal or conservative, Northerner, Southerner, Easterner, or Westerner, Democrat or Republican—was described as "the best congressman in the United States." Having heard it so often, I now accept the description as fact. I am even prepared to believe the same thing (though I cannot claim to have heard it with my own ears) of the members of the Senate. Each of our 435 representatives and 100 senators is, indeed, "the best congressman in the United States." Which is to say that each enjoys a great deal of support and approbation among his or her constituents. Judging by the election returns, this isn't much of an exaggeration. In the recent election, 96 per cent of all House incumbents who ran were re-elected; and 85 per cent of all Senate incumbents who ran were re-elected. These convincing figures are close to the average re-election rates of incumbents for the past ten elections. We do, it appears, love our congressmen.

On the other hand, it seems equally clear that we do not love our Congress. Louis Harris reported in 1970 that only one-quarter of the electorate gave Congress a positive rating on its job performance—while nearly two-thirds expressed themselves negatively on the subject. And we would not be here tonight if there were not considerable concern—dramatized recently by the critical Nader project—for the performance of Congress as an institution. On the evidence, we seem to approve of our legislators a good deal more than we do our legislature. And therein hangs something of a puzzle. If our congressmen are so good, how can our Congress be so bad? If it is the individuals that make up the institution, why should there be such a disparity in our judgments? What follows are a few reflections on this puzzle.

A first answer is that we apply different standards of judgment, those that we apply to the individual being less demanding than those we apply to the institution. For the individual, our standard is one of representativeness—of personal style and policy views. Stylistically, we ask that our legislator display a sense of identity with us so that we, in turn, can identify with him or her—via personal visits to the district, concern for local projects and individual "cases," and media contact of all sorts, for example. On the policy side, we ask only that his general policy stance does not get too frequently out of line with ours. And, if he should become a national leader in some policy area of interest to us, so much the better. These standards are admittedly vague. But because they are locally defined and locally applied, they are consistent and manageable enough so that legislators can devise rules of thumb to meet them. What is more, by their performance they help shape the standards, thereby making them easier to meet. Thus they win constituent recognition as "the best in the United States." And thus they establish the core relationship for a representative democracy.

For the institution, however, our standards emphasize efforts to solve national problems—a far less tractable task than the one we (and he) set for the individual. Given the inevitable existence of unsolved problems, we are destined to be unhappy with congressional performance. The individual legislator knows when he has met our standards of representativeness; he is re-elected. But no such definitive measure of legislative success exists. And, precisely because Congress is the most familiar and most human of our national institutions, lacking the distant majesty of the Presidency and the Court, it is the easy and natural target of our criticism. We have met our problem solvers, and they are us.

Furthermore, such standards as we do use for judging the institutional performance of Congress are applied inconsistently. In 1963, when public dissatisfaction was as great as in 1970, Congress was criticized for being obstructionist, dilatory and insufficiently cooperative with regard to the Kennedy programs. Two years later, Congress got its highest performance rating of the decade when it cooperated completely with the executive in rushing the Great Society program into law. But by the late 1960's and early 1970's the standard of judgment had changed radically—from cooperation to counterbalance in Congressional relations with the Executive. Whereas, in 1963, Harris had found "little in the way of public response to the time-honored claim that the Legislative Branch is . . . the guardian against excessive Executive power," by 1968 he found that three-quarters of the electorate wanted Congress to act as the watchdog of the Executive and not to cooperate so readily with it. The easy passage of the Tonkin Resolution reflects the cooperative standards set in the earlier period; its repeal reflects the counterbalancing standards of the recent period. Today we are concerned about Ralph Nader's "broken branch" which, we hear, has lost—and must reclaim from the Executive—its prerogatives in areas such as war-making and spending control. To some degree, then, our judgments on Congress are negative because we change our minds frequently concerning the kind of Congress we want. A Congress whose main job is to cooperate with the Executive would look quite different from one whose main job is to counterbalance the Executive.

Beneath the differences in our standards of judgment, however, lies a deeper dynamic of the political system. Senators and representatives, for their own reasons, spend a good deal more of their time and energy polishing and worrying about their individual performance than they do working at the institution's performance. Though it is, of course, true that their individual activity is related to institutional activity, their first-order concerns are individual, not institutional. Foremost is their desire for re-election. Most members of Congress like their job, want to keep it, and know that there are people back home who want to take it away from them. So they work long and hard at winning re-election. Even those who are safest want election margins large enough to discourage opposition back home and/or to help them float further political ambitions. No matter what other personal goals representatives and senators wish to accomplish—increased influence in Washington and helping to make good public policy are the most common—re-election is a necessary means to those ends.

We cannot criticize these priorities—not in a representative system. If we believe the representative should mirror constituency opinion, we must acknowledge that it requires considerable effort for him to find out what should be mirrored. If we believe a representative should be free to vote his judgment, he will have to cultivate his constituents assiduously before they will trust him with such freedom. Either way we will look favorably on his efforts. We come to love our legislators, in the *second* place, because they so ardently sue for our affections.

As a courtship technique, moreover, they re-enforce our unfavorable judgments about the institution. Every representative with whom I traveled criticized the Congress and portrayed himself, by contrast as a fighter against its manifest evils. Members run *for* Congress by running *against* Congress. They refurbish their individual reputations as "the best congressman in the United States" by attacking the collective reputation of the Congress of the United States. Small wonder the voters feel so much more warmly disposed and so much less fickle toward the individuals than toward the institution.

One case in point: the House decision to grant President Nixon a spending ceiling plus authority to cut previously appropriated funds to maintain that ceiling. One-half the representatives I was with blasted the House for being so spineless that it gave away its power of the purse to the President. The other half blasted the House for being so spineless in exercising its power of the purse that the President had been forced to act. Both groups spoke to supportive audiences; and each man enhanced his individual reputation by attacking the institution. Only by raising both questions, however, could one see the whole picture. Once the President forced the issue, how come the House didn't stand up to him and protect its crucial institutional power over the purse strings? On the other hand, if economic experts agreed that a spending ceiling was called for, how come the House didn't enact it and make the necessary budget cuts in the first place? The answer to the first question lies in the proximity of their re-election battles, which re-enforced the tendency of all representatives to think in individualistic rather than institutional terms. The answer to the second question lies in the total absence of institutional machinery whereby the House (or, indeed, Congress) can make overall spending decisions.

Mention of the institutional mechanisms of Congress leads us to a *third* explanation for our prevailing pattern of judgments. When members of Congress think institutionally—as, of course they must—they think in terms of a structure that will be most congenial to the pursuit of their individual concerns—for re-election, for influence, or for policy. Since each individual has been independently designated "the best in the United States," each has an equal status and an equal claim to influence within the structure. For these reasons, the members naturally think in terms of a very fragmented, decentralized institution, providing a maximum of opportunity for individual performance, individual influence, and individual credit.

The 100-member Senate more completely fits this description than the 435-member House. The smaller body permits a more freewheeling and creative individualism. But both chambers tend strongly in this direction, and representatives as well as senators chafe against centralizing mechanisms. Neither body is organized in hierarchical—or even well-coordinated—patterns of decision making. Agreements are reached by some fairly subtle forms of mutual adjustment—by negotiation, bargaining, and compromise. And interpersonal relations—of respect, confidence, trust—are crucial building blocks. The members of Congress, in pursuit of their individual desires, have thus created an institution that is internally quite complex. Its structure and processes are, therefore, very difficult to grasp from the outside.

In order to play out some aspects of the original puzzle, however, we must make the effort. And the committee system, the epitome of fragmentation and decentralization, is a good place to start. The performance of Congress as an institution is very largely the performance of its committees. The Nader project's "broken branch" description is mostly a committee-centered description because that is where the countervailing combination of congressional expertise and political skill resides. To strengthen Congress means to strengthen its committees. To love Congress means to love its committees. Certainly when we have not loved our Congress, we have heaped our displeasure upon its committees. The major legislative reorganizations, of 1946 and 1970, were committee-centered reforms—centering on committee jurisdictions, committee democracy, and committee staff support. Other continuing criticisms—of the seniority rule for selecting committee chairmen, for example—have centered on the committees.

Like Congress as a whole, committees must be understood first in terms of what they do for the individual member. To begin with, committees are relatively more important to the individual House member than to the individual senator. The representative's career inside Congress is very closely tied to his committee. For the only way such a large body can function is to divide into highly specialized and independent committees. Policy-making activity funnels through these committees; so does the legislative activity and influence of the individual legislator. While the Senate has a set of committees paralleling those of the House, a committee assignment is nowhere near as constraining for the career of the individual senator. The Senate is more loosely organized, senators sit on many more committees and subcommittees than representatives, and they have easy access to the work of committees of which they are not members. Senators, too, can command and utilize national publicity to gain influence beyond the confines of their committee. Whereas House committees act as funnels for individual activity, Senate committees act as facilitators of individual activity. The difference in functions is considerable—which is why committee chairmen are a good deal more important in the House than in the Senate and why the first modifications of the seniority rule should have come in the House rather than the Senate. My examples will come from the House.

Given the great importance of his committee to the career of the House member, it follows that we will want to know how each committee can affect such careers. . . .

Where a committee's members are especially interested in pyramiding their individual influence, they will act so as to maintain the influence of their committee (and, hence, their personal influence) within the House. They will adopt procedures that enhance the operating independence of the committee. They will work hard to remain relatively independent of the Executive Branch. And they will try to underpin that independence with such resources as specialized expertise, internal cohesion, and the respect of their House colleagues. Ways and Means and Appropriations are committees of this sort. By contrast, where a committee's members are especially interested in getting in on nationally controversial policy action, they will not be much concerned about the independent influence of their committee. They will want to ally themselves closely with any and all groups outside the committee who share their policy views. They want to help enact what they individually regard as good public policy; and if that means ratifying policies shaped elsewhere—in the Executive Branch particularly—so be it. And, since their institutional independence is not a value for them, they make no special effort to acquire such underpinnings as expertise, cohesion, or chamber respect. Education and Labor and Foreign Affairs are committees of this sort.

These two types of committees display quite different strengths in their performance. Those of the first type are especially influential. Ways and Means probably makes a greater independent contribution to policy-making than any other House committee. Appropriations probably exerts a more influential overview of executive branch activities than any other House committee. The price they pay, however, is a certain decrease in their responsiveness to noncommittee forces—as complaints about the closed rule on tax bills and executive hearings on appropriations bills will attest. Committees of the second type are especially responsive to noncommittee forces and provide easy conduits for outside influence in policy-making. Education and Labor was probably more receptive to President Johnson's Great Society policies than any other House committee; it successfully passed the largest part of that program. Foreign Affairs has probably remained as thoroughly responsive to Executive Branch policies, in foreign aid for instance, as any House committee. The price they pay, however, is a certain decrease in their influence—as complaints about the rubber-stamp Education and Labor Committee and about the impotent Foreign Affairs Committee will attest. In terms of the earlier discussions of institutional performance standards, our hopes for a cooperative Congress lie more with the latter type of committee; our hopes for a counterbalancing Congress lie more with the former.

So, committees differ. And they differ to an important degree according to the desires of their members. This ought to make us wary of blanket descriptions. Within the House, Foreign Affairs may look like a broken branch, but Ways and Means does not. And, across chambers, Senate Foreign Relations (where member incentives are stronger) is a good deal more potent than House Foreign Affairs. With the two Appropriations committees, the reverse is the case. It is not just that "the broken branch" is an undiscriminating, hence inaccurate, description. It is also that blanket descriptions lead to blanket prescriptions. And it just might be that the wisest course of congressional reform would be to identify existing nodes of committee strength and nourish them rather than to prescribe, as we usually do, reforms in equal dosages for all committees.

One lesson of the analysis should be that member incentives must exist to support any kind of committee activity. Where incentives vary, it may be silly to prescribe the same functions and resources for all committees. The Reorganization Act of 1946 mandated all committees to exercise "continuous watchfulness" over the executive branch—in the absence of any supporting incentive system. We have gotten overview activity only where random individuals have found an incentive for doing so—not by most committees and certainly not continuously. Similarly, I suspect that our current interest in exhorting all committees to acquire more information with which to combat the executive may be misplaced. Information is relatively easy to come by—and some committees have a lot of it. What is hard to come by is the incentive to use it, not to mention the time and the trust necessary to make it useful. I am not suggesting a set of reforms but rather a somewhat different strategy of committee reforms—less wholesale, more retail.

Since the best-known target of wholesale committee reform is the seniority rule, it deserves special comment. If our attacks on the rule have any substance to them, if they are anything other than symbolic, the complaint must be that some or all committee chairmen are not doing a good job. But we can only find out whether this is so by conducting a committee-by-committee examination. Paradoxically, our discussions of the seniority rule tend to steer us away from such a retail examination by mounting very broad, across-the-board kinds of arguments against chairmen as a class—arguments about their old age, their conservatism, their national unrepresentativeness. Such arguments produce great cartoon copy, easy editorial broadsides, and sitting-duck targets for our congressmen on the stump. But we ought not to let the arguments themselves, nor the Pavlovian public reactions induced by our cartoonists, editorial writers, and representatives, pass for good institutional analysis. Rather, they have diverted us from that task.

More crucial to a committee's performance than the selection of its chairman is his working relationship with the other committee members. Does he agree with his members on the functions of the committee? Does he act to facilitate the achievement of their individual concerns? Do they approve of his performance as chairman? Where there is real disagreement between chairman and members, close analysis may lead us to fault the members and not the chairman. If so, we should be focusing our criticisms on the members. If the fault lies with the chairman, a majority of the members have the power to bring him to heel. They need not kill the king; they can constitutionalize the monarchy. While outsiders have been crying "off with his head," the members of several committees have been quietly and effectively constitutionalizing the monarchy. Education and Labor, Post Office, and Interior are recent examples where dissatisfied committee majorities have subjected their chairmen to majority control. Where this has not been done, it is probably due to member satisfaction, member timidity, member disinterest, or member incompetence. And the time we spend railing against the seniority rule might be better spent finding out, for each congressional committee, just which of these is the case. If, as a final possibility, a chairman and his members are united in opposition to the majority party or to the rest of us, the seniority rule is not the problem. More to the point, as I suspect is usually the case, the reasons and the ways individual members get sorted onto the various committees is the critical factor. In sum, I am not saying that the seniority rule is a good thing. I am saying that, for committee performance, it is not a very important thing.

What has all this got to do with the original puzzle—that we love our congressmen so much more than our Congress? We began with a few explanatory guesses. Our standards of judgment for individual performance are more easily met; the individual member works harder winning approval for himself than for his institution; and Congress is a complex institution, difficult for us to understand. The more we try to understand Congress—as we did briefly with the committee system—the more we are forced to peel back the institutional layers until we reach the individual member. At that point, it becomes hard to separate, as we normally do, our judgments about congressmen and Congress. The more we come to see institutional performance as influenced by the desires of the individual member, the more the original puzzle ought to resolve itself. For as the independence of our judgments decreases, the disparity between them ought to grow smaller. But if we are to hold this perspective on Congress, we shall need to understand the close individual–institution relationship—chamber by chamber, party by party, committee by committee, legislator by legislator.

This is not counsel of despair. It is a counsel of sharper focus and a more discriminating eye. It counsels the mass media, for example, to forego "broken branch" type generalizations about Congress in favor of examining a committee in depth, or to forego broad criticism of the seniority rule for a close look at a committee chairman. It counsels the rest of us to focus more on the individual member and to fix the terms of our dialogue with him more aggressively. It counsels us to fix terms that will force him to think more institutionally and which will hold him more accountable for the performance of the institution. "Who Runs Congress," asks the title of the Nader report, "the President, Big Business or You?" From the perspective of this paper, it is none of these. It is the members who run Congress. And we get pretty much the kind of Congress they want. We shall get a different kind of Congress when we elect different kinds of congressmen or when we start applying different standards of judgment to old congressmen. Whether or not we ought to have a different kind of Congress is still another, much larger, puzzle.

POINTS TO PONDER

1. Why is there a disjuncture between voters' evaluations of Congress as an institution and of their own representatives in Congress?
2. According to Fenno, what is necessary in order to transform Congress?
3. Careful responsiveness to constituents marks the modern Congress, according to Fenno. Why does Fiorina see this as a problem?

13

"CONGRESS-BASHING FOR BEGINNERS"
Nelson W. Polsby

In this selection, Nelson Polsby of the University of California–Berkeley offers a counterbalance to much of the contemporary bashing of Congress by describing previous eras of public discontent with the institution. The foremost critics of Congress in the late twentieth century have been conservatives frustrated that the agendas of Republican presidents have not been fully implemented. But in the 1950s the primary critics were liberal Democrats who felt that Congress was the graveyard of progressive public policy initiatives. In this article from The Public Interest *(1990), Polsby cautions against constitutional change, such as the item veto, that would increase presidential power at the expense of Congress. He also offers a critique of the current wave of public support for proposals to limit the terms of members of Congress to twelve years. In his critique, Polsby explains the complexity of the congressional job and the weakening of Congress that would occur if skilled and experienced members were forced to give up their seats after twelve years.*

On a shelf not far from where I am writing these words sit a half a dozen or so books disparaging Congress and complaining about the congressional role in the constitutional separation of powers. These books date mostly from the late 1940s and the early 1960s, and typically their authors are liberal Democrats. In those years, Congress was unresponsive to liberal Democrats and, naturally enough, aggrieved members of that articulate tribe sought solutions in structural reform.

In fact, instead of reforms weakening Congress what they—and we—got was a considerably strengthened presidency. This was mostly a product of World War II and not the result of liberal complaints. Before World War II Congress would not enact even the modest recommendations of the Brownlow Commission to give the president a handful of assistants with "a passion for anonymity," and it killed the National Resources Planning Board outright. After World War II everything changed: Congress gave the president responsibility for smoothing the effects of the business cycle, created a Defense Department and two presidential agencies—the NSC and the CIA—that enhanced the potential for presidential dominance of national security affairs, and laid the groundwork for the growth of a presidential branch, politically responsive to both Democratic and Republican presidents.

Congress and the Goring of Oxen

Though it took time for the presidential branch to grow into its potential, the growth of this branch, separate and at arm's length from the executive branch that it runs in the president's behalf, is the big news of the postwar era—indeed, of the last half-century in American government. It is customary today to acknowledge that Harry Truman's primary agenda, in the field of foreign affairs, was quite successfully enacted even though Congress was dominated by a conservative coalition, and what Truman wanted in the way of peacetime international involvement was for the United States quite unprecedented. Dwight Eisenhower's agenda was also largely international in its impact. Looking back, it seems that almost all Eisenhower really cared about was protecting the international position of the United States from diminution by Republican isolationists. Everything else was expendable.

Congress responded sluggishly and in its customary piecemeal fashion. It was right around John Kennedy's first year in office that liberals rediscovered that old roadblock in Congress, a "deadlock of democracy," as one of them put it. It was Congress that had thwarted the second New Deal after 1937, the packing of the Supreme Court, and Harry Truman's domestic program; it was Congress that had stalled civil rights and buried Medicare; it was Congress that had sponsored the Bricker Amendment to limit the president's power to make treaties. Are memories so short that we do not recall these dear, departed days when Congress was the graveyard of the forward-looking proposals of liberal presidents? Then, Congress was a creaky eighteenth-century machine unsuited to the modern age, and Congress-bashers were liberal Democrats.

To be sure, Congress had a few defenders, mostly Republicans and Dixiecrats, who found in its musty cloakrooms and windy debates a citadel (as one of them said) of old-time legislative virtues, where the historic functions of oversight and scrutiny were performed, where the run-away proposals of the presidency could be subjected to the sober second thoughts of the people's own elected representatives, and so on.

Why rehash all this? In part, it is to try to make the perfectly obvious point that Congress-bashing then was what people did when they controlled the presidency but didn't control Congress. And that, in part, is what Congress-bashing is about now. Today, Republicans and conservatives are doing most (although not all) of the complaining. It is worth a small bet that a fair number of editorial pages claimed that the separation of powers made a lot of sense during the Kennedy-Johnson years—but no longer say the same today. On the other side, backers of FDR's scheme to pack the Court have turned into vigorous defenders of the judicial status quo since Earl Warren's time.

There is nothing wrong with letting the goring of oxen determine what side we take in a political argument. In a civilized country, however, it makes sense to keep political arguments civil and not to let push come to shove too often. There is something uncivil, in my view, about insisting upon constitutional reforms to cure political ailments. What liberal critics of Congress needed was not constitutional reform. What they needed was the 89th Congress, which, in due course, enacted much of the agenda that the Democratic party had built up over the previous two decades. History didn't stop with the rise of the presidential branch and the enactment of the second New Deal/New Frontier/Great Society. President Johnson overreached. He concealed from Congress the costs of the Vietnam War. He created a credibility gap.

This, among other things, began to change Congress. The legislative branch no longer was altogether comfortable relying on the massaged numbers and other unreliable information coming over from the presidential branch. They began to create a legislative bureaucracy to cope with this challenge. They beefed up the General Accounting Office and the Congressional Research Service. They created an Office of Technology Assessment and a Congressional Budget Office. They doubled and redoubled their personal staffs and committee staffs.

Sentiments supporting this expansion began, oddly enough, after a land-slide election in which the Democratic party swept the presidency and both houses of Congress. So mistrust between the branches in recent history has by no means been entirely a partisan matter. Nevertheless, Richard Nixon's presidency, conducted entirely in unhappy harness with a Democratic Congress, did not improve relations between the two branches of government. Johnson may have been deceitful, but Nixon, especially after his reelection in 1972, was positively confrontational.

It was Nixon's policy to disregard comity between the branches. This, and not merely his commission of impeachable offenses, fueled the impeachment effort in Congress. That effort was never wholly partisan. Republicans as well as Democrats voted articles of impeachment that included complaints specifically related to obstruction of the discharge of congressional responsibilities.

It is necessary to understand this recent history of the relations between Congress and the president in order to understand the provenance of the War Powers Act, the Boland Amendment, numerous other instances of congressional micromanagement, the unprecedented involvement of the NSC in the Iran-*contra* affair, and like manifestations of tension and mistrust between Congress and the president. These tensions are, to a certain degree, now embedded in law and in the routines of responsible public officials; they cannot be made to disappear with a wave of a magic wand. They are, for the most part, regrettable in the consequences they have had for congressional-presidential relations, but they reflect real responses to real problems in these relations. Congressional responses, so far as I can see, have been completely legal, constitutional, and—in the light of historical circumstances—understandable. The best way to turn the relations between the legislative and the presidential branches around would be for the presidential side to take vigorous initiatives to restore comity. As head of the branch far more capable of taking initiatives, and the branch far more responsible for the underlying problem, this effort at restoration is in the first instance up to the President.

President Bush and the Item Veto

In this respect, President Bush is doing a decent job, giving evidence of reaching out constructively. It is not my impression that the Bush administration has done a lot of Congress-bashing. After all, what Bush needs isn't a weakened Congress so much as a Republican Congress. Over the long run (though probably not in time to do Bush much good) Republicans are bound to regret despairing of the latter and therefore seeking the former. We have seen enough turns of the wheel over the last half-century to be reasonably confident that sooner or later Republicans will start to do better in congressional elections. The presidential item veto, the Administration's main Congress-bashing proposal, won't help Republicans in Congress deal with a Democratic president when the time comes, as sooner or later it will, for a Democrat to be elected president.

The item veto would effectively take congressional politics out of the legislative process, and would weaken Congress a lot. It would encourage members of Congress, majority and minority alike, to be irresponsible and to stick the president with embarrassing public choices. It would reduce the incentives for members to acquire knowledge about public policy or indeed to serve.

By allocating legislative responsibilities to Congress, the Constitution as originally (and currently) designed forces representatives of diverse interests to cooperate. Because what Congress does as a collectivity matters, legislative work elicits the committed participation of members. The item veto would greatly trivialize the work product of Congress by requiring the president's acquiescence on each detail of legislation. Members would lose their independent capacity to craft legislation. Their individual views and knowledge would dwindle in importance; only the marshalling of a herd capable of overturning a veto would matter in Congress.

The item veto is, in short, a truly radical idea. It is also almost certainly unconstitutional. To espouse it requires a readiness to give up entirely on the separation of powers and on the constitutional design of the American government. There are plenty of people, some of them well-meaning, who are ready to do that. I am not, nor should people who identify themselves as conservatives or liberals or anywhere in the political mainstream.

The separation of powers is actually a good idea. It gives a necessary weight to the great heterogeneity of our nation—by far the largest and most heterogeneous nation unequivocally to have succeeded at democratic self-government in world history. It would take a medium-sized book to make all the qualifications and all the connections that would do justice to this argument. The conclusion is worth restating anyway: the item veto is a root-and-branch attack on the separation of powers; it is a very radical and a very bad idea.

Term Limitations

Less serious in its impact, but still destructive, is the proposal to limit the terms of members of Congress. This proposal relies heavily for its appeal upon ignorance in the population at large about what members of Congress actually do. For in order to take seriously the idea of limiting congressional terms, one must believe that the job of a representative in Congress is relatively simple, and quickly and easily mastered. It is not.

The job of a member of Congress is varied and complex. It includes: (1) Managing a small group of offices that attempt on request to assist distressed constituents, state and local governments, and enterprises in the home district that may have business with the federal government. This ombudsman function gives members an opportunity to monitor the performance of the government in its dealings with citizens and can serve to identify areas of general need. (2) Serving on committees that oversee executive-branch activity on a broad spectrum of subjects (such as immigration, copyright protection, telecommunications, or health policy) and that undertake to frame issues of national scope for legislative action. This entails mastering complicated subject matter; working with staff members, expert outsiders, and colleagues to build coalitions; understanding justifications; and answering objections. (3) Participating in general legislative work. Members have to vote on everything, not merely on the work of their own committees. They have to inform themselves of the merits of bills, and stand ready to cooperate with colleagues whose support they will need to advance their own proposals. (4) Keeping track of their own political business. This means watching over and occasionally participating in the politics of their own states and localities, and mending fences with interest groups, friends and neighbors, backers, political rivals, and allies. (5) Educating all the varied people with whom they come in contact about issues that are high on the agenda and about reasonable expectations of performance. This includes the performance of the government, the Congress, and the member.

Plenty of members never try to master the job, or try and fail, and these members would be expendable. The objection might still be raised that constituents, not an excess of constitutional limitations, ought to decide who represents whom in Congress. But that aside, what about the rather substantial minority of members who learn their jobs, do their homework, strive to make an impact on public policy, and—through long experience and application to work—actually make a difference? Can we, or should we, dispense with them as well?

It is a delusion to think that good public servants are a dime a dozen in each congressional district, and that only the good ones would queue up to take their twelve-year fling at congressional office. But suppose they did. In case they acquired expertise, what would they do next? Make money, I suppose. Just about the time that their constituents and the American people at large could begin to expect a payoff because of the knowledge and experience that these able members had acquired at our expense, off they would go to some Washington law firm.

And what about their usefulness in the meantime? It would be limited, I'm afraid, by the greater expertise and better command of the territory by lobbyists, congressional staff, and downtown bureaucrats—career people one and all. So this is, once again, a proposal merely to weaken the fabric of Congress in the political system at large, and thereby to limit the effectiveness of the one set of actors most accessible to ordinary citizens.

The standard objection to this last statement is that members of Congress aren't all that accessible. Well, neither is Ralph Nader, who has long overstayed the dozen years that contemporary Congress-bashers wish to allocate to members. Neither is the author of *Wall Street Journal* editorials in praise of limitations. And it must be said that a very large number of members take their representational and ombudsman duties very seriously indeed. This includes holders of safe seats, some of whom fear primary-election opposition, some of whom are simply conscientious. A great many of them do pay attention—close attention—to their constituents. That is one of the reasons—maybe the most important reason—that so many of them are reelected. Much Congress-bashing these days actually complains about high reelection rates, as though a large population of ill-served constituents would be preferable.

Congressional Salaries

While we have Ralph Nader on our minds, it is certainly appropriate to pay our disrespects to his completely off-the-wall effort, temporarily successful, at the head of a crazed phalanx of self-righteous disk jockeys and radio talk-show hosts, to deprive members of Congress of a salary increase. The issue of congressional salaries is a straightforward one. Many members, being well-to-do, don't need one. But some do. The expenses of maintaining two places of residence—in Washington and at home—make membership in Congress nearly unique and singularly expensive among upper-middle-class American jobs. Here is the point once more: it is a job requiring skill and dedication to be done properly. Moreover, membership in Congress brings responsibilities. National policy of the scope and scale now encompassed by acts of the federal government requires responsible, dedicated legislators. People with far less serious responsibilities in the private sector are ordinarily paid considerably better than members of Congress. Think, for example, how far down the organizational chart at General Motors or at CBS or at some other large corporation one would have to go before reaching executives making what members of Congress do, and compare their responsibilities with those of Congress and its members. Actually, most corporations won't say what their compensation packages are like. But at a major auto company, people who make around $100,000 a year are no higher than upper middle management, and certainly don't have responsibilities remotely comparable to those of members of Congress.

There is a case for decent congressional salaries to be made on at least two grounds: one is the rough equity or opportunity-cost ground that we ought not financially to penalize people who serve, and the second is the ground of need for those members who have the expense of families or college educations to think of, and who have no extraordinary private means. The long-run national disadvantage of failing to recognize the justice of these claims is of course a Congress deprived of people for whom these claims are exigent, normal middle-class people with family responsibilities and without money of their own. These are not the sorts of people a sane electorate should wish to prevent from serving.

Members of Congress, knowing very well of the irrational hostilities that the proposal of a congressional pay raise can stir up, have taken the unfortunate precaution of holding hostage the salaries of federal judges, who are now ludicrously underpaid by the admittedly opulent standards of the legal profession, and senior civil servants. An unhealthy impasse has been created owing, at bottom, to Congress-bashing of the most unattractive kind, which exploits the ignorance of ordinary citizens of the dimensions of the members' working lives, and incites citizens to a mindless social envy, in which it is assumed that paying a decent professional salary to professional officeholders is automatically some sort of rip-off.

Members of Congress now make about $98,000. The bottom salary for major-league baseball players is $100,000. Some law firms in New York start new graduates of good law schools at $90,000 or more. How can we argue that members of Congress and others at the top of the federal government should not be paid at least a modest premium above these beginners' wages? There is, evidently, no talking sense to the American people on this subject.

I believe we can dismiss out of hand the charge that large numbers of members individually, or Congress collectively, live in a world all their own, divorced from realities of everyday life. The sophomores who have written attacks of this sort in recent years in the *Atlantic, Newsweek,* and elsewhere simply don't know what they are talking about. They abuse their access to large audiences by neglecting to explain the real conditions that govern the lives of members, conditions that provide ample doses of everyday life.

No doubt scandals involving various members have in recent times made Congress as an institution vulnerable to criticism. But much of this criticism is irresponsible and irrelevant. Suppose we were to discover instances of cupidity, unusual sexual activity, and abuses of power among the rather sizable staff of an important daily newspaper? Or a symphony orchestra? Or, God forbid, a university? I suppose that would shake our confidence in at least part of the collective output, but one would hope for relevant discriminations. One might distrust the ticket office, perhaps, but not the symphony's performance of Mozart; the stock tips, perhaps, but not the Washington page; the basketball program, but not the classics department. I do not think that the existence of scandal excuses us from attempting to draw sensible conclusions about institutions and their performance.

This sort of balanced and discriminating analysis isn't what proposals for item vetoes, limitations on terms of service, or depressed rates of pay are all about. They are about the ancient but now slightly shopworn American custom of Congress-bashing.

POINTS TO PONDER

1. Why has the source of criticisms of Congress changed over the years?
2. Why is Polsby against the item veto?
3. According to Polsby, what would be the effect of term limits?

Chapter 4

THE PRESIDENCY

One of the basic issues of any system of governance is the scope and extent of the power of the chief executive. Although the presidency at the end of the twentieth century is *the* towering center of American national government and politics, it was not always thus. The role of the president in the American political system has depended on dynamic leadership, on whether the United States was facing a crisis or war, and on the institutional growth of the office. The first two factors are recurring, though unpredictable. On the other hand, the growth of the office since Franklin Roosevelt's presidency has been steady and accompanied by increasing expectations by the American people.

Establishing the Presidency

In creating the presidency, the Framers faced a dilemma. Their experience with the Articles of Confederation convinced them that they needed an independent executive who would be responsible for administering the government and reacting quickly to any national security crisis. Yet the oppression of the colonies at the hands of King George III of England made most citizens of the states very skeptical of executive power. They needed an institution that would provide coherent leadership but would not degenerate into a tyranny.

The initial Virginia Plan called for an executive who would be selected by the legislature and might even consist of more than one person. After a summer of deliberation, the Framers finally decided that the presidency would consist of only one person who would not be chosen by (and thus dependent on) the Congress, but neither would the president have the independent power that would follow from election by popular vote. Rather, the president would be selected by an electoral college whose members would be designated by state legislatures for each election. Congress would become involved only if there were no majority in the electoral college balloting.

Thus the vision of the Framers for the presidency was shaped by the need to balance the conflicting concerns of the colonists: legislative control versus executive independence, popular selection versus the judgment of men of character, and the power to lead versus the dangers of tyranny.

Exercise of Presidential Powers

In the nineteenth century presidents actively exercised their constitutional powers as commander in chief and director of foreign policy. In domestic policy presidents were often followers of Congress and did not actively pursue agendas of their own. But the twentieth century has seen the transformation of the presidency into the dominating force in the national government. The debate over the extent of presidential powers between President Taft, who advocated presidential restraint, and Theodore Roosevelt, who championed an aggressive posture of presidential activism, has been decisively won by Roosevelt. Taft argued that presidents had only those powers explicitly granted in the Constitution and should not step beyond them. Roosevelt felt that presidents could take action in any area not explicitly forbidden in the Constitution.

But even Theodore Roosevelt would have been surprised at the role of the presidency pioneered by his distant cousin. Franklin Roosevelt began the era of the modern presidency with his historic legislative agenda in the first "100 days," his leadership in World War II, and his groundwork for the institutional presidency in the creation of the Executive Office of the President in 1939.

The Institutional Presidency

Since Franklin Roosevelt, the scope of presidential power has broadened to match the scope of activity of a greatly enlarged federal government. The White House staff has become institutionalized, with separate units carrying out functions that used to be handled in the executive branch departments and agencies or by the political parties. The national security bureaucracies of the departments of Defense and State, the Central Intelligence Agency (CIA), and the National Security Agency (NSA) are led and coordinated by the National Security Council staff located in the Executive Office of the President. Major domestic policy initiatives are now formulated by the White House domestic policy staff rather than by the departments and agencies. Political parties used to recruit political appointees and build political coalitions. Now these functions are performed by the Office of Presidential Personnel, the Office of Public Liaison, and the Political Affairs Office—all in the White House. The White House staff now includes about 500 professionals in a total of about 2000 people in the Executive Office of the President (EOP).

Presidential Leadership

The legacy of the activism of modern presidential leadership includes rising expectations by the electorate about what presidents can accomplish. Presidential leadership helped bring the nation through the Great Depression and

World War II, and the modern presidential office with its impact on virtually all aspects of public policy seems to be in the news every day. Overpromising by presidential candidates also encourages unrealistic expectations by the public. For example, presidential candidates of both parties promise to cure the U.S. economy of its ills despite the fact that presidents can do very little by themselves to control that economy.

In the end, presidential accomplishment depends on a combination of personal character and historical circumstance. Franklin Roosevelt was able to demonstrate his leadership through the depths of the Great Depression and the adversity of World War II. Lyndon Johnson was a brilliant legislative leader and made historic gains for social justice in the United States but became mired in the war in Vietnam. Richard Nixon was a gifted foreign policy leader but was brought down by Watergate. Jimmy Carter had a fine mind but had organizational problems in his administration and was a victim of hostage takers in Iran, about which he could do very little. Ronald Reagan began his administration with visionary leadership but ended up tripling the national debt. George Bush had little interest in domestic policy but was impressive in knitting together the coalition of allies for the Persian Gulf War. Bill Clinton, in contrast, tackled some of the most pressing domestic problems facing the country but had a mixed record in foreign policy.

The Readings

In some senses the president of the United States is the most powerful person in the world. The economic and military strength of the United States ensures that, when the nation is acting in concert, great things can be accomplished. Within the U.S. political system, the president can dominate the policy agenda, and individual presidents have pushed their powers beyond that of their predecessors. The institutional capacity of the White House has steadily expanded in the twentieth century.

But the readings in this section also make clear that presidential power is limited by the countervailing power of Congress, and that a president cannot govern successfully if this reality is ignored. The American political system is so porous and fragmented that, even within the executive branch, presidential power is not absolute. Thus the presidency is a paradoxical office, extremely powerful in some ways, but vulnerable to political opposition in other ways.

Even though the presidency, including the EOP, involves about 2000 people, the authority of the office is focused in the individual who has been elected president. Everybody in the White House Office and the many more in the other units of the EOP serve at the pleasure of the president, but more important they are all responsible in their duties to the president.

Thus Alexander Hamilton's principle, articulated in *Federalist* No. 70, of unity in the executive is preserved in the modern presidency, despite the size of its offices. In both houses of Congress each member has one vote. In the presidency and the executive branch the president is the final arbiter of all policy decisions, subject, of course, to public law.

The modern presidency is much greater in the scope of its reach and its institutional capacity than it was before the 1930s. But the separation of powers system still operates. Despite the increasing capacity of the institutionalized presidency, presidents do not always get their way in the political system. In one of the classic analyses of the presidency, Richard Neustadt argued that the real power of the president is the power to persuade. In trying to persuade others in the political system to do their will, presidents have many advantages, but the power to command is very limited.

The area of broadest presidential discretion is that of foreign and national security policy, and, as Arthur Schlesinger, Jr., has argued, modern presidents have expanded their power considerably. Schlesinger has argued that Presidents Johnson and Nixon pushed their prerogatives beyond constitutional bounds. Eventually, however, the political system created a counterreaction in which Johnson decided against running for reelection in 1968, and Nixon chose to resign rather than continue to fight his battle against impeachment in the House of Representatives. Congress also provides a powerful counterbalance and often dominates domestic policy, despite active presidential agendas.

Schlesinger's essay confronts the basic question of governance raised by the overreaching of President Nixon in Watergate. Congress's reaction was to reassert congressional prerogatives to the point that some felt the presidency was "imperiled." Schlesinger, however, argues that, despite the institutional weakness of the presidency, the office is a dynamic one when it is occupied by the right incumbent. He does not see the reassertion of Congress as a basic threat to the U.S. system of governance.

One source of presidential power is the president's leadership of the executive branch. Presidential leadership is exercised through presidential appointments, particularly cabinet secretaries. Cabinet officers are the primary line officers of the government who exercise authority over their departments specified in public law and who carry out the policy directives of the president.

While it would seem that cabinet appointees would be unquestionably loyal to the president who appointed them, the reality of the American political system is that other forces, such as Congress, interest groups, and the civil servants who work in cabinet departments, also exert significant influence. One reason the White House staff has grown in size and power in the past several decades is to counter these centrifugal pressures. The selection by James Pfiffner analyzes the reasons for the friction that often develops between cabinet secretaries and the White House staff.

But ensuring discipline in the executive branch is a small problem for presidents compared with trying to get their way with Congress. Modern presidents have been legislative activists, sending to Congress annual legislative agendas since the early 1950s. Presidents now have professionals working in the Office of Legislative Liaison in the White House Office to help them curry favor with Congress. Nevertheless, Congress often resists presidential leadership, and only a few presidents (FDR, Lyndon Johnson, and Ronald Reagan) have had striking success with Congress in the modern era. The article by Robert Loevy presents a case study of a presidential victory. But in analyzing how Lyndon Johnson was able to persuade Congress to pass the Civil Rights Act of 1964, Loevy shows how difficult it was for even a master of the legislative process like Lyndon Johnson to get his way with Congress. The issue of governance illustrated in this case is that a determined minority can use parliamentary tactics in Congress to prevent changes in policy that it opposes.

KEY TERMS

cabinet: the heads (secretaries) of the major departments of the executive branch (numbering 14 in 1993) who report to the president individually but who also meet collectively as the president's cabinet

conservative coalition: a group of conservative Democrats (Dixiecrats) and Republicans in Congress in the middle of the twentieth century who often voted together to defeat any legislation they deemed too liberal, especially civil rights legislation

Executive Office of the President (EOP): the collection of offices that serve the president directly and are separate from the rest of the executive branch departments and agencies. Includes the Office of Management and Budget, the Council of Economic Advisers, the Office of the U.S. Trade Representative, and others, making a total of about 2000 people.

impeachment: the constitutional provision that the president may be removed from office for "high crimes and misdemeanors" by being accused or indicted (impeached) by the House of Representatives and then convicted by the Senate. Impeachment is the House's formal charging of the president. The president must leave office only if convicted by the Senate. Only one president, Andrew Johnson, has been impeached, but he was not convicted by the Senate and thus stayed in office. Richard Nixon resigned from office rather than continue to fight probable impeachment by the House and possible conviction by the Senate for his actions during Watergate.

power to persuade: the idea that the president's power to command obedience in the American government is limited and that to prevail a president must often persuade others rather than command them. This stems from the reality that power is fragmented in the U.S. separation of powers system.

White House Office: one unit within the EOP that contains the president's closest advisers, including the chief of staff, and the assistants to the president for national security affairs, domestic policy, economic policy, and so forth, with a total of 400 to 500 people.

14

FEDERALIST NO. 70
Alexander Hamilton

In Federalist No. 70, *one of a series of* Federalist *essays on the presidency, Hamilton argues that a strong, independent executive is essential to a republic and that "energy in the executive is a leading character in the definition of good government." He spends much of this excerpt taking issue with critics of the Constitution who proposed that the executive power be split among more than one person or who would have required the president to consult with an executive council.*

To the People of the State of New York:

There is an idea, which is not without its advocates, that a vigorous Executive is inconsistent with the genius of republican government. The enlightened well-wishers to this species of government must at least hope that the supposition is destitute of foundation, since they can never admit its truth without at the same time admitting the condemnation of their own principles. Energy in the Executive is a leading character in the definition of good government. It is essential to the protection of the community against foreign attacks; it is not less essential to the steady administration of the laws; to the protection of property against those irregular and high-handed combinations which sometimes interrupt the ordinary course of justice; to the security of liberty against the enterprises and assaults of ambition, of faction, and of anarchy. Every man the least conversant in Roman history knows how often that republic was obliged to take refuge in the absolute power of a single man, under the formidable title of Dictator, as well against the intrigues of ambitious individuals who aspired to the tyranny and the seditions of whole classes of the community whose conduct threatened the existence of all government, as against the invasions of external enemies who menaced the conquest and destruction of Rome.

There can be no need, however, to multiply arguments or examples on this head. A feeble Executive implies a feeble execution of the government. A feeble execution is but another phrase for a bad execution; and a government ill executed, whatever it may be in theory, must be, in practice, a bad government.

Taking it for granted, therefore, that all men of sense will agree in the necessity of an energetic Executive, it will only remain to inquire what are the ingredients which constitute this energy? How far can they be combined with those other ingredients which constitute safety in the republican sense? And how far does this combination characterize the plan which has been reported by the convention?

The ingredients which constitute energy in the Executive are, first, unity; secondly, duration; thirdly, an adequate provision for its support; fourthly, competent powers.

The ingredients which constitute safety in the republican sense are, first, a due dependence on the people; secondly, a due responsibility.

Those politicians and statesmen who have been the most celebrated for the soundness of their principles and for the justice of their views have declared in favor of a single Executive and a numerous legislature. They have, with great propriety, considered energy as the most necessary qualification of the former, and have regarded this as most applicable to power in a single hand; while they have, with equal propriety, considered the latter as best adapted to deliberation and wisdom, best calculated to conciliate the confidence of the people and to secure their privileges and interests.

That unity is conducive to energy will not be disputed. Decision, activity, secrecy, and despatch will generally characterize the proceedings of one man in a much more eminent degree than the proceedings of any greater number; and in proportion as the number is increased, these qualities will be diminished.

This unity may be destroyed in two ways: either by vesting the power in two or more magistrates of equal dignity and authority; or by vesting it ostensibly in one man, subject, in whole or in part, to the control and co-operation of others in the capacity of counsellors to him. Of the first, the two Consuls of Rome may serve as an example; of the last, we shall find examples in the constitutions of several of the States. New York and New Jersey, if I recollect right, are the only States which have intrusted the executive authority wholly to single men. Both these methods of destroying the unity of the Executive have their partisans; but the votaries of an executive council are the most numerous. They are both liable, if not equal, to similar objections, and may in most lights be examined in conjunction.

* * * *

The idea of a council to the Executive, which has so generally obtained in the State constitutions, has been derived from that maxim of republican jealousy which considers power as safer in the hands of a number of men than of a single man. If the maxim should be admitted to be applicable to the case, I should contend that the advantage on that side would not counterbalance the numerous disadvantages on the opposite side. But I do not think the rule at all applicable to the executive power. I clearly concur in opinion, in this particular, with a writer whom the celebrated Junius pronounces to be "deep, solid, and ingenious," that "the executive power is more easily confined when it is ONE"; that it is far more safe there should be a single object for the jealousy and watchfulness of the people; and, in a word, that all multiplication of the Executive is rather dangerous than friendly to liberty.

A little consideration will satisfy us that the species of security sought for in the multiplication of the EXECUTIVE is unattainable. Numbers must be so great as to render combination difficult, or they are rather a source of danger than of security. The united credit and influence of several individuals must be more formidable to liberty than the credit and influence of either of them separately. When power, therefore, is placed in the hands of so small a number of men as to admit of their interests and views being easily combined in a common enterprise, by an artful leader it becomes more liable to abuse, and more dangerous when abused, than if it be lodged in the hands of one man; who, from the very circumstance of his being alone, will be more narrowly watched and more readily suspected, and who cannot unite so great a mass of influence as when he is associated with others. The Decemvirs of Rome, whose name denotes their number, were more to be dreaded, in their usurpation than any ONE of them would have been. No person would think of proposing an Executive much more numerous than that body; from six to a dozen have been suggested for the number of the council. The extreme of these numbers is not too great for an easy combination; and from such a combination America would have more to fear than from the ambition of any single individual. A council to a magistrate, who is himself responsible for what he does, are generally nothing better than a clog upon his good intentions, are often the instruments and accomplices of his bad, and are almost always a cloak to his faults.

I forbear to dwell upon the subject of expense; though it be evident that if the council should be numerous enough to answer the principal end aimed at by the institution, the salaries of the members, who must be drawn from their homes to reside at the seat of government, would form an item in the catalog of public expenditures too serious to be incurred for an object of equivocal utility. I will only add that, prior to the appearance of the Constitution, I rarely met with an intelligent man from any of the States, who did not admit, as the result of experience, that the UNITY of the executive of this State was one of the best of the distinguishing features of our constitution.

Publius.

POINTS TO PONDER

1. According to Hamilton, what are the essential ingredients to "energy in the executive"?
2. Why does Hamilton argue against a plural executive?
3. Why was Hamilton against creating an executive council?

15

"THE POWER TO PERSUADE"

Richard Neustadt

In 1960 Richard Neustadt, a scholar who had worked in the Truman White House, wrote Presidential Power, *a classic of the modern presidency. Neustadt, now a political scientist at Harvard, took a behavioral rather than a legalistic or an institutional perspective on the office. He argued that a president's power is more dependent on the skillful exercise of political judgment than on the constitutional powers of office. One of Neustadt's greatest insights is that the president must operate in a political system of separated institutions* sharing *powers and thus must persuade others that the president's wishes are also in their self-interest.*

The limits on command suggest the structure of our government. The Constitutional Convention of 1787 is supposed to have created a government of "separated powers." It did nothing of the sort. Rather, it created a government of separated institutions *sharing* powers. "I am part of the legislative process," Eisenhower often said in 1959 as a reminder of his veto. Congress, the dispenser of authority and funds, is no less part of the administrative process. Federalism adds another set of separated institutions. The Bill of Rights adds others. Many public purposes can only be achieved by voluntary acts of private institutions; the press, for one, in Douglass Cater's phrase, is a "fourth branch of government." And with the coming of alliances abroad, the separate institutions of a London, or a Bonn, share in the making of American public policy.

What the Constitution separates our political parties do not combine. The parties are themselves composed of separated organizations sharing public authority. The authority consists of nominating powers. Our national parties are confederations of state and local party institutions, with a headquarters that represents the White House, more or less, if the party has a President in office. These confederacies manage presidential nominations. All other public offices depend upon electorates confined within the states. All other nominations are controlled within the states. The President and congressmen who bear one party's label are divided by dependence upon different sets of voters. The differences are sharpest at the stage of nomination. The White House has too small a share in nominating congressmen, and Congress has too little weight in nominating presidents for party to erase their constitutional separation. Party links are stronger than is frequently supposed, but nominating processes assure the separation.

The separateness of institutions and the sharing of authority prescribe the terms on which a President persuades. When one man shares authority with another, but does not gain or lose his job upon the other's whim, his willingness to act upon the urging of the other turns on whether he conceives the action right for him. The essence of a President's persuasive task is to convince such men that what the White House wants of them is what they ought to do for their sake and on their authority. (Sex matters not at all; for *man* read *woman*.)

Persuasive power, thus defined, amounts to more than charm or reasoned argument. These have their uses for a President, but these are not the whole of his resources. For the individuals he would induce to do what he wants done on their own responsibility will need or fear some acts by him on his responsibility. If they share his authority, he has some share in theirs. Presidential "powers" may be inconclusive when a President commands, but always remain relevant as he persuades. The status and authority inherent in his office reinforce his logic and his charm.

Status adds something to persuasiveness; authority adds still more. When Truman urged wage changes on his secretary of commerce while the latter was administering the steel mills, he and Secretary Sawyer were not just two men reasoning with one another. Had they been so, Sawyer probably would never have agreed to act. Truman's status gave him special claims to Sawyer's loyalty or at least attention. In Walter Bagehot's charming phrase "no man can *argue* on his knees." Although there is no kneeling in this country, few men—and exceedingly few cabinet officers—are immune to the impulse to say "yes" to the President of the United States. It grows harder to say "no" when they are seated in his Oval Office at the White House, or in his study on the second floor, where almost tangibly he partakes of the aura of his physical surroundings. In Sawyer's case, moreover, the President possessed formal authority to intervene in many matters of concern to the secretary of commerce. These matters ranged from jurisdictional disputes among the defense agencies to legislation pending before Congress and, ultimately, to the tenure of the secretary, himself. There is nothing in the record to suggest that Truman voiced specific threats when they negotiated over wage increases. But given his formal powers and their relevance to Sawyer's other interests, it is safe to assume that Truman's very advocacy of wage action conveyed an implicit threat.

A President's authority and status give him great advantages in dealing with the men he would persuade. Each "power" is a vantage point for him in the degree that other men have use for his authority. From the veto to appointments, from publicity to budgeting, and so down a long list, the White House now controls the most encompassing array of vantage points in the American political system. With hardly an exception, those who share in governing this country are aware that at some time, in some degree, the doing of *their* jobs, the furthering of *their* ambitions, may depend upon the President of the United States. Their need for presidential action, or their fear of it, is bound to be recurrent if not actually continuous. Their need or fear is his advantage.

A President's advantages are greater than mere listing of his "powers" might suggest. Those with whom he deals must deal with him until the last day of his term. Because they have continuing relationships with him, his future, while it lasts, supports his present influence. Even though there is no need or fear of him today, what he could do tomorrow may supply today's advantage. Continuing relationships may convert any "power," any aspect of his status, into vantage points in almost any case. When he induces other people to do what he wants done, a President can trade on their dependence now and later.

The President's advantages are checked by the advantages of others. Continuing relationships will pull in both directions. These are relationships of mutual dependence. A President depends upon the persons whom he would persuade; he has to reckon with his need or fear of them. They too will possess status, or authority, or both, else they would be of little use to him. Their vantage points confront his own; their power tempers his.

Persuasion is a two-way street. Sawyer, it will be recalled, did not respond at once to Truman's plan for wage increases at the steel mills. On the contrary, the secretary hesitated and delayed and only acquiesced when he was satisfied that publicly he would not bear the onus of decision. Sawyer had some points of vantage all his own from which to resist presidential pressure. If he had to reckon with coercive implications in the President's "situations of strength," so had Truman to be mindful of the implications underlying Sawyer's place as a department head, as steel administrator, and as cabinet spokesman for business. Loyalty is reciprocal. Having taken on a dirty job in the steel crisis, Sawyer had strong claims to loyal support. Besides, he had authority to do some things that the White House could ill afford. Emulating Wilson, he might have resigned in a huff (the removal power also works two ways). Or, emulating Ellis Arnall, he might have declined to sign necessary orders. Or he might have let it be known publicly that he deplored what he was told to do and protested its doing. By following any of these courses Sawyer almost surely would have strengthened the position of management, weakened the position of the White House, and embittered the union. But the whole purpose of a wage increase was to enhance White House persuasiveness in urging settlement upon union and companies alike. Although Sawyer's status and authority did not give him the power to prevent an increase outright, they gave him capability to undermine its purpose. If his authority over wage rates had been vested by a statute, not by revocable presidential order, his power of prevention might have been complete. So Harold Ickes demonstrated in the famous case of helium sales to Germany before the Second World War.

The power to persuade is the power to bargain. Status and authority yield bargaining advantages. But in a government of "separated institutions sharing powers," they yield them to all sides. With the array of vantage points at his disposal, a President may be far more persuasive than his logic or his charm could make him. But outcomes are not guaranteed by his advantages. There remain the counter pressures those whom he would influence can bring to bear on him from vantage points at their disposal. Command has limited utility; persuasion becomes give-and-take. It is well that the White House holds the vantage points it does. In such a business any President may need them all—and more.

This view of power as akin to bargaining is one we commonly accept in the sphere of congressional relations. Every textbook states and every legislative session demonstrates that save in times like the extraordinary Hundred Days of 1933—times virtually ruled out by definition at midcentury—a President will often be unable to obtain congressional action on his terms or even to halt action he opposes. The reverse is equally accepted: Congress often is frustrated by the President. Their formal powers are so intertwined that neither will accomplish very much, for very long, without the acquiescence of the other. By the same token, though, what one demands the other can resist. The stage is set for that great game, much like collective bargaining, in which each seeks to profit from the other's needs and fears. It is a game played catch-as-catch-can, case by case. And everybody knows the game, observers and participants alike.

The concept of real power as a give-and-take is equally familiar when applied to presidential influence outside the formal structure of the federal government. The Little Rock affair may be extreme, but Eisenhower's dealings with the governor—and with the citizens—became a case in point. Less extreme but no less pertinent is the steel seizure case with respect to union leaders, and to workers, and to company executives as well. When he deals with such people a President draws bargaining advantage from his status or authority. By virtue of their public places or their private rights they have some capability to reply in kind.

In spheres of party politics the same thing follows, necessarily, from the confederal nature of our party organizations. Even in the case of national nominations a President's advantages are checked by those of others. In 1944 it is by no means clear that Roosevelt got his first choice as his running mate. In 1948 Truman, then the President, faced serious revolts against his nomination. In 1952 his intervention from the White House helped assure the choice of Adlai Stevenson, but it is far from clear that Truman could have done as much for any other candidate acceptable to him. In 1956 when Eisenhower was President, the record leaves obscure just who backed Harold Stassen's efforts to block Richard Nixon from renomination as vice president. But evidently everything did not go quite as Eisenhower wanted, whatever his intentions may have been. The outcomes in these instances bear all the marks of limits on command and of power checked by power that characterize congressional relations. Both in and out of politics these checks and limits seem to be quite widely understood.

Influence becomes still more a matter of give-and-take when Presidents attempt to deal with allied governments. A classic illustration is the long unhappy wrangle over Suez policy in 1956. In dealing with the British and the French before their military intervention, Eisenhower had his share of bargaining advantages but no effective power of command. His allies had their share of counterpressures, and they finally tried the most extreme of all: action despite him. His pressure then was instrumental in reversing them. But had the British government been on safe ground at home, Eisenhower's wishes might have made as little difference after intervention as before. Behind the decorum of diplomacy—which was not very decorous in the Suez affair—relationships among allies are not unlike relationships among state delegations at a national convention. Power is persuasion, and persuasion becomes bargaining. The concept is familiar to everyone who watches foreign policy.

In only one sphere is the concept unfamiliar: the sphere of executive relations. Perhaps because of civics textbooks and teaching in our schools, Americans instinctively resist the view that power in this sphere resembles power in all others. Even Washington reporters, White House aides, and congressmen are not immune to the illusion that administrative agencies comprise a single structure, "the" executive branch, where presidential word is law, or ought to be. Yet we have seen . . . that when a President seeks something from executive officials his persuasiveness is subject to the same sorts of limitations as in the case of congressmen, or governors, or national committeemen, or private citizens, or foreign governments. There are no generic differences, no differences in kind and only sometimes in degree. The incidents preceding the dismissal of MacArthur and the incidents surrounding seizure of the steel mills make it plain that here as elsewhere influence derives from bargaining advantages; power is a give-and-take.

Like our governmental structure as a whole, the executive establishment consists of separated institutions sharing powers. The President heads one of these; cabinet officers, agency administrators, and military commanders head others. Below the departmental level, virtually independent bureau chiefs head many more. Under midcentury conditions, federal operations spill across dividing lines on organization charts; almost every policy entangles many agencies; almost every program calls for interagency collaboration. Everything somehow involves the President. But operating agencies owe their existence least of all to one another—and only in some part to him. Each has a separate statutory base; each has its statutes to administer; each deals with a different set of subcommittees at the Capitol. Each has its own peculiar set of clients, friends, and enemies outside the formal government. Each has a different set of specialized careerists inside its own bailiwick. Our Constitution gives the President the "take-care" clause and the appointive power. Our statutes give him central budgeting and a degree of personnel control. All agency administrators are responsible to him. But they also are responsible to Congress, to their clients, to their staffs, and to themselves. In short, they have five masters. Only after all of those do they owe any loyalty to each other.

"The members of the cabinet," Charles G. Dawes used to remark, "are a president's natural enemies." Dawes had been Harding's budget director, Coolidge's vice president, and Hoover's ambassador to London; he also had been General Pershing's chief assistant for supply in World War I. The words are highly colored, but Dawes knew whereof he spoke. The men who have to serve so many masters cannot help but be somewhat the "enemy" of any one of them. By the same token, any master wanting service is in some degree the "enemy" of such a servant. A President is likely to want loyal support but not to relish trouble on his doorstep. Yet the more his cabinet members cleave to him, the more they may need help from him in fending off the wrath of rival masters. Help, though, is synonymous with trouble. Many a cabinet officer, with loyalty ill rewarded by his lights and help withheld, has come to view the

White House as innately hostile to department heads. Dawes's dictum can be turned around.

A senior presidential aide remarked to me in Eisenhower's time: "If some of these cabinet members would just take time out to stop and ask themselves, 'What would I want if I were President?' they wouldn't give him all the trouble he's been having." But even if they asked themselves the question, such officials often could not act upon the answer. Their personal attachment to the President is all too often overwhelmed by duty to their other masters.

Executive officials are not equally advantaged in their dealings with a President. Nor are the same officials equally advantaged all the time. Not every officeholder can resist like a MacArthur, or like Arnall, Sawyer, Wilson, in a rough descending order of effective counterpressure. The vantage points conferred upon officials by their own authority and status vary enormously. The variance is heightened by particulars of time and circumstance. In mid–October 1950, Truman, at a press conference, remarked of the man he had considered firing in August and would fire the next April for intolerable insubordination:

> Let me tell you something that will be good for your souls. It's a pity that you . . . can't understand the ideas of two intellectually honest men when they meet. General MacArthur . . . is a member of the Government of the United States. He is loyal to that Government. He is loyal to the President. He is loyal to the President in his foreign policy. . . . There is no disagreement between General MacArthur and myself.

MacArthur's status in and out of government was never higher than when Truman spoke those words. The words, once spoken, added to the general's credibility thereafter when he sought to use the press in his campaign against the President. And what had happened between August and October? Near victory had happened, together with that premature conference on postwar plans, the meeting at Wake Island.

If the bargaining advantages of a MacArthur fluctuate with changing circumstances, this is bound to be so with subordinates who have at their disposal fewer powers, lesser status, to fall back on. And when officials have no powers in their own right, or depend upon the President for status, their counterpressure may be limited indeed. White House aides, who fit both categories, are among the most responsive men of all, and for good reason. As a director of the budget once remarked to me, "Thank God I'm here and not across the street. If the President doesn't call me, I've got plenty I can do right here and plenty coming up to me, by rights, to justify my calling him. But those poor fellows over there, if the boss doesn't call them, doesn't ask them to do something, what *can* they do but sit?" Authority and status so conditional are frail reliances in resisting a President's own wants. Within the White House precincts, lifted eyebrows may suffice to set an aide in motion; command, coercion, even charm aside. But even in the White House a President does not monopolize effective power. Even there persuasion is akin to bargaining. A former Roosevelt aide once wrote of cabinet officers:

Half of a President's suggestions, which theoretically carry the weight of orders, can be safely forgotten by a Cabinet member. And if the President asks about a suggestion a second time, he can be told that it is being investigated. If he asks a third time, a wise Cabinet officer will give him at least part of what he suggests. But only occasionally, except about the most important matters, do Presidents ever get around to asking three times.

The rule applies to staff as well as to the cabinet, and certainly has been applied *by* staff in Truman's time and Eisenhower's.

Some aides will have more vantage points than a selective memory. Sherman Adams, for example, as the assistant to the President under Eisenhower, scarcely deserved the appelation "White House aide" in the meaning of the term before his time or as applied to other members of the Eisenhower entourage. Although Adams was by no means "chief of staff" in any sense so sweeping—or so simple—as press commentaries often took for granted, he apparently became no more dependent on the President than Eisenhower on him. "I need him," said the President when Adams turned out to have been remarkably imprudent in the Goldfine case, and delegated to him, at least nominally, the decision on his own departure. This instance is extreme, but the tendency it illustrates is common enough. Any aide who demonstrates to others that he has the President's consistent confidence and a consistent part in presidential business will acquire so much business on his own account that he becomes in some sense independent of his chief. Nothing in the Constitution keeps a well-placed aide from converting status into power of his own, usable in some degree even against the President—an outcome not unknown in Truman's regime or, by all accounts, in Eisenhower's.

The more an officeholder's status and his powers stem from sources independent of the President, the stronger will be his potential pressure on the President. Department heads in general have more bargaining power than do most members of the White House staff; but bureau chiefs may have still more, and specialists at upper levels of established career services may have almost unlimited reserves of the enormous power which consists of sitting still. As Franklin Roosevelt once remarked:

> The Treasury is so large and far-flung and ingrained in its practices that I find it almost impossible to get the action and results I want—even with Henry [Morgenthau] there. But the Treasury is not to be compared with the State Department. You should go through the experience of trying to get any changes in the thinking, policy, and action of the career diplomats and then you'd know what a real problem was. But the Treasury and the State Department put together are nothing compared to the Na-a-vy. The admirals are really something to cope with—and I should know. To change anything in the Na-a-vy is like punching a feather bed. You punch it with your right and you punch it with your left until you are finally exhausted, and then you find the damn bed just as it was before you started punching.

In the right circumstances, of course, a President can have his way with any of these people. . . . But one need only note . . . that as between a President and his "subordinates," no less than others on whom he depends, real power is reciprocal and varies markedly with organization, subject matter, personality, and situation. The mere fact that persuasion is directed at executive officials signifies no necessary easing of his way. Any new congressman of the Administration's party, especially if narrowly elected, may turn out more amenable (though less useful) to the President than any seasoned bureau chief "downtown." *The probabilities of power do not derive from the literary theory of the Constitution.*

POINTS TO PONDER

1. What does Neustadt mean by distinguishing a government of "separated powers" from a government of "separated institutions sharing powers"?
2. In what way is the exercise of a veto or the firing of a subordinate a failure of presidential power?
3. Why do presidents have to use persuasion in the exercise of their power?

16

"AFTER THE IMPERIAL PRESIDENCY"
Arthur Schlesinger, Jr.

In the following selection from his book The Cycles of American History *(1986), Arthur Schlesinger, Jr., historian and former aide to President John Kennedy, provides a historical perspective on the power of the presidency. The title of this selection comes from Schlesinger's 1973 book* The Imperial Presidency, *in which he argued that President Nixon's exercise of foreign policy powers exceeded the scope of presidential power intended by the Framers. In this retrospective view of the presidency since that 1973 book, Schlesinger takes issue with those who think that the presidency was seriously weakened by the reaction of the political system, particularly Congress, to the Nixon presidency. He argues that the right person can use the office to accomplish what the country needs without any constitutional changes.*

Some years ago I was responsible for unleashing a phrase on the language— "the Imperial Presidency." This is the title of a book written in the latter days, hectic and ominous, of the Presidency of Richard M. Nixon. The book argues that the Constitution intends a strong Presidency within an equally strong system of accountability. The title refers to the condition that ensues when the constitutional balance between presidential power and presidential accountability is upset in favor of presidential power.

The perennial threat to the constitutional balance, I suggested, comes in the field of foreign policy. Confronted by presidential initiatives at home, Congress and the courts—the countervailing branches of government under the constitutional separation of powers—have ample confidence in their own information and judgment. They do not lightly surrender power to the executive. In domestic policy, the republic is all Missouri: it has to be shown. But confronted by presidential initiatives abroad, Congress and the courts, along with the press and the citizenry too, generally lack confidence in their own information and judgment. In foreign policy the inclination is to let the Presidency have the responsibility—and the power.

"It is chiefly in its foreign relations," as Tocqueville noted long ago, "that the executive power of a nation finds occasion to exert its skill and its strength. If the existence of the American Union were perpetually threatened, if its chief interests were in daily connection with those of other powerful nations, the executive would assume an increased importance." But the nation that Tocqueville visited in the 1830s subsisted in happy isolation from world power conflicts. So, he wrote, "the President of the United States possesses almost royal prerogatives which he has no opportunity of exercising." In modern times, international crisis, real, contrived or imagined, has given Presidents the opportunity to exercise these almost royal prerogatives. Hence the Imperial Presidency.

I

Presidential aggrandizement under the spur of international crisis was visible from the start. "Perhaps it is a universal truth," Madison wrote Jefferson during the administration of John Adams, "that the loss of liberty at home is to be charged to provisions against danger, real or pretended, from abroad."

Foreign perplexities tempted, sometimes forced, even the earliest Presidents to evade constitutional limitations. As Professor A. D. Sofaer (later a federal judge, still later legal adviser for Ronald Reagan's State Department) showed in his magistral work *War, Foreign Affairs and Constitutional Power: The Origins*, Jefferson himself, the apostle of strict construction, sent a naval squadron to the Mediterranean under secret orders to fight the Barbary pirates, applied for congressional sanction six months later and then misled Congress as to the nature of the orders. He unilaterally authorized the seizure of armed vessels in waters extending to the Gulf Stream, engaged in rearmament without congressional appropriations, developed "a system of secrecy largely immune from legislative check" and invoked the Lockean doctrine of emergency prerogative to justify presidential action beyond congressional authorization. The broad discretionary powers Madison as President obtained from Congress led on to the War of 1812. Long before there was a Central Intelligence Agency, Madison sent Joel R. Poinsett as a secret agent to Latin America and winked at his clandestine revolutionary adventures in Argentina and Chile; Madison's Secretary of State removed Poinsett's despatches from State Department files lest Congress request them. The Madison and Monroe administrations used covert action to facilitate the annexation of Florida.

When perplexities exploded into war, the flow of power to the executive accelerated. During the Mexican War, John C. Calhoun warned Congress that, with foreign conquest, "this Union would become imperial. . . . All the added power and added patronage which conquest will create, will pass to the Executive. In the end you put in the hands of the Executive the power of conquering you." "We elect a king every four years," Secretary of State William H. Seward told Louis Jennings of *The Times* (London) during the Civil War, "and give him absolute power within certain limits, which after all he can interpret for himself." Abraham Lincoln, as Bryce wrote twenty years later, "wielded more authority than any single Englishman has done since Oliver Cromwell."

Peace brought a reaction against executive excess. Jennings observed three years after Appomattox that no American statesman would now defend the Seward theory of an elective kingship. The nation entered the period famously characterized by Woodrow Wilson as one of "congressional government." Congressional encroachment into foreign affairs drove Henry Adams to the conclusion that the Secretary of State existed only to recognize "obligations which Congress repudiates whenever it can." But the flow to the Presidency resumed once the Spanish-American War brought the United States back into the great world. In his preface to the fifteenth edition in 1901, the author of *Congressional Government* himself called attention to "the greatly increased power . . . given the President by the plunge into international politics." When foreign policy becomes a nation's dominant concern, Wilson said, the executive "must of necessity be its guide: must utter every initial judgment, take every first step of action, supply the information upon which it is to act, suggest and in large measure control its conduct."

Disenchantment with the First World War restored congressional activism in foreign affairs. In the 1930s, Franklin Roosevelt, a mighty domestic President, could not prevent Congress from enacting a rigid neutrality law that put American foreign policy in a straitjacket while Hitler ran amok in Europe. Since Pearl Harbor, however, Americans have lived under a conviction of international crisis, sustained, chronic and often intense. We are at last in the age foreseen by Tocqueville: American interests are in daily connection with those of other powerful nations, the republic itself seems perpetually threatened and Presidents freely exercise their almost royal prerogatives.

The most palpable index of executive aggrandizement is the transfer of the power to go to war from Congress, where the Constitution expressly lodged it, to the Presidency. In June 1940, when the last prime minister of the Third Republic in France pleaded for American aid against Hitler's *Blitzkrieg*, Franklin Roosevelt, after saying that the United States would continue supplies so long as the French continued resistance, took care to add: "These statements carry with them no implication of military commitments. Only the Congress can make such commitments." In 1941 Roosevelt sent naval forces into an undeclared war in the North Atlantic. He did so in a penumbra of consent generated by the congressional enactment of Lend-Lease: if it was national policy to give goods to Britain, it was inferentially national policy to make sure they got there. But Roosevelt relied on a murky proclamation of "unlimited national emergency" and on the public response to Nazi aggression to justify his forward policy. He did not claim inherent power as President or as Commander-in-Chief to send the Navy into combat without congressional authorization.

Nine years later, after North Korea invaded South Korea in June 1950, Harry Truman committed American forces to the war on his own authority. When Senator Robert A. Taft proposed a joint resolution sanctioning military intervention, Truman was persuaded by Dean Acheson, his Secretary of State and an eminent lawyer, that congressional approval was unnecessary. This idea of inherent presidential power to send troops into combat was unwisely defended at the time by some historians, including this one. In its acquiescence, Congress surrendered the war-making power to the executive and has never reclaimed it since.

The Imperial Presidency reached its culmination under Nixon. "I felt," Nixon wrote in his memoirs, "that we were at a historical turning point. My reading of history taught me that when all the leadership institutions of a nation become paralyzed by self-doubt and second thoughts, that nation cannot long survive unless those institutions are either reformed, replaced, or circumvented. In my second term I was prepared to adopt whichever of these three methods—or whichever combination of them—was necessary."

Historically Congress had maintained the rough balance of the Constitution because it retained three vital powers: the war-making power; the power of the purse; and the power of oversight and investigation. By 1950 it had relinquished the war-making power. Johnson fought in Vietnam and Nixon in Cambodia without the explicit congressional authorization required by the Constitution. In 1969–1974 the Nixon administration tried systematically and, until Watergate, successfully to nullify the other two powers: countering the power of the purse by the doctrine of unlimited impoundment of appropriated funds; countering the power of oversight and investigation by the doctrine of unreviewable executive privilege and the extension of the presidential secrecy system. Had Nixon succeeded in imposing these doctrines on top of his amplified claims for the presidential war-making power, he would have effectively ended Congress as a serious partner in the constitutional order.

His further contribution to the Imperial Presidency was to take emergency powers the Presidency had accumulated in order to save the republic from foreign adversaries and to turn these powers against his political opponents—"enemies," he called them—at home. Invoking "national security" as an all-purpose justification for presidential criminality, he set up a secret White House posse to burgle offices, forge historical documents and wiretap officials, embassies, newspapermen and "enemies." The Presidency was above the law, and national crisis justified extreme methods.

Whether a conscious or unconscious revolutionary, Nixon was carrying the Imperial Presidency toward its ultimate form in the plebiscitary Presidency—with the President accountable to the voters only once every four years, shielded by his quadrennial mandate from congressional and public interference between elections, empowered by his mandate to make war or to make peace, to spend or to impound, to give out information or to hold it back, to pursue and punish the opposition, all in the name of a majority whose choice must prevail till it makes another choice four years later. It was Seward's old dream of an elective kingship. It was hardly what the Founding Fathers had in mind.

Events frustrated Nixon's revolution. The press and the courts exposed his methods as furtive and lawless. Congress, at last bestirring itself, acted to save the Constitution. The House of Representatives prepared articles of impeachment, charging Nixon, in words too soon forgotten, with acting "in a manner contrary to his trust as President and subversive of constitutional government, to the great prejudice of the cause of law and justice and to the manifest injury of the people of the United States."

Nixon resigned to avoid impeachment and jail. Subsequently, I might add, he became my neighbor over the back fence in New York City. I had been on Nixon's Enemies List; and, when his Secret Service agents, their salaries paid by me and other taxpayers, tried to stop my children from their time-honored habit of climbing on the fence, it seemed to be carrying harassment a little far. Since then Nixon has made with astonishing dexterity the transition from disgraced politician to respected elder statesman. One thinks of William Cullen Bryant's obituary comment on Nicholas Biddle, the president of the Second Bank of the United States. Biddle, Bryant wrote, "passed the last of his days in elegant retirement, which, if justice had taken place, would have been spent in the penitentiary."

II

Nixon's attempt to institutionalize the Imperial Presidency failed. By the 1970s, Vietnam had shattered public trust of the Presidency in foreign affairs, Watergate in domestic affairs. A pervasive cynicism spread about Presidents. In 1959, when pollsters asked which knew best, the President or Congress, 61 percent of respondents had voted for the President, only 17 percent for Congress. A comparable question in 1977 almost reversed the proportions, favoring Congress by 58 to 26 percent.

Congress, seized by a temporary passion to prevent future Vietnams and Watergates, enacted laws designed to reclaim lost powers, to dismantle the executive secrecy system and to ensure future presidential accountability. The War Powers Resolution of 1973 was meant to restrain the presidential inclination to go to war. A variety of laws limited presidential resort to paramilitary and covert action. Congress set up select committees to monitor the Central Intelligence Agency. It gave the Freedom of Information Act new vitality. It imposed its own priorities—human rights and nuclear nonproliferation, for example—on the executive foreign policy. The Congressional Budget Act of 1974 restricted presidential impoundment. The National Emergencies Act of 1976 terminated existing presidential emergency authority and established congressional review for future national-emergency declarations. Legislative vetoes and reporting requirements curtailed presidential freedom of action in a diversity of fields.

A few scholars had feared during the Watergate crisis that too zealous an investigation might cripple the presidential office. Some formed a committee in defense of the Presidency, its eminent members claiming that their interest lay in the preservation not of Richard Nixon but of an office indispensable to the republic. The Luce Professor of Jurisprudence at the Yale Law School actually argued that, if Nixon turned over his White House tapes to Congress and the courts, it would raise the "danger of degrading or even destroying the Presidency" and constitute a betrayal of his "successors for all time to come."

After Congress began its mild post-Watergate effort to restore the constitutional balance, scholarly pessimism intensified. Some saw the once mighty Presidency tied down, like Gulliver, by a web of debilitating statutory restraints. A theory arose about the fragility of the American Presidency. Not only Congress but history itself seemed, as political scientists saw it, to be conspiring against Presidents. The job was overwhelmed by insuperable problems—inflation, energy shortages, urban decay, the nuclear arms race, the Communists. The national consensus on which Presidents had relied since the war for domestic as well as foreign policy was disintegrating. The party system, which had long supplied the connective sinews of government, was in decay. Lobbies were importunate. Single-issue fanaticisms were distorting the political process.

Presidents, it was added, had compounded their problems by personifying the government in themselves, promising miracles they could not work and exciting hopes they could not fulfill. "The president," said Theodore Lowi, "is the Wizard of Oz." The inevitable gap between popular expectation and presidential delivery guaranteed both presidential failure and popular resentment. Vice President Walter Mondale, defending Jimmy Carter in 1979, cited an observation John Steinbeck had made in the previous decade in defense of Lyndon Johnson: "We give the President more work than a man can do, more responsibility than a man should take, more pressure than a man can bear. . . . We wear him out, use him up, eat him up. . . . He is ours and we exercise the right to destroy him."

The Presidency appeared in rout. Vietnam drove Johnson from the White House. Nixon drove himself. Nixon's successors—the hapless Gerald Ford and the hapless Jimmy Carter—proved incapable of mastering the discordant frustrations of the day. Failure, it seemed, had passed the point of coincidence. These recent Presidents, a veteran political reporter noted in a book on the Presidency, came from a variety of political backgrounds and from all sections of the country; they ran the spectrum in personal temperament and social philosophy. "Their combined experience suggests that the chronic failings of the presidency" sprang not from personal characteristics but from "the political and governing system to which presidents must respond." "When five consecutive men . . . all fail to operate an office, when their tasks seem to get progressively more and more difficult with the passing of time," wrote an intelligent English journalist in his own book on the subject, "then the fault can hardly be in the individuals. It must be in the institution."

"Never has so powerful a leader," the English commentator added, "been so impotent to do what he wants to do, what he is pledged to do, what he is expected to do." Columnists wrote of "the Presidency in decline." Scholars mobilized their colleagues to join in producing books under such titles as *The Tethered Presidency, The Post-Imperial Presidency, The Impossible Presidency*. Pundits confidently predicted an age of one-term Presidents. The impression arose at the end of the 1970s of a beleaguered and pathetic fellow sitting forlornly in the Oval Office, assailed by unprecedentedly intractable problems, paralyzed by the constitutional separation of powers, hemmed in by congressional and bureaucratic constraints, pushed one way and another by exigent interest groups, seduced, betrayed and abandoned by the mass media. "Presidential government is an illusion," proclaimed one political scientist in 1980, "—an illusion that misleads presidents no less than the media and the American public, an illusion that often brings about the destruction of the very men who hold the office. Presidential government is the idea that the president, backed by the people, is or can be in charge of governing the country. . . . Far from being in charge or running the government, the president must struggle even to comprehend what is going on." In 1980 ex-President Ford said to general applause, "We have not an imperial presidency but an imperiled presidency."

III

There is a sense in which the Presidency has always been weak. The President's power over policy is great; for the power to set the nation's course derives from the constitutional prerogatives of the office. But the President's power over execution is incomplete; for the power to manage the vast, whirring machinery of government derives from individual skills as persuader, bargainer and leader. Even Franklin D. Roosevelt, who possessed all those skills to a high degree, had his problems. "Half a President's suggestions, which theoretically carry the weight of orders," one of his assistants, Jonathan Daniels, later recalled, "can be safely forgotten by a Cabinet member." "He'll sit here," Harry Truman said in contemplation of Eisenhower, "and he'll say, 'Do this! Do that!' *And nothing will happen*." Even when the Imperial Presidency culminated in Nixon, the President lived in a state of chronic and profane frustration, unable to command Congress, the judiciary, the press, the universities, unable even to get the FBI, the CIA and the Internal Revenue

Service to do his bidding. This, I take it, was Richard Neustadt's point when he said that the underlying theme of his brilliant book of 1960, *Presidential Power*, was presidential weakness.

But presidential power is more than Neustadt's "power to persuade"; and the exercise of administrative authority is only part of the President's task. Neustadt's illuminating concern was with the way Presidents defend themselves against choices pressed by others with interests of their own. The capacity for presidential self-defense is a personal variable. But the constitutional and institutional strengths of the Presidency endure. I cannot confess to a moment's worry during the lamentations of the 1970s about the fragility of the office. Whatever political scientists, lawyers and journalists may think, historians know that the American Presidency is indestructible.

This is partly so for functional reasons. A governing process based on the separation of powers among three supposedly equal and coordinate branches has an inherent tendency toward stalemate and inertia. One of the three branches must take the initiative if the system is to move. The executive branch alone is structurally capable of taking that initiative. The Founding Fathers intended that it should do so. "Energy in the Executive," said Hamilton in the 70th *Federalist*, "is a leading character in the definition of good government."

Moreover, the growth of presidential initiative resulted not from presidential capacity for power but from the necessities of governing an increasingly complex society. As a tiny agricultural country, straggling along the Atlantic seaboard, turned into a mighty continental, industrial and finally world power, the problems assailing the national polity increased vastly in size, number and urgency. Most of these problems could not be tackled without vigorous executive leadership. Through American history, a robust Presidency kept the system in motion. The President remains, as Woodrow Wilson said, "the only national voice," the Presidency "the vital place of action in the system."

A further reason for the indestructibility of the Presidency lies in the psychology of mass democracy. Once again Tocqueville provides the text. "Our contemporaries," he wrote, "are constantly excited by two conflicting passions: they wanted to be led, and they wish to remain free. . . . By this system the people shake off their state of dependency just long enough to select their master and then relapse into it again." Americans have always had considerable ambivalence about the Presidency. One year they denounce presidential power. The next they demand presidential leadership. While they are quite capable of cursing out Presidents, they also have a profound longing to believe in and admire them.

The political irritations assailing the Presidency in the 1970s were hardly unprecedented. Belligerent Congresses, greedy lobbies, wild-eyed single-issue movements—all were old hat in American history. They were no more the cause of the plight of the Presidency than they were of the decay of the party system. Most preposterous of all is the theory that the Presidency did itself in when recent Presidents started personalizing the office, appealing over the heads of Congress to the people and arousing expectations beyond hope of fulfillment. Radio and especially television, it is suggested, are responsible for the corruption of what had presumably been up till a few years before an impersonal, modest, well-behaved office. Personalization, the plebiscitary stance and presidentially induced mass expectations, we are told, began with John Kennedy or, at the earliest, with Franklin Roosevelt.

This notion springs from a curiously foreshortened view of American history. In fact, the Presidency has been a personalized office from the start, both for political reasons—the interests of the President—and for psychological reasons—the emotional needs of the people. The office would not even have taken the form it did "had not" as one member of the Constitutional Convention wrote, "many members cast their eyes toward General Washington as President; and shaped their ideas of the Powers to be given the President, by their opinions of his Virtue." Washington exploited his advantage and helped create his own myth. The admiring Garry Wills (better as scholar than as journalist) portrays him as "constantly testing public opinion and tailoring his measures to suit it"; and the even more admiring Douglas Southall Freeman found him on occasion "too much the self-conscious national hero." The Father of his Country did not need television in order to personify the nation in the Presidency. Parson Weems (Wills praises his "cinematic vigor") was sufficient.

When Andrew Jackson made his "grand triumphal tour" of the northeastern states in the late spring of 1833, it was "an emotional debauch," as Jackson's most recent biographer describes it; a continuous experience of cheering crowds, booming cannon, popular frenzy. "I have witnessed enthusiasms before," the Hero of New Orleans wrote his son after two days in New York, "but never before have I witnessed such a scene of personal regard as I have today, and ever since I left Washington. I have bowed to upwards of two hundred thousand people to day." Every commanding President in the nineteenth century was guilty of personalizing the office and appealing over the heads of Congress to the people, from Old Hickory through Father Abraham to Teddy Roosevelt at the turn of the century, with his bully pulpit and his highly publicized personality and family.

Nor was the backlash against Presidents an innovation of the 1960s. Dickens anticipated Steinbeck by more than a century. "You no sooner set up an idol firmly," he observed of the American people in 1842, "than you are sure to pull it down and dash it into fragments. . . . Any man who attains a high place among you, from the President downwards, may date his downfall from that moment."

Nor is the expectations gap, so widely invoked to explain the troubles of the contemporary Presidency, a novel phenomenon. The Presidency by its very existence excites expectations. It has always been a target of popular hope and supplication. "I am applied to almost daily," Polk wrote in 1846. ". . . The idea seems to prevail with many persons that the President is from his position compelled to contribute to every loafer who applies." When a friend said to Lincoln that he must get tired of shaking hands, Lincoln supposedly replied that "the tug of the hand was much easier to bear than that upon the heartstrings for all manner of favors behind his power to grant." Benjamin Harrison, who reported this remark, added that letters imploring help "come from every part of the land, and relate to every possible subject. . . . Many people greatly enlarge the powers of the President, and invoke his interference and protection in all their troubles."

William Howard Taft can hardly be accused of seeking to personalize the office or to rouse excessive expectations. But, long before FDR, JFK or television, Taft wrote of the President that "the whole government is so identified in the minds of the people with his personality, that they make him responsible for all the sins of omission and of commission of society at large." Taft complained bitterly of those who "visit the President with responsibility for everything that is done and that is not done," adding that "the President cannot make clouds to rain, he cannot make the corn to grow, he cannot make business to be good." Gabriel has always hovered over the White House.

The expectations-gap thesis rests on the assumption that voters really believe campaign promises and are consequently overcome with astonishment and anger when those promises are not thereafter fulfilled. It assumes, in other words, that the electorate is a pack of fools. But voters are on the whole as intelligent as you or I. They do not take it literally when presidential candidates say they will make the clouds rain, abolish poverty and usher in utopia. They regard campaign oratory as campaign oratory—that is, not as a solemn covenant with the people but as a clue to the candidate's values, priorities and character. They are not greatly bothered by "over-promising." They understand with Emerson that "nothing great was ever achieved without enthusiasm."

The situation today is far from one of voters deluded by excessive expectations. It is, on the contrary, one of voters depressed by absence of expectation. Too many think it makes little difference who is President. They doubt that any President can do what he promises. This is another reason for the steady decline in turnout.

As for the idea that overwhelming historical forces conspire against the contemporary Presidency, obviously the substantive problems of the 1970s and 1980s were not easy. But do we really face tougher problems than our forefathers did? Tougher problems than independence? slavery? the Civil War? the Great Depression? the Second World War? The substantive problems confronting contemporary Presidents are, nuclear weapons aside, relatively manageable compared to those that confronted Washington or Lincoln or Franklin Roosevelt. Let us avoid the fallacy of self-pity that leads every generation to suppose that it is peculiarly persecuted by history. Historical forces have always conspired against the Presidency. The Presidency has survived.

POINTS TO PONDER

1. Why does the president generally have broader discretion in foreign policy than in domestic policy?
2. In what ways did President Nixon assert powers more broadly than had previous presidents, according to Schlesinger?
3. How did the balance of constitutional power between the president and Congress shift in the 1970s?
4. What dimensions of presidential power does Schlesinger add to Neustadt's idea of the power to persuade?

17

"WHITE HOUSE STAFF VERSUS THE CABINET: CENTRIPETAL AND CENTRIFUGAL ROLES"
James P. Pfiffner

Charles G. Dawes, the first director of the Bureau of the Budget and vice president to Calvin Coolidge, once said that "cabinet secretaries are vice presidents in charge of spending, and as such are the natural enemies of the President." His point, though exaggerated, was that members of the president's cabinet, as heads of major departments, are almost inevitably advocates for the programs for which they are responsible. This is one reason for the increase in size and importance of the White House staff. The centrifugal tugs of Congress, interest groups, and bureaucracies are strong and fragmenting forces. White House staffers tend to have a presidential perspective and provide the centripetal force that tries to rein in the executive branch bureaucracies to the purposes of the president. In this 1986 article from Presidential Studies Quarterly, *James Pfiffner, a political scientist at George Mason University, analyzes the often conflicting roles of these two sets of presidential appointees who are both on the president's team but whose underlying roles often bring them into conflict.*

The first task of any new administration must be the organization of the White House and the establishment of the role the cabinet will play. If these central issues are not settled, the President will have trouble pursuing any of his political or governmental priorities. And if there are problems within or between these two central institutions in an administration, much valuable time can be lost until the tensions are settled. The early months of an administration are particularly crucial to a new president because they provide a narrow window of opportunity to accomplish his goals.

If the president does not designate early who will be first among his White House staff, it is an invitation to struggle; for much is at stake. The President's program will necessarily wait while the battle for who is in charge is settled. The Carter administration lost a lot of time while the relative positions of Hamilton Jordan and Jack Watson were established. This struggle helped to negate some of the other elaborate preparations the administration had undertaken during the transition. Time was also lost and energy misspent in the Ford and Carter presidencies while each president experimented with a "spokes of the wheel" model of White House organization and refused to designate a chief of staff.

Presidents must also set early ground rules for the role that cabinet members will play in the administration and the appropriate relationship between the White House staff and the Cabinet. It must be clear what is and is not delegated before cabinet secretaries get established in their departments. If this is not done it will be very difficult to call presumed delegations back in. Presidents Nixon and Carter both felt that they had delegated too much to their cabinet secretaries personnel selection. Both administrations later found this to be an expensive mistake when they finally resorted to firing and replacing several cabinet members in order to regain control, Nixon after the 1972 election and Carter in the summer of 1979. . . .

Organizing the White House

Presidents choose their White House staffs primarily from those who have worked with them on their campaigns for very good reasons. Those who have worked closely with the new president on the campaign understand best the personality and values of the president. More importantly, the president has confidence in the judgment of the people who have weathered the storms of campaigning with him and, according to John Ehrlichman, "The president's confidence is the only qualification for working in the White House." In addition, "you use your own campaign organization because people know each other" and are used to working together.

This natural choice of campaign aides, however, may lead to problems, because the nature of governing is substantially different from the nature of political campaigns. Bradley Patterson, with fourteen years working experience in the White House, argues that "The virtues needed in the crucible of a campaign—are almost the opposite of the preparation needed for life within the White House."

* * * *

Eisenhower and Kennedy Models Contrasted

The two main models of White House organization in the contemporary presidency are the Eisenhower and the Roosevelt-Kennedy models. Recent presidents have seemed to want to imitate President Eisenhower's system of cabinet organization but not necessarily his White House organization. Eisenhower's participation in staff advisory systems in the military led him to the conclusion that the White House must be organized much more formally than Truman and

Roosevelt had organized theirs. While good organization would not guarantee good advice, according to Eisenhower it would enhance the likelihood of efficiency. "Organization cannot make a genius out of an incompetent. On the other hand, disorganization can scarcely fail to result in inefficiency." Eisenhower insisted that as many issues as possible be settled below the Presidential level and that issues be presented for his consideration on one page memoranda.

The driving force behind the Eisenhower White House staff system was Sherman Adams who came to dominate the White House with an iron hand. Adams said that his job was "to manage a staff that would boil down, simplify and expedite the urgent business that had to be brought to Eisenhower's personal attention and to keep as much work of secondary importance as possible off his desk." . . .

When John Kennedy was elected he was strongly urged by his advisors to reject the Eisenhower model of White House organization and to adopt a system closer to that of Franklin Roosevelt. In his memorandum, "Staffing the President-Elect," Richard Neustadt described the type of organization Kennedy might adopt:

> You would be your own "chief of staff." . . . For if you follow my advice you will commit yourself not to each detail of Rooseveltian practice . . . but to the *spirit* of his presidential operation; whereby *you* would oversee, coordinate, and interfere with virtually everything your staff was doing. A collegial staff has to be managed; competition has to be audited.

Clark Clifford also urged Kennedy to reject the Eisenhower model with its dominant chief of staff. In a memorandum to Kennedy he argued: "A vigorous President in the Democratic tradition of the Presidency will probably find it best to act as his own chief of staff, and to have no highly visible majordomo standing between him and his staff, (and, incidently [sic], between him and the public). It is important that all the senior professional persons on the staff should have access to the President, and the staff should consist of no more persons than can conveniently have such access on a day-to-day basis."

Kennedy followed the advice of Clifford and Neustadt and ran a loosely structured White House with several senior aides having access to the president. . . .

The White House under Johnson was so unstructured that when a new aide reported for duty and asked for an organization chart he was told by an amused career official who had been in the White House for thirty years: "We don't have any organization chart at the White House because we don't have any organization."

Nixon's White House

In contrast to the Kennedy and Johnson loosely structured styles, President Nixon began his administration with a clear cut White House organization. While staff members would change, the lynchpin of the organization, H.R. Haldeman, maintained the same tight control over the White House. According to Haldeman "You've got to establish a clear cut organizational structure" in order to keep staff rivalries and competition for the President's ear from dominating the policy process. "We all knew where we fit. There were five of us that were equal, but as Bryce Harlow said: There was a first among equals, and it was clearly me. Nobody questioned it. I never asserted it; I never argued it. I never had to."

While others saw Haldeman as a barrier between them and the president and suspected that the White House staff was arrogating much power to itself, Haldeman saw his role as merely acting at the direction of the President. "If I told someone to do something, he knew it wasn't me—he knew exactly what it was; it was an order from the President. They knew an appeal wouldn't get anywhere." According to this view every President needs someone who will make the tough decisions about protecting the President's time and who will shield the president from having to make unpleasant face-to-face decisions about personnel. Haldeman characterized himself: "Every President needs a son of a bitch, and I'm Nixon's. I'm his buffer and I'm his bastard. I get done what he wants done and I take the heat instead of him." . . .

The reaction in the country to the Watergate scandals was so strong that the next two Presidents felt a need to distance themselves and their administrations from the Nixon legacy. This led Presidents Ford and Carter to begin their terms with promises of open access to the President and a spokes of the wheel structure of White House organization. Each was forced to admit failure after a period of attempting to run the White House without a chief of staff.

The Ford and Carter Reactions

Upon succeeding to the Presidency after Nixon's resignation, President Ford took pains to distinguish his administration from Nixon's. He spoke of a return to "cabinet government" and an open presidency that would not have a powerful White House staff standing between the President and his advisors or cabinet members. "A Watergate was made possible by a strong chief of staff and ambitious White House aides who were more powerful than members of the Cabinet but who had little or no practical experience in judgement. I wanted to reverse the trend. . . ."

Thus Ford began his administration with nine people reporting to him and with the intention of running his White House without a chief of staff who might evoke the specter of H.R. Haldeman. But in order to lend some sort of coherence to a White House staff of over 500 people, Ford designated Donald Rumsfeld to be "Staff Coordinator." And after several months in office even Ford had to admit that something akin to a chief of staff was necessary in order to run the White House. Ford explained: "Someone, I decided, had to be responsible for scheduling appointments, coordinating the paper flow, following up on decisions I had made and giving me status reports on projects and policy development. I didn't like the idea of calling this person chief of staff, but that was the role he would fill." . . .

Carter, like Ford, was reacting to Watergate and the Nixon Presidency and promised Cabinet Government with no powerful White House staff. "I believe in Cabinet administration of our government. There will never be an instance while I am President when the members of the White House staff dominate or act in a superior position to the members of our cabinet."

Carter also started out with nine advisors reporting to him, and he intended to be his own chief of staff. This came naturally for Carter who prided himself as a good manager and who enjoyed (or was obsessed with) the details of policy and management. This led to a situation in which it was difficult in the executive branch to determine who was in charge, and from the perspective of Congress it was not clear who were the key actors and decision makers in the White House. The situation was also aggravated by the transition conflict between the Watson and Jordan staffs. Valuable time was lost in waiting for the dispute to be resolved; and while Jordan was unquestionably the winner, Carter refused to give him unambiguous authority over the White House staff.

Carter tolerated the lack of any formal chief of staff until July of 1979 when he finally admitted the obvious need and officially appointed Jordan to the post. Later, when Jordan moved to work on the 1980 campaign, Jack Watson took over the title. In retrospect both Jack Watson and Stuart Eizenstat have concluded that it is important to have one person in charge of the White House staff.

The Reagan White House

The Reagan administration came to office with the conscious intention of avoiding the mistakes they thought that President Carter had made. One of the ways they did this was that Edwin Meese, who had run the transition, was put in charge of policy, the cabinet and national security. But Meese was not the president's only top staff aide. He shared his primacy with Michael Deaver and James Baker. Thus Reagan's White House was organized in a modified spokes of the wheel and chief of staff system. . . .

The White House organization of domination by Troika (or Quadrumvirate when Clark was there) seemed to work very well for the first part of the administration. The first year victories seemed to be engineered quite well by the functional separation of duties among the three top advisors. They all had direct access to the President, and they coordinated their work with daily meetings and a minimum of friction. In late 1983, however, reports began to surface that some of the traditional problems of lack of monocratic hierarchy were being felt.

The problems stemmed from the fact that no one staff member was clearly in charge and the president was not closely enough engaged in policy making and administration to settle disputes quickly. One White House official who had served other presidents said: "I've never worked in an organization like this. There is no one person to give orders, except the President. This lends itself to jockeying for position and not letting anyone else get too far ahead." Despite these scattered complaints, the triumvirate continued to dominate the White House throughout President Reagan's first term.

In the second term Baker moved out of the White House to take over the Treasury while Treasury Secretary Donald Regan came to the White House to be chief of staff. With Meese at the head of the Justice Department, Regan proceeded to centralize control of the White House in himself. The process was facilitated by the departure of first term Reagan advisors Max Friedersdorf and Ed Rollins, as well as OMB Director David Stockman. The experiment with the troika was abandoned to revert to a system with the strongest chief of staff since H.R. Haldeman and Sherman Adams. Regan's control over the Reagan White House might even exceed that of these two strong predecessors.

The Holy Grail of "True" Cabinet Government

Every president since Lyndon Johnson has come to office promising to give his cabinet a large voice in the running of the government. President Nixon began his administration by giving his department secretaries broad leeway in personnel and policy, but ended up drawing tight control into the White House. President Ford promised to abandon the domination by a strong White House staff and guaranteed personal access to his cabinet secretaries. President Carter promised true cabinet government, but in the end felt he had given away too much power to the cabinet and tried to take it back in the summer of 1979. President Reagan promised cabinet government and developed a system of cabinet councils that was used in innovative ways to coordinate administration policy.

There is a major tug of war in every administration (between the cabinet secretaries and the White House staff) over control of administration policy. There is no way to avoid a strong White House staff in the modern presidency; the challenge is to see that it does not overwhelm the legitimate prerogatives of the cabinet. . . .

Cabinet selection processes and criteria guarantee that members will not be chosen only for their personal and ideological loyalty to the president. Other factors tend to dominate cabinet choices, such as partisan concerns, symbolic statements, expertise, management experience, and clientele concerns. Thus the way members of a cabinet are chosen leads us to expect that they will not always see eye to eye with the White House. And once in office there are also strong centrifugal forces at work pulling the cabinet secretary away from the president. These forces include the cabinet secretary's duties to the law and to Congress and their dependency on their career bureaucracies and the constituencies their departments represent.

* * * *

On the one hand cabinet members owe their allegiance to the President who appointed them and who can remove them at his pleasure. But on the other hand cabinet members have constitutional duties to the law and to Congress as well as dependencies on the career bureaucracy and their clientele groups. It must be stressed that these nonpresidential pulls are legitimate claims on the allegiance of cabinet members. Presidents should be able to expect loyalty from their cabinet members, but to expect the sort of rigid, literal obedience that the Nixon administration came to expect is asking too much from the American separation of power system and is not in the best interests of the presidency. Presidents should realize that they are acting in a system of shared powers, not a unitary state with an executive structure of monocratic hierarchy.

The Eisenhower Cabinet Model

When Eisenhower was elected to the Presidency he came to office with strong ideas about the way it should be organized that stemmed from his military experience and previous contact with the White House. . . . He was also critical of the use to which previous presidents put their cabinet meetings. So Eisenhower resolved to organize his presidency much more formally than had his two immediate predecessors. He did this through his formal staff system tightly run by Sherman Adams and through the use of his cabinet and the cabinet secretariat. . . .

While Eisenhower delegated as much as possible to his cabinet secretaries individually, he wanted to use the cabinet collectively as a deliberative body. As he told his newly selected cabinet before he took office, "My hope will be to make this a policy body, to bring before you and for you to bring up subjects that are worthy of this body as a whole." But the cabinet was not meant to be a decision making body, and Eisenhower did not take votes on issues. In fact many issues had already been decided by the time they were brought before the Cabinet.

Cabinet meetings were relatively formal, with fixed agendas and focussed discussions and follow through. Much of the organization of the Cabinet meetings was due to Eisenhower's introduction of the Cabinet Secretariat in 1954. The function of the Cabinet Secretariat, as described by Bradley Patterson who was a member of it, was to circulate cabinet papers prepared by the departments so that they could be considered by members before the meetings and to assure that important matters were included on the agenda. This was not always easy since cabinet members did not necessarily want to air their problems in front of the whole cabinet. "The Cabinet Secretary had to dig, wheedle, persuade and finesse Cabinet members to bring to the common table what were clearly common matters, but which the department heads, in their century-and-a-half-long tradition, would much prefer to bring privately to the Oval Office. It was only because they knew that Eisenhower wanted it this way and no other that they reluctantly acceded [sic] to the Cabinet Secretary's or Sherman Adams' agenda-planning."

The Eisenhower model of cabinet government is the standard against which future presidents would measure their intentions for the presidency.

Kennedy and Johnson consciously reacted against what they thought was a too rigid system. Nixon and Carter, however, both promised delegation and consultation with their cabinets, but were unable to avoid major conflicts between their cabinets and White House staffs. Reagan promised cabinet government and instituted a system of cabinet councils, an alternative to the Eisenhower model.

Kennedy and Johnson

Just as President Kennedy rejected the Sherman Adams model of White House organization, so he also rejected the Eisenhower model of cabinet organization. . . .

While Eisenhower used organizational channels to delegate and keep decisions out of the White House, Kennedy followed Neustadt's advice and drew matters into the White House so that he and his staff could be actively involved in governmental decisions. He felt the presidency ought to be "the vital center of action in our whole scheme of government . . . the President *must* place himself in the very thick of the fight."

In line with Kennedy's desire to be personally in charge of the government rather than presiding over the institutions of government, he held few cabinet meetings, preferring to deal with his departmental secretaries one at a time. Kennedy felt "cabinet meetings are simply useless. Why should the Postmaster General sit there and listen to a discussion of the problems of Laos?"

Lyndon Johnson, like Kennedy, ran the government from the White House, relying on his White House staff. He held cabinet meetings more regularly than Kennedy, but used them as briefing forums rather than as consultative mechanisms. Toward the end of his administration he relied increasingly on those involved with his national security decision making process, and became distrustful of those outside his immediate circle. As he told President-elect Nixon when they met at the White House in December 1968: "Let me tell you, Dick, I would have been a damn fool to have discussed major decisions with the full Cabinet present, because I knew that if I said something in the morning, you could sure as hell bet it would appear in the afternoon papers."

The Nixon Administration

Richard Nixon began his administration with the intention of reversing the personalized White House control of the government that had developed in the Kennedy-Johnson years and returning to a cabinet centered government. He intended to concentrate his efforts as president on foreign affairs and delegate domestic policy to his cabinet. "I've always thought this country could run itself domestically without a President. All you need is a competent cabinet to run the country at home. You need a president for foreign policy. . . ."

At a meeting of his newly designated cabinet members the day after he presented them on television he exhorted them to seize control of their departments and not cave in to the bureaucrats. It sounded as if he intended to let them run their departments with a minimum of White House interference. At one of the first cabinet meetings in 1969 he delegated to his Cabinet secretaries authority to choose their own subordinates based on the criteria of ability first and loyalty second. In the beginning he had the general notion that the Cabinet would serve a collegial and advisory function, but soon changed to view secretaries primarily as managers of their departments.

According to John Ehrlichman, Nixon was either quite optimistic or naive. But disillusionment soon set in. Nixon believed "all these wonderful guys would help him and all he would do is take the 'big plays.' But it doesn't work that way. The news summary comes in and Wally Hickle has been putting his foot in his mouth. You can't give these guys carte blanche." After only a few weeks into the administration Nixon began to reverse his earlier stance on delegation and give orders to his cabinet secretaries through his White House staff. . . .

If Nixon was disappointed in his cabinet, the feeling was often mutual. Members of the Cabinet often felt that they did not have enough direct access to the President and that he was overly insulated by his White House staff. Some of them complained, even publicly, of their lack of access. They included Secretary of Transportation John Volpe, Secretary of the Interior Walter Hickle, and Budget Director Mayo. According to Jeb Stuart Magruder, they were not all wrong.

> From our perspective in the White House, the cabinet officials were useful spokesmen when we wanted to push a particular line — on Cambodia, on Carswell, or whatever. From their perspective, however, it was often a rude awakening to have Jeb Magruder or Chuck Colson calling up and announcing, "Mr. Secretary, we're sending over this speech that we'd like you to deliver." But that was how it was. Virtually all the cabinet members had to accept that they lacked access to the president and that their dealings would be with Haldeman and his various minions.

Because of these factors there was constant friction between Cabinet members and the White House staff.

Given these developments and Nixon's perception of them, he did three things to deal with the unacceptable situation: he relied more heavily on his White House staff, particularly H.R. Haldeman; he juggled his Cabinet to appoint members with greater loyalty to himself; and he attempted to reorganize the executive branch in order to make it more responsive to the President. After the 1972 election Nixon demanded resignations from all of his cabinet members. In his second term he chose cabinet members of whose loyalty he could be certain. . . .

Nixon and his aides saw the Executive branch as a hierarchy akin to the military with the President as Commander in Chief; violations of the chain of command were intolerable. They saw other opposing forces in the governmental system as illegitimate. Congressional opposition was seen as obstructionist. Cabinet officials' responsiveness to interest groups and their agencies were seen as undermining the President.

While Presidents have a right to expect loyalty from their appointees in the executive branch, they must also realize that compelling pressures from clientele groups and the career bureaucracy are inevitable, and that many of the attempts to affect governmental policy by the Congress are legitimate. Presidents have the right and duty to resist these pressures with all of the legitimate, constitutional means at their disposal (and these are considerable); but they ought not to be so frustrated by their inevitable defeats that they resort to illegitimate means to enforce their prerogatives. . . .

Jimmy Carter's Cabinet Government

Jimmy Carter's vision for his presidency was formed in reaction against what he saw as the abuses of the Nixon administration. Carter would have no chief of staff, and he would rely heavily on his Cabinet and remain accessible to them. In meetings with his newly designated Cabinet members in Georgia during the Christmas holidays in 1976 Carter told them he wanted to "restore the Cabinet to its proper role as the President's first circle of advisors" and that there would be "no all-powerful palace guard in my White House, no anonymous aides, unelected, unknown to the public, and unconfirmed by the Senate, wielding vast power from the White House basement." Carter wanted to be his own chief of staff on the Kennedy and Roosevelt model and refused to designate a chief of staff. He would be the hub at the center of the wheel and all White House staff members would report to him.

His Cabinet would also advise him and have access to him. "I believe in Cabinet administration of our government. There will never be an instance while I am President when the members of the White House Staff dominate or act in a superior position to the members of our Cabinet." He, as Nixon before him, initially intended to delegate much of domestic policy making to his cabinet. Hamilton Jordan, his principal advisor, said: "The problem is too many presidents have tried to deal with all of the problems of the country from the White House. . . .

Carter's early Cabinet meetings were useful as an introduction of the new members to each other and as a means of getting information out. Each secretary would be asked to report on the past week and what would likely come up the next week in their areas of responsibility. But after a year or so of this type of meeting, often without an agenda, attendees began to tire of them. Hamilton Jordan felt they were a waste of time. One Cabinet member said the meetings "were tedious, boring and virtually a waste of time." At a Cabinet meeting at Camp David Juanita Kreps said, "The Cabinet meetings are fairly useless." The meetings were not used for decision making, and tough problems were discussed in smaller meetings with the President.

The tension and friction between the Carter White House and Cabinet came to a head in the spring and summer of 1979 when Carter decided that something had to be done. The White House staff felt there was no discipline in the administration and that Carter had to take charge forcefully. The experiment with cabinet government and spokes of the wheel organization had not worked.

To respond to concerns about the conduct of his administration, Carter went to Camp David in July 1979 to consult with advisors and prominent people from around the country. When he came back he had decided to name Hamilton Jordan to be chief of staff. He told the cabinet at a meeting that they were not working for him but for themselves and that he was going to make some changes. He demanded written resignations from each member of the Cabinet. Despite objections that this would seem too much like President Nixon's demand for resignations in 1972, he went forward with it and told cabinet members to fill out evaluation forms on their immediate subordinates to evaluate their loyalty to the administration. The resignations were dutifully turned in and Carter accepted five of them.

Reagan's Cabinet Councils

Ronald Reagan came to office with a remarkably coherent agenda and set of policy priorities. His priorities to significantly increase defense spending and cut spending in virtually all domestic policy areas lent themselves to a narrow focus and simple set of values for his administration. This simple set of priorities served as a litmus test and guide to action that was a great help in recruiting personnel for the administration. Personal and ideological loyalty were the primary criteria for appointees. The coherence of values led to an administration with much more unity than has marked recent administrations with more disparate policy agendas and personnel.

Reagan also came to office with the notion that he wanted his administration to be run through some form of "cabinet government." Delegating significant authority to the Cabinet fit well into his style of leadership and was consciously different from President Carter's tendency to become embroiled in the details of decisions. What was not intended for a Reagan approach to cabinet government, however, was delegation to cabinet secretaries of authority over their budgets or selection of personnel.

Initial budget decisions were made by the White House staff and David Stockman. Except for defense, the budgets included significant cuts in most agencies, and newly designated cabinet members were brought into the White House to sign off on the proposed cuts. They were called to a meeting with Stockman, the President, and several White House aides and given a chance to react to the proposed cuts, but it was difficult because "they're in the position of having to argue against the group line. And the group line is cut, cut, cut," according to David Stockman's account. The newly designated secretaries were at an added disadvantage because they did not have their management teams together yet and had not yet had a chance to get to know their career executives.

The Reagan White House felt that Carter and Nixon had lost the personnel battle to their Cabinet Secretaries and worked hard to keep tight control of subcabinet appointments in the White House. They were successful, and the Reagan administration kept closer control of administration personnel in the White House than any other recent administration. The slowness of the appointments process resulted in many delays in appointing the subcabinet. This put the new secretaries at an added disadvantage in disagreeing with the White House staff if they had wanted to. . . .

Given this tight White House control of the budget, personnel, and the legislative agenda, how could the Reagan system be considered "cabinet government"? Edwin Meese explained that the "cabinet concept" intended that cabinet members would be the President's principal advisors and that they would not be undercut by other members of the White House staff. He further explained that President Reagan had an eighteen member cabinet: the heads of major departments as well as Meese as counselor to the President, the directors of OMB and CIA, the U.S. Trade Representative, and the U.S. representative to the United Nations.

Meese explained that no major administration decision was made without at least one member of the cabinet present, and this ensured that the President would have input from the cabinet. This is an expansive concept of cabinet government that corresponded with Reagan's expanded cabinet membership. But the tight Reagan White House control of administration policy and its legislative agenda was a far cry from previous attempts at "cabinet government," whether Eisenhower's, Nixon's (first term), or Carter's. . . .

The creation of the Cabinet Councils was announced by the White House on February 26, 1981 with five councils: Economic Affairs (CCEA), Commerce and Trade (CCCT), Human Resources (CCHR), Natural Resources and Environment (CCNRE), and Food and Agriculture (CCFA). The following year the Cabinet Council on Legal Policy (CCLP) and Cabinet Council on Management and Administration (CCMA) were added. The purpose of the councils according to the White House was to act as a "means for deliberate consideration of major policy issues which affect the interests of more than one department or agency."

The purpose of the Cabinet Council approach was to provide a forum for cabinet participation and deliberation on issues that cut across cabinet jurisdictions but still not include secretaries whose jurisdictions had nothing to do with the policies being considered. It also was to provide for interaction and integration of Cabinet views with those of the White House staff and avoid the strains that had marked so many earlier administrations. The system would also allow second level policy issues to be dealt with below the presidential level and it would help keep the focus of the administration on the central Reagan agenda. The cabinet councils were to be the focus of a policy network that integrated both Cabinet and White House resources and input. . . .

During the first term of the Reagan administration the cabinet council system worked well as a means of getting cabinet and White House input and developing issue analysis in an orderly way, though as has been pointed out, the councils themselves enjoyed varying success. Such a cabinet council system entails certain prerequisites for it to accomplish its coordinating goals. First of all, there has to be a commitment by the White House and the Cabinet to play by the rules; the main rule being that issues are not to be brought up to the President on a bilateral basis, but that all issues are to be "roundtabled" by discussing them at a cabinet council meeting. Each cabinet member's policy proposals are to be subjected to the scrutiny and criticism of peers in the cabinet and White House staff. . . .

Early in Reagan's second term all of the cabinet councils were eliminated except one on economic policy and one on domestic policy. The president would thus receive policy advice primarily from these two councils and the National Security Council. The two new councils would be chaired by officials playing two roles. James Baker would chair the council on economic affairs while he was Treasury Secretary, and Edwin Meese would chair the domestic council along with carrying out his duties as Attorney General.

Conclusion: What Have We Learned?

No one questions the need for an active White House staff in the modern presidency. Cabinet members may complain, and certain staffers may abuse their power, but the president cannot operate without a staff to protect his political interests and keep the administration's focus on the central agenda. Stuart Eizenstat argues that departments and agencies are inherently incapable of coordinating themselves. "Agencies simply do not trust each other. . . . This lack of trust means that, when we have to deal with cross–cutting, conflicting, complex issues of the day that involve more than one agency, it is very difficult, if not impossible, to entrust to one agency the responsibility to coordinate the development of policy that affects several agencies. . . . Without a centralized, strong, and effective White House staff, it is simply impossible to assure the neutrality of the policymaking process because agencies bring their own biases to the process. . . . Due process cannot occur without a strong centralized White House staff." . . .

But a strong White House staff is not without its dangers. There will inevitably be complaints from the Cabinet and others that the White House staff is isolating the President and limiting their access to him. This will be so even though it will often be the President's personal decision not to see a cabinet member. There will also be criticisms of the White House staff that are intended for the President. Of course, the function of lightning rod is an important one for the staff in any White House. The other danger is that the President may come to depend too heavily on his staff and limit his sources of information. This may have happened in the Johnson and Nixon presidencies when the wagons were circled because of the Vietnam War and Watergate, respectively. Bowman Cutter argues that a president should keep his staff off balance by not letting them get too confident of their positions in the White

House. But this can be carried to extremes as it sometimes was by Presidents Franklin Roosevelt and Lyndon Johnson.

There is also a developing consensus that in the White House staff someone must unequivocally be in charge. In the words of one Kennedy aide: "Everybody believes in democracy until he gets to the White House and then you begin to believe in dictatorship, because it's so hard to get things done." On this issue we have the informed opinions of H.R. Haldeman, Richard Cheney, and Jack Watson. Each of them has concluded that if the President does not designate someone to control the rivalries and competition for the President's ear, chaos will result. The Reagan experience, with its troika of differentiated jurisdictions, has brought into question whether there must be one person in charge, but during the first term there were complaints from within the administration about the lack of clear leadership.

It is still possible that a President may be elected with the skills and intelligence of a Franklin Roosevelt or a John Kennedy who can act as the hub of a wheel and be his own chief of staff. But experience in the Ford, Carter, and Reagan presidencies has brought into question whether we can return to the less formal days of the 1930s or even 1960s. The consequences of failing to pull it off (Ford and Carter) are apparent and present a serious risk for any president who tries it. . . .

With respect to the cabinet, presidential experience over the past several decades has taught us some lessons. We know that there will inevitably be conflicts between the Cabinet and the White House staff; it is inherent in their differing functions. The trick is to make the interface into a dynamic tension rather than letting it degenerate into a destructive hostility. This can be done by a recognition on each side of the legitimate functions of the other side. It is particularly important the White House recognize that the legitimate, constitutional roles of Cabinet members along with profound political pressures give them perspectives not always in line with those of the White House. As the Carter Presidency taught us, legitimate pressures must be used to extract loyalty and coherence from the cabinet. But as the Nixon Presidency demonstrates, expecting a rigid discipline and subordination to the White House is both unrealistic and harmful.

POINTS TO PONDER

1. Describe the two main styles of organizing the White House: the collegial model (with no chief of staff) and the hierarchical model (using a chief of staff).
2. Why is "true cabinet government" compared to the "Holy Grail"?
3. Why is an active White House staff necessary in the modern presidency, according to the author?
4. What dimension of presidential power does the author add to the perspectives of Neustadt and Schlesinger?

18

"THE PRESIDENCY AND DOMESTIC POLICY: THE CIVIL RIGHTS ACT OF 1964"
Robert D. Loevy

Although presidents have maximum discretion in formulating foreign policy, they are often constrained by Congress in their domestic policy initiatives. In this case study of the historic Civil Rights Act of 1964, Robert Loevy, a political scientist at Colorado College, illuminates both the ability of Congress to thwart a president and the power of the conservative coalition in Congress in the middle of the twentieth century. Lyndon Johnson's wiles as a legislative strategist and his determination to get his bills through Congress are demonstrated in his narrow victory. The broader point of this article from The American Presidency *(1985) is that presidential power in domestic policy is severely constrained by Congress. It took all the considerable skills of a master legislative strategist to win this crucial victory for racial justice in the United States.*

An almost perfect illustration of the relative powerlessness of the United States president in domestic matters is the history of civil rights legislation prior to 1964. From the time of the withdrawal of Union troops from the southern United States in 1876 until the passage of the Civil Rights Act of 1957, Congress refused to pass any civil rights legislation whatsoever. The 1957 act is considered an historic breakthrough because it was the first civil rights bill to get through Congress since Civil War Reconstruction, but the new law was so watered down to meet the criticisms of southern Democrats in the Senate that it had little or no effect on racial segregation in the United States. A 1960 Civil Rights Act, equally watered-down to meet southern requirements, was regarded as equally ineffectual.

On February 28, 1963, President John F. Kennedy sent Congress a strong message on the immediate need for civil rights legislation: "The Negro baby born in America today . . . has about one-half as much chance of completing high school as a white baby born in the same place on the same day—one-third as much chance of completing college—one-third as much chance of becoming a professional man—twice as much chance of becoming unemployed . . . a life expectancy which is seven years less—and the prospects of earning only half as much."

This forthright statement was not backed up with a strong civil rights legislative proposal. President Kennedy limited his recommendations to minor improvements in voting rights laws (none of which were very effective in the South), technical assistance to school districts desegregating voluntarily, and an extension of the Civil Rights Commission, a government body which could study civil rights problems but had no power to remedy them.

Why were the president's words so strong and his proposed legislation so weak? "President Kennedy was never one to demand congressional action on need alone. His sense of timing told him he could not overcome the legislative roadblocks in the way of civil rights legislation, and defeat, no matter how gallant, had no appeal for him." As had happened so often in American political history, a United States president was bowing to the reality that a strong civil rights bill, one that would really end racial segregation and racial oppression in the southern United States, was simply not politically achievable, no matter how much of his political will and his political strength a president might throw into the battle.

The Southern Civil Rights "Veto"

The obstacles to passing a civil rights bill were truly formidable in early 1963. In the House of Representatives, regular legislative committees such as the House Judiciary Committee do not report bills directly to the House floor for a vote. Because debate is limited in the House of Representatives, committee bills first go to the House Rules Committee, where the length of time the bill will be debated and the manner in which the bill will be debated is decided. Many bills that make it through the regular committees, however, often are not reported out of the Rules Committee at all, and usually when this happens the particular bill is dead for the remainder of that session of Congress.

In 1963 the chairman of the House Rules Committee was Howard Smith, a conservative southern Democrat from Virginia. Smith was ardently opposed to all civil rights legislation, and it was clear he would use his power as chairman of the Rules Committee to delay any civil rights bill as long as possible. If Democratic President Kennedy wanted a tough civil rights bill, he would have to blast it past Democratic Rules Committee Chairman Smith.

Over in the Senate, the situation was even more difficult. The chairman of the Senate Judiciary Committee was James O. Eastland, a Democrat from Mississippi and, as one would expect, a staunch opponent of civil rights. Eastland had used his powers as Judiciary Committee chairman to kill more than one hundred proposed civil rights bills throughout the late 1950s and early 1960s. If Democrat Kennedy wanted a civil rights bill, he would have to find a way around Democrat Eastland and his Judiciary Committee.

The big obstacle to a civil rights bill in the Senate, however, was the filibuster. Senate rules provide for unlimited debate, which means that a group of senators can kill a bill by simply talking it to death. Over the years southern Democratic senators had clearly established the idea they would filibuster any strong civil rights proposal. In fact, the reason the 1957 and 1960 Civil Rights Acts were so weak was that southern filibusters had succeeded. Rather than wait-out a lengthy filibuster, liberal senators supporting civil rights had compromised on both bills to the point where the southern Democrats would stop talking and let the bill come to a vote and, eventually, final passage.

President Kennedy's real problem with civil rights, however, was the crucial role of the South in the Democratic party. In 1963, the Democratic party was made up of an uneasy coalition of conservative southern Democrats on the one hand and liberal northern and western Democrats on the other. The only way Kennedy could hope to get a major tax-cut bill and other economic programs through the Congress was to keep the southerners in the Democratic fold. Pushing hard for civil rights, however, would have antagonized the southern Democrats.

In addition, there was the political problem of keeping the support of southern Democratic voters in the upcoming 1964 presidential election. Kennedy had defeated Richard Nixon in 1960 in one of the closest presidential races in American history. The electoral votes of several southern states, particularly Texas, had been essential to Kennedy's victory. Kennedy was going to need that southern Democratic support again in the 1964 presidential race. Similar to all Democratic presidents, Kennedy knew that, as of 1963, no Democrat had ever been elected president of the United States without carrying a substantial portion of the South. To antagonize the South with a strong push for civil rights could well be presidential political suicide.

The president also was aware that a civil rights battle could harm his foreign policy proposals and weaken his position in international affairs. Overseas problems such as the Soviet construction of the Berlin Wall and the Cuban missile crisis could be handled more successfully if public opinion in the United States was united behind the chief executive. Kennedy was currently negotiating a nuclear test ban treaty with the Soviet Union that would require a two-thirds vote of ratification in the Senate. The President knew that "to provoke a bitter national controversy (over civil rights) without achieving any gain would divide the American people at a time when the international scene required maximum unity." As had so often been the case in the past, Kennedy elected to press forward in the international field, where the Constitution gave him much greater freedom of movement, and go slow in the domestic field, where presidential options are much more limited.

Thus it was that, when dealing with civil rights, President Kennedy faced all the crippling constraints that hamper a president's ability to act on domestic policy. Clearly it would be better to forget about civil rights legislation and only do for black Americans those things which a president can do without congressional approval—appoint large numbers of blacks to important government jobs and order the Justice Department to help black and white integrationists arrested in civil rights demonstrations.

The Leadership Conference on Civil Rights

Shortly after President Kennedy's recommended civil rights bill was released to the press and public, the leaders of more than seventy civil rights organizations, operating under the name of the Leadership Conference on Civil Rights, met to discuss the Kennedy proposal. They were dismayed. "The consensus was clear; President Kennedy had yielded on civil rights legislation before the fighting had even begun. The proposed bill was hardly worth the fight. Such comfort as there was came from the hope that (if Kennedy were reelected in 1964) the second Kennedy administration would be different."

Birmingham

As so often happens to American presidents, unexpected external events totally changed the picture and completely undid Kennedy's political strategy. In May of 1963, Martin Luther King and his Southern Christian Leadership Conference began a series of nonviolent demonstrations protesting the rigid segregation of public facilities in Birmingham, Alabama. The city police chief, T. Eugene (Bull) Connor, was an avowed segregationist and brought out police dogs, fire hoses, and, most shocking of all in every sense of the word, electric cattle prods ordinarily used to drive reluctant cattle from the holding pen into the slaughter house.

Newspaper photographs and evening television reports of the violence in Birmingham brought about an immediate change in national public opinion on civil rights, particularly in the North and the West. The nation had seen first hand the worst aspects of Southern white oppression of blacks. Demands for action began pouring into the White House and the Congress from across the country.

President Kennedy was well aware that it was Birmingham that had forced him to change his position on civil rights. At a White House strategy meeting with civil rights leaders, one of those present referred in a hostile way to Bull Connor. Kennedy responded that "Bull Connor has done more for civil rights than anyone in this room." Thereafter the president was often heard to say, "The civil rights movement should thank God for Bull Connor. He's helped it as much as Abraham Lincoln."

Suddenly John F. Kennedy and his White House advisers were flooded with advice on what form a new administration proposal for civil rights legislation should take. The leadership conference on civil rights sent message after message to the president detailing needed civil rights reforms. At the president's weekly breakfasts with the Democratic congressional leadership, Senate Democratic Whip Hubert Humphrey of Minnesota advised and urged the president to send up to Capitol Hill a really strong bill. Kennedy responded by having his brother Robert, the attorney general, draw up the most sweeping civil rights proposal that any president has ever presented to Congress.

The Kennedy Civil Rights Bill

The civil rights bill which President Kennedy sent to Congress in June of 1963 included a strong provision giving black Americans equal access to all public accommodations throughout the United States. It would make illegal the segregated restaurants, cocktail lounges, hotels, and motels which were the most visible forms of racial discrimination in the American South. It also provided for the cut-off of any U.S. government aid programs in the South that were administered in a racially discriminatory fashion.

Perhaps most important of all, the new Kennedy civil rights package gave the attorney general of the United States the power to sue southern state governments that operated segregated schools. This "power to sue" would free the individual black citizen in the South from having to publicly stand up and file a suit in the local court to desegregate the local school system. Such personal attempts to gain civil rights by southern blacks were too frequently met by covert white reprisals, the most violent and brutal of which were beating and lynching.

Because a northern Democrat, Emanuel Celler of New York, was chairman of the House Judiciary Committee, the Kennedy civil rights proposals received a very favorable hearing at the committee level in the House of Representatives. From the president's point of view, in fact, the hearings were too favorable. Liberal Democrats and Republicans on the Judiciary Committee combined to press for a fair employment practices section of the bill that would ban racial discrimination in the hiring of employees by private industry. There also was support for empowering the attorney general to intervene in all civil rights cases in the South rather than only in school desegregation cases. The president was forced to become directly involved. Calling civil rights leaders and the Democratic and Republican House leadership together for five days of high-pressure negotiations, the president emerged with a compromise. A Fair Employment Practices section would be added to the bill, but the power of the attorney general to intervene in civil rights cases in the South would remain limited.

The compromise civil rights bill was reported out of the House Judiciary Committee in late November of 1963. It immediately went to the House Rules Committee, where Chairman Howard Smith had announced his firm intention of bottling up the bill, forever if possible. As the nation's capital prepared itself for the inevitable Rules Committee fight, President Kennedy boarded Air Force One to fly to Dallas. It was to be the first step in his campaign for re-election. It was symptomatic of the problems of Democratic presidents that Kennedy was taking his re-election bid first to Texas, the key southern state that had to be kept in the Democratic party if the Democrats were to retain the White House in 1964.

"To Write It in the Books of Law"

The assassin's bullet that killed President Kennedy in Dallas changed many things, but nothing quite so much as the political situation concerning civil rights. Kennedy's successor, Vice-President Lyndon Johnson, was a Democrat from Texas. At first civil rights supporters believed this would doom the civil rights bill, but actually the reverse was the case. As a southerner, Lyndon Johnson was mainly concerned with winning political support in the North. Similar to Kennedy, he would have to run for re-election in 1964, and he had less than a year to convince skeptical northern and western liberals that a southerner was an acceptable leader for the national Democratic party.

Johnson seized on the civil rights bill as the perfect instrument for establishing his credentials with northern and western liberals. Five days after Kennedy's assassination, the new president told a joint session of the House and Senate: "We have talked long enough in this country about equal rights. . . . It is time now to write the next chapter—and to write it in the books of law." Johnson then asked the Congress to adopt the civil rights bill in memory of his slain predecessor, John F. Kennedy.

If Kennedy's behavior on civil rights was a case study in a president trying to avoid a divisive domestic issue that could not be avoided, Johnson's behavior was a case study in what a president can do when he throws himself and the vast powers of his office totally into the fight. Johnson's first move was to call black leaders and civil rights leaders to well-publicized meetings in the oval office at the White House.

As Johnson himself told it: "I spoke with black groups and with individual leaders of the black community and told them that John Kennedy's dream of equality had not died with him. I assured them that I was going to press for the civil rights bill with every ounce of energy I possessed."

Johnson spoke out in favor of the civil rights bill at every suitable occasion— press conferences, public speeches, messages to Congress, and so on. Knowing that civil rights advocates feared this civil rights bill would be compromised and watered down the way all the previous ones had, Johnson took the position that he and his administration would not compromise with the segregationist southern Democrats in any way. "So far as this administration is concerned," Johnson told a press conference, "its position is firm." There would be no room for bargaining. Johnson would win his spurs as a pro–civil rights president by getting the newly strengthened civil rights bill past the House Rules Committee, the House, the Senate Judiciary Committee, and the Senate filibuster. Furthermore, he would get the bill through substantially intact.

Unlike Kennedy, who had been something of an outsider when he was in the House and the Senate, Lyndon Johnson had been the Senate majority leader when he was elected vice-president in 1960. Johnson thus was a congressional insider, a man with a detailed knowledge of the way things work on Capitol Hill and with an abundance of contacts and friendships. President Kennedy's funeral was hardly ended when the telephones began ringing in the House of Representatives. Members of Congress in key positions began hearing first-hand from the president about how he wanted the civil rights bill moved out of the House Rules Committee and on to the House floor.

The Discharge Petition

On December 9, 1963, House Judiciary Chairman Emanuel Celler filed a petition to discharge the civil rights bill from the Rules Committee. If a majority of the members of the House signed the discharge petition, the civil rights bill would move directly from the Rules Committee to the House floor. Signatures were hard to obtain at first, mainly because senators and representatives believe in the committee system of reviewing legislation and are hesitant to ever bypass a committee or its chairman. By the time of the Christmas recess, the discharge petition still was more than fifty signatures short.

The situation changed immediately after the Christmas recess. Members of Congress had found strong support for the civil rights bill when they went home to their districts for the holidays. President Johnson's constant referrals to the civil rights bill were having a dramatic effect on home town public opinion. Voters suddenly had become aware of the bill and knew that the president wanted it moved quickly through the House and Senate. The number of signatures on the discharge petition began nearing a majority, and a sizable number of signatures were from Lyndon Johnson's fellow Texans in the House of Representatives. Both the Democratic and Republican leadership in the House joined the president in pressuring Chairman Smith to release the bill.

Finally the pressure became too great and Chairman Smith gave in, saying, "I know the facts of life around here." Rather than suffer the embarrassment of having a bill discharged from his committee without his consent, Smith allowed the bill to be reported out to the House floor.

Lyndon Johnson was never one to miss any opportunity to increase the public awareness of civil rights. The president repeatedly linked the civil rights bill to Abraham Lincoln and the fact that the nation had just celebrated (in July of 1963) the hundredth anniversary of the Emancipation Proclamation. In response to a reporter's question about the civil rights bill at a White House press conference, Johnson said: "I hope it is acted upon in the House before the members leave to attend Lincoln Day birthday meetings throughout the nation, because it would be a great tribute to President Lincoln to have that bill finally acted upon in the House before we go out to celebrate his birthday."

Throughout a ten-day debate on the House floor, President Johnson and his congressional allies beat back every attempt to weaken the civil rights bill by amending it. Johnson had pledged he would pass the Kennedy bill, and that was essentially what occurred. In fact, the only major amendment to the bill actually furthered the cause of civil rights. It outlawed discrimination on the basis of sex as well as race in all the major provisions of the bill. On a Monday night, February 10, 1964, the House passed the civil rights bill by a vote of 290 to 130 and sent it to the Senate.

No Rest with Lyndon

Ordinarily, the hard-working lobbyists for the Leadership Conference on Civil Rights might have expected to have a moment of rest once the civil rights bill had been passed by the House. There was no rest, however, with Lyndon Johnson running the show. Clarence Mitchell, Washington director of the National Association for the Advancement of Colored People, recalls that the bill had just passed the House when a message came to call the president. "What are you fellows doing about the Senate," the commander-in-chief had called to say, very much at his post. "We've got it through the House, and now we've got the big job of getting it through the Senate!"

Bypassing the Senate Judiciary Committee

With President Johnson's support, the Democratic leadership in the Senate made short work of Senator Eastland and his Senate Judiciary Committee. Senate Democratic leader Mike Mansfield of Montana moved, on February 26, to place the civil rights bill directly on the Senate calendar, thereby by-passing the Judiciary Committee completely. Although this procedural move provoked a small filibuster of its own from the southern Democrats in the Senate (labeled by Senate insiders as a "mini-buster"), by March 30 the civil rights bill was on the floor of the Senate and the main event, an extended southern filibuster, was underway.

President Johnson had skillfully arranged for the Senate to pass every piece of legislation he considered critical before the civil rights filibuster began. Thus the Kennedy tax-cut bill and a wheat and cotton bill had both been moved out of the Senate before the civil rights bill arrived. "President Johnson had made it clear . . . that he would not care if the Senate did not do another thing for three months until the civil rights bill was enacted. This removed the filibusterers' greatest weapon—that they could hold out until other needed legislation required the Senate to put aside the civil rights bill."

Johnson's strategy was to let the southerners talk and talk until it became clear to everyone that a small minority was frustrating the majority will in the Senate. As the debate droned on through the month of April and then into early May, the president kept the pressure on with a regular weekly statement that he wanted a bill, and he wanted a strong bill. One week the president was quoted as saying he was "committed" to the bill with "no wheels and no deals." Another week he stated: "I believe at the proper time, after all members have had a chance to present their viewpoints both pro and con, the majority of the Senate will work its will and . . . we will pass the bill." Late in April the president said: "We need a good civil rights bill, and the bill now pending in the Senate is a good bill. I hope it can be passed in a reasonable time."

The Wallace Candidacy for President

Early in 1964, Alabama Governor George Wallace announced that he was a candidate for the Democratic nomination for president of the United States and that he would run on a platform of all-out opposition to the civil rights bill. Governor Wallace would be a formidable candidate running on the anti–civil rights issue. He had gained tremendous national publicity by personally "barring the school house door" at the University of Alabama in a futile attempt to prevent integration of the university by U.S. marshals. Although

Wallace had been forced to stand aside and let the university be integrated, he had emerged from the fracas as a southern segregationist hero and as the national symbol of opposition to school integration and black civil rights.

The Wallace candidacy called for quick action on President Johnson's part, and such action was soon forthcoming. Unwilling to permit "open season" on his presidential administration by running against Wallace himself, Johnson set to work recruiting stand-in candidates to run against Wallace in three crucial Democratic presidential primaries—Wisconsin, Indiana, and Maryland.

The Wallace threat to the civil rights bill was serious. Everywhere he went Wallace stated that his presidential candidacy was a referendum on the civil rights bill then being filibustered in the Senate. If Wallace could win only one presidential primary outside the old South, President Johnson's chance of beating the filibuster would be seriously jeopardized. Johnson himself noted that the Wallace campaign "stiffened the southerners' will to keep on fighting the civil rights measure until the liberal ranks (in the Senate) began to crumble."

After Governor Wallace polled 33.9 percent of the vote in the Wisconsin primary and did almost as well in Indiana, political analysts began writing that Wallace just might win the Democratic presidential contest in Maryland. Maryland had not seceded from the Union during the Civil War, but it was, after all, a former slave state and south of the Mason-Dixon line. If Wallace could get more than 30 percent of the vote in a northern state like Wisconsin, he could conceivably get 50 percent or more in a border state like Maryland.

Johnson pulled out all the stops in his support of his Maryland stand-in, U.S. Senator Daniel Brewster. A key White House aide, Clifton Carter of the Democratic National Committee, was dispatched to help Brewster in every way possible. Money for the Brewster campaign was raised and spent freely by the Democratic National Committee. Johnson even arranged for a top campaign publicist to come to Maryland and help Brewster with his campaign speeches and press releases.

Although the president never officially endorsed any of his stand-in candidates in the 1964 Democratic presidential primaries, Johnson skillfully scheduled a trip to western Maryland to study "Appalachian regional problems." The president saw to it that Brewster was at his side every minute he was in Maryland.

Thanks to the president's all-out support, Brewster defeated Wallace in Maryland with more than 57 percent of the vote. A combination of black votes in Baltimore coupled with upper-income suburban white votes in the Maryland suburbs produced a clear-cut majority for civil rights. Wallace and his anti–civil rights campaign had been stopped in their tracks. The filibusterers' hope that Wallace would win Maryland and start a national groundswell of opposition to the civil rights bill quickly faded.

Is the president's position with regard to domestic policy so tenuous that he has to intervene in presidential primary elections in order to get what he wants out of Congress? In the case of the Civil Rights Act of 1964, it appears clear that such action was required. In this case, the president and his political allies proved equal to the challenge.

Cloture

Senate rules provided that extended debate (a filibuster) could be brought to a close by two-thirds vote of those present and voting. Such a vote is called a cloture vote. Although cloture votes had been attempted many times in the past on civil rights bills, none had ever succeeded. The main reason was that senators from small states, mainly in the midwestern and western United States, viewed the filibuster as the only instrument by which small states could protect themselves from the large states. Even if they believed firmly in civil rights, midwestern and western senators, most of them Republicans, did not want to weaken the idea of the filibuster by voting for cloture.

It thus was clear from the beginning that a small group of Republican senators, mainly from small midwestern and western states, would be the key to getting a two-thirds vote for cloture. It was equally clear that the man who could persuade these small-state Republicans to vote for cloture was Everett McKinley Dirksen of Illinois, the Republican leader in the Senate. Dirksen had worked hard to gain the confidence of his fellow party members in the Senate, and it was believed that his support for the civil rights bill would bring along the necessary Republican votes to put the two-thirds cloture vote over the top.

President Johnson saw from the very first that Dirksen was the key to getting the civil rights bill out of the Senate. Shortly after President Kennedy's assassination, Johnson telephoned Dirksen and asked him to convey to his Republican colleagues in the Senate that the time had come to forget partisan politics and get the legislative machinery of the United States moving forward. As Johnson recalled the phone conversation: "There was a long pause on the other end of the line and I could hear him (Dirksen) breathing heavily. When he finally spoke, he expressed obvious disappointment that I would even raise the question of marshaling his party behind the president. 'Mr. President,' he said, 'you know I will.' "

Turning Senator Dirksen's general statement of support for the president into support for a cloture vote on the civil rights bill was something else again. The strategy designed by Johnson was to give Dirksen the opportunity to be a "hero in history!" Johnson noted: "I gave to this fight everything I had in prestige, power, and commitment. At the same time, I deliberately tried to tone down my personal involvement in the daily struggle so that my colleagues on the Hill could take tactical responsibility—and credit so that a hero's niche could be carved out for Senator Dirksen, not me."

The lion's share of the task of winning Everett Dirksen over to the civil rights bill fell to Hubert Humphrey, the Democratic whip in the Senate.

Humphrey recalls a telephone call from Johnson just as the civil rights bill was arriving in the Senate. "Now you know that this bill can't pass unless you get Ev Dirksen," the President told Humphrey. "You and I are going to get him. You make up your mind now that you've got to spend time with Ev Dirksen. You've got to let him have a piece of the action. He's got to look good all the time."

Early in May, Senator Dirksen invited Senator Humphrey to his office to begin negotiating amendments to the civil rights bill that would make the new legislation acceptable to Dirksen and his band of midwestern and western Republicans. Representatives from the Justice Department as well as other Democratic and Republican senators began attending these meetings. In some areas Dirksen's amendments actually strengthened the bill. As a general rule, however, Dirksen pressed to have the bill affect only those states and those business organizations where a "pattern or practice" of racial discrimination could be shown. Dirksen did not want the U.S. government interfering in isolated personal instances of discrimination, and his view eventually prevailed with the civil rights supporters. By mid-May Humphrey and Dirksen emerged from Dirksen's office with an amended bill that had both Dirksen's support and the approval of the Leadership Conference on Civil Rights.

In retrospect, everyone realized that the meetings in Dirksen's office to write amendments for the bill had, in effect, been the Senate committee meetings on the civil rights bill. The Senate had bypassed the regular channel, consideration by the Senate Judiciary Committee, but Everett Dirksen succeeded in seeing that the equivalent of the committee work took place in his office.

Once Dirksen and Humphrey had negotiated an amended bill, the outcome was inevitable. On June 10, 1964, for the first time in its history, the U.S. Senate voted cloture on a civil rights bill. Soon afterward the Senate adopted the Dirksen-Humphrey amendments, and then the final bill as amended. The House of Representatives quickly agreed to the Senate amendments, and on July 2, 1964, before an audience of more than one hundred senators, representatives, cabinet members, and civil rights leaders, President Lyndon Johnson signed the Civil Rights Act of 1964 into law.

Conclusions

The Civil Rights Act of 1964 clearly demonstrates the constraints on the president of the United States in the general area of domestic policy. Both President Kennedy and President Johnson had to deal with opposition in Congress, opposition within the Democratic party, and the political realities of their prospective campaigns for re-election.

It is important to note that, in the case of Congress, the two presidents were forced, almost every step of the way, to support extraordinary measures to get the civil rights bill passed. President Kennedy had to set up special negotiating sessions at the White House to get an acceptable compromise bill out of the House Judiciary Committee. President Johnson had to support a discharge petition to get the bill out of the House Rules Committee. The Judiciary Committee had to be bypassed in the Senate, and the ultimate extraordinary measure, a cloture vote, had to be used to end the filibuster in the Senate. The fact that such unusual and rarely used techniques were required to get the bill passed is a measure of the severe constraints facing any presidential effort to enact a civil rights bill.

Although the Civil Rights Act of 1964 illustrates the constraints on the president vis-à-vis domestic policy making, the act also illustrates what is required for the president to successfully achieve domestic changes. Clearly the crisis created by the white violence in Birmingham against black demonstrators was required for this legislation to get the push needed to move through Congress. This clear relationship between violent crisis and the president's ability to act raises a real question for American democracy, however. Can a governmental system long survive if a major crisis, often involving violence, is required every time conditions on the domestic front are going to change?

Above all, the Civil Rights Act of 1964 illustrates the effective powers the president has at his disposal once he commits himself to a particular course of action. Both Kennedy's and Johnson's use of television to dramatize the nature of the civil rights crisis to the American people was outstanding—and in both cases effective. Johnson also demonstrated how the president, making effective use of the telephone, can put the most intense kinds of personal pressure on members of Congress. Never underestimate the psychological impact, and the excitement and self-esteem, that comes from receiving a phone call from the principal resident of the White House.

The Civil Rights Act of 1964 also revealed that Congress really can change conditions in the United States if it truly wishes to do so. The act ended virtually immediately and completely all forms of public segregation in the nation, both North and South. The threat of cutting off U.S. funds to government programs and business concerns that discriminate against minorities has made "equal employment opportunity" and "affirmative action in hiring" fixed institutions in American life. The act empowered the attorney general of the United States to sue for the desegregation of schools, a program which has resulted in the use of school busing to achieve racial balance in the nation's schools. The act was the first national law to guarantee significant equal rights for women, and it set the precedent for using cloture to stop a filibuster on a civil rights bill—a precedent that was used in 1965 to pass a national law guaranteeing equal housing opportunity.

The Civil Rights Act of 1964 finally illustrates that there are times in a president's career when a domestic issue cannot be avoided, regardless of the final outcome. A politician who also happened to be a good poker player once told Lyndon Johnson that there comes a time in every president's career when he has to throw caution to the winds and bet his entire stack of chips. President Johnson studied the political tumult surrounding the civil rights bill and "decided to shove in all my stack on this vital measure." The president gambled, and that time around he won—big!

POINTS TO PONDER

1. What were the main tactics used by the opponents of the 1964 Civil Rights Act?
2. How was President Lyndon Johnson able to overcome these obstacles?
3. What lessons about presidential power does this case study teach us?

Chapter 5

THE EXECUTIVE BRANCH BUREAUCRACIES

The problem of the power of bureaucracy is faced by all modern systems of governance. Bureaucracies are essential for much of the economic wealth and conveniences of modern life that we enjoy. But bureaucracies are also sources of power independent of the governments that establish them. In the United States, presidents and members of Congress often suspect that governmental bureaucracies are out of control, but the readings in this section argue that Congress and the president have sufficient levers of control to keep our governmental bureaucracies in check.

The Establishment and Development of the U.S. Bureaucracy

The Framers of the Constitution did not spend much time worrying about public administration; they were much more concerned with balancing the sources of political power in the government they were establishing. This was understandable at a time before the industrial revolution when there were only several million people in the nation.

For most of the nineteenth century the executive branch of the government was relatively small. The largest organizations were the army, the navy, and the postal service. The only cabinet departments were those of State, War, and the Treasury. It wasn't until 1849 that the next cabinet agency, the Interior Department, was created.

From the time of Andrew Jackson, the control of most agencies was exercised through the spoils system. When a new president was elected he would bring with him into the government supporters from the political party that elected him. Jackson argued that most government jobs were so simple that they required no special training.

But toward the end of the nineteenth century, as the industrial revolution began to take hold, the corruption spawned by the spoils system and the inefficiency generated by hiring a new set of workers for every new president became evident. When President Garfield was assassinated by a disappointed office seeker in 1881 it was enough to galvanize the Congress to pass the Pendleton Act of 1883. The act established the merit system in which government workers would be hired and promoted on the basis of their own abilities, not their political service. The personnel system set up through the Pendleton Act would govern the development of the twentieth-century bureaucracies that compose the modern U.S. government.

Modern Industrialized Societies

Domination by bureaucracy is the hallmark of modern, industrialized societies, including the United States. Modern economies depend upon mass production and the intricate cooperation of thousands of workers to make possible high levels of productivity. Modern nation-states are also dependent on large-scale organizations to coordinate governmental and economic infrastructures—roads, phone systems, telecommunications, court systems, air traffic control, environmental management, and so on—upon which modern economies depend. Thus the presence of large-scale bureaucracy goes hand in hand with all modern economies.

Bureaucracy is the systematic coordination of hundreds or thousands of individuals, all of whom possess different skills and specialties, to accomplish one focused task, such as a military mission or the management of unemployment compensation. It was the great insight of the German sociologist Max Weber who lived at the turn of the century that bureaucracy is the most efficient way to perform any large-scale function over a sustained period of time. People must be coordinated with hierarchy and division of labor; specialized workers must be recruited; files of actions and institutional memory must be kept; and the succession of leadership must be planned.

But Weber was ambivalent about the considerable power generated by this specialized organization of people, resources, and skills. How can it be controlled? Any elected leader from outside the bureaucracy will be at a disadvantage facing the coordinated intricacy of the large bureaucracy—a new leader will be as a dilettante versus the experts who constitute the bureaucracy.

So bureaucratic organization gives us the blessings of modern life, but it also presents us with the problem of making it accountable to the rest of society. In the United States the rigors of competition and governmental regulation are expected to keep large business bureaucracies in check. Large governmental bureaucracies are controlled through the rule of law and the leadership of elected public officials and their representatives.

The Power and Accountability of Bureaucracies

In the U.S. constitutional system bureaucratic power presents special problems of legitimacy. The large executive branch bureaucracies in the United States exercise considerable governmental power that must be legitimated through the Constitution. The justification for their existence and actions is based on laws passed by Congress and by presidential leadership.

The problem is that, in the United States as in other countries, these large bureaucracies possess the capacity for action independent of their political superiors and the motivation to resist any policies not in their own interests. In implementing the policy directives of Congress and the president, bureaucracies have the money, expert personnel, and institutional memory needed to carry out their missions. But they often develop an institutional culture or esprit that leads them to believe that, being the experts, they know what is best for the country in their own policy area.

Most of the bureaucracies that perform the many functions of the contemporary U.S. government are in the executive branch and thus subject to policy direction from the president. The president usually exercises this policy leadership through political appointees who occupy the top executive positions in each agency and department.

But presidential control is incomplete due to a number of factors. First, presidential appointees usually stay in office for only about two years, far shorter periods than the career bureaucrats they oversee. In addition, the clientele groups in American society that the agencies serve often take a proprietary interest in the programs from which they benefit, narrowing the range of presidential flexibility in dealing with the agencies.

Congress also worries about bureaucratic responsiveness to its directives and laws. Even though Congress creates all agencies and appropriates money for all programs, there are sometimes fears in Congress that executive branch agencies are evading congressional controls, either at the direction of the president or on their own. When this happens Congress can use its control of budgets to enforce its will or it can launch investigations to expose wrongdoing.

Although we want government agencies to be responsive to legitimate political direction, we do not want government agencies to be at the disposal of politicians who might abuse their power. Thus a certain amount of independence on the part of the career professionals in the executive branch is reassuring. For instance, we want the Internal Revenue Service and the FBI to resist any political influence in carrying out their duties.

The executive branch bureaucracies in the United States exist in a dynamic balance among the forces exerted by the president, Congress, their clientele groups, and their own professional independence. The readings in this section illustrate the dynamics of bureaucratic responsiveness to political direction.

The Readings

The following selections deal with the responsiveness of executive branch bureaucracies to democratically elected, political leadership. They challenge the easy stereotype of governmental bureaucracy that many Americans hold. The authors argue that bureaucracies in the federal government, rather than being "out of control," are in fact responsive to political leadership. But this does not mean that presidents always get what they want or that political leaders are never frustrated in the implementation of public policy. The U.S. political system is very porous and fragmented, and the bureaucracy often plays a powerful role in the formulation and implementation of public policy. The point is that our national political institutions have ways of ensuring bureaucratic responsiveness and that bureaucracies acting alone cannot easily resist political direction. In concert, however, with other political forces—Congress, interest groups, and so forth—the bureaucracy can be a formidable opponent of presidential policy preferences.

In the first selection, Francis Rourke argues that, since the growth of large-scale U.S. bureaucracies after the New Deal, the three branches of U.S. government have transformed themselves in order to assure that bureaucracies are responsive to political direction. The presidency now has a large White House staff to formulate policy and oversee implementation to assure bureaucratic compliance. Congress has significantly increased its staff resources, and the courts have delved into the details of bureaucratic operations.

James Q. Wilson presents a case study of what some saw as an "out of control" Federal Bureau of Investigation (FBI) when its agents in a "sting" operation offered bribes that members of Congress accepted and for which they were later prosecuted. Wilson argues that in reality the FBI had made major changes in its priorities in response to congressional direction and pressure. The "Abscam" convictions were merely a consequence of those changes and not a special effort to get back at Congress.

In another article Wilson takes up the issue of bureaucratic efficiency. The popular image is of large, governmental bureaucracies that are wasteful of resources and take much more time and money to accomplish what private businesses could do more efficiently. Wilson argues that public administrators are under many more constraints than are private businesses and that these constraints—for example, strict financial accountability, democratic responsiveness, and equity—are important democratic values that we probably would not want to sacrifice in the name of efficiency.

KEY TERMS

bureaucracy: any large group of human beings organized in a hierarchical arrangement of specialized tasks to achieve a central purpose

civil service: the collectivity of most government workers who are hired through the merit system, not including the uniformed military services

merit system: the system of recruiting, selecting, and promoting government workers on the bases of ability and performance rather than political loyalty

political appointees: people loyal to a president who are selected to help lead government agencies in accomplishing an administration's agenda. They may be presidential appointments requiring Senate confirmation, presidential appointments not requiring confirmation, or lower-level appointments made by agency heads.

19

"BUREAUCRACY IN THE AMERICAN CONSTITUTIONAL ORDER"
Francis E. Rourke

According to Francis Rourke, a political scientist at Johns Hopkins University, the tremendous growth in the size of the executive branch bureaucracies has not fulfilled the worst fears of its critics of either the left or the right. The usual fears concerning large-scale bureaucracies in the United States are that they will develop independent power unresponsive to democratic political institutions and that they will use that power to manipulate the political system and oppress citizens. But the real story, according to Rourke in this 1987 Political Science Quarterly *article, is how the three branches of the national government have changed themselves to cope with the increasing size and influence of bureaucracy.*

Recent presidents have increased the size and influence of the White House staff to make the executive branch responsive to presidential policy direction. Congress has increased its staff resources to deal with the expertise of the executive branch. And the courts have imposed limits and obligations on bureaucracies that have forced them to change their policies. The overall picture is not one of bureaucracies out of control but rather one of responsiveness to political direction.

The development of national bureaucracy in the United States since the 1930s in what can be called its modern era has been a truly remarkable phenomenon. Many more people now work for the government than did then. Bureaucratic organizations in Washington spend far more money today than was the case fifty years ago. They provide more services and their rules and regulations affect a much wider range of human activities. The impact of the decisions made by government agencies upon the lives of ordinary citizens covers not only the familiar trip from the cradle to the grave, but extends even beyond those traditional limits of the human experience, as survivors of the deceased struggle with the Veterans Administration or the Social Security system over death benefits, or as government officials begin to concern themselves with what happens to the fetus before he or she even becomes a citizen.

This growth in the size of bureaucracy and the simultaneous expansion in the scope of its involvement in human affairs has generated a very strong resentment against bureaucrats and the agencies in which they work. There has been a general assumption that what is very big must also be very powerful, the lesson of the dinosaurs to the contrary notwithstanding, and the myth of an all-powerful bureaucracy has become firmly fixed in the American political imagination since World War II. It has been increasingly reflected in those television spectaculars through which American society is periodically "born-again," the election of a president every four years. After being nominated as presidential candidates, Richard Nixon and George Wallace in 1968, Jimmy Carter in 1976, and Ronald Reagan in 1980 all ran against the bureaucracy or in Wallace's phrase, "pointy-headed" bureaucrats. Nixon, Carter, and Reagan won election after such a campaign, and Wallace established himself as the strongest third-party candidate in modern American history. In short, opposition to bureaucracy and its power has been a winning strategy in recent national elections in the United States.

The hostility toward bureaucratic power has been bipartisan, and it has been highly visible in all segments of the ideological spectrum. On the right it has been a product of the traditional animosity of conservatives toward government intervention in the domestic economy—whether in the form of extensive and expensive welfare programs to help the needy and the disadvantaged or the enforcement of regulatory statutes that private individuals or business organizations regard as a burdensome infringement upon their inalienable right to make their own decisions. On the left the resentment against bureaucracy is focused on the national security apparatus where invisible bureaucrats in the Pentagon, the CIA and more recently the National Security Council (NSC) ply their trade. Perhaps just because so much secrecy prevails in national security matters, it is possible to believe virtually anything about what bureaucrats are doing in this sector of government. And sometimes, as in the case of the secret arms dealings with Iran during the Reagan administration, reality outruns even the wildest imaginings of bureaucracy's critics.

But what is commonly overlooked in these hostile reactions to the growth of bureaucracy in the American constitutional order is that this development has triggered other changes in the character and operation of the national government, and that many of these changes have worked to limit the extent to which the expanding scope of bureaucratic activity has actually brought about a commensurate increase in the power of bureaucrats themselves. Indeed, it can be argued that the growth of national bureaucracy in the United States since the 1930s has been a far less important phenomenon than the simultaneous emergence of new ways by which the traditional institutions of American national government — the presidency, Congress, and the courts — have been able to meet and contain the challenge of a bureaucracy that many people prior to World War II anticipated would actually become a fourth branch of government in the postwar period.

Hence, the real story of contemporary American bureaucracy is not, as widely expected to be the case, about the emergence of an imperial government of career officials threatening constitutional norms. It is rather the story of how a traditional political system modified itself to cope with the arrival of a new competitor for power — a set of bureaucratic organizations that was created to carry out the directives of the president and Congress but which had the promise of becoming a power in its own right. This modification process has resulted in major changes in the ways in which American political institutions now function, and these changes represent the most significant impact that the arrival of a large-scale bureaucracy has had upon the American political system in modern times. The change most often predicted in the aftermath of World War II — that the arrival of a large-scale bureaucracy would derange the American constitutional order in fundamental ways — has not occurred at all.

Reshaping the Presidency

Consider, for example, the case of the presidency. During recent decades there has been constant apprehension in the White House that the bureaucracy will obstruct presidential plans and programs and substitute its own preferences for those of a president chosen in a free election to put into effect the policies and programs for which the people have just voted. Fear of bureaucratic usurpation of power was most pronounced at the White House during the Nixon years, but in one form or another it has been a conspicuous feature of all administrations since World War II.

This fear has endured in spite of the fact that genuine cases of bureaucratic challenge to presidential authority since the war have been a rare occurrence — so much so as to command widespread attention when they become public knowledge. Such cases have commonly been regarded as deviating from the norm — justified, if at all, only by the exceptional circumstances in which they occurred. Witness, for example, General Douglas MacArthur's defiance of President Harry Truman during the Korean War, or the unauthorized bombing runs conducted by the air force in Vietnam during the Johnson administration. These cases of bureaucrats acting independently or in opposition to presidential orders only drew what limited justification they possessed from the fact that they occurred during controversial wars, when the legitimacy of presidential authority itself came into question in American society.

But regardless of whether the record supports these White House fears of bureaucratic sabotage, what cannot be denied is the fact that many of the ways in which the presidency has changed in recent years represent adaptations designed to cope with the growing presence of bureaucracy within the governmental structure in the United States. Not the least of these changes has been the shift toward a collegial or collective presidency — a White House in which the chief executive's power to decide and to act is exercised not only by the president, but also by a host of other White House aides and assistants lodged within the White House staff or the executive office of the president. Thus, a power that the framers of the constitution thought they were placing in the hands of a single person has now been parcelled out among a varied set of individuals who serve on the White House staff.

The principal factor forcing this pluralization of the presidency — its transformation into a collegial office — has been the desire of the White House to maintain the hegemony of the president within the executive branch in the face of what it perceives as a bureaucracy threatening constantly to spin out of control. Hence, a major task of the White House staff, and of the many offices into which this staff is now clustered, is to provide the president with information and advice about how to deal with the wide range of problems that executive institutions now confront. Otherwise the president would be entirely at the mercy of whatever data or policy suggestions the administrative agency most directly involved in a policy operation might choose to supply. During the Nixon administration it became standard practice for White House staff members rather than Cabinet officials to draw up major proposals affecting individual executive departments. Nixon and his chief advisers assumed that Cabinet members would be far too much under the influence of their own bureaucrats to be trusted with responsibility for the development of major administration policies.

So while it may narrow the circle of his advisers in disadvantageous ways, the White House staff can protect the president from becoming the prisoner of any bureaucratic information system in shaping his policy initiatives. The pluralized presidency also provides the chief executive with a cadre of aides whose policy suggestions are sensitive to his own interests, rather than simply reflecting the goals and needs of some administrative agency or of the outside groups in whose behalf that agency generally acts. On occasion — as was true in both the Nixon and Reagan presidencies — his staff may even serve the chief executive as an instrument for taking actions that he does not want the rest of the government or the public to know about. History suggests that this use of the staff may lead a president to glory — as in Nixon's opening to China — or to catastrophe — as in Nixon's Watergate caper.

In addition to the assistance it provides in policy development, the White House entourage also plays a major role for the presidency today in monitoring the actions of bureaucratic organizations and officials within the executive branch charged with carrying out policy decisions. This monitoring is designed to insure that the policies that agency bureaucrats are pursuing on a daily basis are those of the president, and that they have not been altered to conform to the preferences of the bureaucracy or its clients. It also enables the White House to identify emerging issues with which they may have to deal in the future, or "big-ticket" items that are being handled in a dilatory way by the bureaucracy when they should be receiving priority attention from the White House.

Such monitoring activity may also have incidental political value for a president. The Office of Public Liaison (OPL) within the White House has the responsibility for cultivating good relations with the various national organizations and groups on which the president depends for political support. From the knowledge this White House office gleans about pending bureaucratic decisions through its monitoring role, the OPL can be used to alert outside groups that the administration is cultivating to the fact that certain decisions affecting their interests are about to be made by a government agency. Providing this kind of advance information can help to bind these groups even more tightly to the president's cause. As is the case with individual members of Congress, the White House can thus derive considerable political benefit from its ability to play an intermediary role in the relations between the public, or at least the organized segments of it, and the bureaucracy.

Changing Presidential Styles

Over the course of recent history, individual presidents have varied a great deal in the way in which they have tried to use the collegial presidency. But they have all shared a common purpose — to create in their staffs an effective counterweight to the power of the departmental bureaucracies. John F. Kennedy, for example, in a strategy that was later to be imitated by Lyndon B. Johnson, tried to bring what he regarded as highly talented people into the White House, a group that David Halberstam was later to describe somewhat sardonically as "the best and the brightest." Kennedy and his associates made a point of denigrating the executive office system that they inherited from Dwight Eisenhower on the grounds that its highly organized structure impeded its effectiveness. He believed that it was the people in the White House who determined the success of public policy and not the character of the organizational system in which it was made. This initial Kennedy disdain for proper organization and procedure contributed to the disaster early in his administration at the Bay of Pigs, since it led him to eliminate organizational procedures that might well have generated warnings sufficient to prevent the error of ever launching this ill-fated expedition. The possibility that elaborate organizational procedures for making decisions might have an error-correction function is not always clear to activist presidents like Kennedy when they take office.

But behind Kennedy's strategy of bringing talented people to the White House lay the belief that the permanent government was stodgy and unimaginative and that new ideas would have to come from outside the bureaucracy. If the White House staff could not by itself generate such innovative approaches to the social and economic problems that beset American society, then experts in the private sector would also have to be recruited to help the president cope with these problems. The institution that was created to forge cooperation between the White House staff and outside experts was the presidentially appointed task force. During the Kennedy and to an even greater extent the Johnson administrations, presidential task forces wrestled with issues that under prior presidents the bureaucracy itself would have handled. This novel approach to the task of making public policy was described by Henry Fairlie as "guerilla government — a kind of "hit-and-run" warfare by outsiders upon the permanent government.

This strategy of trying to develop public policy with a minimal reliance on the bureaucracy was adopted and refined by the Nixon administration. While the Kennedy White House had looked upon the bureaucracy as being far too timid in its approach to tough public policy issues, too reluctant to strike out in the bold new directions that Kennedy's New Frontier philosophy demanded, the Nixon administration saw the problem from a quite different perspective. In its eye the permanent bureaucracy was a wily and aggressive champion of policies and programs that the voters had repudiated in the 1968 election. Bureaucracy was forever trying to nullify White House initiatives by dragging its feet in implementing presidential directives, or, even worse, by leaking information to the outside world in an effort to rally public opposition to plans or policy changes that the administration was considering.

In any event, the bureaucracy was certainly regarded as an enemy by the Nixon White House — perhaps not at the top of the "enemies list" compiled by the White House that the Watergate investigations brought to light, but certainly well up on the list along with the television networks and the other news organizations that were so odious to the administration. There is a striking resemblance between the negative attitude that White House courtiers in the Nixon administration, like John Ehrlichman and H.R. Haldeman, took toward departmental bureaucrats and the contempt or hostility toward bureaucracy visible in the memoirs of Kennedy aides like Arthur Schlesinger, Jr. or Theodore Sorensen.

From Nixon's perspective, it made sense to concentrate control over policy development in the White House whenever possible. This strategy was most prominent in the field of foreign affairs, where the White House National Security staff achieved an ascendancy over foreign policy decision making that no NSC staff has attained before or since the Nixon days. This ascendancy embraced not only the framing of foreign policy but even its implementation, as evident in the leading role that NSC Adviser Henry Kissinger played in executing the opening to China or carrying on peace negotiations with North Vietnam in Paris. It relegated the national security bureaucracies at the State and Defense departments to their lowest estate in the foreign policy process during the postwar period.

The Nixon administration made several attempts to achieve a similar kind of domination over domestic policy making, but without any notable success. The chief of these attempts was the establishment of the Domestic Council in the White House in 1970. It was intended to be the domestic equivalent of the NSC — a vantage point from which the President and his staff could oversee the development of policy in areas other than foreign affairs. Unfortunately for Nixon, however, domestic policy proved highly resistant to such operation by remote control from the White House. The opposition came not only from the bureaucracy, which the Nixon people had anticipated, but also from the very executives they had chosen to run these domestic agencies. These political appointees tended to see the involvement of White House aides in their agency's activities as an infringement upon their own executive prerogatives.

In addition, these agencies were closely tied to the congressional committees under whose jurisdiction they fell, as well as to a variety of domestic constituencies for whom they provided services or whose interests were affected by their decisions. They were thus locked into "iron triangles" — the coalition of executive agencies, interest groups, and congressional committees that have historically dominated major sectors of domestic policy making. It was not easy for a White House institution like the Domestic Council to move into an area of policy already occupied by these formidable political coalitions. It was especially difficult when, as was true under Nixon, Congress was controlled by the Democrats and the iron triangles were centers of power in which the opposition party was strongly entrenched.

The Nixon administration was no more successful when it abandoned its effort to attain comprehensive control over all domestic policy making through an institution like the Domestic Council and sought instead to shape the development of a single area of policy through a White House office. One policy area that greatly interested and at times seemed to obsess Nixon was the field of communications policy. This field lies under the jurisdiction of the Federal Communications Commission (FCC), a highly independent regulatory agency that has among its responsibilities the task of overseeing the operation of radio and television stations. Throughout its years in office the Nixon administration was firmly convinced that a chief source of its political troubles was the strong bias against it within the media organizations that reported the news about the administration's activities. This fear of the power of the media over its own political fortunes gave the Nixon administration a strong incentive to move control over communications policy from the FCC to the White House, where the President could then use threats like antitrust suits to stifle media criticism.

In 1970, the administration made what many of its critics regarded as a strong move in this direction. Through a presidential reorganization plan, it established an Office of Telecommunications Policy (OTP) — an organization created ostensibly to administer some traditional White House responsibilities in the communications area, but also assigned the mission of monitoring decisions in all other government communications agencies. The director of the OTP ultimately became a thorn in the flesh of the media when he began to launch broadsides against what he alleged was their ideological slant in a liberal direction, "ideological plugola" as he put it; but his office never succeeded in exercising much influence over the FCC itself, the agency with the real regulatory power in the communications field. The chairman of the commission, Dean Burch, was a staunch conservative and a Nixon loyalist, but he was also a strong chairman, who wanted to run his own agency and was not about to allow any White House aide to override his authority.

When the Carter administration took office in 1977, it tried in many ways to distance its own governing style from that of the Nixon White House. As part of this strategy, Carter went out of his way to underline the fact that in his presidency Cabinet members rather than the White House staff would be at the center of policy making. However, as time wore on in his administration, Carter — like his predecessors — discovered that many problems could not be dealt with by a single department and the even more painful fact that many departments did not approach policy issues with his own political priorities in mind.

So power inevitably gravitated toward the White House staff during the Carter years, especially to the Domestic Policy Staff (DPS), which Carter had established as a successor agency to Nixon's Domestic Council. To be sure, Carter's DPS never attained the hegemony over policy development that the White House staff enjoyed in Nixon's first term. But its power was certainly greater than Carter initially anticipated would be the case. The DPS played a major role in prodding departments into action on issues the President considered important. It also tried to settle disputes between departments — as, for example, the conflict that erupted between the Health, Education and Welfare Department (HEW) and the Labor Department over the direction that welfare reform should take.

The Reagan administration followed the lead of the Carter presidency in accenting the role of the Cabinet in policy development and downplaying that of the White House staff. Except in the case of the arms deal with Iran in 1986, the NSC staff never reached the heights of power under Reagan that it enjoyed in previous administrations. The fact that Reagan has had so much more success than Carter in diminishing the role of the White House staff can be traced in good part to the much shorter length of his policy agenda as president. He had many fewer promises to keep than Carter. The constituency from which Reagan drew his support by and large wanted the government to do less rather than more. However, it should be noted that it was a presidential agency, the Office of Management and Budget (OMB), that led the way in the achievement of Reagan's chief policy goal when he took office — a drastic cutback in the growth of the national government's domestic expenditures. The director of the OMB, David Stockman, served as the administration's point man in its ultimately successful effort to prune domestic spending programs. There is also the revealing fact that when Reagan began to involve himself in Middle Eastern policy during his second term, because of his personal and political concern over the plight of the American hostages held in Lebanon, he suddenly revived the NSC staff and gave it a major role in the foreign policy process.

What the experience of the White House in modern times strongly suggests is that a president's ability to practice as well as preach Cabinet government largely depends on how active a role he intends to play in the development and implementation of national policy. The more a president wishes to shape the character of his administration's policy goals, the more likely he is to accent the role of the White House staff rather than the Cabinet in the governing process, however pious may be his protestations about the virtues of Cabinet government when he first takes office. This ascendancy by the White House staff has the inevitable effect of reducing bureaucratic influence over national policy decisions, since bureaucrats have much better access to Cabinet officials and much more opportunity to shape their views of policy issues than they do with respect to the president's own staff aides, who are usually isolated in the remote precincts of the White House. The lesson of the last half-century of American politics has thus been unmistakable — as the power of the White House staff grows, the power of departmental bureaucrats recedes.

Bureaucracy as Change Agent

The central conclusion that emerges from this analysis of the operation of the presidency in modern times is that bureaucracy's unsung role in the evolution of modern American government has been that of an unwitting change agent. As we have seen, the expansion in the number and activities of bureaucratic organizations within the executive branch has been a major factor underlying the ascending power of the presidency in the contemporary constitutional order. A variety of efforts have been made during this period to help the president cope with an ever-expanding bureaucracy, and each of these efforts has added another increment of power to the presidential office. This is true of all the reorganizations the executive branch has experienced since the late 1930s, the changes that have been made in the budgetary system, and the reforms that have taken place in executive personnel procedures. The position of the imperial presidency today is in no small measure a product of a widely perceived need to prevent the emergence of an imperial bureaucracy. Moreover, presidents themselves have been quite willing to play on fears of bureaucracy to justify expanding the power of their own office. The real power of bureaucracies today thus lies not with bureaucrats but with the members of a new "political class" — the policy entrepreneurs the president has appointed to run these organizations and to shape their programs in his behalf.

The influence that bureaucracy has exerted as a change agent has been very visible in the development of the legislative and judicial as well as the executive branches of the government in modern times. In the case of Congress one of the most significant changes that a proliferating bureaucracy has triggered is an expansion in the size and proficiency of the legislative staff. This expansion has taken a variety of forms — in the size of the staffs that now serve individual members of Congress, in the number of professional experts presently attached to legislative committees in both the House and the Senate, and, finally, in the establishment or strengthening of four staff agencies that currently serve Congress as a collective body: the General Accounting Office, the Congressional Research Service, the Congressional Budget Office, and the Office of Technology Assessment.

The chief purpose, as well as the most important result, of this development has been to enable Congress to close the "expertise" gap that had opened up between itself and the presidency in the years immediately preceding and following World War II, when presidents began to benefit enormously from the bureaucratic apparatus that emerged at the White House during that period of time. Members of Congress are now able to draw upon the same high level of professional staff assistance that presidents command in handling complicated technical issues in both foreign and domestic policy making. Noteworthy also is the extent to which the reports and forecasts of the Congressional Budget Office are now given as much if not more credence than those of the president's own Office of Management and Budget. In net effect, therefore, the rise of bureaucracy can be said to have led not to a usurpation of legislative power, as many members of Congress feared would be the case when bureaucratic expansion first began, but to an enhancement of the legislature's capacity to do its own job.

Moreover, as Morris Fiorina has shown, the growth of bureaucracy has been of benefit to individual legislators as well as to the overall position of Congress as a legislative institution. Members of the House of Representatives have come to enjoy increased success in running for reelection, and Fiorina attributes this success to the fact that they are able to solidify political support in their own districts by helping them to resolve problems that their constituents are having with the Social Security system, the Veterans Administration, or other government agencies. (According to the *Congressional Quarterly*, the number of House incumbents defeated in 1986 in both the primary and general elections was the smallest in history.) The rise of bureaucracy has thus enabled legislators to provide valuable services for the people in their districts, even if, as some critics contend, such casework activity distracts Congress from playing the part it should play in attacking major national policy issues.

The impact that the growth of bureaucracy has had upon the judicial system has been no less striking. In a variety of areas, but particularly in the field of social regulation, judges have now become major actors in the policy process, largely as a result of statutes that provide broader opportunities for private parties to challenge the decisions of executive agencies in the courts in such areas as environmental and civil rights policy. Thus agencies like the Environmental Protection Agency (EPA) or the Equal Employment Opportunity Commission (EEOC) frequently find themselves being either prodded into action or having their decisions reversed by the courts. Through *Sierra Club v. Ruckelshaus* and other decisions, the courts have pushed EPA toward framing a much more stringent policy to prevent significant deterioration in air quality than the agency originally intended to pursue. In the case of EEOC, court decisions helped persuade the agency to take much stronger action in defense of the position of women in the workplace than it seemed initially prepared to undertake, since the EEOC originally viewed its mission as primarily that of dealing with the employment problems of blacks and other disadvantaged minorities.

In any case, there are clearly areas of policy today in which the old-fashioned iron-triangle paradigm no longer serves to explain the way in which policy is made. Hugh Heclo makes a very compelling argument that in many highly technical policy areas — arms control, for example, or the field of monetary policy — the iron triangle has been supplanted by an "issue network," where expertise rather than economic interest determines who participates in decision making. It can also be argued that even in fields where the old-fashioned iron-triangle structure still stands, it has been greatly altered by the arrival of the courts as major actors in the policy process. Martin Shapiro suggests that this development has created a new iron-triangle system made up of "agency, court, and interest groups" in areas of policy where statutes have created rights or entitlements to governmental assistance for groups like the aged or physically handicapped. Alternatively, in fields of social regulation like civil rights and environmental protection, the iron triangle appears to have broadened into a quadrilateral, as the courts join pressure groups, Congressional committees, and executive agencies as partners in these highly autonomous subgovernment compartments within which public policy is so frequently made in the United States.

But whether it is part of a triangular or a quadrilateral policy-making structure, there can be no denying the fact that the judiciary has extended its authority and stature as an institution because of its ability to monitor and reverse the decisions of administrative agencies in numerous fields of social regulation. In the eyes of some critics, the courts have actually become an imperial judiciary in carrying out this task, as sweeping in the exercise of arbitrary power as any bureaucracy could ever hope to be. In their view, it is from the jurocracy and not the bureaucracy that the constitutional order has the most to fear.

But there is perhaps nowhere in American political life where the rise of bureaucracy has been accompanied by more changes than in the operation of the federal system. Since the 1930s state, local, and national agencies have been laced together by intricate bureaucratic networks carrying on domestic programs that are federally financed and locally administered. Some observers see this development as centralizing in its effect — transferring power from state and local to national agencies. Others argue that it has opened up authentic opportunities for decentralization, as opposed to the illusory opportunities that had previously existed, by providing states and localities with the resources to undertake many activities they could not otherwise afford. But both sides would certainly agree that the bureaucratization of intergovernmental relationships within the political system represents a fundamental change in the character of the American federalism.

Legitimizing American Bureaucracy

Clearly, the evolution of modern American politics has not borne out the worst fears of those who saw the emergence of large-scale bureaucracy in the 1930s as a grave danger to constitutional government. Bureaucracy has, however, been a significant instrument of change in the structure and operation of the three national institutions specifically established by the Constitution: the presidency, Congress, and the courts. And many of the changes it has wrought have strengthened these traditional institutions in ways that reduced the likelihood that bureaucracy would ever threaten their power. It is not unreasonable to conclude, therefore, that looked at in terms of institution building, bureaucracy in the United States has done far more for the other institutions of government in this country than it has done for itself. In so doing, it has reinforced the ability of the American constitutional system to cope with the burdens of modern government.

In light of these developments, what is the constitutional status of bureaucracy today? How, if at all, does it fit into the tripartite scheme of government that the framers of the Constitution devised? Is the power that bureaucracies wield legitimate power, in the sense that it is accepted by those subject to it as being rightfully exercised? In our day, bureaucracy has become an indispensable instrument of government in action. Virtually all government policies depend upon some bureaucratic organization for their enforcement. While bureaucracy does not enjoy that status of explicit mention in the constitutional document itself, this is a deficiency it shares with other institutions and practices that are integral parts of the unwritten Constitution in the United States, including the preeminent position of the Cabinet and the White House staff in the executive branch, the role of political parties in the election process, and the power of judicial review that the Supreme Court has come to exercise. Certainly the written Constitution does assume the presence of a bureaucratic apparatus in government sufficient to carry out the varied tasks it assigns to the president, Congress, and the courts.

Nevertheless, there is a certain aura of illegitimacy about bureaucracy — a suspicion that its presence and activities in the governmental structure are not altogether in accord with the American constitutional order. Partly, this has been a procedural concern — focused on the way bureaucracies do things. Prior to the enactment of the Administrative Procedure Act of 1946 and to a lesser extent since then, a great deal of criticism has been directed at bureaucracy on the grounds that the administrative role in both adjudication and rulemaking frequently violates the constitutional rights of individuals affected by the agency decisions that flow from these processes. While passage of the Procedure Act and the growing role of administrative law judges in agency adjudication have done much to dispel that fear, it has never been completely dispelled.

But quite apart from these long-standing doubts about the constitutional propriety of the procedures that bureaucratic organizations follow in enforcing government policies, there has also been strong criticism of bureaucracy on the grounds that the policies it carries out are unconstitutional in their very nature. Critics on the right who regard the free-enterprise system as part of the American constitutional convenant have questioned the legitimacy of a wide range of government policies regulating the affairs of business organizations or distributing financial or other benefits to a variety of domestic groups.

Critics on the left are equally vehement in their objections to many bureaucratic activities in the national security sector that in their view are carried on by executive agencies like the CIA in violation of constitutional norms. Bureaucracies can thus be attacked on both the right and left as lacking in constitutional legitimacy in the United States because they perform governmental functions that are themselves regarded as inappropriate for the government to undertake. At the root of bureaucracy's problem in this regard is the fact that an expansive role for the national government in the affairs of society still lacks a certain constitutional credibility in American political culture.

Efforts have been made in modern times to relieve bureaucracy of this burden of illegitimacy. James O. Freedman has written "that governmental power in a constitutional democracy can be legitimated in only two ways: Either it must be created by the Constitution or it must be exercised by officials directly accountable to the people through the political process." It is a little late in the day for any effort to be made to repair bureaucracy's omission from the written Constitution and highly questionable whether it would succeed. So that particular door to legitimation can be regarded as permanently closed as far as bureaucracy is concerned.

The other door, however, remains at least half open. Bureaucracy can be said to make a significant contribution to the process of self-government in the United States by providing opportunities for groups of citizens to be more intimately involved in government decision making than the traditional election system permits. Norton Long, for example, makes the argument that "important and vital interests in the United States are unrepresented, underrepresented, or mal-represented in Congress. These interests receive more effective and more responsible representation through administrative channels than through the legislature." Long comes to this conclusion because the bureaucracy more closely mirrors the country from a purely demographic perspective. As he puts it: "Through the breadth of the interests represented in its composition, the bureaucracy provides a significant constitutionalizing element of pluralism in our government." In Long's view many interests that are neglected in the legislature find their only voice in the bureaucracy.

In a recent and very comprehensive analysis of the legitimate place of bureaucracy in the American constitutional order, John Rohr makes a similar and very persuasive argument. In his view "the administrative state heals a defect in the Constitution" — the fact that it does not make adequate provision for public participation in government decision making. The growing role of bureaucracy in government opens an opportunity for many more people to become actively involved in the work of government. They may do so as civil servants, as citizens attending public hearings, or by taking advantage of other opportunities to participate in the everyday activities of administrative agencies.

The weight of this argument was greatly reinforced when citizen participation in government became the order of the day in the 1960s during President Lyndon Johnson's administration as part of the overall design of Great Society programs. When citizen participation democratized bureaucracies by allowing ordinary people to have more influence over their decisions, it also served to legitimate the role of these organizations in the governmental process. Equally important in this regard was the tendency of Great Society programs to be decentralized — directly administered by state and local rather than national agencies.

Since then even longer steps in this direction have been taken by handing programs over to private organizations or groups for their administration. This is the "third-party" or "private-federalism" approach to the implementation of government policies that has become increasingly fashionable. Of course, as it develops, this democratization movement not only legitimizes bureaucracy but also diminishes its power. It thus represents another of the "countervailing forces," which, as previously indicated, have helped American democracy weather the challenge posed by the rise of bureaucracy.

But in any case, what all these varied efforts to involve the public more directly in the administration of government programs reflect is a deep-seated belief on the part of legislative and executive officials that bureaucratic power can best be legitimized by being democratized, by bringing the decisions of public bureaucrats much more closely under the control of private citizens.

A somewhat different approach to legitimizing the role of bureaucracy in the constitutional order was initiated by Woodrow Wilson in the late nineteenth century. In his celebrated essay on the *Study of Administration*, Wilson avoided any claim that bureaucracy has attributes that contribute to the achievement of democratic values. Paralleling the view of Max Weber, he argued that bureaucracy could become as useful a tool in democratic as it already was in nondemocratic societies — helping to make each of these very different political systems more efficient as instruments of governance than they might otherwise be. What bureaucrats actually provide in the governmental process are technical skills that can be used to run any society. As far as political systems are concerned, bureaucracy was value-neutral in Wilson's view. It did not further the values of democracy, but neither did its presence in the governmental structure jeopardize any of these values.

The Wilsonian view, as enunciated in the 1880s, ultimately became a central article of faith in the reform creed in the United States. At the turn of the century the Progressives in Wisconsin and elsewhere saw administrative experts as the saviors of democracy, insofar as they provided the people with a means of offsetting the growing power of giant business organizations in American society. Among New Dealers in the 1930s, belief in the saving power of administrative expertise was as pronounced as it was in the Progressive era. At the state and local level of government, faith in such expertise is still very strong in some parts of the United States. It underlies the strong support given by civil-service reform groups to the proposition that even leadership and policy-making positions in state or local bureaucracies should be filled on the basis of merit rather than election or political appointment.

The courts at first resisted the notion that administrative agencies were endowed with any knowledge superior to their own, but during the early years following World War II they came increasingly to see the legitimate role of bureaucracy in government from precisely this Wilsonian or Weberian perspective. A growing number of judges began to reason that administrative agencies brought a high level of expertise to the task of making or carrying out public policies that the courts could not provide and that effective government required. In their view bureaucrats performed an indispensable function in twentieth-century American government, and the courts were obliged to give a measure of respect and even finality to decisions that rested on their expertise. Divisions and disputes among experts, and the somewhat diminished stature of expertise in contemporary American society have begun to weaken this judicial deference to bureaucrats in recent years. Yet to take hold is the argument Nelson Polsby makes that power is only exercised in a legitimate way in the United States when it rests on a consensus among a variety of elites including the higher civil service. But there can be no disputing the fact that the knowledge and skills that bureaucrats bring to the policy process have given them an indispensable place, if not a legitimate role, in the American constitutional order. The central paradox of modern American bureaucracy thus lies in the fact that it is at one and the same time altogether indispensable and, at least in the eyes of many citizens, somewhat illegitimate.

POINTS TO PONDER

1. How has the presidency changed in recent decades in order to deal with the power of the executive branch bureaucracies?
2. How has Congress responded to the increasing scope and power of executive branch bureaucracies?
3. Government bureaucracies certainly have power. Why is the legitimacy of that power a problem for a democracy?

20

"THE CHANGING FBI—
THE ROAD TO ABSCAM"
James Q. Wilson

In the 1970s several members of Congress were caught in an FBI "sting" operation in which FBI agents posing as businessmen offered them bribes, which were accepted. The members guilty of accepting the bribes were convicted and sent to jail. There were a number of public comments at the time that the operation indicated that the FBI was out to get even with some of its critics in Congress and that the FBI was "out of control." But in this careful analysis UCLA political scientist James Q. Wilson argues that in fact the FBI was actively following congressional direction in shifting its emphasis to white-collar crime. In this article from The Public Interest *(1980), he details the bureaucratic changes necessary to produce the new direction in policy demanded by Congress; ironically, some of its members were caught in the new war on white-collar crime.*

It is inconceivable that J. Edgar Hoover would ever have investigated members of Congress to gather evidence for possible prosecution. Hoover's FBI learned a great deal about congressmen, and may have gone out of its way to collect more information than it needed, but all this would have been locked discreetly away, or possibly leaked, most privately, to a President or attorney general whose taste for gossip Hoover wished to gratify or whose personal loyalty he wished to assure. The Bureau's shrewd cultivation of congressional and White House opinion, effective for decades, was in time denounced as evidence that the FBI was "out of control," immune from effective oversight.

Today, of course, the Bureau is again being criticized, albeit circumspectly, by various congressmen who complain of the manner (and possibly also the fact) of its investigation of possible legislative bribery. Congressmen wonder whether the FBI is launched on a "vendetta" against its erstwhile allies turned critics. Once again there are angry mutterings that the Bureau is "out of control," this time because it is using its most powerful technique—undercover operations—to discover whether congressmen are corrupt.

It would be tempting to ascribe the changes in the Bureau's relations with Congress to nothing more than personal pique amplified into organizational vengeance. After years of congressional adulation of Hoover and the FBI, the mood suddenly turned nasty with revelations of how far the Bureau was prepared to go in using its investigative powers to maintain political support. The list of Bureau excesses is long, familiar, and dismaying; the wrath visited upon it by several congressional committees combined a proper outrage at abuse of power with a hint of romance gone sour. For the FBI now to turn on those who had turned on it would be precisely the sort of thing one might suppose a Hoover-style agency might relish.

This is not what has happened. No doubt there are some FBI agents who are enjoying the sight of congressmen scurrying for cover, but that was not the motive for "Operation Abscam." The Bureau has in fact changed, and changed precisely in accordance with the oft-expressed preferences of Congress itself. Congressional and other critics complained that the Bureau in the 1960's was not only violating the rights of citizens, it was wasting its resources and energies on trivial cases and meaningless statistical accomplishments. Beginning with Director Clarence Kelley, the Bureau pledged that it would end the abuses and redirect its energies to more important matters. This is exactly what has happened.

This rather straightforward explanation is hard for official Washington to accept, and understandably so. Bureaucracies are not supposed to change, they are only supposed to claim to have changed. It tests the credulity of a trained congressional cynic to be told that a large, complex, rule bound organization such as the FBI would or could execute an about-face.

But the FBI is not just any bureaucracy, and never has been. Next to the Marine Corps, it is probably the most centrally controlled organization in the federal government. Its agents do not have civil service or union protection, its disciplinary procedures can be swift and draconian, and despite recent efforts to decentralize some decision making, the director himself, or one of his immediate subordinates, personally approves an astonishingly large proportion of all the administrative decisions made in the Bureau. Not long ago, a decision to install sanitary-napkin dispensers in women's lavatories in Bureau headquarters could not be made until Director William Webster endorsed the recommendation. FBI agents have complained for decades about the heavy-handed supervision they received from headquarters; though that has begun to change, the visit of an inspection team to an FBI field office continues to instill apprehension bordering on terror in the hearts of the local staff. The inspectors sometimes concentrate on the minutiae at the expense of the important, but whatever its defects, nit-picking insures that field offices will conform to explicit headquarters directives pertaining to observable behavior.

But even for the Bureau, the change in investigative strategy that culminated in Operation Abscam was no easy matter. For one thing, much of what the Bureau does is not easily observable and thus not easily controlled by inspection teams and headquarters directives. Law enforcement occurs on the street in low-visibility situations that test the judgment and skill of agents but do not lend themselves to formal review. Many laws the FBI enforces—particularly those pertaining to consensual crimes such as bribery—place heavy reliance on the skill and energy of agents and field supervisors who must find ways of discovering that a crime may have been committed before they can even begin the process of gathering evidence that might lead to a prosecution. Relations between an agent and an informant often lie at the heart of the investigative effort, but these are subtle, complex, and largely unobservable. Finally, what the Bureau chooses to emphasize is not for it alone to decide. The policies of the local United States Attorney, who though nominally an employee of the Justice Department is in reality often quite autonomous, determine what federal cases will be accepted for prosecution and thus what kinds of offenses the local FBI office will emphasize.

Changing the Bureau

Given these difficulties, the effort to change the investigative priorities of the Bureau was a protracted, controversial, and difficult struggle. Several things had to happen: New policies had to be stated, unconventional investigative techniques had to be authorized, organizational changes had to be made, and new incentives had to be found.

As is always the case, stating the new policies was the easiest thing to do. Attorney General Edward Levi and Director Kelley pledged that the Bureau would reduce its interest in domestic security cases, especially of the sort that led to such abuses as COINTELPRO, and in the investigation of certain routine crimes (such as auto theft or small thefts from interstate shipments) that had for years generated the impressive statistics that Hoover was fond of reciting. The domestic security cases were constitutionally and politically vulnerable; the criminal cases that produced evidence of big workloads but few significant convictions were unpopular among the street agents. The man Kelley brought in to close down virtually all the domestic security investigations was, ironically, Neil Welch, then in charge of the Bureau's Philadelphia office and later to be in charge of the New York office and of Operation Abscam. In a matter of months, thousands of security cases were simply terminated; hundreds of security informants were let go; domestic security squads in various field offices were disbanded and their agents assigned to other tasks. New attorney-general guidelines clarified and narrowed the circumstances under which such cases could be opened in the future. The number of FBI informants in organizations thought to constitute a security risk became so small that it was kept secret in order, presumably, to avoid encouraging potential subversives with the knowledge that they were, in effect, free to organize without fear of Bureau surveillance.

Kelley also announced a "quality case program" authorizing each office to close out pending investigative matters that had little prosecutive potential and to develop priorities that would direct its resources toward important cases. Almost overnight, official Bureau caseloads dropped precipitously, as field offices stopped pretending that they were investigating (and in some cases, actually stopped investigating) hundreds of cases—of auto thefts, bank robberies, and thefts from interstate commerce and from government buildings—where the office had no leads, the amounts stolen were small, or it was believed (rightly or wrongly) that local police departments could handle the matter.

Headquarters made clear what it regarded as the "priority" cases that the field should emphasize: white-collar crime, organized crime, and foreign counterintelligence. But saying that these were the priorities, and getting them to *be* the priorities, were two different things. Permitting field offices to stop reporting on high-volume, low-value cases did not automatically insure that the resources thereby saved would be devoted to, say, white-collar crime. For that to occur, some important organizational changes had to be made.

The most important of these was to reorganize the field-office squads. Traditionally, a field office grouped its agent personnel into squads based on the volume of reported criminal offenses—there would be a bank robbery squad, an interstate theft squad, an auto theft squad, and so on. These squads reacted to the incoming flow of reported crimes by assigning an agent to each case. What we now call white-collar crime was typically the province of a single unit—the "accounting squad"—composed, often, of agents with training as accountants, who would handle bank complaints of fraud and embezzlement. Occasionally, more complex cases involving fraud would be developed; many offices had individual agents skilled at detecting and investigating elaborate political, labor, or business conspiracies. But attention to such matters was not routinized because the internal structure of a typical field office was organized around the need to respond to the reports of crimes submitted by victims. Elaborate conspiracies often produced no victims aware of their victimization or enriched the participants in ways that gave no one an incentive to call the FBI. Taxpayers generally suffer when bribes are offered and taken, and innocent investors may be victimized by land frauds, but either the citizen is unaware he is a victim or the "victim" was in fact part of the conspiracy, drawn in by greed and larcenous intent.

Again Neil Welch enters the scene. The Philadelphia office was one of the first to redesign its structure so that most of its squads had the task, not of responding to victim complaints, but of identifying ("targeting") individuals, groups, and organizations for intensive scrutiny on the grounds that they were suspected of being involved in organized crime, major conspiracies, labor racketeering, or political corruption. Though almost every FBI field office would from time to time make cases against corrupt politicians or businessmen, the cases made in Philadelphia were spectacular for their number and scope. Judges, state legislators, labor leaders, businessmen, police officers, and government officials were indicted and convicted. The more indictments that were handed down, the more nervous accomplices, frightened associates, or knowledgeable reporters would come forward to volunteer more information that spurred further investigations.

During the period when Welch and the Philadelphia office were making headlines (roughly, 1975 to 1977), the rest of the Bureau was watching and waiting. Experienced FBI officials knew that under the Hoover regime, the only safe rule was "never do anything for the first time." Taking the initiative could result in rapid promotions but it could also lead to immediate disgrace; innovation was risky. What if the allies of the powerful people being indicted (one was Speaker of the Pennsylvania House of Representatives) complained? Hoover had usually rebuffed such complaints, but you could never be certain. More important, how would Bureau headquarters react to the fact that the *number* of cases being handled in Philadelphia had dropped owing to the reassignment of agents from the regular high-volume squads to the new "target" squads? In the past, resources—money, manpower—were given to field offices that had high and rising caseloads, not to ones with declining statistics.

Kelley's response was clear—he increased the number of agents assigned to Philadelphia and gave Welch even more important responsibilities (it was at this time that Welch was brought to headquarters to oversee the winding down of the domestic security program). There were still many issues to resolve and many apprehensive supervisors to reassure, but the momentum was growing: more and more field offices began to reorganize to give structural effect to the priority-case program, and thus to an aggressive stance regarding white-collar crime.

Emphasizing Priority Offenses

The incentives to comply with the emphasis on priority offenses came from within and without the Bureau. Inside, the management information system was revised so that investigations and convictions were now classified by quality as well as number. The criminal offenses for which the FBI had investigative responsibility were grouped into high- and low-priority categories, and individual offenses within these categories were further classified by the degree of seriousness of the behavior under investigation (for example, thefts were classified by the amount stolen). It is far from clear that the statistics generated were used in any systematic way by Bureau headquarters—in the FBI as in many government agencies, such data are often perceived as a "numbers game" to be played and then forgotten—but at the very least these statistics reinforced the message repeated over and over again in the statements of the director, first Kelley and then William H. Webster: Go after white-collar and organized crime.

Outside the Bureau, key congressmen were pressing hard in the same direction. Nowhere was this pressure greater than in the chambers of the Subcommittee on Civil and Constitutional Rights of the House Judiciary Committee, chaired by Congressman Don Edwards of California—who had once been, briefly, a member of the FBI. This Subcommittee had become one of the centers of congressional attacks on the Bureau. Kelley and Webster spent hours answering questions put by its members, who included in addition to Chairman Edwards, Elizabeth Holtzman of New York and Robert Drinan of Massachusetts. The attack on the FBI's performance began with criticism of the domestic security programs, but came to include criticisms of the Bureau's weaknesses in the area of white-collar crime. This latter concern reflected, in part, the Subcommittee members' genuine conviction that white-collar offenses were serious matters. But it also reflected the Subcommittee members' suspicion that the FBI was "soft" on "establishment" crimes while being excessively preoccupied with subversion, and thus inclined merely to go through the motions when investigating the former and to put its heart and resources into inquiries regarding the latter. Thus, getting the Bureau to emphasize white-collar crimes was not only good in itself, it was a way, the Subcommittee seemed to think, of keeping it out of domestic security work.

In 1977, staff members of the Subcommittee toured various FBI field offices and spoke as well to several U.S. Attorneys. Their report sharply criticized the FBI for continuing to devote manpower to street crimes such as bank robberies and hijacking—all of which, in the opinion of the staff, could better be handled by the local police. In some cases, the staff claimed, the FBI's idea of white-collar crime was welfare cheating and other examples of individual, and presumably small-scale, frauds against the government. The staff lamented the "reluctance on the part of FBI personnel, particularly at the supervisory level, to get involved in more complex investigations that may require significant allocation of manpower for long periods of time." And the report criticized the field offices for not mounting more undercover operations.

Whatever shortcomings the FBI may have, indifference to congressional opinion has never been one of them. The pressure inside the Bureau to develop major white-collar-crime cases mounted. The Bureau had always thoroughly investigated reported violations of federal law whatever the color of the collar worn by the suspects. Businessmen, politicians, and labor leaders had been sent to prison as a result of FBI inquiries. But most of these cases arose out of a complaint to the Bureau by a victim, followed by FBI interviews of suspects and an analysis of documents. Sometimes wiretaps were employed. The number, scope, and success of such investigations depended crucially on the skill and patience of the agents working a case. One legendary FBI agent in Boston was personally responsible for making several major corruption cases as a result of his tenacity, his ability to win the confidence of reluctant witnesses and accomplices, and his knowledge of complex financial transactions. But finding or producing large numbers of such agents is difficult at best. Far easier would be the development of investigative techniques that could generate reliable evidence in large amounts without having to depend solely on an agent's ability to "flip" a suspect, who then would have to testify in court against his former collaborators.

Undercover Operations

One such method was the undercover operation. Narcotics agents in the Drug Enforcement Administration and in local police departments had always relied extensively on undercover agents buying illegal drugs in order to produce evidence. Traditionally, however, the FBI had shied away from these methods. Hoover had resisted any techniques that risked compromising an agent by placing him in situations where he could be exposed to adverse publicity or tempted to accept bribes. Hoover knew that public confidence in FBI agents was the Bureau's principal investigative resource and that confidence should not be jeopardized by having agents appear as anything other than well-groomed, "young executive" individuals with an impeccable reputation for integrity. From time to time, an agent would pose as a purchaser of stolen goods, but these were usually short-lived operations with limited objectives. For most purposes, the FBI relied on informants—persons with knowledge of or connections in the underworld—to provide leads that could then, by conventional investigative techniques, be converted into evidence admissible in court in ways that did not compromise the informant.

The FBI's reliance on informants rather than undercover agents had, of course, its own costs. An informant was not easily controlled, his motives often made him want to use the FBI for personal gain or revenge against rivals, and either he would not testify in court at all or his testimony would be vulnerable to attacks from defense attorneys. Moreover, it is one thing to find informants among bank robbers, jewel thieves, and gamblers with organized crime connections; it is something else again to find informants among high-level politicians, business executives, and labor leaders. An undercover operation came to be seen as a valuable supplement to the informant system: Though created with the aid of an informant, it could be staffed by FBI agents posing as thieves, fences, or businessmen, carefully monitored by recording equipment, used to develop hard physical evidence (such as photographs of cash payoffs), and operated so as to draw in high-level suspects whose world was not easily penetrated by conventional informants.

In 1974 the Law Enforcement Assistance Administration (LEAA) began supplying money to make possible the now-famous "Sting" operations in which stolen property would be purchased from thieves who thought they were selling to criminal fences. LEAA insisted initially that a Sting be a joint federal-local operation, and so the FBI became partners in these early ventures, thereby acquiring substantial experience in how to mount and execute an undercover effort in ways that avoided claims of entrapment. In 1977, the FBI participated in 34 Sting operations. Soon, however, the requirement of federal participation was relaxed and the Sting became almost entirely a state and local venture (albeit often with LEAA money). After all, most of the persons caught in a Sting were thieves who had violated state, but not federal, law.

The experience gained and the success enjoyed by the FBI in the Stings were now put in service of undercover operations directed at the priority crimes—especially white-collar crimes and racketeering. During fiscal year 1978, the Bureau conducted 132 undercover operations, 36 of which were aimed at white-collar crime. They produced impressive (and noncontroversial) results, and led to the indictment of persons operating illegal financial schemes, trying to defraud the government, engaging in union extortion, and participating in political corruption.

Each of these operations was authorized and supervised by FBI headquarters and by the local United States Attorney or by Justice Department attorneys (or both). Among the issues that were reviewed was the need to avoid entrapment. In general, the courts have allowed undercover operations—such as an agent offering to buy illegal narcotics—as a permissible investigative technique. In *Hampton v. United States*, the Supreme Court held in 1976 that the sale to government agents of heroin supplied to the defendant by a government informant did not constitute entrapment. In an earlier case, Justice Potter Stewart tried to formulate a general rule distinguishing a proper from an improper undercover operation: "Government agents may engage in conduct that is likely, when objectively considered, to afford a person ready and willing to commit the crime an opportunity to do so." It is noteworthy that this formulation appeared in a dissenting opinion in which Stewart argued that the case in question *had* involved entrapment; thus, it probably represents the opinion of many justices who take a reasonably strict view of what constitutes entrapment. As such, it affords ample opportunity for undercover operations, especially those, such as Abscam, in which lawyers can monitor agent activity on almost a continuous basis.

Congress was fully aware that the FBI was expanding its use of undercover operations. The House Appropriations Committee, as well as others, were told about these developments—without, of course, particular cases then in progress being identified. Moreover, Congress by law had to give permission for the Bureau to do certain things necessary for an undercover operation. These prerequisites to FBI undercover operations involve the right to lease buildings or to enter into contracts in ways that do not divulge the fact that the contracting party or the lessee are government agents, and that permit advance payment of funds. Indeed, one statute prohibits a government agency from leasing a building in Washington, D.C., without a specific appropriation for that purpose having first been made by Congress. If that law had been in force, the FBI would not have been able to lease the Washington house in which Operation Abscam was conducted. At the request of the FBI, however, Congress exempted the Bureau from compliance with statutes that might have impeded such operations. The proposed FBI Charter, now before Congress, would specifically authorize undercover operations and would grant a continuing exemption, whenever necessary, from the statutes governing contracts and leases.

Though the FBI learned a great deal about undercover operations by its early participation in Stings, Operation Abscam is not, strictly speaking, a Sting at all. In a Sting, a store is opened and the agents declare their willingness to buy merchandise from one and all. Much of what they buy involves perfectly legitimate sales; some of what they buy is stolen, and when that is established, the ground is laid for an arrest. Operation Abscam followed a quite different route. It resulted from the normal exploitation of an informant who had been useful in locating stolen art works. The informant apparently indicated that he could put agents in touch with politicians who were for sale; the agents accepted, and set up Abscam by having an agent pose as a wealthy Arab interested in buying political favors to assist his (mythical) business enterprises. Several important congressmen, or their representatives, were brought to the house used for Abscam and their negotiations with the agents recorded. The operation is no different in design from those used in many other cases that earned praise for the Bureau. What is different is that in this case congressmen were apparently involved and the operation was leaked to the press before indictments were issued.

Congress, Law Enforcement, and the Constitution

For congressmen to be in trouble with the law is nothing new. During the 95th Congress alone, 13 members or former members of the House of Representatives were indicted or convicted on criminal charges. Most if not all of these cases resulted from the use of conventional investigative methods—typically, a tip to a law enforcement officer or reporter by a person involved in the offense (bribery, payroll padding, taking kickbacks) who then testified against the official. Law enforcement in such cases is ordinarily reactive and thus crucially dependent on the existence and volubility of a disaffected employee, businessman, or accomplice. Operation Abscam was "proactive"—it created an opportunity for persons to commit a crime who were (presumably) ready and willing to do so.

Congress has never complained when such methods were used against others; quite the contrary, it has explicitly or implicitly urged—and authorized—their use against others. There is no small element of hypocrisy in the complaints of some congressmen that they did not mean a vigorous investigation of white-collar crime to include *them*.

But it is not all hypocrisy. It is worth discussing how such investigations should be conducted and under what pattern of accountability. An unscrupulous President with a complaisant FBI director could use undercover operations to discredit political enemies, including congressmen from a rival party. Hoover was a highly political FBI director, but he saw, rightly, that his power would be greater if he avoided investigations of Congress than if he undertook them. Clarence Kelley and William H. Webster have been sternly nonpartisan directors who would never consider allowing the Bureau's powers to be put in service of some rancid political purpose. But new times bring new men, and in the future we may again see partisan efforts to use the Bureau. What safeguards can be installed to prevent schemes to embarrass political enemies by leaked stories is worth some discussion.

But there is a dilemma here: the more extensive the pattern of accountability and control, the greater the probability of a leak. The only sure way to minimize leaks is to minimize the number of persons who know something worth leaking. In the case of Operation Abscam, scores of persons knew what was going on—in part because such extensive efforts were made to ensure that it was a lawful and effective investigation. In addition to the dozens of FBI agents and their supervisors, there were lawyers in the Justice Department and U.S. Attorneys in New York, Newark, Philadelphia, and Washington, D.C., together with their staffs, all of whom were well informed. Any one of them could have leaked. Indeed, given their partisan sponsorship and what is often their background in political activism, U.S. Attorneys are especially likely to be sources of leaks—more so, I should surmise, than FBI agents. If, in order to prevent abuses of the Bureau's investigative powers, we increase the number of supervisors—to include, for example, members of the House or Senate ethics committees—we also increase the chances of leaks (to say nothing of other ways by which such investigations could be compromised).

In the meantime, the debate will not be helped by complaints that the Bureau has launched a "vendetta" against Congress or that it is "out of control." It is nothing of the kind. It is an organization that is following out the logic of changes and procedures adopted to meet the explicit demands of Congress.

POINTS TO PONDER

1. Why did the FBI change the orientation of its law enforcement efforts?
2. Why would potential congressional wrongdoers be an unlikely target of law enforcement efforts under the FBI of J. Edgar Hoover?
3. What is entrapment? Why did some members of Congress feel that the FBI sting operation was unfair?

21

"BUREAUCRACY"
James Q. Wilson

In this short selection from his book Bureaucracy: What Government Agencies Do and Why They Do It *(1989), UCLA political scientist James Q. Wilson describes how a private business owner successfully built an ice-skating rink for the city of New York after the city government failed to accomplish the task after years of trying. Wilson analyzes the reasons underlying the private developer's ability to do the job more quickly and for less money than could the city. One of Wilson's main points is that, in addition to efficiency, governments must take into account other important values, such as equity, accountability, and fiscal integrity. He also notes that the public policy-making process is slow and cumbersome because it assures access to all interested parties. Wilson concludes that government may be less efficient than private business in some areas, but that our democratic values are often worth the price in efficiency.*

On the morning of May 22, 1986, Donald Trump, the New York real estate developer, called one of his executives, Anthony Gliedman, into his office. They discussed the inability of the City of New York, despite six years of effort and the expenditure of nearly $13 million, to rebuild the ice-skating rink in Central Park. On May 28 Trump offered to take over the rink reconstruction, promising to do the job in less than six months. A week later Mayor Edward Koch accepted the offer and shortly thereafter the city appropriated $3 million on the understanding that Trump would have to pay for any cost overruns out of his own pocket. On October 28, the renovation was complete, over a month ahead of schedule and about $750,000 under budget. Two weeks later, skaters were using it.

For many readers it is obvious that private enterprise is more efficient than are public bureaucracies, and so they would file this story away as simply another illustration of what everyone already knows. But for other readers it is not so obvious what this story means; to them, business is greedy and unless watched like a hawk will fob off shoddy or overpriced goods on the American public, as when it sells the government $435 hammers and $3,000 coffeepots. Trump may have done a good job in this instance, but perhaps there is something about skating rinks or New York City government that gave him a comparative advantage; in any event, no larger lessons should be drawn from it.

Some lessons can be drawn, however, if one looks closely at the incentives and constraints facing Trump and the Department of Parks and Recreation. It becomes apparent that there is not one "bureaucracy problem" but several, and the solution to each in some degree is incompatible with the solution to every other. First there is the problem of accountability—getting agencies to serve agreed-upon goals. Second there is the problem of equity—treating all citizens fairly, which usually means treating them alike on the basis of clear rules known in advance. Third there is the problem of responsiveness—reacting reasonably to the special needs and circumstances of particular people. Fourth there is the problem of efficiency—obtaining the greatest output for a given level of resources. Finally there is the problem of fiscal integrity—assuring that public funds are spent prudently for public purposes. Donald Trump and Mayor Koch were situated differently with respect to most of these matters.

Accountability

The Mayor wanted the old skating rink refurbished, but he also wanted to minimize the cost of the fuel needed to operate the rink (the first effort to rebuild it occurred right after the Arab oil embargo and the attendant increase in energy prices). Trying to achieve both goals led city hall to select a new re-frigeration system that as it turned out would not work properly. Trump came on the scene when only one goal dominated: get the rink rebuilt. He felt free to select the most reliable refrigeration system without worrying too much about energy costs.

Equity

The Parks and Recreation Department was required by law to give every con-tractor an equal chance to do the job. This meant it had to put every part of the job out to bid and to accept the lowest without much regard to the repu-tation or prior performance of the lowest bidder. Moreover, state law forbade city agencies from hiring a general contractor and letting him select the sub-contractors; in fact, the law forbade the city from even discussing the project in advance with a general contractor who might later bid on it—that would have been collusion. Trump, by contrast, was free to locate the rink builder with the best reputation and give him the job.

Fiscal Integrity

To reduce the chance of corruption or sweetheart deals the law required Parks and Recreation to furnish complete, detailed plans to every contractor bidding on the job; any changes after that would require renegotiating the contract. No such law constrained Trump; he was free to give incomplete plans to his chosen contractor, hold him accountable for building a satisfactory rink, but allow him to work out the details as he went along.

Efficiency

When the Parks and Recreation Department spent over six years and $13 mil-lion and still could not reopen the rink, there was public criticism but no city official lost money. When Trump accepted a contract to do it, any cost overruns or delays would have come out of his pocket and any savings could have gone into his pocket (in this case, Trump agreed not to take a profit on the job).

Gliedman summarized the differences neatly: "The problem with govern-ment is that government can't say, 'yes' . . . there is nobody in government that can do that. There are fifteen or twenty people who have to agree. Govern-ment has to be slower. It has to safeguard the process."

Inefficiency

The government can't say "yes." In other words, the government is con-strained. Where do the constraints come from? From us.

Herbert Kaufman has explained red tape as being of our own making: "Every restraint and requirement originates in somebody's demand for it."

Applied to the Central Park skating rink Kaufman's insight reminds us that civil-service reformers demanded that no city official benefit personally from building a project; that contractors demanded that all be given an equal chance to bid on every job; and that fiscal watchdogs demanded that all contract specifications be detailed as possible. For each demand a procedure was established; viewed from the outside, those procedures are called red tape. To enforce each procedure a manager was appointed; those managers are called bureaucrats. No organized group demanded that all skating rinks be rebuilt as quickly as possible, no procedure existed to enforce that demand, and no manager was appointed to enforce it. The political process can more easily enforce compliance with constraints than the attainment of goals.

When we denounce bureaucracy for being inefficient we are saying something that is half true. Efficiency is a ratio of valued resources used to valued outputs produced. The smaller that ratio the more efficient the production. If the valued output is a rebuilt skating rink, then whatever process uses the fewest dollars or the least time to produce a satisfactory rink is the most efficient process. By this test Trump was more efficient than the Parks and Recreation Department.

But that is too narrow a view of the matter. The economic definition of efficiency (efficiency in the small, so to speak) assumes that there is only one valued output, the new rink. But government has many valued outputs, including a reputation for integrity, the confidence of the people, and the support of important interest groups. When we complain about skating rinks not being built on time we speak as if all we cared about were skating rinks. But when we complain that contracts were awarded without competitive bidding or in a way that allowed bureaucrats to line their pockets we acknowledge that we care about many things besides skating rinks; we care about the contextual goals—the constraints—that we want government to observe. A government that is slow to build rinks but is honest and accountable in its actions and properly responsive to worthy constituencies may be a very efficient government, *if* we measure efficiency in the large by taking into account *all* of the valued outputs.

Calling a government agency efficient when it is slow, cumbersome, and costly may seem perverse. But that is only because we lack any objective way for deciding how much money or time should be devoted to maintaining honest behavior, producing a fair allocation of benefits, and generating popular support as well as to achieving the main goal of the project. If we could measure these things, and if we agreed as to their value, then we would be in a position to judge the true efficiency of a government agency and decide when it is taking too much time or spending too much money achieving all that we expect of it. But we cannot measure these things nor do we agree about their relative importance, and so government always will appear to be inefficient compared to organizations that have fewer goals.

Put simply, the only way to decide whether an agency is truly inefficient is to decide which of the constraints affecting its action ought to be ignored or discounted. In fact that is what most debates about agency behavior are all about. In fighting crime are the police handcuffed? In educating children are teachers tied down by rules? In launching a space shuttle are we too concerned with safety? In building a dam do we worry excessively about endangered species? In running the Postal Service is it important to have many post offices close to where people live? In the case of the skating rink, was the requirement of competitive bidding for each contract on the basis of detailed specifications a reasonable one? Probably not. But if it were abandoned, the gain (the swifter completion of the rink) would have to be balanced against the costs (complaints from contractors who might lose business and the chance of collusion and corruption in some future projects).

Even allowing for all of these constraints, government agencies may still be inefficient. Indeed, given the fact that bureaucrats cannot (for the most part) benefit monetarily from their agencies' achievements, it would be surprising if they were not inefficient. Efficiency, in the large or the small, doesn't pay.

But some critics of government believe that inefficiency is obvious and vast. Many people remember the 1984 claim of the Grace Commission (officially, the President's Private Sector Survey on Cost Control) that it had identified over $400 billion in savings that could be made if only the federal government were managed properly. Though the commission did not say so, many people inferred that careless bureaucrats were wasting that amount of money. But hardly anybody remembers the study issued jointly by the General Accounting Office and the Congressional Budget Office in February 1984, one month after the Grace Commission report. The GAO and CBO reviewed those Grace recommendations that accounted for about 90 percent of the projected savings, and after eliminating double-counting and recommendations for which no savings could be estimated, and other problems, concluded that the true savings would be less than one-third the claimed amount.

Of course, $100 billion is still a lot of money. But wait. It turns out that about 60 percent of this would require not management improvements but policy changes: for example, taxing welfare benefits, ending certain direct loan programs, adopting new rules to restrict Medicare benefits, restricting eligibility for retirement among federal civilian workers and military personnel, and selling the power produced by government-owned hydroelectric plants at the full market price.

That still leaves roughly $40 billion in management savings. But most of this would require either a new congressional policy (for example, hiring more Internal Revenue Service agents to collect delinquent taxes), some unspecified increase in "worker productivity," or buying more services from private suppliers. Setting aside the desirable goal of increasing productivity (for which no procedures were identified), it turns out that almost all of the projected savings would require Congress to alter the goals and constraints of public agencies. If there is a lot of waste (and it is not clear why the failure to tax welfare benefits or to hire more IRS agents should be called waste), it is congressionally directed waste.

Military procurement, of course, is the biggest source of stories about waste, fraud, and mismanagement. There cannot be a reader of this book who has not heard about the navy paying $435 for a hammer or the air force paying $3,000 for a coffeepot, and nobody, I suspect, believes Defense Department estimates of the cost of a new airplane or missile. If ever one needed evidence that bureaucracy is inefficient, the Pentagon supplies it.

Well, yes. But what kind of inefficiency? And why does it occur? To answer these questions one must approach the problem just as we approached the problem of fixing up a skating rink in New York City: We want to understand why the bureaucrats, all of whom are rational and most of whom want to do a good job, behave as they do.

To begin, let us forget about $435 hammers. They never existed. A member of Congress who did not understand (or did not want to understand) government accounting rules created a public stir. The $3,000 coffeepot existed, but it is not clear that it was overpriced.* But that does not mean there are no problems; in fact, the real problems are far more costly and intractable than inflated price tags on hammers and coffemakers. They include sticking too long with new weapons of dubious value, taking forever to acquire even good weapons, and not inducing contractors to increase their efficiency. . . .

When the military buys a new weapons system—a bomber, submarine, or tank—it sets in motion a procurement bureaucracy comprised of two key actors, the military program manager and the civilian contract officer, who must cope with the contractor, the Pentagon hierarchy, and Congress. To understand how they behave we must understand how their tasks get defined, what incentives they have, and what constraints they face.

POINTS TO PONDER

1. What constraints did the government bureaucracy have to deal with that Donald Trump's company did not?
2. Why is the high price of some items procured for defense systems, such as the "$435 hammer," misleading?
3. What are the values of American government that sometimes slow down or decrease the efficiency of government building projects?

* This is what happened: The navy ordered a package of maintenance equipment. One of the items was an inexpensive hammer; some of the others were very expensive test devices. Under the accounting rules then in effect, the supplier was allowed to allocate overhead costs in equal percentages to each item. This was simpler than trying to figure out how much overhead should be attributed to each individual item (in which case the difficult-to-make items would, of course, have acconted for more of the overhead than the easy-to-make ones such as a hammer). As a result, the bill showed the hammer as costing several hundred dollars in "overhead," for a total of $435. When a sailor unpacked the box, he found this bill and, not understanding the equal-allocation formula, called his congressman. A myth was born. . . . The "coffeepot" did cost about $3,000, but it was purchased to make coffee for the more than three hundred soldiers who would be carried on a C-5A transport. Commercial airlines often pay that much for coffeemakers on their jumbo jets. . . .

Chapter 6

THE SUPREME COURT: THE LEAST DANGEROUS BRANCH

The Supreme Court has had a profound impact on the political development of the United States. The potential for this important role was created when the Framers made the Supreme Court a co-equal branch of government, along with Congress and the president. Its role as interpreter of the law was assured by this inclusion, but the role that developed in authoritatively interpreting the Constitution, and even declaring laws enacted by Congress unconstitutional, was only established over time.

The issue of governance amounts to who is to be the final arbiter in disputes over the meaning of the Constitution. It is very useful to have broad agreement that one body, such as the Supreme Court, will have the final say on constitutional decisions. But the Supreme Court has always been self-consciously aware of the vague limits to its authority and the need to pay close attention to the legitimacy of its actions.

Establishing the Judiciary

Article III of the Constitution provides that the judicial power shall be vested in the Supreme Court and that its power shall extend to all cases and controversies arising under the Constitution and the laws of the federal government. The Article also provides that Congress can create inferior federal courts, such as the federal district courts and Circuit Courts of Appeals, which are now part of the federal judiciary. The Framers clearly intended that the courts should be independent of the other two branches by providing judges lifetime tenure during good behavior and prohibiting their salaries from being decreased while they are in office.

The roots of the U.S. judiciary reach back to the legal traditions in England, which, in important ways, stem from the Magna Carta of 1215. This document limited the power of the king and provided for trial by a jury of peers and protection against the loss of life, liberty, or property without due process of law.

The inclusion of the judiciary as a co-equal branch of government in the Constitution reflects the thinking of French political philosopher Montesquieu, whose writings about the separation of powers in government were familiar to the Framers. The idea of the courts as independent checks upon the other branches also reflected the colonial experience of being subject to the seemingly arbitrary rule of the king of England and the Parliament.

In addition to seeing the courts as protectors of individual rights against the new central government, wealthy Americans also may have seen a judiciary independent of the other branches as a protection of their property rights against attacks by debtors or those with no property.

Judicial Review

The role of the Supreme Court in deciding cases interpreting the Constitution and the laws is fairly straightforward, and the need to have a final arbiter when state laws conflict with federal laws is evident. The right of the Court, however, to extend its decisions to declaring actions of Congress or the president unconstitutional was much more tenuous and controversial, though it has become firmly established. The Constitution does not address directly the question of judicial review of congressional and state legislative acts, perhaps because raising the issue explicitly might have made ratification more difficult.

Though there is no explicit language in the Constitution authorizing judicial review, the Supreme Court asserted its own authority in the landmark case of *Marbury v. Madison* (1803). At the very end of John Adams's term as president, after Thomas Jefferson had been elected but had not yet taken office, Adams appointed William Marbury justice of the peace for the District of Columbia. The appointment documents were signed and sealed but were not actually delivered, which was the duty of the secretary of state. James Madison, Jefferson's newly appointed secretary of state, refused to deliver the papers, and Marbury sued in Court for a writ of mandamus to force Madison to deliver the appointment papers.

Chief Justice John Marshall delivered the opinion of the Court and judged that the appointment was proper and that Marbury had a right to the commission. In addition, a writ of mandamus was a proper remedy for the injustice to Marbury. The Supreme Court, however, could not help Marbury because it could not issue the writ of mandamus. Congress had passed a law giving the Supreme Court original jurisdiction to issue writs of mandamus, but that law came into conflict with the Constitution's provision that the Supreme Court would have "original jurisdiction in all cases affecting ambassadors, other public ministries and counsels, and those in which a state shall be a party. In all other cases, the Supreme Court shall have appellate jurisdiction." Thus the law giving the Supreme Court original jurisdiction was unconstitutional, and Marbury had no remedy in the Supreme Court.

The specific circumstances of the *Marbury* case, although interesting, were mundane, but the broader implications of Marshall's opinion were historic.

Marshall declared that "an act of the legislature, repugnant to the Constitution, is void. . . . It is emphatically the province and duty of the judicial department to say what the law is." Although the power of judicial review established by Marshall in *Marbury* is profound and firmly established, it has been used sparingly by the Supreme Court, with only about one hundred laws having been declared unconstitutional.

The Court has been hesitant to exercise its power of judicial review for several reasons. First, the Court, having neither the power of the purse nor the power of the sword, cannot enforce its own decisions; it must depend on the executive branch for implementation. Thus it must be careful to limit itself to decisions that will be heeded. This is one reason the Court often refuses to get into disputes between the president and Congress on the grounds that they are "political" questions.

Another reason the Supreme Court has chosen to exercise its power of judicial review sparingly is deference to the democratically elected popular branches. In a democratic republic the legitimacy of the policy-making role of appointed judges with life tenure is inherently suspect. Thus the extent of the reach of judicial review and the appropriate role of the Supreme Court have been issues of perennial controversy.

U.S. courts are also slow to make sudden changes because they operate in the common law tradition in which each new decision is limited by previous decisions on the same issues. The overriding principle of this approach is *stare decisis*—that is, "let the decision stand." Decisions in new cases thus depart only marginally from previous decisions of the Supreme Court. Even when the Court changes a policy direction, it is justified with previous Court decisions, and special arguments must be made to justify any significant deviation from precedent. This does not mean the Supreme Court does not change policy direction, but changes are mostly marginal and must be justified by other values of the Court.

Judicial Activism and Restraint

Although Hamilton's *Federalist* No. 78 clearly states that he expected the Supreme Court to pass judgment on acts of Congress that violated the Constitution, the position of appointed judges with life terms making far-reaching decisions has been debated throughout our history. Those who want judges to minimize their role in public policy favor judicial "self-restraint"; those who argue that judges must inevitably use their best judgment to apply the laws and Constitution to contemporary circumstances are said to favor "judicial activism."

To shore up the legitimacy of unelected judges making important decisions about public policy, it has been argued that judges merely interpret or discover law; they do not create law or make policy. The classic statement of this maxim is Justice Owen Roberts's dictum that in constitutional adjudication the role of the judge is "to lay the article of the Constitution which is involved beside the statute which is challenged and to decide whether the latter squares with the former." Those who argue that the role of judges in constitutional adjudication should not extend beyond the specific words in the Constitution are referred to as "strict constructionists."

Contemporary strict constructionists argue that for judges to do more than narrowly apply the literal text of the Constitution would usurp the proper rights of the elected branches, federal or state. Insofar as judges reach beyond the text of the Constitution in making decisions, they insert their own values into public policy, and in a democracy choosing among alternative values is properly the province of elected officials.

Others, however, argue that it is not that simple. Many words and phrases of the Constitution are inherently ambiguous. Any case that works its way up to the Supreme Court inevitably entails differences of interpretation between articulate and forceful adversaries. Searching for the original intentions of the Framers may be illuminating but the search seldom settles the issue cleanly, because the drafters of the Constitution did not always make their intentions clear, and the motives of those who ratified the Constitution are even more difficult to determine. In addition, the specific provisions of a document written in the eighteenth century may not cover all the changing circumstances in technology or human values that have occurred since then.

Those who take a more activist approach to the judicial role argue that interpreting the law inherently entails using value judgments to make policy. There is no way to avoid it. They recall Chief Justice Marshall's admonition from *McCulloch v. Maryland*: "We must never forget, that it is a *Constitution* that we are expounding." The implication is that a constitution is a broad charter for government meant to last for centuries and must therefore be flexible enough to accommodate political and economic change, in contrast to a statute, which might be interpreted more narrowly.

From the activist perspective, judges ought to remain faithful to the principles behind the words of the Constitution and apply those principles to the evolving sense of justice in our polity. Although many who espouse an activist role for the courts are contemporary political liberals in the United States, there are also prominent political conservatives who do not believe a literalist approach to constitutional construction is possible or desirable.

The Role of the Supreme Court in American History

Decisions of the Supreme Court have profound and lasting effects on U.S. public life, and the major eras of U.S. history have been marked by decisions that have changed the course of our history. The Court may occasionally get out of sync with the prevailing political consensus, but political forces and new appointments to the Court have eventually brought it back to majority values. During the first third of the twentieth century, the Supreme Court struck down many laws intended to regulate the economy and moderate the effects of the extremes of laissez faire capitalism. But with the vast popular support for Franklin Roosevelt and the New Deal, the Court switched its tack in 1937 and began to accept many laws of economic regulation as constitutional.

During the activist era of the Warren Court (1953–1969), the Supreme Court extended constitutional protection to the rights of African Americans and criminal defendants as well as enforced the principle of one person, one vote (forcing many states to reapportion legislative districts). But after the retirement of Chief Justice Warren, the Court began to moderate its direction under the stewardship of Chief Justices Warren Burger and William Rehnquist.

The Readings

The selections represent a range of commentary on the role of the Supreme Court in the United States. Several selections deal with the perennial issue of the role of the Court in public policy-making and how active that role should be. Historically there is no doubt that the Supreme Court has played a major role in the U.S. system of governance, from the protection of business from governmental regulation at the turn of the century to the civil rights revolution at mid-twentieth century. The readings emphasize the interaction of the Court with the other two branches through the review of laws of Congress and presidential appointments of Supreme Court justices.

Alexander Hamilton's *Federalist* No. 78 makes it clear that he expected the Court to make the final determination of constitutionality where there was a dispute. He argued that one of the purposes of the Constitution was to set limits on the legislative authority and that those limits were to be maintained by the courts "whose duty it must be to declare all acts contrary to the manifest tenor of the Constitution void." Thus the courts would be "bulwarks of a limited Constitution against legislative encroachments."

Other Framers also favored judicial review during the Constitutional Convention, but the concept was not explicitly included in the text of the Constitution. There was general agreement among the Framers that, as a co-equal branch of government, the Supreme Court would act as a check on the other two branches, and Hamilton mentions the danger of "legislative encroachments" that the Court might help curb.

One of the most outspoken critics of the judicial activism of the mid-twentieth century is Judge Robert Bork, the defeated Supreme Court nominee of President Ronald Reagan. Bork argues in his selection that there is no justification for judges ever moving beyond the literal text of a law or the text and original intent of the Framers of the Constitution.

He asserts that a judge gets political values from the "social class or elite with which he identifies." He further argues that the values of judges are likely to be in conflict with majority sentiment in the country, which is reflected in legislation. When judges base their decisions on what they think is best for the country, they are usurping the legitimate role of the legislature. Thus the appropriate behavior for judges is to restrain themselves from any decision beyond the literal text of the Constitution.

In contrast with Bork, Laurence Tribe argues that strict construction of the Constitution is impossible. Although some parts of the Constitution are unambiguous—for example, the length of terms of members of Congress—others are inherently indeterminate, such as the prohibition against unreasonable searches and seizures" or "cruel and unusual punishment." Judges must, of necessity, interpret these phrases in light of their own understanding of the principles embodied in the Constitution.

Tribe also argues that a "slavish adherence to the constitutional text" would allow judges to abdicate their duty to apply the principles of the Constitution to changing times. He argues, for instance, that tapping a person's telephone line has been appropriately included in the Constitution's prohibition of unreasonable searches, though the Framers had no conception of a telephone. Similarly Tribe approves of the Supreme Court's 1954 reversal of the "separate but equal" decision on education for African Americans in *Brown v. Board of Education.*

Tribe concludes that the principles enacted in the Constitution should be the guidelines of the justices and that the temptation of strict construction is that it seems easy, but in reality amounts to the avoidance of important and necessary choices.

An additional dimension to the nonliteralist position is articulated by Supreme Court Justice Ruth Bader Ginsburg in her selection. She seems to take a middle ground between the positions of Bork and Tribe. Ginsburg maintains that the appropriate role of the Supreme Court when a federal or state law is of questionable constitutionality is to engage in a "dialogue" with the popularly elected legislatures. If the Court judges a law to be constitutionally suspect, it should invite the legislature to rethink the matter by issuing an incremental decision rather than by stepping "boldly in front of the political process" by a sweeping decision to invalidate a law. One way to do this would be for the Court to decide that a law is defective, but not to define from the bench exactly what the policy ought to be. This gives more leeway to the elected branches to make policy decisions and narrows the role of the Court.

In the selection, Ginsburg applies her reasoning about the appropriate role of the Court to the *Roe v. Wade* decision that invalidated many state laws prohibiting women from having abortions. She argues that the decision was too sweeping and that it would have been better to allow state legislatures more leeway to formulate acceptable alternatives. Thus Ginsburg's formulation of the role of the Supreme Court would provide for appropriate deference to popularly elected legislatures without giving up an important role for judges in establishing public policy.

One of the enduring questions in American politics is how closely the Supreme Court reflects or leads popular opinion about public policy. In his selection, David O'Brien presents a survey of the constitutional revolution brought about by the Warren Court (1953–1969). During those years Supreme

Court decisions brought about far-reaching expansions in the rights of those accused of crime and the rights of African Americans.

O'Brien argues that Chief Justice Warren Burger (1969–1986), though more conservative than Chief Justice Earl Warren, did not engineer a reversal in direction of the Court. In contrast, the Court under William Rehnquist (1987–   ) is decidedly more conservative than either of his two predecessors because of his leadership and because of the appointment of Justices Anthony Kennedy, Sandra Day O'Connor, and Antonin Scalia by President Reagan and Justices David Souter and Clarence Thomas by President Bush. President Carter did not have the opportunity to appoint a Supreme Court justice. But how far the Court will go in a conservative direction may be tempered by the 1993 appointment of Justice Ginsburg by President Clinton.

But any attempt by presidents to "pack" the Court with justices who agree with their own political values is inherently uncertain, as argued by Chief Justice Rehnquist. Even though presidents are usually successful in appointing justices in general sympathy with their political philosophy, it is difficult to predict the appointees' actions on the Court. It may be possible to predict how a justice will vote on one set of issues, but one cannot predict what other issues will face the Court in future years. Also, upon being elevated to the Supreme Court a person may change his or her perspective on legal issues. One famous example is President Eisenhower's choice of Republican California Governor Earl Warren to be chief justice. No one would have predicted that Warren would lead the Court in a revolution of the constitutional protection of civil rights and liberties in the United States.

KEY TERMS

judicial activism: the idea that courts must interpret the Constitution and adapt constitutional principles to contemporary times

judicial restraint: the idea that courts should not make any decisions that go beyond the literal text of the Constitution

judicial review: the authority for a court to declare laws or actions by the president unconstitutional

jurisprudence: the philosophy of law

22

FEDERALIST NO. 78

Alexander Hamilton

In Federalist *No. 78, Alexander Hamilton makes an argument for the Supreme Court as proposed in the Constitution. He argues that it will be the "least dangerous" of the branches because it does not control the power of the purse or the sword, but can only render its judgment. He also argues that it is the role of the Court "to declare all acts contrary to the manifest tenor of the Constitution void." In performing this judicial review of acts of the legislature, the Court will act as a constitutional bulwark "against legislative encroachments." This power of judicial review was not made explicit in the Constitution, and it wasn't until the case of* Marbury v. Madison *in 1803 that judicial review became an accepted part of constitutional practice.*

To the People of the State of New York:

We proceed now to an examination of the judiciary department of the proposed government.

In unfolding the defects of the existing Confederation, the utility and necessity of a federal judicature have been clearly pointed out. It is the less necessary to recapitulate the considerations there urged, as the propriety of the institution in the abstract is not disputed; the only questions which have been raised being relative to the manner of constituting it, and to its extent. To these points, therefore, our observations shall be confined.

The manner of constituting it seems to embrace these several objects: 1st. The mode of appointing the judges. 2nd. The tenure by which they are to hold their places. 3rd. The partition of the judiciary authority between different courts, and their relations to each other.

First. As to the mode of appointing the judges; this is the same with that of appointing the officers of the Union in general, and has been so fully discussed in the two last numbers that nothing can be said here which would not be useless repetition.

Second. As to the tenure by which the judges are to hold their places: this chiefly concerns their duration in office; the provisions for their support; the precautions for their responsibility.

According to the plan of the convention, all judges who may be appointed by the United States are to hold their offices *during good behavior,* which is conformable to the most approved of the State constitutions, and among the rest, to that of this State. Its propriety having been drawn into question by the adversaries of that plan is no light symptom of the rage for objection which disorders their imaginations and judgments. The standard of good behavior for the continuance in office of the judicial magistracy is certainly one of the most valuable of the modern improvements in the practice of government. In a monarchy it is an excellent barrier to the despotism of the prince; in a republic it is a no less excellent barrier to the encroachments and oppressions of the representative body. And it is the best expedient which can be devised in any government to secure a steady, upright, and impartial administration of the laws.

Whoever attentively considers the different departments of power must perceive that, in a government in which they are separated from each other, the judiciary, from the nature of its functions, will always be the least dangerous to the political rights of the Constitution; because it will be least in a capacity to annoy or injure them. The Executive not only dispenses the honors, but holds the sword of the community. The legislature not only commands the purse, but prescribes the rules by which the duties and rights of every citizen are to be regulated. The judiciary, on the contrary, has no influence over either the sword or the purse; no direction either of the strength or of the wealth of the society; and can take no active resolution whatever. It may truly be said to have neither FORCE nor WILL, but merely judgment; and must ultimately depend upon the aid of the executive arm even for the efficacy of its judgments.

This simple view of the matter suggests several important consequences. It proves incontestably that the judiciary is beyond comparison the weakest of the three departments of power; that it can never attack with success either of the other two; and that all possible care is requisite to enable it to defend itself against their attacks. It equally proves that though individual oppression may now and then proceed from the courts of justice, the general liberty of the people can never be endangered from that quarter; I mean so long as the judiciary remains truly distinct from both the legislature and the Executive. For I agree that "there is no liberty, if the power of judging be not separated from the legislative and executive powers." And it proves, in the last place, that as liberty can have nothing to fear from the judiciary alone, but would have everything to fear from its union with either of the other departments; that as all the effects of such a union must ensue from a dependence of the former on the latter, notwithstanding a nominal and apparent separation; that as, from the natural feebleness of the judiciary, it is in continual jeopardy of being overpowered, awed, or influenced by its co-ordinate branches; and that as nothing can contribute so much to its firmness and independence as permanency in office, this quality may therefore be justly regarded as an indispensable ingredient in its constitution, and, in a great measure, as the citadel of the public justice and the public security.

The complete independence of the courts of justice is peculiarly essential in a limited Constitution. By a limited Constitution I understand one which contains certain specified exceptions to the legislative authority; such, for instance, as that it shall pass no bills of attainder, no *ex post facto* laws, and the like. Limitations of this kind can be preserved in practice no other way than through the medium of courts of justice, whose duty it must be to declare all acts contrary to the manifest tenor of the Constitution void. Without this, all the reservations of particular rights or privileges would amount to nothing.

Some perplexity respecting the rights of the courts to pronounce legislative acts void, because contrary to the Constitution, has arisen from an imagination that the doctrine would imply a superiority of the judiciary to the legislative power. It is urged that the authority which can declare the acts of another void must necessarily be superior to the one whose acts may be declared void. As this doctrine is of great importance in all the American constitutions, a brief discussion of the ground on which it rests cannot be unacceptable.

There is no position which depends on clearer principles than that every act of a delegated authority, contrary to the tenor of the commission under which it is exercised, is void. No legislative act, therefore, contrary to the Constitution can be valid. To deny this would be to affirm that the deputy is greater than his principal; that the servant is above his master; that the representatives of the people are superior to the people themselves; that men acting by virtue of powers may do not only what their powers do not authorize, but what they forbid.

If it be said that the legislative body are themselves the constitutional judges of their own powers, and that the construction they put upon them is conclusive upon the other departments, it may be answered that this cannot be the natural presumption where it is not to be collected from any particular provisions in the Constitution. It is not otherwise to be supposed that the Constitution could intend to enable the representatives of the people to substitute their *will* to that of their constituents. It is far more rational to suppose that the courts were designed to be an intermediate body between the people and the legislature, in order, among other things, to keep the latter within the limits assigned to their authority. The interpretation of the laws is the proper and peculiar province of the courts. A constitution is, in fact, and must be regarded by the judges, as a fundamental law. It therefore belongs to them to ascertain its meaning, as well as the meaning of any particular act proceeding from the legislative body. If there should happen to be an irreconcilable variance between the two, that which has the superior obligation and validity ought, of course, to be preferred; or, in other words, the Constitution ought to be preferred to the statute, the intention of the people to the intention of their agents.

Nor does this conclusion by any means suppose a superiority of the judicial to the legislative power. It only supposes that the power of the people is superior to both; and that where the will of the legislature, declared in its statutes, stands in opposition to that of the people, declared in the Constitution, the judges ought to be governed by the latter rather than the former. They ought to regulate their decisions by the fundamental laws, rather than by those which are not fundamental.

This exercise of judicial discretion, in determining between two contradictory laws, is exemplified in a familiar instance. It not uncommonly happens that there are two statutes existing at one time, clashing in whole or in part with each other, and neither of them containing any repealing clause or expression. In such a case it is the province of the courts to liquidate and fix their meaning and operation. So far as they can, by any fair construction, be reconciled to each other, reason and law conspire to dictate that this should be done; where this is impracticable, it becomes a matter of necessity to give effect to one in exclusion of the other. The rule which has obtained in the courts for determining their relative validity is, that the last in order of time shall be preferred to the first. But this is a mere rule of construction, not derived from any positive law, but from the nature and reason of the thing. It is a rule not enjoined upon the courts by legislative provision, but adopted by themselves, as consonant to truth and propriety, for the direction of their conduct as interpreters of the law. They thought it reasonable that between the interfering acts of an *equal* authority, that which was the last indication of its will should have the preference.

But in regard to the interfering acts of a superior and subordinate authority, of an original and derivative power, the nature and reason of the thing indicate the converse of that rule as proper to be followed. They teach us that the prior act of a superior ought to be preferred to the subsequent act of an inferior and subordinate authority; and that accordingly, whenever a particular statute contravenes the Constitution, it will be the duty of the judicial tribunals to adhere to the latter and disregard the former.

It can be of no weight to say that the courts, on the pretense of a repugnancy, may substitute their own pleasure to the constitutional intentions of the legislature. This might as well happen in the case of two contradictory statutes; or it might as well happen in every adjudication upon any single statute. The courts must declare the sense of the law; and if they should be disposed to exercise WILL instead of JUDGMENT, the consequence would equally be the substitution of their pleasure to that of the legislative body. The observation, if it prove anything, would prove that there ought to be no judges distinct from that body.

If, then, the courts of justice are to be considered as the bulwarks of a limited Constitution against legislative encroachments, this consideration will afford a strong argument for the permanent tenure of judicial offices, since nothing will contribute so much as this to that independent spirit in the judges which must be essential to the faithful performance of so arduous a duty.

POINTS TO PONDER

1. Why does Hamilton refer to the Supreme Court as "the least dangerous branch"?
2. Why were judges given life tenure?
3. Why did Hamilton argue that the Supreme Court should be able to declare laws passed by Congress unconstitutional?

23

"THE SUPREME COURT AND THE TEMPTATIONS OF POLITICS"
Robert H. Bork

Judge Robert H. Bork of the U.S. Court of Appeals is one of the most outspoken proponents of the strict constructionist approach to interpreting the Constitution. He was nominated to the Supreme Court by President Reagan, but in a bitter battle he failed to be confirmed by the Senate. In this selection from his book The Tempting of America *(1990), Judge Bork lays out his argument against judicial activism. He argues that judicial review is a powerful tool of government and for judges to base their decisions on anything but the literal text of the Constitution and the original intent of the Framers is to open the door to the application of the personal values of judges in determining judicial outcomes. Because judges are part of an intellectual elite, their opinions ought not to prevail over the wishes of a democratically elected legislature.*

A popular style in complaining about the courts is to contrast modern judges with those of a golden or, at least, a less tarnished age. Many people have a fuzzy impression that the judges of old were different. They did things like "follow precedent" and "apply the law, not make it up." There is a good deal to be said for that view. The practice of judicial lawmaking has certainly accelerated spectacularly in this century, particularly in the past four or five decades. Nevertheless, the whole truth is rather more complicated.

From the establishment of the federal judiciary at the end of the eighteenth century, some judges at least claimed the power to strike down statutes on the basis of principles not to be found in the Constitution. Judges who claimed this power made little or no attempt to justify it, to describe its source with any specificity, or to state what principles, if any, limited their own power. No more have the activist judges of our time. Justifications for such judicial behavior had, for the most part, to await the ingenuity of modern law faculties. But the actions of the federal judiciary, and in particular those of the Supreme Court, have often provoked angry reaction, though rarely a systematic statement of the appropriate judicial role. The appropriate limits of judicial power, if such there be, are thus the center of an ancient, if not always fruitful, controversy. Its confused and unfocused condition constitutes a venerable tradition, which is one tradition, at least, modern scholarship leaves intact. This part of the book traces the history of judicial revisions of the Constitution, identifies the social values revisionism served, and evaluates such justifications as were offered.

In a single volume, it is possible to examine only the most obvious or the most explicit revisions of the Constitution. But it is important to keep in mind that any court seen engaging in overt revisionism will, in all probability, have engaged in many more instances of disguised departures from the Constitution. A court that desires a result the law does not allow would rather, whenever possible, through misuse of materials or illogic, publish an opinion claiming to be guided or even compelled to its result by the Constitution than state openly that the result rests on other grounds. That is because popular support for judicial supremacy rests upon the belief that the court is applying fundamental principles laid down at the American founding. We would hardly revere a document that we knew to be no more than an open warrant for judges to do as they please.

Disguised or not, the habit of legislating policy from the bench, once acquired, is addictive and hence by no means confined to constitutional cases. The activist or revisionist judge, as we shall see, can no more restrain himself from doing "good" in construing a statute than when he purports to speak with the voice of the Constitution.

The values a revisionist judge enforces do not, of course, come from the law. If they did, he would not be revising. The question, then, is where such a judge finds the values he implements. Academic theorists try to provide various philosophical apparatuses to give the judge the proper values. We may leave until later the question of whether any of these systems succeed. The important point, for the moment, is that no judge has ever really explained the matter. A judge inserting new principles into the Constitution tells us their origin only in a rhetorical, never an analytical, style. There is, however, strong reason to suspect that the judge absorbs those values he writes into law from the social class or elite with which he identifies.

It is a commonplace that moral views vary both regionally within the United States and between socio-economic classes. It is similarly a commonplace that the morality of certain elites may count for more in the operations of government than that morality which might command the allegiance of a majority of the people. In no part of government is this more true than in the courts. An elite moral or political view may never be able to win an election or command the votes of a majority of a legislature, but it may nonetheless influence judges and gain the force of law in that way. That is the reason judicial activism is extremely popular with certain elites and why they encourage judges to think it the highest aspect of their calling. Legislation is far more likely to reflect majority sentiment while judicial activism is likely to represent an elite minority's sentiment. The judge is free to reflect the "better" opinion because he need not stand for reelection and because he can deflect the majority's anger by claiming merely to have been enforcing the Constitution. Constitutional jurisprudence is mysterious terrain for most people, who have more pressing things to think about. And a very handy fact that is for revisionists.

The opinions of the elites to which judges respond change as society changes and one elite replaces another in the ability to impress judges. Thus, judicial activism has had no single political trajectory over time. The values enforced change, and sometimes those of one era directly contradict those of a prior era. That can be seen in the sea changes constitutional doctrine has undergone in our history. There will often be a lag, of course, since judges who have internalized the values of one elite will not necessarily switch allegiances just because a new elite and its values have become dominant. When that happens, when judges are enforcing values regarded by the dominant elite as passé, the interim between the change and the replacement of the judges will be perceived as a time of "constitutional crisis." The fact of judicial mortality redresses the situation eventually, and new judges enforce the new "correct" values. This has happened more than once in our history. The intellectuals of the newly dominant elite are then highly critical of the activist judges of the prior era for enforcing the wrong values while they praise the activist judges of their own time as sensitive to the needs of society. They do not see, or will not allow themselves to see, that the judicial performances, judged as judicial performances, are the same in both eras. The Supreme Court that struck down economic regulation designed to protect workers is, judged as a judicial body, indistinguishable from the Court that struck down abortion laws. Neither Court gave anything resembling an adequate reason derived from the Constitution for frustrating the democratic outcome. So far as one can tell from the opinions written, each Court denied majority morality for no better reason than that elite opinion ran the other way.

. . . The Supreme Court's activism was at various times enlisted in the protection of property, the defense of slave owners, the protection of business enterprise in an industrializing nation, the interests of groups in the New Deal coalition, and, today, the furtherance of the values of the elite or cluster of elites known as the "new class" or the "knowledge class." The point ought not be overstated. We are discussing a strong tendency, not invariable conduct. No Court behaves in this way all of the time, in every case. Few judges are so willful as that. The structure of the law does have force, and, in any event, most cases do not present a conflict between elite morality and the law's structure. Yet such occasions arise in important matters, and it is those occasions that give the Court of each era its distinctive style.

Part of any revisionist Court's style, in addition to the nature of the nonconstitutional values enforced, is the rhetoric employed. The Court of each era is likely to choose different provisions of the Constitution or different formulations of invented rights as the vehicles for its revisory efforts. These are different techniques for claiming that what is being done is "law." The shifts in terminology do not alter the reality of the judicial performance as such. Still, the rhetoric employed will often disclose what values are popular with the elites to which the Court responds. Thus, the Court's shift from the use of the word "liberty" in the due process clause, popular in the closing decades of the last century and the opening decades of this century, to the idea of equality in the equal protection clause signified a shift in dominant values. It also signified a change in the social groups to which the Court responded, a decline in the influence of the business class and a rise in that of the New Deal political coalition and its intellectual spokesmen. Similarly, the change from "liberty of contract," used in striking down economic reform legislation, to the "right of privacy" employed to guarantee various aspects of sexual freedom, signals a change in dominant values from capitalist free enterprise to sexual permissiveness, and, again, a change in dominant elites from the business class to the knowledge class, though now with less concern than previously for the social values of those who made up the New Deal coalition.

* * * *

The Constitution has been many things to Americans. It has been and remains an object of veneration, a sacred text, the symbol of our nationhood,
the foundation of our government's structure and practice, a guarantor of our
liberties, and a moral teacher.

But the Constitution is also power. That is why we see political struggle
over the selection of the judges who will wield that power. In our domestic
affairs and even to some degree in our foreign dealings, the Constitution provides judges with the ultimate coercive power known to our political arrangements. In the hands of judges, words become action: commands are issued by
courts, obeyed by legislatures, and enforced by executives. The reading of the
words becomes freedoms and restrictions for us; the course of the nation is
confirmed or altered; the way we live and the ways we think and feel are
affected.

It will not do to overstate the matter. We are an incredibly complex and intricate society and no power is without checks, some obvious and direct in
operation, some subtle and intangible. But a major check on judicial power,
perhaps the major check, is the judges' and our understanding of the proper
limits to that power. Those limits may be pressed back incrementally, case by
case, until judges rule areas of life not confided to their authority by any provision of the Constitution or other law. We have, in fact, witnessed just that
process. The progression of political judging, judging unrelated to law, has
been recounted in this book. This progression has greatly accelerated in the
past few decades and now we see the theorists of constitutional law urging
judges on to still greater incursions into Americans' right of self-government.

This is an anxious problem and one that can be met only by understanding
that judges must always be guided by the original understanding of the Constitution's provisions. Once adherence to the original understanding is weakened or abandoned, a judge, perhaps instructed by a revisionist theorist, can
reach any result, because the human mind and will, freed of the constraints of
history and "the sediment of history which is law," can reach any result. As we
have seen, no set of propositions is too preposterous to be espoused by a judge
or a law professor who has cast loose from the historical Constitution.

The judge's proper task is not mechanical. "History," Cardinal Newman reminded us, "is not a creed or a catechism, it gives lessons rather than rules."
No body of doctrine is born fully developed. That is as true of constitutional
law as it is of theology. The provisions of the Constitution state profound but
simple and general ideas. The law laid down in those provisions gradually
gains body, substance, doctrines, and distinctions as judges, equipped at first
with only those ideas, are forced to confront new situations and changing circumstances. It is essential, however, that the new developments always be
weighed in the light of the lessons history provides about the principles meant
to be enforced. Doctrine must be shaped and reshaped to conform to the
original ideas of the Constitution, to ensure that the principles intended are

those which guide and limit power, and that no principles not originally meant are invented to deprive us of the right to govern ourselves. The concept of original understanding itself gains in solidity, in articulation and sophistication, as we investigate its meanings, implications, and requirements, and as we are forced to defend its truths from the constitutional heresies with which we are continually tempted.

Among the stakes is the full right of self-government that the Founders bequeathed us and which they limited only as to specified topics. In the long run, however, there may be higher stakes than that. As we move away from the historically rooted Constitution to one created by abstract, universalistic styles of constitutional reasoning, we invite a number of dangers. One is that such styles teach disrespect for the actual institutions of the American nation. A great many academic theorists state explicitly, and some judges seem easily persuaded, that elected legislators and executives are not adequate to decide the moral issues that divide us, and that judges should therefore take their place. But, when Americans are morally divided, it is appropriate that our laws reflect that fact. The often untidy responses of the elected branches possess virtues and benefits that the "principled" reactions of courts do not. Our popular institutions, the legislative and executive branches, were structured to provide safety, to achieve compromise when we are divided, to slow change, to dilute absolutisms. They both embody and produce wholesome inconsistencies. They are designed, in short, to do the very things that abstract generalizations about moral principle and the just society tend to bring into contempt. That is a dangerous civics lesson to teach the citizens of a republic. As Edmund Burke put it:

> All government, indeed every human benefit and enjoyment, every virtue, and every prudent act, is founded on compromise and barter. We balance inconveniences; we give and take; we remit some rights, that we may enjoy others; and, we choose rather to be happy citizens, than subtle disputants.

It may be significant that this passage is from Burke's speech on *Moving His Resolutions for Conciliation With the Colonies*, delivered to Parliament in 1775. The English government elected to stand on abstract principles of sovereignty and lost the American colonies.

The attempt to define individual liberties by abstract moral philosophy, though it is said to broaden our liberties, is actually likely to make them more vulnerable. I am not referring here to the freedom to govern ourselves but to the freedoms from government guaranteed by the Bill of Rights and the post–Civil War amendments. Those constitutional liberties were not produced by abstract reasoning. They arose out of historical experience with unaccountable power and out of political thought grounded in the study of history as well as in moral and religious sentiment. Attempts to frame theories that remove from democratic control areas of life our nation's Founders intended to place there can achieve power only if abstractions are regarded as legitimately able to displace the Constitution's text and structure and the history that gives our legal rights life, rootedness, and meaning. It is no small matter to discredit the foundations upon which our constitutional freedoms have always been sustained and substitute as a bulwark only the abstract propositions of moral philosophy. To do that is, in fact, to display a lightmindedness terrifying in its frivolity. Our freedoms do not ultimately depend upon the pronouncements of judges sitting in a row. They depend upon their acceptance by the American people, and a major factor in that acceptance is the belief that these liberties are inseparable from the founding of the nation. The moral systems urged as constitutional law by the theorists are not compatible with the moral beliefs of most Americans. Richard John Neuhaus wrote that law is "a human enterprise in response to human behavior, and human behavior is stubbornly entangled with beliefs about right and wrong." Law will not be recognized as legitimate if it is not organically related to "the larger universe of moral discourse that helps shape human behavior." Constitutional doctrine that rests upon a parochial and class-bound version of morality, one not shared by the general American public, is certain to be resented and is unlikely to prove much of a safeguard when crisis comes.

Robert Bolt's play about Thomas More, *A Man For All Seasons*, makes the point. When More was Lord Chancellor, his daughter, Margaret, and his son-in-law, Roper, urged him to arrest a man they regarded as evil. Margaret said, "Father, that man's bad." More replied, "There is no law against that." And Roper said, "There is! God's law!" More then gave excellent advice to judges: "Then God can arrest him. . . . The law, Roper, the law. I know what's legal not what's right. And I'll stick to what's legal. . . . I'm *not* God. The currents and eddies of right and wrong, which you find such plain sailing, I can't navigate. I'm no voyager. But in the thickets of the law, oh, there I'm a forester."

Roper would not be appeased and he leveled the charge that More would give the Devil the benefit of law.

> MORE. Yes. What would you do? Cut a great road through the law to get after the Devil?
>
> ROPER. I'd cut down every law in England to do that!
>
> MORE. . . . Oh? . . . And when the last law was down, and the Devil turned round on you—where would you hide, Roper, the laws all being flat? . . . This country's planted thick with laws from coast to coast—man's laws, not God's—and if you cut them down— . . . d'you really think you could stand upright in the winds that would blow then? . . . Yes, I'd give the Devil benefit of law, for my own safety's sake.

This is not a romanticized version of the man, for the historic More is reported to have said of his duty as a judge: "[I]f the parties will at my hands call for justice, then, all were it my father stood on the one side, and the Devil on the other, his cause being good, the Devil should have right." It is a hard saying and a hard duty, but it is the duty we must demand of judges.

Judges will always be tempted to apply what they imagine to be "God's law," cutting a great road through man's law. When they have done, when man's law has been thoroughly weakened and discredited, and when powerful forces have a different version of God's law or the higher morality, we may find that the actual rights of the Constitution and the democratic institutions that protect us may have all been flattened.

The difference between our historically grounded constitutional freedoms and those the theorists, whether of the academy or of the bench, would replace them with is akin to the difference between the American and the French revolutions. The outcome for liberty was much less happy under the regime of the abstract "rights of man" than it has been under the American Constitution. What Burke said of the abstract theorists who produced the calamities of the French Revolution might equally be said of those, judges and professors alike, who would remake our Constitution out of moral philosophy: "This sort of people are so taken up with their theories about the rights of man that they have totally forgotten his nature." Those who made and endorsed our Constitution knew man's nature, and it is to their ideas, rather than to the temptations of utopia, that we must ask that our judges adhere.

POINTS TO PONDER

1. According to Bork, where do judges get their own political values?
2. How do the roles of legislatures and judges differ?
3. Why does Bork argue that even the Devil ought to be afforded the protections of the law?

24

"THE MYTH OF THE STRICT CONSTRUCTIONIST: OUR INCOMPLETE CONSTITUTION"

Laurence H. Tribe

Harvard law professor Laurence Tribe takes issue with those (like Judge Bork) who espouse strict constructionism. In this excerpt from his book, God Save This Honorable Court *(1985), Tribe argues that determining original intent from the text of the Constitution is impossible in principle because "words are inherently indeterminate—they can often be given more than one plausible meaning." Tribe argues that judges should strive to expound the principles embodied in the language of the Constitution. In this way the Supreme Court can apply the original principles of the Constitution to the vastly changed circumstances and technology of the twentieth century. The Court can also apply the enduring principles of the Constitution to our evolving understanding of human rights, such as in the 1954 Brown decision that declared separate educational facilities for African Americans to be inherently unequal.*

Some would argue that one Justice or two would not make that much difference—and that even the many 5–4 splits would gradually disappear—if the Supreme Court were staffed, as they believe it should be, with men and women who understand that constitutional adjudication is simply the job of correctly reading the Constitution. If the Justices interpret our great charter in a straightforward manner—if they pay close attention to its words and avoid twisting or stretching their meanings—there will be few occasions for controversies that can be manipulated by well-chosen appointments. All that the President and the Senate need do is stop appointing "activist" judges who impose their own philosophies upon the document they are sworn to uphold, and appoint instead properly "restrained" jurists who know, and will not exceed, a judge's proper place. So the argument goes. It is simple, appealing, and plainly wrong.

Strict Constructionism Explained

In 1717 Bishop Benjamin Hoadly told the King of England that, in his opinion, "whoever hath an absolute authority to interpret any written laws is truly the Lawgiver to all intents and purposes, and not the person who first wrote them." Thus began a controversy that has continued unabated for the last two hundred and fifty years. Not everyone has agreed that the power of judicial review gives the Supreme Court wide discretion in reading the law. Justice Joseph Story argued in 1833 that the Court must give to the constitutional text only its ordinary and natural meaning: "Constitutions are instruments of a practical nature, founded on the common business of human life, adapted to common wants, designed for common use and fitted for common understanding." A century later Justice Owen Roberts described the Supreme Court's task in an even more limited and mechanical way: "to lay the article of the Constitution which is involved beside the statute which is challenged and to decide whether the latter squares with the former."

This approach to judicial review is usually known as strict constructionism, and its guiding principle is exclusive attention to the constitutional text. The Supreme Court's Justices must take the Constitution as they find it, and not make things up as they go along. Even if the Justices are appalled by the results this method produces, or believe that the Constitution's literal commands are severely out of step with the times, it is not their job to rewrite it. That prerogative belongs to the Congress and the President—and ultimately to the people, who retain the power to *amend* the Constitution. The watchword of strict constructionism is "restraint." The continuing popularity of this approach to constitutional interpretation is revealed by the fact that President

Nixon announced a policy of appointing only strict constructionists to the Supreme Court; the same "judicial philosophy" appears to be a sine qua non for nomination under President Reagan as well.

Why It Doesn't Work

The central flaw of strict constructionism is that words are inherently indeterminate—they can often be given more than one plausible meaning. If simply *reading* the Constitution the "right" way were all the Justices of the Supreme Court had to do, the only qualification for the job would be literacy, and the only tool a dictionary. But the meanings of the Constitution's words are especially difficult to pin down. Many of its most precise commands are relatively trivial—such as the requirement that the President be thirty-five years old—while nearly all of its important phrases are deliberate models of ambiguity. Just what does the Fourth Amendment prohibit as an "unreasonable search"? What exactly is the "speech" whose freedom the government may not "abridge"? What is it that we gain by being guaranteed the "equal protection of the laws"? And what, in heaven's name, is "due process"? Such vague phrases not only invite but *compel* the Supreme Court to put meaning *into* the Constitution, not just to take it out. Judicial construction inevitably entails a major element of judicial creation.

This is not to say that the Court is free to take the position of Humpty Dumpty, that "a word means just what I choose it to mean—neither more nor less." The Justices may not follow a policy of "anything goes" so long as it helps put an end to what they personally consider to be injustice. But the constitutional text is not enough—we need to search for, and explain our selection of, the *principles behind* the words.

Consider the First Amendment to the Constitution. Beyond dispute, it prohibits the Congress from dictating official religious beliefs, censoring newspapers, or punishing criticism of the government. The words of the First Amendment—which command that "Congress shall make no law respecting an establishment of religion, or prohibiting the free exercise thereof; or abridging the freedom of speech, or of the press"—could be read no other way. Yet not one word in the entire Constitution says that the *President* cannot do those things, even though such a notion seems unthinkable. What are we to make of this omission? A resort to the Constitution's text and *only* its text for an answer is a shortcut to a dead end. We must ask *why* the Congress is prohibited from violating our rights but the President is not. Is the President to be considered less of a threat to our liberty? Even if such a thought might have been plausible in 1791, when the First Amendment was ratified, it is certainly not plausible today: the modern American President is the repository of perhaps the world's greatest concentration of power; and that power is growing. We must look deeper than the surface of the Constitution's words.

The principle that animates the Bill of Rights, including the First Amendment, is that there are certain freedoms that are fundamental in determining the kind of society we wish to be. These freedoms must be protected from political compromise, and even democratically elected governments must fully respect them. In light of this principle, it is perfectly sensible to see the shield of the First Amendment as a bulwark of freedom against presidential as well as congressional acts. Indeed, it would be indefensible *not* to.

One of the most important problems of constitutional interpretation has been the question of the "incorporation" of the Bill of Rights into the Fourteenth Amendment, which declares that the states may not "deprive any person of life, liberty, or property, without due process of law." After the ratification of that amendment in 1868, the Supreme Court gradually recognized a glaring inconsistency in the constitutional scheme. The Bill of Rights, with its litany of fundamental liberties, had originally been understood and long been held to provide a shield only against intrusion by the *federal* government. Yet it seemed intolerable to declare that although the President and the Congress had no power to take our private property without compensation, to break into our homes and spy on us at will, or to condemn us to prison or the gallows in trials before kangaroo courts, the states remained perfectly free to do so. That position was particularly intolerable after we fought the Civil War and added the Thirteenth, Fourteenth and Fifteenth Amendments to the Constitution, in part to protect some among us from the governments of the states in which we live. Therefore, over the course of a hundred years, the Supreme Court has gradually read into the Fourteenth Amendment's Due Process Clause most of the liberties guaranteed by the Bill of Rights. Even Justice Hugo Black, who is often considered the strictest constructionist who ever served on the Court, vigorously advocated this very practice.

Another problem emerged with the passage of the Fourteenth Amendment. That amendment, in addition to guaranteeing *due process* of law, prohibits the states from denying to anyone the *equal protection* of the laws. This latter provision was the basis of the Court's decision to strike down racially segregated public schools in *Brown v. Board of Education*. On the same day in 1954 that it upheld Brown's challenge to Topeka's segregated schools, and another student's attack on segregation in Prince Edward County, Virginia, the Court was presented with an identical challenge to the segregated schools of the District of Columbia. The problem was that the Fourteenth Amendment requires only the *states*, and not the federal government, to provide equal protection of the laws; there is no parallel provision in the Bill of Rights.

A unanimous Supreme Court recognized the absurdity of denouncing racism in Virginia while condoning it across the Potomac River in Washington, D.C., and did not hesitate to read into the Fifth Amendment's Due Process Clause—which *does* apply to the federal government—a guarantee of equal protection of the laws. The literal result of this judicial innovation was to

make the Equal Protection Clause of the Fourteenth Amendment wholly re-
dundant, for if the Fifth Amendment's Due Process Clause includes protection
of equality, so must the identically worded Due Process Clause of the Fourteenth Amendment. This reading of the Constitution may seem odd indeed if
one looks only at the language of the document. But the reading is perfectly
logical and laudable if one examines the principles embodied in that language,
for there is no defensible reason to allow the national government to run
roughshod over fundamental liberties that the fifty states and their cities are required to respect.

Chief Justice Marshall once wrote that we must remember that "it is a *Constitution* we are expounding." It is the grand charter of a democratic republic,
the philosophical creed of a free people, and it was written in broad, even majestic language because it was written to evolve. The statesmen who wrote the
Constitution meant the American experiment to endure without having to be
reinvented with an endless series of explicit amendments to its basic blueprint.
There is a message in the common adage "Ours is a Constitution of limited
powers." The Tenth Amendment makes that maxim a reminder that the federal government in particular may exercise only the powers ceded to it by the
people in the Constitution. Perhaps even more important, the Ninth Amendment expressly states that even the Bill of Rights itself is not to be understood
as an exhaustive list of individual liberties. The Ninth Amendment thereby
invites us, and our judges, to expand on the panoply of freedoms that are
uniquely our heritage. Thus the Constitution tells us, both implicitly and
explicitly, that what it does *not* say must also be interpreted, understood, and
applied.

A Related Fallacy: The Intent of the Framers

Another school of constitutional interpretation takes as its lodestar the intent
of the authors of the Constitution. The task of the Supreme Court, when
confronted by ambiguous or open-ended language, is simply to divine what
the Framers and the authors of the amendments had in mind. This method
employs historical research in addition to textual analysis. One obvious
problem with asking "what they meant" is that we must first determine who
"they" are. In the case of the Bill of Rights, do we defer to the intentions of
the men—yes, it was men only—who drafted it and saw it as an essential safeguard against encroachment on fundamental freedoms, or the intentions of
those among them who saw the Bill of Rights as unnecessary and unwise, but
acceded to its passage because otherwise some states might never have ratified
the Constitution? And how should we understand the purpose of the Slave
Trade Clause of Article I of the Constitution, which prohibits Congress from
restricting the importation of slaves until 1808? Did the Framers mean by this
provision that when they said, in the Declaration of Independence, "all men
are created equal," they really meant "all *white* men"? Was this, too, merely a
bargaining chip, a concession to the slaveholding states to entice them into the

Union? Or did the Founding Fathers mean to give the South a two-decade grace period in which to phase out slavery before Congress did it for them? And how was this clause understood by the Southern legislators who ratified the Constitution?

The nagging doubt prompted by inquiries like these is that no collective body—be it the Congress or the Constitutional Convention or the aggregate of state legislatures—can really be said to have a *single*, ascertainable "purpose" or "intent." And even if such a mythical beast could be captured and examined, how relevant would it be to us today? Should the peculiar opinions held, and the particular applications envisioned, by men who have been dead for two centuries *always* trump contemporary insights into what the living Constitution means and ought to mean? Should we permit others to rule us from the grave not only through solemn enactments democratically ratified, but through hidden beliefs and premises perhaps deliberately left unstated?

Consider the Equal Protection Clause as an example. It was clearly intended to restrict racial discrimination against the recently emancipated slaves, but just what did the authors of the Fourteenth Amendment "count" as discrimination? Does a state deny equal protection by forcing blacks to attend segregated schools, use separate bathrooms, and sit only at the back of the bus? In *Plessy v. Ferguson* in 1898 a Supreme Court much closer to the source than we are today answered "no": separate but equal facilities are permissible. Half a century later a different group of Justices unanimously disagreed, because they recognized that, in a society dominated by white men, separate facilities for blacks were not likely ever to be "equal," and that, even if they were, enforced apartheid itself declared white supremacy and automatically denied equality to blacks. That decision may be hard to square with the specific, if for various reasons never expressed, agenda of those who gave us the Fourteenth Amendment. Historical evidence as to what "they" collectively had in mind is inconclusive, but it is quite possible that they had no objection to segregated schools as such. Schools even in some Northern states had been segregated for years. But public education in 1868 was not the crucial institution that it has since become. The right to own property was considered central to individual liberty, as was the right to make contracts, and we can safely say that the authors of the Equal Protection Clause "meant" to extend these rights to blacks as well as whites. In *Brown v. Board of Education* and the cases that followed it the Supreme Court was—and rightly so—less interested in the ways in which the phrase "equal protection" was implemented in the nineteenth century than in the sorts of inequalities which that *principle* should tolerate in the twentieth century.

Abdicating Responsibility for Tough Choices

The most serious flaw in both slavish adherence to the constitutional text and the inevitably inconclusive inquiry into the intent of those who wrote it is not just that these methods of judicial reasoning ask the wrong questions, but that they abdicate responsibility for the choices that constitutional courts *necessarily* make. The Supreme Court just cannot avoid the painful duty of exercising judgment so as to give concrete meaning to the fluid Constitution, because the constitutional rules and precepts that it is charged with administering lack that certainty which permits anything resembling automatic application. Strict constructionism in all of its variants is thus built on a conceit—which through the years has become a full-blown myth—that the Supreme Court does not *make* law, but *finds* law ready-made by others. In this mythology, the Justices do not really render their own opinions in deciding cases, for they are the mere mouthpieces of oracles beyond themselves; just as God spake by the prophets, so the Constitution speaketh by Supreme Court Justices. Even those who say they know it's not so—who claim, when wishing to sound sophisticated, that they realize some measure of choice is unavoidable—fall back on the myth when they criticize "activist" judicial decisions without specifying just *why* a particular "activist" interpretation strikes them as wrong.

Thus the members of the Court themselves occasionally duck responsibility for their substantive decisions about what the Constitution should be taken to mean by shoving the blame—or the credit—onto the document's supposedly plain words or onto the supposedly evident intentions of the people who penned those words two hundred years ago. When Chief Justice Taney declared that blacks were an "inferior class of beings" that could "justly and lawfully be reduced to slavery for the white man's benefit," he claimed that this was not *his* opinion but a conclusion dictated by the language of the Constitution and the obvious intent of the men who wrote it.

But disclaimers that "the Constitution made me do it" are rarely more persuasive than those that blame the devil. When Justice Black refused in 1967 to agree with the majority of the Court in *Katz v. United States* that the Fourth Amendment restricts the government's power to put a tap on your telephone line, it was not because *he* thought that electronic eavesdropping was acceptable, but because the plain language of the Fourth Amendment prohibits only "unreasonable *searches*," not unreasonable *wiretaps*. Naturally, such electronic invasions of privacy were not anticipated by men who knew neither telephones nor tape recorders. Such are the unwholesome fruits of what it sometimes called strict constructionism. Indeed, as the wiretap example suggests, a Constitution frozen in eighteenth-century ice would soon become obsolete; as the centuries pass, and technology changes basic patterns of life, that kind of Constitution would melt into meaningless words signifying nothing.

Not all advocates of primary devotion to the Constitution's literal text or to its authors' historical purpose adhere resolutely to the description of those methods given here. Some searchers after the "original understanding" of the Constitution allow a radical change in circumstances over the last two hundred years to enter into the analysis; and some who seek answers to questions about the Constitution's meaning only among its clauses occasionally give weight to the way that words were used by the Framers, or to the special significance that the law has invested in certain terms. But such exceptions and variations are to no avail because, in the end, the quest for a strict constructionist remains as futile as Diogenes' search for an honest man. The judge capable of fulfilling the duty to make the Constitution meaningful to our lives, and who can accomplish this task by simply "discovering" the meanings that someone else has put there, exists only in myth. Nor does it matter whether we label the preferred method of passive discovery with such law professors' terms as "strict constructionism," "originalism," "literalism," or "mild interpretivism"; a delusion by any other name would sound as hollow. Regardless of how one labels the technique or tries to fine-tune the mechanism, there is simply no getting around the fact that whenever the Supreme Court turns to the Constitution, it must inject a lot of substantive meaning into the words and the structure, and thus the overall message, of that majestic but incomplete document. That there is much a judge could *not* properly do in the document's name is true enough. But that fact should not obscure the wide range of choices that always remain in giving the Constitution contemporary meaning.

It may be that the most subtle danger of nearsighted examination of the Constitution's text or of its authors' intentions is that, by making extremely difficult choices seem easy, such examination stops the judicial inquiry just when it becomes clear that more questions should be asked. Those crucial questions ask both *how* particular legal issues should be resolved and *who* should be trusted to resolve them. The allure of strict constructionism and of those who claim to practice it—their ability to make complicated issues sound simple and tough decisions easy—is precisely what should make us suspicious of it. For it threatens to put us to sleep at the very moments when we must be most alert to the choices that are in fact being made about the Constitution and its impact on our daily lives—choices whose shape is necessarily prefigured by the sorts of men and women we permit our Presidents to place on our nation's highest court.

POINTS TO PONDER

1. According to Tribe, why is strict construction impossible?
2. In Tribe's judgment are there any limits to judicial interpretation?
3. Are Tribe's ideas consistent with those of Hamilton in *Federalist* No. 78?

25

"SPEAKING IN A JUDICIAL VOICE"
Ruth Bader Ginsburg

In this speech delivered in 1993 at the New York University Law School, Justice Ginsburg (before she was nominated to the Supreme Court by President Clinton) criticizes the 1973 Roe v. Wade *decision that invalidated many state laws restricting a woman's right to have an abortion. Her criticisms do not stem from a belief that abortion is wrong, but rather from the scope of the Court's decision. Ginsburg's position on the role of the Supreme Court thus seems to fall between the poles of judicial activism and judicial restraint. According to Ginsburg, the role of the judge is to "persuade, and not to pontificate" and to engage "in a dialogue with, not a diatribe against, co-equal departments of government." Ginsburg's criticisms of* Roe v. Wade *are particularly striking because of her personal conviction that restrictions on abortion violate women's rights and because of her own career in litigating women's rights issues.*

James Madison's forecast still brightens the spirit of federal judges. In his June 1789 speech introducing to Congress the amendments that led to the Bill of Rights, Madison urged:

> [If a Bill of Rights is] incorporated into the [c]onstitution, independent tribunals of justice will consider themselves in a peculiar manner the guardians of those rights; they will be an impenetrable bulwark . . . naturally led to resist every encroachment upon rights . . . stipulated for in the [c]onstitution by the declaration of rights.

Today's independent tribunals of justice are faithful to that "original understanding" when they adhere to traditional ways courts realize the expectation Madison expressed.

In *Federalist* No. 78, Alexander Hamilton said that federal judges, in order to preserve the people's rights and privileges, must have authority to check legislation and acts of the executive for constitutionality. But he qualified his recognition of that awesome authority. The judiciary, Hamilton wrote, from the very nature of its functions, will always be "the least dangerous" branch of government, for judges hold neither the sword nor the purse of the community; ultimately, they must depend upon the political branches to effectuate their judgments. Mindful of that reality, the effective judge, I believe and will explain why in this lecture, will strive to persuade, and not to pontificate. She will speak in "a moderate and restrained" voice, engaging in a dialogue with, not a diatribe against, co-equal departments of government, state authorities, and even her own colleagues.

* * * *

Judges play an interdependent part in our democracy. They do not alone shape legal doctrine but, as I suggested at the outset, they participate in a dialogue with other organs of government, and with the people as well. "[J]udges do and must legislate," Justice Holmes "recognize[d] without hesitation," "but they can do so," he cautioned, "only interstitially"; "they are confined from molar to molecular motions." Measured motions seem to me right, in the main, for constitutional as well as common law adjudication. Doctrinal limbs too swiftly shaped, experience teaches, may prove unstable. The most prominent example in recent decades is Roe v. Wade. To illustrate my point, I have contrasted that breathtaking 1973 decision with the Court's more cautious dispositions, contemporaneously with Roe, in cases involving explicitly sex-based classifications, and will further develop that comparison in this lecture.

The 7–2 judgment in Roe v. Wade declared "violative of the Due Process Clause of the Fourteenth Amendment" a Texas criminal abortion statute that intolerably shackled a woman's autonomy; the Texas law "except[ed] from criminality only a *life-saving* procedure on behalf of the [pregnant woman]." Suppose the Court had stopped there, rightly declaring unconstitutional the most extreme brand of law in the nation, and had not gone on, as the Court did in Roe, to fashion a regime blanketing the subject, a set of rules that displaced virtually every state law then in force? Would there have been the twenty-year controversy we have witnessed, reflected most recently in the Supreme Court's splintered decision in Planned Parenthood v. Casey? A less encompassing Roe, one that merely struck down the extreme Texas law and went no further on that day, I believe and will summarize why, might have served to reduce rather than to fuel controversy.

In the 1992 Planned Parenthood decision, the three controlling Justices accepted as constitutional several restrictions on access to abortion that could not have survived strict adherence to Roe. While those Justices did not closely consider the plight of women without means to overcome the restrictions, they added an important strand to the Court's opinions on abortion—they acknowledged the connection between a woman's "ability to control [her] reproductive li[fe]" and her "ability . . . to participate equally in the economic and social life of the Nation." The idea of the woman in control of her destiny and her place in society was less prominent in the Roe decision itself, which coupled with the rights of the pregnant woman the free exercise of her physician's medical judgment. The Roe decision might have been less of a storm center had it both homed in more precisely on the women's equality dimension of the issue and, correspondingly, attempted nothing more bold at that time than the mode of decisionmaking the Court employed in the 1970s gender classification cases.

In fact, the very term Roe was decided, the Supreme Court had on its calendar a case that could have served as a bridge, linking reproductive choice to disadvantageous treatment of women on the basis of their sex. The case was Struck v. Secretary of Defense; it involved a Captain the Air Force sought to discharge in Vietnam War days. Perhaps it is indulgence in wishful thinking, but the Struck case, I believe, would have proved extraordinarily educational for the Court and had large potential for advancing public understanding. Captain Susan Struck was a career officer. According to her commanding officer, her performance as a manager and nurse was exemplary. Captain Struck had avoided the drugs and the alcohol that hooked many service members in the late 1960s and early 1970s, but she did become pregnant while stationed in Vietnam. She undertook to use, and in fact used, only her accumulated leave time for childbirth. She declared her intention to place, and in fact placed, her child for adoption immediately after birth. Her religious faith precluded recourse to abortion.

Two features of Captain Struck's case are particularly noteworthy. First, the rule she challenged was unequivocal and typical of the time. It provided: "A woman officer will be discharged from the service with the least practicable delay when a determination is made by a medical officer that she is pregnant." To cover any oversight, the Air Force had a back-up rule: "The commission of any woman officer will be terminated with the least practicable delay when it is established that she . . . [h]as given birth to a living child while in a commissioned officer status."

A second striking element of Captain Struck's case was the escape route available to her, which she chose not to take. Air Force regulations current at the start of the 1970s provided: "The Air Force Medical Service is not subject to State laws in the performance of its functions. When medically indicated or for reasons involving medical health, pregnancies may be terminated in Air Force hospitals . . . ideally before 20 weeks gestation."

Captain Struck argued that the unwanted discharge she faced unjustifiably restricted her personal autonomy and dignity; principally, however, she maintained that the regulation mandating her discharge violated the equal protection of the laws guarantee implicit in the Fifth Amendment's due process clause. She urged that the Air Force regime differentiated invidiously by allowing males who became fathers, but not females who became mothers, to remain in service and by allowing women who had undergone abortions but not women who delivered infants to continue their military careers. Her pleas were unsuccessful in the lower courts, but on October 24, 1972, less than three months before the Roe decision, the Supreme Court granted her petition for certiorari.

At that point the Air Force decided it would rather switch than fight. At the end of November 1972, it granted Captain Struck a waiver of the once unwaivable regulation and permitted her to continue her service as an Air Force officer. The Solicitor General promptly and successfully suggested that the case had become moot. Given the parade of cases on the Court's full calendar, it is doubtful that the Justices trained further attention on the Struck scenario. With more time and space for reflection, however, and perhaps a female presence on the court, might the Justices have gained at least these two insights? First, if even the military, an institution not known for avant-garde policy, had taken to providing facilities for abortion, then was not a decision of Roe's muscularity unnecessary? Second, confronted with Captain Struck's unwanted discharge, might the Court have comprehended an argument, or at least glimpsed a reality, it later resisted—that disadvantageous treatment of a woman because of her pregnancy and reproductive choice is a paradigm case of discrimination on the basis of sex? What was the assumption underlying the differential treatment to which Captain Struck was exposed? The regulations that mandated her discharge were not even thinly disguised. They declared, effectively, that responsibility for children disabled female parents, but not male parents, for other work—not for biological reasons, but because society had ordered things that way.

Captain Struck had asked the Court first to apply the highest level of scrutiny to her case, to hold that the sex-based classification she encountered was a "suspect" category for legislative or administrative action. As a fall back, she suggested to the Court an intermediate standard of review, one under which prescriptions that worked to women's disadvantage would gain review of at least heightened, if not the very highest, intensity. In the course of the 1970s, the Supreme Court explicitly acknowledged that it was indeed applying an "intermediate" level of review to classifications it recognized as sex-based. . . .

Until 1971, women did not prevail before the Supreme Court in any case charging unconstitutional sex discrimination. In the years from 1971 to 1982, however, the Court held unconstitutional, as violative of due process or equal protection constraints, a series of state and federal laws that differentiated explicitly on the basis of sex.

The Court ruled in 1973, for example, that married women in the military were entitled to the housing allowance and family medical care benefits that Congress had provided solely for married men in the military. Two years later, the Court held it unconstitutional for a state to allow a parent to stop supporting a daughter once she reached the age of 18, while requiring parental support for a son until he turned 21. In 1975, and again in 1979, the Court declared that state jury-selection systems could not exclude or exempt women as a class. In decisions running from 1975 to 1980, the Court deleted the principal, explicitly sex-based classifications in social insurance and workers' compensation schemes. In 1981, the Court said "nevermore" to a state law designating the husband "head and master" of the household. And in 1982, in an opinion by Justice O'Connor, the Court held that a state could not reserve for women only admission to a state college for nurses.

The backdrop for these rulings was a phenomenal expansion, in the years from 1961 to 1971, of women's employment outside the home, the civil rights movement of the 1960s and the precedents set in that struggle, and a revived feminist movement, fueled abroad and in the United States by Simone de Beauvoir's remarkable 1949 publication, *The Second Sex*. In the main, the Court invalidated laws that had become obsolete, retained into the 1970s by only a few states. In a core set of cases, however, those dealing with social insurance benefits for a worker's spouse or family, the decisions did not utterly condemn the legislature's product. Instead, the Court effectively opened a dialogue with the political branches of government. In essence, the Court instructed Congress and state legislatures to rethink ancient positions on these questions. Where the coordinate branches determined that special treatment for women was warranted, i.e., compensatory legislation because of the entrenched social and economic bias or disadvantages women encounter, the Court left a corridor in which they could still move. But the Court required that classifications be refined, adopted for remedial reasons, and not rooted in prejudice about "the way women (or men) are." In the meantime, the Court's decrees removed no benefits; instead, they extended to a woman worker's husband, widower, or family benefits Congress had authorized only for members of a male worker's family.

The ball, one might say, was tossed by the Justices back into the legislators' court, where the political forces of the day could operate. The Supreme Court wrote modestly, it put forward no grand philosophy; but by requiring legislative reexamination of once customary sex-based classifications, the Court helped to ensure that laws and regulations would "catch up with a changed world."

Roe v. Wade, in contrast, invited no dialogue with legislators. Instead, it seemed entirely to remove the ball from the legislators' court. In 1973, when Roe v. Wade was issued, abortion law was in a state of change across the nation. As the Supreme Court itself noted, there was a marked trend in state legislatures "toward liberalization of abortion statutes." That movement for legislative change ran parallel to another law revision effort then underway—the change from fault to no-fault divorce regimes, a reform that swept through the state legislatures and captured all of them by the mid-1980s.

No measured motion, the Roe decision left virtually no state with laws fully conforming to the Court's delineation of permissible abortion regulation. Around that extraordinary decision, a well-organized and vocal right-to-life movement rallied and succeeded, for a considerable time, in turning the legislative tide in the opposite direction.

Constitutional review by courts is an institution that has been for some two centuries our nation's hallmark and pride. Two extreme modes of court intervention in social change processes, however, have placed stress on the institution. At one extreme, the Supreme Court steps boldly in front of the political process, as some believe it did in Roe v. Wade. At the opposite extreme, the Court in the early part of the twentieth century found—or thrust—itself into the rearguard opposing change, striking down as unconstitutional laws embodying a new philosophy of economic regulation at odds with the nineteenth century's laissez-faire approach. Decisions at both of these poles yielded outcries against the judiciary in certain quarters. The Supreme Court, particularly, was labeled "activist" or "imperial," and its precarious position as final arbiter of constitutional questions was exposed.

I do not suggest that the Court should never step ahead of the political branches in pursuit of a constitutional precept. Brown v. Board of Education, the 1954 decision declaring racial segregation in public schools offensive to the equal protection principle, is the case that best fits the bill. Past the midpoint of the twentieth century, apartheid remained the law-enforced system in several states, shielded by a constitutional interpretation the Court itself advanced at the turn of the century—the separate but equal doctrine.

In contrast to the legislative reform movement in the states, contemporaneous with Roe, widening access to abortion, prospects in 1954 for state legislation dismantling racially segregated schools were bleak. That was so, I believe, for a reason that distances race discrimination from discrimination based on sex. Most women are life partners of men; women bear and raise both sons and daughters. Once women's own consciousness was brought to bear on the unfairness of allocating opportunity and responsibility on the basis of sex, the education of others—of fathers, husbands, and sons as well as daughters—could begin, and could be reinforced at home. When blacks were confined by law to a separate sector, there was no similar prospect for educating the white majority.

It bears emphasis, however, that Brown was not an altogether bold decision. First, Thurgood Marshall and those who worked with him in the campaign against racial injustice carefully set the stepping-stones leading up to the landmark ruling. Pathmarkers of the same kind had not been installed prior to the Court's decision in Roe. Second, Brown launched no broadside attack on the Jim Crow system in all its institutional manifestations. Instead, the Court concentrated on segregated schools; it left the follow-up for other days and future cases. A burgeoning civil rights movement—which Brown helped to propel—culminating in the Civil Rights Act of 1964, set the stage for the Court's ultimate total rejection of Jim Crow legislation.

Significantly, in relation to the point I just made about women and men living together, the end of the Jim Crow era came in 1967, thirteen years after Brown; the case was Loving v. Virginia; the law under attack was a state prohibition on interracial marriage. In holding that law unconstitutional, the Court effectively ruled that with regard to racial classifications, the doctrine of "separate but equal" was dead—everywhere and anywhere within the United States.

The Framers of the Constitution allowed to rest in the Court's hands substantial authority to rule on the Constitution's meaning; but the Framers, as I noted at the outset, armed the Court with no swords to carry out its pronouncements. President Andrew Jackson in 1832, according to an often-told legend, said of a Supreme Court decision he did not like: "The Chief Justice has made his decision, now let him enforce it." With prestige to persuade, but not physical power to enforce, with a will for self-preservation and the knowledge that they are not "a bevy of Platonic Guardians," the Justices generally follow, they do not lead, changes taking place elsewhere in society. But without taking giant strides and thereby risking a backlash too forceful to contain, the Court, through constitutional adjudication, can reinforce or signal a green light for a social change. In most of the post-1970 gender-classification cases, unlike Roe, the Court functioned in just that way. It approved the direction of change through a temperate brand of decisionmaking, one that was not extravagant or divisive. Roe v. Wade, on the other hand, halted a political process that was moving in a reform direction and thereby, I believe, prolonged divisiveness and deferred stable settlement of the issue. The most recent Planned Parenthood decision notably retreats from Roe and further excludes from the High Court's protection women lacking the means or the sophistication to surmount burdensome legislation. The decision may have had the sanguine effect, however, of contributing to the ongoing revitalization in the 1980s and 1990s of the political movement in progress in the early 1970s, a movement that addressed not simply or dominantly the courts but primarily the people's representatives and the people themselves. That renewed force, one may hope, will—within a relatively short span—yield an enduring resolution of this vital matter in a way that affirms the dignity and equality of women.

Conclusion

To sum up what I have tried to convey in this lecture, I will recall counsel my teacher and friend, Professor Gerald Gunther, offered when I was installed as a judge. Professor Gunther had in mind a great jurist, Judge Learned Hand, whose biography Professor Gunther is just now completing. The good judge, Professor Gunther said, is "openminded and detached, . . . heedful of limitations stemming from the judge's own competence and, above all, from the presuppositions of our constitutional scheme; th[at] judge[s] . . . recognize[s] that a felt need to act only interstitially does not mean relegation of judges to a trivial or mechanical role, but rather affords the most responsible room for creative, important judicial contributions."

POINTS TO PONDER

1. Why does Justice Ginsburg criticize the *Roe v. Wade* decision?
2. How can you square her criticism of *Roe v. Wade* with her personal political opinion that a woman ought to have the right to decide whether to have an abortion?
3. Place Bork, Tribe, and Ginsburg along a spectrum of judicial restraint and activism. Where do they fall in relation to each other?

26

"THE SUPREME COURT: FROM WARREN TO BURGER TO REHNQUIST"
David M. O'Brien

Change on the Supreme Court usually comes slowly as prevailing political coalitions and public opinion shift and as the membership of the Court alters when presidents fill vacancies. In this selection David O'Brien, a political scientist at the University of Virginia, traces the change in the Supreme Court from the liberal era and egalitarian jurisprudence of Chief Justice Earl Warren (1953–1969) to the beginnings of the Rehnquist Court (1987–   ). He argues in this 1987 Political Science article that Chief Justice Warren Burger (1969–1986), though a conservative, did not reverse the major direction of the Warren era. He further argues that Rehnquist, with his conserva-

tive ally Antonin Scalia, has the potential to forge a conservative majority on the Court over the longer term, but that opportunity will be affected by the addition of Justices David Souter, Clarence Thomas, and Ruth Bader Ginsburg.

Changes in the composition of the Supreme Court perhaps inevitably invite speculation about whether and how the Court will change, and what direction it will take in the future. The move of William Rehnquist from associate justice to chief justice and the addition of Antonin Scalia certainly alters the chemistry of the Court. These changes may also have a profound impact on the Court's place in American government during the rest of this century.

There is no doubt that the court will change. Differences are already apparent during oral arguments. Rehnquist is sharper, more thoughtful, more commanding and wittier than his predecessor in the center chair. And from the far right of the bench, Scalia almost bubbles over with energy and questions for counsel. No less revealing is that in the week before the start of the 1986–87 term on the first Monday in October, Rehnquist managed to get the justices to dispose of over 1,000 cases (granting 22 and denying or otherwise disposing of the rest). He did so in only two days, whereas it usually took Burger more than twice as long to get through about the same number.

It nevertheless seems fair to say that we will not see an abrupt break with past rulings, in the near term at least. There is likely to be more of the same— more continuity than change in developing constitutional law. On the major controversial issues, the Court is likely to remain as in the past five years divided 6–3 or 5–4. Whether the Court makes a sharp turn to the right, as those in the Reagan administration anticipate, depends not only on the leadership skills of our 16th chief justice and our 103rd justice, but on which and when one or two more seats become vacant.

The Supreme Court, of course, in a sense is always in transition. Within the marble temple, the justices are a close-knit group whose personal relations evolve and change. The docket each year brings new cases, affording fresh perspectives on old problems and opportunities for further reflection and negotiations. And the law clerks come and go, even if the justices remain the same.

From a broader political perspective, the Court swings back and forth with the country—much like a pendulum on a clock. For most of our history, the Court has been in step with major political movements, except during transitional periods or critical elections. The swing of electoral politics—through the power of presidential appointment—controls the composition of the bench and may temper the speed, if not shift the direction, of the Court. Public opinion also touches the justices' lives and may serve to curb them when they threaten to go too far or too fast in their rulings. But changes in the direction of the Court are ultimately moderated by its functioning as a collegial body, in which all nine justices share power and compete for influence.

The Court thus generally shifts direction gradually—on a piecemeal basis, incorporating and accommodating the views of new appointees. There are times, to be sure, when the Court makes rather sharp breaks with the past and charts a new course in constitutional law. This occurred in 1937 during the battle over FDR's "court-packing plan," and then again during the latter years of the Warren Court. The future of the Rehnquist Court, I will argue, holds the potential for as great a change, and perhaps for greater change than at any other time in the recent past. This is clear from the history of the Warren and Burger Courts and how the Rehnquist Court could differ.

The House That the Warren Court Built

The Warren Court (1953–1969) revolutionized constitutional law and American society. First, the unanimous and watershed school desegregation ruling, *Brown v. Board of Education*, in 1954 at the end of Warren's first year on the bench. Then, in 1962 *Baker v. Carr* announced the "reapportionment revolution" guaranteeing equal voting rights. And throughout the 1960s, the Court handed down a series of rulings on criminal procedure that extended the rights of the accused and sought to ensure equal access to justice for the poor. *Mapp v. Ohio* (1961), extending the exclusionary rule to the states, and *Miranda v. Arizona* (1966), sharply limiting police interrogation of criminal suspects, continue to symbolize the Warren Court's revolution in criminal justice.

These rulings became identified with an "egalitarian jurisprudence" that indelibly marks an era in the Court's history and elevated Warren above the ranks of most justices and to the status of one of our "great chief justices." The record of Warren and his Court remains, of course, riddled with irony and controversy. But, Warren did ultimately take command of his Court. Whether they agreed with him or not, as Justice Potter Stewart put it, "We all loved him." A big bear of a man with great personal charm, a real politician, he had the interest and capacity to lead the Court. Though by no means a legal scholar, he grew intellectually with the chief justiceship and won the Court over to his concern with basic principles of equality and fairness.

Still, like other chief justices, Warren could not lead until the others were willing to follow. Change comes slowly to the Court and we tend to forget that a chief justice is only first among equals. Even the force of a powerful intellect or personality may not overcome this basic fact of life in the marble temple.

The unanimity of *Brown v. Board of Education* tends to overshadow the fact that the "Warren Court" did not emerge for almost another decade. During that time in case after case involving criminal procedure, for example, Warren frequently found himself in dissent, along with liberal Justices Hugo Black, William O. Douglas and, after 1956 his close friend and advisor, Justice William J. Brennan, Jr. Justices Felix Frankfurter and John Harlan, apostles of judicial self-restraint, tended to hold sway over, if only to moderate at times, the brethren.

Not until the appointment of Justice Arthur Goldberg in 1962, and later those of Abe Fortas and Thurgood Marshall, was there a critical mass to support a liberal-egalitarian philosophy that placed individual rights above states' rights and boldly challenged the political process. The Warren Court then rather quickly forged new law with a rather broad brush, seeking "bright lines" when limiting the coercive powers of government, ensuring principles of equality, and opening up the electoral process.

The directions in which the Warren Court pushed the country remain controversial. Republican President Dwight Eisenhower himself later regretted his appointment of Warren as "the biggest damn-fool mistake" he ever made. From public opposition and campaigns to "Impeach Earl Warren," Vice President Richard Nixon eventually forged a successful 1968 presidential campaign based on the theme of returning "law and order" to the country. He promised to appoint "strict constructionists" and advocates of judicial self-restraint who would resurrect a Frankfurterian view of the role of the Court.

Interior Redecorating and Minor Remodeling: The Burger Court Years

With his four appointments, Nixon achieved remarkable success in remolding the Court; if not in his own image, then in the ghost of Justice Frankfurter. Burger came to the Court with the agenda of reversing the "liberal-egalitarian jurisprudence" of the Warren Court. The era of the Warren Court came to an end. But, it left behind a series of landmark rulings that profoundly changed our constitutional landscape and a legacy that the Burger Court would not undo or overshadow.

As chief justice, Burger proved a considerable disappointment for conservatives. For one thing, though a devoted Republican, he came from the liberal wing of the party, in the mold of fellow-Minnesotan Harold Stassen. Quite simply, he proved too moderate for California Republicans like Nixon and Reagan.

Even more troubling was that Burger could not lead the Court intellectually. More of a lawyer than Warren, he was by no means a legal scholar and lacked a well-developed judicial philosophy. As one of his colleagues on the Court observed, Burger does not have a "legal mind" or a "taste for the law" outside of the area of criminal procedure. Rather than a coherent judicial philosophy, Burger tended to take positions on various issues on a case-by-case basis.

Moreover, he lacked the charisma of Warren and the demeanor and sharpness of mind of Chief Justice Charles Evans Hughes. With personal charm and a sense of humor, but also a temper, Burger did about all he could to promote collegial relations within the Court. Yet, his lack of precision in directing conference discussions occasionally led to confusion and frequently failed to flush out differences among the justices that needed to be hammered out. While this enhanced Burger's power in assigning opinions, and permitted him to later switch his votes, it troubled the brethren. Ironically, in spite of his interest in court management and basically managerial approach, Burger's personality and style was such that he had a hard time delegating responsibility and compromising with others. In the end, he was more interested (and his great accomplishments lie) in improving the administration of federal and state courts. Burger presided over the Court's functions, but did not lead the Court.

For the most part, centrists on the Court held sway. Eisenhower-appointee Potter Stewart, Kennedy-appointee Byron White, and Nixon-appointee Lewis F. Powell, Jr., in one way or another had all been touched by Frankfurter's philosophy of judicial self-restraint. And they provided the swing votes and moderating influence on the Burger Court.

More independent and less team players than some of the others are Justices Harry Blackmun and John Paul Stevens. Blackmun came to the Court as "the most conservative judge from the most conservative court of appeals in the country," at the urging of his high school buddy, Chief Justice Burger. He remains perhaps the hardest working, most self-consciously brooding justice, and perhaps Nixon's biggest disappointment. In his first years he voted almost 90 percent of the time with Burger but, after writing the abortion opinion in *Roe v. Wade* (1973), he has come to vote over 70 percent of the time with the liberal wing of the Court: Justices Brennan and Marshall. Likewise, Stevens, an appointee of President Gerald Ford in 1975, has demonstrated strong independent judgment. He considers himself a judicial conservative but without the political agenda of Nixon and Reagan appointees.

So it fell to Rehnquist to stake out the Court's conservative philosophy. He came to the Court in 1971 from the Department of Justice in the Nixon administration, though he had established his own conservative credentials years earlier. On the Court, he did not just stand his ground. Rehnquist articulated a consistent and well-developed judicial philosophy that turned out to be more compatible with the Reagan administration than that of Reagan's first appointee, Justice O'Connor (who was also considered for the post of chief justice, but had angered conservatives with her opinions on school prayer, libel, and affirmative action).

During Burger's tenure, the Court thus pretty much went its own way, pulled in different directions on different issues by either its most liberal or most conservative justices. There was no "constitutional counter-revolution" during the Burger Court, as some had predicted. Instead of a transformation, there were only modest "adjustments," as Burger noted when announcing his resignation. From the perspective of the Reagan administration, the Court headed by Burger accomplished little; it eschewed "bright lines" but lacked clear direction and appeared to drift from case to case.

In the final analysis, the Burger Court was one of transition, moderation, and self-restraint: a troubled and fragmented Court in the image of Felix Frankfurter. The legacy of the Burger Court (from 1969 to 1986) is likely to amount to little more than that of "a transitional Court": A Court divided between what the Warren Court accomplished and what the Rehnquist Court achieves and leaves behind. While the Court headed by Chief Justice Burger broke some new ground (as in tackling the problems of affirmative action and reverse discrimination), by and large it confined itself to minor remodeling—with a few new additions (as with the ruling on abortion)—in the house built by the Warren Court.

From Minor to Major Remodeling? The Rehnquist Court

By contrast, the Court that potentially could take shape under Chief Justice Rehnquist could be self-confident, relaxed, and decidedly more conservative. This is already evident in the atmosphere of the courtroom. In the long run, much depends on Rehnquist's willingness to compromise in order to bring others along without reinforcing past divisions among the brethren, or sacrificing his own well-developed judicial philosophy; and, again, on when the Court's composition changes again.

Where a Rehnquist Court ultimately goes is necessarily a matter of speculation. That is no reason, however tempting, to conclude that there will not be changes or that they won't matter. Rehnquist has already proved to be quite a different chief justice and the Court will be different with Scalia. Both are more conservative and ideologically committed than Burger. Recent trends in the rightward direction will certainly continue.

How the Court May Change Under Chief Justice Rehnquist

Unlike Burger, Rehnquist has the intellectual and temperamental wherewithal to be a leader. He is a shrewdly articulate advocate of his views, who also has the sense of humor of a practical joker—and this is readily apparent during oral arguments, despite the quite different impression he gave during his confirmation hearings.

Even liberals on the Court think he will make a "splendid" chief justice. This is largely because Burger was not equipped to lead. His presentation of cases at conference was poor, votes all-too-tentative, and virtually everything turned on how opinions were written. As chief justice, he had the power—when in the majority at conference—to assign opinions for the Court. This allowed Burger to control over 90 percent of all assigned opinions, even though he would subsequently change his views and even votes. Other justices were understandably angered. Rehnquist will be more candid and firm when discussing and voting on cases.

Even if conferences improve under Rehnquist, he must still mass a majority. In a good number of areas he can count on Justices Byron White, Sandra Day O'Connor and Scalia. White may align himself even more often with Rehnquist than did Burger, while O'Connor may well continue down a path toward greater independence and moderation. To pick up one more vote, Rehnquist may moderate some views and exercise the power of assigning opinions in strategic ways. This will test Rehnquist's willingness and ability to compromise—traits rarely shown in the past. When staking out his often extreme positions as an associate justice, he wrote more solo dissents (54) on a broader range of issues than any of his colleagues.

Depending on the issues, Justices Stevens or Blackmun might swing over, but they have been increasingly inclined to align with the liberal wing: Justices Brennan and Thurgood Marshall. That leaves Lewis F. Powell, Jr. at the fulcrum of power in the near term. As a centrist, his vote will prove even more crucial than in the past. Last term, for example, the justices divided five-to-four in 46 cases. (In 35 cases there was a sharp 5–4 split and in another 11 cases four justices wrote separately to reject the majority's rationale.) Powell was most often in the majority (35 times), with the conservative wing winning about three times as often as the liberals. But Powell is an independent and pragmatic jurist who believes in precedent and self-restraint. He remains pivotal in upholding the Court's abortion decision and to rulings in a number of other areas as well.

In What Ways May the Court Change?

The most important change may bear on which cases are granted review. The cornerstone of the Court's operation is the power to decide what to decide. Over 5,000 cases annually arrive, yet only about 170 are given full consideration—oral argument and decision by written opinion.

The power to deny cases enables more than managing a heavy caseload. It is the power to set the Court's substantive agenda as well. Ideological differences inevitably come to play. Indeed, setting the agenda is the first battleground in the war over the direction of the Court.

The importance of ideological changes in the Court's composition is clear. The Warren Court took a large number of cases involving the rights of the accused in order to extend the guarantees of the Bill of Rights to individuals in state as well as federal courts. By contrast, the Burger Court increasingly selected cases so as to cut back, if not reverse, the direction in which the Warren Court pushed constitutional law.

That and other trends are certain to continue with the Rehnquist Court. In recent years the Court has taken cases involving the rights of the accused at the behest of the government, rather than at the request of individuals challenging governmental action. Whereas the Warren Court was sympathetic to cases brought by indigents, the Burger Court became more and more hostile to their claims. In 1969–1972, 30 such cases were granted on average each term. After

Nixon's last two appointments, the average dropped to 16 during 1972–1980. Since Reagan's naming of O'Connor in 1981, the number further dropped to 13 cases per term.

When ruling on claims of individual rights, the Burger Court was generally inhospitable. The Warren Court sided with the individual against the government 66 percent of the time, while the Burger Court only 44 percent. The percentage could well drop further with Rehnquist, whose record of voting for the government is unsurpassed.

As chief justice, Rehnquist has a greater role in structuring the Court's agenda. And he will have more interest and success in doing so than Burger. In addition, the way in which cases are granted could work to his advantage as well.

Prior to each weekly conference, the chief justice circulates two lists of cases that establish the basis for conference discussions. On the first—the Discuss List—are those few deemed worthy of conference time. Attached is a second much longer list—the Dead List—containing those considered too unworthy, and which are simply denied. Any justice may request a case be put on the conference agenda. But the justices no longer individually review every case. They all delegate initial screening of cases to law clerks, who write memos recommending action on each case. Brennan, Marshall and Stevens have each of their clerks screen cases. The others—including, notably, all the conservatives—share memos prepared by a pool of their 23 clerks. With the benefit of those memos and the first crack at putting a limited number of cases on the Discuss List, Rehnquist could not be better positioned to get consideration of the cases he wants reviewed.

What happens at conference determines which cases are granted. As chief justice, Rehnquist has the opportunity to lead discussions. But no less crucial is how the justices vote to grant cases review. Cases are granted on the vote of only four justices, even though in all other respects majority rules. This so-called informal "rule of four" was adopted over 60 years ago, in order to cut back on the workload while allowing review of cases that some justices feel especially strongly about.

The rule of four takes on greater significance with ideological realignments within the Court. In the early years of the Burger Court, for example, less than 20 percent of the cases granted were on the basis of only four votes, but in recent years as many as 30 percent were selected that way. When there were only four votes for taking a case, they often came from those who pool their clerks and share the same ideological orientation. Rehnquist, along with Scalia, O'Connor and White, are now in a position to dictate the Court's agenda.

The advantages of the chief justiceship and the rule of four give greater weight to Rehnquist's personal skills in getting the Court to adopt his agenda. In the short run he may not always have the final say on the outcome of those cases granted review. But controlling the court's agenda is the first step in altering the direction of the Court and redefining its role in American society.

Some recent trends will be perpetuated. In addition to being unsympathetic to claims of the poor and more favorably disposed to the government, the Rehnquist Court will likely take more cases involving federalism and separation of powers. In the area of criminal justice, prominent issues will revolve around fair trial procedures, double jeopardy, and others bearing on the factual guilt of the accused—such as whether a "harmless error" occurred in prosecution and conviction. The Fourth and Fifth Amendments will increasingly be viewed in a dim light. When cases raising these claims are taken, especially those involving the "exclusionary rule" and *Miranda*, the aim will be to carve out exceptions or to cut back on Warren Court rulings expanding those guarantees. Other civil rights cases will tend to fall in the areas of freedom of speech and the electoral process, governmental liability, abortion and reverse discrimination.

What Justice Scalia Adds to the Chemistry of the Court

For the Court to shift direction in the short run at least, it may well fall to Scalia to move Justices Lewis Powell and Byron White—the centrists—and forge a majority with Rehnquist and O'Connor. And, given the way the Court works, Scalia's personal style and skills will prove as important as his judicial philosophy.

Next to Rehnquist and fellow appellate court judge Robert Bork, no other legal scholar has been as close to the Reagan "inner circle" or had as much influence in shaping the judicial and political agenda of the administration. With his energy and comparative youth (at age 50), Scalia will be able to continue this agenda long after Reagan has left office.

Ideology and judicial philosophy, however, is not all that the administration is banking on. By naming the first Italian Catholic, the religious right wing may be appeased and an appeal made to ethnic voters, in the same way that O'Connor was a gesture to women. But, even more importantly, Scalia enjoys a reputation as a team player and consensus builder. And, his personal skills are what the Reagan administration is really betting on.

"Nino," as he is known to his family and friends, is highly sociable, hardworking and profoundly conservative. He brings a good deal of color to the Court with his quick wit, a street-wise sense about him, and the kind of engaging and incisive mind that one finds among New York intellectuals.

More than charm and conviviality, however, will be needed to win others over. Whether Scalia proves successful depends on his willingness to compromise and accommodate others. Rehnquist has often preferred to stand alone. Scalia is more open-minded to the extent that he enjoys kibbitzing and debating. But, once he has decided, he also tends to give no quarter and to stubbornly hold fast—earning him yet another nickname, "Ninopath," on the Court of Appeals for the District of Columbia Circuit. Whether Scalia is willing to temper his language—and often condescending and even sarcastic, tone—as well as bend on some of his hard line views remains to be seen.

These personal skills and Scalia's own judicial and political philosophy should not be underestimated. It is tempting to say, for instance, that Burger is simply being replaced by Scalia—one conservative vote for another—and so not much will change. In the 35 cases that the justices divided 5 to 4 last term, if Scalia instead of Burger had been on the Court, the outcome of only one case might have been changed. That was *Goldman v. Weinberger* (1986) in which Burger sided with Rehnquist in holding that an Orthodox Jewish captain in the Air Force could be forbidden from wearing a yarmulke while on duty; whereas, on the appellate court Scalia indicated that he leaned the other way.

Over the years, Scalia has developed a homespun but trenchant philosophy of aggressive judicial conservatism that distinguishes him from Burger and endeared him to the Reagan administration: a limited view of freedom of expression; antagonism toward affirmative action and the "liberal jurisprudence" that undergirds past judicial activism; a corresponding deference to broad presidential power and control; as well as a respect for a rigid separation of powers, and for limited governmental intervention into the economy based on free-market capitalism.

His views on the First Amendment, for example, are so extreme that conservative columnist William Safire calls him "the worst enemy of free speech in America today." He not only favors making it easier to win libel awards, but cutting back protection for picketing, demonstrations and other forms of "symbolic speech." Constitutional law in the last 50 years simply got it all wrong, according to Scalia. Nor is the Freedom of Information Act spared his ascerbic pen. Too much data is released to the public and, in his view, the Act "is the Taj Mahal of the Doctrine of Unanticipated Consequences, the Sistine Chapel of Cost-Benefit Analysis Ignored."

Even Rehnquist appears more moderate on some issues of civil rights. "Without question," he observed last term in *Meritor Savings Bank v. Vinson* (1986), "when a supervisor sexually harrasses [*sic*] a subordinate because of the subordinate's sex, that supervisor 'discriminates' on the basis of sex." By contrast, in that same case in the lower court, Scalia sided with Judge Robert Bork in rejecting the claim and stressing "the awkwardness of classifying sexual advances as 'discrimination.'"

Although Scalia will prove a powerful ally of Rehnquist and O'Connor, he is not as taken by the latter's brand of judicial self-restraint based on "strict constructionism" and pays less deference to states' rights. He is certainly more aggressive and ideologically committed than Burger.

Much will thus depend on whether Scalia changes and how he adapts to his new responsibilities on the highest court in the land. If he helps forge a majority with the centrists during conferences, the new chief justice will be in a position to assign opinions for the Court. Otherwise, the balance could tip at conference, giving senior Associate Justice Brennan the power to assign opinions. Even if Rehnquist has the opportunity to assign opinions, Justices Powell, White or O'Connor—all respected, more experienced and more moderate conservatives than Scalia—could still take the lead in opinion writing. Certainly, when writing opinions, Rehnquist and Scalia may have to moderate some of their views in order to hang on to a majority.

To capture and hold the centrists on the Court, Rehnquist and Scalia must match wit and wisdom with that of the old consensus builder, Justice Brennan. Scalia's personal style and approach is more closely matched to that of Brennan than any of the others, and this is what makes him so formidable in the long run. Though one is a conservative Italian Catholic and the other a liberal Irish Catholic, both are sons of immigrants, students of the art of politics who work well and wear well with others, and know how to shape opinions and forge coalitions. Still, Scalia's ideological fervor and energy may well initially limit his ability to compromise, whereas Brennan has proven over the years that he knows how to both sway and yield so as to consolidate power and maintain his principles. The challenge for Scalia will be to master Brennan's style and approach without sacrificing his own agenda.

Conclusion

Whether and how far the Rehnquist Court carries forth the "Reagan revolution" in dismantling the house built by the Warren Court, and in charting a truly new course in constitutional law, ultimately turns on the competition for influence among the justices and whether President Reagan has the opportunity to pack the Court with still more "true believers."

The Court is likely, in the near term at least, to continue down the paths trod by the Burger Court—no sharp change in direction, though perhaps a slightly more conservative tone in its rulings. In the long run, however, the Rehnquist Court could set its agenda so as to redefine radically its institutional role, and this is precisely what the Reagan administration hopes and why it was so meticulous in moving Rehnquist to the center chair and elevating Scalia.

How might the Rehnquist Court redefine its institutional role in the long run as envisioned by those in the Reagan administration? In the last 50 years, the Court has stood as guardian of individual rights. The Warren Court, in particular, forged an egalitarian revolution that opened up the democratic process, strengthened the rights of the accused, and sought to safeguard the rights of minorities. By contrast, the Rehnquist Court would no longer look to the vindication of civil liberties and civil rights, but instead to the arbitration of political disputes between the President and Congress and between federal and state governments. The Court's agenda would expand governmental power over claims of individual rights, enlarge presidential power at the expense of Congress, and at the same time elevate states' rights above that of federal legislation.

Whether and how much and fast the Supreme Court changes remains to be seen. But the Court will certainly change under Chief Justice Rehnquist and the direction of that change will not be toward more self-restraint. The trend toward judicial activism will continue but may well push, as the Reagan administration anticipates, in a counter-revolutionary and reactionary direction—toward reclaiming constitutional values that were overshadowed by the revolutions forged by the Warren Court and preserved during the Burger Court years. Still, whether and how far the Rehnquist Court goes down this road depends on when and which seats on the high bench become vacant and whether Reagan or some other (Republican or Democratic) President has the opportunity to fill those seats.

POINTS TO PONDER

1. What was "liberal" or "egalitarian" about the jurisprudence of Chief Justice Earl Warren?
2. According to O'Brien, what is the role of the chief justice and how influential is the chief justice in the overall direction of the Court?
3. Within the confines of *stare decisis*, how much leeway does the Supreme Court have to change policy direction?

27

"PRESIDENTIAL APPOINTMENTS: THE MIXED RECORD OF COURT PACKING"

William H. Rehnquist

In his first term in office Franklin Roosevelt had been frustrated by a Supreme Court that declared a number of New Deal laws unconstitutional because the laws overstepped congressional authority to regulate business. After his landslide reelection in 1936, Roosevelt proposed to Congress that the president be allowed to appoint a new justice to the Supreme Court for each justice over the age of 70. There were six sitting justices over 70 and, if passed, the law would have given Roosevelt a majority of justices sympathetic to his programs. The proposal was rejected by Congress and seen by many in the country as a power grab.

Chief Justice William Rehnquist notes in the following selection from his book The Supreme Court *(1987) that a little patience would have saved Roosevelt the embarrassment of the defeat of his plan in Congress, for in the natural course of events FDR got to appoint six of the nine justices to the Court. Rehnquist goes on to analyze the success of presidents in appointing justices who agree with their own political philosophies. He concludes that predicting judicial behavior on the bench is uncertain, and presents some historical examples of presidents who have been surprised or dismayed at the judicial behavior of their Supreme Court appointees.*

Had Franklin Roosevelt only been more patient—had he but recognized the great wisdom in Henry Ashurst's advice to him—"Time is on your side; *anno domini* is your invincible ally"—he could have avoided the defeat for himself personally and for the Democratic party when the Senate rejected his Court-packing plan, and still have accomplished his goal. Before elaborating on this point, it may be well to define the use of the word *pack*, which seems to me the best verb available for the activity involved despite its highly pejorative connotation. It need not have such a connotation when used in this context; the second edition of Webster's unabridged dictionary defines the verb *pack* as "to choose or arrange (a jury, committee, etc.) in such a way as to secure some advantage, or to favor some particular side or interest." Thus a president who sets out to pack the Court does nothing more than seek to appoint people to the Court who are sympathetic to his political or philosophical principles.

There is no reason in the world why a president should not do this. One of the many marks of genius that our Constitution bears is the fine balance struck in the establishment of the judicial branch, avoiding subservience to the supposedly more vigorous legislative and executive branches on the one hand, and avoiding total institutional isolation from public opinion on the other. The performance of the judicial branch of the United States government for a period of nearly two hundred years has shown it to be remarkably independent of the other coordinate branches of that government. Yet the institution has been constructed in such a way that due to the mortality tables, if nothing else, the public will in the person of the president of the United States—the one official who is elected by the entire nation—have something to say about the membership of the Court, and thereby indirectly about its decisions.

Surely we would not want it any other way. We want our federal courts, and particularly the Supreme Court, to be independent of popular opinion when deciding the particular cases or controversies that come before them. The provision for tenure during good behavior and the prohibition against diminution of compensation have proved more than adequate to secure that sort of independence. The result is that judges are responsible to no electorate or constituency. But the manifold provisions of the Constitution with which judges must deal are by no means crystal clear in their import, and reasonable minds may differ as to which interpretation is proper. When a vacancy occurs on the Court, it is entirely appropriate that that vacancy be filled by the president, responsible to a national constituency, as advised by the Senate, whose members are responsible to regional constituencies. Thus, public opinion has some say in who shall become judges of the Supreme Court.

Whether or not it is, as I contend, both normal and desirable for presidents to attempt to pack the Court, the fact is that presidents who have been sensible of the broad powers they have possessed, and have been willing to exercise those powers, have all but invariably tried to have some influence on the philosophy of the Court as a result of their appointments to that body. Whether or not they have been successful in their attempts to pack the Court is a more difficult question. I think history teaches us that those who have tried have been at least partially successful, but that a number of factors militate against a president's having anything more than partial success. What these factors are can best be illustrated with examples from the history of presidential appointments to the Court.

Very early in the history of the Court, Justice William Cushing, "a sturdy Federalist and follower of Marshall" died in September 1810. His death reduced the seven-member Court to six, evenly divided between Federalist appointees and Republican appointees. Shortly after Cushing's death, Thomas Jefferson, two years out of office as president, wrote to his former secretary of the treasury, Albert Gallatin, in these unseemingly gleeful words:

> I observe old Cushing is dead. At length, then, we have a chance of getting a Republican majority in the Supreme Judiciary. For ten years has that branch braved the spirit and will of the nation. . . . The event is a fortunate one, and so timed as to be a godsend to me.

Jefferson, of course, had been succeeded by James Madison, who, though perhaps less ardently than Jefferson, also championed Republican ideals. Jefferson wrote Madison, "It will be difficult to find a character of firmness enough to preserve his independence on the same Bench with Marshall." When he heard that Madison was considering Joseph Story and Ezekiel Bacon, then chairman of the Ways and Means Committee of the House of Representatives, he admonished Madison that "Story and Bacon are exactly the men who deserted us [on the Embargo Act]. The former unquestionably a Tory, and both are too young."

President Madison seems to have been "snakebit" in his effort to fill the Cushing vacancy. He first nominated his attorney general, Levi Lincoln, who insisted that he did not want the job and after the Senate confirmed him still refused to serve. Madison then nominated a complete dark horse, one Alexander Wolcott, the federal revenue collector of Connecticut, whom the Senate rejected by the mortifying vote of 24 to 9. Finally, in the midst of a Cabinet crisis that occupied a good deal of his time, Madison nominated Joseph Story for the Cushing vacancy, and the Senate confirmed him as a matter of routine three days later. Story, of course, fulfilled Jefferson's worst expectations about him. He became Chief Justice John Marshall's principal ally on the great legal issues of the day in the Supreme Court, repeatedly casting his vote in favor of national power and against the restrictive interpretation of the Constitution urged by Jefferson and his states' rights school. And

Joseph Story served on the Supreme Court for thirty-four years, one of the longest tenures on record.

Presidents who wish to pack the Supreme Court, like murder suspects in a detective novel, must have both motive and opportunity. Here Madison had both, and yet he failed. He was probably a considerably less partisan chief executive than was Jefferson, and so his motivation was perhaps not strong enough. After having botched several opportunities, he finally preferred to nominate someone who would not precipitate another crisis in his relations with the Senate, rather than insisting on a nominee who had the right philosophical credentials. The lesson, I suppose, that can be drawn from this incident is that while for Court-watchers the president's use of his appointment power to nominate people for vacancies on the Supreme Court is the most important use he makes of the executive authority, for the president himself, the filling of Supreme Court vacancies is just one of many acts going on under the "big top" of his administration.

John Marshall was not the only member of the Court to have been appointed in the more than usually partisan atmosphere of a lame-duck presidential administration. In 1840, after the "hard cider and log cabin" campaign, William Henry Harrison, the Whig candidate for president, was elected over Martin Van Buren, the Democratic incumbent. Little more than a week before Harrison would take his oath on March 4, 1841, Justice Phillip Pendleton Barbour of Virginia died suddenly. Two days after Barbour's death Van Buren appointed Peter V. Daniel to be associate justice of the Supreme Court of the United States. A few days later, Martin Van Buren described in a letter to Andrew Jackson, his mentor and predecessor, the appointment of Daniel: "I had an opportunity to put a man on the bench of the Supreme Court at the moment of leaving the government who will I am sure stick to the true principles of the Constitution, and being a Democrat *ab ovo* is not in so much danger of a falling off in the true spirit."

After frantic last-minute maneuvering between the Whig and Democrat factions in the Senate, Daniel was confirmed, and remained an ardent—nay, obdurate—champion of states' rights until his death in 1860.

Abraham Lincoln had inveighed against the Supreme Court's 1857 decision in the *Dred Scott* case during his famous debates with Stephen A. Douglas in 1858 when both sought to be elected United States senator from Illinois. Lincoln lost that election, but his successful presidential campaign two years later was likewise marked by a restrained but nonetheless forceful attack on this decision and by implication on the Court's apparent institutional bias in favor of slaveholders. Within two months of his inauguration, by reason of the death of one justice and the resignation of two others, Lincoln was given three vacancies on the Supreme Court. To fill them he chose Noah Swayne of Ohio, David Davis of Illinois, and Samuel F. Miller of Iowa. All were Republicans who had rendered some help in getting Lincoln elected President in 1860; indeed, Davis had been one of Lincoln's principal managers at the Chicago Convention of the Republican party.

In 1863, by reason of expansion in the membership of the Court, Lincoln was enabled to name still another justice, and he chose Stephen J. Field of California, a War Democrat who had been the chief justice of that state's supreme court. In 1864, Chief Justice Roger B. Taney finally died at the age of eighty-eight, and Lincoln had an opportunity to choose a new chief justice.

At this time, in the fall of 1864, the constitutionality of the so-called "greenback legislation," which the government had used to finance the war effort, was headed for a Court test, and Lincoln was very much aware of this fact. He decided to appoint his secretary of the treasury, Salmon P. Chase, who was in many respects the architect of the greenback legislation, saying to a confidant, "We wish for a Chief Justice who will sustain what has been done in regard to emancipation and the legal tenders. We cannot ask a man what he will do, and if we should, and he should answer us, we should despise him for it. Therefore, we must take a man whose opinions are known" (2 Warren 401).

In all, then, Lincoln had five appointments. How successful was Lincoln at packing the Court with these appointments? The answer has to be, I believe, that he was very successful at first. In the all-important *Prize Cases*, 2 Black 635 (1863), decided in 1863, the three Lincoln appointees already on the Court—Swayne, Miller, and Davis, joined with Justices Wayne and Grier of the Old Court to make up the majority, while Chief Justice Taney and Justices Nelson, Catron, and Clifford dissented. It seems obvious that this case would have been decided the other way had the same justices been on the Court who had decided the *Dred Scott* case six years earlier. Charles Warren, in his *The Supreme Court in United States History*, describes these cases as being not only "the first cases arriving out of the Civil War to be decided by [the Court], but they were far more momentous in the issue involved than any other case; and their final determination favorable to the government's contention was almost a necessary factor in the suppression of the war."

But immediately after the war, a host of new issues arose which could not really have been foreseen at the time Lincoln made his first appointments to the Supreme Court. The extent to which military tribunals might displace civil courts during time of war or insurrection was decided by the Supreme Court in 1866 in the famous case of *Ex Parte Milligan*, 4 Wall. 2. While the Court was unanimous as to one aspect of this case, it divided 5 to 4 on the equally important question of whether Congress might provide for trial by military commissions during time of insurrection even though the president alone could not. On the latter question, the Lincoln appointees divided two to three.

During the postwar Reconstruction Era, three new amendments to the United States Constitution were promulgated, and the construction of those amendments was also necessarily on the agenda of the Supreme Court. The first important case involving the Fourteenth Amendment to come before the Court was that of the Slaughterhouse Cases, in which the applicability of the provisions of that amendment to claims not based on racial discrimination was taken up by the Court. Of the Lincoln appointees, Justice Miller wrote the majority opinion and was joined in it by Justice Davis, while Chief Justice Chase and Justices Field and Swayne were in dissent.

The ultimate irony in Lincoln's effort to pack the court was the Court's first decision in the so-called Legal Tender Cases, *Hepburn v. Griswold*, 8 Wall. 603. In 1870 the Court held, in an opinion by Chief Justice Chase, who had been named Chief Justice by Lincoln primarily for the purposes of upholding the greenback legislation, that this legislation was unconstitutional. Justice Field joined the opinion of the Chief Justice, while the other three Lincoln appointees—Miller, Swayne, and Davis—dissented. Chief Justice Chase's vote in the Legal Tender Cases is a textbook example of the proposition that one may look at a legal question differently as a judge from the way one did as a member of the executive branch. There is no reason to believe that Chase thought he was acting unconstitutionally when he helped draft and shepherd through Congress the greenback legislation, and it may well be that if Lincoln had actually posed the question to him before nominating him as Chief Justice, he would have agreed that the measures were constitutional. But administrators in charge of a program, even if they are lawyers, simply do not ponder these questions in the depth that judges do, and Chase's vote in the Legal Tender Case is proof of this fact.

In assessing Lincoln's success in his effort to pack the Court, it seems that with regard to the problems he foresaw at the time of his first appointments— the difficulties that the Supreme Court might put in the way of successfully fighting the Civil War—Lincoln was preeminently successful in his efforts. But with respect to issues that arose after the war—the use of military courts, the constitutionality of the greenback legislation, and the construction of the Fourteenth Amendment—his appointees divided from one another regularly. Perhaps the lesson to be drawn from these examples is that judges may think very much alike with respect to one issue, but quite differently from one another with respect to other issues. And while both presidents and judicial nominees may know the current constitutional issues of importance, neither of them is usually vouchsafed the foresight to see what the great issues of ten or fifteen years hence are to be.

* * * *

Although Franklin D. Roosevelt was understandably disappointed that he had had no opportunities to fill a vacancy on the Supreme Court during his first term in office, the vacancy occasioned by the retirement of Justice Van Devanter to which he appointed Justice Black was the first of eight vacancies that Roosevelt would have the opportunity to fill during his twelve years as President. There is no doubt that Roosevelt was keenly aware of the importance of judicial philosophy in a justice of the Supreme Court; if he were not, he never would have taken on the institutional might of the third branch with his Court-packing plan.

* * * *

In rapid succession, as the so-called nine old men retired or died, Franklin Roosevelt appointed first Senator Hugo Black of Alabama, then Solicitor General Stanley Reed of Kentucky, then Professor Felix Frankfurter of Massachusetts, then SEC Chairman William O. Douglas of Connecticut and Washington, then Attorney General Frank Murphy of Michigan. During his third term Roosevelt appointed Attorney General Robert H. Jackson of New York, Senator James F. Byrnes of South Carolina, and law school dean Wiley B. Rutledge of Iowa to the Court. As I have indicated earlier, five of these justices—Black, Reed, Frankfurter, Douglas, and Jackson—remained on the Court at the time of the Steel Seizure Case in 1952.

In the short run the effect of the change in membership on the Court's decisions was immediate, dramatic, and predictable. Social and regulatory legislation, whether enacted by the states or by Congress, was sustained across the board against constitutional challenges that might have prevailed before the Old Court. When Franklin Roosevelt in 1941 elevated Harlan F. Stone from associate justice to Chief Justice in place of Charles Evans Hughes, the periodical *United States News* commented, "The new head of the Court also will find no sharp divergence of opinion among his colleagues." *The Washington Post* echoed the same sentiment when it foresaw "for years to come" a "virtual unanimity on the tribunal."

These forecasts proved to be entirely accurate in the area of economic and social legislation. But other issues began to percolate up through the judicial coffee pot, as they have a habit of doing. The Second World War, which occupied the United States from 1941 until 1945, produced numerous lawsuits about civil liberties. During the war, the Court maintained a fair degree of cohesion in deciding most of these cases, but quite suddenly after the war, the predicted "virtual unanimity" was rent asunder in rancorous squabbling the like of which the Court had never seen before.

A part, but only a part, of the difference was of judicial philosophy. Understandably, seven justices who agreed as to the appropriate constitutional analysis to apply to economic and social legislation might not agree with one another in cases involving civil liberties. These differences manifested themselves infrequently during the war years, but came into full bloom shortly afterward. In a case called *Saia v. New York*, 334 U.S. 558 (1948), the Court held by a vote of 5 to 4 that a local ordinance of the city of Lockport, New York, regulating the use of sound trucks in city parks, was unconstitutional. Four of the five justices in the majority were appointees of Franklin Roosevelt, but so were three of the four justices in the minority. Seven months later the Court all but overruled the *Saia* case in *Kovacs v. Cooper*, 336 U.S. 53 (1949), with one of the *Saia* majority defecting to join the four dissenters for the *Kovacs* majority. These two cases provide but one of abundant examples of similar episodes in the Court's adjudication during the period from 1945 to 1949.

Thus history teaches us, I think, that even a "strong" president determined to leave his mark on the Court—a president such as Lincoln or Franklin Roosevelt—is apt to be only partially successful. Neither the president nor his appointees can foresee what issues will come before the Court during the tenure of the appointees, and it may be that none has thought very much about these issues. Even though they agree as to the proper resolution of current cases, they may well disagree as to future cases involving other questions when, as judges, they study briefs and hear arguments. Longevity of the appointees, or untimely deaths such as those of Justice Murphy and Justice Rutledge, may also frustrate a president's expectations; so also may the personal antagonisms developed between strong-willed appointees of the same president.

All of these factors are subsumed to a greater or lesser extent by observing that the Supreme Court is an institution far more dominated by centrifugal forces, pushing toward individuality and independence, than it is by centripetal forces, pulling for hierarchical ordering and institutional unity. The well-known checks and balances provided by the framers of the Constitution have supplied the necessary centrifugal force to make the Supreme Court independent of Congress and the president. The degree to which a new justice should change his way of looking at things when he "puts on the robe" is emphasized by the fact that Supreme Court appointments almost invariably come one at a time, and each new appointee goes alone to take his place with eight collegues who are already there. Unlike his freshman counterpart in the House of Representatives, where if there has been a strong political tide running at the time of a particular election there may be as many as seventy or eighty new members who form a bloc and cooperate with one another, the new judicial appointee brings no cohorts with him.

A second series of centrifugal forces is at work within the Court itself, pushing each member to be thoroughly independent of his colleagues. The chief justice has some authority that the associate justices do not have, but this is relatively insignificant compared to the extraordinary independence that each justice has from every other justice. Tenure is assured no matter how one votes in any given case; one is independent not only of public opinion, of the president, and of Congress, but of one's eight colleagues as well. When one puts on the robe, one enters a world of public scrutiny and professional criticism which sets great store by individual performance, and much less store upon the virtue of being a "team player."

James Madison, in his pre-presidential days when he was authoring political tracts, said in *The Federalist*, No. 51:

But the great security against a gradual concentration of the several powers in the same department, consists in giving to those who administer each department the necessary constitutional means and personal motives to resist encroachments of the others. The provision for defense must in this, as in all other cases, be made commensurate to the danger of attack. Ambition must be made to counteract ambition. The interest of the man must be connected with the constitutional rights of the place.

Madison, of course, was talking about the principles necessary to secure independence of one branch of the government from another. But he might equally well have been talking about principles, at least in the case of the Supreme Court of the United States, designed to weaken and diffuse the outside loyalties of any new appointee, and to gradually cause that appointee to identify his interests in the broadest sense not merely with the institution to which he is appointed, but to his own particular place within the institution. Here again, this remarkable group of fifty-some men who met in Philadelphia in the summer of 1787 seems to have created the separate branches of the federal government with consummate skill. The Supreme Court is to be independent of the legislative and executive branch of the government; yet by reason of vacancies occurring on that Court, it is to be subjected to indirect infusions of the popular will in terms of the president's use of his appointment power. But the institution is so structured that a brand-new presidential appointee, perhaps feeling himself strongly loyal to the president who appointed him, and looking for collegues of a similar mind on the Court, is immediately beset with the institutional pressures I have described. He identifies more and more strongly with the new institution of which he has become a member, and he learns how much store is set by his behaving independently of his colleagues. I think it is these institutional effects, as much as anything, that have prevented even strong presidents from being any more than partially successful when they sought to pack the Supreme Court.

POINTS TO PONDER

1. What does it mean to "pack" the Supreme Court?
2. Why is choosing Supreme Court justices an inherently unpredictable undertaking?
3. How does the nomination of justices by the president and confirmation by the Senate affect the legitimacy of judicial decisions?

Chapter 7

Chapter 7

CHECKS AND BALANCES: ECHOES OF THE FRAMERS

Previous sections have dealt with each of the three branches and how they operate; this section shifts the focus from the individual components to the dynamics of the whole system of governance. What is striking about the system is that it has operated in many different historical circumstances with vastly different national leaders and has endured for more than two centuries. The selections in this section bring out the positive effects of the system in ensuring that no one branch achieves tyrannical power. But the system is not without drawbacks; sometimes it is difficult to move the government to take concerted action in the face of pressing public problems, such as the growing national debt. In our system of governance we enjoy protections against the rise of tyranny, but we also suffer the danger of gridlock.

Establishing Checks and Balances

The American Revolution against the British was fought to throw off the shackles that held the colonies to England and made them subject to the arbitrary rule of King George III. In many important matters, such as taxation, the colonists had no say in their own governance. Thus, in designing their own government, the Framers wanted to assure that power could not be concentrated enough to result in tyranny. Being careful students of history, they believed that the tendency to accumulate power was a universal aspect of human nature and would be as tempting to their own elected leaders as it was to the British.

To prevent the concentration of power, the Framers decided to separate powers and provide each branch with checks upon the others. According to Madison in *Federalist* No. 47, "the accumulation of all powers, legislative, executive, and judiciary, in the same hands, whether one, a few, or many, and whether hereditary, self-appointed, or elective, may justly be pronounced the very definition of tyranny." But a strict and complete separation of the powers, with each branch able to act in only one sphere, was not their intention either. Each branch must be "connected and blended," according to Madison (*Feder-*

alist No. 48), or, in the words of presidential scholar Richard Neustadt, the Framers created a system of "separate institutions sharing powers."

Checks and Balances in the Constitution

The ambitions of people sharing power would give teeth to the "parchment barriers" (*Federalist* No. 48) of the Constitution, and the means of exercising their powers would be the checks and balances built into the Constitution. The formal checks include presidential participation in the legislative process by proposing legislation and being able to veto bills passed by Congress, with Congress being able to override the veto with a two-thirds majority of both houses.

The president can appoint officers of the executive branch and federal judges, but the Senate must confirm the appointments. In foreign policy the president can receive ambassadors (recognize foreign nations), negotiate treaties, and act as commander in chief of the armed forces. But the Senate must ratify treaties, and the president's power of the sword is checked by the congressional power to raise armies and navies and to declare war. The power of the purse is split in that all money spent must be appropriated by Congress, but the president uses discretion in actually spending the money. Federal courts can interpret legislation and decide on the constitutionality of acts of Congress and the president. But judges are appointed by the president with the consent of the Senate.

Checks and Balances in Operation

The dynamics of the system of checks and balances are engaged not so much in the operation of each of these separate powers, but rather in their cumulative effect in allowing the ambitions of politicians in the Congress and the presidency to act as a counterweight to each other. For instance, in the twentieth century after presidential power had been enhanced in the 1930s and World War II, Congress played an important restraining role in domestic policy with Presidents Truman, Eisenhower, and Kennedy. In national security matters after World War II presidential power was enhanced because of the Cold War with the Soviet Union. President Truman used his power as commander in chief to initiate the war in Korea without congressional approval, and President Kennedy confronted the Soviet Union in the Cuban Missile Crisis.

President Johnson fought the war in Vietnam on the authority of the Gulf of Tonkin Resolution of 1964, but, as public opinion turned against the war, Johnson decided not to run for reelection. When President Nixon continued to pursue the war, Congress used its power of the purse to force the administration to negotiate with the North Vietnamese to end the war. In 1973 Congress passed the War Powers Resolution in order to assert its constitutional role in deciding on issues of war and peace. Presidents, however, have refused to recognize the resolution's legitimacy, though they generally have gone along with its major provisions.

Although the federal courts have generally refused to make decisions on the congressional authority to declare war, the Supreme Court has occasionally made decisions against a sitting president, as it did in ruling against President Truman's seizure of the steel mills during the Korean War and in forcing President Nixon to release the Watergate tapes in 1974.

An example of checks and balances in action is the dispute between President Nixon and Congress over the spending power. In the early 1970s Congress appropriated more money for water pollution control than President Nixon thought wise. Nixon decided to impound part of the money by ordering his executive branch officials not to spend it. The administration was sued in federal court for not carrying out the law, and the Supreme Court finally decided that the president did not have the constitutional authority to refuse to spend money provided in legislation. This is an example of a president asserting unprecedented power over federal spending against the will of Congress as embodied in public law. In this case the Supreme Court stepped in to settle the matter.

In foreign relations the president can negotiate treaties, as President Carter did with the treaty that turned over control of the Panama Canal to Panama. The Senate, however, refused to ratify the treaty until Carter had negotiated changes in the original draft to satisfy their concerns. When President Carter decided to open formal relations with the People's Republic of China, he broke the treaty the United States had with Taiwan. Senator Barry Goldwater sued the president in court, arguing that the President could not abrogate a treaty without Senate approval. The Supreme Court, however, decided that presidential renunciation of a treaty does not require Senate approval.

The Readings

The readings in this section focus upon the interaction among the three branches, but particularly upon the inherent tensions between the primary policy-making branches—the president and Congress. The emphasis is on how the separate institutions act together and the dynamic balance of the system of governance embodied in the Constitution.

In his classic defense of the separation of powers system, James Madison in *Federalist* No. 51 argues that in order to prevent the accumulation of power and potential tyranny, a government must be structured so that power is divided. The purpose of this sharing or blending was to enable the government to act but also to ensure that each branch would prevent the other from accumulating too much power. This was to be accomplished by "giving to those who administer each department the necessary constitutional means and personal motives to resist encroachments by the others. . . . Ambition must be made to counteract ambition."

The power sharing and checking devices have produced a government that is able to make major policy changes only if the separate branches agree on the direction of change. In times of national unity or crisis, action can be achieved, but in normal times concerted action by the whole government is unusual. The system was not designed for quick action because the checks and balances are effective in their operation, as the Framers intended.

In the second half of the twentieth century there occurred another significant overlay on the separation of powers: the increasing occurrence of divided government, when control of Congress and the presidency is split between the two political parties. In his selection, James Sundquist argues that, although divided government has occurred in the past, its increasing incidence amounts to an important new, and destructive, factor in American government. He points out that, though the Framers were antiparty (faction), the dynamics of twentieth-century American politics and the rise of the presidency have made political parties the glue that holds together a governing coalition across the branches that the Framers intentionally separated.

From Sundquist's perspective the destructive rivalries of divided government have prevented the country from being able to face up to its most important policy crises, such as the huge budget deficits of the 1980s and 1990s. Sundquist suggests several constitutional amendments that might mitigate the problems of divided government. Sundquist's position on the desirability of unified government, however, must be tempered by the experiences of Presidents Carter and Clinton, neither of whom had smooth relations with Congresses controlled by their own parties.

We often focus on current public policy issues and the temporary imbalances in the system when either Congress or the president pushes constitutional prerogatives too far. Hugh Heclo steps back from the tight focus to notice that "the most important and least commented upon feature about our separation of powers system" is its durability. In describing the rise of the presidency and the broad delegation of powers from Congress, Heclo observes that Congress has left many strings attached to its delegations of power to the president. Much of what has been called the "micromanagement" of the executive branch by Congress has resulted from the loss of comity, that is, the trust created by mutually agreed–upon rules of self-restraint between the branches.

The separation of powers has been exacerbated by the "combination of deceit and mistrust, competitive staffing, divided government, and ideological activism in the past 25 or so years." Heclo argues that an imbalance developed in the national security area with the presidency asserting greater control of the war power than the Framers intended or is healthy for the system.

But Heclo's overall perspective is that the separation of powers has worked remarkably well in creating an enduring government that brought the United States through two centuries of tremendous change. In Heclo's judgment, "the Founders' mixed view of human nature seems to have gotten it about right: people are bad enough not to be trusted with power but virtuous enough to govern themselves within properly designed constitutional institutions for allocating power."

KEY TERMS

checks and balances: provisions in the Constitution that allow one branch to check or limit the exercise of power by another branch

1974 Budget Act: reform legislation that limited the president's authority to impound (to not spend) funds provided by Congress. The law also reformed the congressional budget process. Full title: Congressional Budget and Impoundment Control Act of 1974

power of the purse: authority to spend money from the treasury. The executive branch actually spends the money, but only for purposes authorized by Congress and only in amounts appropriated by Congress.

power of the sword: authority to control the military services, split between the president and Congress

28

FEDERALIST NO. 51
James Madison

In Federalist No. 51 James Madison presents a cogent and concise argument for the separation of governmental powers among three branches ("departments") of government. This separation is necessary, Madison asserts, because men are not angels and are continually tempted to aggrandize power for themselves. The way to control this very human lust after power is to let the ambition of one set of rulers counter the ambitions of others in the struggle to control governmental policy. Thus the government will be obliged to control itself.

To the People of the State of New York:
    To what expedient, then, shall we finally resort, for maintaining in practice the necessary partition of power among the several departments, as laid down in the Constitution? The only answer that can be given is, that as all these exterior provisions are found to be inadequate, the defect must be supplied, by so contriving the interior structure of the government as that its several constituent parts may, by their mutual relations, be the means of keeping each other in their proper places. Without presuming to undertake a full development of this important idea, I will hazard a few general observations, which may perhaps

place it in a clearer light, and enable us to form a more correct judgment of the principles and structure of the government planned by the convention.

In order to lay a due foundation for that separate and distinct exercise of the different powers of government, which to a certain extent is admitted on all hands to be essential to the preservation of liberty, it is evident that each department should have a will of its own; and consequently should be so constituted that the members of each should have as little agency as possible in the appointment of the members of the others. Were this principle rigorously adhered to, it would require that all the appointments for the supreme executive, legislative, and judiciary magistracies should be drawn from the same fountain of authority, the people, through channels having no communication whatever with one another. Perhaps such a plan of constructing the several departments would be less difficult in practice than it may in contemplation appear. Some difficulties, however, and some additional expense would attend the execution of it. Some deviations, therefore, from the principle must be admitted. In the constitution of the judiciary department in particular, it might be inexpedient to insist rigorously on the principle: first, because peculiar qualifications being essential in the members, the primary consideration ought to be to select that mode of choice which best secures these qualifications; secondly, because the permanent tenure by which the appointments are held in that department must soon destroy all sense of dependence on the authority conferring them.

It is equally evident, that the members of each department should be as little dependent as possible on those of the others, for the emoluments annexed to their offices. Were the executive magistrate, or the judges, not independent of the legislature in this particular, their independence in every other would be merely nominal.

But the great security against a gradual concentration of the several powers in the same department, consists in giving to those who administer each department the necessary constitutional means and personal motives to resist encroachments of the others. The provision for defense must in this, as in all other cases, be made commensurate to the danger of attack. Ambition must be made to counteract ambition. The interest of the man must be connected with the constitutional rights of the place. It may be a reflection on human nature that such devices should be necessary to control the abuses of government. But what is government itself but the greatest of all reflections on human nature? If men were angels, no government would be necessary. If angels were to govern men, neither external nor internal controls on government would be necessary. In framing a government which is to be administered by men over men, the great difficulty lies in this: you must first enable the government to control the governed; and in the next place oblige it to control itself. A dependence on the people is, no doubt, the primary control on the government; but experience has taught mankind the necessity of auxiliary precautions.

This policy of supplying, by opposite and rival interests, the defect of better motives, might be traced through the whole system of human affairs, private as well as public. We see it particularly displayed in all the subordinate distributions of power, where the constant aim is to divide and arrange the several offices in such a manner as that each may be a check on the other—that the private interest of every individual may be a sentinel over the public rights. These inventions of prudence cannot be less requisite in the distribution of the supreme powers of the State.

But it is not possible to give to each department an equal power of self-defense. In republican government, the legislative authority necessarily predominates. The remedy for this inconveniency is to divide the legislature into different branches; and to render them, by different modes of election and different principles of action, as little connected with each other as the nature of their common functions and their common dependence on the society will admit. It may even be necessary to guard against dangerous encroachments by still further precautions. As the weight of the legislative authority requires that it should be thus divided, the weakness of the executive may require, on the other hand, that it should be fortified. An absolute negative on the legislature appears, at first view, to be the natural defense with which the executive magistrate should be armed. But perhaps it would be neither altogether safe nor alone sufficient. On ordinary occasions it might not be exerted with the requisite firmness, and on extraordinary occasions it might be perfidiously abused. May not this defect of an absolute negative be supplied by some qualified connection between this weaker department and the weaker branch of the stronger department, by which the latter may be led to support the constitutional rights of the former, without being too much detached from the rights of its own department?

If the principles on which these observations are founded be just, as I persuade myself they are, and they be applied as a criterion to the several State constitutions, and to the federal Constitution, it will be found that if the latter does not perfectly correspond with them, the former are infinitely less able to bear such a test.

There are, moreover, two considerations particularly applicable to the federal system of America, which place that system in a very interesting point of view.

First. In a single republic all the power surrendered by the people is submitted to the administration of a single government; and the usurpations are guarded against by a division of the government into distinct and separate departments. In the compound republic of America, the power surrendered by the people is first divided between two distinct governments, and then the portion allotted to each subdivided among distinct and separate departments. Hence a double security arises to the rights of the people. The different governments will control each other, at the same time that each will be controlled by itself.

Second. It is of great importance in a republic not only to guard the society against the oppression of its rulers, but to guard one part of the society against the injustice of the other part. Different interests necessarily exist in different classes of citizens. If a majority be united by a common interest, the rights of the minority will be insecure. There are but two methods of providing against this evil: the one by creating a will in the community independent of the majority—that is, of the society itself; the other, by comprehending in the society so many separate descriptions of citizens as will render an unjust combination of a majority of the whole very improbable, if not impracticable. The first method prevails in all governments possessing an hereditary or self-appointed authority. This, at best, is but a precarious security; because a power independent of the society may as well espouse the unjust views of the major, as the rightful interests of the minor party, and may possibly be turned against both parties. The second method will be exemplified in the federal republic of the United States. Whilst all authority in it will be derived from and dependent on the society, the society itself will be broken into so many parts, interests, and classes of citizens, that the rights of individuals, or of the minority, will be in little danger from interested combinations of the majority. In a free government the security for civil rights must be the same as that for religious rights. It consists in the one case in the multiplicity of interests, and in the other in the multiplicity of sects. The degree of security in both cases will depend on the number of interests and sects; and this may be presumed to depend on the extent of country and number of people comprehended under the same government. This view of the subject must particularly recommend a proper federal system to all sincere and considerate friends of republican government, since it shows that in exact proportion as the territory of the Union may be formed into more circumscribed Confederacies, or States, oppressive combination of a majority will be facilitated; the best security, under the republican forms, for the rights of every class of citizens will be diminished; and consequently the stability and independence of some member of the government, the only other security, must be proportionally increased. Justice is the end of government. It is the end of civil society. It ever has been and ever will be pursued until it be obtained, or until liberty be lost in the pursuit. In a society under the forms of which the stronger faction can readily unite and oppress the weaker, anarchy may as truly be said to reign as in a state of nature, where the weaker individual is not secured against the violence of the stronger; and as, in the latter state, even the stronger individuals are prompted, by the uncertainty of their condition, to submit to a government which may protect the weak as well as themselves; so, in the former state, will the more powerful factions or parties be gradually induced, by a like motive, to wish for a government which will protect all parties, the weaker as well as the more powerful. It can be little doubted that if the State of Rhode Island was separated from the Confederacy and left to itself, the insecurity of rights under the popular form of government within such narrow limits would be displayed by such reiterated oppressions of factious majorities that some power altogether independent of the people would soon be called for by the voice of the very factions whose misrule had proved the necessity of it. In the extended republic of the United States, and among the great variety of interests, parties, and sects which it embraces, a coalition of a majority of the whole society could seldom take place on any other principles than those of justice and the general good; whilst there being thus less danger to a minor from the will of a major party, there must be less pretext, also, to provide for the security of the former, by introducing into the government a will not dependent on the latter, or, in other words, a will independent of the society itself. It is no less certain than it is important, notwithstanding the contrary opinions which have been entertained, that the larger the society, provided it lie within a practical sphere, the more duly capable it will be of self-government. And happily for the *republican cause*, the practicable sphere may be carried to a very great extent by a judicious modification and mixture of the *federal principle*.

Publius.

POINTS TO PONDER

1. What are the implications of Madison's assertion that men are not angels?
2. How does the separation of powers operate to control the government?
3. What ensures that the separation of powers embodied in the Constitution will amount to more than "parchment barriers"?

29

"NEEDED: A POLITICAL THEORY FOR THE NEW ERA OF COALITION GOVERNMENT IN THE UNITED STATES"

James Sundquist

In this 1988 Political Science Quarterly *article, James Sundquist, a political scientist at the Brookings Institution, analyzes the problems presented by divided government, when control of the presidency and of both houses of Congress is split between the two major political parties. He argues that this condition leads to policy stalemate and to a lack of responsibility in which each branch of government—Congress and the president—blames the other for the inability of the government to deal with major public policy problems, such as the national debt.*

Sundquist further argues that political parties are the only institution that can bridge the gap across the separate branches that the Framers created. He suggests several possible constitutional amendments that might make cooperation between the two branches more likely and thus allow the formulation of coherent public policy.

On 8 November 1988, when the American voters decreed that Republican George Bush would succeed Ronald Reagan in the White House but the opposition Democratic Party would control both houses of the Congress, it was the sixth time in the last nine presidential elections that the electorate chose to split the government between the parties. As in 1988, so in the earlier elections of 1956, 1968, 1972, 1980, and 1984, the people placed their faith in Republican presidential leadership but voted to retain Democratic majorities in the House of Representatives and in the first three of those elections (as well as in 1988), Democratic majorities in the Senate also.

This is something new in American politics. When Dwight D. Eisenhower took his second oath of office in 1957, he was the first chief executive in seventy-two years—since Grover Cleveland in 1885—to confront on Inauguration Day a Congress of which even one house was controlled by the opposition party. Sometimes the opposition would win majorities in the House or the Senate, or both, at the midterm election, but even such occasions were relatively rare. In the fifty-eight years from 1897 through 1954, the country experienced divided government during only eight years—all in the last half of a presidential term—or 14 percent of the time. Yet in the thirty-six years from 1955 through 1990, the government will have been divided between the parties for twenty-four years—exactly two-thirds of that period.

A generation ago, then, the country passed from a long era of party government, when either the Republican or the Democratic Party controlled both the presidency and the Congress almost all of the time, to an era when the government was divided between the parties most of the time. Under these circumstances, the United States has its own unique version of coalition government—not a coalition voluntarily entered into by the parties but one forced upon them by the accidents of the electoral process.

It is the argument of this article that the advent of the new era has rendered obsolete much of the theory developed by political scientists, from the day of Woodrow Wilson to the 1950s, to explain how the United States government can and should work. That theory identified the political party as the indispensable instrument that brought cohesion and unity, and hence effectiveness, to the government as a whole by linking the executive and legislative branches in a bond of common interest. And, as a corollary, the party made it possible for the president to succeed in his indispensable role as leader and energizer of the governmental process; it accomplished that end because the congressional majorities, while they would not accept the president's leadership by virtue of his constitutional position as chief executive—institutional rivalry would bar that—would accept it in his alternate capacity as head of the political party to which the majorities adhered.

The generations of political scientists who expounded this theory paid little attention to how the government would and should function when the president and the Senate and House majorities were not all of the same party. They could in good conscience disregard that question because intervals of divided government in their experience had been infrequent and short-lived. Whenever the midterm election brought a division of the government, anyone concerned about that could take a deep breath and wait confidently for the next presidential election to put the system back into its proper alignment. As late as 1952 it had always done so in the memory of everybody writing on the subject. But since 1956, that has no longer been a certainty. It has not even been the probability. And that represents a momentous change in the American governmental system, for institutional processes and relationships are profoundly altered when the unifying bond of party disappears.

* * * *

The Theory of Party Government and Presidential Leadership

Madison did not expound a new theory to supplant the one that he had been so instrumental in embedding in the Constitution. But without benefit of much explicit doctrine, the nation's political leaders developed in practice the system of party government—as distinct from nonpartisan government—that settled into place in the Jacksonian era and prevailed throughout the next century and a quarter. In each presidential election two national parties sought exactly what the Madisonian theory written into the Constitution was supposed to forestall: the capture of all three of the policy-making elements of the government—the presidency, Senate and House—by the same faction or party, so that the party could carry out its program.

No major party has ever said, "We want only the presidency," or only the Senate or the House. They have always said, "give us *total* responsibility." Since early in the nineteenth century, they have presented their programs formally in official party platforms. Asking for total power in the two elected branches, they have been eager to accept the total responsibility and accountability that would accompany it.

That was the theory of party government; and not only the politicians, but the people accepted it. The parties lined up naturally on opposite sides of whatever were the great issues of the day—creating a national bank, opening the West with turnpikes and railroads and canals financed by the national government, prohibiting slavery in the western territories, raising or lowering tariffs, mobilizing the national government to help the victims of the Great Depression, and so on. The people listened to the arguments of the two parties and made their choices. And when they did, the party they had elected had a full opportunity to carry out its mandate, because when the voters chose a president each four years they normally entrusted control of the Congress to the president's party, thus making it fully responsible. From Andrew Jackson's time until the second election of Dwight Eisenhower in 1956, only four presidents—Zachary Taylor elected in 1848, Rutherford B. Hayes in 1876, James A. Garfield in 1880, and Grover Cleveland in 1884—had to confront immediately upon inauguration either a House of Representatives or a Senate organized by the opposition. In the nineteenth century these results may have been largely an artifact of the election process itself. The parties printed separate ballots listing their slates, and the voter selected the ballot of the party he preferred, marked it, and dropped it in the box. Yet after the government-printed, secret ballot came into universal use early in this century, straight-ticket voting and the resultant single-party control of the government continued to prevail. The voters gave the Republican Party responsibility for the entire government in the 1900s, again in the 1920s, and finally in 1952; and they chose the Democratic Party in the 1910s, 1930s, and 1940s. No president in the first half of this century ever had to suffer divided government upon taking office, and few had the problem even after the normal setback to the president's party in the midterm election.

As soon as political science emerged as a scholarly discipline, its adherents began to pronounce and elaborate the theoretical foundation of the system of party government that was in being. Parties were not only natural, since people were bound to organize to advance their differing notions as to the goals and programs of government, but the scholars concluded that they were useful and necessary too. Among their uses was the one that is the concern of this paper: their utility in unifying a government of dispersed powers and thereby making it effective.

In his review of the literature on political parties in the late nineteenth century, Austin Ranney found that Woodrow Wilson "was perhaps the first American scholar in his period to attack the principle and deplore the effects of separation of powers, and to consider methods for by-passing it." The primary method was to accept the political party as the unifier of the separate powers. "The organization of parties," wrote Wilson, "is, in a sense, indistinguishable from the legislature and executive themselves. The several active parts of the government are closely united in organization for a common purpose, because they are under a common direction and themselves constitute the machinery of party control." And they had to be united because, wrote Wilson, "our government is a living, organic thing, and must . . . work out a close synthesis of active parts which can exist only when leadership is lodged in some one man or group of men. You cannot compound a successful government out of antagonisms."

* * * *

And how is that degree of party discipline and responsibility achieved? In the national government, political scientists proclaim with virtual unanimity that it is through presidential leadership. When the party serves its unifying function, it is because the members of the president's party in the Congress recognize the president as not merely the head of the executive branch but as the leader of the band of "brothers in the same political lodge." In enacting as well as in administering the laws, the government cannot move dynamically and prudently without a recognized and accepted prime mover, a leader. And that leader is logically and necessarily the man chosen by the whole national party to carry its standard, and who has done so successfully in the most recent presidential election. Besides, the president has the resources of the entire executive branch to help him to develop coordinated programs. "The President proposes and the Congress disposes" long ago became the catch phrase to describe the legislative process.

Austin Ranney notes that, of the "various devices by which American presidents and other politicians have tried to join together, for purposes of getting the government to work, what the Constitution so successfully put asunder," most "fall under the general heading of 'presidential leadership of Congress.'" He summarizes:

> The ideas underlying all of them are that America, like every other country, must sometimes take swift, coherent, and purposeful action . . . that Congress . . . cannot by itself initiate such action; the president . . . is the only official who can take the lead; and that the basic problem of American government is finding and perfecting institutions that will enable the president to lead Congress with maximum effectiveness.

Political scientists played no small role in creating those devices of presidential leadership. They refined and embellished, if they did not originate, the concepts of the executive budget that were enacted in the Budget and Accounting Act of 1921. They dominated the task forces of the President's Committee on Administrative Management, whose report in 1937 laid the basis for expanding the executive office of the president and giving the chief executive the mechanisms for serving effectively as the general manager of the government. And they heartily acclaimed the assertion by the president of leadership in the legislative process. The identification of the president as chief legislator has been traced back to Howard Lee McBain's *The Living Constitution*, published in 1927. By the 1940s, no textbook on American government failed to highlight the president's legislative role, usually in a section carrying the phrase "chief legislator" in the title.

* * * *

By the 1960s, political science had developed a dominating theory as to how the American constitutional system should—and at its best, did—work. The political party was the institution that unified the separated branches of the government and brought coherence to the policy-making process. And because the president was the leader of his party, he was the chief policy maker of the entire government, presiding directly over the executive branch and indirectly working through and with his party's congressional leadership over the legislative branch as well.

The Old Theory in a New Era

This established theory presupposed one essential condition: there would in fact be a majority party in control of both branches of government. Rereading the literature of the midcentury, one is struck with how easily this condition was taken for granted. The writers could well do so, for in the twentieth century until 1955, the government had been divided between the parties only for four periods of two years each, and in each case in the last half of a presidential term—those of Taft, Wilson, Hoover, and Truman. A scholar who happened to be writing during or immediately after one of these intervals (or who was commenting on state governmental systems) might observe in parenthetical style that divided government could sometimes obscure responsibility, impede leadership, and thus thwart the fulfillment of the party government ideal. But the aberration was passed over quickly, without interrupting the flow of the basic argument. In the normal state of affairs, one party would have control of the policy-making branches of government; the other would be in opposition. . . .

Divided government invalidates the entire theory of party government and presidential leadership, both elements of it. Divided government requires that the United States "construct a successful government out of antagonisms," which Wilson warned could not be done, and renders impossible the "close synthesis of active parts" that he found necessary. How can a party cast its web over the dispersed organs of government to bring a semblance of unity, in Key's phrase, if it controls but one of the branches? How can the majority party fulfill Burns's "vital function of integration," or rally the government's elements behind Penniman's "common purpose," or provide Rossiter's "bridges across the gaps," or Sorauf's "unifying force" if there is no majority party? How can the president lead the Congress if either or both houses are controlled by the party that fought to defeat him in the last election and has vowed to vanquish him, or his successor as his party's candidate, in the next one? But if the president cannot lead, Rossiter has told us, "weak and disorganized government" must follow. Our "toughest problems," Hyneman has admonished, will in that circumstance remain unsolved.

The question at once arises: In our twenty-two years thus far of forced coalition government, have those gloomy forecasts been fulfilled? Eleven Congresses during the administrations of four presidents would appear to have given ample time for putting the established theory to the test. Unfortunately, however, the test results are bound to be uncertain and would still be so if another two score years of experience were added. There will not be agreement on whether, and to what extent, and during what periods the government has in fact been "weak and disorganized," or even on whether those characteristics are wholly undesirable. "That government is best which governs least" is still an aphorism of wide appeal, and the weaker and more disorganized the government the less governance it can inflict. Moreover, to rest a theoretical proposition on concrete examples from history is to invite debate on the merits of each example and to call forth counterexamples. And when the instances are so recent that they involve current personalities or groups—Democrats and Republicans, conservatives and liberals—the debate is distorted by the emotional attachments of the debaters. Moreover, almost any failure or success can be ruled out of consideration as attributable to accidents of personality or to circumstances beyond the control of the institutions however organized. So, in the absence of proven and acceptable methodology for evaluating the performance and success of governments, any judgment about institutional structures will necessarily embody the biases and the values of whomever is the judge. But if that is the best that can be done, so be it. If there is any worth at all to the contention that a government cannot function without the unifying web of party, as Key held, the judgment must be made on whatever is the soundest basis that can be contrived.

My own conclusion is that the predictions of the sages of the earlier generation have been borne out in this modern era of divided or coalition government. True, in the administrations of the four Republican presidents who had to make their peace with House Democratic majorities—and usually Democratic Senate majorities as well—there were significant accomplishments. President Dwight D. Eisenhower achieved a successful bipartisan foreign policy, and President Ronald Reagan managed to carry enough Democrats with him to enact for better or worse the essentials of his economic program in 1981. In subsequent Reagan years, the Congress and the administration collaborated across party lines to enact measures to bring illegal immigration under control, rescue social security, and reform the tax code. But Eisenhower and the Democratic Congress were stalemated on domestic measures throughout his six years of coalition government; the Nixon-Ford period was one of almost unbroken conflict and deadlock on both domestic and foreign issues; and the last seven years of Reagan found the government immobilized on some of the central issues of the day, unwilling to follow the leadership of the President or anyone else and deferring those issues in hope that somehow the 1988 election would resolve matters and render the government functional again.

By common consent, the most conspicuous among the urgent but unresolved problems has been, of course, the federal budget deficit, which has been running at between $150 billion and $200 billion a year since the great tax cut of 1981 took effect. The national debt now stands at well over $2 trillion, more than doubled in seven years of divided government. The United States has suffered the shock of falling from the status of a great creditor nation to the world's largest debtor nation, living on borrowing from abroad. The huge trade deficit, the shortfall in investment, and high interest rates are all blamed on the inability of the government to get the budget deficit under control. For all these reasons, virtually all of the country's responsible leaders—the president, the congressional leaders, and members of both parties in both houses—have for nearly over half a dozen years been proclaiming loudly and in unison that the nation simply cannot go on this way. The experts from outside—in the academic world, the Federal Reserve System, on Wall Street, in foreign countries—likewise agree that these deficits are economically perilous, whether or not they can be termed morally outrageous as well.

But during all that time that the country has seen a virtual consensus on the urgency of this problem, its governmental institutions have floundered in trying to cope with it. President Reagan sent the Congress his program, but the Congress flatly rejected it. The legislators in turn floated suggestions, but the President killed them by promising a veto if they were passed. The congressional leaders and others pleaded for a summit meeting between the executive and legislative branches to hammer out a common policy. Finally, in November 1986, the meeting took place. But it is a measure of the national predicament that it took a half-trillion-dollar collapse in the stock market—a five-hundred-billion-dollar panic—before the two branches of the U.S. government would even sit down together. It was easier for Mikhail Gorbachev to get a summit meeting with the President of the United States than it was for the Speaker of the United States House of Representatives. And even the domestic summit that was finally held essentially papered over the problem rather than solved it.

Or we can draw examples of the failure of coalition government from international affairs. The country lost a war for the first time in history—in Vietnam—after another period of floundering in search of a policy, with the president pulling in one direction and the Congress in another. And the situation in Nicaragua was throughout the Reagan years almost a replica of Vietnam. The government could adopt no clear and effective policy at all; it could neither take measures strong enough to force the Sandinista government out of power, as the President and his administration wished to do, nor accept that government and make peace with it, as many in the Senate and the House would like. Then there is the Iran-contra debacle. President Reagan in his own summation of that episode spoke of the "failure" of his policy, of "a policy that went astray," of "the damage that's been done," and he blamed it all on mistrust between the executive and legislative branches.

But, some will argue, even if these or other instances can indeed be considered governmental failures attributable to mistrust between the unwilling partners of a forced coalition, the performance of recent unified government has been no better. The Kennedy and Carter years cannot claim overwhelming success, they will maintain, and while Lyndon Johnson proved to be a spectacular presidential leader of the Congress in the enactment of his Great Society measures in 1964 and 1965, he also led the country into the quagmire of Vietnam that in turn launched a devastating spiral of inflation. This is the difficulty of arguing from cases, as I suggested earlier.

Nor is it any more profitable to look abroad for answers to the effectiveness of unified compared to coalition government. It is easy to demonstrate that Britain's unified governments have not always been successful, and that in continental countries coalition governments (which, it is important to note, are quite different from ours) have not always failed. For better or worse, the discussion of the relative merits of unified over divided government has to be pursued in abstract terms, as it was for the most part in the political science literature cited earlier.

The essence of the theoretical argument in favor of the unified government has been and is: For coherent and timely policies to be adopted and carried out—in short, for government to work effectively, as the established theory held—the president, the Senate, and the House must come into agreement. When the same party controls all three of these power centers, the incentive to reach such agreement is powerful despite the inevitable institutional rivalries and jealousies. The party *does* serve as the bridge or the web, in the metaphors of political science. But in divided government, it is not merely the separated institutions of government that must overcome their built-in rivalries but the opposing parties themselves. And that is bound to be a difficult, arduous process, characterized by conflict, delay, and indecision, and leading frequently to deadlock, inadequate and ineffective policies, or no policies at all.

Competition is the very essence of democratic politics. It gives democracy its meaning, and its vitality. The parties are the instruments of that competition. They are and should be organized for combat, not for collaboration and compromise. They live to win elections in order to advance their philosophies and programs. Therefore, each party strives and must strive to defeat the opposing party. But in a divided government, this healthy competition is translated into an unhealthy, debilitating conflict between the institutions of government themselves. Then, the president and Congress are motivated to try to discredit and defeat each other. Yet these are the institutions that, for anything constructive to happen, simply have to get together.

The average citizen reacts by simply condemning all politicians as a class. "Why don't those people in Washington stop playing politics and just get together and do what's right?" But that is not in the nature of things. Political parties, as the textbooks have always told us, are organized because people have genuine, deep disagreements about the goals and the programs of their societies. If a coalition government is to work, the leaders of committed groups have to be willing to submerge or abandon the very philosophies that caused them to organize their parties in the first place. They have to set aside the principles that are their reason for seeking governmental power. And they will do that only under compulsion of clear and grave necessity—usually, in other words, after deadlock has deteriorated into crisis.

In the American form of coalition government, if the president sends a proposal to Capitol Hill or takes a foreign policy stand, the opposition-controlled House or houses of Congress—unless they are overwhelmed by the president's popularity and standing in the country—simply *must* reject it. Otherwise they are saying the president is a wise and prudent leader. That would only strengthen him and his party for the next election, and how can the men and women of the congressional majority do that, when their whole object is to defeat him when that time arrives? By the same token, if the opposition party in control of Congress initiates a measure, the president has to veto it—or he is saying of his opponents that they are sound and statesmanlike, and so is building them up for the next election.

So when President Reagan sent his budgets to the Congress, the Democrats who controlled both houses had to pronounce them "dead on arrival," as they did. And when they came up with their alternatives, the President had to condemn them and hurl them back. Eventually, when the stream of recrimination and vetoes ran dry each year, some kind of budget was necessarily adopted; but it did not reflect the views of either party, and in terms of the consensus objective of deficit reduction it was a pale and ineffective compromise. Neither party would take responsibility, neither could be held accountable, each could point the finger at the other when things went wrong.

In such circumstances, the people in their one solemn, sovereign act of voting cannot render a clear verdict and thus set the course of government. Elections lose their purpose and their meaning. The President, all through 1988, was saying, "Don't blame me for the budget deficit. It's those Democrats in Congress." And the Democrats were replying, "Don't blame us. Blame that man in the White House for not giving us the proper leadership." In November, the voters were not able to hold anybody clearly responsible, because, in fact nobody had been.

Our struggles with coalition government have demonstrated also the truth of the established wisdom concerning presidential leadership: in the American system there is simply no substitute for it. The Congress has 535 voting members, organized in two houses and in innumerable committees and subcommittees; every member is in principle the equal of every other member, and nobody can give directions to anybody else and make them stick. Such a body is simply not well designed for making coherent, decisive, coordinated policy. As the old theory told us, the system works best when the president proposes and the Congress disposes, when the president sets the agenda and leads, as everyone expects him to.

But how can leaders lead if followers don't follow? In divided government, presidential leadership becomes all but impossible. The president is not the leader of the congressional majority. He is precisely the opposite—the leader of their opposition, the man they are most dedicated to discredit and defeat. With great fanfare and immense hope, the people elect a president each four years. But then, most of the time these days, they give him a Congress a majority of whose members tried their best to beat him in the last election and will do so again in the next. To lead in those circumstances would be beyond the capability of any mortal. No one should blame presidents when they fail in a time of coalition government. It is the system that is at fault.

Nobody planned it this way. The country in no way made a conscious decision thirty years ago to abandon the responsible-party system that had served it well for almost the whole life of the nation. It was simply an accident of the electoral system. Almost unique in the world, the United States has an electoral process that permits people to split their tickets—to vote one way for president and the other way for Congress, if they so choose. And that is what enough of them have done to produce a divided outcome most of the time of late.

Re-reconciling Theory and Practice

Today there is a disjunction between theory and practice, between the long-accepted and not-yet-abandoned ideas about how the government of the United States should work and the way in which it is now compelled to try to work. How can theory and practice once again be synchronized?

First, can the practice be altered to fit the therapy? In other words, is there any way to restore party government as the normal, rather than abnormal, state of affairs? Theoretically, there is. But only by altering the electoral system that lets ticket-splitting determine the composition of the government. That would mean fundamental change in the Constitution, and it only takes a split second of reflection to convince anyone that politically and practically it cannot be done. It would take the utter collapse of government to make such change possible.

The constitutional amendment might take any of several forms, the simplest of which would be a revision of the ballot to make ticket-splitting impossible in national elections. That would in effect return the country to the nineteenth-century mode, when straight-ticket ballots were printed and handed out by the parties—except that the ballots would now be government-printed and the secrecy of the vote protected. The voters would select one from among two or more party slates or "team tickets" that included each party's candidates for president, vice president, Senate, and House. This is not a totally outlandish idea, because voters now choose between team tickets for president and vice president. If that principle were extended to Senate and House candidates as well, it would be almost a certainty that every incoming president would have a Congress of his own party to work with and to lead. A subtle variant of this scheme would be to require a party's candidates for Congress to be its candidates for the electoral college also, so that a voter could cast a ballot for president only by casting it for the congressional candidate as the elector. A different approach would be to create bonus seats in the House and Senate, to be awarded to the president's party in sufficient number to give it control of the Congress.

But any of those ideas would be anathema to the members of Congress, who under normal constitutional amendment procedures would have to initiate the change. Because the amendment process requires extraordinary majorities—two-thirds of the House and Senate and three-fourths of the state legislatures—it demands in effect bipartisan agreement. Therefore, both parties would have to see benefit in the change. But since redistribution of power is a zero-sum game that creates both winners and losers, one party is bound to lose. In the current case it would be the Democrats, for any of these proposals would have given the Republicans control of the Congress during much or all of the time that they have held the presidency. The Democrats in the Congress would never take a second look at any team ticket scheme that would make them stand or fall with a George McGovern or a Walter Mondale, and that would convert their majorities into minorities every time their candidate for president was beaten. And the Republicans would not perceive the advantage for their party, however obvious that advantage may have been throughout the past twenty years. Faced with a team ticket proposal, they would remember how many seats they would have lost with Barry Goldwater back in 1964 and play it safe.

If practice cannot be changed to fit the established theory of party government, then what are the prospects for the development of new theory? If coalition government is what the United States must live with most of the time, can political leadership and political science produce an alternative theory that tells us how that kind of government can be made to work?

On this question, today's political scientists, who would appear to have the primary obligation to make suggestions, fall into three groups. The first consists of those who are happy with the way the government works now. They simply reject the party-government and presidential-leadership theories of the preceding generation. They find divided government acceptable enough, and maybe even better than party government, for it more certainly safeguards individual liberties and assures that rash and impulsive actions can be forestalled—in domestic affairs, at least. This is the position of traditional conservatives who still echo the fears of government that dominated the eighteenth century, and is a wholly arguable and defensive position. But ironically, these conservatives are joined now by their exact opposites—the typical liberal Democrats, whose gut reaction is, "Thank God for divided government under President Reagan. It saved us from Judge Robert Bork, and war in Nicaragua, and all kinds of other follies." These liberals were *for* party government and presidential leadership when their man—FDR or John Kennedy or another Democrat—was in the White House, but they were against it when the President was Ronald Reagan.

The second group is made up of the intellectual heirs of the dominant school of the midcentury, still true believers in party government and presidential leadership. It includes such survivors of that school as James MacGregor Burns, who was a leader in the formation of two current reform organizations, the Committee on the Constitutional System and the Committee for Party Renewal, both of which attempt to bridge the separate worlds of academic science and practical politics. The Democrats in this group had to swallow hard in the Reagan era, but forced their reason to overcome their emotions so that they could say, "We're willing to let the Republicans have their day—even under Reagan—because they will be held accountable, they will discredit themselves, and then we will have our day." The Democrats are now joined, too, by some of their exact opposites—the new breed of conservative activists who have found that divided government can frustrate them too, when the public mood swings their way. Those in this group in both parties believe that in the long run a government that is able to act, even if it makes mistakes, is less dangerous than one that is rendered impotent by deadlock and division. A government with the capability to act will also have the capability to correct its errors (or its successor can) but there is no recourse when a government is inert, lethargic, paralyzed. Accordingly, scholars in this group believe that reform measures are in order, but they are apt to put the question aside because of the hopelessness of advocating changes in the Constitution.

The third block of political scientists and apparently the largest, even among specialists in American national government, is made up of those who have not found it necessary to take a stand at all. This group can be charged with evading what is surely one of the most crucial intellectual questions facing students of American government—one that the previous generation of political scientists explicitly asked and answered.

There are many reasons that scholars of government might prefer to evade the question. One was mentioned earlier—methodology. How is the general performance of a government to be evaluated, anyway? How can the effects of divided government be separated from the effects of all the other factors that influence outcomes—the temperaments and capabilities of individual leaders, the economic and social circumstances of a given time, and the actions of the other peoples and nations that share the globe—so that one can render a quasi-scientific judgment as to whether unified or divided government is the superior model for America? These are daunting questions, but no one needs precise quantitative answers. Informed judgments are needed based on the best methods of analysis that are available, as rough as those may be.

Some of the other reasons for evading the issue are less respectable. It is not satisfactory to argue that an intellectual effort is unnecessary because the new era will shortly end and the country will return to party government of its own accord. A third of a century has already elapsed since 1955, and the tendency of the voters to elect Republican presidents and Democratic Senates most of the time, and Democratic Houses all of the time, appears to be as firmly fixed as anything in national politics, reinforced rather than weakened from election to election. Those who would rely on this argument should provide a convincing explanation for predicting an automatic restoration of the previous order.

Nor is it satisfactory to contend, as many do, that a basic principle of democracy forbids questioning the desirability of coalition government: that of majority rule. A majority of the people evidently want divided government, runs this argument, and therefore they are entitled to have it, whether it is good for them or not. After all, the people rule. But this argument assumes that divided government is the people's intent, more or less conscious, rather than the essentially chance outcome of the electoral system that was not designed by those who use it. Clearly the latter is the case: divided government is a historical and procedural accident. The era of coalition government was not ushered in three decades ago by the sudden appearance of an overwhelming popular demand for that form of government as such. In 1956, the first presidential election year of the new era, a majority of voters liked Eisenhower and a majority wanted to retain their incumbent Democratic congressmen; but those were not the same majorities. In that year and in every one of the divided-government elections since, a large majority of the voters in fact voted a straight ballot, either Republican or Democratic, for national offices. It was the ticket-splitting *minority*, often a small minority, that gave the country its divided government. There is no evidence from electoral behavior that the public at large has deliberately rejected the long-accepted doctrine of party government; reliable public opinion polling data on the abstract question do not exist.

In short, fence straddling on this issue is not intellectually defensible. Either the dominant pre-1954 view of the desirability of party government and presidential leadership as the model and the ideal was right or it was wrong. That two systems so diametrically opposite as party government and coalition could serve the country equally well is a virtual mathematical impossibility, and that they could come close to equality is highly improbable. One or the other necessarily has to be the superior model for America, and political scientists have a responsibility to determine which it is and inform the country of their judgment.

Not that the discipline would ever speak with a single voice, of course, or even reach the level of agreement that prevailed in the 1940s and 1950s. But political scientists have the responsibility to grapple with the question individually, and by pooling their wisdom and debating opposing views to see whether a broad area of agreement might emerge.

Those who think that the model of party government and presidential leadership was wrong, and who would advance the post-1955 structure of coalition government as the new ideal, have an obligation to provide a new body of theory that will tell us what is the substitute for presidential leadership and congressional followership, how the partners in the American coalition government should relate to one another for that type of government to function well, and how those relationships can be brought about. What is the role of parties in such a system, and will strengthening them simply intensify the confrontation between the branches and render deadlocks more implacable? Should the agitation within the discipline for stronger parties be reversed and should weaker parties be made the goal? How would the weakening of congressional parties affect the efficiency of the Congress and its status vis-à-vis the presidency? Does the answer—or part of it, at least—lie in bipartisan mechanisms such as the one that resolved the social security issue and the National Economic Commission that was created in 1988 to grapple with the budget deficit? Can these be multiplied and regularized to anticipate and forestall crises rather than simply cope with them when they reach the desperation stage? If we are to accept coalition government as ideal, or even as satisfactory, we need a body of theory as fully developed as the one it super-seded, followed by institutional innovation based on the new theory. No such body of theory has even begun to emerge.

By the same token, those who still cherish the idea of party government have an obligation of equal gravity. They must come to grips with the question of how our election system, or the composition of powers of the branches of government, should be altered to restore unified government as the normal state of affairs. And if that means—as it surely does—that the Constitution itself should be changed, how can that be brought about? That question obviously is not one for the faint-hearted. But for any serious student of American government to contend that all of the issues raised by coalition government can simply be set aside, because whatever is is best, is not an answer. The times demand a more responsible political science than that.

POINTS TO PONDER

1. What is divided government and what are its main causes?
2. What is responsible-party government, and why is it incompatible with divided government?
3. Why does Sundquist argue that divided government is bad for the country?

30

"WHAT HAS HAPPENED TO THE SEPARATION OF POWERS?"
Hugh Heclo

In this selection from The Separation of Powers and Good Government *(Bradford Wilson, ed. 1991), Hugh Heclo, a political scientist at George Mason University, takes a broad, historical view of the separation of powers. He argues that, despite the swings of the pendulum of power between the president and Congress and the resulting temporary imbalances, the most striking aspect of the system is the fact that it has survived the historical changes of the past two centuries. Heclo examines the shifting balance among the branches in recent years, noting that, while the federal courts have played a limited role in constitutional review, "they have become increasingly active in review of statutory provisions." He notes that the tendency of Congress to micromanage executive branch administration has resulted from the breakdown of trust between the branches and that the presidency has come to dominate the war-making power at the expense of the constitutional role of Congress.*

Introduction

The separation of powers is a subject that invites compartmentalized thinking. Protagonists proclaim the unfettered or hamstrung condition of this or the other branch of government. If one side is up, the other must be down; one side more powerful, the other less so. The clarity of a development in one part of the system easily obscures the reverberations set off in other parts of the government web. It is very difficult to gain a view of the whole, steadily and with perspective.

The discussion that follows begins with one of the most neglected "holistic" aspects of the separation of powers: its durability. We then turn to what *has* been discussed at extensive (and, some might say, banal) length: the growing overall role of the Presidency in the separation of powers. The picture becomes more complex and hopefully less banal as we move on to show how congressional delegation of power to the executive and legislative strings of control have grown hand in hand. And because institutions in our system of government are inescapably interconnected, our discussion reaches out to include the often limited (in terms of "constitutional review") and increasingly extensive (in terms of "statutory review") role of the courts in the unfolding development of the separation of powers. The final sections offer evidence and analysis relevant to thinking about the important question of whether or not the system works. On the whole there is reason to feel sanguine about what appears as a moving balance of overlapping and separate powers. When it comes to the particular issue of the President's war-making powers, however, there are trends that should give Americans more cause for worry.

The Forgotten Success

Political writers have fallen into the habit of using shorthand labels to characterize the state of our national institutions. One hears about the "Imperial Presidency," or the "Resurgent Congress," the "Fettered Presidency," or the "Imperial Congress." Above all, in recent years we hear about a government of "Stalemate," "Gridlock," and "Immobilism."

Leaving aside for the moment how accurate these labels might be, they all miss the most important and least commented upon feature about our separation of powers system. That feature is its durability. Granted, durability is not something that many people today are likely to become excited about. Endurance is a seemingly humdrum, "unsexy" affair. With the basic constitutional design of separated powers still in place after 200 years, durability is something we simply take for granted.

It was not always so. The minds of the Founders—both those who designed the American Constitution and the larger, diverse groups who debated its ratification—were preoccupied with the problem of durability. Of course, institutional survival was "only" a means to the larger ends of government. The chief object in the separation of governing power was liberty—a safeguarding of each person's unalienable rights from arbitrary power. And too, contrary to some more recent interpretations, efficiency was also an important objective. Having lived through the chaos of government-by-committee in the Continental Congress, as well as having witnessed the upheavals in domestic affairs resulting from executive feebleness in state governments, many of the Founders saw the separation and balancing of different powers as essential to efficient government. A bumbling, ineffective government could threaten liberty as surely as could an unrepresentative government of concentrated powers. As Justice Robert Jackson would later put it,

> While the Constitution diffuses power the better to secure liberty, it also contemplates that the practice will integrate the dispersed powers into a *workable* government. It enjoins upon its branches separateness but interdependence, autonomy but reciprocity. (emphasis added)

If goals such as liberty and efficiency were in the back of their minds, the question of viability was in the front of the Founders' thoughts. In those days any college graduate or other person of learning could be expected to have studied the history of the ancient republics and the seemingly inevitable decline of such governments. The one-way life cycle of the republican form of government—from public virtue and liberty, to licentiousness and the corruption of public-mindedness, and thence to anarchy and eventual tyranny—was part of the common currency of late 18th century political thought. Or, as the patriot-orator Thomas Dawes, Jr. put it, "Half our learning is their epitaph."

Given these familiar historical lessons, given their experience with the Articles of Confederation and the accompanying turmoil in state governments, it seems fair to say that those debating the U.S. Constitution were fairly haunted by the fear that such a form of government as they were proposing could not endure.

Hence the first and, historically speaking, most astonishing answer to the question of what has happened to the separation of powers system is that it has survived. The design has proven robust and resilient throughout immense transformations in our national life. For us today it is difficult to grasp the enormity of that achievement. At issue is a government framework that has accommodated the metamorphosis from a seacoast strip of a nation with under 4 million inhabitants to a continental world power with over one quarter billion people. This institutional framework has endured the economic transformation of a pre-capitalist collection of several thousand agrarian, insular communities into a post-industrial, high-tech economy integrated through virtually instantaneous communications. And, while some complain that U.S. politics is still run by privileged insiders, today's mass democracy seems light years away from the early days of the Republic when only one in six Americans was eligible to participate in the political process, and a much smaller proportion could hold public office.

No other political framework in place in the late 18th century managed to survive those sorts of transformations. Ancient history, some may say. Is our separation of governing powers a system that is viable for today? Isn't the separation and balancing of power just another word for stalemate in a modern, complex society? Later we shall examine some evidence on this question, but for the moment it is important not to lose sight of the big picture even in more recent times. While we may grouse about the system and invent labels for our frustrations, we should also recall what the basic separation of powers design has survived just within the memory of living Americans. It has survived a Depression that shook the foundations of the economy and prompted extremist attacks from the fascist Right and communist Left. It has survived the first truly world-wide war from 1939–1945 and the domestic upheavals that this created. It has endured a 40-year Cold War, threats of nuclear annihilation, the self-inflicted madness of McCarthyism, the assassination and attempted assassination of the nation's leaders. The system has come through a transformation in the public agenda during the 1960s and 70s—the first major national attack on over 200 years of racism, the shock of the nation's first major defeat in a war, a presidential challenge to the rule of law followed by the first resignation of a Chief Executive, and the list could go on. All of this, and yet, despite the grousing and criticisms of the system, no one really doubts that after the next election, or ten or twenty years from now, we will still have separate legislative, executive and judicial institutions sparring with each other in Washington. The separation of governing power is a regime that looks robust and durable.

This should not suggest a Pollyannaish view, and later we will examine one area where developments are especially troubling for American constitutionalism. But the enormous and easily overlooked historical fact of regime durability should be the starting point for any such discussion.

How has the separation of powers design managed to be so durable? One may doubt it is because of any unique wisdom or virtue inherent in the American people. The Founders' mixed view of human nature seems to have gotten it about right: people are bad enough not to be trusted with power but virtuous enough to govern themselves with properly designed constitutional institutions for allocating power.

Perhaps we have just been lucky, bearing out Chancellor Bismarck's observation that a special Providence protects fools, drunkards and the United States of America. But the authoritarian Chancellor did not understand much about republics or constitutions. And it has surely been an improbably long streak of luck.

Three other reasons carry more weight in explaining the durability of the separation of powers. For one thing, popular reverence for the Constitution itself—something which the nation's early leaders successfully enshrined as central to Americans' self-identity—has aided regime survival. Although few

Americans have very much detailed knowledge about its contents, reverence for the very idea of the Constitution has served as a huge sheet anchor of stability amid the turmoil of events. Any politician, no matter how popular, incurs immense penalties if he is perceived as somehow playing fast and loose with the Constitution. This is what befell President Franklin Roosevelt and his Supreme Court "packing" plan after the 1936 election landslide, and the results were even more disastrous for President Richard Nixon and the Watergate cover-up after his own landslide victory in 1972.

In the second place, the framework of 1787 has proven durable because the dynamics set up in its allocations of power have usually operated more or less as intended. Ambitions of legislators, with their own electoral base and legislative powers, and ambitions of presidents, with their different electoral base and executive powers, have indeed checked each other and thereby reduced the risk of either branch usurping the functions of the other. Likewise no "faction" has been able to gain control over the whole system and independently work its will. For important things to get done, very large coalitions are needed throughout the dispersed centers of power. From the outset the intention behind the design was not simply to produce self-cancelling vetoes on any action but, by delaying and checking the exercise of power, to facilitate the kind of action that recognizes joint concerns across many interests (*Federalist* no. 51). Something of that hope was operational approximately 100 years later when James Bryce observed that "there is an excessive friction in the American system, a waste of force in the strife of various bodies and persons created to check and balance one another." It is "only when a distinct majority of the people are so clearly of one mind" that concerted action becomes possible. And today on matters such as Social Security reform, the environment, health insurance or educational reform something of the same tendency can be discerned, though we often have to call those common concerns a "crisis."

The third point is that the separation of powers system has proven durable because it has been adaptable. Practical-minded people in and around Washington have kept adjusting to circumstances and acting out of the belief that, as a character in Lampedusa's novel *The Leopard* puts it, "If we're going to keep things the same there are going to have to be some changes made around here." Since this phenomenon of stability-enhancing change is central to what has happened to the separation of powers, the point deserves a fuller discussion.

Improvisation and Joint Construction

Political adjustment and accommodation, events and experience rather than doctrine have been the lifeblood of the separation of powers. It has been so from the beginning. Amid our current confusions one is tempted to assume that the Founders had a clear idea of how the separation of powers would operate. It is more accurate to say that they had a clear idea of the opposite— how the concentration and abuse of power would operate. They knew this from hard experience, and it accounts for some of the provisions in the Constitution that seem obscure today but that the Founders regarded as very important. For example they knew from British politics how executive leaders could dominate the legislature by bribing lawmakers with sinecures. Hence the Constitution prohibits members of Congress from concurrently holding any other civil office and also forbids former congressmen from being appointed to any federal position, the salary of which has been increased during their term in office (Article I, sec. 6). Then too the Founders had also seen from state experiences how legislatures could be inflamed and ride roughshod over executive and judicial officials. Thus the Constitution prohibits Congress from reducing the compensation of the President and federal judges while they are in office as well as makes it difficult for Congress to remove them from office (Article II, sec. 1 & sec. 4; Article III, sec. 1).

As to how the separation of powers would actually function in a more positive way, the Founders were no different from their successors in having to experiment, adjust and, as we would say, work things out. The most famous early improvisation was the matter of the removal powers of the President versus Congress, but there were many others. Thus George Washington had presided and presumably learned about the document's intentions as the Constitution was constructed piece by piece in Philadelphia. But even Washington could only improvise as he pondered what form of communications to adopt in order to carry out the Constitution's "advise and consent" requirement regarding presidential nominations to office and the submission of foreign treaties to the Senate. At first Washington thought it essential to communicate orally and in advance of negotiating the terms of such treaties. Accordingly the President and his Secretary of War came to the floor of the Senate on Saturday, August 22, 1789, and submitted papers for discussing the terms of a new Indian treaty. It was not a happy experiment and was never repeated. Likewise, in the early Congress some members of the House sought to have Cabinet secretaries appear on the floor of the House for discussion and questioning. The House's leader, James Madison, effectively squelched that idea, thereby helping preserve not only the integrity of strictly legislative debate on the floor of Congress but also the President's control over executive departments.

Such political adjustments have continued down to the present day. The ongoing process of interaction by which the executive and legislative branches have tried to work out the practical meaning of the Constitution's separation of powers has sometimes been called coordinate or joint construction (as opposed to strictly judicial constitutional construction). With a few important exceptions, the courts have played a fairly marginal role in sorting out what the Constitution requires with regard to the operation of the separation of executive and legislative powers. Judges have prudently regarded this as a political matter to be worked out between the other two branches. Hence, unlike questions of individual rights or the power of the federal government vis-à-vis the states, there has grown up no extensive body of court-sanctioned doctrine to consult and apply when disputes about the relative roles of the executive and legislative branches arise. As we shall see, some recent Supreme Court decisions have sought, with dubious results, to move in a more doctrinal direction in this matter.

The Rise of Presidentialism

The most obvious development in the 20th century separation of powers is the growth of the President's role as policy leader. By this I mean that presidents, who with a few exceptions were routinely overshadowed in the 19th century by the political presence of Congress, have in this century become routinely expected to be the nation's leading agenda-setter, policy initiator, problem-solver and all-round leader with a "vision." How that occurred in the last 100 years is a complex story that has been told in many presidency textbooks. Here I wish to sketch just a few, sometimes forgotten, highlights.

To say that developments in the separation of powers have been ad hoc, experimental and event-driven is not to suggest that things have just happened without rhyme or reason. The President's growing prominence as policy leader is directly connected to the increasingly complex demands on government that have come in the wake of rapid economic, technological and social changes. Since such an abstract statement may not mean much, we should recall that a little over 100 years ago the United States was a nation where most people still lived in rural areas, large-scale manufacturing had only just begun, most "marketing" was done in general stores and from the backs of horse-drawn wagons; where the frontier of unsettled territory had only just disappeared, few Americans had ever travelled over 45 miles an hour, and the only form of wireless communication was yelling.

As demands grew for government to deal with increasingly complex changes in economic and social conditions, Congress's ability to legislate in sufficient detail was strained. Bureaucracy grew in Washington, as it did in the states and other developed countries, and the President as head of the executive bureaucracy increasingly became a focal point for policy management. It is important to recall that in the early part of this century the Presidency was given new coordinating chores, not to enhance the power of presidents, but to help Congress get on with its work. For example, Congress had traditionally produced a federal budget by summing up the separate budgets negotiated individually with each executive bureau, a process that was proving increasingly unmanageable before the First World War. Finally in 1921 the Budget Control and Accounting Act recognized the inability of a multi-headed Congress to produce a coherent budget for the government without executive leadership. The President, with the aid of a new professional budget staff housed in the Treasury Department, was charged by Congress with the responsibility to prepare a single, coordinated budget proposal for the executive branch as a whole and to submit such a proposal to Congress each year. Today it may be difficult to believe, but the orienting idea in those days was that, by helping the President prepare and execute a unified executive branch budget, such a professional budget staff would enhance the power of Congress, not the Presidency, to effect its will. As Charles G. Dawes, the first Director of the Bureau of the Budget, put it in 1923:

> We have nothing to do with policy. Much as we love the President, if Congress in its omnipotence over appropriations and in accordance with its authority over policy passed a law that garbage should be put on the White House steps, it would be our regrettable duty, as a bureau, in an impartial, nonpolitical and nonpartisan way to advise the Executive and Congress as to how the largest amount of garbage could be spread in the most expeditious and economical manner.

To a significant extent the same motivation of using presidential coordination to facilitate Congress's deliberative ability underlay legislative authorization for the President to negotiate individual tariff rates, reorganize executive branch agencies, and report on the condition of the economy.

The presumption of simply helping Congress do its work did not last long. Although some of the relevant developments were underway before the 1930s, the Depression and Franklin Roosevelt's administration set the mold for the more modern, powerful Presidency. Previous presidents such as Jackson or Lincoln had made vigorous use of presidential power, but these were sporadic, crisis-driven responses that produced few lasting institutional changes. By contrast, developments after 1932 institutionalized the Presidency as the focal point of national government leadership, no matter who held the office and whether or not there was a national crisis. This change became evident in a variety of ways. From the first half dozen special assistants provided to the President in 1939 legislation, the White House Office evolved in a 400- to 500-member complex of specialized staffs looking after presidents' personal political and policy interests. The Executive Office of the President was created in the same year and soon came to house presidential agencies concerned with the budget (the Budget Bureau was transferred from the Treasury Department in 1939 and later renamed the Office of Management and Budget, or OMB, in 1970) and the economy (Council of Economic Advisers, 1946). Eventually Executive Office staffs were added to advise presidents on defense and foreign policy (National Security Council, 1948), science policy (Office of Science and Technology, 1962), trade relations (Special Representative for Trade Negotiations, 1963), the environment (Council on Environmental Quality, 1970) and domestic policy in general (Domestic Council/Office of Policy Development, 1971). By mid-century the President's "legislative program" was expected to set the main agenda for Congress and the nation each year. Executive agency proposals for legislation, their testimony to Congress and their comments on pending legislation had to be "cleared" through the President's OMB staff. After 1981 their proposed regulations had to be cleared as well.

Overarching all of these particular developments was a growing aura, a seeming awesomeness that surrounded the Presidency. The emergence of the U.S. as a world power, the onset of the Cold War against which stood "the leader of the free world," images of the presidential finger on the atomic button—this was the stuff for creating a White House aureole. At the same time, growth of the mass electronic media offered presidents unique advantages for focussing public attention on the presidential persona, advantages which the White House became increasingly expert in exploiting and against which the hydra-headed and usually undramatic work of Congress could not compete. From the late 1940s to the 1980s Americans became bombarded with the symbolism of a Presidency running the government in lonely grandeur, without background detail, beyond politics, communing directly with the People and, it is suggested, even higher powers. As perhaps the leading student of presidential communications has observed, "even in the economic addresses (of Presidents), God is cited more frequently than the Federal Reserve or the Council of Economic Advisers."

Delegation and Control

Although the growing prominence of the President has been a dramatic development, it is scarcely the whole or most of the story about what has happened to the separation of powers. Congress has been far more than a passive participant in or observer of this trend. Like a moving counterweight to what has been happening in the Presidency, congressional adaptations have been made in the ongoing struggle to control policy.

Congress has delegated legislative power not only to the President but also to executive agencies and independent commissions. Partly this has been due to the practical difficulty of legislating complex public policies in sufficient detail and in part it has been a way for Congress to avoid politically tough decisions. Delegations of legislative power accelerated in the 1930s to accommodate the expanding role of government in the economy. After briefly objecting in 1935, the Supreme Court generally sustained such delegations so long as there were fairly clear legislative standards to guide the bureaucracy's actions or procedural safeguards to protect against arbitrary action. In recent decades the courts have tolerated much more vague delegations and increasingly rested content with the latter procedural criteria, especially as extrapolated from the advance notice, hearing, and appeal provisions of the Administrative Procedure Act (1946).

Delegation has certainly not meant that Congress has given free rein to presidents or the executive agencies on the matters so delegated. The familiar theme has continued to be not a neat separation but an overlapping or, as the Founders might have said, "blending" of powers. For example, major delegations of power to regulatory agencies have, even apart from any other congressional "strings," prevented presidents from removing commissioners of these organizations except for "good cause." After much political and legal wrangling, the Supreme Court laid down that the Congress could indeed restrict presidential removals to specified causes—i.e., not simply policy disagreements with commissioners. This has been seen as a way to protect the quasi-legislative, quasi-judicial position of "independent" regulatory commissions from White House policy control. Such interpretations did not prevent FDR and his Committee on Administrative Management from proposing that all such regulatory organizations be brought within the normal executive branch structure under the President. However, efforts to implement this president-centric view of policy management (sometimes called the Brownlow doctrine after Louis Brownlow, chairman of FDR's 1936 Committee) were soundly defeated in Congress, especially in light of the simultaneous congressional and public revulsion over the President's "court-packing" plan. Fifty years later the same idea for a unified executive branch incorporating the regulatory commissions was championed by leading officials in the Reagan administration, with as little result.

Much more pervasive than any fights over the removal of personnel has been Congress's insistence on maintaining a voice and ultimate policy control even while it has authorized the executive bureaucracy to do more and delegated power to that end. At this point we come to the essence of how the separation of powers framework has managed to both change and in some ways stay the same. Beyond the formal congressional power to pass laws authorizing and appropriating funds for federal activities—an immense power in the life of the bureaucracy—the legislature has continued to evolve a vast, informal system (though that term makes it sound too "systematic") of control based on political negotiations and *quid pro quos*. In addition to the requirements it writes into laws, Congress watches, nudges, and in many instances directs executive agency activities in ways that never have or will make the nightly news. The language in committee reports, understandings reached with executive officials in hearings, correspondence and reviews, informal concordants reached between staffs in the two branches—these are the workaday means through which the separation of powers has adapted and survived. Congress has usually found means to combine delegation and control, but doing so is a messy political process that can never satisfy those who wish to see clear bright lines drawn between the branches of government.

The legislative veto is a good example of the way the separation of powers design has been adapted through a combination of delegation and control. Although there were a few early precedents, the modern legislative veto came into major use in the 1930s when executive officials sought authority to take actions that would normally have required congressional legislation. In return for this authority, such executive action was made subject to some form of congressional approval or disapproval before it could take effect. Thus in 1932 President Herbert Hoover obtained congressional authority to reorganize executive departments through reorganization plans that would take effect unless either House of Congress passed a resolution rejecting the President's reorganization plan. Use of the legislative veto soon spread to other policy areas. Congress experimented with provisions requiring a positive vote to sustain the presidential action in question as well as provisions that required merely the absence of a negative vote. Legislative vetoes could sometimes be registered by both Houses, or one House, or even just one committee of Congress. Presidents and their advisers objected to such vetoes as unconstitutional infringements on executive functions, but usually acquiesced and signed the legislation containing veto provisions. As a rule, they wanted the new authority more than they disliked the veto strings.

When executive legislative relations deteriorated from the late Johnson through the Nixon administrations, Congress made increasing use of legislative vetoes to reassert its position in areas such as presidential war powers, agency regulations, and budget impoundments. Both the Carter and the Reagan administrations expressed their determination to raise constitutional challenges to the legislative veto, and in 1983 the Supreme Court responded with the decision *INS* v. *Chadha*. The Court declared that legislative veto provisions were unconstitutional, arguing that the exercise of such congressional actions was the equivalent to law-making and that therefore congressional vetoes should have to follow the normal constitutional requirements of passing both Houses of Congress and being presented to the President for his signature or veto. Although acknowledging that the laws containing legislative veto provisions had themselves been signed by presidents and that such provisions facilitated working relations between the branches, the Court repeated the familiar refrain that "convenience and efficiency are not the primary objectives—or the hallmarks—of democratic government. . . ." According to the 1983 ruling, the Constitution separated government into "three defined categories, Legislative, Executive, and Judicial," and it is the duty of the Court to resist the "hydraulic pressures inherent within each of the separate Branches to exceed the outer limits of its power."

In 1986 the Court reiterated in even stronger language the doctrine of compartmentalized powers by declaring unconstitutional a provision in the Gramm-Rudman-Hollings Budget Act that allowed the Comptroller General to order executive spending cuts if a schedule of deficit reduction targets were not met. Since the Comptroller General is removable only by a congressional joint resolution, these executive duties given to that officer by the Act were said to interfere with the powers of the President in what was "a separate and wholly independent Executive Branch." The Court argued that, apart from impeachment, the President is "responsible not to the Congress but to the people" and that "once Congress makes its choice in enacting legislation, its participation ends. Congress can thereafter control the execution of its enactment only indirectly—by passing new legislation." The Court went on to quote the sweeping language of the 1935 *Humphrey's Executor* case cited above, to the effect that:

The fundamental necessity of maintaining each of the three general departments of government entirely free from the control or coercive influence, direct or indirect, of either of the others, has often been stressed and is hardly open to serious question.

Despite these declarations of the mid-1980s, the legislative veto and equivalent informal arrangements have continued in the practical political world of joint construction. Between the time of the *Chadha* decision in 1983 and the end of 1990, over 200 new legislative veto provisions were passed into law under the signatures of Presidents Reagan and Bush. A legal purist might well wonder what is going on here. The answer is that what has been going on has been an exercise in pragmatic accommodation to political realities, realities created in large part by the constitutional design itself.

One thing Congress did after the *Chadha* decision was to rewrite certain laws to eliminate legislative vetoes, thereby making life more difficult for executive officials seeking discretionary authority to act. For example, statutes on executive branch reorganization were changed to require the President to obtain approval from both Houses of Congress for a reorganization resolution that would then be presented to the President for signature or veto. This was actually a more stringent hurdle for presidents than the earlier pre-*Chadha* situation when presidents had discretion to reorganize unless there was a resolution of disapproval passed by one House.

However, formal amendments to statutes were less important than post-*Chadha* reassertions of informal strings that Congress continued to tie to executive branch activities. For example, congressional Appropriation Committees have threatened to withdraw authority for particular executive agencies to transfer funds or exceed specified spending caps unless prior notification has been given to the Committees and the approval obtained. Executive officials have generally agreed to such informal understandings as the price of the discretion they desire. They have proceeded just as if a legislative veto had been written into the laws. In another example, against objections from the Bush White House, Secretary of State James Baker struck a bargain in 1989 with Congress to provide $50 million in humanitarian aid to the Nicaraguan Contras. By this "gentlemen's agreement," Baker promised that a major part of the funds would be disbursed only with the prior approval of four key congressional committees and the party leaders of both Houses of Congress. In short, political bargaining has continued to produce numerous implicit or explicit legislative vetoes.

The courts have acquiesced to this bypassing of the strict separation of powers doctrine laid down in the *Chadha* and *Bowsher* cases of the mid-1980s. Indeed, in recent decisions the courts have returned to the more traditional, pragmatic approach that accepts the political reality of overlapping powers. thus in a case challenging the "gentlemen's agreement" negotiated by Secretary of State Baker, the appellate court affirmed that "our separation of powers makes such informal cooperation much more necessary than it would be in a pure system of parliamentary government." Likewise, the Supreme Court in 1988 ruled that the Act authorizing the creation of independent counsels to prosecute high level executive branch officials was constitutional, even though the counsels investigating executive personnel are appointed by a panel of judges rather than the President and not removable except for good cause (rather than serving at the pleasure of the Chief Executive). As the Court put it, "We have never held that the Constitution requires that the three Branches of Government 'operate with absolute independence.'" In a case the next year the Court went on to recommend "a flexible understanding of the separation of powers." Unlike the reasoning in the 1983 *Chadha* case, the Justices now observed that "the Framers did not require—and indeed rejected—the notion that the three Branches must be entirely separate and distinct." According to the Court, the Constitution created branches with "a degree of overlapping responsibility, a duty of interdependence as well as independence."

Distrust, Micromanagement and Fudged Legislation

In retrospect we can now see that congressional delegations of rule-making power in the 1930s were accompanied by a good deal of faith in the efficiency of the bureaucracy and confidence that executive officials would carry out Congress's policy intentions. As the story of the legislative veto implies, since the 1960s that faith has largely disappeared and distrust between the two branches has grown. Typically the term used to identify what has been lost is "comity," a kind of mutual, courteous respect. One can catch a whiff of such understanding or sentiment in the 1923 quotation from the President's Budget Director cited earlier. A number of developments came together in the last generation to produce this loss of comity, and there is no need to try to decide here which was the more important.

The basic fact that trust depends on honesty is a good place to begin. Of course a degree of deception and manipulation is nothing new in politics. But, starting with the Johnson administration and intensifying in the Nixon administration, there was a growing perception in Congress that the President and his representatives simply could not be counted on to deal in good faith with the legislature and the American public. This "credibility gap"—a term coined midway through the Johnson Presidency—applied not only to the exceptional circumstances of high stakes politics, but also to the routine facts and numbers from the executive branch which Congress heretofore had counted on in order to do its legislative work. Misinformation and outright lies on conditions in the Vietnam War and, later, surrounding the Watergate affair were only the most dramatic examples. Information on the budget and spending transfers, conditions in the economy, implementation of congressional statutes and a broad variety of other government concerns were seen as subject to self-serving political influences from the White House, and thus suspect. When President Nixon failed to achieve his policy goals in Congress, the White House after 1970 adopted a strategy later dubbed the "Administrative Presidency" by a former presidential advisor. This strategy used presidential appointees and procedures within the executive bureaucracy to shape implementation of the law in the President's preferred policy direction.

Mistrust has in turn fed an explosion in congressional staffing to counter the growing presidential establishment. To enhance its own independent sources of information and give greater scrutiny—or oversight as it is called—to executive branch activities, Congress has produced a virtual revolution in the supply of people to support the work of Congress. New congressional agencies have been created (Office of Technology Assessment, 1974; Congressional Budget Office, 1975), the size of the Congressional Research Service quadrupled between 1960 and 1980 and, most dramatic of all, staff support to congressmen in the personal offices and committees has become a Capitol Hill mob scene. The number of persons employed in congressmen's personal offices rose from 3,556 in 1957 to 11,625 in 1985. The number working for the standing committees of Congress rose from less than 900 to over 3,000 persons in the same period. Moreover these additions to the political scene have been different from the folksy, political generalists that typically staffed the pre-1960s Congresses. The newer types of people are more likely to be young professionals, often well-trained in the ways of policy analysis and interested in the substantive details of government programs. These interests and abilities can, of course, put the newer breed of congressional staffers into competition with the policy expertise claimed by executive branch officials, producing ever more intricate and arcane conflicts between executive and legislative bureaucracies.

Other developments undermining the chances for comity have also been at work. Certainly it has not helped that divided government, with one party controlling the White House and the other the Congress or at least one House of Congress, has become the norm in recent decades. In only four of the last 24 years (the Carter administration) have the Presidency and both Houses of Congress been controlled by the same political party. Nothing like this condition has ever prevailed for so long in American history, and it means that the natural institutional jealousies established in the Constitution's separation of powers are intensified by the overlay of divided partisan control. Then too, the general trend in the same period has been toward a more ideologically strident politics. Evidence indicates that those who are active in the two political parties have increasingly grounded their political involvement in a concern for "the issues" and that the activists' attitudes toward policy issues have become increasingly polarized and "truly antagonistic" between the two parties. To appreciate what has happened to the separation of powers, we need to understand the corrosive impact on working relations between the branches produced by this combination of deceit and mistrust, competitive staffing, divided government and ideological activism in the past 25 or so years.

At the same time, demands on government continued to grow. In order to deal with contemporary concerns about the environment, health, energy, education and many other matters, Congress has still found it necessary to delegate rule-making and other powers. But given the changed political context, Congress has been led to pass statutes and otherwise behave in ways that further intensify the policy-making overlap of separated powers. Chief among these activities is what critics of Congress call "micromanagement." Distrustful that executive officials will vigorously carry out its legislation, Congress has often resorted to detailed instructions telling agencies when and how to enforce its laws.

Some modern conservatives critical of Congress have argued along lines that, knowingly or unknowingly, follow closely the traditional Brownlow doctrine of President-centric administration. They argue that if Congress cannot legislate in sufficient detail on a given issue, then what it is delegating was never legislative power in the first place but rather an attempt to usurp the executive function. This may be a reassuringly tidy view of government, but it immediately runs afoul of political reality. Congress has shown that if it wishes to it can legislate in very great detail indeed, leaving executives little of the discretionary power they so highly value. Trying to find the Essence of the legislative or executive function becomes beside the point, if not positively counterproductive, in the political bargaining over policy. For example, the 1976 Resource Conservation and Recovery Act had delegated broad regulatory powers and general guidelines to the Environmental Protection Agency for protecting the environment against hazardous wastes. After a series of highly publicized disasters such as Love Canal and clear evidence of EPA foot-dragging in implementing the 1976 Act, Congress passed a much different sort of act in 1984. The 1984 Hazardous and Solid Waste Amendments recaptured the regulatory role that had been delegated and did so by enacting a highly detailed policy framework with specific standards of protection, clear deadlines, and an implementation schedule studded with penalties that would take effect if the timetable was not met. All of these so-called "land ban hammers" were meant to counter the prevailing "bury and forget it" mentality in hazardous waste disposal and would strike unless EPA produced acceptable alternatives by a certain date. In the end EPA met the congressional deadlines. Purists, but not politicians, might wonder how a manifestation of the executive power had transmogrified to legislative power and back again.

Techniques for congressional micromanagement are legion. They include not only traditional budget controls and legislative veto-type provisions discussed earlier but also reporting and certification requirements laid on executive agencies, mandated agency reorganizations, grillings of executive officials at congressional hearings, and many other methods. As power in Congress has become more decentralized into committees and subcommittees—a post-1960s reflection of more open participation by increasingly independent political entrepreneurs—the possibilities for more specialized and detailed congressional controls have become very great indeed. And this in turn has been made possible by and helped encourage the growth of congressional staff.

Despite the conventional wisdom, the results of this trend are not necessarily counterproductive for government policy. In the early 1990s a panel of the National Academy of Public Administration selected ten important case studies to illustrate the nature and supposedly deleterious effects of congressional micromanagement. The cases ranged from the "land ban hammer" just mentioned to hospital reimbursement rules under Medicare, foreign arms sales, and international human rights policy. All ten cases showed a shift from an original, broad delegation of authority under legislation passed in the 1940s, 1950s and early 1960s to much more detailed and continuous congressional guidance of the executive in the 1970s and 1980s. Often these changes were made after policy differences erupted between the branches, chronic administrative difficulties or crises occurred, and/or executive officials were perceived as failing to carry out the legislation as Congress had intended. But, to the surprise of the panel of management and academic experts, these cases showed the results of congressional micromanagement to have been more sustained and constructive for the administration of policy than critics assumed. For example, congressional intervention pushed the Federal Aviation Administration to act on a new system for avoiding mid-air collisions, reduced the number of U.S. arms that would have otherwise been sold abroad in volatile situations, and forced the Department of Energy to shift its focus from the production of high-level nuclear waste to public protection and environmental restoration in its disposal. Congress created new reporting and certification requirements that made the State Department give more attention to human rights records in foreign aid decisions and established a new technical capacity to advise on standardized formulae to control Medicare payments.

As a reflection of the increased distrust between the branches, micromanagement is one of two major characteristics more frequently found in legislation of the last 25 years. The second characteristic affecting the overlap and separation of powers is what might be called "fudged legislation." It too is a response to a changed political environment. Since the early 1960s there has been a proliferation and mobilization of interest groups and policy networks, both those favoring and those opposing various forms of government activism. At the same time, legislative power in Congress has become more decentralized in the hands of congressmen whose political careers owe little to their party and almost everything to their personal campaign organizations and fund-raising capacities. The result has been to increase the range of contending groups, the number of available veto points and an every-man-for-himself mentality in the legislative process. In order for anything to pass in this situation, legislation typically has to be "fudged"—i.e., embody a host of concessions that render the statute ambiguous if not contradictory on key points in order to assemble the unpredictable votes and pass through the numerous roadblocks. For example, liberal pro-activist forces are likely to be strong enough to write broad language about purposes of the legislation and "rights" to a clean environment or access of the handicapped to various facilities. But other forces are likely to have to be appeased by special exemptions or qualifying language that sets down ambiguous requirements for administrators' actions to be "reasonable," "cost-effective," "feasible," and the like.

Fudged legislation means that, although Congress has delegated legislative rule-making power, how that power is to be used is often open to a variety of plausible interpretations.

Enter the courts. Challenges to the validity of agency decisions have mushroomed in the past 25 years, especially since much of the domestic legislation passed in this time literally invites disgruntled groups to litigate agency actions. Federal district and appeals courts in particular have become intimately involved in deciding what agency rules should look like, when and how they should apply in areas of education, health, the environment and consumer safety, to mention just a few areas. In the name of assuring a fair rule-making process, judges (particularly in the D.C. Circuit Appeals Court) have required agencies to develop and maintain thorough records of all the information that has gone into making a given rule. This record is then used by judges to take a close look at challenged agency decisions in light of statutes that, being both detailed and ambiguous, almost invariably point in several different directions. By such statutory review—deciding whether an agency action accords with congressional legislation and fair procedures—judges are frequently the final word on what action is "reasonable," and therefore what public policy is to be.

In recent years the Supreme Court has shown its willingness to supervise and enter into such policy-making through rigorous examination of the reasonableness of agency rules constructed under vague laws. Generally speaking it is this statutory review of agency decisions—rather than the constitutional review of statutes under any separation of powers doctrine—that has thrown the Court into the middle of political squabbles about legislative versus executive control over policy.

Whether this trend helps the President or Congress now depends on the ideology and policy preferences of judges as well as the distribution of partisan power in the executive and legislative branches. For example, a traditional constraint on judicial review of agency decision-making has been deference to the presumed administrative expertise in the bureaucracy. But in the contemporary political environment, deference to administrative expertise has become a means for courts to make policy by determining whether agencies have used reasonable means to achieve reasonable results. Abortion counseling is one of many such issues. In adopting the 1970 Public Health Services Act to subsidize low-cost family planning services, Congress prohibited the use of funds to perform abortions but did not mention restricting abortion counseling or referral to any other outside services. Throughout the Nixon, Ford, Carter and most of the Reagan years, the relevant executive agency interpreted this statute allowing non-directive counseling to all outside services, including prenatal care, adoption and abortion. During this time Congress consistently rejected efforts that would have amended the Act so as to prohibit counseling references to abortion services. Late in the Reagan administration,

White House officials successfully urged the agency to issue a new rule requiring physicians and counselors at such federally funded clinics to withhold any information about abortion. Challenged in the courts, the agency's new interpretation was upheld by the Supreme Court (*Rust v. Sullivan*, 1991).

The Court held that since the agency's new interpretation was based on a "reasoned analysis" supplemented by "a shift in attitude against the elimination of unborn children," the Court should "defer to the Secretary's permissible construction of the statute." Critics charged that the Court, rather than making the obvious finding that Congress had never authorized restrictions on counseling and referral, used its own interpretation of what was a reasonable analysis and of shifting public opinion to justify a new policy made within the confines of the bureaucracy. Congress then sought to correct the interpretation of its statute by passing legislation allowing non-directive counseling and referral information on abortion. When this legislation was vetoed by President Bush and the House narrowly failed to override the veto, the regulation became the law of the land, notwithstanding the majority view in the legislature.

Thus if Congress has become more involved in managing administration, it can also be said that the executive and courts have become more involved in law-making. The various threads might be drawn together in the following way. The formal, constitutional separation of powers has in recent years occasionally been affected by legal doctrine expressed by the courts (*Chadha, Bowsher*). But usually a more pragmatic, flexible approach has prevailed as the courts have accommodated the executive/legislative politicking—joint construction—through which the meaning of the separation of powers has developed. Thus despite attacks on the constitutionality of the legislative veto, congressional micromanagement has continued. However, the political incentives to pass "fudged" legislation have brought the courts to engage in widespread statutory review. This and not constitutional review has given judges an important policy-making role by allowing them to decide just what a congressional delegation of rule-making power to the executive requires and allows.

* * * *

Conclusion

Clearly there is no single or simple answer to the question of what has happened to the separation of powers. Where once the defining problem had been the potential instability of our republican political institutions, the problem now is conventionally seen as an excess of stability, to the point of immobilism.

However in this discussion we have seen reasons to be wary of the conventional slogans about stalemate or consistent dominance of one branch by another. No one has ever doubted that it is difficult to get things done in Washington, and it has probably become more difficult in the last 25 or so years. Institutional developments under the separation of powers system are only one complex part of an even larger, more complex picture of our public life. As a sharp observer of American politics observed some 50 years ago,

"Our government works as it does, not entirely because the machinery is cumbersome, but rather because the propelling power is sporadic and the load is heavy." The propelling power is ultimately the will of the people, in all its variegated, contradictory and differently-organized forms. The load is the accumulation of public expectations on government and its congested legacy of policies and programs. To judge if the system is working we need to inquire about something deeper than the matter of whether or not government is "solving" any particular problem that you or I might care about. It is asking us to judge the state of American constitutionalism.

Taking the large view, in the bulk of our affairs, domestic and, to a lesser extent perhaps, foreign developments in the separation of powers seem to have flowed through fairly familiar constitutional channels—so long as we understand those channels in a politically pragmatic rather than narrowly legalistic way. What we find in domestic and much of foreign affairs is neither presidential or congressional dominance but a mixed picture, depending on time and circumstance. Certainly today's executive branch is more prominent in sharing in the legislative power than anything with which the Framers were familiar. And too Congress's and the courts' interventions in "execution" of the law is more extensive than they ever imagined. This should not be surprising or alarming since, as we noted, the Founders were much clearer on what the separation of powers was to prevent and how it was to prevent it than on how such a novel system would positively do its work. But prominent does not mean dominant when we talk about the hands of president and Congress in each other's work. The overall "holistic" picture is one of a moving balance— both a checking and balancing, a separation and overlap between the spheres of government. As the Founders seem to have intended, it is a kinetic design where institutions must practice a relationship.

Where this portrait breaks down, I have suggested, is in the postwar shift in war-making powers toward the President. This is a contentious view. But in a post–Cold War era, when for the first time in its history the U.S. lacks a major foreign military threat—indeed when for the first time in all human history the world has one dominant military power, and that supposedly a government of, by, and for the people—this is an issue to which citizens should pay serious attention.

POINTS TO PONDER

1. Why has the presidency increased in power in the twentieth century?
2. What role have the federal courts played in balancing the power of the two popularly elected branches?
3. What is congressional "micromanagement," and why do some consider it a problem?
4. According to Heclo, how have the national security powers shifted in the twentieth century? Why is Heclo critical of this shift?

Chapter 8

✿

CORRUPTION AND
ABUSE OF POWER

Corruption is the improper use of public office for private purposes. The most common types of corruption stem from greed, and are attempts to enrich the wrongdoer at the expense of others, usually the taxpayers. Common forms of this type of corruption are bribery (a bribe is an inducement to improperly affect the performance of an official duty), embezzlement (the manipulation of accounts to siphon off money), or outright stealing. Abuse of power is using an official position and the power of the government in an improper manner to subvert the political or legal process. The readings in this section illustrate some of the more dangerous threats to our system of governance. These threats are particularly insidious because they undermine the confidence of citizens in the legitimacy of the political process itself.

Petty Corruption

Financial corruption is in a sense petty, even though the sums of money may be large, because its main purpose is to enrich the wrongdoer. It is also the least dangerous form of corruption, because everyone recognizes that it is wrong, and when it is detected, its punishment in our system is straightforward and accepted as just. This petty type of corruption has been found throughout American history at all levels of government, as well as in the private sector. It has even crept up to the vice presidential level. Ulysses S. Grant's vice president, Schuyler Colfax, accepted some railroad stock when he was a member of Congress for the purpose of stopping an investigation into the Credit Mobilier Corporation. Grant's second-term vice president, Henry Wilson, was also implicated in the scheme, though Grant himself was cleared of any wrongdoing. Secretary of the Interior Albert B. Fall was paid about $400,000 by two oil companies for granting them leases for the Teapot Dome oil reserves in California. President Nixon's first vice president, Spiro Agnew, resigned his office and pleaded nolo contendere to receiving money for official acts when he was governor of Maryland. He had continued to receive cash after he became vice president.

Systemic Corruption

A more serious type of corruption, though much more difficult to define, might be called systemic corruption. It is systemic in the sense that it is embedded in the nature of the system, and "everybody does it." It is usually legal, and isolating the individuals who are responsible for it is difficult because the line between what is legitimate and what is illegitimate is so blurred. If a system of governance is to maintain its legitimacy, it must attempt to brighten the line between acceptable behavior and unacceptable behavior.

One type of systemic corruption lies in the area of congressional campaign finance. Here, the tremendous sums of money that must pay for media time and campaign workers are raised through contributions by individuals and organizations. Hundreds of thousands of dollars are necessary to run a campaign without the support that political parties used to provide or without the public funding available in presidential campaigns. The problem, of course, is how to ensure that these contributions to the campaign coffers of candidates for office do not buy undue influence in the conduct of legislative business.

We have tried to solve the problem at the presidential level by providing public money for campaigns, but the amounts deemed necessary by political parties and presidential candidates exceed the public funds. So various dubious practices are used in presidential campaigns, one of which is "soft money" in which donations above the official limits can be accepted if they are used for the political party and not for individual presidential candidates. In contemporary presidential elections, this is a distinction without real meaning.

In congressional campaigns there is no public financing, and all the money must be raised by candidates themselves. Most fund-raising for congressional campaigns is quite legal, but many of the large donations come from organizations, interest groups, and businesses that have a stake in public policies that will be affected by legislation. Most members of Congress feel uneasy raising money from these groups, and very few would let such donations explicitly affect their votes in Congress. But the sums of money necessary for contemporary political campaigns leave congressional candidates little choice but to ask for it from those who are willing to give.

This system might be considered corrupt even though campaign contributions are carefully monitored by the Federal Election Commission, and most members are careful to stay within the bounds of the law. Most members of Congress are morally upstanding and do not engage in any unethical or illegal behavior in raising money for their campaigns. Yet the system as a whole tends to be corrupting because it distorts priorities away from legislating and toward money raising, and because it tempts members to ask for money from those who may be affected by members' official actions.

Elements of systemic corruption were involved in the savings and loan scandal of the 1980s. Savings and loan organizations were formed to take in deposits of money and pay interest to individual depositors. The organizations then loaned out that money at higher interest rates to home buyers. When inflation soared in the 1970s, the savings and loan institutions had to pay higher interest rates in order to attract deposits, but they were stuck with the low interest rate income from the long-term mortgage loans they had made in the past. To solve the problem, savings and loans were given authority to expand their borrowing and lending to commercial loans, where they had little experience.

This expansion of the savings and loans' scope was in line with the deregulation policies of the 1980s, but government auditors also came to take a lenient view of the savings and loans' practices as they became overextended in paying high interest rates justified by dubious commercial investments. Because of bad management, hundreds of these institutions went bankrupt and their depositors were reimbursed for their losses by the federal government. Part of what made the savings and loan debacle possible was the government guarantee of up to $100,000 on each deposit. Individual depositors thus did not have to inquire closely about the solvency of the savings and loan institutions in which they kept their savings.

When the system was collapsing and the government decided to shut down the insolvent savings and loans, the cost of paying the individual depositors for their lost savings amounted to hundreds of *billions* of dollars. Some of the business people went to jail for breaking the law in their stewardship of the savings and loans, but much of the problem was caused by incompetence and recklessness allowed by the system. In one case even U.S. senators became involved when they intervened with government regulators and used their influence to pressure government officials to be lenient with savings and loan operator Charles Keating, who had been a substantial contributor to a number of campaign funds. Despite their argument that they were only doing their job, five senators (the Keating Five) were rebuked or reprimanded by the Senate after an Ethics Committee investigation.

Abuse of Power

The most dangerous kind of corruption and threat to a system of governance, however, is the abuse of power. This type of corruption occurs when power is used, not for personal financial gain, but for the purpose of staying in power or achieving political goals despite the law or constitutional process. Using official governmental power in illegal or unethical ways to stay in power is dangerous because it undermines the democratic process that allows the people to change their political leaders. Such undercutting of democratic processes could easily lead to what the Framers would call tyranny. Achieving policy goals by extra-constitutional methods undermines faith that the system is fair and that it gives all interests a chance to achieve their policy goals through legal and constitutional procedures.

The Readings

The readings in this section discuss examples of corruption in American politics that tend to undermine citizen confidence in our system of governance. Different types of corruption do not have the same impact on the political system. Our systems of campaign finance and congressional representation easily lead to ambiguous situations that are not clearly illegal, yet might be seen as corrupt. More important examples of corruption, such as Watergate or the Iran–Contra scandal, are clearer examples of wrongdoing, but they are so politically charged that punishing the wrongdoing is controversial. Any system of governance must draw lines between legitimate and illegitimate political behavior, but the more areas where the line is uncertain and blurred, the more vulnerable the system is to declining citizen confidence.

The selection by Brooks Jackson describes the congressional fund-raising process from the perspective of Congressman Tony Coelho. The system of campaign finance might be considered corrupt in the sense that members of Congress must spend a large portion of their time asking rich people and organizations for money, rather than doing their jobs as representatives of the people. Even though most of them do not enjoy it and find it demeaning, they feel that there is no choice. Even many scrupulous members cannot help but grant consultations to heavy campaign contributors about legislation in which those contributors have an interest.

The selection by Dennis Thompson lays out a line of reasoning that distinguishes between legitimate and illegitimate congressional actions on the part of constituents. The connection of private savings and loan money with political campaign contributions was corrupting because it distorted the democratic legislative process. There were many other incidents of fraud and corruption in the savings and loan debacle, and most did not involve government officials. Indeed, part of the problem was that government officials did not monitor the solvency of savings and loan institutions closely enough.

In the next selection Michael Genovese describes the types of corruption that were involved in Watergate. Among other things, the Nixon administration used unethical means to undermine the political campaigns of its opponents in the 1972 elections. In addition, the administration abused its power by trying to persuade the CIA to mislead FBI investigators looking into the sources of the administration's campaign funds and by suborning (encouraging) perjury to cover up its misdeeds. Many of these actions, condoned and encouraged by the president, were unprecedented in American history.

Another selection deals with the Iran–Contra affair in the 1980s in which the Reagan administration tried to rescue U.S. citizens held hostage in the Middle East by selling missiles and other arms to Iran. The selection is taken from the congressional investigation of the Iran–Contra affair and lays out the conclusions of the committees. The committees concluded that the administration decided to accomplish its own policy goals of aiding the Contras despite the prohibition in law. It decided to pursue in secret a policy that it failed to obtain through the normal constitutional policy process.

The selections in this section are intended to distinguish the most dangerous types of corruption. Some cynics say that all politicians are corrupt and "they all do it," so why participate in the political process. They believe all politics is corrupt.

But as we can see from these selections, only some individuals actually steal money from the public, and when they are caught they are put in jail. Most of the actions I have termed "systemic corruption" are not illegal and are often hard to distinguish from the legitimate actions of public officials. The way to deal with these problems is through legislative reform—for instance, of campaign financing for congressional and presidential elections. Finally, the instances of Watergate and Iran-Contra are unprecedented in American politics, and the best way for a polity to avoid repeating mistakes is to be aware of them.

KEY TERMS

Iran-Contra: the decision of the Reagan administration to sell arms to Iran in order to obtain the release of U.S. hostages in the Middle East. Some of the money from the arms deals was then sent to the Contras in Nicaragua during a time that this type of aid was forbidden by law. President Reagan approved of sending arms to Iran, but said that he did not know about the diversion of the proceeds of the Iran sales to the Contras.

Watergate: a series of actions by the Nixon administration involving "dirty tricks" in the 1972 presidential campaign and the cover-up of a break-in to the Democratic party national headquarters office in the Watergate building in Washington, D.C. The investigations culminated in the resignation of President Nixon on August 9, 1974.

Keating Five: five U.S. senators who put pressure on federal regulators to lighten their scrutiny of Charles Keating's savings and loan institution. Keating later served time in federal prison for fraud connected with his institution. The senators were rebuked or reprimanded by the Senate Ethics Committee, and three decided not to run for reelection.

31

"HONEST GRAFT: WHY MONEY IS IMPORTANT"
Brooks Jackson

In this selection from his 1988 book, Honest Graft, *journalist Brooks Jackson describes the money-raising activities of Representative Tony Coelho in the mid-1980s. Coelho was chairman of the House Democratic Campaign Committee, in charge of reelecting Democrats to Congress. The "graft" described by Jackson is "honest" because the types of fund-raising in which Coelho engaged were mostly legal, and, in a sense, "everybody does it." That is, both the Republican and Democratic parties raise money for political campaigns in ways that are allowed by the campaign finance laws, and they both exploit loopholes in those laws, such as "bundling" and "soft money." Even though the practices are seldom starkly illegal, they tend to be corrupting because politicians must solicit money from donors who have an interest in laws the members will vote on. Although individual votes are seldom "bought" (for an exception, see James Q. Wilson's article on Abscam in this volume), the strong implication is that donors of campaign money will receive a sympathetic hearing for their concerns about pending legislation. After this selection was written, Tony Coelho resigned his seat as a representative from California because of allegations of conflict of interest.*

I acknowledge that you can't keep an organization together without patronage. Men ain't in politics for nothin'. They want to get somethin' out of it.

But there is more than one kind of patronage.

—George Washington Plunkitt,
Democratic Leader of the
15th Assembly District,
New York City, 1905

Tony Coelho sat at the head of a conference table rimmed by his top staff aides in a glass-walled room in the Democratic party's new headquarters building, beginning a Monday morning strategy session. Outside, visible through the fan-shaped leaves of a ginko tree stirring in a warm June breeze, could be seen the twin smokestacks of a grimy heating plant. The stately Capitol was out of view, three blocks to the north.

Coelho was starting another week of chasing money. He pursued it not for personal gain, though he lived comfortably enough with the help of personal-appearance fees from lobbyists. He solicited money for the power it purchased, power for his party and for himself. Like the old machines that dominated big-city politics in the era before civil-service jobs and television, Coelho's machine ran on patronage. The old system used municipal jobs and contracts; Coelho's patronage was the federal government's array of subsidies, entitlements, tax breaks, and commercial regulation. The machines were paid directly in votes or in electioneering labor by government employees. Coelho's operation reaped money, which he converted to votes through the acquisition of what he called "political technology"—polling, television advertising, and computer-driven mail.

Like the Tammanys of old, Coelho's machine gave incumbents a firm grip on their jobs and reduced the political opposition to frustrated impotence. It viewed attempts at reform with suspicion. Meanwhile, the House remained a soil where scandals sprang up like weeds. But where the old bosses held sway in a single city or county, Coelho's machine straddled the entire nation.

Coelho had already read a thick sheaf of weekly reports from his staff. His finance director, Terence McAuliffe, reported that now, barely midway through 1986, the committee had taken in nearly $2 million. Roughly two-thirds of that was from rich donors, lobbyists, and political action committees, or PACs, run mainly by labor unions, corporations, and business and professional groups. About one-third had come through the mail from rank-and-file Democrats sending in small donations. That $2 million was only the "hard money" raised according to the strictures of the federal election law, which among its many intricate provisions limited party organizations to taking no more than $20,000 per year from any one person, or $15,000 per year from any PAC, and required that donations be fully disclosed. Coelho could use hard money, in amounts also limited by law, for donations to House candidates or for paying their campaign bills, and for meeting the operating expenses of the campaign committee.

Besides the hard money, however, McAuliffe reported that the committee also had received more than $600,000 in soft money from union treasuries, rich backers, and some corporations, sources that technically made it illegal to use the money directly in connection with federal elections. But the law was so full of loopholes and so poorly enforced that Coelho easily used these additional funds to help elect Democrats to the House. Furthermore, much of the income and expenditure of soft money wouldn't have to be disclosed.

McAuliffe was projecting a good haul from a weekend trip during which Coelho planned to parade speaker Thomas P. "Tip" O'Neill through a series of money-raising events in Los Angeles and San Francisco. O'Neill, the most powerful Democrat in Washington, was Coelho's best draw. Rich donors bought $1,000 tickets to have a drink with the big Irishman.

"We are in good shape in California," McAuliffe wrote in his report. "We should bring back $350,000–$400,000. I will be out there all week and I hope to get another $50,000–$75,000 next week."

"*Great!*" Coelho responded, scribbling on McAuliffe's report. His writing, like everything he did, was punctuated with underlinings and exclamation points.

Much of the California money was coming from the movie and real-estate industries, both of which wanted to preserve some lucrative loopholes in the tax code, which Congress was rewriting. Movie mogul Lew Wasserman, chairman of MCA Corp., and multimillionaire real-estate developer Walter Shorenstein were sponsoring events.

McAuliffe pushed Coelho to try for even more movie money. "Have you had an opportunity to call Jack Valenti?" McAuliffe reminded him. Valenti was president of the Motion Picture Association. "No, because we have Lew Wasserman on board," Coelho responded. "But I will!"

This week, as every week, Coelho would devote time to raising money, spending it, trying to cut off his enemy's supply of it. His quest for money never ceased, in both off years and election years. He understood, better than most of his colleagues, the simple reality that politics had become a capital-intensive enterprise. The campaign-money reforms of the 1970s, far from ending the days when lobbyists furtively passed around sacks of cash, had only brought the traffic in campaign money into the open, given it legal sanction, and turned lobbyists and commercial interests into regular collection agents for lawmakers. Favor seekers paid to gain the ear of members of Congress in the hope of influencing their votes. Understanding that reality, Coelho exploited it with the same exuberance with which he attacked everything else.

This morning Coelho was working, as always, to persuade business lobbyists not to give money to Republican candidates. Coelho's rival, the National Republican Congressional Committee, was planning to raise funds from business groups by exploiting the prestige of President Reagan. The Republican committee invited managers of hundreds of business-sponsored political action committees to a cocktail party with the President at a downtown hotel. For $5,000, two people would be admitted. And for $20,000, four PAC officials could enter an inner sanctum, the "President's Circle," where each could line up for a production-line, souvenir photo with the President. Republicans were figuring that the event could bring in $500,000 or more for twenty-four incumbents whom Coelho hoped to defeat.

Coelho was trying to find a way to scare timid corporate executives away from the event. He wanted to plant a news story suggesting that donors might be in legal trouble. Republicans were calling their event a "bundling party," because they would use a legal trick called bundling to get around donation limits in the federal election law. The law allows a PAC to give only $15,000 per year to party organizations such as the Republican campaign committee. But party officials planned to bundle up the checks and deliver them to the candidates, making sure that the PACs wrote the checks directly to the candidates. That way the money wouldn't pass through the party's bank account and wouldn't count against its limits. This was one of the mildest forms of evasion, but such tricks had become so common that limits on donations and spending had become nearly a dead letter and even the President himself aided the process. Still, some potential Republican donors were nervous. The GOP committee included a three-page legal opinion with its invitation.

Coelho saw an opening. "I think we have a real PR opportunity here," wrote his press secretary, Mark Johnson. "At the very least, our good friend Fred Wertheimer should not let this one slide by."

Wertheimer was president of Common Cause, a reform group that pushed for limiting PAC donations. Democrats, however, were far more reliant on the special-interest money than Republicans and got their share of criticism from Wertheimer. Coelho didn't really view him as a "good friend"; Johnson's reference was ironic. Johnson also suggested that, rather than arouse Common Cause, the Democrats might throw a bundling party of their own. "We could just copy the idea," he said. Democrats had lifted many Republican fund-raising ideas before. But no Democrat could match Reagan's drawing power with business PACs, and Coelho decided this time to attack rather than imitate.

At first he proposed a press release denouncing the Republicans directly, but was quickly reminded that Democrats lacked the moral standing from which to criticize.

"Should we mention that it's being questioned legally?" he asked his staff.

"But some of our candidates take bundled checks," warned an aide.

Indeed, bundling was invented by a PAC that gave almost exclusively to Democrats, the anti-nuclear Council for a Livable World. A women's group also bundled donations to female Democratic candidates for the Senate. The name of the group was EMILY, which stood for "Early Money Is Like Yeast": it raises the dough. A direct attack on the legality of bundling would backfire, or just be laughed off.

"One party accusing the other of violating the spirit of the law is like the pot calling the kettle [black]," said Martin Franks, Coelho's chief of staff.

Coelho tried it anyway, indirectly. He wrote to Common Cause and to another public-interest group, the Center for Responsive Politics, saying, "I am sure you will agree" that the GOP event "is indeed a violation of the spirit if not the letter of the law." He added, "I hope you also agree that this matter is worthy of your public denunciation."

But Franks was right. Neither reform group would carry Coelho's water. Common Cause simply kept quiet. The Center for Responsive Politics sent a letter to the Republican committee saying that their bundling event seemed to be a violation, but it also questioned Coelho about his own use of soft money. "We would enjoy an opportunity to meet with you and share our insights on this issue, wrote Ellen Miller, the group's executive director. Coelho was collecting soft-money donations as large as $100,000 each to subsidize a television studio to produce campaign commercials. He dropped the matter and the Republican bundling party went off smoothly.

After the Monday strategy session Coelho spent much of the week, as he did every week, at money-raising events for Democratic House candidates. He agreed to be listed as a "co-sponsor" of many of these events. His name was a valuable commodity. At Coelho's insistence, House Democrats had made the chairman of the campaign committee officially part of the "leadership," the powerful circle that included the Speaker, the Majority Leader, the Majority Whip, and the chairman of the Democratic Caucus, to which all House Democrats belonged. The campaign committee chairmanship formerly carried no official rank. That Democrats would elevate it to such lofty official status showed how tightly special-interest money had become intertwined in the process of government. It also helped make Coelho's name a magnet for the dollars of lobbyists; they tended to treat invitations from high-ranking lawmakers as assessments.

In trying to move one rung up the leadership ladder, to the post of Majority Whip, the number-three spot, Coelho handed out money, night after night, courting the support of his Democratic colleagues. Monday he swung by a hotel near the Capitol to drop off a check for $1,000 for Ralph Hall of Texas. It was drawn on Coelho's personal political action committee, the Valley Education Fund, named for California's Central Valley, which contained his congressional district. It wasn't just corporations, unions, trade groups, and ideological crusaders who maintained PACs; ambitious politicians had their own. Sometimes Coelho carried half a dozen white envelopes in his inside jacket pocket, each containing a Valley Education Fund check for $1,000 or more for a colleague or a struggling newcomer.

Tuesday morning Coelho was receiving money. He spoke to a breakfast meeting of the California Cable Television Association, part of an industry that wanted Congress to restrain the power of local governments to regulate rates charged to subscribers. Coelho nailed down a donation of $1,000 to the Valley Education Fund from the group's president, Spencer R. Kalitz of Castro Valley, California. The congressman's personal PAC was filled with such special-interest money.

A few hours later Coelho co-sponsored a fund-raising luncheon for Rep. Edward Feighan of Ohio at a large home near the Supreme Court building, owned by a wealthy liberal, Stewart Mott, heir to a General Motors fortune. Coelho gave another $1,000 from his PAC. Several blocks away at the Democratic Club, a lobbyists' lair next door to party headquarters, Coelho was simultaneously sponsoring another fund-raiser, this one for David Price, a Duke University political science professor running for the House in North Carolina. Coelho gave Price $1,000 too.

On Tuesday evening four different fund-raising events were scheduled between six and eight o'clock. Coelho co-sponsored three: one for Rep. Larry Smith of Florida on the rooftop of the Hotel Washington, another for Rep. Paul Kanjorski of Pennsylvania, and a third for Rep. Frank McCloskey of Indiana at party headquarters. These functions were such everyday occurrences that Democrats built catering facilities into their new building to accommodate them.

One event wasn't sponsored by Coelho. Rep. Beryl Anthony of Arkansas was a senior member of the tax-writing Ways and Means Committee and hardly needed Coelho's help to attract lobbyists' money. His committee had the power to raise or lower the taxes of specific industries by tens of billions of dollars.

On this busy Tuesday night Coelho gave $1,000 from his PAC to Anthony and $1,000 to Smith. He had donated $1,000 to Kanjorski a few months earlier. He skipped giving to McCloskey, who owed his seat to Coelho anyway. Coelho resurrected McCloskey after Indiana state officials declared him the loser in the 1984 election. He engineered a recount in the House, where Democrats transformed McCloskey into the winner by a party-line vote, leaving Republicans sputtering in impotent rage. In revenge, GOP congressmen refused to allow taxpayers' money to be used to pay legal bills arising from the recount, as had been the custom. Coelho had to divert campaign money into an undisclosed recount fund. McCloskey was supposed to raise labor-union money to replenish the fund but fell short, leaving Coelho stuck for tens of thousands of dollars. So McCloskey got nothing from Coelho's Pac.

On Wednesday Coelho was feeling high; his financial advisers had just told him that dollars were cascading into the campaign committee coffers. "All of our money stuff is doing better than I had expected," he said.

"The only negative has been the media center."

The new television studio in the basement of party headquarters was Coelho's pride, but it had been hemorrhaging money since it opened for business a few months earlier. Coelho had been counting on getting substantial business from his labor-union allies, liberal not-for-profit groups, and political consultants with commercial clients. His budget called for them to throw enough business his way to pay the staff salaries and the mortgage on the elaborate new facility, but that had turned out to be a miscalculation. Of the $630,000 worth of work he had expected by now, only a little better than one-third had actually materialized, and payment had been made for only a fraction of that. Coelho was so upset he had taken to dunning deadbeats personally, even threatening to sue a House colleague who wouldn't pay. The financial troubles of the studio were becoming a serious preoccupation, but Franks and McAuliffe assured him that the losses could be more than offset by the better than expected flow of money from donors. Franks was projecting, among other things, that he'd take in at least $1 million in soft money from several large labor unions, each pledged to give $100,000. "I'm not worried as much," Coelho said.

On Wednesday evening Coelho stopped by yet another fund-raising event, a reception for Rep. Jim Chapman of Texas aboard the yacht *High Spirits*, docked on the Potomac near a row of waterfront restaurants. The 112-foot craft— a small ship, really—was built in the Roaring Twenties and reflected that reckless era's preoccupation with conspicuous display of wealth. A promenade encircled the main salon, which was furnished with plump sofas, oriental rugs, and potted palms. It was launched in 1928, barely a year before the stock-market crash that ushered in the Depression. Now the *High Spirits* was once again maintained in gleaming condition by a full-time crew. It was financed by Donald Dixon, a man with a taste for four-star restaurants and real-estate gambles.

Coelho himself made frequent use of the yacht to entertain donors and lobbyists. He didn't ask how the bills were being paid, an oversight he would later regret. Chapman was also getting free use of the yacht. The normal charter fee was $2,000 per half-day, plus the cost of fuel and food, which came to $1,234 for Chapman's reception. The entire cost was being absorbed, apparently illegally, by Dixon's federally insured savings and loan, Vernon Savings and Loan Association of Texas, to which the yacht skipper remitted the bills. Vernon was in the process of collapsing into insolvency; it would soon be taken over by federal regulators accusing Dixon of plundering and wasting its assets through high living and mismanagement and driving it $350 million into the red. But as the liquor and money flowed at Wednesday night's dockside fund-raiser, Coelho and Chapman were oblivious to their host's legal problems.

When Chapman was later criticized for his free use of the yacht, he insisted that he had never met Dixon or done any favors for him. But he didn't reimburse Vernon. Instead, he amended his campaign finance reports to reflect the reception as a $234 personal contribution from a lobbyist for the Texas savings and loan industry, Durward Curlee, who lived aboard the *High Spirits* when in Washington. Chapman's staff claimed his use of the yacht was authorized under an election-law provision allowing volunteers to donate use of their personal residences.

Chapman, like McCloskey, owed a debt to Coelho. The Texan won it a year earlier in a special election that became a nationally watched showdown. GOP party strategists, hoping to demonstrate that conservative Southern Democrats were ready to defect in big numbers following Reagan's crushing defeat of liberal Walter Mondale in 1984, tried to snatch a solidly Democratic district around Texarkana. Reagan made a federal judge of the Democratic incumbent, opening up the seat for a free-for-all election in 1985. The Republican candidate, Edd Hargett, spent $1.2 million but lost narrowly to Chapman, who spent $540,000. The defeat so demoralized Texas Republicans that now, only one year later, they were giving Chapman a free ride to re-election, having failed to field a candidate.

PACs were donating money to Chapman's campaign fund anyway, to help retire his debts from the special election and to get acquainted with a new House member who was likely to remain for many years. During 1986 Chapman reaped nearly $119,000 from PACs and paid off $130,000 in personal indebtedness, either money he had lent directly to his 1985 campaign or bank loans for which he had guaranteed repayment. Coelho considered giving $1,000 too, but saved the money for campaigns that needed it.

Later on Wednesday Coelho dropped off $1,000 for Rep. Dale Kildee of Michigan. Kildee raised about $19,000 in PAC money at a Coelho-sponsored party at the Democratic Club, including $2,000 each from the Teamsters and the civil-service pensioners' lobby.

At the same time, a couple of blocks away, lobbyists were attending a fundraiser for Benjamin Cardin of Baltimore. Normally they shy away from nonincumbents, but Cardin, who was speaker of the Maryland House of Delegates, was looking like a winner for a vacant seat in a safely Democratic district. His event got $17,000 in PAC money, including $5,000 from the Teamsters and $2,500 from the United Auto Workers. Coelho dispensed another $1,000 check from his Valley PAC.

For Cardin's event the American Trucking Associations provided free use of their building near the Capitol, which they opened routinely for fund-raising receptions. It's illegal for corporations to subsidize congressional campaigns with company funds, but this corporate hospitality wasn't counted as a gift. The truckers said their facility was available free for non-campaign activities as well, such as retirement parties for lawmakers or Capitol staff members and events for credit unions and conservation groups favored by legislators. This exploited a provision allowing campaigns to use corporate facilities open to the general public. It was one of the many loopholes that were being stretched to allow lobbyists to deploy their money more freely.

On Thursday Coelho gave $1,000 for Chicago congressman Frank Annunzio at the Democratic Club. He also signed $1,000 checks to be sent off to two women candidates running in upstate New York districts, Louise Slaughter and Rosemary Pooler, and to Mike Espy, a black candidate running in Mississippi. That made a total of $11,000 given by the Valley Education Fund during the week. It was about average; his one-man PAC provided $513,600 to candidates in 1986.

Friday morning at eight Coelho left National Airport aboard a private plane supplied by the Philip Morris tobacco company, bound for California. The committee got the plane for much less than it cost the company to operate, using yet another loophole in the campaign-finance laws. Philip Morris had millions riding on what Congress would do about the federal tax on cigarettes, so it was happy to pay. How much was it worth for the company's lobbyist to spend four uninterrupted hours with the Speaker of the House?

But Speaker O'Neill didn't make the trip after all. He begged off, saying his wife wasn't feeling well. Later, to his irritation, Coelho heard that O'Neill went golfing. It was the third time in four years that O'Neill had ducked out of a major money-raising tour at the last minute. The Speaker didn't enjoy the big-dollar circuit.

O'Neill's sudden withdrawal left Coelho personally embarrassed. Among the several events that weekend, he had arranged for a group of Taiwanese-Americans to meet O'Neill in a private room at the Beverly Hilton Hotel. The audience with the Speaker was their reward for raising $25,000 for the campaign committee. Finance director McAuliffe was upset because O'Neill canceled a meeting with the same group a year earlier, deeply offending their ethnic pride. "For them, that's an insult," McAuliffe said. "You just can't explain it to them." He tried for hours to telephone the event's main organizer, but couldn't connect. Finally, sixty-five Taiwanese donors arrived at the large suite, where a mortified Coelho broke the news that O'Neill wouldn't show. "It was just a heart-wrenching experience," McAuliffe said later. "They were very, very, very, disappointed."

Without O'Neill the weekend events brought in $100,000 less than Coelho had hoped. McAuliffe knew he could have cashed in the Speaker's prestige for more money. "The Speaker never made a money call for us," he said wistfully. But the California weekend still produced about $300,000.

Coelho's detractors saw only a political opportunist, scooping up special-interest money to perpetuate Democratic power in the House. Years earlier a newspaper quoted an unnamed colleague as saying of Coelho that he had "one foot in the fast lane and one foot on a banana peel."

And yet Coelho saw his job in grand terms, like a bishop raising money for a cathedral. He barely was able to contain his enthusiasm, bursting to explain the sense of mission that he felt.

"Unless you believe that the Democratic party can really help people change their lives and provide some hope, you don't understand what I'm doing," Coelho said one day. "You don't understand my drive, you don't understand why I want to change things. You don't understand why money is important." He radiated a sense of innocence.

Coelho believed he had turned aside a right-wing Republican revolution, fighting money with money. The way he saw it, his new political machine allowed Democrats to stymie GOP designs on the pensions of the elderly and to frustrate plans of hard-line militarists to finance a war in Central America. When Democrats spent money for such noble ends, who cared where it came from. "I have inner peace," he said.

Except for a twist of fate, Coelho would have entered the Roman Catholic priesthood. It wasn't hard to imagine him rising in a totally different hierarchy. For him, the Democratic House was a surrogate church. George Washington Plunkitt, the garrulous Tammany Hall chieftain, said more than eighty years ago that his own political machine "does missionary work like a church." Plunkitt added, "It's got big expenses and it's got to be supported by the faithful. If a corporation sends in a check to help the good work, why shouldn't we take it like other missionary societies?" Coelho's attitude was exactly the same.

POINTS TO PONDER

1. With respect to campaign finance, what is the difference between "hard" and "soft" money?
2. What are the dangers of the present system for financing congressional campaigns?
3. Are there any alternatives to the current campaign finance regulations?

32

"MEDIATED CORRUPTION:
THE CASE OF THE KEATING FIVE"
Dennis F. Thompson

The savings and loan scandal of the 1980s was one of the most costly financial disasters in American history. The causes of the scandal included a combination of incompetence, greed, changing regulations, lax federal oversight of financial institutions, and political influence. In this 1993 American Political Science Review *article, Harvard political philosopher Dennis Thompson analyzes the intervention of five U.S. senators to persuade federal regulators to lighten their scrutiny of one savings and loan institution. Thompson argues that this was in fact a case of corruption even though the senators received no direct benefit and even though their actions were similar to other interventions of members of Congress for their constituents.*

The case of the "Keating Five"—featuring five prominent U.S. Senators and Charles Keating, Jr., a savings-and-loan financier who contributed to their campaigns—has "come to symbolize public distrust of elected officials" and has reinforced the widespread view that many members of Congress and the institution itself are corrupt. The nine months of investigation and seven weeks of hearings conducted by the Senate Ethics Committee that concluded in January 1992 revealed an underside of our system of representation to a depth and in a detail rarely seen before.

The broad shape of this underside is familiar enough: politicians take money from contributors to get elected, then do favors for them. But the deeper significance, theoretical and practical, is to be found in the details and in the relation of those details to principles of democratic representation. Although the case reveals a darker side of our politics, we can still try to recognize degrees of darkness. We should aim for a kind of moral chiaroscuro. More generally, the case can help us better understand a form of political corruption that is becoming increasingly common but has not received the attention it deserves from political scientists or political theorists.

This form of corruption involves the use of public office for private purposes in a manner that subverts the democratic process. It may be called *mediated* corruption because the corrupt acts are mediated by the political process. The public official's contribution to the corruption is filtered through various practices that are otherwise legitimate and may even be duties of office. As a result, both the official and citizens are less likely to recognize that the official has done anything wrong or that any serious harm has been done.

Mediated corruption is still a form of corruption. It includes the three main elements of the general concept of corruption: a public official gains, a private citizen receives a benefit, and the connection between the gain and the benefit is improper. But mediated corruption differs from conventional corruption with respect to each of these three elements: (1) the gain that the politician receives is political, not personal and is not illegitimate in itself, as in conventional corruption; (2) *how* the public official provides the benefit is improper, not necessarily the benefit itself, or the fact that the particular citizen receives the benefit; (3) the connection between the gain and the benefit is improper because it damages the democratic process, not because the public official provides the benefit with a corrupt motive. . . .

What the Keating Five Gave and What They Got

A brief summary of the events in this case will set the stage for examining the competing interpretations. The senators who are forever joined together by the name the Keating Five had never worked together as a group before, and will (it is safe to assume) never work together again. Four are Democrats—Dennis DeConcini (Arizona), Alan Cranston (California), John Glenn (Ohio), and Donald Riegle (Michigan)—and one is a Republican, John McCain (Arizona).

They were brought together by Charles Keating, Jr., now in prison in California, convicted on charges of fraud and racketeering. As chairman of a home construction company in Phoenix, he bought Lincoln Savings and Loan in California in 1984 and began to shift its assets from home loans to high-risk projects, violating a wide variety of state and federal regulations in the process. In 1989, Lincoln collapsed, wiping out the savings of twenty-three thousand (mostly elderly) uninsured customers and costing taxpayers over two billion dollars. It was the biggest failure in what came to be the most costly financial scandal in American history. Lincoln came to symbolize the savings-and-loan crisis.

But to many in the financial community during the years before the collapse, Keating was a model of the financial entrepreneur that the Republican administration wished to encourage through its policy of deregulation. His most visible political lobbying was directed against the new rule prohibiting direct investment by savings-and-loans, which many legitimate financial institutions and many members of Congress also opposed. His most prominent and persistent target was Edwin Gray, the head of the three-member bank board that regulated the industry, himself a controversial figure.

The fateful meeting that would forever link the Keating Five took place on April 2, 1987, in the early evening in DeConcini's office. The senators asked Gray why the investigation of Lincoln and their "friend" Keating was taking so long. Gray said later that he was intimidated by this "show of force." Toward the end of the meeting, he suggested that the senators talk directly to the San Francisco examiners who were handling the Lincoln case. And so they did, a week later, in what was to become the most scrutinized meeting in the hearings. The senators told the examiners that they believed that the government was harrassing [sic] a constituent. After the regulators reported that they were about to make a "criminal referral" against Lincoln, the senators seemed to back off.

After that meeting, McCain, Riegle, and Glenn had no further dealings of significance with Keating. Glenn arranged a lunch for Keating and House Speaker Jim Wright the following January, but the committee concluded that although this showed "poor judgment," Glenn's actions were not "improper." McCain had already broken off relations with Keating, who had called him a "wimp" for refusing to put pressure on the bank board. Cranston and DeConcini continued to act on Keating's behalf.

The Keating Five, particularly DeConcini and Cranston, certainly provided this constituent with good service. Since an act of corruption typically involves an exchange of some kind, we have to ask, What did the Senators get in return? The answer is $1.3 million, all within legal limits. But this figure and this fact, handy for headline writers, obscures some important details (especially the timing and uses of the funds) that should affect our assessment of corruption.

In February 1991, the Ethics Committee rebuked four of the Senators—DeConcini and Riegle more severely, McCain and Glenn less so—and said that further action was warranted only against Cranston. Then in November, after much behind-the-scenes political negotiation, the committee reported to the full Senate that Cranston had "violated established norms of behavior in the Senate." To avoid a stronger resolution by the committee (which would have required a Senate vote), Cranston formally accepted the reprimand. In a dramatic speech on the floor, he also claimed that he had done nothing worse than had most of his colleagues in the senate.

Competition or Corruption?

Cranston's own defense exemplifies, in a cynical form, one of the two standard interpretations of the conduct of the Keating Five. This interpretation holds that the conduct was part of a normal competitive process, in which all politicians are encouraged by the political system to solicit support and bestow favors in order to win elections. We may call this the *competitive politics* theory. On this view, most politicians are not corrupt, nor is the system—even if some citizens like Keating happen to have corrupt designs. The quest for campaign contributions and the provision of service to influential contributors are necessary features of a healthy competitive politics.

The second interpretation also holds that what the Keating Five did is not significantly different from what other members have done but concludes that it is corrupt. On this view (call it the *pervasive corruption* theory), most politicians are corrupt or (more sympathetically) are forced by the system to act in corrupt ways even if they begin with honest intentions. This interpretation is naturally more popular among the press, the public, and academics than it is among politicians. It is consistent with the views both of those who urge radical reforms in the political system (e.g., abolishing campaign contributions completely) and of those who believe that corruption is unavoidable in government (and either accept it or advocate reducing the scope of government).

These two common interpretations seem to be different. Indeed, they seem to be opposites, since one finds corruption where the other does not. But on closer inspection, their concepts of corruption turn out to be fundamentally similar. We can begin to see the similarity in the fact that they both conclude that the conduct of the Keating Five is not morally distinguishable from that of most other politicians. On both accounts, the Keating Five were simply intervening with administrators on behalf of a campaign contributor, a common practice. The competitive politics theory accepts the practice, the pervasive corruption theory condemns it. But on neither theory do the details of the case (e.g., what kind of intervention) make any difference in the moral assessment.

The reason that both theories take this view is that they agree in their fundamental assumptions. The analysis that follows focuses on three of these assumptions (each corresponding to an element in the general concept of corruption) and argues that each is mistaken. Understanding why they are mistaken points toward the need for a concept of mediated corruption.

First, both interpretations assume that corruption requires that the public official receive a personal gain, either directly or indirectly in the form of an advantage that is not distinguished from personal gain. They disagree about whether a campaign contribution should count as personal gain in the required sense, but they agree that some such gain or its moral equivalent is necessary. The image of the self-serving politician acting on base motives contrary to the public interest supplies much of the force of the moralistic reactions to corruption, both the defensiveness of the competitive politics view, and the censoriousness of the pervasive corruption view. This is also the image that most public officials themselves evidently have of the corrupt official: the more personal and the larger the payoff and the less the favor seems part of the job, the more likely is the conduct to be regarded as corrupt. . . . Second, both interpretations assume that corruption requires that the citizen receive a benefit that is not deserved or be threatened with not receiving one that is deserved. More generally, the justice of the constituent's claim is the only aspect of the benefit that is relevant to the determination of corruption. Third, both interpretations assume that corruption requires a corrupt motive. The personal or political gain and the citizen's benefit are *connected* in the mind of the public official. The official knowingly acts for the contributor in exchange for gain to himself or herself.

Personal Gain: The Ambiguity of Self-interest

Is personal gain by an official a necessary element of corruption? Only one of the Keating Five—McCain—ever received anything from Keating for his own personal use, and he (along with Glenn) is generally considered to have been the least guilty of the group. (The McCain family took some vacation trips to Keating's Bahamas home in the early 1980s, for which McCain eventually paid when notified by the company in 1989.) If personal gain is an element of the corruption in the Keating Five case, it must be found in the campaign contributions. Should campaign contributions count as the personal gain that the conventional concept of corruption requires?

This case suggests a negative answer. Cranston received no personal financial benefit, yet his conduct was reasonably regarded as the most flagrant of the Five; he was the only one ultimately reprimanded by the Senate. Most of the $850,000 Keating gave to Cranston went to voter registration groups, which had public-spirited names such as Center for the Participation in Democracy and had the purpose of trying to increase turnout in several different states. One of Cranston's main defenses was that he did not gain personally from these contributions.

But one might say that he did gain politically, or at least he thought he would. Why not count this political advantage as the element of personal gain? This is a tempting move and is commonly made, but it should be avoided. It is a mistake to try to force contributions into the category of personal gain. Doing so obscures a moral difference between personal and political gain. These should be distinguished even if one insists on treating both as forms of self-interest. "Personal gain" refers to goods that are usable generally in pursuit of one's own interest (including that of one's family) and are not necessary by-products of political activity. "Political gain" (which may also be a kind of self-interest) involves goods that are usable primarily in the political process, and are necessary by-products of this process.

The distinction is important because in our political system (and any democracy based on elections) the pursuit of political profit is a necessary element in the structure of incentives in a way that the pursuit of personal profit is not. Our system depends on politicians' seeking political advantage: we count on their wanting to be elected or reelected. Among the advantages that they must seek are campaign contributions. If political gain were part of what makes a contribution corrupt, it would also discredit many other kinds of political support, such as organizational efforts on behalf of a candidate, on which a robust democratic politics depends. This is part of the truth in the competitive politics theory. . . .

Official Favors: The Perils of Constituent Service

Consider now the second element of corruption, the official favors that the senators provided. The Keating Five claimed that there was nothing improper about the help they gave Keating. The benefits that Keating received were all provided in the name of "constituent service," a normal practice in a political system where representatives have to compete for the support of voters and campaign contributors.

The senators—and even the Ethics Committee at times—seemed to assume that if what a member does is constituent service and breaks no law, it is never improper. If the conduct does not involve bribery, extortion, or an illegal campaign contribution, it is not only acceptable but admirable. This is the competitive politics theory in its purest form. But as the hearings progressed, some of the senators came to accept a slightly more moderate view. In effect, they allowed that otherwise proper constituent service could become improper if it were provided unfairly. It would be wrong (and perhaps evidence of corruption) if it were provided only to big contributors. The senators seemed to accept as a reasonable test the question, Does the member typically intervene in this way for other constituents?

DeConcini made it a major part of his defense to show that he responded to virtually any constituent who asked for help. (He brandished a list of 75,000 constituents who could be called to testify, though to everyone's relief he settled for inviting only three—a social worker for Hispanics, a drug-busting sheriff, and a handicapped veteran.) Despite these heroic efforts, the answer to the question in this case is still probably negative: what the Keating Five provided was not typical constituent service. Five senators meeting in private with regulators on a specific case is unusual. During the hearings, no one could cite a sufficiently close precedent.

But even if we were to accept that the senators would do for other constituents what they did for Keating, we should still be concerned about another feature of this case, what may be called "the problem of too many representatives." Only DeConcini and McCain could claim Keating as a constituent in the convention (electoral) sense. The other three count as his representatives mainly by virtue of his business interests in their states. It is true that business interests, like other interests, may deserve representation; and geographical districts need not define the limits of representation, even of constituency service. However, we may reasonably criticize multiple representation if, in practice (as this case suggests), the extra representatives tend to go disproportionately to those with greater financial resources. That this tendency is undesirable is part of the truth in the pervasive corruption theory. A fair system of democratic representation does not grant more representatives to some citizens just because they have more financial resources. . . .

Corrupt Connections:
The Significance of Mixed Motives

In any form of corruption, there must be an improper connection between the benefit granted and the gain received. Otherwise, there would be only simple bias or simple malfeasance. With conventional corruption, we look for the link in the guilty mind of the public official—a corrupt motive. But the question immediately arises, How can we distinguish corrupt motives from other kinds? We have already seen that personal gain is neither a necessary nor a sufficient condition, nor is the impropriety of the benefit. Therefore, the corruption has to be found partly in the nature of the exchange. The difficulty is that corrupt exchanges do not seem obviously different from many of the other kinds of deals that go on in politics—exchanges of support of various kinds, without which political life could not go on at all. Politics is replete with quid pro quos: you vote for my bill, and I'll support yours; you raise funds for my primary campaign, and I'll endorse you in the next election. What is so corrupt about the exchange of campaign contributions for constituent service?

Without an answer to this question, we would be forced either to brand nearly all ordinary politics as corrupt or to excuse much political corruption as just ordinary politics.

The competitive politics theory, fearing a purification of the process that might enervate political life, attempts to contain the concept of corruption. It insists on narrow criteria for what counts as a corrupt link. The connection between the contribution and the service must be close in two senses: proximate in time and explicit in word or deed. In the case of several of the Keating Five, the connection between the contributions and the service were, by these standards, close. The connection was especially close in the case of Cranston, one reason that the committee singled him out for special criticism. He solicited contributions from Keating while he was also working to help Lincoln with its problems. His chief fundraiser combined discussions about regulations and contributions. Favors and contributions were also linked in memos and informal comments. He made the connection explicit in a memorable line delivered at a dinner at the Belair Hotel, where he "came up and patted Mr. Keating on the back and said, 'Ah, the mutual aid society'."

The committee found the contributions and services to be "substantially linked" through an "impermissible pattern of conduct," but they stopped short of finding "corrupt intent." . . . Why did the committee decline to find corruption here? The connection, it would seem, could hardly be closer. For that matter, we might also ask why the committee did not find the pattern impermissible in the case of Riegle and DeConcini. Part of the answer probably is that "corrupt intent" is the language of the bribery statutes, and the committee did not dare suggest that campaign contributions could be bribes. The line between contributions and bribes must be kept bright. . . .

The connection between contributions and benefits is corrupt if it bypasses the democratic process. The corruption here is twofold. It consists, first, in the actual and presumed tendency of certain kinds of contributions to influence the actions of representatives without regard to the substantive merits of issues. This is the corruption of the representative's judgment. The corruption also shows itself in broader effects of the democratic process, namely, in the actual and presumed tendency to undermine substantive political competition and deliberation. This is the corruption of the representative system. . . .

Conclusion

Mediated corruption is not new, but it is newly prospering. It thrives in the world of large, multinational financial institutions that increasingly interact, in closed and complex ways, with governments. Many of the major governmental scandals in recent years have involved a large measure of mediated corruption—the affairs of Iran–Contra, Housing and Urban Development (under Samuel Pierce), the Bank of Credit and Commerce International, and the Banca Nazionale del Lavoro's Atlanta branch, among others. Where private greed mixes easily with the public good, where the difference between serving citizens and serving supporters blurs, where secret funds lubricate the schemes of public officials, there mediated corruption is likely to flourish.

We can better understand the cunning ways of this growing form of corruption if we keep in mind its distinctive characteristics. The concept of mediated corruption serves this purpose. Each of its three elements, it has been argued here, differs from those of conventional corruption, the kind assumed by the competitive politics and pervasive corruption theories.

First, in mediated corruption a public official typically receives a political gain. But, as the pervasive corruption mistakenly denies and the competitive politics theory rightly implies, there is nothing wrong with this gain itself. Mediated corruption, furthermore, does not require that the public official personally gain or otherwise serve his (narrow) self-interest, as conventional corruption typically assumes. The gain contributes to mediated corruption insofar as it damages the democratic process—for example, by influencing a representative to serve private purposes without regard to their substantive merits.

Second, the public official provides a benefit, typically as an intermediary attempting to influence other officials to serve a constituent's private ends. Contrary to both the competitive politics and the pervasive corruption views, the benefit itself may be deserved and may even be something that the official would provide for any constituent. But if the way in which the official provides the benefit damages the democratic process, it still counts as a contribution to the corruption. The way in which the member presses the constituent's claim, not simply the justice of the claim, is relevant to the assessment of the corruption.

Third, the connection between the gain and the benefit is corrupt if it would lead a reasonable citizen to believe that an exchange has taken place that damages the democratic process in specified ways (typically in ways that bypass the process). Mediated corruption thus adds an appearance standard to the corrupt-motive test of conventional corruption. It goes further, and, like the pervasive corruption theory, relates the corruption in any particular case to corruption of the system as a whole. But the standards for determining whether the connection is corrupt are more fine-grained than that theory allows. They permit some connections that might otherwise seem corrupt (e.g., money is not necessarily corrupting) and condemn some connections that otherwise seem legitimate (money can be corrupting independently of the inequalities it perpetuates). The standards ultimately depend on what kind of democratic process we wish to maintain.

The concept of mediated corruption is consistent with a wide range of theories of democracy but is probably best justified from the perspective of a theory that prescribes that officials act on considerations of moral principle, rather than only on calculations of political power. This is sometimes called the deliberative conception of democracy. . . . As we have seen, mediated corruption characteristically attempts to translate private interest directly into public policy, bypassing the democratic processes of political discussion and competition. It thereby blocks our considering the moral reasons for and against a policy. Mediated corruption also prevents *deliberately* adopting a policy even without considering moral reasons: it precludes deliberation about whether to deliberate.

If we accept the concept of mediated corruption (as a supplement to the concept of conventional corruption), at least three implications follow. First, cases like the Keating Five would look different in the future. It would be easier to justify making finer distinctions of kind and degree in judging misconduct. The kind of conduct in which McCain and Glenn engaged, for example, would be more clearly distinguishable from that of the other three; and the kind of conduct in which all five engaged would be more clearly set apart from that of most other senators. More generally, we would hear less talk of motives (whether honest or rationalized), fewer appeals to constituent service as if it excused all sins, and fewer attacks on the appearance standard. We would see more concern about the mixing of private profit and public service, more attention to the merits of constituents' claims, and more worry about the effects of practices of individual representatives on the broader process of democratic representation. This shift of attention from the individual to the system (or, more precisely, to the effects of individual behavior on the system) would require not only new ways of thinking but also new standards of ethics.

The practical change most emphasized by the committee and most often mentioned by observers is campaign finance reform. Reducing the importance of money in campaigns (and politics more generally) is certainly desirable and could be seen as one of the implications of the concept of mediated corruption. But since the dominating role of money in politics is objectionable from the perspective of many different theories, it is worth emphasizing an implication that points toward a different dimension of reform. The concept of mediated corruption helps bring out the fact that money is not the only important source of corruption. Some of the kinds of misconduct to which mediated corruption calls attention depend less on money than do the kinds condemned by conventional corruption. As far as *public officials* are concerned, mediated corruption works its wiles less through greed than through ambition and even a misplaced sense of duty. Even some quite radical campaign finance reforms would not completely eliminate some forms of mediated corruption. Recall that political action committees, the bête noire of many progressive reformers, played almost no role in the case of the Keating Five.

A second implication of adopting the concept of mediated corruption concerns the process by which charges of unethical conduct should be heard and decided. In the Keating Five case, the process was directed by the Ethics Committee of the Senate. Legislatures have traditionally insisted on exclusive authority to discipline their own members, and the ethics committees of both houses have in the past managed to bring some tough judgments against some of their colleagues. But these have almost always been in flagrant cases of wrongdoing, closer to clear violations of rules that resembled the criminal law. It is difficult enough for colleagues who have worked together for years and may have to work together again to bring themselves to judge one another harshly in these cases. It may be almost impossible in cases involving mediated corruption. The less the charge is like conventional corruption, the harder it is to reach a severe judgment. The member implicated in mediated corruption, showing no obvious signs of a guilty mind or especially selfish motives, is often seen as simply doing his job. Under such circumstances, the sympathy of one's colleagues is maximized, their capacity for objectivity, minimized.

Furthermore, the legislature is, in a sense, also judging itself—specifically, its own practices and procedures, through which the corruption is mediated. In these circumstances, we might reasonably wonder whether anybody, including a legislative body, should be a judge in its own case. The clear implication of these considerations, suggested in part by the concept of mediated corruption, is that we should consider establishing an outside body to judge cases of ethics violations. To overcome possible constitutional objections, Congress could ultimately control the body; but it should be established in a way that would have at least the independence and respect of an institution like the Congressional Budget Office.

POINTS TO PONDER

1. According to Thompson, what is "mediated corruption"?
2. What is the difference between a campaign contribution and a bribe?
3. In what ways were the actions of the Keating Five similar to and different from other types of constituent services common to most members of Congress?

33

"WATERGATE AND THE COLLAPSE OF THE NIXON PRESIDENCY"
Michael Genovese

Richard Nixon was a tragic figure in the classical sense that he had the potential for greatness but was brought down by his own actions. Despite the accomplishments of his administration, especially in foreign policy, Nixon will always be remembered as the president who chose to resign rather than face almost certain impeachment by the House and probable conviction by the Senate. In this excerpt from his book The Nixon Presidency *(1990), political scientist Michael Genovese of Loyola Marymount University describes the many actions by the Nixon administration that are subsumed under the broad term* Watergate. *The type of corruption described here is more dangerous than the stealing of money because it involves the use of governmental power to cover up crimes in order to stay in power, thus undermining the rule of law and the premises of democratic government.*

Let us begin by committing ourselves to the truth—to see it like it is, and tell it like it is—to find the truth, to speak the truth, and to live the truth.

Richard Nixon, accepting the Republican
Presidential nomination in 1968

"Watergate" is a generic term that originally referred only to the break-in of the Democratic National Committee (DNC) headquarters located at the Watergate office complex, but has come to be an umbrella term, under which a wide variety of crimes and improper acts are included. Watergate caused the downfall of a president. It led to jail sentences for a number of the highest-ranking officials of the administration. It was a traumatic experience for the nation. Why Watergate? How could it have happened? How could someone as smart and experienced as Richard Nixon behave so criminally *and* so stupidly? How could someone so adroit and practiced in the art and science of politics behave so foolishly? How could a "third-rate burglary" turn into a national disaster? How could Richard Nixon have done it to himself?

In essence, Watergate involved three separate but interconnected conspiracies, centered in four different areas. The first conspiracy was the *Plumbers conspiracy*. This involved a variety of steps taken in the first term to plug leaks and "get" political enemies, illegal wiretapping, the break-in of Daniel Ellsberg's psychiatrist's office, and other acts, done in some instances for ostensible "national security" reasons, and at other times for purely political reasons. The purpose of this conspiracy was to destroy political enemies and strengthen the president's political position.

The second conspiracy was the *reelection conspiracy*. This grew out of lawful efforts to reelect the president, but degenerated into illegal efforts to extort money, launder money, sabotage the electoral process, spy, commit fraud, forgery, and burglary, play "dirty tricks," and attack Democratic front-runners. The purposes of this conspiracy were to (a) knock the stronger potential Democratic candidates (Hubert Humphrey, Ted Kennedy, Edmund Muskie, and Henry (Scoop) Jackson) out of the race; (b) accumulate enough money to bury the Democratic opponent by massively outspending him, and (c) thus guarantee the reelection of Richard Nixon. This conspiracy was conscious, deliberate, organized.

The third conspiracy was the *coverup conspiracy*. Almost immediately after the burglars were caught at the DNC headquarters in the Watergate, a criminal conspiracy began that was designed to mislead law enforcement officers and protect the reelection bid of the president, and then after the election, to keep the criminal investigations away from the White House. To this end, evidence was destroyed, perjury committed, lies told, investigations obstructed, and subpoenas defied. The purpose of the coverup was to contain the criminal charges and protect the president. This conspiracy was less conscious, almost instinctive. It was deliberate but poorly organized.

One can divide Watergate activities into four categories: the partisan arena, the policy arena, the financial arena, and the legal arena. The *partisan* activities include acts taken against those of the opposition party and those deemed to be "enemies" of the administration. They include acts such as wiretapping and break-ins, the establishment of the Huston Plan, the Plumbers, and the enemies list, forged State Department cables, and political dirty tricks.

Policy activities include the stretching of presidential power beyond legal or constitutional limits. Examples include the secret bombing of Cambodia, the impoundment of congressionally appropriated funds, attempts to dismantle programs authorized by Congress, the extensive use of executive privilege, and underenforcement of laws such as the Civil Rights Act of 1964. When Nixon's defenders answer charges against the president by saying that "everybody does it," they are most often referring to this area of behavior.

In the *financial* area, both Nixon's political and personal finances deserve mention. On the political front, the "selling" of ambassadorships, extortion of money in the form of illegal campaign contributions, and laundering of money must be included. In Nixon's personal finances, such things as "irregularities" in income tax deductions and questionable "security" improvements in his private Florida and California homes, paid for with tax dollars, are included.

Finally, in the *legal* arena, illegal activities of the Nixon administration include obstruction of justice, perjury, criminal coverup, interference with criminal investigations, and destruction of evidence. It was the criminal coverup that eventually led to Nixon's forced resignation.

Categorizing and classifying Watergate behavior does a disservice to the drama and suspense of the unfurling of this political mystery. The story of Nixon's rise and fall, of his choices at several important points in the story, of his ultimate collapse, is what makes this drama so poignant and tragic.

Watergate was a series of criminal and unethical acts committed by Richard Nixon and members of his administration that were designed to increase Nixon's political power, punish potential "enemies," sabotage the electoral process, and cover up evidence of crimes. Acts such as obstruction of justice, burglary, conspiracy, lying under oath, wiretapping, misprision of perjury, and dirty tricks were involved. It took a vigilant press, a determined court system, two special prosecutors, House and Senate investigations, a federal grand jury, an aroused public, a good deal of luck, and ultimately, Nixon's own tape-recorded words to finally force the president to resign one step ahead of impeachment in the House and conviction in the Senate.

A number of crimes and "dirty tricks" had taken place before the 1972 reelection bid, but these acts did not become public until after the '72 election. In this sense, a clear and lengthy pattern, some would say policy, of deceit, manipulation, and crimes can be traced back to the early days of the administration. For example, in March of 1969 the United States began four-teen months of secret bombings of Cambodia; in May of 1969, illegal wire-tapping was under way; in June of 1970, the Huston Plan was approved; in June of 1971, the Plumbers were created and they began to act against Daniel Ellsberg, eventually breaking into his psychiatrist's office; and in 1971, the enemies list was created. But these events came to light after and as part of an investigation into a bizarre event that took place at the Democratic National Committee's headquarters located at the Watergate office complex. An examination of the Watergate scandal reveals, as does no other area, the extent to which the paranoid style animated behavior in the Nixon administration.

* * * *

Dirty Money

> I made my mistakes, but in all of my years of public life, I have never profited, never profited from public service. I have earned every cent. And in all of my years of public life, I have never obstructed justice. And I think, too, that I could say that in my years of public life, that I welcome this kind of examination because people have got to know whether or not their President is a crook. Well, I am not a crook, I have earned everything I have got.
>
> Richard M. Nixon, at Walt Disney World, November 17, 1973

"Money," as Jesse Unruh used to say, "is the mother's milk of politics," and the Nixon team collected and spent more money (over $60 million) than any campaign in presidential history. But money was also a sticking point for the president, for in both his political and personal finances, Richard Nixon went afoul of the law, and by being too greedy, helped cause his own downfall. "Remember 1960," Nixon told Haldeman, "I never want to be outspent again."

In his first term, Nixon was the target of allegations of trading influence for money. The "ITT affair" and the dairy lobby money raised serious questions about the sense of propriety of the administration. But it was in the reelection campaign that money became the root of many Nixon evils.

The effort not to be outspent was led by former commerce secretary Maurice Stans, with Nixon's longtime personal lawyer Herbert Kalmbach as chief fund-raiser. The money was collected in two stages, reflecting changes in the campaign reform laws. Money collected *before* April 7, 1971, did not fall under the stricter reporting requirements of the new regulations, so there was a major effort to get the money in "pre–April 7."

In spite of frantic efforts to get as much money as possible before the reporting requirements went into effect, some money came in "late." On April 10, a former Republican state senate majority leader named Harry L. Sears gave Stans an attaché case containing $200,000 in $100 bills. The money was illegally treated as "pre–April 7" money and proved an even greater embarrassment when it was revealed that the money was a contribution from Robert Vesco, the international financier and fugitive from American justice.

Stans and his fundraising associates sought contributions from corporations dependent on the largesse of the government. Campaign contributions from corporations are illegal, but this did not deter Stans. The pitch made to these corporate executives was "finely calibrated, depending on who they were and how much fund-raisers thought they could get."

This approach brought in millions. By politely hinting that corporate contributions would help and that failure to contribute would hurt badly, the president's reelection team was able to extract political tithes from some of the biggest and most respected companies in the nation. Even a partial list is impressive: American Airlines, $55,000; Braniff Airways, $40,000; Ashland Oil, $100,000; Goodyear Tire and Rubber, $40,000; Gulf Oil, $100,000; Northrop, $150,000; and Phillips Petroleum, $100,000. This who's who of corporate America illegally contributed to the Nixon reelection effort, and all were convicted—after the 1972 campaign.

In an effort to hide the money, that is, to prevent tracing it to the source, most of this money was laundered. The laundering took several forms. American Airlines sent money from a U.S. bank to a Swiss account of an agent in Lebanon, back to another U.S. bank, then to CREEP [Committee for the Re-election of the President]. Still other firms gave money from slush funds, and some airlines sold bogus tickets and sent the cash to CREEP. By far the most common route to launder money was through Mexico. In fact, it was to protect the money-laundering operation in Mexico that President Nixon first became actively involved in the criminal conspiracy to obstruct justice on June 23, 1972, less than a week after the Watergate break-in.

Illegal corporate contributions proved to be an excellent source of money, as did the "selling" of ambassadorships. Several big donors were promised ambassadorships in exchange for campaign money. J. Fife Symington gave over $100,000, but the promised post of Spain or Portugal fell through (Herbert Kalmbach pled guilty to a charge of promising a federal job to Symington in exchange for money). Vincent P. de Roulet paid over $100,000 for Jamaica. Walter H. Annenberg received Great Britain after a $250,000 contribution. Mrs. Ruth Farkas, after donating $250,000 and being promised Costa Rica, complained to Kalmbach, saying, according to the grand jury testimony, "Well, you know, I am interested in Europe, I think, and isn't two hundred and fifty thousand dollars an awful lot of money for Costa Rica?" After giving a total of $300,000, Mrs. Farkas was appointed ambassador to Luxembourg. The president was well aware of the "ambassadorial auction," as notes taken by H. R. Haldeman at a meeting with the president and Maurice Stans on March 21, 1972, indicate. Stans and Nixon discussed possible appointments and how much money each donor gave. The notation on Farkas was: "Mrs. Farkas 250?—where's the play on her?"

CREEP was almost literally awash in cash. There was so much money that the Nixon campaign officials were looking for ways to spend it. Besides the normal political expenses, money was used for some abnormal campaign expenses that crossed the line of ethics and legality.

Dirty Tricks

Part of the Nixon predatory strategy involved attempts to sabotage the campaigns of the top Democratic candidates in hopes of destroying their campaigns and thereby running against one of the weaker Democrats in the November general election. The predatory strategy involved the use of political "dirty tricks" that often went far beyond the bounds of ethics and the law. . . .

Perhaps the most amazing and insidious activity in the campaign of dirty tricks and sabotage was what became known as the "Liddy Plan." As chief legal counsel for CREEP, G. Gordon Liddy cast his net over a wide array of activities, most notorious of which was the plan that bears his name. In an effort to further disrupt and divide the Democrats, Liddy was to develop an intelligence-gathering/undercover operation. On January 27, 1972, at four o'clock in the afternoon, Liddy went to the office of the attorney general of the United States, John Mitchell, and presented a plan that was frightening—or should have been.

At the meeting with Liddy and Mitchell were John Dean and Jeb Magruder. Liddy, with charts and an easel, presented a plan that at first the rest of the group could not understand. That was because everything was in code. But as Liddy proceeded to explain, it became clear what "Gemstone" was all about: it was a massive and expensive plan of sabotage and surveillance of unprecedented proportions.

Carrying a $1 million price tag, the Liddy Plan called for mugging squads to beat up demonstrators at the Republican Convention, teams to kidnap leaders of the demonstrations and hijack them to Mexico until the Republican Convention was over, electronic surveillance against the Democrats at their Washington headquarters and convention sites, prostitutes to be employed ("high-class" ones, according to Liddy, "the best in the business") to lure prominent Democrats onto a yacht equipped with hidden cameras and recording equipment, break-ins to obtain and photograph documents, shorting out the air conditioning at the arena in Miami where the Democrats were to have their Convention, and other sordid acts.

John Dean called the plan "mind-boggling." The attorney general, the highest-ranking law enforcement official in the land, rather than throwing Liddy out of his office—as he later admitted he should have done—rejected the plan, not on its merits, but as too expensive, and asked Liddy to draw up a new, scaled-down version. As John Dean testified before the Senate Watergate Committee, Mitchell "took a few long puffs on his pipe," and told Liddy, "the plan . . . was not quite what he had in mind and the cost was out of the question, and suggested to Liddy he go back and revise his plan, keeping in mind that he was most interested in the demonstration problem." Jeb Magruder recalls a similar response from Mitchell: "Gordon that's not quite what we had in mind, and the money you're asking for is way out of line. Why don't you tone it down a little, then we'll talk about it again?"

On February 4, 1972, Liddy returned to Mitchell's office with a scaled-down plan costing only half a million dollars. But again the attorney general demurred. Liddy was to come up with another proposal. Almost two months later, on March 30, 1972, a third meeting with Mitchell was held in Key Biscayne, Florida. Dean and Liddy were not present, but Magruder and Fred LaRue were in attendance. Toward the end of a wide-ranging meeting, Mitchell, who by that time had resigned as attorney general to become director of CREEP, turned to the revised Liddy plan. While everyone at the meeting expressed reservations, Mitchell finally approved the plan, but gave Liddy "only" $250,000. Among the targets was Larry O'Brien, chair of the Democratic National Committee, whose office was located in the Watergate office complex.

Within a week, Liddy was off and running. He received $83,000 in cash from CREEP's Finance Committee, purchased bugging and surveillance equipment, and began planning the first break-in of Watergate. In attempting to figure out why Mitchell approved the revised Liddy plan, and why so many others in the administration and CREEP went along with it, Jeb Magruder offers that it was "the result of a combination of pressures that played upon us at that time." First, Liddy "put his plan to us in a highly effective way"; second, Mitchell was under pressure from the ITT affair and was distracted; third, Mitchell's wife, the high-strung Martha, was putting a strain on her busy husband; and fourth, "Liddy's plan was approved because of the climate of fear and suspicion that had grown up in the White House, an atmosphere that started with the President himself and reached us through Haldeman and Colson and others, one that came to affect all our thinking, so that decisions that now seem insane seemed at the time to be rational." He continued, "It was all but impossible not to get caught up in the 'enemies' mentality."

The Break-in

Out of this atmosphere of dirty tricks, dirty money, and dirty politics came the plan to break into and bug offices in the headquarters of the Democratic National Committee. While the roots of the DNC break-in can be found in the legitimate need for campaign intelligence, things got so out of hand, sank so low, that the dirty tricks and break-ins were eventually seen as a necessary part in the reelection of the president.

Early efforts at gaining political and campaign intelligence led John Dean, at the instruction of Bob Haldeman, to contact Jack Caulfield to set up such a capability. Caulfield developed what he called "Operation Sandwedge," an intelligence-gathering operation that would have "black bag" capability.

Caulfield's plan never got off the ground, and Dean continued to feel the pressure from Haldeman. Dean would later testify before the Senate Watergate Committee that the White House had an insatiable appetite for political intelligence.

As part of Liddy's intelligence-gathering plan, information was to be obtained by what Liddy called a *Nacht und Nebel* (Night and Fog) operation. One such operation was to get information on what the Democrats had on the Republicans, and more specifically on Nixon. The fear was that Larry O'Brien, chairman of the DNC, might possess material that could be particularly damaging to the president. Liddy and his accomplices broke into the Democratic headquarters twice. The first time, the bugging equipment did not work properly, and the information obtained was not useful.

According to Liddy, Jeb Magruder, then deputy director of CREEP, ordered the second break-in on June 12. At a 1987 conference at Hofstra University, Magruder admitted that the break-in was deemed necessary, to "find out what information Larry O'Brien knew." The "primary purpose of the break-in was to see if O'Brien had embarrassing information linking President Nixon's close friend Bebe Rebozo to loans from Howard Hughes" that went to Nixon. "It was a planned burglary," said Magruder. Thus, while most political professionals scoffed at the break-in in its aftermath, suggesting that it had to be a renegade operation because everyone knew that there was nothing of value at the DNC, there was a reason: the fear that Larry O'Brien had the goods on a Hughes-Nixon deal.

As Magruder said at the Hofstra conference: "These people [the Watergate burglars] were hired . . . under the insistence . . . to my recollection when I was in Key Biscayne with John Mitchell and Fred LaRue, in discussions on the phone with Bob Haldeman, that it was important for us to get the information on Larry O'Brien that regarded to the Hughes affair. . . . So the purpose as I understand it for the break-in and the wiretapping was to find out what information Larry O'Brien knew and what information we would then be able to use to keep that under wraps during the election."

To get this information, Liddy and his accomplices first broke into the DNC headquarters on May 27, 1972, and installed wiretaps. When the taps didn't work properly, a second surreptitious entry was required. On the night of June 16 and the morning of the 17th, Liddy and his cohorts returned.

In the early morning hours of Saturday, June 17, 1972, after a call to police by security guard Frank Wills, five men were arrested for illegal entry to the DNC headquarters in the Watergate office complex in Washington, D.C. At first this case was treated as a routine criminal act, but the arrested men were found to have links to the White House and CIA, and one of those arrested, James W. McCord, Jr., was director of security for the Committee for the Re-election of the President (CREEP). Soon two other suspects were linked to the crime, E. Howard Hunt, a former White House aide, and G. Gordon Liddy, a former White House aid currently under the employ of CREEP. The

White House denied any involvement in the burglary, with Press Secretary Ron Ziegler calling it a "third-rate burglary attempt."

Did President Nixon *know* about Gemstone, the Liddy Plan, the effort to bug the DNC? There is no evidence to suggest that he knew of the plan in advance. While Nixon may not have ordered the break-in, he certainly created an atmosphere in which planning such crimes was tolerated and even encouraged. Bob Haldeman gives us an indication of the atmosphere when he recounts an example of what he calls "classic Nixonian rhetorical overkill" when the president ordered him to get the tax files of leading Democrats: "There are ways to get it," Nixon said, "Goddamnit, sneak in in the middle of the night." On January 14, 1971, Nixon did send Bob Haldeman a memo suggesting that they needed more information on DNC chairman Lawrence O'Brien. The memo read in part: "It would seem that the time is approaching when Larry O'Brien is held accountable for his retainer with Hughes," and "perhaps Colson should make a check on this." While Nixon had an interest in O'Brien, there is no direct evidence pointing to the president having advance knowledge of the break-in. But he was actively involved in the coverup from the beginning.

The Coverup Begins

The arrests at the Watergate, occurring less than five months before the 1972 election, might have been a political embarrassment, perhaps even a serious scandal, but the White House quickly went to work on an effort to cover up the crime and contain political damage from the president and his reelection. . . .

June 20 was the first time Nixon had the opportunity to meet with the top people involved in the break-in and coverup. On that day, the president held meetings or discussions with Haldeman, Mitchell, Colson, and others. He discussed Watergate with these aides, and when the White House taping system was revealed, a search for tapes of these meetings proved fruitless. Meetings with Mitchell were, according to a White House spokesman, not recorded; there was a mysterious eighteen-and-a-half-minute gap in a Haldeman conversation on Watergate, and a thirty-eight-second gap in the Dictabelt recording Nixon made of his daily recollections. On this, the most important day for the president, the day when he first discussed Watergate with top principals, the recorded evidence is gone.

By June 23, less than a week after the arrests, the president was directly leading a criminal coverup. In a discussion between Haldeman and Nixon, the substance of which was not revealed until August 5, 1974, the president's chief of staff informed Nixon that the break-in occurred because Liddy was under pressure (probably from Mitchell) to "get more information," to which the president responded, "All right, fine. I understand it all. We won't second guess Mitchell and the rest. Thank God it wasn't Colson." Haldeman then informed Nixon that the FBI was beginning to close in on the source of money used for the illegal activities, saying that "the FBI is not under control," and suggested that "the way to handle this now is for us to have Walters [deputy director, CIA] call Pat Gray [acting director, FBI] and just say 'stay to hell out of this' . . . Pat wants to [end the investigation] . . . he doesn't have the basis for doing it. Given this, he will then have the basis."

The president then ordered Haldeman to tell CIA director Richard Helms that "the President believes that it is going to open the whole Bay of Pigs thing up again. And . . . that they [the CIA] should call the FBI in and [unintelligible] don't go any further into this case period!"

Later that day in another meeting with Haldeman, Nixon orders Haldeman to tell Helms that "Hunt . . . knows too damned much. . . . If it gets out that this is all involved . . . it would make the CIA look bad, it's going to make Hunt look bad, and it is likely to blow the whole Bay of Pigs thing which we think would be very unfortunate—both for the CIA and for the country . . . and for American foreign policy. Just tell him [Helms] to lay off . . . I would just say, lookit, because of the Hunt involvement, whole cover basically this."

At 1:30 p.m. on June 23, Haldeman and Ehrlichman met with Helms and Walters and persuaded them to approach Gray in an effort to limit the FBI investigation into the break-in. Later that afternoon, Haldeman again met with the president to report on his meeting with Helms and Walters. He told the president that while he didn't mention Hunt, he did tell the CIA officials that "the thing was leading into directions that were going to create potential problems because they were exploring leads that led back into areas that would be harmful to the CIA and harmful to the Government," and that Helms "kind of got the picture. He said, he said, 'we'll be very happy to be helpful [unintelligible] to handle anything you want.' . . . Walters is going to make a call to Gray."

At almost the precise moment Haldeman was having this conversation with the president, Vernon Walters called L. Patrick Gray and told him that if the FBI pursued its investigation into Mexico, it would be jeopardizing some of the CIA's covert operations. He suggested that the investigation be limited to the suspects already under arrest. Gray complied. Thus, the criminal conspiracy to obstruct justice, to interfere with an FBI investigation, began less than a week after the arrests in the Watergate. This put the president right in the middle of a criminal conspiracy to obstruct justice. The national security excuse was a ruse. The top people in the administration were covering up a crime. But this was only the beginning. . . .

Indeed, "other reasons" made the coverup so important and necessary. Covering up the break-in itself was not the key; what was important was to keep a lid on all the other illegal and unethical activities that might be revealed if the "can of worms" were opened. The real enemy was an enemy from within. That is what had to be kept hidden, the dirty tricks and dirty money and crimes of the past several years: warrantless wiretaps, the Fielding break-in, the extortion of campaign funds, sabotage of elections, campaign crimes, and a host of other crimes. There simply couldn't *not* be a coverup.

Uncovering the Coverup

On July 6, 1972, Pat Gray warned the president that "people on your staff are tying to mortally wound you by using the CIA and FBI." Gray didn't know that it was the president who was leading the coverup.

In spite of all the problems attendant to keeping a lid on the story and investigations, as the election approached, it appeared that containment was indeed working. Dean had "handled" Watergate, and the reelection was assured. But after the election, the walls came tumbling down.

In an effort to control the Watergate investigation, the president, through John Dean, closely monitored the Justice Department's investigations. Dean was allowed to sit in on questioning of White House and CREEP officials, and as Dean later told the president, "I was totally aware what the bureau was doing at all times. I was totally aware what the grand jury was doing. I knew what witnesses were going to be called. I knew what they were going to be asked." When Nixon asked why Henry Peterson (the assistant attorney general who was in charge of the Watergate investigation) was "so straight with us," Dean replied, "Because he is a soldier."

This of course greatly aided the administration in its efforts to keep the investigation limited. Thus, witnesses could be encouraged to commit perjury and conceal information, and Dean could keep track of how well the coverup was holding together. Additionally, Peterson kept reporting to the president on the status of the investigation. Peterson did not know that the information he gave Nixon was going to aid in the coverup because he did not know that the president was involved in the coverup. At one point Nixon told Ehrlichman and Ziegler, "I've got Peterson on a short leash." Following pressure from Nixon, Peterson and his colleague Earl Silbert kept the investigation on a very narrow course. Again, the coverup seemed to be working. But the defendants were threatening to go "off the reservation." By late December James McCord sent John Caulfield a letter warning: "If the Watergate operation is laid at the CIA's feet, where it does not belong, every tree in the forest will fall. It will be a scorched desert. The whole matter is at the precipice now. Just pass the message that if they want it to blow, they are on exactly the right course. Shortly after the election, the defendants began to fear that they were vulnerable, that Nixon didn't need their silence as much as he did prior to the election, and that they might be "forgotten." Hunt began pressuring Colson. He spoke of financial needs of the defendants. But Colson, who was taping the call, tried to get Hunt to back away. Hunt refused. . . .

Colson gave the tape to Dean, who played it for Haldeman and Ehrlichman. The threat was clear. Dean was told to "tell Mitchell to take care of all these problems." Hunt wrote a nine-hundred-word indictment of the way they were being handled by the administration. The defendants, he wrote, had committed the burglary "against their better judgment," but the administration was guilty of "indecisiveness at the moment of crisis." They failed to "quash the investigation while that option was still open," and a laundry list of other charges, including "failure to provide promised support funds on a timely and adequate basis; continued postponements and consequent avoidance of commitments."

Then Hunt listed some of the potentially damaging information he possessed: "Mitchell may well have perjured himself"; the Watergate crime was "only one of a number of highly illegal conspiracies engaged in by one or more of the defendants at the behest of senior White House officials. These as yet undisclosed crimes can be proved"; that "immunity from prosecution and/or judicial clemency for cooperating defendants is a standing offer"; and that "congressional elections will take place in less than two years." The deadline given Colson was extended until November 27, but the defendants would meet before that time to "determine our joint and automatic response to evidence of continued indifference on the part of those in whose behalf we have suffered the loss of our employment, our futures, and our reputations as honorable men. The foregoing should not be interpreted as a threat. It is among other things a reminder that loyalty has always been a two-way street."

The president of the United States was being *blackmailed*.

The threat worked. Almost immediately, $50,000 was delivered by LaRue to Hunt's lawyer. Shortly thereafter LaRue said he needed more money. Haldeman told Dean to give LaRue "the entire damn bundle, but make sure we get a receipt."

On December 8, Hunt's wife, Dorothy, was killed in a plane crash. She was carrying $10,000 in $100 bills. Hunt became increasingly despondent. Hunt wanted clemency. Charles Colson began to push for clemency to Ehrlichman, who, according to Dean, took the matter up with the president and then gave Colson an assurance that the president had promised clemency for Hunt. A few days later the president and Colson discussed Hunt's clemency.

* * * *

Toward the end of the March 22 meeting, Nixon assured everyone, "We will survive it," and complimented Dean for being a "son-of-a-bitching tough thing," and the president added: "I don't give a shit what happens. I want you all to stonewall it, let them plead the Fifth Amendment, coverup or anything else, if it'll save it—save the plan. That's the whole point."

Then the president, commenting to Mitchell, said, "Up to this point the whole theory has been containment, as you know, John," and Mitchell answered, "Yeah."

The following day everything hit the fan.

On Friday, March 23, an unexpected crack in the coverup developed. In open court, Judge John Sirica dropped a bombshell when he made public a letter written to him by convicted Watergate burglar James McCord. McCord's letter charged that the Watergate defendants were under "political pressure" to plead guilty and remain silent, that perjury had been committed, and that higher-ups were involved. It was the first crack in the coverup wall. Soon, the walls would come tumbling down on Richard Nixon.

The following week McCord testified for four hours in a closed-door session before the Senate Watergate Committee. He declared that Colson, Dean, Magruder, and Mitchell had prior knowledge of the Watergate break-in.

Dean began to feel the noose closing around his neck. The McCord letter and his fear that Nixon was setting him up (taking Dean's own advice and cutting the losses), plus the continued pressure to write a "Dean report," led Dean to consider a trip to the prosecutors in hopes of getting a deal. Finally, on March 26, when Haldeman told Dean that the White House was cutting Magruder and Mitchell loose, he realized that everyone—except the president—was expendable. Dean, fearing that Magruder would crack, called criminal lawyer Charles Shaffer. On April 2, Dean's lawyers told the prosecutors that their client was ready to cooperate. On April 8, John Dean began to talk. Magruder, seeing the writing on the wall, also decided to cooperate with the prosecutors. The coverup continued to crack.

Senator Ervin's Committee

When the Senate Select Committee on Presidential Campaign Activities (usually referred to as the Ervin Committee or Watergate Committee) opened its hearings on May 17, the president was already in a precarious position: Dean, Magruder, and McCord were talking, Haldeman and Ehrlichman had been jettisoned from the administration, the president's popularity was slipping, and the press was pursuing lead after lead on Watergate. The fact that the Senate hearings would be televised nationally only worsened things.

The hearings got off to a slow start, with the committee initially calling witnesses on the periphery of power. Everyone was waiting for John Dean. Finally, on June 25, John Dean took the chair and began to read his prepared opening statement in a monotone voice: "To one who was in the White House and became somewhat familiar with its interworkings, the Watergate matter was an inevitable outgrowth of a climate of excessive concern over the political impact of demonstrators, excessive concern over leaks, an insatiable appetite for political intelligence, all coupled with a do-it-yourself White House staff, regardless of the law."

Thus began a 245-page statement in which Dean blew the lid off the administration. The portrait Dean painted was devastating: wiretapping, burglary, enemies lists, secret funds, money laundering, dirty tricks, Plumbers, intelligence surveillance, character assassination, obstruction of justice, coverup. But all Dean had was his word—no documentation, no corroboration. Dean's assertion that the president was right in the middle of the mess came down to his word against the president's. How would the dilemma be resolved?

The answer fell into the lap of the committee on July 16 after several staff members had questioned Alexander Butterfield in preparation for his appearance before the committee. In that questioning Butterfield revealed the existence of a White House taping system. Butterfield was rushed to give testimony. Minority counsel Fred Thompson asked, "Mr. Butterfield, are you aware of the installation of any listening devices in the Oval office of the President?" "I was aware of listening devices, yes, sir," was Butterfield's reply. "Are you aware of any devices that were installed in the Executive Office Building office of the President?" asked Thompson. "Yes, sir."

The president had secretly tape-recorded all conversations in the Oval Office, the president's office in the Executive Office Building, the Lincoln Room, and at Camp David. Another bombshell. The tapes could confirm or shatter Dean's charges against the president. It was no longer Dean's word against the president's. There was proof.

The Senate immediately requested the tapes, as did the special prosecutor. Nixon refused. The Senate and special prosecutor subpoenaed several of the tapes, and Nixon still refused, citing executive privilege. The Senate Watergate Committee and Archibald Cox took the president to court over the tapes. On August 29, Judge John Sirica ruled that the president must turn over the subpoenaed tapes. The president appealed the ruling, and on October 12, the U.S. Court of Appeals upheld Sirica's order. The president decided to appeal to the Supreme Court.

As the battle for the tapes began, the Senate committee continued to hear from witnesses. Mitchell, Ehrlichman, and Haldeman all contradicted Dean and pointed the finger at Dean as being the real culprit in the coverup. But as the Senate's investigation wound down, the battle for the tapes heated up.

As if things weren't bad enough for President Nixon, the Justice Department was also investigating charges of corruption against Nixon's vice president, Spiro Agnew. Allegedly, Agnew had taken cash payments—bribes—in exchange for government contracts while Agnew was an official and later governor of Maryland. According to the charges, Agnew was accepting bribe money while he was vice president.

An investigation by the U.S. attorney in Baltimore found approximately fifty possible criminal violations, including bribery, extortion, conspiracy, and tax evasion. After reviewing the evidence, Agnew's attorneys negotiated a plea bargain: Agnew would resign as vice president, plead *nolo contendere* (no contest) to a single charge of income tax evasion, the Justice Department would enter the evidence into the public record, and Agnew would escape a prison sentence. Walter Hoffman, the judge in the case, told Agnew that the no-contest plea was "the full equivalent of a plea of guilty." On October 10, 1973, Spiro Agnew resigned as vice president. Two days later, President Nixon nominated Gerald Ford as vice president. Ford was confirmed and was sworn in on December 6, 1973.

The battle for the tapes continued, with the president insisting that Archibald Cox, who was technically part of the executive branch, cease from pressing the president to produce the tapes. In an effort to get a compromise, Nixon offered Cox a surprise deal: the Stennis Plan. Under this plan, Nixon would let the seventy-two-year-old conservative Democrat Senator John Stennis of Mississippi, who was still recovering from a gunshot wound, verify the accuracy of a transcript of the tapes, but not turn them over to Cox. Part of the deal included an insistence that Cox ask for no more tapes.

Cox refused, and on October 20, in what came to be known as the "Saturday Night Massacre," Attorney General Elliot Richardson resigned after refusing to fire Cox. Deputy Attorney General William Ruckelshaus also resigned; and finally Solicitor General Robert Bork was named acting attorney general, and he carried out Nixon's order to fire Cox, abolish the special prosecutor's office, and have the FBI seal Cox's offices to prevent removal of any files.

A tremendous public outcry followed, as did the introduction of twenty-two bills in Congress calling for an impeachment investigation. How much more could the president—and the nation—take? On October 30, the House Judiciary Committee began consideration of possible procedures in the event of an impeachment. Nixon finally agreed to turn over some of the tapes. On November 1, 1972, Leon Jaworski was appointed as new special prosecutor. He too sought the tapes. As pressure on the president mounted, calls for his resignation appeared. On November 17, the president, in a televised press conference, said, "People have got to know whether or not their President is a crook. Well, I'm not a crook."

The president was determined to try one last PR offensive, this one called "Operation Candor." In this operation, Nixon would publicly promise to deliver everything, but stall, stall, stall. Although the president promised on November 20 that there were no more Watergate "bombshells" waiting to explode, on the very next day Nixon's lawyers told John Sirica of a "gap" problem in the tapes. Operation Candor was dead.

The president continued to take a public beating. Within a week of his "I am not a crook" statement, Judge John Sirica revealed that there was an eighteen-and-a-half minute gap in the important June 20, 1972, tape of a conversation between Nixon and Haldeman—a meeting held three days after the Watergate break-in. Although Alexander Haig, Nixon's chief of staff, blamed the gap on "some sinister force," a panel of experts concluded that it was the result of five separate manual erasures. Judge Sirica recommended a grand jury investigation into "the possibility of unlawful destruction of evidence and related offenses," adding that "a distinct possibility of unlawful conduct on the part of one or more persons exists." The eighteen-and-a-half minute gap caused another public outcry. Calls for Nixon's resignation became more frequent—and came from more establishment-oriented, mainstream sources.

As the Ervin Committee and special prosecutor continued to battle Nixon for more tapes, the president announced that he would not hand over any more tapes because it would violate confidentiality and could have an adverse effect on the Watergate trials.

On February 6, with only four dissenting votes, the House of Representatives adopted H. R. 803, which directed the House Committee on the Judiciary to begin an investigation into whether grounds existed for the House to impeach President Nixon.

Watergate was moving closer and closer to the president. On March 1, the federal grand jury indicted seven former top presidential aides—Mitchell, Haldeman, Ehrlichman, Colson, Mardian, Parkinson, and Strachan—for attempting to cover up the Watergate investigation by lying to the FBI and to the grand jury, and for paying hush money to the original defendants. The grand jury also turned a briefcase over to Judge Sirica, the contents of which were kept secret, but which related to the president's role in the scandal. In this briefcase was material based on which the grand jury named Richard M. Nixon, president of the United States, as "unindicted co-conspirator" in the case.

The House joined the Senate and special prosecutor in seeking White House tapes, but the president continued to resist. Finally, on April 29, in a national television address, Nixon announced that he would supply the Judiciary Committee with "edited transcripts" of the subpoenaed conversations. Nixon said that this action would "at last, once and for all, show that what I knew and what I did with regard to the Watergate break-in and coverup were just as I have described to you from the very beginning. As far as the president's role with regard to Watergate is concerned, the entire story is there."

But the entire story *was not* there. The transcripts later proved to be incomplete and inaccurate. At the time, however, they appeared impressive indeed. The president, in his speech, had the camera pan to a table containing stack upon stack of binders that appeared to contain thousands upon thousands of pages. In reality, this was a public relations ploy. Many of the binders contained only a few pages.

Among the many White House omissions is this portion of the March 22, 1973 conversation between Nixon and Mitchell. The president says: "I don't give a shit what happens. I want you all to stonewall it, let them plead the Fifth Amendment, cover up or anything else, if it'll save it—save the plan. That's the whole point. . . . Up to this point, the whole theory has been containment, as you know, John."

This incriminating material *does not* appear in the White House transcript but is in the House Judiciary Committee's version. There were many other inaccuracies. Nixon's sanitized version was not acceptable, and the fight for the tapes themselves continued.

Leon Jaworski was methodically building a criminal case against administration officials, but a problem remained: what to do about the president? The charges against Mitchell, Haldeman, et al. hinged upon a conspiracy in which the president was actively involved. But could the president of the United States be indicted in a criminal case, or was impeachment the only avenue?

Jaworski asked his staff for legal memoranda relating to this question. The conclusion reached was that while there was a question of "propriety," there was "no explicit or implicit constitutional bar to indictment." In the end,

Jaworski, while admitting that there was clearly enough evidence to indict Nixon, could not bring himself to indict a sitting president. Instead, the grand jury unanimously voted to name Richard Nixon an "unindicted co-conspirator."

The House Faces Impeachment

In this highly charged atmosphere of eroding public confidence in the president, in which every day seemed to bring a new, more-damaging revelation, the House Judiciary Committee prepared to open the public phase of its impeachment inquiry. The case against the president had been building for over a year, but the case was made up primarily of circumstantial evidence linking the president to the scandal, with accusations from Dean, Magruder, and others. The direct evidence was still fairly thin.

As committee counsel John Doar accumulated material against Nixon, it became clear that the full weight of the accumulated evidence was devastating. But before impeachment proceedings against the president could begin, a very important question had to be answered: What is an impeachable offense?

At one end of the spectrum of thought (the president's position) was the view that impeachment could *only* be for serious crimes. Nixon's was a strictly *legalistic* view. At a March 6, 1974, press conference, Nixon, answering a question, said that "impeachment should be limited to very serious crimes committed in one's official capacity." Nixon added, "When you refer to a narrow view of what is an impeachable crime, I would say that might leave in the minds of some of our viewers and listeners a connotation which would be inaccurate. It is the constitutional view. The Constitution is very precise. Even Senator Ervin agrees that that view is the right one, and if Senator Ervin agrees, it must be the right one." (Senator Ervin did not hold this view.) At the other end of the spectrum was the view that impeachment was primarily a *political* device for removing a president, and one need not find violations of the law to vote for impeachment.

The Constitution, as it is in many areas, is rather vague regarding impeachment. The Constitution says that public officers "shall be removed from office on impeachment for, and conviction of, treason, bribery, or other high crimes and misdemeanors" (Article II, Section 4). But what are high crimes and misdemeanors?

The Founders' original proposal on impeachment first presented at the Constitutional Convention provided for impeachment for "malpractice or neglect of duty." The Committee on Detail changed the wording to read "treason, bribery, or corruption," and still later changed it to "treason or bribery." George Mason recommended that "maladministration" be added to the list, but James Madison objected on the grounds that it was too vague. Finally, the wording was changed to the old British term "high crimes and misdemeanors." What then, did the Founders understand this phrase to mean?

In general, the Founders, following the British common law tradition, did not understand "high crimes and misdemeanors" in the narrow, legal sense, or in the strictly criminal sense. Constitutional scholar Raoul Berger concludes that the Founders had a fairly wide view of the grounds for impeachment that included misapplication of funds, abuse of official power, neglect of duty, encroachment on or contempt of Parliament's prerogatives, corruption, and betrayal of trust.

The history of impeachment in the United States offers few precedents, as only a handful of cases have reached the Senate. Several of these cases, however, *did not* involve indictable criminal offenses. In the only other attempted case of presidential impeachment, that of Andrew Johnson in 1868, the charges were almost strictly political. Following this view, on February 21, John Doar submitted a report to the committee entitled "Constitutional Grounds for Presidential Impeachment," which reviewed the history of impeachment and its application to the case at hand. Doar concluded that impeachment was a remedy to be applied in cases of "serious offenses against the system of government."

A long, emotional, often heated, sometimes eloquent debate over the evidence against the president ensued. Under the glare of national television, Chairman Peter Rodino of New Jersey guided the hearings through these difficult times with evenhandedness. He knew that if the impeachment of Richard Nixon were to be legitimate and appropriate, it would require a bipartisan vote in favor of impeachment. Would any of the Republicans vote for impeachment?

On July 19, John Doar summarized the case against Nixon for the committee. "Reasonable men," he said, "acting reasonably would find the President guilty." Doar spoke of Nixon's "enormous crimes," and accused the President of "the terrible deed of subverting the Constitution." Minority counsel Albert Jenner supported Doar's conclusion. Would the Republicans on the committee?

On July 27, the committee voted on Article I of impeachment, which accused the president of engaging in a "course of conduct" designed to obstruct justice in attempting to cover up Watergate. This article passed by a 27–11 vote, with 6 Republicans joining all 21 Democrats in the majority. The following day Article II, charging Nixon with abuse of power, passed 28–10, and on the following day, the third article of impeachment, charging the president with unconstitutionally defying a congressional subpoena, passed 21–17. Two other articles, dealing with concealing the bombing of Cambodia and with income tax evasion, both failed by 26–12 votes.

The vote against the president—especially on Articles I and II—was bipartisan (see Table 6). Rodino was able to get enough Republicans to vote against a president of their own party to ensure that the public would see that the case against Nixon crossed party loyalties. The Judiciary Committee would recommend to the full House that it vote to impeach Richard M. Nixon,

Table 6 VOTE ON IMPEACHMENT ARTICLES

		FOR		AGAINST		
	ARTICLE	Dems.	Reps.	Dems.	Reps.	TOTAL
I	Obstruction of Justice	21	6	0	11	27–11
II	Abuse of Power	21	7	0	10	28–10
III	Contempt of Congress	19	2	2	15	21–17
IV	Bombing of Cambodia	12	–	9	17	12–26
V	Income Tax Evasion	12	–	9	17	12–26

Source: Adapted from *Impeachment of Richard Nixon*, Report of the Committee on the Judiciary, House of Representatives, August 20, 1974.

thirty-seventh president of the United States. On only one other occasion, in the impeachment of Andrew Johnson over one hundred years earlier, had the House faced such a situation.

The Battle for the Tapes

Everyone seemed to want Nixon's White House tapes. The Senate, the special prosecutor, then the House, all wanted the recorded record to see who was telling the truth. But the president refused to part with the tapes, citing variously executive privilege, the need for confidentiality, and other reasons.

Judiciary Committee chairman Pete Rodino wanted the tapes, and by a vote of 20–18 (essentially along partisan lines) the Judiciary Committee rejected Nixon's offer of transcripts, and informed the president that he had "failed to comply with the Committee's subpoena." After battles by the Judiciary Committee and Jaworski to get the tapes from the president, the Supreme Court agreed to hear the case.

President Nixon refused to comply with the committee's subpoena, invoking a claim of "executive privilege." While there is no mention of executive privilege in the Constitution, the claim derives from a belief that it is part of the implied power of the executive function of the president. The president's claim was not entirely self-serving. Not only is there a considerable history of presidential claims of privilege and confidentiality, but it is clear that some stages of the policy-making process must remain outside the glare of public scrutiny.

Taking the case placed the Court in the center of a legal *and* political battle. It was not a foregone conclusion that the president would obey a Court ruling. He had already warned that he would only obey a "definitive" ruling, and Charles Alan Wright, Nixon's lawyer, said, "The tradition is very strong that judges should have the last word, but," he added, "in a government organized as ours is, there are times when that simply cannot be the case."

The case, *United States of America v. Richard Nixon*, revolved around the question of who decides whether a president obeys a subpoena, the Congress, the courts, or the president himself? Leon Jaworski argued that the president must comply with a subpoena in a criminal case, that our system of law is based on no man being above the law:

> Who is to be the arbiter of what the Constitution says? Now, the President may be right in how he reads the Constitution. But he may also be wrong. And if he is wrong, who is there to tell him so? . . . This nation's constitutional form of government is in serious jeopardy if the President, any President, is to say that the Constitution means what he says it does, and that there is no one, not even the Supreme Court to tell him otherwise.

Nixon's lawyer, James St. Clair, thought otherwise:

> The President is not above the law. Nor does he contend that he is. What he does contend is that as President the law can be applied to him in only one way, and that is by impeachment.

On July 24, in an 8–10 decision (Justice Rehnquist withdrew from the case), the Supreme Court ruled that President Nixon must give to Judge Sirica (who was presiding in the Watergate coverup trial) the tapes, which were evidence in a criminal case. While acknowledging a heretofore unrecognized constitutional basis for the claim of executive privilege, the Court ruled that in this case, the president was required to turn over the tapes. The decision read in part:

> A President and those who assist him must be free to explore alternatives in the process of shaping policies and making decisions and to do so in a way many would be unwilling to express except privately. . . . The privilege is fundamental to the operation of government and inextricably rooted in the separation of powers under the Constitution. . . . Nowhere in the Constitution . . . is there any explicit relevance to a privilege of confidentiality, yet to the extent this interest relates to the effective discharge of the President's power, it is constitutionally based.

But this privilege was not without limits. As the Court noted:

> Neither the doctrine of separation of powers, nor the need for confidentiality of high level communications, without more, can sustain an absolute, unqualified presidential privilege of immunity from judicial process under all circumstances. The President's need for complete candor and objectivity from advisers calls for great deference from the courts. However, when the privilege depends solely on the broad undifferentiated claim of public interest in the confidentiality of such conversations, a confrontation with other values arises.

On August 5, Nixon finally released the tapes, and his fate was sealed. The June 23, 1972, tape became the "smoking gun," with undeniable evidence of criminal complicity, and when its content became known, it decimated the president's defense. When he released the tapes, the president admitted that some of the tapes "are at variance with certain of my previous statements." Nixon *had* lied, covered up, obstructed justice, not for national security reasons, but to protect himself. There was no way Nixon could survive. Even his staunchest supporters turned on the president. It was over.

Table 7 *PERCENT BELIEVING IN NIXON'S COMPLICITY*

May 11–14	56
June 1–4	67
June 22–25	71
July 6–9	73
August 3–6	76

Source: Gallup polls (adapted from *Congressional Quarterly Weekly Report*, Washington, D.C., 1974).

When the tapes were released, nearly all Nixon's support evaporated. Nixon loyalist Senator Hugh Scott said that the tapes showed "a shabby, disgusting, immoral performance by all those involved." Representative Mann of South Carolina said that "the more that people know about him, it seems the more trouble he's in." Conservative publisher William Randolph Hearst, Jr., said Nixon was "a man totally immersed in the cheapest and sleaziest kind of conniving." Impeachment in the House and conviction in the Senate were now certainties. Public opinion, which had been turning against the president since January, was now overwhelmingly against the president. Gallup Poll data (see Table 7) reveals the quick, sharp shift in public opinion.

The June 23 tape not only revealed that Nixon was directing a criminal coverup in the first week after the break-in, but also showed Nixon to be a small, petty person. This tape, and others, contained revealing personal glimpses into Nixon the man, and much of what was revealed showed a side of Nixon never before shown to the public. Nixon appeared small, petty, political in the worst sense of that word.

But it was not these indications of Nixon's smallness that proved to be his undoing. The tapes also contained irrefutable proof that Richard Nixon had committed indictable crimes, lied about his knowledge and involvement, and obstructed justice and directed the coverup from June of 1972.

The Pardon

Would Nixon, as ex-president, have to face criminal charges? After all, the conspiracy to obstruct justice had Nixon as an "unindicted co-conspirator." The answer came less than a month after Nixon left office.

On Sunday, September 8, 1974, President Gerald Ford called a news conference in which he announced that he had granted former president Nixon "a full, free, and absolute pardon . . . for all offenses against the United States which he, Richard Nixon, has committed, or may have committed, or taken part in during the period" of his presidency.

Some suggested that Ford and Nixon, or Ford and Haig, made some sort of deal: resignation in exchange for a pardon. But no proof exists, and all parties to the decision deny that any deal—implicit or explicit—was made. But the pardon, granted in the absence of criminal charges, leaves unanswered questions and creates disconcerting problems. To what extent was Nixon criminally guilty? Is a president above the law? How does one accept a pardon for acts he claims never to have committed?

The Republicans took a beating in the midterm elections following Richard Nixon's resignation. Fighting an uphill battle against the recent legacy of Watergate, the Republicans had little hope of doing well. In the House, the Republicans lost 48 seats, and in the Senate they lost 5 seats. While numerically this may not seem drastic, one must remember that the Democrats already had large majorities in both chambers. Given their already clear control of the Congress, these numbers are indeed impressive.

The Case Against Nixon

Since Richard Nixon was not brought before the court of justice, some defenders still maintain that while some mistakes were made, Nixon did not "really" commit an impeachable or indictable offense. This view flies in the face of overwhelming evidence to the contrary. What then were the offenses of Richard Nixon? Leaving policy disagreements aside, of what is Richard Nixon guilty? What crimes did Nixon order, tolerate, and encourage?

Richard Nixon is the most investigated president in history. Part of his defense is that other presidents did what he did—but because of the intense investigations, he got caught and they didn't. He also maintains that while he did make some mistakes, the evidence, when looked at in its entirety, shows that he committed no impeachable or indictable offenses, in spite of a grand jury naming him an "unindicted co-conspirator." Bob Haldeman refers to Nixon's own description of his involvement in Watergate as a cry of "innocence," and of Nixon's rationale of this innocence as "ignorance."

Indeed. that *is not* the way it was. Richard M. Nixon, thirty-seventh president of the United States, engaged in a variety of illegal and unethical acts while president. Among them are the following:

(N) *Obstruction of Justice:* On June 23, 1972, just six days after the Watergate burglars were caught, Richard Nixon—as tape recordings prove—instructed Bob Haldeman to have the CIA stop the FBI investigation into the sources of funds used by the burglars (the money came from Nixon campaign funds).

(N) *Conspiracy to Obstruct Justice:* As the March 21, 1973, tape clearly shows, Nixon conspired with others to continue the coverup of Watergate. The following day the president, talking with John Mitchell, discussed "stonewalling," and saving the "plan." The conspiracy to obstruct justice included paying money for the silence of the Watergate defendants, offers of clemency, etc.

(N) *Conspiracy:* In several areas, Nixon conspired with other members of the administration to break the law. The grand jury, convinced of this, named Nixon an "unindicted co-conspirator."

(N) *Conspiracy to Misuse Government Agencies:* The administration sought to have the IRS harass people on Nixon's "enemies list."

(N) *Coverup of Crimes:* Again the June 23, 1972, tape is important. It reveals that at least from that date, Nixon was engaged in covering up crimes. Numerous other examples of Nixon's coverup can be gleaned from the tapes; for example, on September

15, 1972, Nixon tells Dean, "So you just try to button it up as well as you can," on March 21, 1973, Nixon to Dean: "It's better to just fight it out and not let people testify," on March 22, 1973, Nixon to Mitchell: "I want you all to stonewall it, let them plead the Fifth Amendment, cover up or anything else, if it'll save it—save the plan." The coverup took several forms at different times, from a block-the-investigation, to a containment, to a modified-limited-hangout, to a circle-the-wagons, to a give-'em-an-hors-d'oeuvre approach. But the goal was the same: save the president.

(N) *Illegal Wiretaps:* Without obtaining a court order, Nixon approved seventeen wiretaps on newsmen and government officials.

Destruction of Evidence: Apart from the eighteen-and-a-half-minute gap (and other gaps) in the June 20, 1972, tape, examples of destruction of evidence include burning sensitive documents (Magruder) and "deep sixing" incriminating evidence from Hunt's safe (Gray). Relevant CREEP records were also destroyed.

Presentation of False Material to Congress: The transcripts of taped conversations that Nixon submitted contained many discrepancies, with several compromising statements expunged from the Nixon-sanitized version. For example, the White House transcript of a portion of the March 22, 1973, tape has Nixon saying he needed flexibility "in order to get off the coverup line." In the committee transcript the line reads, "in order to get on with the coverup plan."

Election Fraud: A variety of efforts to undermine the Democratic party's leading candidates was undertaken, including theft of campaign material, dissemination of false and libelous material, dirty tricks, misinformation, and political espionage, leading up to the break-in and bugging at the DNC headquarters. This effort successfully undermined the democratic and electoral process.

Forgery: The administration forged State Department cables falsely linking President Kennedy to political assassinations and attempted to get reporters to write stories based on these lies.

(N) *Perjury and Suborning of Perjury:* On several occasions, the president advised potential witnesses to lie or give incomplete answers to the grand jury and congressional committees. He also coached witnesses to give testimony that would not contradict "the plan." On March 21, 1973, he told Dean, who was to meet with prosecutors, "Just be damned sure you say I don't . . . remember, I can't recall, I can't give any honest, an answer to that, that I can recall. But that's it." And on April 14, 1973, he directed Ehrlichman to coach Gordon Strachan in giving testimony before the prosecutors so his story would match Magruder's. Several members of the administration lied before the grand jury.

(N) *Money Laundering:* In order to hide illegal or questionable campaign contributions, money was laundered, usually via Mexico. Nixon was aware of this, as the June 23, 1973, tape confirms.

Extortion of Campaign Funds: Pressure tactics and threats were used to get corporations and individuals to contribute money to the president's reelection campaign.

(N) *Bribery and Hush Money:* Beginning on June 29, 1972, just twelve days after the Watergate break-in, over $450,000 was paid to the burglars to buy their silence. Nixon, as the March 21, 1973, tape indicates, was aware of and discussed the paying of money to the defendants. On that day Nixon told Haldeman of Hunt, "His price is pretty high, but at least, uh, we should, we should buy the time on that, uh, as I, as I pointed out to John." That evening, $75,000 in cash was delivered to Hunt's lawyer.

(N) *Questionable "Security" Improvements in Nixon's Private Homes:* At public expense, a fireplace fan, a heating system, new windows, handrails, a shuffleboard court, a fiberglass flagpole, twelve brass lanterns, furniture, an ice maker, and other nonsecurity improvements were made in Nixon's San Clemente and Key Biscayne homes. The Joint Congressional Committee on Internal Revenue Taxation eventually determined that over $90,000 of nonsecurity improvements were made on Nixon's homes.

(N) *Income Tax Violations:* Back dating of Nixon's donation of his vice presidential papers to the National Archives allowed the President to claim a $482,018 income tax deduction. This was later disallowed after an IRS investigation.

(N) *Money for Favors:* In the ITT, Vesco, Dairy, and other cases, favorable governmental decisions followed contributions to the president's campaign coffers.

Burglary: In the Watergate break-in, there is no direct evidence that the president knew in advance of the crime.

(N) *Huston Plan:* The president approved a domestic intelligence plan even though he was aware that some elements of the plan were clearly illegal. Shortly after approving the plan, it was scrapped.

(N) *Clemency Offers:* Nixon, on several occasions, discussed offering clemency to the Watergate burglars. In fact, the burglars were given the impression that they would be granted clemency.

(N) *Plumbers:* Nixon approved the creation of a private presidential investigation unit, first to plug leaks, but which later engaged in such acts as breaking and entering (Fielding break-in).

(N) *Failure to Fulfill Oath of Office:* Richard Nixon took an oath to faithfully execute the law, but failed, for example, to act when his subordinates informed him that certain crimes had been committed (this is due in part to the fact that the president was involved in some of these crimes).

(N) *Failure to Comply with Subpoenas:* Nixon failed to honor congressional and special prosecutor's subpoenas and withheld information requested by the courts. This resulted in charges of contempt of Congress against the president.

(N) *Interference with Prosecutors:* Henry Peterson, who originally was assigned to handle the Watergate prosecution for the Justice Department, repeatedly fed Nixon information on the status of his investigation, and Nixon used this information to help him and his staff avoid prosecution. "I've got Peterson on a short leash," Nixon once told John Ehrlichman.

(N) *Obstruction of a Congressional Investigation:* Nixon tried to interfere with and influence testimony given by various staff members before the Ervin Committee.

Agnew: The vice president was forced to resign from office as part of a plea bargain for which he avoided prosecution and jail while pleading *nolo contendere* to income tax violation.

(N) *Nixon's Lies:* Repeatedly the president lied in speeches and news conferences about his involvement in and knowledge of Watergate and the coverup. The Judiciary Committee staff compared the information in the tapes with Nixon's public statements and found numerous examples of dishonesty in the president's public claims of innocence and ignorance.

(N) *Betrayal of the Public Trust:* The cumulative impact of Watergate was a legacy of suspicion and distrust. It left a mark on the way we viewed and practiced politics.

While this list is not exhaustive, it highlights some of the main areas in which Nixon went beyond the bounds of law and ethics. By his actions in

Watergate, Nixon undermined the rule of law and the oath of office he took. The House Judiciary Committee laid Watergate squarely at the feet of the president: "From the beginning, the President knowingly directed the cover-up of the Watergate burglary—this concealment required perjury, destruction of evidence, obstruction of justice—all of which are crimes. It included false and misleading public statements as part of a deliberate, contrived, continued deception of the American people." As Arthur Schlesinger has written:

> If he really had not known and for nine months had not bothered to find out, he was evidently an irresponsible and incompetent executive. For, if he did not know, it could only have been because he did not want to know. He had all the facilities in the world for discovering the facts. The courts and posterity would have to decide whether the *Spectator* of London was right in its harsh judgment that in two centuries American history had come full circle "from George Washington, who could not tell a lie, to Richard Nixon, who cannot tell the truth."

The Meaning of Watergate

Watergate, that generic word by which we refer to a range of crimes and improprieties, raised legal issues, political issues, *and* moral issues. It spoke to who we are and what we believe. It tested our system and ourselves.

Would the United States remain a "limited government" under the rule of law, or had we become an imperial nation with an imperial presidency?

For Nixon, the question is, how could someone so smart and seasoned behave so stupidly? It was a "third-rate burglary" made into a first-rate coverup and into a world-class scandal.

In the end, Nixon remains unable or unwilling to admit guilt in Watergate. While he calls his handling of Watergate stupid and a failure, he continues to "stonewall" on his own guilt. In a television interview with David Frost in May of 1977, Nixon told the interviewer, "I did not commit, in my view, an impeachable offense." But he did admit:

> I let down the country. I let down our system of government and the dreams of all those young people that ought to get into government, but who now will think it's all too corrupt. . . .
>
> Yep, I, I, I let the American people down, and I have to carry that burden with me for the rest of my life. . . . And, so, I can only say that in answer to your question, that while technically, I did not commit a crime, an impeachable offense . . . these are legalisms. As far as the handling of this matter is concerned, it was so botched-up. I made so many bad judgments. The worst ones, mistakes of the heart rather than the head.

Watergate spawned a variety of legislative responses. In the aftermath of Nixon's abuses, the Congress went through a period of legislative activism that resulted in the passage of the Budget Control and Impoundment Act (1974), the War Powers Act (1973), the Case Act (1972), the Federal Election Campaign Act (1974), the Ethics in Government Act (1978), the Presidential

Records Act (1978), the National Emergencies Act (1976), the Government in Sunshine Act (1976), the Federal Corrupt Practices Act (1977), the Foreign Intelligence Surveillance Act (1978), plus laws relating to privacy in banking and to setting up a vehicle for creating special prosecutors, and the Freedom of Information Act (1974).

"Everybody Does It"

Was Nixon different in his behavior from other presidents? A refrain one often hears from Nixon's defenders is "Everybody does it, Nixon just got caught!" Is this true? And if everybody does do it, why pick on Nixon? Victor Lasky asks, "Precisely what is Nixon accused of doing, if he actually did it, that his predecessors didn't do many times over?" If "everybody does it" is true, this is the most damning indictment of the United States and its government imaginable. To suggest that every president, or even most presidents, engaged in the voluminous crimes such as those that make up Watergate is to accuse the government of being rotten and corrupt, deceitful and petty, antidemocratic and immoral. Those defenders of Nixon who use the excuse that everybody does it, show contempt for the United States and cynicism about human beings. Everybody *doesn't* do it! Gerald Ford didn't. Jimmy Carter didn't. And while some presidents engaged in some sordid behavior, none can compare to Richard Nixon.

The defense of Nixon that says that it is "just politics," or everybody does it, is both false and dangerous. False because while other presidents *did* engage in immoral and illegal behavior, not one comes close to Nixon in volume, type, or degree of presidential involvement. Nixon's was a systematic abuse of power and subversion of law. It is dangerous because such an attitude breeds disrespect for the government and contempt for our political institutions. Aside from that, the "everybody does it" excuse is no justification for misconduct.

What John Mitchell called the "White House horrors" is without precedent in the United States. The United States is far from perfect, and past presidents are not without sin, but historian C. Vann Woodward sums up the difference between Nixon and his predecessors nicely:

> Heretofore, no president has been proved to be the chief coordinator of the crime and misdemeanor charged against his own administration as a deliberate course of conduct or plan. Heretofore, no president has been held to be the chief personal beneficiary of misconduct in his administration or of measures taken to destroy or cover-up evidence of it. Heretofore, the malfeasance and misdemeanor have had no confessed ideological purpose, no constitutionally subversive ends. Heretofore, no president has been accused of extensively subverting and secretly using established government agencies to defame or discredit political opponents and critics, to obstruct justice, to conceal misconduct and protect criminals, or to deprive citizens of their rights and liberties. Heretofore, no president has been accused of creating secret investigative units to engage in covert and unlawful activities against private citizens and their rights.

One of the primary differences between Watergate and the scandals of previous administrations is that the scandals of the past almost always involved greed for private financial gain, and the president was the unwitting victim. Past presidents were not knowingly a part of the corruption. In Watergate, the greed was for power, and the president was a direct participant in the corruption.

POINTS TO PONDER

1. What was the primary obstruction of justice action that Nixon took regarding the CIA and the FBI?
2. What did the "smoking gun" tape show?
3. Is Nixon's defense that there are precedents for many of the actions in his administration and thus "they all do it" convincing?

34

"REPORT OF THE CONGRESSIONAL COMMITTEES INVESTIGATING THE IRAN-CONTRA AFFAIR"
U.S. Congress

The 1987 congressional report on the Iran-Contra affair argues that the White House operations were flawed from several perspectives. There was a disjunction between the public position of the administration, which abjured negotiating with terrorists, and its secret sales of arms to Iran. The diversion of funds to the Contras demonstrated a "disdain for law" on the part of the administration in which a small group of administration officials decided that they knew the national interest well enough to deceive Congress, the public, and members of their own administration. The selection lays out the findings of the committees and their conclusions of wrongdoing on the part of the Reagan administration. Also included is a selection from the Minority Report that argues that the "mistakes of the Iran-Contra affair were just that—mistakes in judgment, and nothing more." The Minority Report was signed by all the Republican representatives and two Republican senators. The Majority Report was signed by all Democrats and three Republican senators.

Findings and Conclusions

The common ingredients of the Iran and Contra policies were secrecy, deception, and disdain for the law. A small group of senior officials believed that they alone knew what was right. They viewed knowledge of their actions by others in the Government as a threat to their objectives. They told neither the

Secretary of State, the Congress nor the American people of their actions. When exposure was threatened, they destroyed official documents and lied to Cabinet officials, to the public, and to elected representatives in Congress. They testified that they even withheld key facts from the President.

The United States Constitution specifies the process by which laws and policy are to be made and executed. Constitutional process is the essence of our democracy and our democratic form of Government is the basis of our strength. Time and again we have learned that a flawed process leads to bad results, and that a lawless process leads to worse.

Policy Contradictions and Failures

The Administration's departure from democratic processes created the conditions for policy failure, and led to contradictions which undermined the credibility of the United States.

The United States simultaneously pursued two contradictory foreign policies—a public one and a secret one:

—The public policy was not to make any concessions for the release of hostages lest such concessions encourage more hostage-taking. At the same time, the United States was secretly trading weapons to get the hostages back.

—The public policy was to ban arms shipments to Iran and to exhort other Governments to observe this embargo. At the same time, the United States was secretly selling sophisticated missiles to Iran and promising more.

—The public policy was to improve relations with Iraq. At the same time, the United States secretly shared military intelligence on Iraq with Iran and North told the Iranians in contradiction to United States policy that the United States would help promote the overthrow of the Iraqi head of government.

—The public policy was to urge all Governments to punish terrorism and to support, indeed encourage, the refusal of Kuwait to free the Da'wa prisoners who were convicted of terrorist acts. At the same time, senior officials secretly endorsed a Secord-Hakim plan to permit Iran to obtain the release of the Da'wa prisoners.

—The public policy was to observe the "letter and spirit" of the Boland Amendment's proscriptions against military or paramilitary assistance to the contras. At the same time, the NSC staff was secretly assuming direction and funding of the Contras' military effort.

—The public policy, embodied in agreements signed by Director Casey, was for the Administration to consult with the Congressional oversight committees about covert activities in a "new spirit of frankness and cooperation." At the same time, the CIA and the White House were secretly withholding from those committees all information concerning the Iran initiative and the Contra support network.

—The public policy, embodied in Executive Order 12333, was to conduct covert operations solely through the CIA or other organs of the intelligence community specifically authorized by the President. At the same time, although the NSC was not so authorized, the NSC staff secretly became operational and used private, non-accountable agents to engage in covert activities.

These contradictions in policy inevitably resulted in policy failure:

—The United States armed Iran, including its most radical elements, but attained neither a new relationship with that hostile regime nor a reduction in the number of American hostages.

—The arms sales did not lead to a moderation of Iranian policies. Moderates did not come forward, and Iran to this day sponsors actions directed against the United States in the Persian Gulf and elsewhere.

—The United States opened itself to blackmail by adversaries who might reveal the secret arms sales and who, according to North, threatened to kill the hostages if the sales stopped.

—The United States undermined its credibility with friends and allies, including moderate Arab states, by its public stance of opposing arms sales to Iran while undertaking such arms sales in secret.

—The United States lost a $10 million contribution to the Contras from the Sultan of Brunei by directing it to the wrong bank account—the result of an improper effort to channel that humanitarian aid contribution into an account used for lethal assistance.

—The United States sought illicit funding for the Contras through profits from the secret arms sales, but a substantial portion of those profits ended up in the personal bank accounts of the private individuals executing the sales—while the exorbitant amounts charged for the weapons inflamed the Iranians with whom the United States was seeking a new relationship.

Flawed Policy Process

The record of the Iran-Contra Affair also shows a seriously flawed policy-making process.

Confusion

There was confusion and disarray at the highest levels of Government.

—McFarlane embarked on a dangerous trip to Tehran under a complete misapprehension. He thought the Iranians had promised to secure the release of all hostages before he delivered arms, when in fact they had promised only to seek the hostages' release, and then only after one planeload of arms had arrived.

—The President first told the Tower Board that he had approved the initial Israeli shipments. Then, he told the Tower Board that he had not. Finally, he told the Tower Board that he does not know whether he approved the initial Israeli arms shipments, and his top advisers disagree on the question.

—The President claims he does not recall signing a Finding approving the November 1985 HAWK shipment to Iran. But Poindexter testified that the President did sign a Finding on December 5, 1985, approving the shipment retroactively. Poindexter later destroyed the Finding to save the President from embarassment [*sic*].

—That Finding was prepared without adequate discussion and stuck in Poindexter's safe for a year; Poindexter claimed he forgot about it; the White House asserts the President never signed it; and when events began to unravel, Poindexter ripped it up.

—The President and the Attorney General told the public that the President did not know about the November 1985 Israeli HAWK shipment until February 1986—an error the White House Chief of Staff explained by saying that the preparation for the press conference "sort of confused the Presidential mind."

—Poindexter says the President would have approved the diversion, if he had been asked; and the President says he would not have.

—One National Security Adviser understood that the Boland Amendment applied to the NSC; another thought it did not. Neither sought a legal opinion on the question.

—The President incorrectly assured the American people that the NSC staff was adhering to the law and that the Government was not connected to the Hasenfus airplane. His staff was in fact conducting a "full service" covert operation to support the Contras which they believed he had authorized.

—North says he sent five or six completed memorandums to Poindexter seeking the President's approval for the diversion. Poindexter does not remember receiving any. Only one has been found.

Dishonesty and Secrecy

The Iran-Contra Affair was characterized by pervasive dishonesty and inordinate secrecy.

North admitted that he and other officials lied repeatedly to Congress and to the American people about the Contra covert action and Iran arms sales, and that he altered and destroyed official documents. North's testimony demonstrates that he also lied to members of the Executive branch, including the Attorney General, and officials of the State Department, CIA and NSC.

Secrecy became an obsession. Congress was never informed of the Iran or the Contra covert actions, notwithstanding the requirement in the law that Congress be notified of all covert actions in a "timely fashion."

Poindexter said that Donald Regan, the President's Chief of Staff, was not told of the NSC staff's fundraising activities because he might reveal it to the press. Secretary Shultz objected to third-country solicitation in 1984 shortly before the Boland Amendment was adopted; accordingly, he was not told that, in the same time period, the National Security Adviser had accepted an $8 million contribution from Country 2 even though the State Department had prime responsibility for dealing with that country. Nor was the Secretary of State told by the President in February 1985 that the same country had pledged another $24 million—even though the President briefed the Secretary of State on his meeting with the head of state at which the pledge was made. Poindexter asked North to keep secrets from Casey; Casey, North, and Poindexter agreed to keep secrets from Shultz.

Poindexter and North cited fear of leaks as a justification for these practices. But the need to prevent public disclosure cannot justify the deception practiced upon Members of Congress and Executive branch officials by those who knew of the arms sales to Iran and of the Contra support network. The State and Defense Departments deal each day with the most sensitive matters affecting millions of lives here and abroad. The Congressional Intelligence Committees receive the most highly classified information, including information on covert activities. Yet, according to North and Poindexter, even the senior officials of these bodies could not be entrusted with the NSC staff's secrets because they might leak.

While Congress's record in maintaining the confidentiality of classified information is not unblemished, it is not nearly as poor or perforated as some members of the NSC staff maintained. If the Executive branch has any basis to suspect that any member of the Intelligence Committees breached security, it has the obligation to bring that breach to the attention of the House and Senate Leaders—not to make blanket accusations. Congress has the capability and responsibility of protecting secrets entrusted to it. Congress cannot fulfill its legislative responsibilities if it is denied information because members of the Executive branch, who place their faith in a band of international arms merchants and financiers, unilaterally declare Congress unworthy of trust.

In the case of the "secret" Iran arms-for-hostages deal, although the NSC staff did not inform the Secretary of State, the Chairman of the Joint Chiefs of Staff, or the leadership of the United States Congress, it was content to let the following persons know:

—Manucher Ghorbanifar, who flunked every polygraph test administered by the U.S. Government;

—Iranian officials, who daily denounced the United States but received an inscribed Bible from the President;

—Officials of Iran's Revolutionary Guard, who received the U.S. weapons;

—Secord and Hakim, whose personal interests could conflict with the interests of the United States;

—Israeli officials, international arms merchants, pilots and air crews, whose interests did not always coincide with ours; and

—An unknown number of shadowy intermediaries and financiers who assisted with the First and Second Iranian Channels.

While sharing the secret with this disparate group, North ordered the intelligence agencies not to disseminate intelligence on the Iran initiative to the Secretaries of State and Defense. Poindexter told the Secretary of State in May 1986 that the Iran initiative was over, at the very time the McFarlane mission to Tehran was being launched. Poindexter also concealed from Cabinet officials the remarkable nine-point agreement negotiated by Hakim with the

Second Channel. North assured the FBI liaison to the NSC as late as November 1986 that the United States was not bargaining for the release of hostages but seizing terrorists to exchange for hostages—a complete fabrication. The lies, omissions, shredding, attempts to rewrite history—all continued, even after the President authorized the Attorney General to find out the facts.

It was not operational security that motivated such conduct—not when our own Government was the victim. Rather, the NSC staff feared, correctly, that any disclosure to Congress or the Cabinet of the arms-for-hostages and arms-for-profit activities would produce a storm of outrage.

As with Iran, Congress was misled about the NSC staff's support for the Contras during the period of the Boland Amendment, although the role of the NSC staff was no secret to others. North testified that his operation was well-known to the press in the Soviet Union, Cuba, and Nicaragua. It was not a secret from Nicaragua's neighbors, with whom the NSC staff communicated throughout the period. It was not a secret from the third countries—including a totalitarian state—from whom the NSC staff sought arms or funds. It was not a secret from the private resupply network which North recruited and supervised. According to North, even Ghorbanifar knew.

The Administration never sought to hide its desire to assist the Contras so long as such aid was authorized by statute. On the contrary, it wanted the Sandinistas to know that the United States supported the Contras. After enactment of the Boland Amendment, the Administration repeatedly and publicly called upon Congress to resume U.S. assistance. Only the NSC staff's Contra support activities were kept under wraps. The Committees believe these actions were concealed in order to prevent Congress from learning that the Boland Amendment was being circumvented.

It was stated on several occasions that the confusion, secrecy and deception surrounding the aid program for the Nicaraguan freedom fighters was produced in part by Congress' shifting positions on Contra aid.

But Congress' inconsistency mirrored the chameleon-like nature of the rationale offered for granting assistance in the first instance. Initially, Congress was told that our purpose was simply to interdict the flow of weapons from Nicaragua into El Salvador. Then Congress was told that our purpose was to harrass [sic] the Sandinistas to prevent them from consolidating their power and exporting their revolution. Eventually, Congress was told that our purpose was to eliminate all foreign forces from Nicaragua, to reduce the size of the Sandinista armed forces, and to restore the democratic reforms pledged by the Sandinistas during the overthrow of the Somoza regime.

Congress had cast a skeptical eye upon each rationale proffered by the Administration. It suspected that the Administration's true purpose was identical to that of the Contras—the overthrow of the Sandinista regime itself. Ultimately Congress yielded to domestic political pressure to discontinue assistance to the Contras, but Congress was unwilling to bear responsibility for the loss of

Central America to communist military and political forces. So Congress compromised, providing in 1985 humanitarian aid to the Contras; and the NSC staff provided what Congress prohibited: lethal support for the Contras.

Compromise is no excuse for violation of law and deceiving Congress. A law is no less a law because it is passed by a slender majority, or because Congress is open-minded about its reconsideration in the future.

Privatization

The NSC staff turned to private parties and third countries to do the Government's business. Funds denied by Congress were obtained by the Administration from third countries and private citizens. Activities normally conducted by the professional intelligence services—which are accountable to Congress—were turned over to Secord and Hakim.

The solicitation of foreign funds by an Administration to pursue foreign policy goals rejected by Congress is dangerous and improper. Such solicitations, when done secretly and without Congressional authorization, create a risk that the foreign country will expect and demand something in return. McFarlane testified that "any responsible official has an obligation to acknowledge that every country in the world will see benefit to itself by ingratiating itself to the United States." North, in fact, proposed rewarding a Central American country with foreign assistance funds for facilitating arms shipments to the Contras. And Secord, who had once been in charge of the U.S. Air Force's foreign military sales, said "where there is a quid, there is a quo."

Moreover, under the Constitution only Congress can provide funds for the Executive branch. The Framers intended Congress's "power of the purse" to be one of the principal checks on Executive action. It was designed, among other things, to prevent the Executive from involving this country unilaterally in a foreign conflict. The Constitutional plan does not prohibit a President from asking a foreign state, or anyone else, to contribute funds to a third party. But it does prohibit such solicitation where the United States exercises control over their receipt and expenditure. By circumventing Congress' power of the purse through third-country and private contributions to the Contras, the Administration undermined a cardinal principle of the Constitution.

Further, by turning to private citizens, the NSC staff jeopardized its own objectives. Sensitive negotiations were conducted by parties with little experience in diplomacy, and financial interests of their own. The diplomatic aspect of the mission failed—the United States today has no long-term relationship with Iran and no fewer hostages in captivity. But the private financial aspect succeeded—Secord and Hakim took $4.4 million in commissions and used $2.2 million more for their personal benefit; in addition, they set aside reserves of over $4 million in Swiss bank accounts of the Enterprise.

Covert operations of this Government should only be directed and conducted by the trained professional services that are accountable to the President and Congress. Such operations should never be delegated, as they were here, to private citizens in order to evade Governmental restrictions.

Lack of Accountability

The confusion, deception, and privatization which marked the Iran-Contra Affair were the inevitable products of an attempt to avoid accountability. Congress, the Cabinet, and the Joint Chiefs of Staff were denied information and excluded from the decision-making process. Democratic procedures were disregarded.

Officials who make public policy must be accountable to the public. But the public cannot hold officials accountable for policies of which the public is unaware. Policies that are known can be subjected to the test of reason, and mistakes can be corrected after consultation with the Congress and deliberation within the Executive branch itself. Policies that are secret become the private preserve of the few, mistakes are inevitably perpetuated, and the public loses control over Government. That is what happened in the Iran-Contra Affair:

—The President's NSC staff carried out a covert action in furtherance of his policy to sustain the Contras, but the President said he did not know about it.

—The President's NSC staff secretly diverted millions of dollars in profits from the Iran arms sales to the Contras, but the President said he did not know about it and Poindexter claimed he did not tell him.

—The Chairman of the Joint Chiefs of Staff was not informed of the Iran arms sales, nor was he ever consulted regarding the impact of such sales on the Iran-Iraq war or on U.S. military readiness.

—The Secretary of State was not informed of the millions of dollars in Contra contributions solicited by the NSC staff from foreign governments with which the State Department deals each day.

—Congress was told almost nothing—and what it was told was false.

Deniability replaced accountability. Thus, Poindexter justified his decision not to inform the President of the diversion on the ground that he wanted to give the President "deniability." Poindexter said he wanted to shield the President from political embarrassment if the diversion became public.

This kind of thinking is inconsistent with democratic governance. "Plausible denial," an accepted concept in intelligence activities, means structuring an authorized covert operation so that, if discovered by the party against whom it is directed, United States involvement may plausibly be denied. That is a legitimate feature of authorized covert operations. In no circumstance, however, does "plausible denial" mean structuring an operation so that it may be concealed from—or denied to—the highest elected officials of the United States Government itself.

The very premise of democracy is that "we the people" are entitled to make our own choices on fundamental policies. But freedom of choice is illusory if policies are kept, not only from the public, but from its elected representatives.

Disdain for Law

In the Iran-Contra Affair, officials viewed the law not as setting boundaries for their actions, but raising impediments to their goals. When the goals and the law collided, the law gave way:

—The covert program of support for the Contras evaded the Constitution's most significant check on Executive power: the President can spend funds on a program only if he can convince Congress to appropriate the money.

When Congress enacted the Boland Amendment, cutting off funds for the war in Nicaragua, Administration officials raised funds for the Contras from other sources—foreign Governments, the Iran arms sales, and private individuals; and the NSC staff controlled the expenditures of these funds through power over the Enterprise. Conducting the covert program in Nicaragua with funding from the sale of U.S. Government property and contributions raised by Government officials was a flagrant violation of the Appropriations Clause of the Constitution.

—In addition, the covert program of support for the Contras was an evasion of the letter and spirit of the Boland Amendment. The President made it clear that while he opposed restrictions on military or paramilitary assistance to the Contras, he recognized that compliance with the law was not optional. "[W]hat I might personally wish or what our Government might wish still would not justify us violating the law of the land," he said in 1983.

A year later, members of the NSC staff were devising ways to continue support and direction of Contra activities during the period of the Boland Amendment. What was previously done by the CIA—and now prohibited by the Boland Amendment—would be done instead by the NSC staff.

The President set the stage by welcoming a huge donation for the Contras from a foreign Government—a contribution clearly intended to keep the Contras in the field while U.S. aid was barred. The NSC staff thereafter solicited other foreign Governments for military aid, facilitated the efforts of U.S. fundraisers to provide lethal assistance to the Contras, and ultimately developed and directed a private network that conducted, in North's words, a "full service covert operation" in support of the Contras.

This could not have been more contrary to the intent of the Boland legislation.

Numerous other laws were disregarded:

—North's full-service covert operation was a "significant anticipated intelligence activity" required to be disclosed to the Intelligence Committees of Congress under Section 501 of the National Security Act. No such disclosure was made.

—By Executive order, a covert operation requires a personal determination by the President before it can be conducted by an agency other than the CIA. It requires a written Finding before any agency can carry it out. In the case of North's full-service covert operation in support of the Contras, there was no such personal determination and no such Finding. In fact, the President disclaims any knowledge of this covert action.

—False statements to Congress are felonies if made with knowledge and intent. Several Administration officials gave statements denying NSC staff activities in support of the Contras which North later described in his testimony as "false," and "misleading, evasive, and wrong."

—The application of proceeds from U.S. arms sales for the benefit of the Contra war effort violated the Boland Amendment's ban on U.S. military aid to the Contras, and constituted a misappropriation of Government funds derived from the transfer of U.S. property.

—The U.S. Government's approval of the pre-Finding 1985 sales by Israel of arms to the Government of Iran was inconsistent with the Government's obligations under the Arms Export Control Act.

—The testimony to Congress in November 1986 that the U.S. Government had no contemporaneous knowledge of the Israeli shipments, and the shredding of documents relating to the shipments while a Congressional inquiry into those shipments was pending, obstructed Congressional investigations.

—The Administration did not make, and clearly intended never to make, disclosure to the Intelligence Committees of the Finding—later destroyed—approving the November 1985 HAWK shipment, nor did it disclose the covert action to which the Finding related.

The Committees make no determination as to whether any particular individual involved in the Iran-Contra Affair acted with criminal intent or was guilty of any crime. That is a matter for the Independent Counsel and the courts. But the Committees reject any notion that worthy ends justify violations of law by Government officials; and the Committees condemn without reservation the making of false statements to Congress and the withholding, shredding, and alteration of documents relevant to a pending inquiry.

Administration officials have, if anything, an even greater responsibility than private citizens to comply with the law. There is no place in Government for law breakers.

Thus, the question whether the President knew of the diversion is not conclusive on the issue of his responsibility. The President created or at least tolerated an environment where those who did know of the diversion believed with certainty that they were carrying out the President's policies.

This same environment enabled a secretary who shredded, smuggled, and altered documents to tell the Committees that "sometimes you have to go above the written law;" and it enabled Admiral Poindexter to testify that "frankly, we were willing to take some risks with the law." It was in such an environment that former officials of the NSC staff and their private agents could lecture the Committees that a "rightful cause" justifies any means, that lying to Congress and other officials in the executive branch itself is acceptable when the ends are just, and that Congress is to blame for passing laws that run counter to Administration policy. What may aptly be called the "cabal of the zealots" was in charge.

In a Constitutional democracy, it is not true, as one official maintained, that "when you take the King's shilling, you do the King's bidding." The idea of monarchy was rejected here 200 years ago and since then, the law—not any official or ideology—has been paramount. For not instilling this precept in his staff, for failing to take care that the law reigned supreme, the President bears the responsibility.

Fifty years ago Supreme Court Justice Louis Brandeis observed: "Our Government is the potent, the omnipresent teacher. For good or for ill, it teaches the whole people by its example. Crime is contagious. If the Government becomes a law-breaker, it breeds contempt for law, it invites every man to become a law unto himself, it invites anarchy."

The Iran-Contra Affair resulted from a failure to heed this message.

MINORITY REPORT

President Reagan and his staff made mistakes in the Iran-Contra Affair. It is important at the outset, however, to note that the President himself has already taken the hard step of acknowledging his mistakes and reacting precisely to correct what went wrong. He has directed the National Security Council staff not to engage in covert operations. He has changed the procedures for notifying Congress when an intelligence activity does take place. Finally, he has installed people with seasoned judgment to be White House Chief of Staff, National Security Adviser, and Director of Central Intelligence.

The bottom line, however, is that the mistakes of the Iran-Contra Affair were just that—mistakes in judgment, and nothing more. There was no constitutional crisis, no systematic disrespect for "the rule of law," no grand conspiracy, and no Administrationwide dishonesty or coverup. In fact, the evidence will not support any of the more hysterical conclusions the Committees' Report tries to reach.

No one in the government was acting out of corrupt motives. To understand what they did, it is important to understand the context within which they acted. The decisions we have been investigating grew out of:

—Efforts to pursue important U.S. interests both in Central America and in the Middle East;

—A compassionate, but disproportionate, concern for the fate of American citizens held hostage in Lebanon by terrorists, including one CIA station chief who was killed as a result of torture;

—A legitimate frustration with abuses of power and irresolution by the legislative branch, and;

—An equally legitimte frustration with leaks of sensitive national security secrets coming out of both Congress and the executive branch.

Understanding this context can help explain and mitigate the resulting mistakes. It does not explain them away, or excuse their having happened.

The Committees' Report and the Ongoing Battle

The excesses of the Committees' Report are reflections of something far more profound. Deeper than the specifics of the Iran-Contra Affair lies an underlying and festering institutional wound these Committees have been unwilling to face. In order to support rhetorical overstatements about democracy and the rule of law, the Committees have rested their case upon an aggrandizing theory of Congress' foreign policy powers that is itself part of the problem. Rather than seeking to heal, the Committees' hearings and Report betray an attitude that we fear will make matters worse. The attitude is particularly regrettable in light of the unprecedented steps the President took to cooperate with the Committees, and in light of the actions he already has taken to correct past errors.

A substantial number of the mistakes of the Iran-Contra Affair resulted directly from an ongoing state of political guerrilla warfare over foreign policy between the legislative and executive branches. We would include in this category the excessive secrecy of the Iran initiative that resulted from a history and legitimate fear of leaks. We also would include the approach both branches took toward the so-called Boland Amendments. Congressional Democrats tried to use vaguely worded and constantly changing laws to impose policies in Central America that went well beyond the law itself. For its own part, the Administration decided to work within the letter of the law covertly, instead of forcing a public and principled confrontation that would have been healthier in the long run.

Given these kinds of problems, a sober examination of legislative-executive branch relations in foreign policy was sorely needed. It still is. Judgments about the Iran-Contra Affair ultimately must rest upon one's views about the proper roles of Congress and the President in foreign policy. There were many statements during the public hearings, for example, about the rule of law. But the fundamental law of the land is the Constitution. Unconstitutional statutes violate the rule of law every bit as much as do willful violations of constitutional statutes. It is essential, therefore, to frame any discussion of what happened with a proper analysis of the Constitutional allocation of legislative and executive power in foreign affairs.

The country's future security depends upon a modus vivendi in which each branch recognizes the other's legitimate and constitutionally sanctioned sphere of activity. Congress must recognize that an effective foreign policy requires, and the Constitution mandates, the President to be the country's foreign policy leader. At the same time, the President must recognize that his preeminence rests upon personal leadership, public education, political support, and inter-branch comity. Interbranch comity does not require Presidential obsequious-ness, of course. Presidents are elected to lead and to persuade. But Presidents must also have Congressional support for the tools to make foreign policy ef-fective. No President can ignore Congress and be successful over the long term. Congress must realize, however, that the power of the purse does not make it supreme. Limits must be recognized by both branches, to protect the balance that was intended by the Framers, and that is still needed today for ef-fective policy. This mutual recognition has been sorely lacking in recent years.

* * * *

Congress

Congress has a hard time even conceiving of itself as contributing to the problem of democratic accountability. But the record of ever-changing poli-cies toward Central America that contributed to the NSC staff's behavior is symptomatic of a frequently recurring problem. When Congress is narrowly divided over highly emotional issues, it frequently ends up passing intention-ally ambiguous laws or amendments that postpone the day of decision. In for-eign policy, those decisions often take the form of restrictive amendments on money bills that are open to being amended again *every year*, with new, and equally ambiguous, language replacing the old. This matter is exacerbated by the way Congress, year after year, avoids passing appropriations bills before the fiscal year starts and then wraps them together in a governmentwide contin-uing resolution loaded with amendments that cannot be vetoed without threatening the whole Government's operation.

One properly democratic way to ameliorate the problem of foreign policy inconsistency would be to give the President an opportunity to address the major differences between himself and the Congress cleanly, instead of com-bining them with unrelated subjects. To restore the Presidency to the position it held just a few administrations ago, Congress should exercise the self-disci-pline to split continuing resolutions into separate appropriation bills and present each of them individually to the President for his signature or veto. Even better would be a line-item veto that would permit the President to force Congress to an override vote without jeopardizing funding for the whole Government. Matters of war and peace are too important to be held hostage to governmental decisions about funding Medicare or highways. To describe this legislative hostage taking as democracy in action is to turn language on its head.

The Presidency

The Constitution created the Presidency to be a separate branch of govern-ment whose occupant would have substantial discretionary power to act. He was not given the power of an 18th century monarch, but neither was he meant to be a creature of Congress. The country needs a President who can exercise the powers the Framers intended. As long as any President has those powers, there will be mistakes. It would be disastrous to respond to the possibility of error by further restraining and limiting the powers of the office. Then, instead of seeing occasional actions turn out to be wrong, we would be increasing the probability that future Presidents would be unable to act decisively, thus guaranteeing ourselves a perpetually paralyzed, reactive, and unclear foreign policy in which mistake by inaction would be the order of the day.

If Congress can learn something about democratic responsibility from the Iran-Contra Affair, future Presidents can learn something too. The Administration would have been better served over the long run by insisting on a principled confrontation over those strategic issues that can be debated publicly. Where secrecy is necessary, as it often must be, the Administration should have paid more careful attention to consultation and the need for consistency between what is public and what is covert. Inconsistency carries a risk to a President's future ability to persuade, and persuasion is at the heart of a vigorous, successful presidency.

A President's most important priorities, the ones that give him a chance to leave an historic legacy, can be attained only through persistent leadership that leads to a lasting change in the public's understanding and opinions. President Reagan has been praised by his supporters as a "communicator" and criticized by his opponents as an ideologue. The mistakes of the Iran-Contra Affair, ironically, came from a lack of communication and an inadequate appreciation of the importance of ideas. During President Reagan's terms of office, he has persistently taken two major policy themes to the American people: a strong national defense for the United States, and support for the institutions of freedom abroad. The 1984 election showed his success in persuading the people to adopt his fundamental perspective. The events since then have threatened to undermine that achievement by shifting the agenda and refocusing the debate. If the President's substantial successes are to be sustained, it is up to him, and those of us who support his objectives, to begin once again with the task of democratic persuasion.

POINTS TO PONDER

1. What is the difference between a covert operation and a secret policy?
2. What was the "Boland Amendment"?
3. What was Oliver North's justification for lying to Congress about covert aid to the Contras?
4. How does the conclusion of the minority report differ from the conclusion of the majority?

PART III

*Political Behavior
and the Policy Process*

Chapter 9

❧

POLITICAL PARTIES

Political parties, though suspected by the Framers and often derided by contemporary political commentators, perform important functions in our system of governance. They were not even mentioned in the Constitution, yet they have dominated elections to Congress and the presidency for most of our political history. Parties provide essential links between citizens and their government and allow changes in political leadership to take place peacefully. This section of readings examines the positive and negative aspects of political parties in the United States.

The Role of Parties in a Democracy

Political parties are fundamental to the effective operation of a democracy through the establishment of a "loyal opposition" that will remain loyal to the nation, yet endeavor to replace the current governmental leadership. Political parties become vehicles for new ideas to come into the political system and then moderate those ideas enough to prevent a debilitating polarization. The two-party system in the United States integrates individuals with diverse ideas and interests into broad-based coalitions.

The party also recruits political leaders to compete for office and run the government. In the United States, political parties have encouraged upward mobility by integrating new immigrant groups into the political system. At the turn of the century, the political "machines" in large cities provided patronage and occasional welfare in exchange for faithful party-line voting. Perhaps the most important function of political parties is to present the electorate with coherent alternative policies and philosophies for ruling the country. Voters thus have more than personality and image on which to base their choice of a candidate.

Origins of U.S. Parties

The Framers of the Constitution, especially James Madison, were very distrustful of political factions and cabals. They felt that the formation of such alliances would lead to the polarization of politics into competing factions (for instance, property owners versus the less well-off) and that when one faction gained control of the government, it would inevitably oppress the out-of-office minority. Madison in *Federalist* No. 10 argues that the large size of the republic would mitigate the negative effects of faction, and that the national government was carefully designed to make it difficult for any one faction to gain control of all three branches at one time.

Despite this anti-party attitude on the part of the Framers, prototypical parties soon developed, first with the dispute over adoption of the Constitution between the Federalists and the Anti-Federalists. The Jeffersonians soon became the Democratic-Republicans, who remained a party through the election of 1824. In 1828 Andrew Jackson and the newly formed Democratic party came to power and battled the Whigs until the Republican party was formed in the early 1850s. The two-party system of Democrats and Republicans has lasted through the twentieth century.

Looking back, it seems that the creation of political parties was almost inevitable, despite the misgivings of the Framers. In fact, V. O. Key argued that political parties are essential for the operation of democratic government. If government is to be based on the consent of the governed rather than on divine right, heredity, or force, then an organized means must exist for replacing those in power with a different set of leaders. But how can an opposition to current government leaders be organized except by political parties or their functional equivalent? According to Key, the "institutionalization of party warfare" was a major innovation in the art of governance, replacing revolt and insurrection as the means for citizens to control government and establish a peaceful succession of authority.

Development of U.S. Parties

The heyday of political parties was the post–Civil War period of the nineteenth century. Party loyalty ran deep and seldom changed. Party-line voting was encouraged—ballots were provided by the parties rather than by the government. Election turnout was high, with more than 70 percent of the eligible electorate consistently voting in presidential elections. Appeals for support were most often framed in terms of loyalty to the party rather than support for the individual candidate.

Since that heady era, however, the power of the parties and their position as the center for politics in the United States has diminished. The roots of that decline are embedded in the Progressive movement that developed at the turn of the century in reaction to the corruption and abuses of partisan politics common in American governments. Party bosses seemed to control everything from minor patronage jobs to the nomination of presidents. Voters seemed to vote blindly at the dictates of the party.

The Progressives wanted to take politics out of government. They fought for such reforms as the city manager form of municipal government, in which

nonpartisan experts would administer city services. They favored the establishment of independent (bipartisan) regulatory commissions so that important
economic decisions would not be controlled by any one party. They also fostered two direct democracy techniques: the referendum (in which voters
could decide on issues that usually would be decided by legislatures) and the
recall (in which a government official could be removed from office by the
voters).

The innovation of the Progressives that had the most impact on the party
system, however, was the institution of primary elections. These elections
were intended to take the nominating function away from the party professionals and allow the voters to decide who would be nominated for office.
Though primary elections were used early in the twentieth century, they did
not come to dominate electoral politics until the last quarter of the century.

The last surge of importance of the political parties came with the establishment of the New Deal coalition in the Democratic party in the election of
1932. The Republicans, who had dominated the presidency in the 1920s,
were defeated, and a twenty-year reign by the Democratic party began. The
New Deal coalition comprised urban ethnic groups, African Americans, most
of the Solid South, organized labor, and Catholic and Jewish religious groups.
The New Deal coalition was to last through the 1950s, but it began to break
up as the party system began to disintegrate.

The Contemporary Party System

The candidacy of conservative Barry Goldwater began the breakup of the
Solid South; the election of Richard Nixon solidified it. Conservative southerners began to vote Republican in large numbers for the first time since Reconstruction. The election of Ronald Reagan further undermined the New
Deal coalition by attracting the votes of many blue-collar workers who previously had been loyal Democrats. But this shift in voting allegiances did not result in a realigning election similar to that of 1932. Those who left the
Democratic party did not switch their allegiance to the Republican party;
rather, they classified themselves as "independents" along with others who left
the Republican party. Thus the once-firm party identification of many voters
began to erode in a process that has been called *dealignment*.

Another major factor that continued the decline of parties was the proliferation of primary elections after the reforms in the Democratic party following
the 1968 election. The reforms undermined the power of the party professionals and increased the use of primary elections and participatory caucuses to
nominate candidates for office. Thus successful presidential candidates no
longer had to court assiduously the party professionals and "kingmakers," but
instead had to put together their own campaign organizations to capture the
nomination in the primaries and caucuses. To do this they had to raise their
own money with professional fund-raisers rather than turn to the political

parties. This trend has led to the rise of the "personal candidate," who hires a professional consulting firm to run a campaign, and to the corresponding diminution of the role of the party.

The role of political parties as the primary intermediating institution between the citizen and the government has also been undermined by the rise of television. Candidates and government officials can now speak directly to the people. They no longer need the mobilizing functions of political parties. The use of professional public opinion polling by candidates and government officials has also reduced the use of political parties as a means of translating public pressure into governmental action.

The decline of parties has also been marked by an increase in ticket splitting, the practice of casting votes for the candidate of one party for president and the other party for Congress. Ticket splitting has often resulted in divided government, which, in the judgment of some, leads to stalemate and gridlock in which neither party can prevail since each can block initiatives of the other. Divided government undermines one of the primary functions of political parties—to serve as a link between the two branches that the Constitution divides in the separation of powers.

Not all analysts agree that political parties are in their death throes. They point to the roles of the national Democratic and Republican parties in raising money through political action committees (PACs) and the recruitment of candidates to run for congressional seats. They also point to the fiscal health of the national party organizations and their professional staffs. In addition, party voting in Congress (when most members of one party vote against most members of the other party) increased in the 1980s and 1990s.

But the relative health of national party organizations does not entirely make up for the weakness of party in the electorate (that is, party identification) and the weakness of party in government (that is, divided government). In any case, no one argues that political parties have anywhere near the strength they enjoyed in the late nineteenth century or even in the middle of the twentieth century.

Public opinion polls consistently show that Americans are not much concerned with political parties, though they are very concerned with the political and economic health of the country. In fact, voters often express disgust at the political posturing of the parties and with "politics as usual." They feel that the Democratic and Republican parties are part of the problem, not part of the solution.

This feeling of frustration on the part of American citizens that the parties are not facing the issues and creating the solutions to the major problems of the country explains in part the tremendous popularity of Ross Perot in the presidential campaign of 1992. The billionaire business tycoon attacked both parties as part of the governmental gridlock problem and argued that a "common sense" approach and a willingness to "get down to business" were the answers to the huge budget deficits plaguing the country. His appeal was very effective, for even after dropping out and then reentering the race, he won 19 percent of the vote.

What difference does this make to political scientists who are concerned with political parties as essential mediating institutions in a democracy? They would argue that the Perot phenomenon does not present an answer to our deep-seated political problems. His appeal represents the old American yearning to take politics out of politics and turn our problems over to the lone hero riding out of the West who will save us from ourselves. According to this analysis, the narrower and more personalized the appeal of Perot, the less likely he would be able to build the coalitions necessary to deal with broad-based problems. His personality and narrow approach could not hold together the votes in Congress necessary to make the difficult choices that any serious progress entails.

The only way for Perot's movement to succeed would be for him to broaden his appeal and address the wide range of issues facing the country. But the wider he casts his net for voters, the more like a traditional party his group becomes, and the more like "politics as usual" it looks. Thus the only way Perot's anti-party appeal can work in the U.S. political system is for his movement to become more like a genuine political party.

If this does not happen, and voters continue to reject the solutions presented by political parties, the appeals of narrow interests and individual personalities become stronger. Politics becomes more fragmented and the system becomes vulnerable to demagogic appeals. According to Arthur Schlesinger, "without the stabilizing influence of parties, our politics would grow angrier, wilder, and more irresponsible." Whether this happens depends on the ability of the Democratic and Republican parties to renew themselves and respond to the concerns of voting Americans, including those who consider themselves independents.

The Readings

The readings in this section cover the fundamentals of understanding the place of political parties in the United States. First, the functions of political parties in any democratic polity are laid out by V. O. Key, Jr. Arthur Schlesinger, Jr., then provides a historical account of the rise and decline of our two major parties. Finally E. J. Dionne, Jr., argues that citizens are cynical because contemporary liberals and conservatives are paying more attention to ideological rhetoric than to solving political problems.

In the first selection political scientist V. O. Key, in a selection from his classic text, *Politics, Parties, and Pressure Groups*, lays out the basis of a party system and argues that political parties are essential to any system of democratic governance. He then looks for the reasons the United States has only two parties while other countries often have multiple parties. He concludes that two factors are important: single-member congressional districts and the electoral college system in which the plurality of the popular votes commits all the electoral votes for a state.

In the next selection Arthur Schlesinger examines the development of political parties in the United States. He describes the flourishing party system of the late nineteenth century and analyzes the decline of American political parties in the middle of the twentieth century. He argues that some important functions of parties have been taken over by professional political technicians, such as polling professionals, fund-raisers, and campaign organizers.

Schlesinger notes the negative effects of the decline of political parties, but chides those who romanticize the "good old days" when parties flourished. Blind party loyalty and the power of party bosses did not always bring out the best aspects of democracy. But he also argues that political life without parties could produce demagogic personal political movements that would polarize the nation and lead to a dangerous instability.

Contemporary alienation from the political system is the subject of Dionne's selection, "Why Americans Hate Politics." Dionne argues that the two political parties have spent the past several decades posturing about political ideology rather than searching for pragmatic solutions to such basic problems as education, transportation, and the economy.

Significantly, Dionne does not deal specifically with the political parties although his descriptions of the extremes of left and right clearly correspond to the Democratic and Republican parties. But Dionne would argue that neither party is performing the function of moderating its more extreme partisans and focusing on the pragmatic politics for which most Americans yearn. This may explain part of the appeal of "nonpolitical" leaders like H. Ross Perot, with his promises to end politics as usual and solve political problems with a non-partisan, common-sense approach.

KEY TERMS

dealignment: in contrast to realignment when the allegiance of the electorate shifts from one party to the other, in the dealignment of the 1970s and 1980s many voters ceased identifying with the major parties and began identifying themselves as independents

Democratic party: one of the two major political parties in the United States. The party traces its roots to the presidential campaign of Andrew Jackson. Democrat Franklin Roosevelt put together the New Deal coalition that held the majority of American voters from the 1930s through the 1960s.

political machine: a political party organization that effectively controls the government of a city by consistently winning elections and by controlling jobs and public works in the jurisdiction. Political machines controlled some large cities in the early twentieth century and were often associated with corruption, patronage, and voting fraud.

political party: an organization that attempts to achieve power by nominating candidates for election and by taking positions across a broad range of public policy issues

realignment: a shift in political allegiance in which the electorate switches its support from one political party to the other, as happened during the New Deal when the Democrats replaced the Republicans as the majority party

Republican party: one of the two major political parties in the American political system. It was founded in the 1850s, and Abraham Lincoln was the first Republican president. Republicans dominated the presidency in the late nineteenth century and during the 1920s.

single-member districts: a system of legislative representation in which each legislator is chosen to represent one geographic area, in contrast with a proportional representation system in which representatives are chosen by political parties and sent to parliament in proportion to the share of the vote won by the party

35

"THE NATURE AND FUNCTION OF POLITICAL PARTIES"
V. O. Key, Jr.

Political parties are more than interest groups trying to get their own way in the political process. In this excerpt from his book Politics, Parties, and Pressure Groups *(1942, 1964), the late political scientist V. O. Key argues that political parties are essential to the functioning of a democracy. Parties must aggregate a broad array of interests in order to win elections and control the government. Parties are thus the mediating link between voters and the government. Voters are able to hold the government accountable by rewarding incumbents with reelection or by punishing them by electing candidates from the other party. Key also reviews explanations for the two-party system of the United States, in contrast with the multiparty systems of many European nations, whose parties are arrayed along a political spectrum from the far left to the far right.*

Government derives its strength from the support, active or passive, of a coalition of elements of society. That support may be rooted in interest, consent, fear, tradition, or a combination of these and other factors in proportions that vary from society to society. In one instance a comparatively small group with control of instruments of violence may cow the populace into submission. In other instances authority may stem in far greater degree from the consent of the governed. In some states those in power may claim the right to retain their places without challenge; in others, provision may be made for periodic changes in the personnel of government by orderly processes.

In times past, the right to rule was assumed—or grasped—by small groups who based their claim of authority on the rights of religion, birth, family, class, force, wealth. In modern times such narrowly based power has been challenged, if not swept away, by the demand that an ever-larger proportion of the people share in the process of governance. The party politician, rather than the prince, becomes the characteristic contestant for power. The political party becomes the instrument for the organization of support in societies founded on the doctrine of the consent of the governed. Inherent in that doctrine is the idea of popular discharge of governments and their replacement by other rulers preferred by the people. The only way so far contrived by which such popular decisions may be made is through competition between political parties.

Within all sorts of human associations "political parties" exist, although they may not ordinarily be so designated. Affairs of a group—be it a nation, a church, a union, or a chamber of commerce—do not and cannot take care of themselves; small factions of men offer to assume responsibility for handling them. "Ringleaders" propose ways of dealing with group problems and vie for place; they exercise leadership. Although the germ of party may be observed in private clubs, societies, and associations, the party system in the nation possesses its special characteristics. The party system of a fraternity may be organizationally no more intricate than a back-room caucus. A party system for a nation includes means for the conduct of competition for control of the government in contrast with the more common existence in private groups of oligarchies infrequently challenged in their position. Moreover, a party system for the nation (or a state or a large city) must create organization to extend its leadership over considerable areas or over large numbers of people.

* * * *

The Two-Party Pattern

A salient characteristic of the American party system is its dual form. During most of our history power has alternated between two major parties. Although minor parties have arisen from time to time and exerted influence on governmental policy, the two major parties have been the only serious contenders for the Presidency. On occasion a major party has disintegrated, but in due course the biparty division has reasserted itself. For relatively long periods, single parties have dominated the national scene, yet even during these eras the opposition has retained the loyalty of a substantial proportion of the electorate. Most voters consistently place their faith in one or the other of two parties: and neither party has been able to wipe out the other's following.

Concept of party system. Since many of the peculiarities of American politics are associated with the duality of the party system, the significant features of that system need to be set out concretely. An identification of its main operating characteristics will supplement the insights gained about the role of party in the governing process from the earlier excursion into the genesis of party. To speak of a party *system* is to imply a patterned relationship among elements of a larger whole. A pattern or system of relationships exists between, for example, two football teams. Each team has a role to play in the game, a role that changes from time to time. Within each team a subsystem of relationships ties together the roles of each player. Or, if one prefers mechanical figures, the components of an internal combustion engine combine and perform in specified relation to each other to produce the total engine, or system.

Similarly, a party system consists of interrelated components, each of which has an assigned role. The American party system consists of two major elements, each of which performs in specified ways or follows customary behavior patterns in the total system. To remove or alter the role of one element would destroy the system or create a new one. If one ignores for the moment the internal complexities of parties, the broad features of the system as a whole are quite simple. The major parties compete for electoral favor by presenting alternate slates of candidates and differing programs of projected action. It is a basic characteristic of the system that each party campaigns with hope of victory, if not in this election perhaps at the next.

In their relations to the electorate, another element of the system, the parties confront the voters with an either-or choice. Commonly the electoral decision either continues a party in power or replaces the executive and a legislative majority by the slate of the outs. The system, thus, differs fundamentally from a multiparty system which ordinarily presents the electorate with no such clear-cut choice; an election may be followed by only a mild modification of the majority coalition. The dual arrangement assigns to its parties a radically different role from that played by parties of a multiparty system. The multiparty system may present to the electorate a choice ranging between extremes of the political spectrum but the dual system permits more extreme electoral decisions. The voters may throw the old crowd out of power and install a completely new management even if they do not set an entirely new policy orientation. The differences in the roles that their respective systems assign to them make a party of a multiparty system by no means the equivalent of a party of a two-party system.

To be distinguished from the roles of parties in electoral competition are the functions of party in the operation of government. The candidates of the victorious party assume public office. As public officers that may become more than partisans: they are cast in public rather than party roles. Yet the party role remains, for the government is operated under the expectation that the party may be held accountable at the next election for its stewardship. To the minority falls the role of criticism, of opposition, and of preparation for the day when it may become the government itself. These functions belong mainly to the minority members in the representative body but they may also be shared by the party organization outside the government. The minority role constitutes a critical element of the system. The minority may assail governmental ineptitude, serve as a point for the coalescence of discontent, propose alternative governmental policies, and influence the behavior of the majority as well as lay plans to throw it out of power.

In addition to the elements described, the party system includes customary rules which prescribe, often imprecisely, the manner in which the elements of the system shall interact. Of these, the most basic rule is that the government that loses the election shall surrender office to the candidates of the victorious party, a commonplace expectation which becomes significant only by contemplation of the relative infrequency of adherence to such a custom in the history of the government of man. Other rules and customs place limits on the conduct of party warfare. For example, the niceties of the etiquette of parliamentary conflict compel the attribution of good faith, patriotism, and even intelligence to the most despised enemy. Similar limitations, more poorly defined and less effectively sanctioned, apply to party warfare outside the parliamentary chambers.

Such are the rough outlines of the American two-party system described in terms similar to those employed by social theorists in their conception of social systems generally. Real party life does not nicely fit any such neat system of patterned relations among sets of actors. Yet the conception of system alerts the observer to the interrelations of the elements of party institutions.

Why two parties? Foreign observers manifest the utmost bewilderment as they contemplate the American two-party system, and native scholars are not overwhelmingly persuasive in their explanations of it. The pervasive effects on American political life of the dual form make the quest for the causes of this arrangement a favorite topic of speculation. Given the diversity of interests in American society one might expect numerous parties to be formed to represent groups with conflicting aims and objectives. Yet that does not occur. In the less sophisticated explanations of why, the system is attributed to a single "cause." One commentator hits on this cause, another on that, and a third clings to his peculiar interpretation. A more tenable assumption would be that several factors drive toward dualism on the American scene. Whether one of those factors plays a determinative role remains problematic. Nor can one readily assign weights to the several variables.

Persistence of initial form. Human institutions have an impressive capacity to perpetuate themselves or at least to preserve their form. The circumstances that happened to mold the American party system into a dual form at its inception must bear a degree of responsibility for its present existence. They included the confrontation of the country with a great issue that could divide it only into the ayes and the nays: the debate over the adoption of the Constitution. As party life began to emerge under the Constitution, again the issues split the country into two camps that corresponded roughly with the lines of division over the Constitution.

The initial lines of cleavage built also on a dualism of interest in a nation with a far less intricate economic and social structure than that of today. Arthur Macmahon concludes that, in addition to other influences, the two-party division was "induced by the existence of two major complexes of interest in the country." A cleavage between agriculture and the interests of the mercantile and financial community antedated even the adoption of the Constitution. This conflict, with a growing industry allying itself with trade and finance, was fundamental in the debate on the adoption of the Constitution and remained an issue in national politics afterwards. The great issues changed from time to time but each party managed to renew itself as it found new followers to replace those it lost. The Civil War, thus, brought a realignment in national politics, yet it re-enforced the dual division. For decades southern Democrats recalled the heroes of the Confederacy and the Republicans waved the "bloody shirt" to rally their followers. As memories of the war faded new alignments gradually took shape within the matrix of the pre-existing structure, with each party hierarchy struggling to maintain its position in the system.

Institutional factors. A recurring question in political analysis is whether formal institutional structure and procedure influence the nature of party groupings. Though it is doubtful that formal governmental structures cause dualism, certain features of American institutions are congenial to two-partyism and certainly over the short run obstruct the growth of splinter parties.

Some commentators, in seeking the influences that lead to two-partyism, attribute great weight to the practice of choosing representatives from single-member districts by a plurality vote in contrast with systems of proportional representation which are based on multimember districts. In a single-member district only two parties can contend for electoral victory with any hope of success; a third party is doomed to perpetual defeat unless it can manage to absorb the following of one of the major parties and thereby become one of them. Parties do not thrive on the certainty of defeat. That prospect tends to drive adherents of minor parties to one or the other of the two major parties. The single-member district thus re-enforces the bipartisan pattern. Each of the contending groups in such a district must formulate its appeals with an eye to attracting a majority of the electors to its banner.

An essential element of the theory is its plurality-election feature. If, so the hypothesis goes, a plurality—be it only 25 per cent of the total vote—is sufficient for victory in a single-member district the leaders of a group consisting of, say, 15 per cent of the electorate, will join with other such groups before the voting to maximize their chance of being on the winning side. They

assume that if they do not form such coalitions, others will. Moreover, concessions will be made to attract the support of smaller groups. If a majority, instead
of a plurality, is required to elect, a second election to choose between the two
high candidates in the first polling becomes necessary. Such a situation may encourage several parties to enter candidates at the first election, each on the
chance that its candidates may be among the two leaders. Of course, under systems of proportional representation the incentive to form two coalitions, each
approaching a majority, is destroyed by the opportunity to elect candidates in
proportion to popular strength whatever the number of the parties.

The validity of the single-member-district theory has not been adequately
tested against the evidence. Obviously, in those states of the United States in
which third parties have developed fairly durable strength, the institutional situation has stimulated moves toward coalitions and mergers with one or another of the major parties. Yet the single-member-district and plurality
election can at the most encourage a dual division—or discourage a multiparty
division—only within each representative district. Other influences must account for the federation of the district units of the principal party groups into
two competing national organizations.

The popular election of the Chief Executive is commonly said to be another institutional factor that exerts a centripetal influence upon party organization and encourages a dualism. The supposed effect of the mode of choice
of the President resembles that of the single-member constituency. The
winner takes all. The Presidency, unlike a French cabinet, cannot be parceled
out among minuscule parties. The circumstances stimulate coalition within
the electorate before the election rather than within the parliament after the
popular vote. Since no more than two parties can for long compete effectively
for the Presidency, two contending groups tend to develop, each built on its
constituent units in each of the 48 states. The President is, in effect, chosen by
the voters in 48 single-member constituencies which designate their electors
by a plurality vote. The necessity of uniting to have a chance of sharing in a
victory in a presidential campaign pulls the state party organizations together.
The election of the President is paralleled by the popular election of state governors and municipal executives, who are chosen in a manner equivalent in its
effects to the single-member district.

Systems of beliefs and attitudes. Certain patterns of popular political beliefs and
attitudes mightily facilitate the existence of a dualism of parties. In turn, a
two-party system, once in operation, may perpetuate and strengthen those beliefs and attitudes. These patterns of political faith consist in part simply of the
absence of groups irreconcilably attached to divisive or parochial beliefs that in
other countries provide bases for multiparty systems. Although there are racial
minorities in the United States, either they have been politically repressed, as
has the Negro, or they have been, as in most instances, able to earn a niche for

themselves in the nation's social system. Nor do national minorities form irredentist parties. For example, the Germans of Milwaukee do not form a separatist party to return Milwaukee to the Fatherland as did the Germans of Alsace-Lorraine. Nor has any church had memories of earlier secular power and the habit of political action that would lead to the formation of religious political parties. Class consciousness among workers has been weak in comparison with European countries, and labor parties have made little headway. When one group places the restoration of the monarchy above all other values, that group regards the prerogatives of its church as the highest good, another places its faith in the trade unions, and perhaps a fourth group ranks the allocation of estates among the peasants as the greatest good, the foundations exist for a multiparty politics.

The attitudes underlying a political dualism do not consist solely in the absence of blocks of people with irreconcilable parochial faiths. A pattern of attitudes exists that favors, or at least permits, a political dualism. Its precise nature must remain elusive, but it is often described as a popular consensus on fundamentals. Powerful mechanisms of education and indoctrination, along with the accidents of history, maintain broad agreement upon political essentials if not a universal conformity. At times, it can be said, with a color of truth, that we are all liberals; at another time, it may be equally true that we are all conservatives. Breadth of consensus seems to be associated with a disposition to cope pragmatically with problems as they emerge. Standpatters, to be sure, remain who are attached irrevocably to an ancient formula for dealing with all questions, but they soon die off and seem never to be numerous enough to form the basis for a durable third party.

Political dualism is not a necessary result of wide consensus but a powerful, self-perpetuating consensus retards and discourages the growth of population splinters that might form the basis for a multiplicity of deviating parties. Within the context of the general consensus, perhaps dualism has been fostered by the occurrence of a succession of great issues, or complexes of issues, on which the voters could divide in two ways. Often these have not been issues of substance but of means or of timing. The simultaneous occurrence of burning issues that cut across the electorate in different directions might well strain the dual-party structure. A single great problem with a variety of solutions, each attracting the determined support of a sector of the population, could have the same effect.

Explanations of the factors determinative of so complex a social structure as a party system must remain unsatisfactory. It seems clear that several factors conspired toward the development of the American dual pattern. Whatever its origins, once the two-party system became established, the system itself possessed great durability and as a going system it exerted great influence in conditioning behavior. The system adapts new generations to its practices and new movements, new population groups, new causes tend to be assimilated into it.

POINTS TO PONDER

1. Why does Key argue that political parties are essential to any democratic system of governance?
2. Why does the United States have a two-party system when many other democracies have more than two parties?
3. What does Key see as the most important functions of political parties?

36

"THE SHORT, HAPPY LIFE OF AMERICAN POLITICAL PARTIES"

Arthur M. Schlesinger, Jr.

In this overview of political parties from his book, The Cycles of American History *(1986), historian Arthur Schlesinger, Jr., of the City University of New York describes the golden age of U.S. parties in the late nineteenth century. Party loyalty was an article of faith among the voting electorate, which turned out for elections regularly and in high percentages. Schlesinger then lays out the factors that led to the decline of parties, beginning in the Progressive period with its distrust of politics. Television has replaced the party as the link between government and citizen, and public opinion polling has replaced the party as the link between leaders and the people.*

What has happened to the American as political animal? In the nineteenth century visiting Europeans were awed by the popular obsession with politics. Tocqueville in the 1830s thought politics "the only pleasure an American knows." Bryce half a century later found parties "organized far more elaborately in the United States than anywhere else in the world." Voting statistics justified transatlantic awe. In no presidential election between the Civil War and the end of the century did the American turnout—the proportion of eligible voters actually voting—fall below 70 percent. In 1876 it reached nearly 82 percent.

But in no presidential election since 1968 has the American turnout exceeded 55 percent. In 1984, only 52.9 percent voted. In the meantime, turnout in the once awed European democracies is over 75 percent in Great Britain and France, over 80 percent in West Germany, the Low Countries and Scandinavia, over 90 percent in Italy. The United States ranks twentieth among twenty-one democracies in turnout as a percentage of the voting-age population (only

Switzerland is worse). Fifty million additional Americans would have had to vote in 1984 to bring turnout back to nineteenth-century levels.

I

Why have Americans stopped voting? The dutiful citizens of a century ago did not rush to the polls out of uncontrollable excitement over the choices before them. The dreary procession of presidential candidates in these high turnout years moved Bryce to write the famous chapter in *The American Commonwealth* on "Why Great Men Are Not Chosen President," nor did the major parties disagree much on issues.

Changes in the composition of the electorate doubtless contributed to the decline in turnout. The pool of eligible voters was enlarged in 1920 by the Nineteenth Amendment (women), in 1965 by the Voting Rights Act (blacks) and in 1971 by the Twenty-sixth Amendment (eighteen-year-olds). The newly enfranchised tend, for an interval at least, to vote less frequently than adult white males inured to the process. Each enlargement reduced the ratio of turnout. Still, the voting pool was steadily enlarged in the nineteenth century by an influx of immigrants far less habituated to the idea of voting than native-born women, blacks or eighteen-year-olds, and white male immigrants were rather promptly incorporated into the political system.

The agency that seized and indoctrinated the immigrant was the political party. In the twentieth century the party has proved notably less successful in mobilizing women, blacks, the young and even adult white males. The conspicuous difference between the 1880s and the 1980s lies in the decay of the party as the organizing unit of American politics.

II

Parties have always represented the great anomaly of the American political order. The Founding Fathers were reared in an anti-party tradition. The eighteenth century had little use for parties. In France Rousseau condemned those "intriguing groups and partial associations" which, by nourishing special interests, obscured the general will. For Britain party was "faction"—a selfish and irresponsible clique—and "the influence of faction," as Hume wrote, "is directly contrary to that of laws. Factions subvert government, render laws impotent, and beget the fiercest animosities among men of the same nation, who ought to give mutual assistance and protection to each other." Parties were particularly at war with the philosophy, strong in colonial America, of civic republicanism and its emphasis on a public good beyond the sum of individual and group interests.

The American experience exemplified the anti-party philosophy. It was one of self-government without parties. There were no parties in the colonial assemblies or in the Continental Congress or under the Articles of Confederation. The Constitution made no provision for parties. "Such an addiction," Jefferson wrote of party spirit in 1789, "is the last degradation of a free and moral agent. If I could not go to heaven but with a party, I would not go there at all." The republic began under non-party government; and in his Farewell Address the first President issued a "most solemn" warning "against the baneful effects of the spirit of party." That malign spirit, Washington emphasized, "is seen in its greatest rankness" in popular governments "and is truly their worst enemy."

Yet, as Washington spoke, parties were beginning to crystallize around him. Condemned by the Founding Fathers, unknown to the Constitution, they imperiously forced themselves into political life in the early years of the republic. Their extraconstitutional presence rapidly acquired a quasi-constitutional legitimacy. Even Jefferson decided in another decade that he would be willing to go with the right party, if not to heaven, at least to the White House. By the time the first President who was born an American citizen took his oath of office, parties had become, it seemed, the indispensable means of American self-government. (It was fitting that this President, Martin Van Buren, was both the creative architect and the classic philosopher of the role of party in the American democracy.)

This extraconstitutional revolution took place because parties met urgent social and political needs. In the dialect of the sociologists, parties were functional. They contributed in a variety of ingenious ways to the stability of the system.

American parties originated in the diversity of circumstance and aspiration in the new nation. Madison in the 10th *Federalist*, after the customary denunciation of "the mischiefs of faction," went on to observe that the most common source of faction was "the various and unequal distribution of property" and, more surprisingly, to acknowledge that "the regulation of these various and interfering interests . . . involves the spirit of party and faction in the necessary and ordinary operations of the government." The very expanse of the new nation now offered hope, Madison thought, of controlling the baneful effects of party by diluting the influence of the interfering interests.

The expanse of the new nation gave parties another function. The thirteen colonies that had joined precariously to overthrow British rule were divided by local loyalties, by discrepant principles, by diverging folkways, by imperfect communications. Yet they were pledged to establish an American Union—and to do so over nearly a million square miles of territory. The parties as national associations were a force, soon a potent force, against provincialism and separatism. At the same time, they strengthened the fabric of unity by legitimizing the idea of political opposition—a startling development for a world in which that idea had little legitimacy (it has little enough for most of the world today). In 1800–1801 the American parties showed they could solve the most tense of all problems in new nations—the transfer of power from a governing party to its opponents.

"The party system of Government," Franklin D. Roosevelt once said, "is one of the greatest methods of unification and of teaching people to think in common terms." When by the middle of the nineteenth century the growing tensions between North and South split most national institutions, even the churches, party organization, as that brilliant early analyst of American politics, Henry Jones Ford, observed, was "the last bond of union to give way."

III

Parties performed an equally vital function within the national government itself by supplying the means of overcoming one of the paradoxes of the Constitution. The doctrine of the separation of powers, literally construed, warred against the principle of concerted action that is the essence of effective government. The need to make the new Constitution work demanded a mechanism that could coordinate the executive and legislative branches. The party now furnished the connective tissue essential to unity of administration.

The party found other functions in a polity groping to give substance to the implications of democracy. As vehicles for ideas, parties furthered the nation's political education, both defining national purposes and formulating national policies. As instruments of compromise, they encouraged, within the parties as well as between them, the containment and mediation of national quarrels. As agencies of representation, they gave salient interests a voice in national decisions and thus a stake in the national political order. As agencies of recruitment, they brought ambitious men into public service and leadership. As agencies of popular mobilization, they drew ordinary people into political participation. As agencies of social escalation, they opened paths of upward mobility to vigorous newcomers debarred by class or ethnic prejudice from more conventional avenues to status. As agencies of 'Americanization,' they received immigrants from abroad, tending (to quote Henry Jones Ford again) "to fuse them into one mass of citizenship, pervaded by a common order of ideas and sentiments, and actuated by the same class of motives." Thoreau cared little enough for politics, but he saw the point: "Politics is, as it were, the gizzard of society, full of grit and gravel, and the two political parties are its two opposite halves, which grind on each other," digesting and absorbing national differences.

On the local level the party, while generally organized for self-advancement and self-enrichment, prevailed because it also met community needs. Without mistaking the party boss for a sort of early social worker, one may still agree that city machines, with their patronage jobs, food baskets, Thanksgiving turkeys, friendly precinct captains, gave people lost in a frightening economic world a rare feeling of human contact. "There's got to be in every ward," Martin Lomasny of Boston told Lincoln Steffens, "somebody that any bloke can come to—no matter what he's done—and get help. Help, you understand, none of your law and your justice, but help." The machines, said

Steffens, "provided help and counsel and a hiding-place in emergencies for friendless men, women and children who were in dire need, who were in guilty need, with the mob of justice after them."

In an age lacking developed forms of popular amusement, political parties were even an essential source of diversion and fun. "To take a hand in the regulation of society and to discuss it," as Tocqueville noted, "is his biggest concern and, so to speak, the only pleasure an American knows. . . . Even the women frequently attend public meetings and listen to political harangues as a recreation from their household labors. Debating clubs are, to a certain extent, a substitute for theatrical entertainments."

IV

In view of the manifold functions served, it is no surprise that American parties so quickly planted their roots deep into the political culture. The immediate post–Civil War years were, I suppose, the golden age of political parties. Party regularity was higher, party loyalty deeper and party stability greater than at any other time in American history. Bryce, writing in 1888, described American parties as marked by "a sort of military discipline."

Independent voting was scorned, even when, as in 1884, it was urged by the most high-minded spokesmen of the genteel tradition. The young Theodore Roosevelt privately detested James G. Blaine, the Republican nominee, but stuck by the party and denounced his Mugwump friends as suffering "from a species of moral myopia, complicated with intellectual strabismus." "A good party," said the ordinarily sardonic Thomas B. Reed, the despotic Speaker of the House, "is better than the best man that ever lived." Or, in the sonorous language of Senator Ratcliffe in Henry Adams's *Democracy* (1880): "Believing as I do that great results can only be accomplished by great parties, I have uniformly yielded my own personal opinions where they have failed to obtain general assent."

How remote this all sounds! The contrast between the 1880s and the 1980s could hardly be more spectacular. A century after the golden age, all the gauges that measure party efficacy register trouble. Not only has turnout alarmingly declined, but the straight party ticket has become a thing of the past. In 1900 only 4 percent of congressional districts voted one party for Presidents and another for the House of Representatives; in 1984 44 percent of congressional districts split their tickets. In their advertising, candidates minimize when they do not conceal their party affiliations. Voters who designate themselves "independents" in public opinion polls now make up a third of the electorate. The party of nonvoters is almost as large. The classic political machine has generally disappeared, even in Chicago. By every test party loyalty in the old style is nearing extinction. Recent presidential elections have been marked by the rise of personalist political movements—George Wallace in 1968, Eugene McCarthy in 1976, John Anderson in 1980. All these developments are symptoms of a party order in a state of dissolution. The most astute of contemporary political analysts, Samuel Lubell, wrote in 1970 of "the war of the voters against the party system." What in the world has happened?

V

It is currently fashionable to explain recent party decline by citing allegedly novel and untoward developments assailing the system from without—the rise of single-issue movements, the power of lobbies, the fragmentation of Congress.

The historian may find such explanations unsatisfactory. Single-issue movements are hardly the horrifying novelty that our contemporaries, intimidated by the feminists, the environmentalists, the right-to-lifers, the Moral Majority, the anti–gun-controllers, the homosexuals and so on, suppose them to be. What, after all, was Madison writing about in November 1787 when he defined "a faction" as "a number of citizens . . . united and actuated by some common impulse of passion, or of interest"?

The mischiefs of faction has been an abiding theme in American history. Single-issue movements have flickered through the political scene from 1787 to the present, dedicated to the extirpation of Freemasonry, abolition of slavery, discrimination against immigrants, issuance of greenbacks or (one of the most alarmingly successful of all) prohibition of drink. American democracy has taken these movements in stride. When the Native American or Know-Nothing party was at its height, Horace Greeley predicted that it was destined "to run its course, and vanish as suddenly as it appeared. . . . It would seem as devoid of the elements of persistence as an anti-cholera or an anti-potato-rot party would be." The Know-Nothing party, it should be noted, won far more legislative seats than any single-issue movement of our own day has done. It vanished as Greeley predicted.

The same historical discount must be applied to the menace of lobbies. The United States has had lobbies as long as it has had Congresses. And lobbies were never more powerful than in the golden age of parties. Those who suppose lobbies to be some fearful invention of the late twentieth century should read *The Gilded Age* (1873), by Mark Twain and Charles Dudley Warner, or meditate the gaudy career of Sam Ward (1814–1884), the King of the Lobby. What the late twentieth century has raised to new levels of effectiveness is the public-interest lobby. This development somewhat offsets the less benign manipulations of special-interest lobbies. Common Cause and Ralph Nader became the antidote that Colonel Sellers and Sam Ward never had.

Nor is the fragmentation of Congress all that unprecedented. Political commentators write as if present indiscipline represents a lamentable lapse from better times when legislators unquestioningly obeyed their whips. But when were those better times? Even Franklin Roosevelt, in the epoch of 'rubber stamp' Congresses, had to fight hard for every New Deal bill after the Hundred

Days. Congresses controlled by his own party defeated some of FDR's most cherished initiatives, such as discretionary neutrality legislation and the Supreme Court plan.

Nor was legislative indiscipline new in the days of FDR. Woodrow Wilson, writing during the golden age of party regularity, called his book *Congressional Government*. But Wilson did not portray a well-ordered Congress. "Outside of Congress," he observed in 1885, "the organization of the national parties is exceedingly well-defined and tangible . . . but within Congress it is obscure and intangible. Our parties marshal their adherents with the strictest possible discipline for the purpose of carrying elections, but their discipline is very slack and indefinite in dealing with legislation. . . . There are in Congress no authoritative leaders who are the recognized spokesmen of their parties. Power is nowhere concentrated; it is rather deliberately and of set policy scattered amongst many small chiefs."

Legislative indiscipline is inherent in the American Constitution. The separation of powers denies the executive branch any organic means of controlling the legislative majority. Federalism turns national parties into loose coalitions of state parties. Between the commands of the Constitution and the sprawl of the country, strict party discipline has always been alien to Congress. Tocqueville made the point a century and a half ago. In the American democracy, he wrote, "Parties are impatient of control and are never manageable except in moments of great public danger"—and he knew the United States in an age of presidential domination as overweening as in the age of FDR. Tocqueville correctly traced this unmanageability to the dependence of the legislator on his constituents. "A representative," he wrote, "is never sure of his supporters, and, if they foresake him, he is left without a resource." Consequently legislators "think more of their constituents than of their party. . . . But what ought to be said to gratify constituents is not always what ought to be said to serve the party to which representatives profess to belong."

The observation that a legislator's loyalty runs more to his constituents than to his party remains true today; but it is hardly a new truth. And is legislative indiscipline altogether a bad thing? Is the republic better off when legislators give unquestioning obedience to whips? "Reader, suppose you were an idiot," Mark Twain wrote. "And suppose you were a member of Congress. But I repeat myself." Congressional fragmentation in recent times springs in part from the fact that Congress today probably has fewer idiots and more educated and independent-minded legislators than the nation has enjoyed since the early republic. The price democracy pays for independent-minded legislators is precisely their determination to make up their own minds.

Single-issue movements, lobbies, legislative fragmentation: these are the standard and abiding conditions of American politics. They are conditions with which the parties have cheerfully coexisted since the start of the republic. The causes of party decline must be sought elsewhere.

VI

Living as we do amidst the ruins of the traditional party system, we see a great yearning for the golden age of party supremacy. But let us not overdo the historic glory of American political parties. "America has had great parties, but has them no longer," Tocqueville wrote as early as 1835. By this he meant that parties of principle had already given way to parties of ambition and interest.

Far from taking principled positions, our major parties have been at one time or another on all sides of major issues. "Each in turn," wrote Henry Adams, "belied its own principles according as each was in power or in opposition." The Federalists were the party of secession (at the Hartford Convention) as well as of national government; the Democrats have been the party of state rights as well as of centralization; the Republicans, the party of centralization as well as of state rights. "American parties," my father once observed, "have been symbolized by such animals as the elephant and the donkey, but not by the leopard, which never changes its spots." Only minor parties have indulged the luxury of consistency "with the result that they have nearly always stayed minor."

The late nineteenth century was a golden age for the party as an institution. It was not a golden age for Presidents or for public policy or for politics as a profession. The worship of party swallowed up the purposes that had initially called the party into being. Originating as a means to other ends, the party fatally became an end in itself.

As party became king, the quality of men entering public life declined. Not a single notable President led the nation in the forty years between Lincoln and the first Roosevelt; and Lincoln was a minority President and Roosevelt an accident. Politics fell into disrepute. Young Henry Adams, returning from London after the Civil War, "noticed with horror that the grossest satires on the American Senator and politician never failed to excite the laughter and applause of every audience. Rich and poor joined in throwing contempt on their own representatives." The sympathetic Bryce reached the melancholy conclusion that "the ordinary American voter does not object to mediocrity" and that party professionals, "usually commonplace men," positively preferred the mediocre to the brilliant candidate. When politicians were not mediocrities, they were all too often thieves. "It could probably be shown by facts and figures," wrote Mark Twain, "that there is no distinctly native criminal class except Congress."

We are currently admonished to recall the blessings of boss rule. Contemplating the invasion of the parties by amateurs and zealots streaming up through primaries and caucuses, journalists and political scientists insist how much better things were in the good old days when a few bosses retired to the smoke-filled room and came out with a strong candidate and a balanced ticket. Yet bosses rarely proposed candidates they could not control. The typical candidate to emerge from the smoke-filled room was, of course, Warren

G. Harding. The effective Presidents of the twentieth century all won nomination over the prostrate bodies of party bosses. New ideas gain access to politics through hard-to-control reformers like Theodore Roosevelt, Woodrow Wilson, Franklin Roosevelt, John Kennedy and, in his peculiar way, Ronald Reagan. These men were leaders who took their parties away from the bosses and remolded them in their own images. Bosses are responsive to local interest and local boodle; reformers, to national concerns and national aspirations. Boss rule was no blessing.

Moreover, as party loyalty, regularity and discipline solidified, so did the determination of parties to evade pressing issues. The major parties in the golden age scored badly in responding to popular urgencies. The result was increasingly angry resort to third parties (the Greenback party in 1880, the Anti-Monopoly party in 1884, the Labor party in 1888, the Populist party in 1892) and to non-party movements. All pressed issues the major parties ignored—issues the major parties grudgingly coopted (as the Democrats did in 1896) only when necessary to assure their own survival.

The cult of party stifled the art of politics. Walt Whitman, the old Locofoco editor, retained after the Civil War the Jacksonian faith in politics as the method of democracy. In *Democratic Vistas*, he condemned "the fashion among dilletants and fops . . . to decry the whole formulation of the active politics of America, as beyond redemption, and to be carefully kept away from." He urged young men "to enter more strongly yet into politics. . . . Always inform yourself; always do the best you can; always vote." But he added with emphasis: "These savage, wolfish parties alarm me. . . . It behooves you to convey yourself implicitly to no party, nor submit blindly to their dictators, but steadily hold yourself judge and master over all of them."

Party supremacy, in short, bred political frustration. Whitman looked for the redemption of politics to "the floating, uncommitted electors, farmers, clerks, mechanics, the masters of parties—watching aloof, inclining victory this side or that side—such as the ones most needed, present and future." With his usual expansive prescience, Whitman prophesied the steady drift of voters from parties that has characterized the evolution of American politics over the last century.

VII

The parties were their own gravediggers. They were also the victims of changes in the political environment. For the modern history of political parties has been the story of the steady loss of the functions that gave parties their classical role.

The rise of a civil service based on merit largely dried up the reservoir of patronage. The decline (until recently) of mass immigration deprived the city machine of its historic clientele. Social workers and the welfare state took over the work of parties in ministering to the poor and helpless. A more diversified society opened new avenues of upward mobility. The rise of the mass media reduced the centrality of parties as the instrument of national unification. The development of mass entertainment gave people more agreeable diversions than listening to political harangues. The better educated, college-bred, post–GI Bill of Rights, suburban electorate felt no inclination to defer to political bosses. And parties in recent times have conspicuously failed to recognize urgent popular concerns. So many influential movements of our own age have developed outside the party process. Civil rights, women's liberation, the environmental movement, the antinuclear movement, the Moral Majority—all surged up from the grass roots to impose themselves on American politics.

The decomposition of parties has been under way a long time. The Progressive period at the start of the twentieth century mounted a purposeful assault on the party. Herbert Croly, the great Progressive theorist, considered "the overthrow of the two-party system indispensable to the success of progressive democracy," at least in the long run, and hoped to establish forms of direct democracy. This particular assault languished rather quickly.

But erosion continued. "The last twenty years," Calvin Coolidge wrote in 1929, "have witnessed a decline in party spirit and a distinct weakening in party loyalty." The twentieth century had no shrewder politician than the second Roosevelt. FDR was without nineteenth-century illusions about the sanctity of party. A Democrat, he cast his first presidential vote for a Republican, appointed two Republicans to his cabinet when elected President himself (and two more in the shadow of war), and a few months before his death was exploring the possibility of a political alliance with the very man the Republicans had run against him four years earlier. "People tell me that I hold to party ties less tenaciously than most of my predecessors in the Presidency," he told a Jackson Day dinner in 1940. ". . . I must admit the soft impeachment." Parties, FDR added,

> are good instruments for the purpose of presenting and explaining issues, of drumming up interest in elections, and, incidentally, of improving the breed of candidates for public office.
>
> But the future lies with those wise political leaders who realize that the great public is interested more in Government than in politics. . . . The growing independence of voters, after all, has been proven by the votes in every Presidential election since my childhood—and the tendency, frankly, is on the increase.

The tendency that FDR discerned greatly intensified in the next forty years and has landed the parties in the condition of desuetude we gloomily acknowledge today.

It was this situation that produced the zeal some years ago for party reform. That reform movement has been much misunderstood. It is currently fashionable to ascribe the contemporary party crisis to changes in party rules. But the reform movement of the 1960s, unlike the Progressive movement at the turn of the century, was designed not to overthrow but to save the party system.

The theory of the reforms was to tame the new social energies and incorporate them into the party process. In particular, it was to do for women, non-whites and the young what nineteenth-century parties had done for immigrants. Nor can one reasonably argue that the enlargement of citizen participation is such a bad thing in a democracy.

Some of the reforms—the modernization of procedures, for example, the new strength and autonomy conferred on the national committee, and the larger representation of women and of minorities—probably gave parties a somewhat longer life expectancy. Other new rules carelessly or deliberately ignored the interests of party as institutions—for example, in denying preference to party officials and elected representatives. Most of these lapses were subsequently corrected. In any event, the idea that rule changes caused the party crisis, and that repealing those changes will cure it, is akin to the delusion of Rostand's Chantecler that his cock-a-doodle-do made the sun rise. Party reform was not a cause of but a response to organic maladies.

Another blow to the parties came when reforms designed to control the role of money in elections had unexpected consequences in reducing the party's command of campaign finance. The Federal Election Campaign Act of 1974 provided for public funding of presidential elections. It also imposed limits both on political contributions and political spending. In limiting contributions to candidates, the law permitted larger contributions by non-party political action committees (PACs) than by individuals.

The advantage thus conferred on PACs was greatly increased two years later when the Supreme Court in *Buckley v. Valeo* knocked out the spending ceilings in congressional campaigns, doing so on the bizarre ground that political spending was equivalent to speech and therefore protected by the First Amendment. The Court evidently had no doubt that money talks. This ill-considered decision not only stimulated the formation of PACs as well as the appetite of candidates but also sanctioned, even in publicly financed presidential campaigns, "independent expenditures" by PACs—that is, political spending not coordinated with the favored candidate and his campaign. No aggregate limit, moreover, was placed on the amount of money PACs could receive and disburse. With a freer hand to play, PACs lured an increasing share of political money from the parties. By the mid-1980s PACs had increased sevenfold in number since 1974 (from 600 to more than 4000); the money they spent increased tenfold. PAC contributions accounted for 13 percent of congressional campaign funds in 1974; 41 percent in 1984. Because PACs often represented corporate and other particular interests, their expanding role threatened further distortions and corruptions in the democratic process.

VIII

Parties are in trouble, in short, because they failed to meet national needs in their season of supremacy and because they thereafter lost one after another of their historic functions. And today a fundamental transformation in the political environment is further undermining the already shaky structure of American politics. Two modern electronic devices—television and the computerized public opinion poll—are having a devastating and conceivably fatal impact on the party system.

Television has not had all the malign consequences for the political process that some commentators expected. It was predicted, for example, that television would breed candidates endowed with histrionic skills, photogenic profiles and ingratiating personalities. Ronald Reagan is cited as the inevitable product of the television age. But Reagan, one surmises, would have been equally successful in the age of radio, like Franklin D. Roosevelt, or in the age of newsreels, like Warren G. Harding, or in the age of steel engravings and the penny press, like Franklin Pierce. Presidential candidates in the television era—Johnson, Nixon, Humphrey, McGovern, Ford, Carter, Mondale—hardly constitute a parade of bathing beauties calculated to excite Atlantic City. Highly photogenic aspirants, like John Lindsay and John Connally, men qualified by experience and intelligence as well, got nowhere in their presidential quests.

It was feared too that Presidents, with their ready command of television opportunities and ready access to polling data, would use the electronic techniques to enhance the Imperial Presidency. Yet during most of the television era the Presidency has been in an embattled and beleaguered condition. It was feared that the rich men who owned the networks would use the medium to buttress privilege. Yet television has given dissenters and agitators, from the National Organization of Women to the Moral Majority, unprecedented opportunities to influence opinion. While politicians try to use television to manipulate the public, the public is using television to manipulate the politicians.

And television enables voters to know their leaders far better than they did when newspapers were the primary source of political information. Television is more pitiless than the press because the moving image is more revealing than the printed word. In earlier times, as that old political stager Harold Macmillan has recalled, "the public character of any leading politician seldom bore any close relationship to his true nature. It was largely represented or distorted by party bias, by rumor, and above all by the Press. . . . The radio, and especially the television, allow the mass of the public to hear, see and judge for themselves. Indeed, with all its faults—its triviality and superficiality—this medium can be very penetrating." This capacity for demystification—who can forget Nixon's darting, shifty eyes on the tiny screen?—is one reason why television has not filled all the dark expectations pundits had about it.

In some respects television may well have strengthened the checks and balances in the political order. And television, it must be remembered, is a case of multiple personality—one part snapshots of reality, one part commercial manipulation, one part dream factory. Even as collective fantasy television introduces people to new thoughts, habits and possibilities. Very likely, on balance, television shakes people up more than it settles them down, encourages equality more than it does hierarchy and thereby is generally diversifying and liberating in its social effect.

IX

On the other hand, television has dismally reduced both the intellectual content of campaigns and the attention span of political audiences. In the nineteenth century political speeches generally lasted for two or three hours and dealt with issues in systematic and exhaustive fashion. Voters drove wagons for miles to hear Daniel Webster and Henry Clay, Williams Jennings Bryan and Fighting Bob La Follette, and felt cheated if the famous orator did not give them their money's worth. Then radio came along and cut the length of political speeches first to an hour, soon to thirty minutes. It was still possible to develop substantive arguments even in half an hour. But television appeared, and the political talk shrank to fifteen minutes.

In recent years the fifteen-minute talk has given way to the commercial spot. Advertising agencies sell candidates in sixty seconds with all the cynical skill and contrivance they previously devoted to selling mouthwash and detergents. "The idea that you can merchandise candidates for high office like breakfast cereal," Adlai Stevenson said in 1952, "is the ultimate indignity to the democratic process." Stevenson did not foresee that by the 1980s even the spot might begin to give way to the political rock video, replacing all pretense of argument by a dreamlike flow of music and image.

Television, moreover, is the major cause of the appallingly high costs of modern campaigns. Presidential candidates devote more than half their federal campaign funds to television. In contests for lesser offices, where no public funds are available, the cost is even greater. The result is increasingly to limit politics to candidates who have money of their own or who take money from political action committees: in either case, a bad outcome for democracy.

Television is here to stay. But some of the accompanying abuses are not beyond remedy. America is almost alone among the Atlantic democracies in declining to provide political parties free prime time on television during elections. Were the United States to follow the civilized example, it could do much both to bring inordinate campaign costs under control and to revitalize the political parties. The airwaves after all belong to the people. Private operators use them only under public license. The Communications Act of 1934 empowered the Federal Communications Commission to grant licenses to serve the "public convenience, interest, or necessity." A television channel is immensely lucrative. The television barons are not owners of private property with which they can do anything they want. They are trustees of public property obligated to prove their continuing right to the public trust. If anything is central to the public interest, it is to use the airwaves to improve the process by which a people chooses its rulers.

When political parties receive free time, the purchase of additional political time should be prohibited, and the use of free time in less than five-minute segments should also be prohibited. Even advertising men feel that the spot mania has gone too far. "The time has come," the chairman of Foote Cone & Belding has said, "to stop trivializing the electoral process by equating a candidate and a public office with an antiperspirant and an armpit. It is time to stop selling television spots to political candidates."

X

Legislative action can moderate both the financial costs and the intellectual trivialization imposed by television on politics. It is much more difficult, however, to moderate the impact of television and the computer on the structure of the party system.

The old system had three tiers: the politician at one end; the voter at the other; and the party in between. The party's indispensable function was to negotiate between the politician and the voters, interpreting each to the other and providing the links that held the political process together. The electronic revolution has substantially abolished this mediatorial role. It has thereby undermined the traditional party structure.

Television presents the politician directly to the voter, who judges candidates far more on what the box shows him than on what the party tells him. Computerized polls present the voter directly to the politician, who judges the electorate far more on what the polls show him than on what the party tells him. The prime party function that A. Lawrence Lowell classically described as "brokerage" has disappeared in the electronic age. The political organization is left to wither on the vine.

The party has lost control of the lines of information and communication. It has also lost control of the selection of top candidates. This loss is often blamed on the proliferation of presidential primaries. But primaries have been around since the start of the century. It took television to transform them into the ruling force they are today. Television gives candidates the means of appealing to the electorate over the head of the party organization. It also gives voters a sense of entitlement in the political process. Ordinary citizens now nominate presidential candidates long before the professional politicians gather at the quadrennial conventions. The cherished American political drama of the 'dark horse' conjured out of the smoke-filled room has gone, never to return. Presidential conventions, once forums of decision, become in the electronic age ceremonies of ratification. The last year in which a convention required more than one ballot to choose the presidential candidate was 1952, more than a generation ago.

The party, in addition, is losing its control of campaigns. Television and the computer have produced a new class of electronic political specialists. Assembled in election-management firms, working indifferently for one party or the other, media mercenaries usurp the role once played by the party organization. Computers organize mailings and telephone banks. Campaigns abandon the traditional paraphernalia of mass democracy—volunteers, rallies, torchlight processions, leaflets, posters, billboards, bumper stickers. Politics, once labor-intensive, becomes capital-intensive. With elections dominated by signals from the computer and by the insensate pursuit of television opportunities, the voters' new sense of entitlement becomes vicarious. Personal participation ebbs away. Television makes spectators of us all.

Beyond these specific effects, the very atmosphere generated by television is antipathetic to parties. For obvious technical reasons, television focuses on personality, not on organization; on immediate events, not on historical tendencies. The more it monopolizes the presentation of political reality to the electorate, the less will voters conceive of politics in terms of parties. Television, as Austin Ranney points out, is "by its very nature an antiparty medium."

XI

The electronic age threatens the withering away of the traditional political party. Can the party system be saved?

Political scientists propose structural remedies: formal party membership; midterm party conferences; local party caucuses; binding party discipline and accountability; in short, the revitalization of the party through stronger rules and regulations. I must confess skepticism. The effort is to call the old parties from the vasty deep. It is not likely that they will come when we do call for them, even with the incantations of rules and regulations. Proposals to centralize the parties run against the historical grain of American politics as well as against the centrifugal impact of the electronic age. Actually some of the much-abused reforms have already given the parties new institutional and financial strength as national organizations. Yet, for all this, the party continues to decay as a force in politics. Carried too far—the midterm party conference, for example—efforts to discipline the party only speed up the process of dissolution.

Obviously we must avoid weakening the party system further. Such schemes as the direct election of Presidents, a national primary, a national initiative and referendum, might well administer the coup de grace. Even if the quadrennial conventions are not likely to recover the power to nominate, they provide the party an invaluable opportunity to come together after divisive contests for the nomination. As fraternal gatherings, the conventions introduce activists across the country to each other, foster the exchange of ideas, promote discussion and accommodation, produce a common platform, renew the party's sense of national identity. The allocation of a share of public funds and the provision of free television time to national committees during elections would be modestly useful in propping up the parties. But, in an age when the political culture is turning away from parties, structural remedies will have limited effect. The attempt to shore up structure in the face of loss of function is artificial and futile.

The party is simply no longer indispensable as an agency of mass mobilization; or as an agency of information and communication; or as an agency of brokerage; or as an agency of welfare and acculturation; or even as a manager of campaigns. Parties no longer serve as the gizzard of our politics. They no longer supply the links between government and the people. They no longer give jobs to the unemployed and soup to the poor. What use are they?

Yet the alternative to the party system would be a slow, agonized, turbulent descent into an era of what Walter Dean Burnham calls "politics without parties." This is the politics foreshadowed by independent voting, ticket-splitting, non-voting, running without party identification, professional campaign management, the substitution of television for organization, the rise of personalist movements—by the spreading war of the voters against the party system.

Of course "politics without parties" is the way America began. But even in the simpler eighteenth century parties were required to make the Constitution work. One shudders at the consequence for the republic of "politics without parties" in the late twentieth century. The crumbling away of the historic parties would leave political power concentrated in the leaders of personalist movements, in the interest groups that finance them and in the executive bureaucracy, which will supply the major element of stability in an ever more unstable environment.

Political adventurers might roam the countryside, like Chinese warlords, building personal armies equipped with electronic technologies, conducting hostilities against some rival warlords, forming alliances with others, and, if they win elections, striving to govern through ad hoc coalitions. The rest of the voters might not even have the limited entry into and leverage on the process that the party system, for all its manifold defects, has made possible. Accountability would fade away. Without the stabilizing influence of parties, American politics would grow angrier, wilder and more irresponsible.

XII

How to avert this fate? If present tendencies continue, parties will soon have little more to do than collect money, certify platforms and provide labels for the organization of elections and legislatures. What other functions are left in the electronic age?

We might begin by recalling what politics is all about. We are often told that politics is about power, and that is, of course, true. More recently, it is said that politics in the age of the mass media is about image; there is something in that too. But in a democracy politics is about something more than the struggle for power or the manipulation of image. It is about the search for remedy. In a country where citizens choose their own leaders, the leaders must justify themselves by their effectiveness in meeting the problems of their time. No amount of power and publicity will avail if, at the end of the day, policies are not seen to work. A major source of the anxiety and frustration that darken the climate of democratic politics is surely the gnawing fear that our masters are intellectually baffled by and analytically impotent before the long-term crises of our age—that they know neither causes nor cures and are desperately improvising on the edge of catastrophe.

"In a country so full of change and movement as America," Bryce wrote a century ago, "new questions are always coming up, and must be answered. New troubles surround a government, and a way must be found to escape from them; new diseases attack the nation, and have to be cured. The duty of a great party is . . . to find answers and remedies."

Bryce was right; and one way by which these decrepit organizations may acquire a new lease on life would be to revive the parties as incubators of remedies. One wishes that the intellectual energy expended in recent years on procedural reform had been devoted instead to the substance of our problems. Nor are substantive problems going to be solved by large committees with two representatives from every state, Puerto Rico and the District of Columbia. Ideas are produced by individuals working in solitude. They are refined and extended by informal discussions with other individuals. They are disseminated when political leaders, conscious both of the world's problems and their own ignorance, reach out for counsel. The incubation of remedy depends, not on techniques of party organization, but on the intelligence and resourcefulness of people outside the organization and on the receptivity and seriousness of individual politicians, who will then use the parties as vehicles for ideas.

The second hope for party restoration follows in sequence. It lies in the election of competent Presidents who will thereafter act to revitalize their party in the interest of their own more effective command of the political process. The future of the party may well depend on Presidents who, in order to put new programs into effect, invoke the party to overcome the separation of powers in Washington and to organize mass support in the country. A strong President needs a strongish party in order to govern effectively. The serious remaining function for the party is as an instrument of leadership.

It is not necessary to forecast precise institutional changes. One imagines that party names will survive while party structures modulate to fill new needs. The power of American democracy lies in its capacity for adaptation. Democracy has flourished in a succession of social contexts, from the rural rides of the eighteenth century to the urban jungles of today. Every innovation in modes of communication has added to the need for readjustment. Democracy along the way has absorbed the penny press, the telegraph, the movie and the radio. It will doubtless find ways of turning television and the microchip to its purposes.

Electronic techniques may subvert the present but they do not determine the future. In a despotic state, they become weapons of manipulation and controls. In a democracy, the electronic age remains open. The new media have the capacity to strengthen hierarchy or to strengthen equality; to centralize or to decentralize political power; to concentrate or to diffuse power over information; to increase anomie or to increase participation; to invade or to intensify privacy; to clarify the political process or to distort it; to reinforce representative democracy or to undermine it. These choices remain within democracy's power to make. So far the electronic age has not notably weakened the democratic commitment to individual freedom and the constitutional state, nor the American capacity for administrative innovation.

The national penchant for experiment, subdued in the 1980s, will burst out again at the next turn of the cycle. "The sum of political life," Henry Adams wrote, "was, or should have been, the attainment of a working political system. Society needed to reach it. If moral standards broke down, and machinery stopped working, new morals and machinery of some sort had to be invented." This is still the problem for American statecraft a century after—to reinvent the morals, mechanisms and ideas demanded by the harsh challenges of the waning years of the twentieth century. One thing is clear: we will not attain a working political system simply by fiddling with party rules and structure, nor by trying to reclaim a vanished past through act of will. We will attain it only by remembering that politics in the end is the art of solving substantive problems.

POINTS TO PONDER

1. What characterized the "golden age" of political parties in the nineteenth century?
2. Does Schlesinger favor a return to the "golden age"? Why or why not?
3. What are some of the different functions that political parties fulfill in the United States?
4. According to Schlesinger, why have U.S. political parties declined in the late twentieth century?

37

"WHY AMERICANS HATE POLITICS"
E. J. Dionne, Jr.

In this excerpt from his 1991 book of the same title, Washington Post *writer E. J. Dionne, Jr., argues that American politics has become polarized between the "1960s liberals" who value tolerance and compassion and "1980s conservatives" who value hard work and personal responsibility. But the ideological intolerance of the left and the right for each other's values does not reflect the concerns of the majority of middle-class Americans who would prefer pragmatic solutions to real public policy problems (like education, jobs, and roads) rather than the rhetorical battling of the two extreme positions.*

Is it possible for a nation to learn from thirty years of political debate? Can partisans in the debate accept that wisdom is not the exclusive province of one side of the barricades?

The Sixties Left and the Eighties Right had far more in common than either realized. If they shared a virtue, it was their mutual, if differently expressed, hope that politics could find ways of liberating the potential of individuals and fostering benevolent communities. If they shared a flaw, it was expecting far too much of politics. For both the Sixties Left and the Eighties Right, politics became the arena in which moral and ethical questions could be settled once and for all. Partisans of the Sixties Left could not understand how anyone could reject their insistence on tolerance and compassion. Partisans of the Eighties Right could not understand how anyone could reject their insistence on hard work and personal responsibility.

In both their virtues and their flaws, the Sixties Left and the Eighties Right were caught up in the tensions and ironies that have characterized politics throughout American history. As James A. Morone argued in his brilliant book *The Democratic Wish*, American politics is characterized by both "a dread and a yearning." The dread is a "fear of public power as a threat to liberty." The yearning, said Morone, a Brown University political scientist, is "an alternative faith in direct, communal democracy," the idea that Americans could "put aside their government and rule themselves directly." Put another way, Americans yearn simultaneously for untrammeled personal liberty and a strong sense of community that allows burdens and benefits to be shared fairly and willingly, apportioned through democratic decisions.

In their very different ways, the Sixties Left and the Eighties Right reflected both of these honorable impulses—and all of their contradictions. The "if-it-feels-good-do-it" left rejected the imposition of conventional moral norms through force of law. The entrepreneurial right rejected the imposition of compassion through taxation and regulation. The New Left and the more conventional liberals who ran the Great Society believed that the federal government could strengthen and "empower" local communities to organize themselves and act on their own behalf, sometimes by fighting City Hall and the federal government itself on the streets and in the courts. The Eighties Right also took "empowerment" seriously and sought to give individuals and local communities more say, at the expense of the federal government and bureaucrats of all kinds.

In their respective attempts to break with the drabness of bureaucratic and conventional politics, the Sixties Left and the Eighties Right aspired to a higher vision of public life. The paradox of the last thirty years is that their elevated aspirations drove both left and right further and further away from the practical concerns of the broad electorate and blinded both to the challenges facing the United States at the end of the century.

The moralism of the left blinded it to the legitimate sources of middle-class anger. The revolt of the middle class against a growing tax burden was not an expression of selfishness but a reaction to the difficulties of maintaining a middle-class standard of living. Anger at rising crime rates was not a covert form of racism but an expression of genuine fear that society seemed to be veering out of control. Impatience with welfare programs was sometimes the result of racial prejudice, but it was just as often a demand that certain basic rules about the value of work be made to apply to all. Those who spoke of "traditional family values" were not necessarily bigots opposed to "alternative lifestyles." As often as not, they were parents worried about how new family arrangements and shifting moral standards would affect their children. And those who complained about the inefficiency of government programs were not always antigovernment reactionaries; in many cases, the programs really did stop working and the bureaucracies really were unresponsive.

The right was guilty of its own misguided moralism. Feminists demanding equality for women were not selfish souls who put the children second; they were rational human beings responding to a world that had been vastly transformed, and to which they wished to make their own contribution. Gays demanding tolerance were not looking to insult the heterosexual world; they were simply asking that they not be picked on, ridiculed, and discriminated against. The right's worst blind spot was its indifference to economic inequality, an indifference that the politics of the supply side disguised brilliantly. At the heart of the supply-side vision, after all, was a view grounded in common sense: That we get less of what we tax. Supply-siders proposed cutting taxes on work, savings, and investment. But the net result of the Reagan tax program was to *increase* taxes on the work done by the vast majority in the middle; supply-side tax cuts disproportionately favored the savings and investments of the better-off. Social security payroll taxes, along with state and local taxes, kept going up. When the eighties were over, the middle class felt cheated. It had voted for tax relief, but got little of it for itself. The demand for "tax fairness" was thus not class envy or watered-down Marxism; it was simply what the middle class thought it would get when it elected Ronald Reagan.

Because of the particular myopias of left and right, American politics came to be mired in a series of narrow ideological battles at a time when much larger issues were at stake. While Americans battled over the Religious Right, Japanese and German industrialists won ever larger shares of the American market. While left and right argued about racial quotas, the average take-home pay of *all* Americans stagnated. While Michael Dukakis and George Bush discussed Willie Horton and the Pledge of Allegiance, the savings and loan industry moved inexorably toward collapse. While politicians screamed at each other about the death penalty, more and more children were being born into an urban underclass whose life chances were dismal and whose members were more likely to be both the victims and perpetrators of crime. While conservatives and liberals bickered over whether the government or private enterprise was the fountainhead of efficiency, America's health system—a mishmash of public and private spending—consumed an ever larger share of the Gross National Product. While veterans of the sixties continued to debate the meaning of the Vietnam War, communism collapsed and a new world— probably *more* dangerous and certainly less predictable than the old—was born.

Thus, when Americans say that politics has nothing to do with what really matters, they are largely right.

The Sixties Left and the Eighties Right conspired in another way to wage war against public life. Both profoundly mistrusted the decisions that a democratic electorate might arrive at. The left increasingly stopped trying to make its case to the voters and instead relied on the courts to win benefits for needy and outcast groups. The right waged wholesale war on the state and argued that government was *always* the problem and *never* the solution—except when it came to the military buildup. Over time, as Martin Shefter and Benjamin Ginsberg argued, fewer and fewer questions got settled through the electoral process. Instead, political battles were fought out through court decisions, Congressional investigations, and revelations in the media. The result has been a less democratic politics in which voters feel increasingly powerless.

In the meantime, the sheer volume of money that flooded through the electoral process made it an increasingly technocratic pursuit. Democratic politics is supposed to be about making public arguments and persuading fellow citizens. Instead, it has become an elaborate insider industry in which those skilled at fund-raising, polling, media relations, and advertising have the upper hand.

* * * *

The creation of a new political center is also vital to resolving the conflicts surrounding family life and feminism. And that center now exists, if politicians would but find it.

In three decades of argument, we have learned two very significant things; first, that most of the time the best way to bring up children is in what we sometimes (and very misleadingly) call "the traditional family," meaning mothers and fathers who live under the same roof with their children. To want to support that kind of family is *not* to discriminate in favor of one "lifestyle" over others. It is to lend a hand to the *only* institution in society whose main purpose for existing is the full-time nurturing of children. To make this assertion is not to discriminate against other "lifestyle choices." It is simply accepting that it is in society's interest to have our children well cared for and that children are usually better off when they live with a mother and a father who have made more than a passing commitment to each other.

Following from that, liberals should see that many of the proposals conservatives make in defense of the family are, in fact, quite consistent with the liberal agenda. Conservatives who argue that the tax system should be more generous to parents with children are, in effect, arguing for a more progressive tax system that is fairer to the families that most need relief.

But conservatives need to make a comparable concession, and this is the second thing we have learned over the last thirty years: that talk about reestablishing the 1950s-style family in which women would stay home all or most of the time is just that—talk. It is ludicrous to base public policies on the hope that women will give up their social gains. It is foolish to pretend that the economy will grow so quickly that a majority of women will be able to rush back home. Today, roughly 50 percent of families would fall below the poverty line but for the wages earned by women.

As we have seen, feminism did not arise by accident. Nor did it arise suddenly. When the economy changed radically at the turn of the century, so did family life *and* our attitudes toward family life. Work left the household and so did the people who lived there—first men, later women. Over time, society made a series of new commitments to women, including a commitment to providing women with educational opportunities equal to those of men. This transformed many things, most notably women's aspirations. It took until the 1960s for these transformations to have an explosive effect, but those changes had been coming for a long time. It is simply silly to think that a society that puts so much emphasis on work and its creative possibilities will convince half of its members to stay home, just because they happen to be women.

As a society, we are not entirely at ease with all these changes, and for good reason: In our mad rush into the workplace, we have left the children behind. New words and phrases describe our discontent, phrases like "latch-key children" who come home to an empty house because both parents are out earning a living.

These problems will not be resolved easily. But almost none of the answers will come from conservatives if they insist on holding out the 1950s ideal as the solution. The 1950s ideal is, at best, an option for those who can afford to live on one income. Conservatives also render the pro-family rhetoric highly suspect when they oppose requiring businesses to give leave time to the parents of newborns. This suggests that conservative solicitude for their business allies is greater than their concern for what happens to children. Conservatives talk of making it easier for parents to live on one income by changing the tax laws to help middle-income families raising children. But when President Bush offered his major tax-cut proposal, it was not to help these families; it was to cut the capital-gains tax, which would mainly benefit the wealthy. Once again, a conservative administration betrayed where its real bias lay.

What is needed is an approach that is both pro-family and pro-feminist. Such an approach accepts two widely held values in the society: that the family is good, that men and women are equal. For both liberals and conservatives, this approach will mean overcoming a deep mistrust that twenty years of false choices have encouraged. Many traditionalist conservatives really do believe that feminism is "anti-family." Many feminists really do believe that the traditionalists are "anti-woman." Many traditionalists see feminists as having little respect for "homemakers." Many feminists see traditionalists as having little respect for professional or single women.

The truth is that activists on both sides of the traditionalist–feminist debate have far more room for agreement than they realize. In 1989, Susan Moller Okin, a feminist scholar, published a book called *Justice, Gender and the Family*. On its face, the book was radical in its feminism. Okin argued that until the division of labor between men and women within the household was made equal, feminism would be a distant dream. To achieve real equality, she called for an end to all distinctions between men and women in the workplace. Employers, she said, should not assume that the primary responsibility for the care of small children will fall inevitably to women. It was thus vital, she argued, that all leave programs designed to allow parents to spend more time for their children be applied equally to men and women.

Such a proposal would find little support from backers of the Moral Majority. But what is striking is how many of Okin's other ideas would win a hearing from Jerry Falwell's followers. For example, she argues that in divorce cases, the parent without physical custody of the child—usually the father—should be required to contribute to the child's support *"to the point where the standards of living of the two households are the same."* (Her italics.) To do anything else, she contended, was unfair both to the children and to the (usually) female parent who bore responsibility for their care. Thus, in the name of feminist equality, Okin proposed an approach that traditionalists have long sought: an end to "no fault" divorce settlements that left women impoverished. By placing such a heavy burden on the divorcing father, Okin would create a powerful economic incentive for him to consider trying to keep a marriage together.

Okin also offered the intriguing suggestion that employers issue two paychecks "equally divided between the earner and the partner who provides all or most of his or her unpaid domestic services." This idea is surely controversial, but it provides an interesting point of contact between feminists and traditionalists, *both* of whom argue that women's work as mothers and "primary caretakers" is vastly undervalued by the society.

In short, we have reached a point where not all feminist ideas necessarily work against the values of traditionalists, and not all traditionalist ideas work against feminism. Most important, both feminists and traditionalists find common ground in seeing the care of children as taking priority over the narrowest marketplace values. It is around this proposition that a new center could form.

But if any one issue is obstructing the formation of such a center, it is abortion. On its face, abortion is as uncompromisable an issue as the American political system has ever confronted. For advocates of choice, abortion is a fundamental right. For the prolife movement, abortion is murder. Between those two positions there is little room for agreement—and, in fact, the dialogue between the prochoice and prolife movements is almost nonexistent.

Yet the mass electorate sees the issue quite differently from the partisans on either side. There is no single majority on abortion in the country; there are two overlapping majorities. On the one hand, Americans are deeply uneasy with government interference in intimate decisions. Thus, when pollsters pose the abortion issue as a question of whether the choices of individual women or government policy will be binding, the results are a clear prochoice majority. Yet when pollsters put the question differently, they get another majority: Most of the country thinks too many abortions are performed, rejects most of the reasons women give for having abortions, and favors certain restrictions on abortion—such as requiring teenagers to get parental permission. Some polls have produced the rather staggering finding that a majority can support legal abortion, even as a majority *of the same group* considers abortion to be the equivalent of murder.

This mass ambivalence makes itself felt at the polls in a peculiar way. Many voters simply refuse to base their vote on the abortion issue at all. Thus in Iowa, in 1990, Sen. Tom Harkin, running on a prochoice platform was reelected, and so was Gov. Terry Branstad, an ardent right-to-lifer. In 1990, voters handed prochoice candidates the governorships of Florida and Texas—and prolife candidates the governorships of Michigan and Ohio. The 1990 elections, which were once touted as the nation's abortion referendum, turned out to be something far less. An ambivalent country cast an ambivalent vote.

If ever there were an issue on which ambivalence is understandable, it is abortion. The challenge to our politics is to find ways of promoting public policy that speaks to that ambivalence. The problem for the right-to-life movement is that the country as a whole does not accept its absolutist opposition to abortion and is wary of too much government meddling. The problem for the prochoice movement is that the country shares the right-to-lifers' moral uneasiness with abortion and would like to encourage a moral standard that would reduce the number of abortions.

For the rather long short run, the right-to-life movement needs to accept that its primary task is not political but moral: It needs to convince the country that its view of abortion is morally compelling. Even if the right-to-lifers succeeded in their goal of banning all abortions, large numbers of women would continue to seek and get them illegally. Indeed, the polls suggest that younger women are far more prochoice than the rest of the female population, suggesting that the moral trends may be moving away from the right-to-life movement.

Accepting that abortion will remain largely legal indefinitely is not a happy prospect for the right-to-life movement. But the prochoice movement could ease the way toward compromise by accepting that "choice" is not the end of the story, but only the beginning. As Daniel Callahan, a philosopher who supports abortion rights, has argued, "the prochoice movement has tried to make do with a thin, near-to-vanishing idea of personal morality." This, he argues, "serves neither its own long-term interests nor those of the pluralistic proposition."

Thus, on a broad range of issues, from promoting adoption to making it easier for women who want to give birth to do so, there is a broad arena for compromise and cooperation. Also helpful, as Callahan argues, would be "a significant improvement in maternal and child benefits, improved counseling and more effective family planning and contraceptive education and services." Further, accepting restrictions on late abortions except where a mother's life is endangered—there are, in any event, few of these—would speak powerfully to the country's uneasiness with abortion. So, too, would parental notification laws with real escape clauses for teenage girls who have reason to fear the reactions of their parents.

The truth, as Callahan argues, is that abortion is about more than choice. It is, he says, "also about the welfare of families and children, about the obligation of males toward women and toward the children they procreate, and about the family and the place of childbearing within it." Americans are ambivalent about abortion because they take exactly this sort of complex view.

What I am suggesting here will surely not satisfy the right-to-life movement, since my approach assumes that abortion will remain largely legal. It is understandable that from the right-to-lifers' ethical point of view, tolerating abortion for a fixed period is like tolerating slavery for a few more years. And many pro-choice advocates will resist even the suggestion that abortion should be restricted or discouraged. They see this as a threat to a right they cherish.

But the abortion issue could provide us with a powerful example of how to deal politically with a complex moral question. The debate the country most needs on abortion is not political but ethical. The question is as unsettled as it is unsettling, and the political system is never likely to settle the matter entirely.

For three decades we have loaded up the political system with moral debates and cast political foes as moral lepers. The result, judging from the popular revulsion with politics, has not been satisfactory. A genuinely moral politics cannot be narrow and moralistic. The mass of voters understand quite well that complex moral questions do not get settled easily. They accept that both the right-to-life and prochoice movements are animated by people of good will. Many individuals agree with arguments made by *both* sides.

The lesson here goes beyond the abortion issue: If we are to end the cultural civil war that has so distorted our politics, we need to begin to practice a certain charity and understanding. We need politics to deal with the things it is good at dealing with—the practical matters like schools and roads, education and jobs. *Paradoxically, by expecting politics to settle too many issues, we have diminished the possibilities of politics.* After years of battling about culture and morality through the political system, voters are looking for a settlement that combines tolerance with a basic commitment to the values of family and work, compassion and the rule of law. Americans welcomed many of the liberating aspects of the sixties. They also welcomed the rediscovery during the eighties that certain "traditional" rules and values were socially useful and even necessary. In the 1990s, we have a choice: We can join the old battles all over again and set the sixties against the eighties. Or we can try to move on.

If there is a positive sign in the early 1990s, it is that even ideologues are growing impatient with ideological conflict. The death of communism and the end of the Reagan and Thatcher eras all signal a new turn in world politics. And intellectuals on the left and right finally take each other's ideas seriously. There is no more talk of liberalism as America's only serious ideology and much less casual dismissal of the arguments of political opponents. After a decade in power, conservatives are coming to accept that many problems were not created by liberals, and that many of them are hard to solve.

Thus, it was a breath of fresh air when *National Review*, the creator of the ideology of the postwar right, offered a lavishly favorable review of *The American Prospect*, a liberal magazine founded in 1990 that has proven itself refreshingly unorthodox.

Writing in one of the most ideological magazines in America, Richard Vigilante of the libertarian-leaning Manhattan Institute praised *The American Prospect* as "another sign of the welcomed waning of ideology in American politics and the return to a healthier American tradition." Vigilante declared flatly that "the old ideological bundles are breaking up, in part because some of the old issues are passing away, in part because in other areas of dispute experience is overtaking theory and producing consensus, and in part because people got tired of screaming." One can only hope that Vigilante has it right.

* * * *

The 1990s are daunting, but they also offer an opportunity for creative political thinking not seen since the industrial revolution ushered in new intellectual systems that we now call Marxism and capitalism.

The end of Soviet-style socialism creates an enormous opening for American social and political thought since Americans were never much taken with the capitalist-socialist debate. The relative efficiency of markets over bureaucracies was never really questioned here. When Americans made the case for social reform, they did so using a presocialist language of democracy, community, and republicanism. That is precisely the language that is most relevant in the postcommunist world. It also offers an approach that could rescue American politics from its current impasse.

Taken together, the collapse of communism and the affluence of Western market societies would seem to prove conclusively that the choice between rigid state economic control and largely unregulated economic activity is, in truth, no choice at all. When it is market against bureaucracy, market wins.

This comes as a surprise to almost no one—and certainly not to most American liberals or European social democrats, who have always accepted the efficiency of markets. But the argument that the Eastern European experience proves that all bureaucracies and all governments are doomed to the same kinds of inefficiencies is simply wrong. This view, now popular on the right, assumes that all governments and all bureaucracies are more or less the same, and that public endeavor is always inferior to private endeavor.

There is a dangerous moral equivalence at work here that misses the primary difference between the Western societies and communist regimes: Western governments were *democratic*. Our bureaucracies, though at times inefficient and unresponsive, were the creations and creatures of the popular will. Communism's biggest crime was not economic failure or inefficiency but tyranny. Communism was both inefficient *and* repressive.

As Vaclav Havel has reminded us so eloquently, political repression robbed Eastern European nations of a healthy civic life and decent public institutions. Eastern Europe is in trouble today not simply because of a shortage of private investment, but because all the *public* structures, ranging from phones and roads to schools and, yes, the bureaucracy itself, are in such a state of disrepair.

The antisocial nature of the sort of socialism created in the East is most glaring in the way communist regimes treated the environment. Their environmental crimes are almost as outrageous as their crimes against human rights. It is true that the environment is cleaner in the West in part because the West had the money available to clean things up. But the *primary* cause of the West's environmental consciousness is democracy, not the market. A cleaner environment is the product of *public life*. The bureaucrats who ran industry in Eastern Europe had no fear of popular democratic pressure; the capitalists and managers who ran the economies of the West did. If you want to know the difference between communist dictatorship and democracy, it is this: In the East, government officials, *free from public pressure*, nearly destroyed the environment; in the West, government officials, *responding to public pressure*, cleaned up the environment. In the East, bureaucrats were the polluters. In the West, bureaucrats—the people at the environmental protection agencies—were the foes of pollution.

The point here is that government and public life are not abstractions; they are what we make them. The lesson from Eastern Europe is not that we must fear government and public engagement, but that we need a *democratic* public life built on enthusiastic public engagement. The communists were thoroughly wrong in seeing capitalist democracies as doomed to collapsing into dictatorships of the rich. But they were wrong not only because they underestimated capitalism's productive capacities but also because they underestimated democracy's gift for self-correction. It was democracy that fostered the growth of social movements that called attention to those aspects of capitalism that didn't work. Such movements—New Dealism in the United States, democratic socialism and social democracy in Western Europe—insisted on a broad definition of democratic citizenship. In T. H. Marshall's famous formulation, citizenship in a free society consisted not only in civil and legal rights, not only in political rights, but also in social rights. Marshall's insight was that citizens could not fully exercise their basic civil rights and civil liberties without a degree of economic security. The struggle for Marshall's social rights produced the West's social insurance systems, which preserve tens of millions from lives of desperation.

It would be tragic indeed if the welcomed collapse of communist dictatorships were to teach us that the struggle for such "social rights" has become unnecessary. The democratic idea for which the United States and the other Western nations waged a cold war for forty years includes a recognition of both political *and* social rights. The truth is that the progress of the West has depended on the friendly rivalry between the capitalist's insistence on individual initiative and the communitarian's insistence on the broadest possible definition of citizenship and the most inclusive view of the national community. The capitalist and the democratic communitarian needed each other before communism collapsed, and they need each other now.

What is required to end America's hatred of politics is an organizing idea that simultaneously accepts the efficiencies of markets and the importance of a vigorous public life. The American political tradition contains such an idea, an idea that reaches back to the noblest traditions of Western culture. The idea is what the Founding Fathers called republicanism, before there was a political party bearing that name. At the heart of republicanism is the belief that self-government is not a drab necessity but a joy to be treasured. It is the view that politics is not simply a grubby confrontation of competing interests but an arena in which citizens can learn from each other and discover an "enlightened self-interest" in common. Republicanism is based on the realistic hope that, as the political philosopher Michael Sandel has put it, "when politics goes well, we can know a good in common that we cannot know alone."

Republicanism can sound foolishly utopian. When unchecked by the libertarian impulse, republicanism can be oppressive. Rousseau's declaration that "the better the constitution of a state is, the more do public affairs encroach on private in the minds of the citizens" sends a chill up our spines at the thought of republican mind-control.

But we are a very long way from such dangers and face instead the dangers of too little faith in the possibilities of politics. Citizens in a free, democratic republic need to accept that there will always be a healthy tension among liberty, virtue, equality, and community. It is an ancient but still valid idea that liberty without virtue will collapse, and that virtue without liberty will become despotic. And without a sense of community and equity, free citizens will be unwilling to come to the aid and defense of each other's liberty. These notions are broadly accepted by Americans. Our current political dialogue fails us and leads us to hate politics because it insists on stifling yes/no, either/or approaches that ignore the elements that must come together to create a successful and democratic civic culture. Democracy is built on constant struggle among competing goods, not on an absolute certainty about which goods are paramount.

In our efforts to find our way toward a new world role, we would do well to revive what made us a special nation long before we became the world's leading military and economic power—our republican tradition that nurtured free citizens who eagerly embraced the responsibilities and pleasures of self-government. With democracy on the march outside our borders, our first responsibility is to ensure that the United States again becomes a model for what self-government should be and not an example of what happens to free nations when they lose interest in public life. A nation that hates politics will not long thrive as a democracy.

POINTS TO PONDER

1. What are the two opposing ideologies of the left and right that Dionne says make compromise difficult?
2. How do Dionne's ideas relate to political parties?
3. How does Dionne reconcile the efficiency of markets with the need for governmental action?

Chapter 10

❧

CAMPAIGNS AND ELECTIONS

Elections are the central defining feature of democratic governments. Because direct, participatory democracy is impossible except in very small communities, the selection of governmental leaders is the most important way in which governments can be made responsive to the people. And in order for elections to be meaningful there must be some sort of competition for office—that is, a choice among candidates who propose differing policies or approaches to governing. Political campaigns, then, are crucial for presenting options from which voters can choose when they exercise their francise.

Expansion and Exercise of the Franchise

Perhaps the most important constitutional transformation in United States history has been the increasing democratization of the franchise. In the early nineteenth century the franchise was limited by the exclusion of women and African Americans, most of whom were slaves at that time, and by property restrictions imposed by state governments. Blacks were given the franchise after the Civil War through the Thirteenth, Fourteenth, and Fifteenth Amendments to the Constitution, though it was the middle of the twentieth century before federal legislation and concerted action made those Amendments a reality. Women were included as full voting citizens after the Nineteenth Amendment passed in 1920. Finally, the Twenty-sixth Amendment in 1971 reduced the voting age from 21 to 18 years. Property requirements and poll taxes are no longer allowed.

Despite the centrality of voting to self-government and the reputation of the United States as one of the foremost democracies in the world, a smaller proportion of Americans choose to exercise their right to vote than in any other modern democracy (except Switzerland). During the heyday of political parties in the latter half of the nineteenth century, presidential elections consistently drew more than 70 percent of the voters. By the middle of the twentieth century, voter turnout had dropped to around 60 percent of the eligible electorate. In the 1970s participation continued to decline, and by 1988 it had dropped to barely 50 percent, though it bounced back to 54 percent in the 1992 presidential election.

Presidential Campaigns

The campaign for the presidency every four years has been one of the most popular spectator sports in the United States for the past two centuries. Despite important continuities in the nature of the quadrennial contest, a number of changes in recent decades have drastically altered the strategies necessary to be a successful candidate.

In the nineteenth century, presidential nominations were controlled by the leaders of political parties who would use their leverage at national conventions to select acceptable candidates who seemed to have the best chance of winning the general election. At the turn of the century, Progressive reformers argued that ordinary citizens had very little choice because they could vote only for one of two candidates that the party bosses had decided to nominate. The Progressives convinced a number of states to institute primary elections in which voters in each political party could select delegates to the national conventions. Those delegates would then choose the party standard-bearers. Although primary elections were held in a number of states, they did not play the dominant role in determining party nominations, in part because candidates saw party leader endorsement as much more important to winning delegates at the conventions.

Primary Elections

Primaries gained more luster after the Democratic party nomination reforms that followed the 1968 election. In fact, the most far-reaching change in this reform period was the proliferation of primaries. By 1992 forty states had established primary elections to select presidential nominees, and most of the delegates to national conventions were selected through these primaries. This transformation amounted to a victory for the reformers over the party regulars who could no longer control the presidential selection process. The system was thus much more open to "outsiders." The way to the nomination now was through creating one's own campaign organization rather than winning endorsement by the party. Candidates had to organize their own fund-raising and hire their own campaign technicians for direct mail, advertising, and strategy. It was a personal, rather than a party, organization.

The determination of nomination victory by primary elections rather than by conventions increased the importance of the press and the weight of the early contests, especially New Hampshire. The need for large sums of money and the momentum of early victories magnifies the importance of the press in interpreting primary outcomes. Often what is most important is not the percentage of votes a candidate wins but whether the candidate's performance is better or worse than expected. For example, in 1968 President Lyndon Johnson won the New Hampshire primary, but peace candidate Eugene McCarthy's 42 percent of the vote showed that Johnson was vulnerable and convinced him to withdraw from the election.

The General Election

After a candidate wins the nomination, the focus must shift to the general election. While it might seem that the campaign for the general election would be merely a continuation of the primary campaign, an important shift must occur. The typical voter in the general election is not the same as the participant in the nomination process. Even though the vote in the general election is exercised only by slightly more than half the eligible electorate, turnout for primary elections is even more limited. Only 35 to 40 percent of the electorate is committed enough to vote in the primary election. These committed voters tend to be those who are at the ideological ends of their party's political spectrum—Republican conservatives and Democratic liberals.

Thus, when the campaign shifts from the primaries to the general election, the appeal of the candidates must be moderated in order to capture the large number of votes in the middle of the political spectrum. Most presidential candidates are able to make this shift; those who do not can be swamped. Such was the case in 1964 when conservative Barry Goldwater lost in a landslide to Lyndon Johnson, and again in 1972 when liberal George McGovern lost to Richard Nixon. Those who nominated these presidential candidates were not representative of the general electorate.

The Electoral College

Although the expansion of the franchise has democratized presidential elections greatly over the past two centuries, the actual election of the president is determined by the rules of the electoral college established in the Constitution. When voters pull the lever in the voting booth, they are in fact voting for a slate of electors pledged to vote for a particular candidate. Moreover, 48 states have chosen to cast their electoral ballots as a unit. That is, the winner of the plurality vote in the states wins all the electoral votes for that state (equal to the total number of senators and representatives from that state). Effectively, this arrangement gives a slight advantage to small states, which, in a strictly proportional system, would have less influence. At the same time it gives an important advantage to the most populous states, which have the largest chunks of electoral votes at stake. This set of rules heavily influences the campaign strategies of presidential candidates, and it often exaggerates the margin of victory for winners.

But the rules of the electoral college system also present the possibility that no candidate will win a majority and the election will be decided by the House of Representatives. The rules of House voting for president are complicated, and, if the popular winner were not chosen, a crisis of confidence in the legitimacy of the outcome could result. The House has chosen the president only twice in our history. In 1800 it selected Thomas Jefferson, and in 1824 it chose the runner-up, John Quincy Adams, over Andrew Jackson, who had won a plurality of the electoral and popular votes. The system can also result in the runner-up winning the presidency outright, which has happened only once in our history—in 1888 William Henry Harrison was elected over incumbent President Grover Cleveland. There have been more than five hundred proposals to change the electoral college provisions in the Constitution, but none of them has generated sufficient support to be enacted.

Campaign Finance

In an attempt to limit the amount of money spent on presidential campaigns and the special influence that large contributions could buy, Congress passed several laws in the 1970s placing limits on total spending and limiting contributions that could be made by individuals. The Supreme Court, determining that some of those limits violated freedom of speech, invalidated those portions of the laws limiting total expenditures and candidate contributions to political campaigns. The Court, however, did allow acceptance of expenditure limits as a prerequisite for receiving public funds for presidential campaigns. There is no public financing of congressional campaigns and thus no limits on total expenditures, although a number of proposals for public financing have been suggested.

Public financing of presidential campaigns places limits on certain kinds of direct contributions to candidates, but several loopholes have allowed campaign spending to continue to grow. One loophole is "soft money," or money that is donated to be spent on general support for a political party or get-out-the-vote activities. These funds are not to be directly controlled by specific candidates or their organizations. This indirect spending amounted to more than $80 million in 1991–1992, almost as much as was directly spent by candidates. Another loophole allows many small contributions to be "bundled" into one large contribution to a candidate, thus giving a considerable amount of influence to organizations able to raise money in this fashion.

One fertile source of campaign contributions has been political action committees (PACs), which are created to donate money for political campaigns. The number of PACs increased from about 600 in 1974 to more than 4,000 in 1989. At the same time PAC expenditures have increased from less than $20 million in the early 1970s to more than $340 million. PACs were organized to get around the limits on individual donations and are often sponsored by businesses, labor unions, and special interest groups. Of course, the expectation is that contributions to members of Congress will result in access and sympathetic consideration for issues of concern to the donors.

A number of plans for reforming congressional campaign finance have been put forward, but any serious proposal must allow for legitimate sources of funds for financing campaigns. Public financing is one alternative, but taxpayers may very well resist financing congressional campaigns. Public financing would also place limits on spending, and it is difficult to find one set of limits that is appropriate for all elections. One central dilemma is how to ensure that challengers have access to sufficient funds to mount a credible campaign against an incumbent.

The real goal of campaign reform ought to be to contain costs and ensure competition for seats so that voters can have a genuine choice in elections. It is far easier for incumbents to raise money than for challengers, and PACs give much more money to incumbents than to challengers. In fact, after elections PACs often switch sides to help new winners retire their campaign debts. Incumbents have other advantages, including free mailing, name recognition, staff help, and the media visibility that attends public office. Serious campaign reform must also create balances for some of these advantages of incumbency.

The Readings

The articles in this section analyze a number of issues central to campaigns and elections in the United States. Voting behavior has changed over the decades, and political scientists have tried to discover the causes and consequences of party identification, attitudes toward government, and voter turnout. Important changes in the rules of elections and in campaign technology have also had far-reaching consequences for governance in the United States. Campaign finance has been not only an enduring source of frustration for political reformers, but also an essential component of our democracy. The articles in this section address all these issues in looking at our electoral system.

In the first selection, Elaine Kamarck explains the impact of the post-1968 Democratic party reforms on presidential nominating politics. Party leaders could no longer be delegates to conventions *ex officio*, but had to be selected as delegates in caucuses or primaries. Convention delegates had to be pledged to vote for a specific candidate when they were selected. Quotas for women, minorities, and young people were established for conventions. The times and places of caucuses had to be published ahead of time. These changes amounted to a transformation of the nominating system, and since many state legislatures were controlled by the Democrats, the Republican party had no choice but to go along with the changed state laws.

Both presidential and congressional election campaigns have been affected by the dominance of television as a means of reaching voters. This reality of modern campaigns has led to the increasing influence of professional campaign consultants who raise money and develop televised campaign advertisements. The use of the medium lends itself to sophisticated ways to tap into voters' emotions and influence their vote. This has led to some unfair campaign commercials and to "negative campaigning," which attacks an opposing candidate's character rather than argues for policies or principles.

One famous TV ad from the 1964 presidential campaign showed a little girl picking petals off a daisy. As she continued to pick the petals, a man's voice began a countdown that ended with an image of an exploding nuclear bomb. This harsh and unfair ad was meant to associate Barry Goldwater's candidacy with a reckless approach to foreign policy and was intended to frighten voters into backing Lyndon Johnson. The ad was withdrawn after only one airing. In her selection on "Dirty Politics," Kathleen Hall Jamieson examines two television commercials from the 1988 campaign and explains how commercials can be used to distort or ignore the real issues. She also shows how media reporters influence our perceptions by interpreting both the candidates and their ads.

This section ends with an analysis by Gerald Pomper of the 1992 presidential election outcome. Pomper analyzes President Bush's precipitous decline in popularity from unprecedented heights immediately after the 1991 Persian Gulf War to his 1992 loss to Bill Clinton. He also analyzes the striking popularity of billionaire H. Ross Perot, who garnered the largest percentage of presidential votes by a third-party candidate since Theodore Roosevelt in 1912. Pomper puts the election into a broad historical and electoral context.

KEY TERMS

caucus system: the method by which political party members in states with no primary election choose delegates to the national nominating conventions. Party members meet at the local level and vote to send delegates to higher levels who in turn elect delegates to attend the national conventions. Delegates are pledged to support a particular candidate on the first ballot.

electoral college: the system by which the voters in each state vote for president. The voters elect a slate of electors pledged to cast their electoral votes for one of the presidential candidates. The winner of the popular vote in each state usually receives all the electoral votes for that state. The electors meet in each state capital to cast their ballots and then send them to the Congress to be counted.

general election: in contrast to primary elections, the final election that determines who will take office

political action committee (PAC): an organized political interest group that raises money to contribute to candidates for political office

primary election: an election held to select candidates to represent a political party in the general election. Primaries were developed early in the twentieth century to give rank-and-file party members a voice in choosing the party's candidates.

38

"STRUCTURE AS STRATEGY: PRESIDENTIAL NOMINATING POLITICS IN THE POST-REFORM ERA"

Elaine Ciulla Kamarck

In presidential elections the voters elect the president from one of two major parties, with a viable third-party candidate occasionally available. But clearly most of the sifting and winnowing of potential presidential candidates occurs in the nominating process. Elaine Kamarck, a scholar at the Progressive Politics Institute who is also active in presidential politics, argues that the strategies used by presidential candidates in the general election are quite similar to those used by Presidents Roosevelt, Eisenhower, and Kennedy. But the strategies necessary to win the nomination of the party have been profoundly different since the nomination reforms of the Democratic party after 1968.

In this excerpt from The Parties Respond, *edited by Sandy Maisel, Kamarck traces the changes in nomination procedures since 1968 and shows how they have affected the types of candidates who are successful at winning their party's nomination. She argues that the proliferation of primaries has made the national party conventions into "four-day television commercials" rather than the final arbiters of the nomination.*

Imagine for a moment that Franklin Delano Roosevelt, Dwight D. Eisenhower, and John F. Kennedy were to join us once again. Furthermore, imagine that they found themselves in the middle of a political strategy session for a presidential campaign. Strategy for the general election would be quite familiar to them. It would revolve around winning the majority of electoral votes. Each state would be categorized as safe for one party or the other, as a lost cause, or as a possible battleground. Candidates and their surrogates would move around the country giving speeches and holding rallies in an attempt to win the crucial battleground states. Much about the general election would be different, of course, but the underlying strategy for accumulating a majority of electoral votes would be very much the same as it had been in their day.

Suppose, however, that our three returned presidents were to find themselves in the midst of a strategy session for the Democratic or Republican nomination. The goal would be the same as it had been for them—to accumulate enough delegates to win the nod at their party's nominating convention. Beyond that, however, the similarities would end, for the strategy for achieving that goal is very different today from what it was in their time.

Imagine Franklin Roosevelt's bewilderment at the use of the term *momentum*. In his day this term was used to describe activity in the convention hall; now it refers to the boost in attention that a candidate gets from primaries and caucuses that take place months before the convention even opens. Imagine Eisenhower's surprise upon hearing that Senator Howard Baker (R–TN) had given up both his job as majority leader of the Senate and his Senate seat *four years* before the presidential election in order to run for president full time. Ike spent the years before the 1952 Republican Convention in Europe with NATO, arriving home in June to campaign for his nomination in July. Imagine Kennedy's puzzlement over the decision made by Walter Mondale, a former Democratic vice-president and favorite of the Democratic party establishment, to enter every single presidential primary. In his day a candidate avoided presidential primaries unless, like Kennedy, he was young, untested, and eager to prove himself to the party establishment.

What our three returned presidents would soon realize is that the strategies for winning the nomination have changed dramatically as the result of underlying changes in the structure of the nominating system. Until the early 1970s, winning the nomination of a major political party was essentially an inside game. Presidential candidates worked at winning the allegiances of the major party leaders, who controlled the minor party leaders, who in turn became delegates to the nominating convention. Presidential primaries were sometimes important, especially if a candidate had to demonstrate vote-getting ability; but to do that he had to keep favorite sons out and draw other national candidates in, a task that was often very difficult. More often than not, the public portion of the nomination campaign—presidential primaries—was not very important to the eventual outcome.

What was important was the semi-public search for delegates—a search that was difficult to observe and often downright mysterious even to careful observers of the process. The nomination system prior to 1972 was, to use Nelson Polsby's term, "a mixed system." The first stage was public and took place in a few contested presidential primaries. The second stage was semi-public at best and involved intense negotiations between serious national candidates and powerful party leaders. James Reston described this stage as follows: "This presidential election is being fought on several levels. The most important of these, so far as nominating candidates is concerned, is the least obvious . . . the underground battle for delegates." Usually the "underground" battle for delegates was fought in the proverbial smoke-filled rooms. Another political reporter, W. H. Lawrence, described the 1960 nomination race as follows: "With the end of the contested presidential primaries, the struggle for the nomination has moved from Main Street to the backrooms of individual party leaders and state conventions dense with the smoke of cheap cigars."

This process, of courting powerful and not so powerful party leaders in search of a convention majority, was hard to observe and impossible to quantify until the convention itself assembled and started to vote. Thus the race for the nomination used to be very visible during the weeks leading up to and including the convention. More recently, however, the race for the nomination is visible at least a year before the nominating convention and is usually over well before the convention itself ever convenes.

The Post-Reform Nomination System

The presidential nomination system that exists today is the result of two reform movements that occurred at approximately the same time in American politics. Between 1968 and 1972 the Democratic party adopted a series of changes in the process by which delegates to its nominating conventions were chosen. This movement began as a reaction to the contentious 1968 Democratic convention; newcomers opposed to the Vietnam war felt that the party establishment had unfairly thwarted their attempts at participating in the nominating process. At the time, few people (including party professionals) anticipated how profoundly these changes would affect the way that Democrats *and* Republicans elected delegates. Even though the Republican party did not undergo anything even remotely like the reform movement in the Democratic party, so many Democratically dominated state legislatures had to change their laws to comply with the new dictates of the Democratic National Committee that the state Republican parties, more often than not, were inadvertently reformed as well.

The other reform movement begin in 1971 with passage of the Federal Election Campaign Act. This law was amended in 1974 as part of the post-Watergate reforms designed to decrease the influence of money in politics, and again in 1979 when it became clear that the law was having unintended negative effects on party activity. The campaign finance reform laws affected both political parties and, like the reforms in delegate selection, had far-reaching implications for the conduct of presidential elections, particularly primary elections.

The effect of these two reform movements was to transform the nomination system into a totally public system where activity at every step of the process could be observed and quantified. In the post-reform system, the search for delegates was conducted in public primaries or caucuses (which became the "functional equivalent" of highly visible primaries), and the search for money took place under the new election law. By limiting the amount of money that any one individual could contribute to a candidate, the new law transformed the quest for money from a quiet search for a few "fat cats" to a public search for thousands of small- and medium-sized contributions. Changes of this magnitude in the underlying structure of the nomination process eventually affected the strategies of presidential hopefuls seeking their party's nomination, but before we can understand these strategies we must understand the structure of the new nominating system.

Primaries and Their "Functional Equivalents"

In the pre-reform era fewer than half of the convention delegates were elected in primaries contested by the major national candidates. In the post-reform era, however, nearly all delegates are elected as the result of contested primaries. A famous quote by former Vice-President Hubert Humphrey sums up the attitude of many presidential hopefuls in the pre-reform era: "[A]ny man who goes into a primary isn't fit to be President. You have to be crazy to go into a primary. A primary now, is worse than the torture of the rack."

No one who has watched candidates undergo the grueling process of the modern post-reform nomination process would be surprised to hear Walter Mondale, George Bush, or Michael Dukakis express these sentiments. But for these modern candidates, skipping the primaries is akin to skipping the whole ball game.

The Democratic reformers who made up part of the famous McGovern-Fraser Commission did not set out to increase the number of presidential primaries, but just such an increase was the most immediate and dramatic result of the new rules they had proposed for delegate selection to the 1972 convention. In 1968 there were sixteen states that held some form of presidential primary; in 1972, twenty-three states; in 1976, thirty states; in 1980, thirty-five states; in 1984, thirty states; and in 1988, thirty-four states.

Most observers of the nomination process focus solely on the increase in the number of primaries that followed in the wake of the reform movement—but the increase in *number* is not nearly so important as the change in the *nature* of these primaries. The reform rules' requirement that delegates from a state "fairly reflect the division of preferences expressed by those who participate in the presidential nominating process in each state" greatly increased the importance of each primary by linking a presidential candidate's performance in the primary to the number of delegates that he could get from the state. . . .

When delegates to national conventions are not elected in primaries, they are elected in caucus systems. In a caucus system, people meet at the local level and elect representatives to the next level—usually the county level. At the county level, the people elected locally meet and elect representatives to the state convention. The state convention then meets to select those who will attend the presidential nominating convention.

Traditionally, many state parties have held conventions to elect delegates to the presidential nominating convention. These conventions used to be closed; that is, only individuals who already held party office could participate in the selection of delegates. But the party reform movement turned these systems of delegate selection into smaller versions of presidential primaries.

Three new requirements—that party meetings having to do with delegate selection be open to anyone who wished to be known as a Democrat; that every participant in the process as well as every candidate for delegate declare his or her presidential preference; and that all first-tier caucuses (i.e., those at the precinct level) be held on the same day—effectively abolished the party caucus and began the process of turning the caucus system itself into the "functional equivalent of a primary." . . .

Finally, the requirement that first-tier caucuses be held at the same time and on the same day meant that the delegate-selection system, the impact of which had heretofore been difficult to gauge, could now be treated like a primary. When precinct caucuses or county conventions were spread across several weeks or months, most reporters—especially those connected with the national news media—had to wait until the state convention met in order to see which presidential candidate would win the most delegates. Simultaneous precinct caucuses, the requirement that everyone present announce their presidential preference, and, of course, the use of computers and telephones to aggregate lots of data quickly meant that national reporters could descend upon a state such as Iowa and turn their hitherto-ignored precinct caucuses into a primary.

The Iowa precinct caucuses were "discovered" in 1976, when Jimmy Carter "won" them by coming in second to "uncommitted" and beating a field of much better known candidates. Four years earlier most of the press corps had overlooked the Iowa caucuses and in so doing had missed signs that George McGovern was a lot stronger and Senator Edmund Muskie (the reputed frontrunner) a lot weaker than most pundits had assumed. So the press was ready in 1976. As Jules Witcover explains: "For their romance with Muskie the press and television paid heavy alimony after 1972 in terms of their reputation for clairvoyance, let alone clear thinking and evidence at hand. . . . [I]n 1976, if there were going to be early signals, the fourth estate was going to be on the scene en masse to catch them."

The popularity of this new, transformed Democratic caucus system became the envy of the Iowa Republican party. Since its delegate-selection rules were not governed by any state statutes when the Iowa Democratic party was "reformed," the Iowa Republican party wasn't reformed. The result was that, in 1976, the hard-fought battle between President Ford and Ronald Reagan began, as far as the public could see, in New Hampshire, not in Iowa—even though the Iowa Republican caucuses had been held on the same night as the Democratic caucuses that had attracted so much attention. No one paid attention to the Iowa Republican caucuses that year because they were traditional, old-fashioned caucuses that could not be easily counted and interpreted by the national press corps.

The lesson was not lost on the Iowa Republicans who, left out of the limelight in 1976 and eager to share in it in 1980, decided to hold a nonbinding straw poll at each precinct caucus in 1980 and to have the results reported to the Republican State Committee at a location in Des Moines convenient to the national press corps.

Thus, in a relatively short period of time, the process of delegate selection in both political parties was transformed from a process understandable to only the most astute of political observers—and then only toward the end of the process—to a process that was easily quantifiable and therefore accessible to reporters from the earliest moments.

Money and the Need for an Early Start

Reform of the delegate selection system shifted the focus of attention from the convention to the seven or eight months of primaries and caucuses before the convention; reform of the campaign finance laws shifted attention to the year before the primaries even began. Without going into detail on campaign finance reform, I will say simply that, like delegate-selection reform, it transformed the search for money from a private (or at best a semi-public) undertaking to a highly public, easily quantifiable one.

The reasons are simple. In the pre-reform system a few very rich people could and did bankroll entire campaigns. Sometimes the public knew who these people were; often they did not. After campaign finance reform, the most that any one person could contribute to a presidential nomination campaign was $1,000. Thus candidates had to hold countless cocktail parties, dinners, luncheons, and other events in order to amass the millions of dollars needed to run in every caucus and primary in the country.

Another part of the campaign finance reform bill provided that any contribution up to $250 would be matched by the federal treasury. This meant that large numbers of small contributions suddenly became very valuable, especially if they could be raised through the use of direct mail. But in order for direct mail to work well, the presidential candidate signing the letter had to be well known. With money in lots of fairly small chunks doubling in value (due to the federal match), presidential candidates therefore sought ways to become visible and to appear that they were doing well as early as possible—usually one full year prior to the beginning of the primaries and caucuses.

Another provision of the new campaign finance reform laws required that all presidential candidates make quarterly reports of the money they had raised and spent. These quarterly reports, which are made public, have occasioned news stories on how each presidential candidate is doing. A candidate who raises lots of money begins to be taken seriously, whereas a candidate who raises little money tends to get left out of television stories, newspaper columns, and all the other free press that is so important in campaigns. Media coverage then generates more money, and more money generates more media coverage, and so on and on in a self-fulfilling circle.

This is not to say that money equals success. In 1984 Gary Hart tended to win those contests in which he spent a little bit of money and to lose those contests in which he spent a great deal. But early money not only makes a candidate look like a winner; it also allows him to withstand early disappointments once the nomination season begins. George Bush had $10 million in the bank when he placed third in the Iowa caucuses. Losing so early in the season was clearly a disappointment, but he had plenty of resources with which to withstand a loss. In contrast, a candidate like former Arizona Governor Bruce

Babbitt on the Democratic side had such meager cash reserves that his 1988 campaign was over when he failed in Iowa.

Strategies of the Post-Reform Era

Sequence as Strategy

The two reform movements and the changes they wrought in the structure of the nomination system created a set of new strategic imperatives for presidential candidates. The most important of these was understanding the role of sequence in winning the nomination. Once primaries and caucuses became binding, presidential candidates had to contest every single one or risk forfeiting delegates. But the new campaign finance laws limited both the amount of money that could be spent in any one state and the total amount of money that could be spent on the entire nomination race to a sum that was less than the total spending permitted in each state. Thus, even if a presidential candidate could raise enough money to spend the maximum in each state, the campaign finance law forced him to pick and choose between states while the new rules for delegate selection were making it all the more important to contest every state.

The result was to make winning early the key to winning the nomination. If a candidate can win several early contests, he will possess "momentum"—and momentum buys things that money cannot buy, such as free media coverage and the perception that the candidate is a winner. Since 1976, when Jimmy Carter's surprise victories in Iowa and New Hampshire demonstrated the power of momentum in no uncertain terms, media coverage of the early contests (especially those in Iowa and New Hampshire) was vastly out of proportion to the size of those states and the number of delegates elected in each. In recent years the major evening news programs have chosen to move their entire shows to Des Moines, Iowa, and to Manchester, New Hampshire, for the week leading up to the delegate-selection contests in those two states—but they paid nowhere near the same amount of attention to Pennsylvania and California, which (though much bigger states) hold primaries late in the season. One reporter counted the number of journalists in Iowa during the 1984 caucuses and discovered that there was one journalist for every one hundred caucus goers.

This kind of early media coverage tends to have a powerful effect on voters further down the line. As Larry Bartels has demonstrated, momentum itself, or the perception that the candidate is a winner, influences voters in subsequent primaries independent of other factors such as region and ideology. Unlike nomination contests in the pre-reform years, strategy in the post-reform era relies heavily on the sequence of victories. Bartels sums it up as follows: "The key to success, it appeared, was not to enter the nomination with a broad coalition of political support, but to rely on the dynamics of the campaign itself—particularity in its earliest public phases—to generate support." . . .

The importance of winning early in the new nomination system was not lost on individual state parties. As they looked with envy at the attention and money spent on the early contests, more and more states moved their primaries early in the spring in order to get in on the media and candidate attention that went with being early. . . .

The percentage of delegates elected in March went up steadily throughout the post-reform years, but it rose sharply in 1988 due to the creation of the Southern Regional primary. In 1986 a group of southern Democratic legislative leaders, concerned that the Democratic party was nominating candidates (such as Walter Mondale) who were too liberal to carry the South, got together and decided to form a southern Super Tuesday. They did so by moving all the southern states' primaries to the second Tuesday in March, specifically in the hopes of giving these states a decisive role in the selection of the Democratic nominee.

Mobilizing the Ideological Extremes

By all accounts, southern Super Tuesday was a failure. . . . It not only failed to produce a southern, more conservative nominee but it gave a boost to two candidates who were, arguably, the most liberal of the seven in the Democratic field—Massachusetts Governor Michael Dukakis and the Reverend Jesse Jackson. Had the crafters of the southern Super Tuesday been more attuned to the history of voting in presidential primaries, however, they may not have been so quick to predict that their new primary would produce a more centrist nominee for the Democratic party.

Voters in presidential primaries have always been more liberal (in the case of the Democrats) or more conservative (in the case of the Republicans) than the rest of the electorate. This factor was not very important in the days when the nomination was largely in the hands of the party professionals. By and large, these people were in the business of winning elections and they judged potential candidates according to whether they could win, not on ideological grounds.

But in the post-reform era, primaries matter and party leaders do not. Presidential primaries attract a very small percentage of all voters—a percentage of people who tend to be more highly educated, more well to do, and more ideologically committed than most voters. . . .

Because the primary electorates are so small, a candidate who can mobilize a faction of these loyal party voters has a leg up in seeking the nomination. Jesse Jackson's base in the Democratic party among black voters was very important to his successes in 1984 and 1988. Even though black voters made up only 8 percent of the November electorate, they constituted an average 17 percent of the electorate in the primary states. In some states black voters were a very substantial percentage of the primary electorate. In New York they constituted 27 percent of the Democratic primary, and in states with large black populations, such as Mississippi, they constituted nearly half of the Democratic primary electorate.

Being acceptable to the primary electorate is not, however, the same as being acceptable to the general electorate. The successful presidential candidate survives the marathon of primaries and caucuses ever mindful of two audiences: the small audience of party loyalists who participate in the primaries and who hold policy viewpoints far from the center, and the very large and more centrist audience that he will face in the general election.

The preponderance of conservatives in the Republican primary electorates meant that George Bush had to spend most of the year prior to the primaries and caucuses trying to prove his conservative credentials to groups that were suspicious that he was more moderate than Ronald Reagan. Four years earlier Mondale appealed to the liberal wing of the Democratic party when Gary Hart's come-from-behind campaign threatened to derail his campaign. Mondale's counterattack brought Hart's liberal credentials into question and helped him to mobilize the core group in the Democratic electorate.

In recent years Republican candidates have been better able to handle this transition than their Democratic counterparts, in part because conservatives and moderates outnumber liberals in the electorate by margins of three to one. Thus the Republican candidate doesn't need to convert as many liberals and moderates as the Democrat. In the general election Michael Dukakis won the vast majority of self-identified liberals, but he failed to win enough conservative, moderate, and Independent voters to win.

The Delegate Count

Once the initial contests are over, the field of candidates tends to narrow considerably—usually to one or two candidates by the end of March. Presidential candidates continue to receive influxes of federal matching funds as the campaign season progresses; but the law stipulates that, once a candidate fails to win 10 percent of the vote in two consecutive primaries, he can be deemed ineligible for matching funds. Thus candidates who have won very small percentages of the vote have a powerful reason—lack of money—to get out of the race.

Beyond the early contests there are many simultaneous primaries and caucuses, and the delegate count becomes more and more important as a means of interpreting events and of judging who, among the remaining contenders, is closest to winning the nomination. Counting delegates used to be the exclusive domain of party insiders and political professionals who knew all there was to know about the party leaders (major and minor) and could predict how they would behave and whom they would vote for at the nominating convention. At the end of the 1960 primary season John Kennedy had only 134 delegates committed to him, or 18 percent of those he needed to get nominated, as a result of the primaries. Then, as Theodore White described it, the real work began: "Now the rest of the harvest proceeded, state by state, across the nation, fitting itself to the manners and morals of each state's politics like an exercise in the diversity of American life."

In the post-reform era, the delegate count can be conducted even when actual delegates have not been elected. On April 3, 1984, for instance, United Press International reported that Mondale had 729 delegates, Hart had 440, and Jackson had 101. As of that same date, however, if someone had wanted to, he or she could have talked to real live delegates from only six states for a total of 434 delegates—or about one-third the number being reported in the delegate count. But in April no one was interested in talking to real live delegates, so absolute was the certainty that the delegates would simply represent the will of the primary voters.

The translation of the primary vote into a delegate count is accomplished by means of formal allocation rules. Because these rules dictate who wins how many delegates, they have been the source of endless controversy in the Democratic party. Because Republicans do not have centralized rules, and because these rules are often not part of state statutes, the Republican party has not been as affected by the Democratic allocation rules as by some of the Democrats' other rules. Thus there are real and significant differences between the two parties when it comes to the accumulation of a delegate majority.

Simply put, there are two basic ways to award delegates to a presidential candidate: winner take all, and proportional representation. The Republican party tends to use the former and the Democratic party, the latter. Winner-take-all rules award all of the delegates from a state or a congressional district to the candidate who wins the most votes in that state or district. Proportional rules divide the delegates from a state or district as nearly as possible in proportion to the vote that each presidential candidate won in that state or district. The Democratic party has come up with many variations on this theme, but these two rules are the most important for our purposes.

The Democratic party's reform movement encouraged and eventually mandated the use of proportional representation to award delegates to presidential candidates. . . . With the exception of 1972, during which the Democrats encouraged but did not require the use of proportional representation, the Democrats have tended to award delegates to presidential candidates in proportion to the primary vote whereas the Republicans have tended to award delegates to the winner of the state or district.

This difference has important consequences for the two parties. First, proportional representation increases the already-dangerous predisposition of the Democratic party to break down into factions; and, second, it reinforces the importance of a strong showing in the early part of the nomination season for Democratic candidates. Nelson Polsby argues that reform of the delegate-selection process has worked "disproportionately to the disadvantage of the majority party, the Democrats," who, according to Polsby, are disadvantaged in comparison to the Republicans because of their greater ideological diversity.

Unlike losing Republican candidates, a losing Democratic candidate, especially a second-place finisher, can still win delegates. Indeed, a steady accumulation of delegates gives the second-place candidate who is still losing but doing well enough to keep his federal matching funds an incentive to stay in the race for one, two, three, or more rounds, always hoping for a turn in fortunes. As the delegate count of the second- and third-place candidates increases, the delegates pledged to those candidates and the national campaign staff generally urge the candidate to stay in the race until the convention. In other words, proportional representation increases the Democrats' predisposition toward internal disarray.

In 1988 the nomination race in the Republican party was over by the last week in March. Not only had George Bush won an impressive string of primary victories, but the winner-take-all nature of many of those contests meant that no other candidate had accumulated an appreciable number of delegates to the Republican convention. The process of making internal peace and preparing for the general election could begin, in the Republican party, in March—with George Bush the all but annointed nominee.

The story on the Democratic side was quite different. Dukakis did not win by the same margin as Bush on Super Tuesday, even though he had won the two biggest Super Tuesday states, Texas and Florida. Yet, although Bush got nearly every single one of the delegates from those two states, proportional rules dictated that Dukakis had to share the delegates from those states with Jackson. By the end of March Dukakis had accumulated only 21.9 percent of the delegates needed to win the nomination, but George Bush had accumulated 61 percent of the delegates needed to win. It took another month for the delegate count to show a bare majority of delegates for Dukakis. By that time Jackson was firmly committed to staying in the race and had accumulated a large number of delegates—a fact that led him to believe he could use his delegate strength to bargain for the vice-presidential nomination.

Jackson may have been the first second-place finisher to attempt to use his delegate strength to bargain for the vice-presidency, but others have used their accumulation of delegates to bargain for planks in the party platform or for changes in the party rules. In 1984 Gary Hart used his delegate strength to win some victories on both platform and rules, and in 1980 Ted Kennedy filed a record number of platform and rules amendments in an attempt to wrest control of the convention from Carter.

The losing candidate who is steadily accumulating delegates needs a rationale for staying in the race, for during the last few contests, the frontrunner and much of the party leadership are urging the loser to end the race as soon as possible. In the process of seeking such a rationale, minor differences between candidates tend to be enlarged and emphasized. Candidates who are not really very far apart become polarized on issues, and the divisions between factions in the party are accentuated at the very point in time when they should be unified—usually to the detriment of Democrats in the general election.

The second effect of a nominating system dominated by proportional representation is, paradoxically, to reinforce the importance of the earliest contests. In a proportional system an early winner can withstand losses later on in the season because he can continue to win delegates even while losing primaries. There are no late bloomers in proportional systems: A candidate who suddenly starts to win or who enters late will find it very difficult to overtake the front-runner because he can never win large chunks of delegates.

The best example can be found in the 1976 nomination season. Jimmy Carter was the early winner that year, and yet as the spring wore on more and more voters came to have doubts about him (doubts that crystallized in the formation of ABC—Anybody But Carter—groups), and he began to lose primaries. In May and June, Carter suffered a string of defeats, including a defeat in the all-important California primary; but he was still able to accumulate delegates because proportional rules allowed him to claim a share. These delegates, added to those won earlier in the year, gave Carter the nomination in spite of his loss of momentum.

On the Republican side, President Gerald Ford, also an early winner, began (like Carter) to lose contests in the month of May to challenger Ronald Reagan. But due to winner-take-all rules, Ford's losses had serious consequences. In five of the twelve states he had lost to Reagan he won no delegates at all, and in the other states he won very small numbers of delegates. Ford went from being ahead of Reagan in the delegate count to being behind. Even though he eventually won the nomination, Ford was seriously threatened by Reagan all the way up to and including the convention.

In 1976 the controversy was on the Republican side, which lost. And thus we are brought to one final point. Divisive nomination contests in a political party—regardless of the underlying structure—almost always result in the defeat of that party in the general election. . . .

Two lessons are implicit in this aspect of the nominating system. The first is that political parties should try to avoid systems that add to or generate divisiveness. (The Democrats have yet to learn this lesson.) The second is that presidential candidates should seek not only to avoid divisiveness in the primary season but also to reach the "magic number" of delegates as soon as possible. In 1984 Mondale successfully tied up the nomination on the day after he lost the California primary. He did this in a last-minute blitz of still-uncommitted delegates and managed to deflect attention from his California defeat onto the fact that he had enough pledged delegates to win the nomination on a first ballot.

The desire to go over the top as far in advance of the convention as possible requires that, when there are different allocation rules in effect, candidates must spend more time and attention in places where they can win more delegates by winning the primary. In other words, winner-take-all systems of delegate allocation are another way for a state to be important in the nomination system without having to select its delegates first.

The Dukakis Super Tuesday strategy was carefully crafted to win congressional districts in states where the delegate harvest would be greatest. For instance, even though Dukakis lost more primaries than he won on Super Tuesday, his delegate count was slightly higher than anyone else's, thus giving him an important edge in the perceptions of those who were trying to interpret the race.

But the most dramatic use of the delegate count occurred during the Mondale campaign in 1984. Reeling from the unexpected victory by Gary Hart in New Hampshire, Mondale went south amid anticipation that his campaign was about to end and lost several important primaries, including the all-important Florida primary. But the vicissitudes of the delegate-selection process allowed Mondale to emerge from Super Tuesday 1984 with many more delegates than Gary Hart. This fact found its way into the hands of the press, which used it, to the dismay of the Hart campaign, to give new life to Mondale's candidacy.

The Four-Day Television Commercial

Why is it so important to wrap up the nomination before the convention? Because the post-reform convention has a new role. With rare exceptions, it is no longer the place where the nomination is won. As we have seen, the nomination is won in the primaries and in the caucuses, and the nominee is almost always known prior to the convention. In the pre-reform era, the weeks between the last primary and the opening of the convention were times of intense activity as the leading candidates sought to pin down the votes of delegates who were not already pledged to a presidential candidate. . . . During the [pre-reform years], an average of 38 percent of the delegates remained to be wooed in the weeks prior to the convention; during the [post-reform years], that number generally dropped significantly.

Another way to look at the same phenomenon is to compare the delegate count for the eventual nominee at the end of the primary season with the first ballot vote for the nominee at the convention. In the pre-reform years, the nominee had barely 50 percent of what he needed to get nominated by the end of the primary season; in the post-reform years, the count at the end of the season tends to be a pretty good predictor of the vote on the first ballot.

In the modern nominating system, therefore, the actual nomination function is all but gone from the convention; suspense about the identity of the nominee is a thing of the past. It has been many years since either political party has had a convention that went past the first ballot, so effectively have the primaries and caucuses displaced the convention as the place where the most important decision is made. Other matters of importance still go on at conventions—the party platform and party rules are debated and adopted, for instance—but the big decision is generally made weeks if not months before the convention ever opens.

In the post-reform era, then, the convention has become the place where the general election campaign begins. Byron Shafer, whose book *Bifurcated Politics: Evolution and Reform in the National Party Convention* is an excellent treatment of the post-reform convention, sums up the changes as follows: "[T]he role of the convention in inaugurating the general election campaign grew enormously as the nomination receded. . . . [N]ational news media, especially as embodied in full and national coverage, became the means by which public presentations at the convention could be turned explicitly to the task of advertising the candidate, his party, and their program."

Anything that detracts from the party's ability to put its best foot forward—platform fights, rule fights, and ongoing tensions such as those between Ford and Reagan in 1976, Kennedy and Carter in 1980, Hart and Mondale in 1984, and Dukakis and Jackson in 1988—is seen as a major impediment to the use of the convention to begin the general election.

Whereas political parties have become more and more adept at "managing" their conventions, network news executives, under pressure to cut the huge costs involved in covering a convention, have become increasingly reluctant to cover events that are little more than four-day-long advertisements for the party and its nominee. Conventions used to be covered "gavel to gavel," or from the time they opened until the time they closed. In the 1950s and 1960s, in fact, television coverage actually exceeded the amount of time that the convention was in session.

Beginning in 1980, however, coverage by all three networks declined dramatically. When NBC News announced a plan to cut from its prime-time coverage of the Democratic convention to a "convention without walls" that it was producing itself, there was a predictable outcry from party officials. Joe Angotti, executive producer of the news, said that "[o]ur first and primary responsibility is to cover the news. I'd like nothing better than to throw all this out and cover a real breaking story." Threats by the networks to dramatically scale back coverage in the future have become more and more common.

Thus the nominating convention, devoid of its old functions, may have a hard time hanging onto its new functions. The political parties and nominees want to stage the entire affair so as to put the best light on their party, whereas the networks want to cover real news. If some balance is not struck, the conventions could go the way of the electoral college and become a vestigial part of the body politic.

Prospects for Change

The basic characteristics of the post-reform nominating system are not likely to change. For the foreseeable future the nominating process will be dominated by highly visible public contests for money and delegates. Though flawed, this system does have one advantage: People perceive it to be fair and open. When polled on the subject, the public has continually favored more primaries (usually national primaries), not fewer primaries. Any attempt to go back in time and give significantly more power to party officials would most likely be perceived as illegitimate by large numbers of voters accustomed to open presidential primaries.

Aside from Congress, which has traditionally been reluctant to get involved in the nomination process, the only agent of change would be the Democratic party, given that the Republicans do not believe in dictating delegate-selection systems to state Republican parties. Having preached the virtues of openness and wide participation for nearly twenty years, the Democrats, no matter how unhappy they are with the results of their recent nominating contests, can ill afford to return the process to smoke-filled rooms.

But the Democrats have made changes that, at the least, will put some checks and balances into the nomination system. One recent change was to make all major party elected officials (especially governors, senators, and members of Congress) automatic voting delegates to the convention. This change was necessary because one of the consequences of party reform was that elected officials, reluctant to compete with constituents for delegate slots, had dropped out of the convention picture.

The "Super Delegates" have not exercised an independent voice in the nomination process thus far. In 1984 many of them endorsed Mondale early, and in 1988 many members of Congress started out with their fellow House member Richard Gephardt and then switched to Dukakis when Gephardt failed in the primaries.

But the inclusion of the Super Delegates remains popular with the Democratic party for several reasons. Some see them as a centrist force that can serve as a counterbalance to the more ideologically extreme activists who tend to dominate the platform and other forums. Others want them there just in case the primaries fail to produce a winner one day and the nomination actually gets decided on the floor of the convention—an unlikely but still possible scenario. In that case the Super Delegates would be expected to exert a leadership role in bringing the convention to a decision, much as they did in the pre-reform era. And, finally, the Super Delegates can provide an element of "peer review" that the primary voters and ordinary delegates cannot provide, inasmuch as many of them will have known and worked with potential presidential candidates.

Another set of changes that are talked about but have not been incorporated into the Democratic party thus far involve deregulating the party rules. Some students of the rules (this author included) believe that the current rules dictate too many details of the delegate-selection process and that in some instances they have become examples of regulation for the sake of regulation. Indeed, there is no real reason to force every state to elect delegates in exactly the same way so long as the process in each state is clear, open, and easy to participate in. If the Democrats allowed for variations among states, one state could check and balance another, and they could all avoid the unanticipated consequences that have ensued every time they have attempted to "reform" the process by writing yet another rule.

Changes in the nomination process should not be tied to an attempt to recapture some prior moment in history, when nominations were decided in the smoke-filled rooms of party leaders. To the extent that changes do occur in the future, they should be made with the goal of building checks and balances into the current system so that it can work to produce the best nominees—of both parties.

POINTS TO PONDER

1. How has the presidential nominating process changed over the past 50 years?
2. How have candidates' strategies changed in order to adapt to the new system?
3. What is the difference between the primary electorate and the general electorate?

39

"DIRTY POLITICS"
Kathleen Hall Jamieson

The importance and sophistication of television advertising in presidential campaigns have been increasing and contain the potential for distortion as well as illumination of the issues. In this selection from her 1992 book, Dirty Politics, *Kathleen Hall Jamieson, Dean of the Annenberg School for Communication at the University of Pennsylvania, analyzes two television commercials of the 1988 presidential campaign. In examining the televised clip of candidate Dukakis riding in a tank, she shows the impact of the press on the interpretation of campaigns and how the real issues dividing the candidates are often ignored.*

In her analysis of the "Willie Horton" ads of the Bush campaign, Jamieson shows how the use of "visuals" and misleading "facts" can have an emotionally charged impact. She then suggests ways in which television can be more effectively used to encourage presidential candidates to engage each other over the issues that divide them in formats more sustained than 30-second commercial spots.

Michael Dukakis looked "like Patton on his way to Berlin," observed NBC's Chris Wallace (September 13, 1988). "[A] Massachusetts Rambo on the prowl," noted CBS's Bruce Morton the same evening. Footage of that ride was resurrected by a Bush attack ad that pilloried Dukakis's supposed positions. "Dukakis opposed virtually every weapons system developed," declared the ad in the first of its false statements about the Democrat. The Massachusetts Democrat responded with an ad in which he turned off a set showing the Bush ad. "I'm fed up with it," said Dukakis. "George Bush's negative ads are full of lies and he knows it. I'm on record for the very weapons systems his ad says I'm against."

By the campaign's end, the tank ride had appeared in news, the news footage had appeared in a Bush ad, the Bush ad had appeared in a Dukakis ad, and the Bush and Dukakis ads had appeared in news. The *New Yorker* cartoon showing a man watching a television set had prophesied the endless loops through which the image passed. In the set in front of him, the man sees himself watching the television set. In that set is another image of himself watching the set. Images of images damaged Dukakis's candidacy. One poll indicates that "voters who knew about the ride were much more likely to shift against the Democrat than toward him."

It is difficult to explain to someone unfamiliar with the conventions of our political discourse what facets of presidential character a candidate is featuring by marauding about in an armored vehicle. If past is prophet, the vehicle a president is most likely to drive is a golf cart.

So, why the tank? The answer is simple. Visual, dramatic moments are more likely than talking heads to get news play. Accordingly, Ronald Reagan appropriated the monuments in Washington as the backdrop for his first inaugural and regularly dramatized his State of the Union claims with "heroes" who appeared in the House gallery. Indeed, as CBS's Lesley Stahl reported in 1984, the Reagan presidency pioneered the use of visuals to counter the "facts." If support for nursing homes had just been cut, one could contain the fallout by appearing with seniors in a nursing home according to Reagan logic.

The Reagan presidency accustomed the press to believing that there is no substantive relationship between dramatizing visuals and either performance or policy proposals. So it didn't occur to most reporters to ask whether Dukakis's M-1 tank ride was an attempt to focus the press and public on the fact that, unlike his opponent, he favored a conventional build-up in tanks, antitank weapons, and tank supplies. But that was precisely what Dukakis was trying to do.

The tank ride did get the attention of the press. But the message wasn't the one Dukakis intended. Instead of seeing this as a dramatic incarnation of his substantive policy proposals, the press viewed the event as attempted compensation for his weakness. In short, it was regarded as strategic and silly. After talking with the reporters who covered the tank ride, I am convinced that what evoked this interpretation was something less tangible than Dukakis's goofy grin or Rocky the Squirrel–like helmet. If silliness were the bait, then either of George Bush's two past tank trips or his swing in a fire engine would have garnered comparable news time and tone. But, unlike the visual claim that Bush aspired to be Fireman in Chief, Dukakis's tryout as Tank Commander in Chief tied into the dualistic, poll-driven, strategy-saturated structure through which the press views politics.

Seen from this perspective, the Democrat's martial moment reeked of strategic intent. Here, after all, was a candidate trailing his opponent by a widening margin and perceived in the polls as "weak" on defense. By demonstrating both the Democrat's "attempt" to counter his "weakness" and signalling the incompetence of his failing campaign, the tank ride could do double duty. "The idea," explained CBS's Bruce Morton, "is pictures are symbols which tell the voter important things about the candidate. If your candidate is seen in the polls as weak on defense, put him in a tank."

Bush's appropriation of odd modes of transport went unridiculed because in the context set by the polls they could not be read as acts of desperation or signs of a campaign in disarray. Indeed, the news report that shows him prepared to battle the next Great Chicago Fire confirms that he was "buoyed by his own latest poll showing him leading in Illinois for the first time" (CBS Evening News, October 9, 1988). So nothing was made of the fire truck ride as nothing had been made of his political posturing in a tank of his own at the Illinois State Fair in late August or of an attempt earlier in his second vice-presidential term to tie his foreign policy credentials to a picture of himself in a tank.

The tank ride invited reporters to play out the full range of strategic interpretation. Dukakis wants you to believe he is strong on defense, said the reports, but the polls show that the public perceives he is instead weak. Appearance versus reality. Here the reality is not the positions the Democrat has articulated but rather the perception of him in the polls. The story also gave journalists a chance to explain how politics works. Politicians craft visuals to create false impressions. Reporters, by contrast, reveal "what's actually going on."

Once this frame of reference was imposed on the tank ride, its place in the network news lineup was secure. And since the "news hole" is limited, something else had to give up space. The frame also ensured that the news reports would not focus on the actual substance of Dukakis's positions on defense. "Not only was this [Dukakis in the tank] a foolish image but it crowded out any coverage that night on any of the networks of his foreign policy speech," recalls NBC's Andrea Mitchell. "That episode became an emblem of Dukakis's bad campaign."

Now constructed as evidence of Dukakis's weakness on defense, the tank ride could easily be appropriated by the Republican ad team. The resulting ad reduced the complex positions both candidates had taken on new weaponry to simplistic, inaccurate appositions and identifications: Dukakis as the risky commander in chief, Bush as risk free; Dukakis opposed to "virtually every weapons system we've developed," Bush presumably in favor of them all.

The ad suffers from the weaknesses that pervade contemporary campaigning. It tells us what Dukakis is against but not what Bush is for. It assumes but does not argue that the listed weapons systems are vital to our national defense. It suppresses discussion of all the weapons systems the Democrat supports and focuses on those he presumably opposes. And it leaps from specific claims to a broad and unwarranted inference. "America can't afford that risk." Moreover, as reporters finally pointed out in the final weeks of the campaign, three of the claims in the ad are false. The Democrat did not oppose "virtually every defense system we developed." He opposed two not "four missile systems," the MX and the Midgetman. He did not oppose the Stealth bomber but favored using it as a bargaining chip if conditions with the Soviet Union warranted. In short, the ad fails to argue, fails to engage the Democratic and Republican positions, and fails to accept the accountability that comes with making claims.

Lost in press coverage of the tank ride and in the subsequent ad war was the relation between the M-1 and Dukakis's military proposals. The tank ride built upon the speech Dukakis delivered that same day and forecast the speech he would deliver the next morning. On September 14, 1988, the Democrat argued:

> In Central Europe today, the most serious danger we face is the two-to-one Warsaw Pact advantage in modern tanks. Yet the Republicans have already cut our tank production and want to slash it almost in half again next year. And after eight years in office, they have still failed to deploy an infantry anti-tank missile that can take out modern Soviet tanks. A recent government report estimated that *up to 85 percent* of the infantry soldiers using today's anti-tank weapons to stop a Soviet tank attack in Europe would be dead after firing a single round! And that round would bounce off the Soviet tank.

By reducing "military issues" to the presupposition that Dukakis was "weak on defense," a claim visually incarnated in the tank ride, reporters obscured a fundamental philosophical difference between the Republican and Democratic contender. Where one favored a nuclear build-up, the other favored a conventional build-up.

Lest reporters miss the relationship between his positions and the tank ride, the Democrat told them, "We'd better do something about our conventional forces instead of spending billions and billions on fantasies in the sky." Dukakis also reminded those assembled at the General Dynamics tank facility in Sterling Heights, Michigan, that in 1987 Bush had lauded the superiority of Soviet tank mechanics. "Mr. Bush," proclaimed the Democrat, "I'd rather have mechanics from Michigan." One of the few print reporters to point out the relationship between the tank ride and Dukakis's defense plan was Carl Leubsdorf of the *Dallas Morning News*. "It was commonsense reporting," he recalls. "He told us why he was doing it. That's what I reported."

Reporters failed to translate the tank ride into coverage of the candidates' policy differences. The Republican ad then locked in the perception that the Democrat was weak on defense. As a result, few now realize how prescient Dukakis's positions were. No nuclear weapons were used in "Desert Storm," the only military action the United States undertook during Bush's first term. Instead the M-1, in which Dukakis had ridden in his much-ridiculed effort to stress his conventional commitments, battled it out with the Soviet T-62 and T-72. Indeed, in February 1991, the M-1 tank backed by the Apache helicopter—two weapons the Reagan-Bush administration had tried to cut—functioned as the military's workhorses. And in Desert Storm, Dukakis's concerns about communication in the field proved well placed. Claiming that the Army may have covered up communication problems between U.S. helicopters and U.S. tanks that contributed to deaths by "friendly fire" in the Gulf War, in November 1991 congressional investigators on the House's Subcommittee on Oversight and Investigations called for a criminal inquiry.

Also ironic is the fact that President Bush abolished two of the weapons systems the tank ad indicted Dukakis for opposing. Republican support documents accurately list the MX and the Midgetman as missile systems Dukakis opposed. On the stump, Bush declared, "I will not do what my opponent has suggested. I will not get rid of the MX, get rid of the Midgetman. . . . I will not make those unilateral cuts in our defense." Yet in October 1991, that is precisely what Bush did. And he did it unilaterally. He then followed up in January by shutting down the last nuclear weapon assembly line still running. That move ended production of the Trident missile warheads that Dukakis had placed in the "negotiable" category.

But the ironies don't end there. Dukakis had argued in September 1987 that he would consider giving up the Stealth if conditions in the Soviet Union were right. Not I, replied candidate Bush. Yet, in November 1991, after learning of "flaws in the radar-evading ability of the Stealth," Congress denied Bush the funding he requested for more of the planes. The same bill earmarked nearly a billion dollars in Pentagon money for humanitarian aid to our new friend, the Soviet Union. And in his January 1992 State of the Union address, Bush ended production of the Stealth—after completion of only 20 of the original 132 he had sought.

Conventional wisdom says that Dukakis's tank ride in the 1988 general election campaign was an instance of consummate incompetence, a failed attempt to establish that the Democrat was "strong on defense." Instead I would argue that that staged event synopsized an important, far-ranging difference between the Republican and Democratic candidates. At the same time it showed the extent to which the traditional genres of campaign discourse are being reduced to visually evocative ads, with the boundaries between news and ads blurring in the process. Finally, it signals much of what was wrong with the press coverage and advertising of the 1988 campaign.

* * * *

Campaign discourse is failing the body politic in the United States not because it is "negative" or bodied in paid ads but because it has conventionalized genres of candidate and press discourse that minimize argumentative engagement and ignore the responsibility that all parties should shoulder for the claims they make. When all discourse becomes adlike, argument, engagement, and accountability are lost.

* * * *

Voters Are Pack Rats

The role that ads, Bush rhetoric, news, and audience psychology played in transforming William Horton's name for some into a symbol of the terrors of crime and for others of the exploitation of racist fears shows the powerful ways in which messages interact and the varying responses they evoke in individuals. Like pack rats, voters gather bits and pieces of political information and store them in a single place. Lost in the storage is a clear recall of where this or that "fact" came from. Information obtained from news mixes with that from ads, for example.

Although Bush had been telling the tale on the stump since June, in the second week in September 1988, the Horton story broke into prime time in the form of a National Security Political Action Committee (NSPAC) ad. The ad tied Michael Dukakis to a convicted murderer who had jumped furlough and gone on to rape a Maryland woman and assault her fiancé. The convict was black, the couple white.

The ad opens with side-by-side pictures of Dukakis and Bush. Dukakis's hair is unkempt, the photo dark. Bush, by contrast, is smiling and bathed in light. As the pictures appear, an announcer says "Bush and Dukakis on crime." A picture of Bush flashes on the screen. "Bush supports the death penalty for first-degree murderers." A picture of Dukakis. "Dukakis not only opposes the death penalty, he allowed first-degree murderers to have weekend passes from prison." A close-up mug shot of Horton flashes onto the screen. "One was Willie Horton, who murdered a boy in a robbery, stabbing him nineteen times." A blurry black-and-white photo of Horton apparently being arrested appears. "Despite a life sentence, Horton received ten weekend passes from prison." The words "kidnapping," "stabbing," and "raping" appear on the screen with Horton's picture as the announcer adds, "Horton fled, kidnapping a young couple, stabbing the man and repeatedly raping his girlfriend." The final photo again shows Michael Dukakis. The announcer notes "Weekend prison passes. Dukakis on crime."

When the Bush campaign's "revolving door" ad began to air on October 5, viewers read Horton from the PAC ad into the furlough ad. This stark black-and-white Bush ad opened with bleak prison scenes. It then cut to a procession of convicts circling through a revolving gate and marching toward the nation's living rooms. By carefully juxtaposing words and pictures, the ad invited the false inference that 268 first-degree murders were furloughed by Dukakis to rape and kidnap. As the bleak visuals appeared, the announcer said that Dukakis had vetoed the death penalty and given furloughs to "first-degree murderers not eligible for parole. While out, many committed other crimes like kidnapping and rape."

The furlough ad contains three false statements and invites one illegitimate inference. The structure of the ad prompts listeners to hear "first-degree murderers not eligible for parole" as the antecedent referent for "many." Many of whom committed crimes? First-degree murderers not eligible for parole. Many of whom went on to commit crimes like kidnapping and rape? First-degree murderers not eligible for parole.

But many unparoleable first-degree murderers did not escape. Of the 268 furloughed convicts who jumped furlough during Dukakis's first two terms, only four had ever been convicted first-degree murderers not eligible for parole. Of those four not "many" but one went on to kidnap and rape. That one was William Horton. By flashing "268 escaped" on the screen as the announcer speaks of "many first-degree murderers," the ad invites the false inference that 268 murderers jumped furlough to rape and kidnap. Again, the single individual who fits this description is Horton. Finally, the actual number who were more than four hours late in returning from furlough during Dukakis's two and a half terms was not 268 but 275. In Dukakis's first two terms, 268 escapes were made by the 11,497 individuals who were given a total of 67,378 furloughs. In the ten-year period encompassing his two completed terms and the first two years of his third term (1987–88), 275 of 76,455 furloughs resulted in escape.

This figure of 275 in ten years compares with 269 who escaped in the three years in which the program was run by Dukakis's Republican predecessor, who created the furlough program.

Still the battle of drama against data continued. After the Bush campaign's furlough ad had been on the air for two and a half weeks, in the third week of October, PAC ads featuring the victims of Horton began airing. One showed the man whose fiancé had been raped by the furloughed Horton. "Mike Dukakis and Willie Horton changed our lives forever," said Cliff Barnes, speaking in tight close-up. "He was serving a life term, without the possibility of a parole, when Governor Dukakis gave him a few days off. Horton broke into our home. For twelve hours, I was beaten, slashed, and terrorized. My wife, Angie, was brutally raped. When his liberal experiment failed, Dukakis simply looked away. He also vetoed the death penalty bill. Regardless of the election, we are worried people don't know enough about Mike Dukakis."

The second ad was narrated by the sister of the teenager killed by Horton. "Governor Dukakis's liberal furlough experiments failed. We are all victims. First, Dukakis let killers out of prison. He also vetoed the death penalty. Willie Horton stabbed my teenage brother nineteen times. Joey died. Horton was sentenced to life without parole, but Dukakis gave him a furlough. He never returned. Horton went on to rape and torture others. I worry that people here don't know enough about Dukakis's record." The words that recur in the two ads are: "liberal," "experiment," "rape," worry that "people don't know enough about Dukakis," "vetoed the death penalty."

Taken together the ads created a coherent narrative. Dukakis furloughed Horton (PAC ads), just as he had furloughed 267 other escapees (Bush revolving door ad). Horton raped a woman and stabbed her fiancé (crime-quiz and victim PAC ads). Viewers could infer what must have happened to the victims of the other 267 escapees.

The narrative was reinforced by print and radio. The "get out of jail free courtesy of Dukakis" card reappeared in 400,000 fliers mailed by the Bush campaign to Texans. "He let convicted rapists, murderers and drug dealers out of prison on weekend passes," said the flier. "And even after—while out on furlough—they raped and tried to kill again."

ALAMO PAC, a political action committee based in San Antonio, Texas, produced one ad that paralleled the claims of the furlough ad but focused on drugs. While showing a drug dealer at a high school, the ad noted that Dukakis had vetoed mandatory prison terms for convicted drug dealers, had fought the death penalty for drug "murderers," and supported weekend furloughs for drug convicts. A second ALAMO PAC ad showed a burglar, presumably freed under a furlough program, creeping into a darkened bedroom.

Clips from Bush's speeches that appeared in the news reinforced the Horton-Dukakis link. In Xenia, Ohio, in early October, Bush talked in what the *New York Times* described as "vivid detail . . . about the notorious case of Willie Horton." Press accounts vivified the case by supplying details and occasional pictures of Horton. The *New York Times* described Horton as "the murderer who left the Massachusetts prison system on a weekend furlough, only to be caught a year later after he raped a Maryland woman and brutally beat her fiancé." At a rally in Medina, Ohio, Bush referred to the Massachusetts governor as "the furlough king." In Trenton, New Jersey, Bush noted that "the victims of crime are given no furlough from their pain and suffering."

The sister of one of Horton's victims and the man Horton had assaulted while on furlough began holding press conferences just as PAC ads featuring them were beginning to air. In Texas, newspapers devoted front-page space to Donna Fournier Cuomo, whose seventeen-year-old brother Horton supposedly killed, and Cliff Barnes, then the fiancé of the woman the escapee had raped. The press tours were underwritten by a two-million dollar fund raised by the Committee for the Presidency, the pro-Bush Political Action Committee that sponsored the "victim" ads.

In 1988, broadcast news stories allied segments from three ads to create new congeries of images. The ads included clips from the furlough ad, still photos of furloughed convict William Horton, close-ups of the sister of a man Horton "murdered," and the husband of a woman Horton raped. Horton's victims and the murdered teenager's sister recounted their stories. Since Robert McClure and Thomas Patterson's pioneering study of the relationship of ads and news, we have known that viewers import segments of one story into another, a phenomenon McClure and Patterson call "meltdown."

This phenomenon is well explained by former NBC president Robert Mulholland. "I think during the campaign the average viewer starts to get a little confused. I'm expecting any day now to see Willie Horton endorse a line of jeans. . . . Some of the ads start to look like news stories, they're the same length, 30 seconds. . . . Television is not just separated in the minds of the viewer between this is news, this is commercial, and this is entertainment. Sometimes it all gets fuzzed up because it all comes into the home through the same little piece of glass."

The "melting down" of these images explains the controversy surrounding the Bush campaign's use of William Horton. In late fall 1988 a rising chorus of Democrats condemned George Bush and his Republican handlers for the "Willie Horton" ad. Feigning cherubic innocence, Bush's surrogates pointed out that no picture of the black murderer and rapist Horton had ever appeared in a Bush-sponsored ad.

From Bush strategist Lee Atwater to Bush media advisor Roger Ailes, Bush's aides were telling the literal truth. The scowling convict's mug shot appeared only in the ads of presumably independent political action committees. But the psychological impact was similar. In his stump speeches, Bush routinely raised the case of the furloughed convict without mentioning his race. But once a viewer had seen the PAC ad or a news clip about it, the images of Horton, his victims, and the circling convicts were likely to meld into a coherent narrative reinforced almost daily by Bush's recounting of it in his campaign speeches.

Not All Information Is Created Equal

Democratic nominee Michael Dukakis both opposed the death penalty and favored furloughs. It is no accident that the image chosen by the Republicans to symbolize the Massachusetts furlough system was a black male. By explaining that they used Horton not because he was black but because he "slashed" a Maryland man and raped his fiancée, the Republicans tacitly acknowledged the atypicality of the case. No other furloughed first-degree murderer—white or black—either murdered or raped while out. During the primaries a double murderer did jump furlough but was caught and returned. As one of the authors of the Lawrence, Massachusetts *Eagle-Tribune's* series notes, the Bush campaign could have selected a white criminal had it wanted. "We did a page 1 story on a white murderer," recalls Sue Forrest. "He was a former cop who was furloughed. My colleagues wrote a story on five furlough cases. Four were white. The fifth was Horton." Former trooper Armand Therrein killed his business partner and a policeman. On December 11, 1987, he jumped work detail. A month later, he was recaptured. The Republicans opted for a street crime involving strangers and a black villain over the story of a white cop-gone-bad who killed a friend for insurance money. Since the Bush campaign relied on the *Eagle-Tribune* for its information on the fur-lough program, it presumably knew of these cases.

Horton was not a representative instance of the furlough program. Nor were his crimes typical of crime in the United States, where murder, assault, and nearly nine out of ten rapes are intraracial, not interracial.

Yet by late October, Bush was observing that the Horton case had "come to symbolize, and represent—accurately, I believe—the misguided outlook of my opponent when it comes to crime." In my judgment, a single aberrational incident was taken by the Republicans, the press, and the public to be typical of crime, and Dukakis's handling of it seen as symptomatic of the failures of liberalism because dramatic, personalized evidence carries more weight psy-chologically than do statistics. Moreover, the Horton case played both into the widely held presupposition that Democrats are "soft on crime" and into the conventions of network news.

* * * *

An Assessment of the Best and Worst of Times

Asking what it was about the 1960 and 1980 campaigns that produced en-gagement on policy and useful predictions about governance is instructive. Both were close elections. And in close elections, the press and the candidates behave differently. Both candidates see advantage in providing the press and public with access. Increased as a result are well-publicized news conferences with the national press, participation in interview shows, and willingness to debate. At the same time, when the race is close the press makes better use of the access it is given. Press questions are more likely to focus on substance than strategy; and one candidate is not burdened with a greater percent of strategy questions than the other.

When an opponent begins to close in the polls, the "front runner" be-comes more accessible. So, for example, in the final weeks of both the 1968 and 1988 campaigns Nixon and Bush, who had been ducking such press con-tact, agreed to network interviews, Nixon on the Sunday interview shows, Bush on network morning and evening news. Close races also create incen-tives for candidates to engage in a broader range of discourse and to employ engaged forms more frequently.

If the matters at issue are central to governance, differentiating one's stands from those of the opponent is a useful means of informing voters. The longer the statement, the more likely it is to compare and contrast candidates' posi-tions, providing either oppositional evidence discrediting the opponent's stand or supportive evidence for one's own side or both. So, for example, speeches are more likely to engage than spots, the longer soundbites of "MacNeil/ Lehrer" more likely to engage than those on other network evening news. Unfortunately, the number of nationally broadcast general election messages fifteen minutes or longer had declined dramatically in recent years as has public attention to programs, speeches and discussions about campaigns, the number of hours of convention programming aired on the three commercial networks, and viewed there, and the number of hours of candidate sponsored programming on election eve.

The presidents elected in 1960 and 1980 did so with campaigns filled with five-minute not thirty- and sixty-second ads. In these campaigns, the contenders delivered major nationally broadcast policy speeches. And the greater press access that came with the closeness of the race meant that the clash of opposing positions both advanced arguments and deepened understanding of their rationale and implications. At the same time, enhanced contact with press and public caught and corrected distortions that candidates put out about their records or recommendations.

Since there is no way to engineer close races, how can we encourage the argument, engagement, and accountability that come with longer forms of communication and with access to the press? And how can we invite the press to use access to the candidates to advance our understanding of the who, what, and how of governance rather than the "why" and "with what effect" of campaigning?

Some of the answers are structural. By throwing candidates into states as dissimilar as Georgia, Colorado, and Maryland in a single week, we ensure that the messages reaching the national audience will fragment. Because the South Dakota primary was unpaired with that of any other agricultural state, the farm policies the candidates discussed in that debate seemed irrelevant to most of the rest of the nation. They were lost, as well, in media reports that covered strategy because there was not enough similarity in policy focus across the primary states to build stories on substance.

When the resources of the entire candidate field are concentrated on one homogeneous state such as New Hampshire, the discourse naturally focuses on that state's concerns. With New Hampshire in economic crisis in winter 1992, the candidates had no choice but to lay out their economic plans. There was little room for distraction. The quality of the discourse was high. Ads inched upward in length. Thirty-minute ads re-emerged. Three of the candidates distributed detailed print policy statements. The debates were substantive and distraction was low.

When the candidates' focus shifted to campaigning in a handful of states with no marked similarities, the discourse quickly became meaner and more meaningless. With resources spread across the larger number of media markets and no single natural policy focus upon which to build the redundancy that is central to retention, the sensible strategic thing to do is exactly what the candidates did: roll out the unengaged attacks.

One way to increase the amount of focused, engaged discourse in the primaries would be to cluster states that share similar problems and challenges. One set of primaries might occur in states grappling with decaying cities (e.g.,

Pennsylvania could be added to Michigan and Illinois). This would solve a problem for the candidates and the press.

If one week's primaries were in states that raise cotton, cows, and corn, the candidates could focus their debates, speeches, ads, interviews, and press conferences for that week on farm policy. The interests of voters in those states would invite candidates to concentrate their resources on discussing parity pricing, subsidies, the relationship between farm policy and international trade, use of agri-products as alternative fuels, and combatting U.S. and world hunger through use of American-produced grain.

The level of engaged oppositional advertising would undoubtedly be high but in an environment in which all forms of communication are focused on the same topic so too would candidate accountability for distortion. And the shared topic area would make it easier for the press to structure stories on problems and solutions rather than strategy.

In 1980, Ronald Reagan argued that we were creating a disincentive to work by taxing wealth. Momentarily adopting his philosophy might lead us to ask, How do we reward candidates for engaging in a broad menu of discourse and, as a result, for accessibility to public and press? Since broadcast speeches attract small audiences, we must find a way to provide an incentive for candidates to deliver such speeches, accept invitations to be interviewed and conduct press conferences and also provide incentives for voters to watch. Elsewhere, I have proposed that the press, civil organizations, and schools set the expectation that citizens will watch two thirty-minute speeches by each candidate, one delivered on national television on Labor Day, the other on election eve. In the intervening time, the candidates would participate in four debates in various formats, and appear in nationally telecast press conferences after each debate. They would also appear weekly in five-minute time slots provided to major party candidates who agree to deliver a statement on a specified weekly topic. The topics would be determined by non-candidate polls. So, for example, the topic for the first week after Labor Day would be the topic listed by the largest percentage of the surveyed public as most important to it. By noting major items on the congressional agenda, experts could add to the list of topics.

Because the airwaves are publicly owned, the networks, their affiliates, and the unaffiliated stations could contribute a powerful incentive by providing free national airtime for these rhetorical acts. In 1988, both presidential candidates accepted offers to be interviewed in morning and evening news although the front runner ducked CBS and "Nightline." Similarly, in March 1992, three of the Democrats and one Republican accepted the offer by the Discovery Channel of twenty minutes of time to deliver a speech. One might also tie acceptance of federal campaign financing to an agreement to participate in debates.

However, if debates are to engage and hold candidates accountable for the statements they make, the format has to change. To minimize risk, both

Democratic and Republican candidates have insisted on short answers with no press follow-up. Longer answers with provision for reporters to follow up would do much to eliminate the debate-ads that now masquerade as debates. Because the 1976 debates followed a three-minute first answer, two-minute second answer with follow-up by the questioner, reporter Jack Nelson could say to candidate Jimmy Carter, "Governor, I don't believe you answered my question about the kinds of people you would be looking for [on the] Court, the type of philosophy you would be looking for?" Where Carter had ducked the question the first time, when pressed he responds that in the Burger-Warren tradition he would appoint those who tip the balance toward human rights.

Banning the studio audience would help as well. Alternatively, if the experiments undertaken in the primaries of 1980 and 1984 are any indication, removing the buffer of the press panel would also increase engagement and accountability in debates.

To ensure that the candidates both address each other and the issues of primary concern to the public, the press would cover campaigns in ways that increase candidate accountability and decrease the rewards for pseudo-answers, pseudo-events, and for transforming all available forms of communication into ads. The importance of reporters in the equation was acknowledged by the man who choreographed the visuals for the Reagan presidency, Michael Deaver, who noted: "The candidates aren't going to change. The media are going to have to force the change by the type of coverage they do, they insist upon."

The portents are varied. On the one hand, on a live radio interview show *San Francisco Examiner* reporter Chris Matthews asked Bill Clinton, "What was it like having an outhouse." Laughing, Clinton responded, "It was O.K. except in the winter when it was cold, and in the summer sometimes when there were snakes down the hole." An inveterate seeker of insight about primal candidate experiences, Matthews inquired, "How did you go at night with those snakes?" "You made real sure you wanted to go bad," responded the candidate to audience laughter. "I don't believe I agreed to do this." (May 29, 1992, San Francisco).

On the other, in the Democratic candidates' debate on PBS (January 31, 1992), Jim Lehrer asked: "Senator Tsongas, the experts say that all of the discussions that you and everybody else have about health care in the United States always avoid the real issue, which is allocation of resources, rationing, or whatever. In other words, we cannot afford to pay for the health care system that our science and medical profession can provide. Are they right?" His follow-up questions asked Tsongas to define managed competition, queried Kerrey about the mandated nature of his proposal, pursued the question, "How do you manage costs under your plan?", and parried an answer by asking "But that's going to lead to rationing and allocation, is it not?" The exchanges clarified the different approaches the two candidates would take to national health insurance.

By giving voters the information they need to judge candidates' messages on their accuracy, fairness, and contextuality and relevance to governance, reporters also make it possible to penalize sleaze and reward substance. So, for example, in the 1992 Georgia primary, voters surprised those who had assumed that the South surfeits with "Bubbas" eager to vote their prejudices. Viewers penalized Republican hopeful Patrick Buchanan for an unfair attack on incumbent president George Bush.

The ad showed scenes from the film *Tongues Untied* as print scrolled up the screen saying, "In the past three years the Bush Administration has invested our tax dollars in pornographic and blasphemous art, too shocking to show." Voters spotted the irony. "If it's so shocking, what his business in showing it in my living room?" asked an angered focus group member. "He's using my money to put that junk on the air just like what he says George Bush did," noted another. What the voters are referring to are the semi-clad men in leather shown dancing on the screen.

"This so-called art has glorified homosexuality, exploited children, and perverted the image of Jesus Christ," says the ad. "He thinks we're going to vote for him because we are Christians," said a middle-aged man in one of the groups. "And because some of us believe that homosexuality is wrong," added another. "I know George Bush is a good Christian," noted the first. "He would not have approved of anything that profaned Jesus Christ."

"Even after good people protested, Bush continued to fund this kind of art," states the ad. "I heard on television that that wasn't true," said a seventy-three-year-old retired school teacher. "I even made it on tape and freeze frome (*sic*) [laughter] my television set. When you go up and look I don't even know what it is. All I saw was a bunch of butts [laughter]." "The thing that really offended me," said a college student, "was putting George Bush's picture right on the film as if he had made it himself." "What matters to me," said a middle-aged male construction worker, "is that that ad doesn't tell the truth." "Bush didn't support that film. It happened under Reagan. This kind of advertising is what's wrong with politics." "But it does tell you a lot about Buchanan," said the college student. "Yeah," responded the construction worker. "He's a low life." "If that's all he's got to say about what he'd want to do when he is president, he hasn't got much more to say," commented a secretary.

"How, what makes you think the ad is untrue?" asked the focus group leader. "It was on the news," said the construction worker. "CNN," said the school teacher. "No, it was one of the other ones," added the construction worker. "It said that that film was funded by someone else while Reagan was president and that what the agency [National Endowment for the Arts] does now is funds symphonies and opera." "I just didn't believe junk like that. Who would believe that the president would attack Jesus Christ," observed a cop. "That's interesting," said the woman who had tried to get a better look at the ad. "I believe if you can't say something nice, don't say something at all."

The thirty voters in these three groups had been selected to ensure that their demographics matched those of the state; all said they were undecided three weeks before the primary. The night before balloting, each group was asked whether the Buchanan ad had made them more or less likely to support Buchanan or hadn't changed their inclination at all. Seven said that the ad had made them less likely to support the Republican insurgent. A week after the balloting in Georgia, a CNN-Gallup poll confirmed that the NEA ad had created a backlash against Buchanan. Indeed, 23 percent said that the ad had increased the likelihood that they would vote for Buchanan's opponent, George Bush. A misleading ad by Democratic contender Paul Tsongas created a similar effect.

Ten chapters ago, I argued that in 1988 the Republicans exploited quirks in the electorate and conventions of the press to give an atypical instance—the "drama" of William Horton—a power unwarranted by the data. By 1992, the press had learned one lesson of 1988. As a result voters rejected a drama-filled but atypical instance of arts funding that played on fears of gays.

Where the press had abetted the Horton story, it discredited the tale of a president funding pornography. On CNN (February 28, 1992), Brooks Jackson pointed out that the film had been funded by the Reagan, not the Bush, administration at a total cost to the tax payers of $5000. NBC's Lisa Myers went a step further (March 3, 1992) to note that the film was not typical of NEA projects.

As she made this claim, Myers displaced the ad's images with shots of the Chicago Symphony and Pavarotti on PBS. These, she argued, were more representative of the Endowment's mission and expenditures. Both NBC and CNN distanced audiences from the ad by boxing it on the screen and dampened the power of the ad's visuals by imposing the words "misleading" or "false" over the ad copy in appropriate places.

Data had triumphed over drama, substance over strategy. Argumentation, engagement, and accountability had other noteworthy moments in 1992 as well.

Earlier I argued that the 1988 general election debates were worrisomely ad-like. By contrast, the 1992 MacNeil–Lehrer, Jennings, and Donahue primary debates proved more substantive than any in recent memory. The educator-philosopher John Dewey would have been pleased with the extent to which, occasionally with the gentle encouragement of the moderators, each Democratic contender "follow[ed] an argument, grasp[ed] the point of view of another, expand[ed] the boundaries on understanding, [and] debate[d] the alternative purposes that might be pursued."

The bad news is that the audiences for these exchanges were equaled by those for "trash" television. In the low point of the primary campaign, a woman who claimed, without persuasive evidence, to have been Bill Clinton's mistress told a tabloid TV interviewer that she rated the Democrat a nine on a ten-point scale of lovers.

Tabloid television was not the only new genre added to the traditional political mix in 1992. As my earlier discussion of the gubernatorial candidacy of David Duke noted, live radio and television talk shows now provide candidates with access to large and, some fear, largely uncritical, audiences.

Responding to the competition provided by "Oprah" and "Geraldo," by 1992 the once serious talk shows have moved to include "sex" and "scandal." Of Jerry Brown, Phil Donahue asked, "You went to Africa with Linda Ronstadt. Did you go anywhere else with anybody else?" Donahue's questions of Bill Clinton focused on whether the Arkansan had or hadn't had affairs.

Midway through Donahue's assault on Clinton, an exasperated candidate and an audience member both said, "Enough." "We're going to sit here a long time in silence, Phil. I'm not going to answer any more of these questions," said Clinton to rising audience applause. "I've answered 'em until I'm blue in the face. You are responsible for the cynicism in this country. You don't want to talk about the real issues." As the crowd voiced its approval, an audience member agreed. "Given the pathetic state of most of the United States at this point . . . ," she said, "I can't believe you spent half an hour of air time attacking this man's character. I'm not even a Bill Clinton supporter, but I think this is ridiculous."

In penance, Donahue devoted his last show before the New York primary to an uninterrupted discussion between Democratic contenders Jerry Brown and Bill Clinton. The worst of times had given way to the best. The exchange proved as substantive and more civil than any in the campaign. And it reached an audience not usually attracted by PBS and C-SPAN.

The emergence of the talk show as a site of both substance and silliness suggests a system in transition. By providing callers and audience members with direct access to candidates, the format enfranchises. Participation rather than spectatorship is invited by its interactive form. Moreover, it attracts an audience otherwise largely inaccessible to candidates.

But because the hosts range from dedicated partisans to entertaining lightweights, a skillful candidate can transform many of these opportunities into interview- or news-ads. And while callers ask useful and often important questions, most are unskilled in follow-up. The opportunity to ask a second question is usually not provided, in any event. In other words, while potentially productive, the talk show form is not likely, of itself, to elicit a high level of argument, engagement, and accountability. And on the horizon is a candidacy capitalizing on public disdain for the traditional news media and disaffection with the forms of politics as usual.

Whether the rise of H. Ross Perot is a symptom of the problem or a solution remains to be seen. But if history is a guide, such questions can best be answered by campaigns that engage in argumentation rather than assertion, differentiation rather than vilification, substantive engagement rather than storytelling. The public and the body politic are ill-served if discourse is driven by drama rather than data and if reporters concentrate on fathoming the candidate's strategic intent and its effect rather [than] on the problems facing us, the qualifications of those who would lead and the legitimacy of the solutions they offer.

All of this is possible if the public will adopt the posture of the angered member of the Donahue audience and insist that candidates and reporters restore the relationship between campaign discourse and governance.

POINTS TO PONDER

1. What differences between candidates Bush and Dukakis did the reaction to the Dukakis tank ride obscure?
2. How can visual images be used to convey to the viewer more than what is claimed in audio statements?
3. In what ways was the Willie Horton ad of the Bush campaign misleading?
4. Do the types of campaign commercials discussed by Jamieson have anything to do with the increased voter alienation or decline in turnout?

40

"THE PRESIDENTIAL ELECTION OF 1992"

Gerald M. Pomper

The election of Bill Clinton and Al Gore in 1992 could not easily have been predicted in 1991. President Bush enjoyed unprecedented popularity after the U.S. victory in the Persian Gulf War, and the Republicans seemed to have a "lock" on the presidency. In this excerpt from his edited book, The Election of 1992, *Gerald Pomper of Rutgers University analyzes the outcome of the 1992 election, its historical context, and its broader implications. He sees the surprising Perot vote of 19 percent as a generalized protest against the political system, which did not give either Clinton or Bush a clear advantage. Pomper concludes that Clinton's victory was clear, but tentative, and that his performance in office is more important than the overall partisan balance in the electorate.*

On 3 November, the floodtides of American politics elected Governor Bill Clinton president of the United States and Senator Al Gore vice-president. On a secondary wave, Ross Perot roiled the electoral waters. Submerged in the political wake were President George Bush and a corps of timid or inexpert Democratic politicians.

The presidential election tides carved sharp changes in the contours of the American political landscape. Clinton gained the first Democratic win in sixteen years and only the second convincing party victory (including 1964) since World War II. Clinton and Gore personified change—as explicit revisionists within their party, as the only successful all-southern ticket since 1828, and as the first of their generation to assume power.

Perot demonstrated the openness, even the vulnerable porousness, of the American political system. After an eccentric and lavish self-financed campaign, he won more votes than all but one independent candidate (Theodore Roosevelt in 1912) in American history. Without any party organization, he won a place on the ballot in every state, topped his publicly subsidized rivals in direct campaign spending, and raised the possibility of a constitutional crisis, the election of the president by the House of Representatives.

Most astonishing was the defeat of the incumbent president. George Bush had been easily elected in 1988 as the heir of a popular and innovative leader, Ronald Reagan. He had led the United States to its overwhelming military victory in the Persian Gulf, the only clear national triumph of arms in nearly fifty years. He had presided over the even more astounding fulfillment of American strategic goals—the end of the cold war and the dissolution of the Soviet Union. By March 1991, nearly 90 percent of the public commended Bush's performance in office, the highest level ever recorded in opinion polls.

Ironically, these very successes were the root causes of Bush's defeat in the 1992 election. Inheriting the Reagan legacy, . . . Bush confined himself to the role of understudy, dismissing what he ridiculed as "the vision thing." The end of the cold war allowed voters to concentrate on domestic problems, even as it opened fissures within the Republican party. Bush's unprecedented standing in opinion polls made him complacent, as he ignored the growing economic distress at home.

President Bush appropriately characterized the events occurring during his administration as changes of biblical proportions. Scripture also provides an explanation of his failure to win reelection. Like the mighty pharaoh of ancient Egypt, Bush failed to hear the distress of his people, leading eventually to the drowning of his legions.

The Democratic Victory

The election results present a bundle of anomalies. The Democratic tide swept across a nation that had become habituated to Republican presidents. The Democrats won decisively, yet gained a smaller share of the vote than in their stunning defeat in 1988. Social alignments resembled the established party cleavages, but new patterns emerged. An electorate disillusioned with politicians paid rapt attention to the political process. An independent candidate captured nearly a fifth of the vote, yet had no direct impact on the outcome.

The Electoral Map

Clinton's victory was national, encompassing 370 of the 538 total electoral votes. As seen on the electoral map . . . the Arkansas governor carried states in all regions of the country: all of the Northeast (eleven states plus the District of Columbia), six of the fourteen states of his native South and the border region, seven of the twelve Midwest and Plains states, and eight of the thirteen mountain and Pacific states.

Although Clinton won only a minority of the popular vote, his margin of 5.6 percentage points over George Bush was comfortable—almost identical, on a two-party basis, to the Republican's own victory in 1988. Even on a three-party basis, Clinton did better than his Democratic ancestor Woodrow Wilson in 1912. He also did as well as Richard Nixon in 1968, the most recent race with a major independent candidate in the running.

The victory of 1992 was the culmination of previous growth in Democratic electoral strength. Capturing thirty-two states, Clinton carried the ten won and all but one of the states narrowly lost by Michael Dukakis in 1988, while adding new strength, particularly in the south and the border region. The Arkansas governor extended the Democratic coalition; he did not transform the political map. George Bush's support, in contrast, shrank. Of the forty states he had carried four years earlier, fewer than half remained loyal in 1992.

Continuity in the parties' geographical support is demonstrated by some simple statistics. The average change in the states' (two-party) vote was only 6.8 percentage points, and most states clustered around this average. The shift reached ten points only in nine states; the Democratic candidates' home states, the northern tier of New England, and four other scattered locales (California, Delaware, Georgia, Nevada). Consequently, there was a very close relationship between the vote in 1992 and that in 1988, as well as between 1992 and the four previous elections (a correlation of .89 in both cases).

The Clinton victory potentially had a deeper impact on the parties' futures. In their victories in the 1980s, Reagan and Bush appeared to have created a new majority coalition, which held a "lock" on the Electoral College. This presumed dominance was based on Republican strength in the South and West. There the party had won six straight elections in twenty-one states having 191 electoral votes; its strength was reinforced by seventeen additional states, casting 217 electoral votes consistently Republican during the 1980s.

The asserted Republican "lock" had always been somewhat of a statistical artifact, ignoring the popular vote breakdown within states. Even while consistently losing California, for example, the Democrats had remained within striking distance, averaging 45 percent of the vote since 1976. In 1992, the Democrats successfully scaled the walls of Republican strongholds. On the map on the inside back cover, the states are classified into three equal groups, on the basis of the shift in their 1992 vote from the average Democratic proportion in the four previous presidential contests. The greatest changes came in the areas of previous party weakness, particularly the West, with other significant gains in the South and industrial states. These shifts provide reasons for Democratic optimism in future elections—and for caution in future electoral analyses.

An important effect of the election results was to demonstrate the virtues of the Electoral College. The system has been frequently condemned as antiquated and antidemocratic. Throughout American history, many have sought to replace the Constitutional mechanism with direct election of the president or other schemes. In 1992, these alternatives could have led to serious problems. The direct election of a president without a popular majority would have undermined the legitimacy of the office or forced a second, and wearisome, runoff between Clinton and Bush. A proportional division of electoral votes would probably have meant a deadlock or even corrupt bargaining in the Electoral College and uncertain selection of the president by the House of Representatives. The existing system, while hard to justify in democratic philosophy, gave the nation a clear, immediate, and legitimate verdict.

* * * *

Parties, Principles, and Perot

Party and ideology also affected the vote. Past loyalties largely held, Clinton winning the overwhelming proportion of Democrats and liberals, Bush gaining the bulk of Republicans and conservatives. Between these two factors, party was the greater influence; Clinton won a majority even among conservative Democrats, just as Bush did among liberal Republicans. More important than these typical, overall patterns were the shifts in the vote from 1988.

Here Clinton was notably more successful in holding past support and adding new voters to his cause. Even in the face of the Perot candidacy, Clinton was able to keep the Democratic vote close to the levels reached by Dukakis. Particularly important were the ideological moderates, the largest bloc, who showed a large shift, on a two-party basis, toward the Arkansan. Bush, by contrast, lost in all groups, and most substantially among moderate Republicans and both moderate and conservative Independents. These losses came despite a Republican campaign aimed at winning votes on grounds of "traditional values" considered important by these constituencies.

. . . Bush's vote was almost totally composed of persons who had voted for him four years earlier. Clinton had a much broader appeal, holding almost all of those who reported a 1988 vote for Dukakis . . . and winning converts from previous Bush voters, as well as a large proportion of those "recruits" who did not vote four years earlier. Perot drew far more heavily from those who had once supported the president than from the Dukakis vote, and gained about a fourth of the new entrants to the polling booths.

The vote for Ross Perot was large, but hazy in character. Typically, a third-party or independent candidate will draw strong support from particular groups, such as the southern segregationists who supported George Wallace in

1968 or the liberal Republicans drawn to John Anderson in 1980. Perot, by contrast, drew his fraction of the vote from almost all groups. He gained at least a tenth of the ballots in every state but Mississippi, and similar percentages in every region. His steady vote denied Clinton a popular majority in every state but Arkansas, even as he deprived Bush of a majority in every state but Mississippi. But by running a consistent third everywhere but Maine and Utah, Perot was completely shut out in the Electoral College.

In a two-man race, the Perot vote would have divided evenly, 38 percent each to Clinton and Bush, with the rest choosing minor candidates or abstaining. No state's electoral vote was obviously affected. His backers also equally divided their congressional ballots between Republicans and Democratic candidates. Perot took votes from Bush in the South, but the president still carried the region. The independent took votes from Clinton in the Northeast, but the governor still won all these states. In the other regions, Perot equally affected the two major candidates. With or without the billionaire, Clinton and Gore would have won the election.

Moreover, the Texan independent's support was fairly similar among most social groups, approximating his national share of 19 percent. Only some ethnic minorities—African Americans and Jews—clearly resisted his appeal, while some reservations were evident among the retired elderly, unmarried women, and Hispanics. Just as there was no clear Perot platform, there was no discernible ideological base to his vote; he drew about the same among liberals, moderates, and conservatives.

Threading through the quilt of Perot support is an unfocused discontent with the political and economic system. Among self-declared Independents, the unaffiliated candidate came close to his partisan rivals, winning 30 percent. He did better among those with the most shallow political roots; first-time voters, especially young white men; those not voting for House candidates; and those in insecure economic positions. His appeal was greatest to those who distrusted politicians, whether they evaluated Clinton's honesty on the draft, Bush's honesty on taxes and secret payments to Iran, or everyone's honesty on the federal budget deficit.

The Perot vote was a generalized protest, not a specific program. Indeed, it was in some ways a protest against politics itself, the latest expression of a desire that "deep in our democracy has always yearned for the immaculate conception of a president, delivered to us unsmeared by the messy afterbirth of most campaigns." Because of its lack of political roots, the Perot candidacy had no immediate political effect. Without his personal attraction and personal fortune, his movement lacks the social or organizational basis for a persistent impact on American politics. Yet, Perot certainly contributed to the sharp increase in voter turnout, affected the conduct of the campaign, and will have a substantial indirect and long-lasting impact on politics beyond 1992.

Using innovative techniques, Perot's campaign hastened the continuing change in American politics toward a plebiscitarian democracy, where voters communicate directly to politicians, without the help or hindrance of intermediaries such as political parties, mass media, or opinion leaders. He evidenced the vulnerabilities of unmediated politics in his unregulated spending, authoritarian conduct, and disregard for representative institutions. At the same time, he helped make the election a more serious discussion of national problems, particularly jobs and the federal deficit.

The Effects of the Election

What's next? Clinton and Gore did not capture the hearts of the nation, or even the votes of a majority of Americans. They did speak their country's mind with sufficient precision to claim a mandate for change. The electoral decision in 1992 was not only a choice among candidates; it was also a judgment on the basic philosophical and policy differences between the major parties. Beyond a Democratic victory, it provides a Democratic opportunity.

The Parties' Futures

There is no party realignment evident in the election, but there is an opportunity to consolidate Democratic gains and to move beyond their 1992 electoral minority. No new party coalition emerges from the vote, but rather a shift among all groups, based on discontent with existing conditions and uncertain expectations for the future. Partisan identification is virtually unchanged since 1988 (38 percent Democratic, 35 percent Republican), although there are glimmers of change among the youngest voters. Democratic party prospects will rise or fall with the achievements or failures of the Clinton administration.

Even without realignment, however, the major parties face vital challenges. The Perot vote clearly underlines voters' willingness to abandon partisan loyalties and receptivity to new appeals. The new campaign technologies of the 1992 election, by circumventing the party organizations, cast new doubt on their role in the political process and even raise the question of their viability in an era of direct communication between candidates and voters.

The major parties did remain important in 1992 as organizational shells and financial conduits for the candidates. Including their direct spending and "soft money" contributions, they each outspent Perot by a 2-to-1 margin. Viable parties, however, need more; they must have heads and hearts, not only deep pockets in empty clothes. Both Democrats and Republicans need to foster loyalties by clarifying their beliefs.

The Democratic party has been riven for decades on issues of international involvement, social liberalism, and the competing claims of economic redistribution and economic growth. That debate was muted in 1992 by the year's unique circumstances. With a limited field, Clinton's Democratic moderates could capture the party nomination quickly and without major damage. The end of the cold war cast foreign policy issues aside. Social liberals were willing to dampen their demands in order to forestall the final conservative capture of the judiciary. Given the economic failures of the Bush administration, the pacified Democrats achieved victory.

The rifts remain and may become evident as Clinton seeks support of his programs from a Democratic Congress. He will have advantages: the power of the presidency, his political skills, and the Democrats' need to prove their competence in government. Yet he must also deal with entrenched interests in and near the Capitol and with a party structure that facilitates factional conflict. As president, assured of renomination, he may be able to move his party toward both organizational and policy coherence.

Republicans face similar problems of ideological incohesion, and now without leaders in office to give direction. Factions within the party will debate "Who lost the White House?" with the fervor of cold-war controversies over "Who lost China?" Social conservatives and abortion rights advocates will battle within state and local organizations, as others argue economic theories. The resulting debate will be contentious yet helpful in marking the underlying ideologies within and between the major parties.

Principles and Parties

The basic party difference, at least since the New Deal, has been in the two parties' attitudes toward government. Republicans distrust government, even when they control it. They rely on the private sector, and particularly the accumulation of private capital, to meet social needs. It was not by whim that Ronald Reagan put Calvin Coolidge's portrait in a place of honor in the White House. Reagan often declared his party's basic philosophy, that government itself was the problem and could not be the solution to the nation's problems.

The Democratic party since the New Deal, by contrast, has looked on government as a potentially benign force, which can take action—at the very least to stimulate the private sector and, more ambitiously, to redistribute the national wealth. When Franklin Roosevelt, in his first Inaugural Address, found one-third of the nation "ill-fed, ill-clothed, ill-housed," he sought the remedy in government programs, not in the invisible beneficence of the marketplace.

That basic philosophical distinction was evident in this election campaign, in the party platforms and television debates, and in the contrasting programs offered by Bush and Clinton. They often acknowledged the same national needs, but they presented different solutions. Each candidate pointed, for example, to the need to provide basic health care, particularly for the 37 million Americans without medical insurance. President Bush showed the consistent Republican aversion to government in his plan to give tax benefits to businesses providing insurance for their employees and to individuals buying private health plans. President Clinton will be using the power of government to require some degree of universal coverage.

The same distinction is evident on other issues. In regard to family leave, Bush again wanted to give tax breaks to businesses that allowed new parents to take time off from their jobs without losing their positions; Clinton promised to sign legislation requiring most employers to provide unpaid leaves. Bush would stimulate the economy by reducing capital gains taxation; Clinton proposed to prime the economic pump through government spending on infrastructure. Bush expected to improve education by giving parents vouchers to "buy" better schools in a competitive educational marketplace; Clinton preferred to set national goals and provide federal financial aid.

To be sure, the differences are not absolute or always consistent. Bush and most Republicans do support the basic elements of the welfare state, such as social security, just as Democrats are increasingly willing to use market incentives, as in Clinton's endorsement of urban enterprise zones. Neither party has ever come close to socialist programs of government ownership. Both use the language of American individualism, whether in Quayle's simplistic analysis of the evils of single parenthood or in Clinton's rhetorical emphasis on personal responsibility in his welfare-reform program.

Nevertheless, the basic distinction remains. America has a complex political belief system, which tries to balance a commitment to individual liberty with a commitment to social equality, to balance the pursuit of our private interests with our search for a public community. We engage in a perpetual personal and national debate asking, to paraphrase John Kennedy, *both* what we can do for ourselves and what we can do for others in our country. In that debate, Republicans are more likely to raise the banner of individualism: Pursuit of individual goals will add up to the common good. Democrats are more likely to raise the banner of community: Pursuing the social good will be better for each of us individually.

Prospects for the Future

Clinton and Gore's success is built on a revival of Democratic commitments, not their replacement. Their program accepts much of the social liberalism of their own young years, the 1960s, most notably women's liberation. Yet, in an important sense, it also returns to earlier values, seeking the votes of those erstwhile Democrats who "came to see the party as indifferent, if not hostile, to their moral sentiments and not much interested in their economic struggles." From the Madison Square Garden convention to the Old State House victory celebration, Clinton stressed this new and old appeal to "those who do the work, pay the taxes, raise the kids and play by the rules . . . the hardworking Americans who make up our forgotten middle class."

The party's predominance had been based on its commitment to governmental action aimed at economic growth and the interests of those at risk in the private marketplace. Previously, that commitment focused on the poor and industrial working class and was effective when these groups were a majority of the electorate. Clinton did not change the appeal; he modernized it for a nation with higher average incomes expectations.

The United States is now a middle-class, suburban nation with a service-oriented economy, but differences in wealth and opportunity are as evident today as in the industrial age. Clinton's campaign can be seen as a rhetorical echo of FDR, with an upscale appeal, speaking of a nation ill educated, ill healed, ill transported. By renewing the traditional Democratic stress on economic disadvantages, he brought his party back to power.

It remains to be seen if he can keep it there. Voters are still skeptical of government—proposals to limit the terms of senators and representatives passed in all fourteen states considering the issue. At the same time, voters retain some trust in their government—all but 6 of 116 Congressmen were reelected in these same states. Despite their discontent, . . . voters returned most incumbents to office. The Clinton victory was clear, but tentative, an electoral plurality within a possible majority. He won not a personal mandate but a chance to prove himself. Clinton differed from Bush more in his potential than his popularity; the distinction was "that one man has exhausted the possibilities of office . . . while the other has hardly begun."

Politics in a democracy, wrote Emerson, is always a contest between "the party of memory" and "the party of hope." The Democrats had become too committed to their memories, too dependent on the waning coalition established earlier, New Deal generations, and too committed to statist programs. Now the Democrats have full control of the national government, but also full responsibility for the public welfare. With a leader appropriately born in "a place called Hope," they have a chance to rebuild confidence in their party—and in their nation's future.

POINTS TO PONDER

1. To what part of the electorate did Ross Perot appeal? What types of people voted for him?
2. How important were political parties to the 1992 outcome?
3. What are the implications of the Perot candidacy for American governance? That is, what does the 19 percent vote for Perot tell us about the governability of the country?

Chapter 11

✧⟡✧

INTEREST GROUPS

It is ironic that the Framers of the Constitution considered the dangers of faction to be one of the greatest threats to a stable and just government, yet the power and proliferation of special-interest groups has been one of the hallmarks of two centuries of American politics. This section takes up the roles that interest groups play in the American system of governance. From one perspective, interest groups exercise constitutional rights of representation and have a positive effect on public policy-making; but from another perspective, they present threats to the ability of the political system to respond to the broader public interest.

Origins of Interest Groups in the United States

In *Federalist* No. 10 Madison recognized that the formation of factions was inevitable, and one of the main features of the Constitution was an attempt to assure that no faction could capture control of the whole government. The separation of powers ensured fragmentation of governmental power, and the different sources of power and personnel in the three branches make it very difficult for one faction to form a majority that could control the whole government. Of course, this guard against the aggregation of interests also makes it difficult to formulate coherent policies to deal with major societal or economic problems—the problem of gridlock.

Madison felt that, in addition to the separation of powers, the most effective safeguards against the evils of faction were a representative form of government and the size of the republic. As the country increased in size and the number of interests diversified, it would become less likely that any one faction would be able to dominate the whole.

Despite the Framers' distrust of factions, the First Amendment to the Constitution protects the rights of groups to try to influence governmental policy. The right of "the people peaceably to assemble" necessarily allows associations of all kinds; "freedom of speech" allows them to publicly press for whatever cause they please; and the guarantee of the people "to petition the Government for redress of grievances" certainly allows groups to lobby the government for their favorite cause.

These constitutional guarantees are consistent with the American tendency to join groups of people with similar interests. Two of the most astute foreign observers of American politics, Alexis de Tocqueville (French) and Lord James Bryce (British), both remarked in their writings (*Democracy in America* and *The American Commonwealth*, respectively) that Americans seem to be much more a nation of joiners than were European societies.

Development of Interest Groups

Americans associate with each other for many purposes—religious, recreational, financial—and the desire to influence governmental policy is one important reason for group associations. From the beginning of the Republic there were always individual lobbyists, facilitators, fixers, peddlers of influence, and others who made their living by attempting to influence the direction of public policy. It was natural for some groups wanting to influence the government to hire these people to press their causes by talking with members of Congress in the lobbies of the Capitol.

Later in the nineteenth century, as large-scale economic interests formed during the Industrial Revolution, large corporations hired their own lobbyists to watch over their interests in Washington. Whether it was the railroads fighting for public land, manufacturing firms arguing for protective tariffs, or veterans' groups in search of pensions, lobbying was an active profession in the nineteenth century. Much of this lobbying was perfectly legal, but there was no lack of attempts to buy influence, including outright bribery as in the Crédit Mobilier scandal in the 1880s.

With the growing involvement of the national government in the economy of the twentieth century, the numbers and range of interest groups continued to increase. But a striking jump in the numbers occurred after 1960 as the national government became a focal point for policy-making that affected more aspects of American life.

The number of registered lobbyists in Washington, D.C., increased from 3400 in 1975 to 7200 in 1985. But that number is only the tip of the iceberg of interest representation in Washington. While the number of business corporations maintaining offices in Washington increased from 50 in 1961 to 545 in 1982, many more businesses and other groups have hired law firms and professional firms to represent them in Washington. Another indicator of interest representation is the number of lawyers belonging to the District of Columbia Bar Association, whose membership increased from about 11,000 in 1973 to 34,000 in 1981. Estimates of the total number of people engaged in some way in representing interests and lobbying in Washington range from 50,000 to 90,000. Regardless of who you count or how you count them, the traditional occupation of lobbying in Washington has undergone a boom in the late twentieth century.

Types of Interest Groups

Many groups formed to influence policy were based on traditional economic interests, such as business corporations, labor unions, and trade and professional groups. One of the largest interest groups in the country, with 31 million members, is the American Association of Retired Persons (AARP), which is very active in public policy issues that affect the elderly. Its power stems from its large membership, its fiscal resources, and its ability to mobilize members on issues of interest to them.

In addition to groups organized for economic self-interest, there are other groups that claim to have the broader public interest in mind. Some of these are associations of governments with common interests in public policy, especially federalism issues. These organizations include the National League of Cities, the National Association of Counties, the National Governors Association, and the National Conference of State Legislatures.

There are also organizations formed to be advocates for the public interest, such as the Sierra Club, an advocate for environmental issues, or groups that represent consumers. There are advocacy groups for people interested in sports or leisure-time activities as well as groups organized to represent the disadvantaged, the poor, or minorities.

Single-issue interest groups focus narrowly on only one issue and use their resources to support only that cause. Anti-abortion groups fall into this category, as does the National Rifle Association, which has hundreds of paid staffers who oppose any type of law that might control access to guns.

Theories of Interest Groups

Viewed in isolation, the number of lobbyists in Washington can seem alarming. The broader questions, however, are how they affect the policy process and how much power they have. There is an important distinction between political parties and interest groups. Political parties try to form broad coalitions whose goal is to capture control of the government. By definition, interest groups are concerned with a narrow range of policies—those that affect them directly—and thus their claims on public policy are self-limited.

Students of American politics are ambivalent about the role of interest groups in public policy-making. In one sense, interest groups are destructive in that they are advocates for their own interests and thus often in conflict with the general public interest. With many groups intent on influencing policy in their own favor, who will be the advocate for the broader public interest? The opposing point of view is the pluralist school of democracy.

The pluralist approach to understanding the role of interest groups holds that any interest of significance has the ability to form a group to protect that interest in the policy arena. If business interests came to have heavy influence, labor unions would develop their own lobbying efforts. If commercial groups gained power in business regulation, so would farm groups organize to have a say in farm policy. If one sector of the economy was particularly well organized, groups representing other sectors would soon spring up to balance its power. Thus there would be a pluralistic marketplace of group representation that would assure all legitimate interests a chance to influence public policy.

One criticism of this school of thought argued that no groups existed to protect the poor, the disadvantaged, or minority groups. But in recent decades scores of organized interest groups have sprung up to lobby for the poor, the handicapped, women, gays, and other groups not traditionally represented in American politics. The criticism still remains, however, that the power and influence of groups is highly correlated with the amount of money they can devote to lobbying and to the status of their membership. Thus, although most interests can be articulated, some groups are clearly more powerful than others.

Although powerful sectors of the U.S. economy undoubtedly have an important influence on policies that affect them, the pluralist school of thought argues that competing interests tend to balance each other, and the outcome does not undermine the public interest. Reinforcing this benign view of the influence of interest groups are analyses demonstrating that much of the activity of organized interests is spent on information exchange, informing members of Congress about conditions in various sectors of the economy and warning group members when their interests will be affected by legislation under consideration. This activity is seen as facilitating the policy process and aiding governance rather than buying influence.

The Readings

The readings in this section cover a range of issues about interest groups, beginning with Madison's analysis of factions. More contemporary issues are then taken up, from the proliferation of interest groups to contrasting styles of lobbying. Differing perspectives are presented on the effect of lobbying and interest groups on our system of governance, from the reassuring arguments of Robert Salisbury to the disturbing interpretation of Jonathan Rauch.

In *Federalist* No. 10, Madison argues that factions originate in the differences of interests within a society and are thus inevitable. Trying to remove them would destroy the liberty essential to a just republic and would do more harm than good. But the number of groups organized to influence public policy has increased greatly as the size and scope of government have grown.

The explosion in numbers of formal interest groups in Washington is reported in the selection by Robert Salisbury, though he is not alarmed at this development. He argues that, although there are undoubtedly more groups trying to influence policy, the modern economy is so complex that it is not obvious how any given change will affect different economic interests. He argues further that different parts of the same sector of the economy may not have the same economic interests. Thus when health policy is considered, the interests of private doctors may not be the same as those of public hospitals. The interests of publicly financed hospitals may differ from those of for-profit hospitals, and they both may differ from the interests of health maintenance organizations. Salisbury argues that in the contemporary economy most economic interests are so fragmented that they do not pose a major threat to the commonweal.

There is still enough truth, however, in the popular image of the influence-buying lobbyist to make people suspicious of the way influence is wielded in Washington. Even if the broad contours of public policy are carved out by electoral coalitions rather than by lobbying interests, the details of policy are often influenced by those who have enough access and clout to have their special needs represented.

Hedrick Smith analyzes the changing nature of the way the clout of interests groups is wielded in the nation's capital. Washington has always been home to those who make their living by trying to influence the direction of public policy. The classic image of traditional lobbying is the cigar-chomping pol socializing with members of Congress or their Gucci-clad descendants applying pressure and money to grease the legislative machine.

Smith contrasts this traditional style with "new-breed" lobbying in which a client hires a professional firm to orchestrate a "campaign" to affect public policy. The new techniques tend to be "wholesale" in that they often entail the use of sophisticated public relations techniques, such as targeted mailing, to mobilize constituents or those affected by policies to apply pressure to members of Congress. These new techniques are focused much more on broad electoral pressures than are the personal favors and threats of traditional lobbyists.

Jonathan Rauch in his article "Demosclerosis" takes a broader, systemic perspective. While there may be many groups that are interested in only a narrow aspect of public policy, he argues that eventually every significant benefit provided by the government generates a group protective of those benefits. It may take time to establish the group and generate the resources to make it viable, but once it is established, it never goes away, and it will fight fiercely to protect the program that provides the benefits.

The implication is that the cumulation of all these vested interests and their skill in protecting their own piece of the governmental pie leads to a hardening of the arteries of political and economic renewal. Even though the United States is the richest nation on earth, our politics seem to revolve around scarcity. What is scarce is not resources, but the implications of their distribution. With each interest protecting its own benefits, there is little flexibility to make public policy changes. Even in the face of huge deficits and the realization that the long-term viability of the U.S. economy is being damaged by the increasing portion of the federal budget devoted to interest payments, there is not enough political flexibility to cut the deficit significantly.

Taxpayers will not accept the elimination of tax breaks for themselves or a sufficient increase in taxes to eliminate the deficit. Benefit recipients, such as those receiving Social Security or Medicare, will not stand for the scaling back of any of their benefits. This rigidity and the growth in cost of these programs prevent switching new resources into other areas of need, such as caring for the large number of children living in poverty or rebuilding our infrastructure. From Rauch's perspective the cumulative effect of these many interest groups is a real threat to governance because of their effect on the ability of the nation to change.

As in the past, ambivalence toward interest groups and lobbying will continue to produce public controversy. People like Ross Perot will continue to rail against the special interests that prevent the public interest from being achieved. From this perspective the evil lobbyists in expensive suits and Gucci loafers will continue to walk the corridors of power in Washington in their endless quest for special consideration for the rich and powerful. This image will continue to be countered by the many hard-working, public-spirited people supporting good causes in Washington and performing valuable mediating and facilitating services to help our fragmented system of government function. That interest groups are inevitable in our system of governance is clear; the question is how abuses of the system can be regulated without endangering our valued freedoms.

KEY TERMS

demosclerosis: the hardening of the arteries of economic and political renewal by each group's careful protection of the benefits it receives from the government. This leaves the whole system much less flexible and less able to respond to economic and political change.

interest group: a group of people who have a common stake in some aspect of public policy and who take political action, such as lobbying, to protect that stake

lobbyist: a person who represents a group and tries to influence public policy in its favor

pluralism: a theory of government that holds that the U.S. political system is made up of a broad variety of different interests and that each legitimate interest is represented by a group that will protect its political interests

public interest: that which benefits the polity as a whole rather than a narrower, special interest. In any area of public policy there will be sharp disagreement over what policies in fact represent the public interest.

public-interest group: a group that claims to represent interests that are not narrowly defined by economic self-interest, such as associations of governments or consumer advocates

single-issue interest group: a group devoted to only one public policy issue, often ideologically oriented. If their members are numerous and committed, these groups can have a significant effect on the voting of members of Congress in their area of interest.

41

FEDERALIST NO. 10
James Madison

In their attempt to protect the liberties of citizens, the Framers were very sensitive to the dangers presented by groups of people who might combine for their own interest and who might deprive others of their rights. The greatest danger would result from control of the government by a faction of citizens who constituted a majority and thus could use their power to oppress the minority.

The only cure for the evils of faction, according to Madison, is controlling their effects, since eliminating the causes would produce more harm than good. Mitigating the effects of faction can be done first by delegating governing to representatives of the people as in all republics. But the second defense against the negative effects of faction is to "extend the sphere" by increasing the size of the polity. The larger the size the less likely it is that any one faction will amount to a majority of the whole and oppress the rest of the citizenry.

To the People of the State of New York:

Among the numerous advantages promised by a well-constructed Union, none deserves to be more accurately developed than its tendency to break and control the violence of faction. The friend of popular governments never finds himself so much alarmed for their character and fate as when he contemplates their propensity to this dangerous vice. He will not fail, therefore, to set a due value on any plan which, without violating the principles to which he is attached, provides a proper cure for it. The instability, injustice, and confusion introduced into the public councils, have, in truth, been the mortal diseases under which popular governments have everywhere perished; as they continue to be the favorite and fruitful topics from which the adversaries to liberty derive their most specious declamations. The valuable improvements made by the American constitutions on the popular models, both ancient and modern, cannot certainly be too much admired; but it would be an unwarrantable partiality, to contend that they have as effectually obviated the danger on this side, as was wished and expected. Complaints are everywhere heard from our most considerate and virtuous citizens, equally the friends of public and private faith, and of public and personal liberty, that our governments are too unstable, that the public good is disregarded in the conflicts of rival parties, and that measures are too often decided, not according to the rules of justice and rights of the minor party, but by the superior force of an interested and overbearing majority. However anxiously we may wish that these complaints had no foundation, the evidence of known facts will not permit us to deny that they are in some degree true. It will be found, indeed, on a candid review of our situation, that some of the distresses under which we labor have been erroneously charged on the operation of our governments; but it will be found, at the same time, that other causes will not alone account for many of our heaviest misfortunes; and, particularly, for that prevailing and increasing distrust of public engagements, and alarm for private rights, which are echoed from one end of the continent to the other. These must be chiefly, if not wholly, effects of the unsteadiness and injustice with which a factious spirit has tainted our public administrations.

By a faction, I understand a number of citizens, whether amounting to a majority or minority of the whole, who are united and actuated by some common impulse of passion, or of interest, adverse to the rights of other citizens, or to the permanent and aggregate interests of the community.

There are two methods of curing the mischiefs of faction: the one, by removing its causes; the other, by controlling its effects.

There are again two methods of removing the causes of faction: the one, by destroying the liberty which is essential to its existence; the other, by giving to every citizen the same opinions, the same passions, and the same interests.

It could never be more truly said than of the first remedy, that it was worse than the disease. Liberty is to faction what air is to fire, an ailment without which it instantly expires. But it could not be less folly to abolish liberty, which is essential to political life, because it nourishes faction, than it would be to wish the annihilation of air, which is essential to animal life, because it imparts to fire its destructive agency.

The second expedient is as impracticable as the first would be unwise. As long as the reason of man continues fallible, and he is at liberty to exercise it, different opinions will be formed. As long as the connection subsists between his reason and his self love, his opinions and his passions will have a reciprocal influence on each other; and the former will be objects to which the latter will attach themselves. The diversity in the faculties of men, from which the rights of property originate, is not less an insuperable obstacle to a uniformity of interests. The protection of these faculties is the first object of government. From the protection of different and unequal faculties of acquiring property, the possession of different degrees and kinds of property immediately results; and from the influence of these on the sentiments and views of the respective proprietors, ensues a division of the society into different interests and parties.

The latent causes of faction are thus sown in the nature of man; and we see them everywhere brought into different degrees of activity, according to the different circumstances of civil society. A zeal for different opinions concerning religion, concerning government, and many other points, as well of speculation as of practice; an attachment of different leaders ambitiously contending for pre-eminence and power; or to persons of other descriptions whose fortunes have been interesting to the human passions, have, in turn, divided mankind into parties, inflamed them with mutual animosity, and rendered them much more disposed to vex and oppress each other than to co-operate for the common good. So strong is this propensity of mankind to fall into mutual animosities, that where no substantial occasion presents itself, the most frivolous and fanciful distinctions have been sufficient to kindle their unfriendly passions and excite their most violent conflicts. But the most common and durable source of factions has been the various and unequal distribution of property. Those who hold and those who are without property have ever formed distinct interests in society. Those who are creditors, and those who are debtors, fall under a like discrimination. A landed interest, a manufacturing interest, a mercantile interest, a moneyed interest, with many lesser interests, grow up of necessity in civilized nations, and divide them into different classes, actuated by different sentiments and views. The regulation of these various and interfering interests forms the principal task of modern legislation, and involves the spirit of party and faction in the necessary and ordinary operations of the government.

No man is allowed to be a judge in his own cause, because his interest would certainly bias his judgment, and, not improbably, corrupt his integrity. With equal, nay, with greater reason, a body of men are unfit to be both judges and parties at the same time; yet what are many of the most important acts of legislation but so many judicial determinations, not indeed concerning the rights of single persons, but concerning the rights of large bodies of citizens? And what are the different classes of legislators but advocates and parties to the causes which they determine? Is a law proposed concerning private debts? It is a question to which the creditors are parties on one side and the debtors on the other. Justice ought to hold the balance between them. Yet the parties are, and must be, themselves the judges; and the most numerous party, or, in other words, the most powerful faction must be expected to prevail. Shall domestic manufactures be encouraged, and in what degree, by restrictions on foreign manufactures? are questions which would be differently decided by the landed and the manufacturing classes, and probably by neither with a sole regard to justice and the public good. The apportionment of taxes on the various descriptions of property is an act which seems to require the most exact impartiality; yet there is, perhaps, no legislative act in which greater opportunity and temptation are given to a predominant party to trample on the rules of justice. Every shilling with which they overburden the inferior number is a shilling saved to their own pockets.

It is vain to say that enlightened statesmen will be able to adjust these clashing interests, and render them all subservient to the public good. Enlightened statesmen will not always be at the helm. Nor, in many cases, can such an adjustment be made at all without taking into view indirect and remote considerations, which will rarely prevail over the immediate interest which one party may find in disregarding the rights of another or the good of the whole.

The inference to which we are brought is, that the *causes* of faction cannot be removed, and that relief is only to be sought in the means of controlling its *effects*.

If a faction consists of less than a majority, relief is supplied by the republican principle, which enables the majority to defeat its sinister views by regular vote. It may clog the administration, it may convulse the society; but it will be unable to execute and mask its violence under the forms of the Constitution. When a majority is included in a faction, the form of popular government, on the other hand, enables it to sacrifice to its ruling passion or interest both the public good and the rights of other citizens. To secure the public good and private rights against the danger of such a faction, and at the same time to preserve the spirit and the form of popular government, is then the great object to which our inquiries are directed. Let me add that it is the great desideratum by which this form of government can be rescued from the opprobrium under which it has so long labored, and be recommended to the esteem and adoption of mankind.

By what means is this object attainable? Evidently by one of two only. Either the existence of the same passion or interest in a majority at the same time must be prevented, or the majority, having such co-existent passion or interest, must be rendered, by their number and local situation, unable to concert and carry into effect schemes of oppression. If the impulse and the opportunity be suffered to coincide, we well know that neither moral nor religious motives can be relied on as an adequate control. They are not found to be such on the injustice and violence of individuals, and lose their efficacy in proportion to the number combined together, that is, in proportion as their efficacy becomes needful.

From this view of the subject it may be concluded that a pure democracy, by which I mean a society consisting of a small number of citizens, who assemble and administer the government in person, can admit of no cure for the mischiefs of faction. A common passion or interest will, in almost every case, be felt by a majority of the whole; a communication and concert result from the form of government itself; and there is nothing to check the inducements to sacrifice the weaker party or an obnoxious individual. Hence it is that such democracies have ever been spectacles of turbulence and contention; have ever been found incompatible with personal security or the rights of property; and have in general been as short in their lives as they have been violent in their deaths. Theoretic politicians, who have patronized this species of government, have erroneously supposed that by reducing mankind to a perfect equality in their political rights, they would, at the same time, be perfectly equalized and assimilated in their possessions, their opinions, and their passions.

A republic, by which I mean a government in which the scheme of representation takes place, opens a different prospect, and promises the cure for which we are seeking. Let us examine the points in which it varies from pure democracy, and we shall comprehend both the nature of the cure and the efficacy which it must derive from the Union.

The two great points of difference between a democracy and a republic are: first, the delegation of the government, in the latter, to a small number of citizens elected by the rest; secondly, the greater number of citizens, and greater sphere of country, over which the latter may be extended.

The effect of the first difference is, on the one hand, to refine and enlarge the public views, by passing them through the medium of a chosen body of citizens, whose wisdom may best discern the true interest of their country, and whose patriotism and love of justice will be least likely to sacrifice it to temporary or partial considerations. Under such a regulation, it may well happen that the public voice, pronounced by the representatives of the people, will be more consonant to the public good than if pronounced by the people themselves, convened for the purpose. On the other hand, the effect may be inverted. Men of factious tempers, of local prejudices, or of sinister designs, may, by intrigue, by corruption, or by other means, first obtain the suffrages, and then betray the interests, of the people. The question resulting is, whether small or extensive republics are more favorable to the election of proper guardians of the public weal; and it is clearly decided in favor of the latter by two obvious considerations:

In the first place, it is to be remarked that, however small the republic may be, the representatives must be raised to a certain number, in order to guard against the cabals of a few; and that, however large it may be, they must be limited to a certain number, in order to guard against the confusion of a multitude. Hence the number of representatives in the two cases not being in proportion to that of the two constituents, and being proportionally greater in the small republic, it follows that, if the proportion of fit characters be not less in the large than in the small republic, the former will present a greater option, and consequently a greater probability of a fit choice.

In the next place, as each representative will be chosen by a greater number of citizens in the large than in the small republic, it will be more difficult for unworthy candidates to practice with success the vicious arts by which elections are too often carried; and the suffrages of the people being more free, will be more likely to center in men who possess the most attractive merit and the most diffusive and established character.

It must be confessed that in this, as in most other cases, there is a mean, on both sides of which inconveniences will be found to lie. By enlarging too much the number of electors, you render the representative too little acquainted with all their local circumstances and lesser interests; as by reducing it too much, you render him unduly attached to these, and too little fit to comprehend and pursue great and national objects. The federal Constitution forms a happy combination in this respect; the great and aggregate interests being referred to the national, the local and particular to the State legislatures.

The other point of difference is, the greater number of citizens and extent of territory which may be brought within the compass of republican than of democratic government; and it is this circumstance principally which renders factious combinations less to be dreaded in the former than in the latter. The smaller the society, the fewer probably will be the distinct parties and interests composing it; the fewer the distinct parties and interests, the more frequently will a majority be found of the same party; and the smaller the number of individuals composing a majority, and the smaller the compass within which they are placed, the more easily will they concert and execute their plans of oppression. Extend the sphere, and you take in a greater variety of parties and interests; you make it less probable that a majority of the whole will have a common motive to invade the rights of other citizens; or if such a common motive exists, it will be more difficult for all who feel it to discover their own strength, and to act in unison with each other. Besides other impediments, it may be remarked that, where there is a consciousness of unjust or dishonorable purposes, communication is always checked by distrust in proportion to the number whose concurrence is necessary.

Hence, it clearly appears, that the same advantage which a republic has over a democracy, in controlling the effects of faction, is enjoyed by a large over a small republic—is enjoyed by the Union over the States composing it. Does the advantage consist in the substitution of representatives whose enlightened views and virtuous sentiments render them superior to local prejudices and to schemes of injustice? It will not be denied that the representation of the Union will be most likely to possess these requisite endowments. Does it consist in the greater security afforded by a greater variety of parties, against the event of any one party being able to outnumber and oppress the rest? In an equal degree does the increased variety of parties comprised within the Union increase this security? Does it, in fine, consist in the greater obstacles opposed to the concert and accomplishment of the secret wishes of an unjust and interested majority? Here, again, the extent of the Union gives it the most palpable advantage.

The influence of factious leaders may kindle a flame within their particular States, but will be unable to spread a general conflagration through the other States. A religious sect may degenerate into a political faction in a part of the Confederacy; but the variety of sects dispersed over the entire face of it must secure the national councils against any danger from that source. A rage for paper money, for an abolition of debts, for an equal division of property, or for any other improper or wicked project, will be less apt to pervade the whole body of the Union than a particular member of it; in the same proportion as such a malady is more likely to taint a particular county or district, than an entire State.

In the extent and proper structure of the Union, therefore, we behold a republican remedy for the diseases most incident to republican government.

And according to the degree of pleasure and pride we feel in being republicans, ought to be our zeal in cherishing the spirit and supporting the character of Federalists.

Publius.

POINTS TO PONDER

1. Why were the Framers suspicious of factions?
2. According to Madison, how can a government avoid the evils of faction?
3. Is there any difference between a faction and a political party?
4. Is there any difference between a faction and an interest group?

42

"THE PARADOX OF
INTEREST GROUPS IN WASHINGTON—
MORE GROUPS, LESS CLOUT"
Robert H. Salisbury

All analysts agree that the number of lobbyists and firms that specialize in representing interests in Washington has grown greatly over the past several decades. It would seem to follow that their power has also increased. Certainly this is our image of highly paid lobbyists trying to influence a legislative outcome.

But in his chapter from Anthony King's The New American Political System *(1990), political scientist Robert Salisbury of Washington University in St. Louis challenges this common-sense approach by arguing that the policy context has changed considerably over the years. As government activity in the economy has grown, the consequences of specific policies for large sectors of the economy have become more complex. Thus the impact of any one group may not be obvious, and there is no single interest for different groups within an industry; economic interests have become fragmented. Thus the clout of interest groups has become fragmented—they often spend more time monitoring how public policy changes may affect their interests than trying to influence outcomes.*

One of the most startling events in the history of public policy in the United States was the Tax Reform Act of 1986. It was startling not so much because of its content or its possible impact as, first, because it happened at all, contrary to the forecasts of all knowledgeable observers and, second, because it was fashioned and passed while virtual armies of lobbyists looked on in distress and frustration, unable to intervene to affect the outcome. The "Battle of

Gucci Gulch" was fought by members of Congress, mindful, to be sure, of the needs and concerns of organized interests but operating in a context shaped mainly by broader policy, partisan, and institutional considerations. It seemed a heavy irony indeed that, just when the number and variety of organized interests represented in Washington were at an all-time high—with unprecedented numbers of lobbyists using high personal skill supplemented by elaborate modern technologies of analysis, communication, and mobilization —and in a policy area, taxation, that had acquired many of its bizarre existing contours from the pressures and demands of narrowly based interest groups, the ultimate decision process should largely screen out those interests.

This paradox of more interest groups and lobbyists wielding less influence over policy results does not manifest itself all the time, to be sure. The paradox, however, is substantially valid, if not in quite this stark form, then at least in more nuanced forms. In this chapter I argue the case that the growth in the number, variety, and sophistication of interest groups represented in Washington has been associated with, and in some measure has helped to bring about, a transformation in the way much public policy is made and, further, that this transformed process is not dominated so often by a relatively small number of powerful interest groups as it may once have been. I certainly do not want to be understood as saying that interest groups as a whole have weakened in the way, say, that party organizations have lost control over the nomination of candidates. Nor would I deny that in particular instances the old ways are still intact—the "veterans' system" comes to mind—with triangular symbioses linking groups, congressional committees, and executive agencies in nearly impregnable policy success. Moreover, policies such as social security may be quite rigid and largely beyond amendment, not so much because of organized group pressure as such as from the fear among policy makers that such pressure is potentially mobilizable and would soon follow any adverse policy revision. Still, I contend that a great many interest group representatives seek information more than influence, that in many ways they have become dependent on and are sometimes exploited by government officials rather than the other way around, and that much of what contemporary lobbyists do is to be understood as a search for order and a measure of predictability in a policy-making world that has been fundamentally destabilized by developments of the past twenty years.

Changes since 1960

The Explosion in Numbers.

The number of organizations directly engaged in pursuing their interests in Washington, D.C., has grown dramatically since about 1960. We have no reliable base line of observation, but the following items suggest the magnitude of expansion in the interest group universe.

- The number of registered lobbyists increased from 3,400 in 1975 to 7,200 in 1985.
- The annual publication *Washington Representatives* managed to find and list more than 5,000 people in 1979; by 1988 it listed nearly 11,000.
- The proportion of U.S. trade and professional associations headquartered in and around Washington grew from 19 percent in 1971 to 30 percent in 1982.
- The number of lawyers belonging to the District of Columbia Bar Association (a requirement for practice in Washington) increased from 10,925 in 1973 to 34,087 in 1981.
- The number of business corporations operating offices in Washington increased from 50 in 1961 to 545 in 1982.
- Some 76 percent of the citizens' groups and 79 percent of the welfare groups in Washington in 1981 had come into existence since 1960.

* * * *

The Fragmentation of Interest Sectors

In the "old days"—the 1950s, say—it was characteristic of many policy sectors for a few organizations, sometimes only one, to have hegemony. The American Medical Association (AMA) dominated health policy, the American Farm Bureau Federation (AFBF) was far and away the most influential group on agricultural matters, the American Petroleum Institute led the list of energy interests, and so on. In the late 1980s these are still substantial organizations, actively involved in making policy pronouncements and using the tactics of influence, but in most policy domains such quasi-monopoly power has been undermined by a process of interest fragmentation that has greatly changed the distribution of influence.

This fragmentation process has two distinct components. First, the self-interested groups have increased in number, variety, and specificity of policy concerns. In agriculture the National Farmers Union gained a position as liberal Democratic rival to the conservative Republican AFBF, only to be challenged on specific issues by the National Wheat Growers Association, the Soy Bean Association, the Corn Growers Association, and dozens of commodity-based trade associations. Some, like the National Milk Producers Federation, had been around for decades but as relatively peripheral players. Others, like the corn growers, were newly organized, drawing on more self-conscious and, because of changes in farming technology, more differentiated groups of producers. But not just producers. Many of the groups now active in agricultural issues include corporations engaged in other stages of the chain linking the farmer to the consumer. The Grocery Manufacturers Association is one example, but there are scores of others in which farmers play little or no role. Commodity organizations and trade associations have been joined by numerous individual corporations, including giant agribusiness firms like Cargill or Archer-Daniels-Midland and firms like Coca-Cola or Pizza Hut, concerned about the prices they must pay for commodities they use.

In the mid-1980s William P. Browne identified well over 200 interests involved in shaping farm legislation. With this massive expansion of private interest group participants, it has been necessary since at least the late 1950s to construct quite elaborate coalitions of these groups to get the support necessary to enact major farm legislation. In agriculture the farm bills still take broad multipurpose form and are enacted for terms of three to five years, after which there is another round of negotiation. The complexity of these negotiations defies quick summary, but it is clear that the peak associations no longer guide the process.

A similar story can be told of the health policy domain. There no single legislative enactment brings into focus the full extent of interest fragmentation, although efforts to achieve national health insurance and sometimes medical cost containment issues have come close. Issues concerning hospital construction, medical research, veterans' health care, and drug regulation, however, have long been treated separately. Whatever the question, the AMA, once so imperiously powerful, is no longer the dominant voice even of organized medicine. The hospital associations now speak with quite independent voices. So do many organizations of medical specialists. Medical insurance interests, medical schools, corporations engaged in medical technology research and manufacturing, and of course the drug companies all get involved. Again, complex coalitions among diverse interests are necessary to enact legislation and secure its continued funding.

* * * *

Uncertain Structures of Power

The destabilization argument I have been developing affects the pattern of policy outcomes at two levels. In the formulation of legislation and the implementing of regulations it means that it is no longer accurate to account for outcomes by reference to the familiar metaphor of iron or cozy triangles wherein interest groups, congressional committees or subcommittees, and executive agencies operate in symbiotic interdependence. For some time, indeed, attentive observers have doubted the validity of the triangle interpretation. Charles O. Jones suggested that "sloppy hexagon" might come closer to expressing the shape of the policy subsystem. Hugh Heclo abandoned geometric tropes entirely in favor of the notion of "issue network." The quest for a suitably evocative phrase will no doubt continue, but it will be difficult indeed to capture in simple terms the shifting, almost kaleidoscopic configurations of groups involved in trying to shape policy.

At a more highly aggregated level, destabilization challenges the value of what for two decades has been the dominant conception of most U.S. policy, interest group liberalism. Theodore Lowi's view, embraced in at least substantial part by most observers, was that in the United States, since the 1930s at least, the major thrusts of policy decision reflected the demands of particularistic groups, opposed weakly if at all by competitors and enacted without much reference to standards of judgment drawn from outside the interest-dominated arenas of politics. In a destabilized world of fragmented interests and multidimensional challenges from externality groups it becomes impossible for policy makers to identify which interests, if any, they can succumb to without grave political risk. They find themselves with choice and discretion, able to select policy alternatives and take positions knowing that almost any position will have some group support and none can prevent opposition from arising. We can easily carry this interpretation too far, denying all policy effect to organized groups, and this would be quite unwarranted. Nevertheless, as was illustrated by the Gucci Gulch example I began with, the presumption has been significantly altered: where interest groups were seen as the prime motive force pressing politicians to make policy decisions in their favor, now the officials very often exploit the groups.

This partial reversal in the flow of influence is not simply a product of the expansion in size and fragmentation in purpose of interest sectors. It is also closely linked with changes in the institutional configurations of Congress and the executive branch. I need not detail these developments here but merely identify those that have especially affected the position and practice of interest group politics.

First has been the diffusion of power in Congress. The weakening of seniority, the empowering of subcommittees, and the expansion of congressional staffs have all contributed to the result that many members are in a position to participate actively and meaningfully on a much larger number of issues than once was possible. Specialization is not so much required to gain substantive expertise—and not so much deferred to by others in any case. On any particular set of policy concerns there are multiple points of potentially relevant access as groups seek support in the Congress, but the depressing corollary for the groups is that none of them is likely to carry decisive weight in shaping policy. Indeed, the position-taking and credit-claiming competition among these many focal points may well mean that ultimately no action is possible in any direction.

Diffusion of power within Congress has been accompanied by the widely remarked increase in the electoral success of incumbents. Incumbents' electoral safety further undermines dependence on interest groups. As John Mark Hansen has shown with reference to the growth of interest triangles in agriculture, the influence of farm groups developed in the late 1920s as members of Congress gradually learned that farm issues were a perennial part of the legislative agenda and farm organizations were therefore continually active and more reliable sources of electoral support than the political parties. Farm belt Republicans therefore defected from their party and forged independent, mutually supportive links with the farm groups. But what was learned can be unlearned. As members of Congress today find themselves increasingly secure beneficiaries of pork, casework, and name recognition, they learn that they can afford to stand aloof from many interest groups. There are important exceptions, but my argument is that in the Congress of the late 1980s interest groups are virtually awash in access but often subordinate in influence.

In the executive branch the most significant development affecting established interest triangles has been the centralization of policy initiatives within the Executive Office of the President and particularly the White House staff. Interest group access in the past has been greatest and most productive with line agencies and independent commissions. The White House is a much more difficult target for lobbyists to reach, and even though White House decisions will necessarily favor some interests over others, it will rarely be, in any direct sense, because of the groups' skill or power. The groups report regular contact with the White House only about one-third as often as with the leaders of their most significant cabinet departments; this reflects a difference in accessibility, not power. The groups go where they can; but ever since Franklin D. Roosevelt executive authority has been brought more and more fully within the White House orbit, and most organized interests have been disadvantaged accordingly.

* * * *

The inside strategic options for interest groups have crystallized in recent years as the principal means of action have become more clearly differentiated and better documented. I will look in some detail at several of these options as they have been used by business corporations. Since some of the data reported are nearly ten years old and corporate organization has been extremely volatile in many respects, changes have surely taken place in the use of these strategies. Nevertheless, these data allow us to examine systematically not only the frequency with which business firms employ one method or another but the factors that help explain their strategic selections.

A time-honored method of securing representation in Washington is to hire an agent. Washington has no shortage of people with formal credentials as lawyers, public relations advisers, or consultants with substantive policy expertise to whom groups can turn for assistance. Indeed, the supply of independent lobbying agents has increased massively in recent years. Nearly every really large manufacturing firm engages at least one such agent (98 percent of the leading 100 firms in sales volume do so), and organizations that can afford to often employ ten or a dozen for various purposes. Nevertheless, only about one-fifth of the interest representatives examined by Nelson and his colleagues were independent agents, and many of these are used for specialized tasks—

litigation, for example—that are on the periphery of the interest group's policy agenda.

Despite the very sizable hourly rates charged by many Washington representatives, it is generally cheaper for a group to employ them ad hoc than to staff a Washington office all year round. The rapid growth of corporate offices in Washington therefore signifies a major increase in the investment that firms have found it useful to make in the tasks of policy representation. To be sure, some companies, often under pressure from Wall Street, have decided that a permanent D.C. establishment is too expensive and have closed down, but especially among the larger firms the proportion with Washington offices remains very substantial.

* * * *

The most striking change, however, in cooperative interest representation strategy reflects the inherent limitation of nearly every trade or professional association. More and better coalitions are required by the complexity of effects of federal policy on the institutions of society. Not all widget-making corporations or banks or universities will be affected in the same way by what the government does. Peer-reviewed research grants from the National Science Foundation are greatly admired by large research universities but are not much help to the colleges; the leading dozen or so private universities have somewhat different concerns from the public institutions, and so on. Some of these differences are reflected in different voluntary associations, of course; the Association of American Universities (AAU) is distinct from both the National Association of State Universities and Land Grant Colleges and the National Association of Independent Colleges and Universities. In addition, however, several smaller working groups of university lobbyists exchange information and try to orchestrate their actions for maximum, highly targeted effect. . . .

Are big firms more actively represented simply because they can afford it, or are other factors involved? A number of possibilities come to mind. Craig Humphries finds that the extent of government regulation of a firm's industry strongly affects whether the firm establishes itself in Washington. Among regulated industries, those that are more concentrated (that is, with a smaller number of firms) are more actively represented. So also are firms with more diversified product lines. The threat of imports has some effect, but the degree of unionization is not very important, at least not for the entire array of 1,000 firms. Having government contracts is associated with establishing a Washington office but not with the hiring of an independent agent or the creation of a PAC.

A significant relationship exists among those three strategic forms. That is, if a firm has a Washington office or uses independent agents, it is likely also to create a PAC. Using agents is strongly related to establishing a D.C. office. The forms of action go together, reinforcing one another and to some extent creating the necessity for one another. A company needs a Washington office in part to supervise its agents and direct its PAC's selection of the candidates it will favor. But the office can seldom cover all the politically relevant bases it can identify; hence the agents. And without a PAC to finance attendance at fund raisers, a corporate presence in Washington may be dismissed by officials as worthless. This interdependence among strategic forms of action leads to the recognition that interest group representation is a dynamic phenomenon, driven not only by the "objective" needs of rational actors affected by what the government does to them or for them but also by the internal logic of the association or the institution. It also points up the importance of examining such highly publicized matters as PACs in the context of other forms of interest group action.

* * * *

In the electoral process generally, the PAC phenomenon, so often denounced in the media and by reformers everywhere, has seemed to move from one tack to another with little assurance of where, if anywhere, a stable equilibrium may be found. Labor had long employed PACs, of course. Ever since the creation of the CIO-PAC in 1943 unions had used this device to assemble campaign funds and had increasingly dispensed them almost entirely to Democrats. After the 1971–1974 changes in the law unambiguously legitimated PACs for all interests, the rapid expansion of corporate, trade association, and unaffiliated (mostly politically conservative) committees seemed likely for a time to overwhelm labor's efforts, giving most of their money to Republicans. Especially in 1978 and 1980 Republican candidates, including challengers as well as incumbents, benefited enormously from PAC assistance. Great dangers to balanced electoral competition were prophesied, and proposals for public funding of congressional elections, usually advanced by Democrats, were accordingly dismissed out of hand by Republicans. Since then, however, the balance has shifted. Unaffiliated PACs continue to back conservative candidates, but their funding has not kept pace, and their influence has therefore provoked fewer anxieties. Business PACs meanwhile have redirected their contributions quite sharply in favor of incumbents. Inasmuch as a solid majority of the House and, since 1986, of the Senate are Democrats, they have been the beneficiaries. The pragmatism that has guided PAC contributions by business interests to congressional candidates is in sharp contrast to the ideological fervor displayed by interests active in presidential campaigns. PAC pragmatism is an important indictor of the power of incumbent congressmen—interest groups that depend on them for help on narrow but vital issues give them campaign support, regardless of the broader policy orientation that the incumbent members display.

Away from the electoral process, a broad array of activities may be undertaken by Washington-based lobbyists. The usual characterization of lobbying has emphasized the tasks of making formal and informal contacts with officials and presenting them with information and argument. Schlozman and Tierney found that virtually every group did these things and did them more now than before. Other research shows, however, that this direct lobbying is not the most time-consuming or often the most important concern. Thirty years ago Lester Milbrath found that lobbyists spent a large part of their working time in their own offices, not on Capitol Hill or elsewhere, making contact with officials. This remains true today. The tasks that are both the most time consuming and the most important are concerned not so much with persuading government officials to act one way or another as with keeping track of what is happening in the policy process, alerting the client organizations to developments relevant to their interests, and developing appropriate strategies of response or adaptation. Advocacy of one's cause continues to require attention, of course, and the ways and means of gaining influence over outcomes are in no sense ignored. Schlozman and Tierney are quite right in saying that groups do more of everything than they did two or three decades ago. Even litigation, one of the less highly valued modes of action, is reported to have been undertaken by nearly two-thirds of the interest organizations surveyed by Heinz and others. Nevertheless, there appears to have been a significant shift in the balance among the lobbyists' tasks, and that shift is closely related to the broad movement of groups toward a full-time presence in Washington.

Recall a "classic" model of lobbying. A group sends a representative to Washington to press its case for or against some policy option, or it hires one of the many would-be agents already located in the nation's capital, waiting like defense lawyers in the courthouse corridors for a paying client to come into view. The presumption in this model is that the group knows what its policy interest is. If the group is big enough to have great voting strength, it may expect to gain its ends through the electoral process. If it is small and its needs are limited, it may need only to add lobbying expertise to secure the desired result. Many of these group concerns, richly illustrated in the case study literature, have been ad hoc and discontinuous, adequately served by a single lobbying campaign. Others require continuing attention but may still be very stable with respect to the policy interests sought. Thus for many years the big oil companies maintained a firm lobbying commitment to the depletion allowance, home builders have never wavered in their defense of deducting interest on home mortgages, and veterans' groups have kept up the pressure to maintain Veterans Administration hospitals.

The great expansion in the scope of federal programs since World War II, however, has meant that many more elements of the society are far more extensively affected by what the government does and must, in their own interests, become more involved in trying to optimize those effects. This sea change has been accompanied by two other changes of great importance. One is essentially intellectual: we acknowledge far more fully than we once did that there are profound interdependencies and interaction effects such that any policy decision is likely to be seen as having a major effect not just on its primary target population but on diverse other areas of life. The second is that these external concerns have been the basis of substantial group formation and political action. In consequence, a widespread destabilization of many of the old influence relationships has occurred. But there has been another level of destabilization. In today's world of complex, interdependent interests and policies, it is often quite unclear what the "true interests" of a group or an institution may be. The policy that will be maximally advantageous to an association often cannot even be framed without prolonged and searching analysis involving extensive discussion among those who are knowledgeable about both the technical substance of the issue and the feasibilities of the relevant political situation.

Uncertainty concerning the substance of group interests, as well as about how best to achieve them, forces those we call lobbyists to shift much of their energy away from lobbying, that is, away from advocating policies and influencing government officials. Before they can advocate a policy, they must determine what position they wish to embrace. Before they do this, they must find out not only what technical policy analysis can tell them but what relevant others, inside government and outside, are thinking and planning. Often, indeed, a group may not even know that it has a policy interest requiring attention until it discovers the plans of an agency to propose new regulations or of a congressional subcommittee to hold hearings on a subject. Information, timely and accurate, is absolutely vital to the lobbyist.

This point is nicely captured in the opening paragraph of Edward Laumann and David Knoke's analysis of the organizational networks involved in energy and health policies:

> The executive director of a major petroleum-industry trade association was leafing through the Federal Register, his daily ritual of scanning the Washington scene. Buried in the fine print was an apparently innocuous announcement by the Federal Aviation Administration of its intent to promulgate new regulations that would require detailed flight plans to be filed by pilots of noncommercial aircraft. Recently, several planes had gone down, and search and rescue efforts had been hampered by lack of information on the pilots' intended routes. The trade association director muttered, "We've got a problem," and spent a frantic morning on the phone alerting his group's membership to apply pressure on the FAA to set aside the regulation. The executive realized that once detailed flight plans were on record with the FAA, the open-disclosure provisions of the Freedom of Information Act would allow anyone to learn where his member companies' planes were flying on their aerial explorations for oil, gas, and minerals. The alert director's quick mobilization of collective response saved the corporations potentially millions of dollars worth of secret data that might have fallen into the laps of their competitors.

Laumann and Knoke treat information as a resource of central importance in the policy process and, as I do, see policy interests as "continuously constructed" social phenomena. Their emphasis is on the conversion of information resources into influence over policy outcomes, however, and while it would be extremely foolish to ignore this element, it is important also to recognize that information may often be necessary to adjust one's own behavior sensibly. A corporation that knows the intentions of the Federal Aviation Administration may decide to change its own policies rather than try to persuade the agency to change.

The point of my argument is that the descent on Washington of so many hundreds of associations, institutions, and their agents does not mean that these private interests have acquired greater sway or even a more articulate voice in the shaping of national policy. In many ways the opposite is true. Washington is, after all, the main source of information about what government officials are doing or planning to do. To get that information in a timely way, a continuous and alert presence in the capital is vital. Moreover, in this quest for information the interest representatives are very often in a position of profound dependence. They need access to officials not so much to apply pressure or even to advocate policy as to be told when something important to them is about to happen.

Specialized newsletters are often helpful in this situation, and these expensive aids have multiplied in recent years. Coalitions and trade associations are, among other things, means of enhancing the exchange of information, although trade associations must be careful not to circulate more data about members' intentions than the antitrust laws permit. Withal, the centrality of the need for information and its use by interests groups to help define interests and policy preferences, structure the workday, and adapt organizational behavior to emerging political conditions are clearly reflected in the findings of Heinz and others regarding how lobbyists spend their time. . . . Formal interaction with government ranks well below more informal contacts. Information exchanges claim a higher priority than position taking, and intraorganizational efforts along with monitoring of the political environment are of central importance.

One further consequence of the lobbyists' overriding need to know is that in their contacts with government officials they display considerably less specialization than might have been expected. Rather than focusing on a particular committee or administrative agency, interest representatives report making regular contacts with an average of four or five government units. More often than not these contacts are in both the executive and the legislative branches and include both Republicans and Democrats. Their dependence on information requires the interest representatives to go wherever they can learn something useful. This may well mean that watchful attendance at hearings and markup sessions is more the modal lobbying task than position taking or policy advocacy in any form.

Conclusion

I come back to the apparent paradox with which I began, to the Tax Reform Act of 1986 in which the members of Congress made the choices, excluding the scores of interest group representatives from the process and forcing them to wait outside until it was over. The interpretation I have offered suggests that, rather than being a paradox, this situation simply registered important changes that have been taking place. Many of the old symbioses have given way, destabilized as a result of expanded group participation, of greater electoral security, increased staff, and lessened need or inclination to specialize on the part of Congress, and of more centralized control of the executive branch, which leaves the specialized agencies less able to create their own triangular policy deals.

The uncertainty generated by this political destabilization is compounded by the problematic nature of policy interests. Organizations are often unsure which among the live policy options might be most to their advantage; indeed, they are often in doubt about what the options are. They are engaged in a never-ending process of learning, assessment, and calculation; and timely information, much of it available only from government, is the sine qua non of this process. It would be too much to claim that interest group lobbyists have been wholly subordinated to public officials, but we would surely misread the American political process if we ignored the extent to which these groups have come to Washington out of need and dependence rather than because they have influence.

POINTS TO PONDER

1. Why has the number of groups with representatives in Washington increased so markedly in recent decades?
2. Why is Salisbury not alarmed at the significantly increased number of lobbyists and lobbying groups in Washington?
3. What are the primary activities of most groups that represent interests in Washington?

43

"OLD-BREED LOBBYING
AND NEW-BREED LOBBYING"

Hedrick Smith

According to journalist Hedrick Smith, "old-breed" lobbying thrives on the personal relationships of lobbyists with the movers and shakers in Washington. It is retail lobbying in the sense that it is conducted person to person, often over a minor provision of an important piece of legislation that will make a big difference to the client. In this selection from his book, The Power Game *(1988), Smith illustrates this style of lobbying and contrasts it with "new style" lobbying, which relies on public relations techniques aimed at the constituencies of members of Congress.*

In the abstract, lobbying kindles an image of wickedness only barely less disreputable than the skullduggery of the Mafia. It conjures up Upton Sinclair's exposés of the beef and sugar trusts or Thomas Nast's oils of robber barons closeted in back rooms, their corpulent figures framed in thick black strokes against a backdrop in red. It has the illicit aroma of cigar smoke, booze, and money delivered in brown envelopes. Or it smacks of big labor muscling congressional minions. But that is a caricature, for lobbying has changed immensely with the rise of mass citizen protests in the 1960s over civil rights and the Vietnam War. It changed further with the breakup of the old power baronies, the arrival of new-breed politicians, and the intrusion of campaign techniques.

Of course, plenty of lobbyists still practice old-fashioned lobbying. At heart, the old-breed game is inside politics. That is why so many lobbyists are former members of Congress, former White House officials, former legislative staff aides, former cabinet officers. Their game thrives on the clubbiness of the old-boy network. It turns on the camaraderie of personal friendships, on expertise born of experience. It taps old loyalties and well-practiced access. It draws on the common bond of old battles and the certain knowledge that you may lose on this year's tax bill, but you'll be back to revise it next year, and that yesterday's foe may be tomorrow's ally. It depends on relationships for the long haul.

The superlobbyists of the old-breed game are people such as Clark Clifford, a courtly, genteel former White House counsel to Harry Truman and secretary of Defense to Lyndon Johnson; Robert Strauss, the wisecracking former Democratic party chairman and Mr. Everything for Jimmy Carter; and Howard Baker, between stints as Senate majority leader and White House chief of staff. Close behind are Tommy Boggs, the able, likable, paunchy son of Representative Lindy Boggs and the late House Democratic Majority Leader Hale Boggs; Charls Walker, an astute, drawling Texas-born tax attorney with high Treasury experience in the Nixon years; and Robert Gray, secretary to the Eisenhower cabinet, who got to know the Reagans in California. These inside fixers cannot do what was possible a generation ago. Yet in a game where access and reputation are the coin of the marketplace, king rainmakers still have influence.

For the essence of the old-breed game is *retail* lobbying: the one-on-one pitch. It is Bob Strauss's note to Treasury Secretary Jim Baker to help a friend seek appointment to the World Bank. It is Howard Baker's contact with an old Senate colleague to see that some client gets a break on the "transition rules" of a tax bill. It is Bob Gray's phone call to the White House to ask the president to address some convention or to wrangle an invitation to a state dinner for an industrial big shot. It is breakfast with a committee staff director who is drafting intricate legislation. It is little favors such as tickets to a Washington Redskins football game or helping Ed Meese's wife get a job. It is knowing which buttons to push.

"The best lobbyists' work is basically just socializing," former Speaker O'Neill's spokesman, Chris Matthews, advised me. "They know members of Congress are here three nights a week, alone, without their families. So they say, 'Let's have dinner. Let's go see a ballgame.' Shmooze with them. Make friends. And they don't lean on it all the time. Every once in a while, they call up—maybe once or twice a year—ask a few questions. Call you up and say, 'Say, what's Danny going to do on this tax-reform bill?' Anne Wexler [a former Carter White House official, now a lobbyist] will call up and spend half an hour talking about left-wing politics, and suddenly she'll pop a question, pick up something. They want that little bit of access. That's what does it. You can hear it. It clicks home. They'll call their chief executive officer, and they've delivered. That's how it works. It's not illegal. They work on a personal basis."

An inside tip can be gold. Right after Reagan's inauguration in 1981, John Gunther, executive director of the U.S. Conference of Mayors, got a tip from a cabinet staff aide that the Reagan administration was planning to kill the revenue-sharing program which funneled billions to states, counties, and cities. The timing was serendipitous. The next day a mayor's delegation was scheduled to lunch with the president. Over lunch, the mayors of Peoria, Indianapolis, Denver, and Columbus, lobbied Reagan and top aides. The program escaped the guillotine for several years, though it was ultimately reduced.

In another case, a former Reagan White House official turned lobbyist told me that a Washington lawyer telephoned him on behalf of a businessman who had a $497,000 cost overrun on a contract with the Department of Housing and Urban Development. In one telephone call, my lobbyist source learned that HUD had already decided to pay the contractor $350,000 and would tell him in about two weeks. My friend phoned the lawyer back, but before he could speak, the lawyer said his client was willing to pay the lobbyist ten percent of whatever he got. My source stopped in mid-sentence and replied, "Well, let me see what I can do." With some misgivings, but rationalizing that the contractor or the lawyer could have made the same phone call, my source waited a couple of days and then called back to report that the contractor would get $350,000. He never claimed to have fixed the deal, but he got a check for $35,000—simply for knowing whom to ask.

"A lot of it is direct contact," Christopher Matthews commented. "You see Tip, he'll be out at a country club playing golf [usually Burning Tree Country Club], and some lobbyist will walk up to him just as he's about ready to tee up his ball and say, 'Tip, you know, I got to tell you one thing. Do me one favor. Just don't push that state-and-local tax thing through on the tax bill.' You don't think that has an impression? Of course it does. They know what they're doing. Tip's mood can be affected by who the heck he's seen over the weekend. And these guys do their homework. They know right where these members socialize. You think it's an accident some guy walks up and talks to Tip on the golf tee? No. It's smart. It's natural. It's easy."

That is classic old-breed lobbying, and as an old-breed politician, Tip O'Neill was particularly susceptible. Indeed, practically no politician is immune to the flattery and personal attention that are the essence of old-breed lobbying. I remember an article in 1978 about Tongsun Park, a Korean lobbyist who had been close to O'Neill and who wound up getting several other congressmen indicted for taking illegal campaign contributions from a foreigner. But the article, by William Grieder in *The Washington Post*, was emphasizing something else: Park's simple but shrewd understanding that politicians need to feel loved.

"Park exploited this weakness with his Georgetown parties and gifts, but that hardly makes him unique," Greider wrote.

> The most effective lobbies on Capitol Hill, whether it is the Pentagon or the Farm Bureau, have always been the ones that played most skillfully to the Congressmen's egos. The military treats them like generals, flies them around in big airplanes and fires off rocket shows to entertain them. The Farm Bureau awards them plaques and holds banquets in their honor. Politicians are not different in this respect from the rest of us, except that many of them have a stronger personal need for ego gratification. It's what drew them into politics in the first place, the roar of the crowd and all that.
>
> Now, picture a scrambling politician who works his way up the local ladder, who finally wins a coveted seat in Congress and comes to Washington to collect his glory. The first thing he discovers is that glory gets spread pretty thin in this town. . . . He hardly ever sees his name in the daily newspaper unless he gets into trouble or creates an outrageous media stunt which the press can't resist. When he opens the mail from home, it is a hot blast of complaints, demands, threats. In the last decade, his status has declined considerably, displaced by the new celebrities who dominate Washington's glitter: movie stars, cause advocates, rock musicians, even members of the news media. In this environment, politicians, some of them anyway, will behave like the rest of us—they will devote their attention to people who appreciate them. Lobbyists appreciate Congressmen. They thank them constantly for their hard work. They provide them with the trappings, however phony, of exalted status. They protect a Congressman, with small favors, while the rest of the world beats up on him.

Old-breed lobbying also thrives on an aura of influence, a promise of the inside track, the hint of priceless contacts. A certain amount of this promise of influence is hokum. There is no year-in, year-out box-score, but even the big-name lobbyist "rainmakers" lose major battles or settle for much less than they had hoped for. "One of the great myths around is that wheelers and dealers can come in there and write policy and have their way in whatever they want—it's simply not the case," asserts Norm Ornstein, one of the best-known scholars on Congress, who is at the American Enterprise Institute for Public Policy Research. "You pick any big shot, and you're dealing with *some* wins and losses. Any sophisticated person is going to know that you hire a Tommy Boggs, and that doesn't mean you buy victory. What you buy with a Tommy Boggs is access. Very few people are gonna say they won't see him. You buy acumen. This is somebody who understands how the process works."

Ornstein's skepticism is well taken, for lobbyists are prone to oversell their influence; but his assertion that lobbyists do not write policy is too sweeping. Their effectiveness, suggested David Cohen, codirector of the Advocacy Institute, depends largely on the public visibility of issues. Large issues like the MX missile, environmental legislation, the Voting Rights Act, or broad provisions of tax law are "less susceptible to the superlobbyists because they are highly visible," Cohen argues—correctly, I think. "But when you're dealing with invisible issues and the narrower details of legislation, you can still use the superlawyers and the superlobbyists."

Access is the first arrow in any lobbyist's quiver, especially lobbyists of the old breed. Scores of times I have been told that votes are won simply by gaining an audience with a time-harassed congressman, so he could hear your case. In this access game, the lobbyist's first rule is to make his own services so reliable and indispensable that officeholders become dependent on him—for his information, his contacts, his policy advice, not to mention his money. "A good lobbyist is simply an extension of a congressional member's staff," I was told by Terry Lierman, an energetic health lobbyist and former staff aide for the Senate Appropriations Committee. "If you're a good lobbyist and you're working something, all the members know where you're coming from," Lierman said. "So if they want information and they trust you, they'll call *you* for that information."

That takes expertise. For instance, Representative Tony Coelho, a California Democrat, pointed out how lobbyists work hand in glove with the members and staffs of the highly specialized subcommittees of the House Agriculture Committee. They help craft legislation that covers their own sector. "There are lobbyists who are extremely influential in the subcommittees," Coelho asserted. "They know more about the subject than the staff or the committee members. The Cotton Council will be writing legislation for the cotton industry in the cotton subcommittee."

A top real estate lobbyist explained the premium value of expertise in the final stages of writing a tax bill and why lobbyists gather by the score outside the committee room. "There are very arcane, very turgid, complicated sections of the tax code, and members and their staffs often are not as familiar with how they apply to the industry as we are," explain Wayne Thevnot, president of the National Realty Committee. "So if you've got entrée there and you understand the process and you're present, you can influence the specific drafting of these proposals. Staff and others will come out and seek you out in the halls and say, 'We're on the passive-loss provision, and this is the material-participation test that the staff is proposing. Does that work? Does that solve your problem? And, if not, how can we correct it?' "

AIPAC has institutionalized its influence through this technique. Tom Dine and other staffers draft speeches and legislation for many members of both House and Senate, offering detailed rundowns on the Arab-Israeli military balance, or doing spot checks on Middle Eastern visitors. "We'll get a call from a congressional staffer, say at nine in the morning, and they want a speech on an issue," one midlevel AIPAC legislative assistant disclosed. "By ten-thirty, they'll have a speech." AIPAC has a research staff of fifteen people, well-stocked with papers on many topical issues. Practically every senator or House member known as a spokesman on Israeli issues and scores of lesser lights have leaned on this service or gotten AIPAC's staff to ghostwrite or edit op-ed articles on Middle East issues.

Charles Peters, in his slim and knowing handbook on Washington, *How Washington Really Works*, argues that the name of the game for politicians and administration officials is survival, and lobbyists work to become an integral part of the survival networks of people in power. "The smart lobbyist knows he must build networks not only for himself, but for those officials he tries to influence," Peters wrote. "Each time the lobbyist meets an official whose help he needs, he tries to let that official know—in the most subtle ways possible—that he can be an important part of that official's survival network."

Ultimately, that urge to prove a vital part of an officeholder's network gets into campaign money and demonstrating clout with the voters. And that begins to bridge from the old inside game of lobbying to the new inside game.

New-Breed Lobbying

The new-breed game reflects the organic changes in American politics and the institutional changes in Congress. Its medium is mass marketing, its style is packaging issues; its hallmark is wholesale lobbying. New-breed lobbying borrows heavily from the techniques of political campaigns, with their slick P.R., television advertising, orchestrated coalitions, targeted mass mailings, and their crowds of activists. It is the National Rifle Association generating three million telegrams in seventy-two hours and blanketing Capitol Hill with so many phone calls that members cannot make outgoing calls. It is the "gray lobby" dumping up to fifteen million postcards and letters on Jim Wright in one day to warn Congress not to tamper with Social Security cost-of-living adjustments. It is legions of insurance or real estate lobby agents swarming Capitol Hill as a tax markup nears a climax. It is political consultants and campaign strategists elbowing superlawyers aside, to generate grass-roots support for their lobbying clients or to do public-relations campaigns.

For example, when Jonas Savimbi, the Angolan rebel leader, wanted to push his cause in Washington in late 1985 and to bring pressure on Congress and the administration to supply him with missiles to combat Soviet tanks and jets, he paid a fancy $600,000 fee to Black, Manafort, Stone, and Kelly, a hot-shot lobbying firm set up by a group of young political campaign managers and consultants. The firm, whose campaign work gave it ties to the Reagan White House and influential Republican senators, not only arranged entrée at the highest levels of the administration and Congress, but it orchestrated a massive public-relations blitz for Savimbi. In his two-week visit, the jaunty, bearded anti-Communist rebel had scores of press interviews and television appearances. Suddenly Savimbi became a cause célèbre, which helped him get the weapons.

There are literally hundreds of deals like these, tapping the ranks of political campaign specialists for lobbying. That is an important shift away from reliance on lawyers and former government officials for lobbying—a shift symptomatic of how the new politics have altered the Washington power game.

The essence of the new-breed game is grass-roots lobbying. It developed in the 1960s with the advent of citizen protest. The civil rights movement, mass marches against the Vietnam War, and then Ralph Nader and public-interest groups such as Common Cause opened up mass lobbying. These movements spawned a new generation, a new cadre of players trained in grass-roots activism, many of whom settled into the Washington power game. Business was initially slow to react, but it arrived with a vengeance to play on the new terrain in the late 1970s and gained the upper hand in the 1980s. Now old-breed and new-breed lobbyists jostle, borrowing techniques from each other.

The new game has made lobbying a boom industry. It takes a lot more money and manpower than it did in the old days to touch all the power bases in Congress, and the campaign techniques of working the grass roots shoot costs up exponentially. The swarm of lobbyists in Washington seem to reach new highs every year: from 5,662 registered with the secretary of the Senate in 1981 to 23,011 in mid-1987 (registration is required to work the halls of Congress legally), plus another fifty or sixty thousand more lobbyists and workers in law firms and trade association offices. In the new Washington, practically no big client will settle these days for a single lobbying firm. The style now is "team lobbying" to make all the necessary contacts and to handle all aspects of the influence game: a law firm, a public-relations outfit, a lobbying firm, plus grass-roots political specialists.

One hallmark of new-breed lobbying is its strange political bedfellows. With Congress split for six of the past eight years between a Democratic-controlled House and a Republican-dominated Senate, bipartisan lobbying coalitions became a necessity. Even in 1978, when the Chrysler Corporation was looking for a government bailout loan, it pulled together a big Democratic law firm (Patton, Boggs and Blow) and a big Republican lobbying firm (Timmons and Company). The latest pattern is for each firm to have its own in-house bipartisan coalition. For example, Bill Timmons—who regularly runs Republican national conventions—hired Democratic lobbyists such as Bill Cable from the Carter White House staff and Howard Paster, formerly with the United Auto Workers union.

It is not unusual for lobbying partners to wind up on opposite sides of political campaigns. One striking example is the highly respected firm of Wexler,

Reynolds, Harrison & Schule, which principally pairs Anne Wexler, a liberal Democrat from the Carter White House, and Nancy Reynolds, a close confidante and White House aide to Nancy Reagan. In the hot 1986 Senate campaign, their rivalries stretched across the country; Wexler and Reynolds ran fund-raisers for rival candidates in Senate races from Florida and Maryland to Idaho and Nevada. "We don't think anything of it," Anne Wexler told me. "Our having contacts on both sides benefits our clients."

The swarm of lobbyists is so great that members of Congress have grown jaded—quick to challenge Washington lobbyists for evidence that their case has real pull among the voters. Danny Rostenkowski, chairman of the House Ways and Means Committee, told me that while his committee was drafting the 1986 tax bill, he refused to see Washington lobbyists—though he would grant time to constituents from home. And Tom Korologos, an old-breed lobbyist who learned the power game in the 1960s under Utah Senator Wallace Bennett and as congressional liaison in the Nixon White House, concedes: "We have a different breed of congressman who is more active, more publicity prone, more responsive to his district. . . .

"On the Senate side in the old days you could go talk to two or three committee chairmen," Korologos recalled, "you could talk to John Stennis and Russell Long and Allen Ellender and Warren Magnuson, and you had a policy. You had a defense bill. You had an oil policy. Now, you've got to talk to fifty-one guys. So you fly in the Utah plant manager to see Orrin Hatch and Jake Garn [Utah's two senators], and the Utah plant manager gets in to see 'em. If he doesn't get in, he goes back home and goes to church on Sunday and bowling on Monday and to coffee on Tuesday and says, 'I was in Washington, and the son of a bitch wouldn't see me.' And let that spread around for a while. Political graveyards are filled with statesmen who forgot the folks back home."

"The logistics of trying to persuade Congress have changed enormously," agreed Jim Mooney, for years a top House Democratic staff aide and now chief lobbyist for the cable-television industry. "What's changed is there are so many more groups now and simultaneously a diminution of power in the power centers of Congress. You've got to persuade members one by one."

In the new game, another maxim is that lobbyists must demonstrate that the home folks are with them to prove their political legitimacy. "There's a suspicion on the part of elected officials toward paid lobbyists," acknowledged David Cohen, the public-interest lobbyist. "They often sense a gap between leaders and the rank and file, whether labor unions or other organizations like church groups. I don't think you're a player unless you have a constituency to mobilize."

In an earlier era, labor unions had a near monopoly on lobbying with a mass base. Disgruntled farmers also rolled their tractors onto the Capitol Mall to demonstrate mass anger. Business has now entered that game. Mass-marketing techniques are being used even by people like Charls Walker, a traditional Washington insider whose normal style is lobbying at intimate dinners for selected members of Congress. After serving as an inside tax adviser to the 1980 Reagan campaign, Walker got important tax write-offs for business written into the 1981 tax bill. But more recently he has enlisted help from new-breed lobbyists.

"When a member says to you, 'Go convince my constituents,' then you are thrown into those arenas," Walker explained to me. "You get into targeted mail and all that sort of stuff. The lobbying business is moving toward a full service which will include not just your legislative experts and administration experts, but your public-relations experts, experts in grass-roots communications, targeted communications, cluster-group approaches, grass-roots coalition building." Charls Walker was talking the lingo of the modern political campaign, and in fact, the old-breed lobbyists are turning increasingly to campaign consultants.

POINTS TO PONDER

1. What is the difference between "old-breed" lobbying and "new-breed" lobbying?
2. What are the major techniques of "wholesale" lobbying?
3. How are members of Congress affected by the two different styles of lobbying?

44

"DEMOSCLEROSIS"
Jonathan Rauch

In this short 1992 article, journalist Jonathan Rauch of the National Journal *lays out some of the implications of interest group activity in modern economies. He argues that, whenever the government creates a program, those who benefit from that program will organize to protect it against any change. As these groups accumulate political power, it becomes increasingly difficult to eliminate a program, even if its original purpose has been accomplished. In this manner existing programs tend to soak up all available resources, leaving little room for change or for new programs, especially with a stagnant economy. This "creeping special-interest gridlock" is systemic and not dependent on any particular group of politicians. Thus, overcoming its negative effects is a challenge to any developed economy.*

On April 10, a group of kamikaze Senators marched to the chamber floor with an alternative budget. What they got back was a stark demonstration of the forces that are petrifying postwar democracy.

"We do not seek to end entitlements, or even to reduce them," Sen. Charles S. Robb, D-Va., told the Senate that day. "We do, however, believe that it is necessary to restrain their growth. That is, first and foremost, what this amendment does."

Entitlement programs are check-writing machines whose subsidies are mandatory under law: social security, medicare, farm supports, welfare, countless more. Today they account for a staggering three-fourths of all federal domestic spending. And so Sen. Pete V. Domenici, R-N.M., was doing nothing more than acknowledging reality when he told the Senate, "If we do not do anything to control the mandatory expenditures, the deficit will continue skyrocketing."

The bipartisan group—Domenici and Robb, Sam Nunn, D-Ga., and Warren Rudman, R-N.H.—proposed phasing in a cap on over-all entitlement growth. To avoid bringing the roof down on their heads, they exempted social security. The other entitlement programs would collectively grow to account for inflation and demographic changes, but no more.

Within two hours of the four Senators' first detailed discussion of their proposal, they were receiving telegrams, Domenici told the Senate, "from all over the country, saying that this is going to hurt a veterans' group, this is going to hurt people on welfare, this is going to hurt seniors on medicare."

"We were inundated," G. William Hoagland, the Senate Budget Committee's Republican staff director, recalled during a recent interview. "Just about every interest group you can think of was strongly opposed. It was very dramatic how quickly they all came to the defense."

The American Association of Retired Persons (AARP) called the proposal a "direct attack"; the National Council of Senior Citizens, "outrageous"; the Children's Defense Fund, "unacceptable"; the Committee for Education Funding, "unconscionable"; the Food Research and Action Center, "devastating"; the American Federation of Government Employees, AFL-CIO, "unfair and unconscionable"; the Veterans of Foreign Wars of the United States, "totally unjust"; the Disabled American Veterans, "unconscionable"; the American Legion, "incredible"; the Paralyzed Veterans of America, "inherently unfair"; the National Cotton Council of America, the U.S. Rice Producers' Group and the National Farmers Organization, "unfair"; the American Postal Workers Union, AFL-CIO, "irresponsible, simple-minded," and so on.

On the floor of the Senate, the amendment's opponents moved to exempt disabled veterans from the entitlement cap. The exemption passed, 66-28. "We were going to exclude every Tom, Dick and Harry organization out there before we were finished," Hoagland said. Rather than face death by amendment, Domenici and the others withdrew their plan. That ended it.

The Domenici group's effort fell victim to demosclerosis—postwar democratic government's progressive loss of the ability to adapt. Demosclerosis is the most important governmental phenomenon of our time. No surprise, then, that it is also the most explained.

Liberals blame conservatives. "Government has stopped addressing accumulated public problems," wrote the liberal journalist Robert Kuttner in *The New Republic* recently: "a deliberate strategy of laissez-faire Republicans, who don't believe in government."

Conservatives blame liberals, alleging that left-wing ideology drives liberals to cling brainlessly to every program ever adopted. "Reactionary liberalism," the conservatives call it.

Populists and business-bashers, such as the liberal journalist William Greider, blame moneyed elites and corporate lobbying. Political analysts blame the current state of the political system: divided control of the government, the early-1970s reforms that dispersed power in Congress, the breakdown of strong political parties, the rise of a professional political class and so forth.

The public blames, above all, "leadership," or the lack of it. A strong leader (runs the theory), uncorrupted by politics as usual, could shake the barnacles from the system. Thus the wave of support for Ross Perot.

Many of the explainers' standard explanations are partly right. Yet there are grounds to believe that none of the above fully comprehends what is going on.

People used to fear that democracy would dither fatally while dictators and totalitarians swept the field. That fear turned out to be mistaken. Now it appears that the vulnerabilities of democracy—at any rate, of the postwar style of democracy, with its professional activists and its large and fairly powerful government—are mundane and close to home.

One such vulnerability is the tendency to rob the future to pay for consumption today—but that's another story. The other vulnerability is creeping special-interest gridlock: that is, progressive sclerosis.

Here in Washington, people like to think that sclerosis is temporary, or at least is treatable with political reforms. Maybe not. If postwar government is petrifying, the causes may be deep rather than superficial and fundamental rather than merely partisan. In other words, demosclerosis may be inherent and irreversible.

Getting Organized

In 1982, a University of Maryland economist published a scholarly book called *The Rise and Decline of Nations* (Yale University Press). Mancur Olson set out to explain, or partially explain, why societies tend to ossify and stagnate as they age. Few people outside of academia took much note of Olson and his ideas. To return to his book today, however, is an eerie experience, for the theory of 1982 foreshadows 1992's politics of frustration.

In every society, Olson said, there are two ways for people to improve their lot and grow rich. One is to produce more; the other is to capture more of what others produce. Doing the latter is possible, but requires political pull or marketplace power; attaining either of those requires that people band together to form either interest groups or cartels.

Interest groups can make their members better off by seeking subsidies, tax breaks, monopolies, favorable regulations and so on. Postal workers seek a monopoly on first-class mail; dairy farmers seek production controls to jack up prices; and so on. Private cartels can make their members better off by raising prices and barring newcomers from the market. Olson called such beggar-thy-neighbor groups "distributional coalitions."

So far, so obvious. Then Olson went on to the less obvious. Despite what you might think, to organize an interest group or cartel is difficult. The organizer will bear most of the start-up costs, and yet can expect only a fraction of the benefits, which must be shared among the members. Members, in turn, will be reluctant to join until they see that the group is successful. Even then, they may stay out and let others do the work.

As a result, Olson wrote, "organization for collective action takes a good deal of time to emerge." Trade unions did not appear, for instance, until almost a century after the Industrial Revolution. Farmers' groups didn't appear in America until after World War I. Social security dates back to 1935, but the AARP didn't appear until 1958.

Once groups organize, however, they almost never disappear. Instead, Olson wrote, "they usually survive until there is a social upheaval or other form of violence or instability" Furthermore, over time the interest groups professionalize. This makes them still less likely to go away: Amateur activists can always drop the cause and go home, but for professionals, the cause pays the mortgage.

The result, Olson concluded, is this rule: "Stable societies with unchanged boundaries tend to accumulate more collusions and organizations for collective action over time." Look at the AARP's membership curve, multiply it by countless interest groups, and you get the idea.

Cartels have not proved to be the problem that Americans once expected, thanks mainly to foreign competition. If cartels organize the domestic market, as some say the Big Three automakers did informally through the 1970s, fat profits lure in imports to bust the trust.

But political pressure groups have the added power of the law, and are not so easily undermined. These groups' effects are of two kinds, economic and governmental.

Economically speaking, entrenched interest groups slow the adoption of new technology and ideas by clinging to the status quo. They distort the economy, and so reduce its efficiency, by locking out competition and locking in subsidies. As they grow, they suck more of society's top talent into the redistribution industry. All in all, the economic costs can be very large.

The other kind of effect is on government. The accretion of interest groups, and the rise of bickering over scarce resources, Olson feared, can "make societies ungovernable."

Now the theory's darker implications come into view. "The logic of the argument implies that countries that have had democratic freedom of organization without upheaval or invasion the longest will suffer the most from growth-repressing organizations and combinations," Olson wrote. If he is right, then the piling up of entrenched interest groups, each clinging to some favorable deal or subsidy, is an inevitable process as democracies age.

However, occasionally some cataclysmic event—war, perhaps, or revolution—may sweep away an existing government and, with it, the countless cozy arrangements that are protected by interest groups.

If his theory is right, Olson concludes, "it follows that countries whose distributional coalitions have been emasculated or abolished by totalitarian government or foreign occupation should grow relatively quickly after a free and stable legal order is established."

Look at Japan and West Germany, where authoritarian regimes and then foreign occupations swept away entrenched interest groups and anticompetitive deals. "Economic miracles" followed in both countries as resources were freed from groups that had captured and monopolized them. (Catch-up growth, Olson says, can explain only a part of Japan's and Germany's success.) By contrast, "Great Britain, the major nation with the longest immunity from dictatorship, invasion and revolution, has had in this century a lower rate of growth than other large, developed democracies."

Even in the United States, Olson said, the pattern applies. Statistical tests comparing the 50 states showed that "the longer a state has been settled and the longer the time it has had to accumulate special-interest groups, the slower its rate of growth."

His hypothesis suggested a social cycle:

A country emerges from a period of political repression or upheaval into a period of stability and freedom. If other conditions are favorable, rapid growth ensues. (South Korea and Taiwan, both emerging from dictatorships and both showing rapid growth, would be in this stage today; China might be next.) Gradually, interest groups organize and secure anticompetitive deals. These deals accumulate, each being jealously defended. Over time, growth slows and paralysis sets in.

Although Olson was concerned mainly with the sapping of economic vigor, his theory also has profound implications for the sapping of governmental vigor. To see why, look at Washington in 1992.

Paralysis

Look, for instance, at what happened to the entitlement-cap proposal. Anyone who doubts that today's professional interest groups can mobilize almost instantly to defend their favorable deals need only consider the fate of the move by Robb, Domenici and the others.

Another case in point, one of many, is banking reform. The law that regulates the U.S. banking system goes back 50 years or more and is largely archaic. Banks are barred from a variety of money-making activities (underwriting securities or mutual funds, selling insurance, branching across state lines) that their modern competitors perform with impunity. Thus hobbled, banks have difficulty finding profits. Weak banks, in turn, weaken the whole financial system.

In 1991, the Bush Administration sent Congress a banking reform package. It was shot to pieces in what the *New York Times* called "a frenzied attack by lobbyists. . . . Small bankers, fearing competition, tore away interstate banking. Insurance firms, fearing competition, tore away insurance underwriting. Securities firms, fearing competition, tore away the proposal to let banks sell stocks and bonds."

In the end, *National Journal* reported, "every Administration proposal for permitting banks to widen their business horizons—every single one—was picked off in the carnage." The result is surely one of the most bizarre policies of our time: As the 21st century approaches, the country limps along with New Deal banking laws.

What happens when you try to attack an anticompetitive arrangement? A classic example of such an arrangement protects public school employees, who enjoy a monopoly claim on tax dollars for education. Recently, two provisions of the Bush Administration's watery education reform package attempted to nibble at this monopoly.

Bush wanted to finance 535 new "break-the-mold" schools, both public and private, to be chosen competitively in Washington; he also proposed incentives for localities to try voucher plans, which let parents spend public money at private schools. The idea in both cases was to stimulate innovation by bypassing the entrenched establishment of public school employees.

On Capitol Hill, the voucher measure was demolished under ferocious opposition from groups representing public school teachers and administrators. Under pressure from the National School Boards Association and others, the "break-the-mold" schools turned mostly into block grants for state education agencies and local school districts; in other words, more money for the existing system and its officials.

Whichever way you feel about the Bush proposals, their fate is indicative. "In the politics of education, what you have to recognize right from the start is that the [public school] educational establishment has tremendously more resources than anybody else," said Stanford University political scientist Terry M. Moe, who advocates vouchers and other reforms. "And that's not unique to education. You can't get anything past these groups."

If there is a single sad symptom of demosclerosis, however, it is bogus national poverty.

People often talk as though the country has become too poor to afford federal initiatives. In fact, the United States is now wealthier than any other country in human history, including its prior self. In 1990, real per capita disposable income was twice as high as in 1960, when the federal government could "afford" almost anything; real wealth per capita was 62 per cent higher than in 1960 and real output was 80 per cent higher. "Poor" is the one thing America is not.

Is the government poor? It collects and spends more, in inflation-adjusted dollars, than at any time in history, far more even than at the peak of World War II. Its tax base, measured as a share of the economy, is at the high end of the postwar norm, and above the level of the "wealthy" 1950s and 1960s.

If government is "poor," it is only because of its inability to reallocate resources for new needs. In other words, government is not poor, it is paralyzed.

Trial and Error

What is going on here? Why has government become so ossified and immobile?

In large, complex systems, the key to successful adaptation is the method of trial and error. In the large, complex system of biological evolution, species undergo mutations, the vast majority of which fail. A few, however, succeed brilliantly, and those proliferate by out-competing the others. That is how life adapts to changing environments.

Similarly with a capitalist economy: The key to its adaptability is that it makes many mistakes but corrects them quickly. Entrepreneurs open businesses; many fail, but every so often someone hits on a brilliant innovation. The more-successful strategies will proliferate by out-competing the others. Capitalism adapts through trial and error.

Similarly with science: It tries out countless hypotheses every day and abandons most of them. The knowledge base adapts through trial and error.

Government is another big, complex social system. The way for governments to learn what works in a changing world is to try various approaches and quickly abandon or adjust the failures: trial and error. However, something has gone badly wrong.

For fiscal 1993 alone, the Bush Administration proposed ending 246 federal programs and 4,192 federal projects. How many of those will die? Approximately none. The Reagan Administration made a fetish of trying to eliminate federal programs. Despite President Reagan's high popularity and his effective control of Congress in 1981–82, during his eight years in office a grand total of two major programs—general revenue sharing and urban development action grants—actually got killed.

One reason is that people disagree about which programs failed, and even about what "failing" means. Another reason is that as soon as a program is set up, the people who depend on it—both the direct beneficiaries and the program's employees and administrators—organize to defend it ferociously. These groups are, of course, none other than Olson's "distributional coalitions"— what others have for years described as part of an "iron triangle." They have money, votes and passion. They can be defied, but only at serious political risk.

In the period beginning with the New Deal and peaking with President Johnson's Great Society, Washington seemed one of society's most adaptive and progressive forces—which, at the time, it was. What Franklin D. Roosevelt's and LBJ's visionary policy makers did not foresee was that every program generates an entrenched lobby that never goes away. The result is that virtually every program lasts forever.

And so, although no one disputes that the Rural Electrification Administration has largely fulfilled its New Deal mission of bringing power and telephones to rural America, the program keeps right on going. The rural electric cooperatives' 65,000 employees and 10,000 local directors vigorously defend it, with the help of their interest group, the National Rural Electric Cooperative Association, whose budget for programs and administration runs to $11 million a year.

In 1955, Congress set up a program to subsidize the production of wool, which in those days was a vital military commodity. Along came synthetics, which by 1960 knocked wool off the Pentagon's strategic commodities list. But in 1992, more than three decades later, the wool program will spend $180 million. It is ably defended by the small but devoted group of people who benefit from it, in some cases richly (in 1989, more than 60 farmers got subsidy checks for more than $100,000).

Not only are policies hard to kill, they are also hard to change. Every wrinkle in the law produces a winner who will resist reform. That is why the United States operates under an anachronistic banking law from the early 20th century. Years ago, scholars understood that some provisions of the program of aid to families with dependent children, a mainstay of the welfare system, encourage fathers to leave home. Yet key corrections have still not been made.

And so programs are impossible to kill and very difficult to correct. The implications of this are profound.

Imagine an economy in which every important business enterprise is kept alive by an interest group with political clout. Over time, the world would change, but the businesses wouldn't. Obsolescent companies would gobble up resources, crowding out new companies. The economy would cease to adapt.

That is what happened to the Soviet economy. Which imploded.

In principle, the U.S. government's situation is like the Soviet economy's. In both, the method of trial and error has collapsed.

In Washington, every program is quasi-permanent, every mistake is written into a law that some vested interest will defend furiously. The result is that as the old clutter accumulates, government cannot adapt.

First, old programs and policies cannot be gotten rid of, and yet continue to suck up money and energy. And so there is little money or energy for new programs and policies. The old crowds out the new.

Second, and at least as important: When every program is permanent, the price of failure becomes extravagant. The key to experimenting successfully is knowing that you can correct your mistakes and try again. But what if you are stuck with your mistakes forever, or at least for decades? Then experimentation becomes extremely risky.

Everyone agrees that the nation's current health care system makes no sense. Yet any reform will produce vested winners (hospitals? doctors? drug companies? left-handed dentists?) who will fight further change. A Canadian-style system or a voucher system, once adopted, would be hard to adjust and almost impossible to get rid of. Policy makers, fearful of making a mess they cannot clean up, become rightly reluctant to innovate.

Underlying the breakdown of the method of trial and error is an ironic cycle, based on the fact that every new program creates a permanent interest group. The same programs that made government a progressive force from the 1930s through the 1960s also created swarms of dependent special interests whose defensive lobbying made government rigid and brittle in the 1990s. In effect, the rise of government activism immobilized activist government. Yesterday's innovations became today's prisons.

No one starting anew today would think to subsidize wool farmers, banish banks from the mutual fund business, forbid United Parcel Service to deliver letters, grant massive tax breaks for borrowing. Countless policies are on the books not because they make sense in 1992, but merely because they cannot be gotten rid of. They are dinosaurs that will not die. In a Darwinian sense, the universe of federal policies is ceasing to evolve.

Happy Ending?

"Maybe the message is: Cheer up, things are getting worse," Olson said.

In person, Olson is more optimistic than his theory. Ten years ago, he ended his book with a sentence carefully crafted to leave room for optimism. Is it reasonable to expect, he wondered, that awareness of the damage done by special interests "will spread to larger and larger proportions of the population? And that this wider awareness will greatly limit the losses from special interests? That is what I expect, at least when I am searching for a happy ending."

He is still searching for that happy ending, and he reports being optimistic three days out of five. If the public becomes angry enough, politicians may risk the wrath of the special interests. Thus, if things get worse, action might be taken.

"We do see growing recognition of the problem," he said, "and history does show examples of thoroughgoing reform." Mexico, for instance, which has long been hogtied by cozy deals between special interests and the ruling party, is opening its economy. Even the obstinate government of India is opening up. In America, the 1986 Tax Reform Act demonstrated that an anti-special-interest package can succeed if the political leadership pushes hard enough and the payoff is big enough.

However, hope can be matched stride for stride by doubt. Tax reform was remarkable precisely because it was so rare and so difficult, and the steady accumulation of interest groups implies that such reform will become harder, not easier. Moreover, India, Mexico and, for that matter, the old Soviet Union turned to reform only after approaching, or actually crossing, the brink of calamity, a fact that gives little comfort.

Short of calamity, suppose American voters do get angry? So what? Generalized voter anger against "the system" does not translate into votes against particular programs or groups; no one gets reelected to Congress for voting against maritime subsidies or wool farmers. "In Congress, we don't get to vote on the abstraction," retiring Rep. Vin Weber, R-Minn., told *Time* magazine in June. "We have to vote for or against actual programs."

What about reforms of the political process? Limits on politicians' terms and on campaign contributions, for example? Process reforms might make some difference, but probably not much. In a free society, groups will always find ways to defend their interests, as is their right.

At intervals, windows may open for reform. If the 1992 elections shake up both Congress and the White House, 1993 might provide such a window. However, the processes that Olson described are fundamental. They are in the system, not the people; new politicians will face the same pressures that their predecessors faced. Weber implied as much when he told *Time*, "I don't know what comes next after we have this tremendous cleaning-out election and then the Congress gets together next year and people find we still are not going to reduce the deficit, we still are not going to reform health care."

Weber added: "I'm not by nature a pessimist. I like to think that our system works and is going to right itself. But I see it decaying."

In any case, reforms' effects are likely to be temporary. Special-interest groups will always tend to accumulate over time; if shaken off, they will re-accumulate. "The termites are always there," Olson said. "The clock keeps ticking."

If government tends to calcify, this does not necessarily mean the country will also calcify. It depends on how other institutions compensate. Corporations, for instance, are delivering education that the public schools are not.

Nor does calcification mean that the federal government is, or will be, wholly unable to pass laws, adopt policies and expand programs. It means, rather, that new reforms and policies and programs will tend to be piled on top of old ones, so that the whole accumulated mass becomes steadily less rational and less flexible—as though you had to build every new house on top of its predecessor.

What demosclerosis means for conservatives is that there is no significant hope of scraping away outmoded or unneeded or counterproductive liberal policies, because nothing old can be jettisoned. What it means for liberals is that there is no significant hope of using government as a progressive tool, because the method of trial and error has broken down.

For Washington and for the broad public, demosclerosis quite possibly means that the federal government is rusting solid and, in the medium and long term, nothing can be done about it. The disease of democratic government is not heart failure but hardening of the arteries.

POINTS TO PONDER

1. What does the age of democracies have to do with the number of interest groups?
2. How does the increasing number of interest groups affect the ability of the country to make changes in public policy?
3. Why does Rauch's pessimistic conclusion differ from Salisbury's more optimistic conclusion?

Chapter 12

❖

THE MEDIA
AND PUBLIC OPINION

The media—print (newspapers, magazines, and so on) and electronic (radio, television, and so forth)—play crucial roles in American politics and government. After all, the Framers made their case for the ratification of the Constitution by publishing their arguments (the *Federalist* Papers) in New York newspapers. In addition, the First Amendment to the Constitution assures freedom of speech and freedom of the press to journalists of all sorts. The articles in this section cover a number of issues concerning the appropriate role of the media and public opinion in the United States. They emphasize the increasing impact of the media on our politics and comment on the implications of this impact for governance.

Development of the Media

The free press has always played an important role in the American style of democracy. If the government is to be responsive to the will of the governed, voters cannot make wise choices unless they have adequate information upon which to base their judgments. The press plays a valuable role in governance by informing citizens about the activities of the government and the issues of political campaigns. But despite the generally agreed-upon benefits of a free press, Americans harbor an ambivalence about the media, fearing that at times those who control the media insert their own value judgments rather than objectively report the facts. In addition, there is also the suspicion that those in powerful positions in government are able to manipulate the press to their own advantage. For their part, government officials often feel that the press is out to get them by digging for scandal and reporting any embarrassing incident, regardless of its relevance to public policy.

No one can doubt the pervasive influence of the media in American life and politics. Before the rise of the electronic media, newspapers and magazines were read by leaders whose opinions influenced those with whom they exchanged information. Word about the government was either read by citizens or learned secondhand from those who had read the papers. With the advent of radio, political leaders were able to speak directly to the people in broadcast speeches or in the famous "fireside chats" of President Franklin Roosevelt.

Television is capable of creating major changes in American politics. Moving visual images are more power than sound alone and can produce a significant emotional impact. Combine this with the facts that virtually all households in the United States have television sets and that most people receive most of their information about politics and government through television and the potential force of the medium becomes enormous.

Role of the Media

In political campaigns the role of TV has been growing in importance, and correspondingly in cost. But there is no better alternative for communicating effectively with a "media market" than television. Political campaigns are often dominated by professional media experts who carefully craft visual images to support their candidate and attack the opposition. Aside from the need for increasing amounts of money to conduct political campaigns, the emotional potential of television advertising is great. Several of the more dubious examples of the impact of television commercials were analyzed by Kathleen Hall Jamieson in a previous selection in this volume. She examined the infamous "Willy Horton" ads that President Bush's 1988 campaign ran against his opponent, Michael Dukakis. The ad is a case study in the subtle ways that TV ads can distort "facts" to make a point. Jamieson also looked at an ad that backfired when the image of Dukakis riding in a tank was turned against him by the Republicans.

In addition to paid political advertising, candidates can also benefit from the "free" coverage of televised news programs. Thus candidates will go to great lengths to get on the news and will often stage events and organize their campaigns around television schedules.

The Media and Governance

The media, particularly television, are the most important mediators between political candidates and the public. Thus the quality of political coverage is of prime concern. Certainly the potential of TV for comprehensive coverage of candidates for office is great. Visual images can convey the subtlety of body language and expression as well as aids such as charts or graphs in ways that radio cannot.

There is a symbiotic relationship between political candidates and the press, because each needs the other to perform effectively. The press needs stories about political conflict, and the candidates need the press for exposure and for publicizing their message. The relationship of the press with the government is similar. There are many legitimate and important ways in which the press informs the public about governmental activities, and each government agency has a press office that specializes in providing information about their programs to the press. There are problems of a constrained perspective on both sides of the public affairs offices. Agencies want to make themselves look good and hope the press will overlook any negative information. The press does not often cover programs that operate effectively and efficiently, but will jump on any story that smacks of scandal or inefficiency.

Impact of the Media on Politics

Because the media are so powerful in their influence on public opinion, politicians and public officials tend to complain often about "bias" in reporting. Of course, we might expect public officials to believe that any criticism of them in the press results from bias rather than from an objective evaluation of a situation.

Conservative presidential administrations often accuse the press of a liberal bias, and they point to opinion surveys indicating that more reporters consider themselves liberal than conservative. Reporters counter that their professionalism compels them to do their best to report issues as objectively as possible. They also point out that more editors than reporters tend to be conservative and provide a check on any obviously biased reporting. But probably the most effective counter to charges of a liberal press bias is to examine closely press treatment of Democratic presidents and candidates. Lyndon Johnson suffered from a "credibility gap" with the press and the public. Jimmy Carter certainly did not believe that the press was sympathetic to him in the 1980 election. President Clinton often felt that the press was unfair to him in the primaries, and suffered a number of very critical press coverage episodes in his first year in office.

Liberals and conservatives, Democrats and Republicans, complain about press bias, and in a sense they are right. For government officials, especially presidents and members of Congress, press coverage in the 1990s is more critical than it was several decades ago. This changing role of the press is due in part to the effects of Watergate, in which corruption in the presidency was exposed by two investigative reporters. But public standards of conduct about money, sex, and the use of political influence are now much more stringent than they were in the past.

The point here is that, although any liberal personal values of reporters do not bias the overall coverage of politicians, this does not mean the press is not biased, because it is. But the directions of bias do not run along a liberal/conservative dimension. In a very broad sense the mass media accept mainstream American values and cannot be expected to provide radical critiques of the status quo. The press is also biased by its need to attract readers and viewers, and this often makes it seem biased against politicians and government officials when it looks for scandal.

At the mundane level of attracting readers and viewers, the media will focus on those aspects of politics and government that are flashy and "newsworthy." Conflict and confrontation are more interesting than bland agreement, and reporters will seek out controversy or even try to provoke it by asking pointed questions. The press will tend to cover political campaigns as horse races, that is, who is ahead of whom, rather than spend a lot of time laying out the pros and cons of complex policy issues.

Reporters feel the need to simplify issues to fit into a format of several paragraphs or a television sound bite. They will tend to focus on human interest rather than on dry analyses of underlying causal factors. There are important exceptions in the print and electronic media to this shallowness, but the reality is that most viewers and readers do not have the attention span necessary for in-depth reporting, and the media are heavily influenced by their markets.

These underlying biases of the media may lead politicians and public officials to see sinister motives. We can expect the press to be sympathetic to underdogs and critical of those in power. It is the temptation of presidents to take press criticism personally and to see the press as their enemy. When this attitude reaches the point of obsession, the president almost always suffers. Both Presidents Johnson and Nixon suffered from their feelings that the press was persecuting them, and there is no doubt that the national media were critical of both administrations.

But presidential complaining in public is seen as whining, and actions taken against the press in secret do not often remain secret. The use of lie detector tests or other extreme measures to plug leaks are seen as invasions of privacy or restrictions on freedom of speech or of the press and make the administration seem as if it has something to cover up. The best perspective a president can have about critical press coverage is that it is like the weather—it fluctuates arbitrarily and is often frustrating, but to complain about it is futile and just makes you look bad.

With a view toward influencing public opinion, presidential administrations have devoted considerable resources to dealing with the press. Most twentieth-century presidents have had press secretaries, and as television has increased in importance, more time has been spent getting the administration's story to the people. Presidents, feeling that the Washington press corps will not give them an even break, have devoted considerable resources to circumventing the major media outlets and getting their unfiltered message directly to the people. A special unit in the White House, the Office of Communications, was established for this purpose in the 1970s and has increased its importance since then. The Office of Communications puts out press releases and makes available taped statements from the president and other administration officials to local media outlets throughout the country. These officials feel that local reporters will be more sympathetic to them than will a national press corps, which will ask tough follow-up questions and try to score points by tripping them up.

The Readings

As Kiku Adatto points out, the amount of time television devotes to allowing candidates to speak for themselves on news programs has been decreasing over the past several decades to the point where the average "sound bite" of uninterrupted talk from a presidential candidate in 1988 had shrunk to less than ten seconds. Thus the role of the press in choosing what to cover and which sound bite to broadcast is crucial.

If candidates hope to get their image broadcast on network news shows (which all candidates want), they have to speak in effective sound bites, often at the expense of the complex reality of public policy issues. The imperatives of television broadcasters thus determine the quality of coverage of candidates and also influence politicians who change their behavior to conform to the dictates of the medium.

David Gergen was one of the early shapers of the White House communications operation in the 1970s and has drawn some lessons from his experiences. In his selection, he warns that television coverage of foreign affairs can influence public opinion toward a short-term and reactive U.S. foreign policy rather than toward a measured approach to long-term foreign policy interests. He then argues that presidents need to fully explain U.S. military actions to the American public in order to secure support for actions in our long-term interests.

Most modern presidents put a lot of effort into trying to control the image of their administrations in the media and thus influence public opinion in their favor. Presidents have always known that public opinion is an important source of their power. President Lincoln declared: "Public sentiment is everything. With public sentiment nothing can fail, without it nothing can succeed." With the development of modern polling technology using computers and telephone interviews, presidents can keep weekly or even daily track of how they are doing with the public.

The selection by Charles Kenney provides some guidelines for understanding public opinion polling. He emphasizes the importance of the technical aspects of polling to the validity of the results. If the sample is not random or the questions are biased, we cannot have confidence in the results. It is certainly true that any major governmental direction, whether it be a foreign war or a broad-ranging social policy initiative, depends on support among the public. And it is also true that presidents who are popular in the country have an easier time getting what they want from Congress.

KEY TERMS

leak: an unauthorized disclosure of information about a governmental plan or policy

media: a plural noun denoting the means of publicly disseminating news—for example, newspapers and magazines (print media), radio, television, and computers (electronic media)

sound bite: a series of spoken words that is uninterrupted by comment from the reporter presenting the report. The implication is that, to effectively get your point across, your statements must be concise and pithy.

45

"THE INCREDIBLE SHRINKING SOUND BITE"
Kiku Adatto

Television coverage of political campaigns underwent a transformation between the 1960s and the 1980s. In this analysis scholar Kiku Adatto contrasts the television coverage of the 1968 presidential campaign between Nixon and Humphrey with the 1988 contest between Bush and Dukakis. The title of this 1990 article in The New Republic *comes from the length of time, measured in seconds, that network news shows allowed candidates to speak without interruption. Adatto argues that coverage of the issues and substance of policy is being overshadowed by increasing coverage of the techniques of the campaigns and the "media gurus" that run them.*

One of the ironies of television coverage of campaign technique, rather than of substantive issues, is that if a candidate publicly calls attention to a misleading commercial of the opposition, he or she risks having that same commercial being replayed on news programs, giving more free air time to the misleading ad.

Standing before a campaign rally in Pennsylvania, the 1968 Democratic vice presidential candidate, Edmund Muskie, tried to speak, but a group of anti-war protesters drowned him out. Muskie offered the hecklers a deal. He would give the platform to one of their representatives if he could then speak without interruption. Rick Brody, the students' choice, rose to the microphone where, to cheers from the crowd, he denounced the candidates that the 1968 presidential campaign had to offer. "Wallace is no answer. Nixon's no answer. And Humphrey's no answer. Sit out this election!" When Brody finished, Muskie made his case for the Democratic ticket. That night Muskie's confrontation with the demonstrators played prominently on the network news. NBC showed fifty-seven seconds of Brody's speech, and more than a minute of Muskie's.

Twenty years later, things had changed. Throughout the entire 1988 campaign, no network allowed either presidential candidate to speak uninterrupted on the evening news for as long as Rick Brody spoke. By 1988 television's tolerance for the languid pace of political discourse, never great, had all but vanished. An analysis of all weekday evening network newscasts (over 280) from Labor Day to Election Day in 1968 and 1988 reveals that the average "sound bite" fell from 42.3 seconds in 1968 to only 9.8 seconds in 1988. Meanwhile the time the networks devoted to visuals of the candidates, unaccompanied by their words, increased by more than 300 percent.

Since the Kennedy-Nixon debates of 1960, television has played a pivotal role in presidential politics. The Nixon campaign of 1968 was the first to be managed and orchestrated to play on the evening news. With the decline of political parties and the direct appeal to voters in the primaries, presidential campaigns became more adept at conveying their messages through visual images, not only in political commercials but also in elaborately staged media events. By the time of Ronald Reagan, the actor turned president, Michael Deaver had perfected the techniques of the video presidency.

For television news, the politicians' mastery of television imagery posed a temptation and a challenge. The temptation was to show the pictures. What network producer could resist the footage of Reagan at Normandy Beach, or of Bush in Boston Harbor? The challenge was to avoid being entangled in the artifice and imagery that the campaigns dispensed. In 1988 the networks tried to have it both ways—to meet the challenge even as they succumbed to the temptation. They showed the images that the campaigns produced—their commercials as well as their media events. But they also sought to retain their objectivity by exposing the artifice of the images, by calling constant attention to their self-conscious design.

The language of political reporting was filled with accounts of staging and backdrops, camera angles and scripts, sound bites and spin control, photo opportunities and media gurus. So attentive was television news to the way the campaigns constructed images for television that political reporters began to sound like theater critics, reporting more on the stagecraft than the substance of politics.

When Bush kicked off his campaign with a Labor Day appearance at Disneyland, the networks covered the event as a performance for television. "In the war of the Labor Day visuals," CBS's Bob Schieffer reported, "George Bush pulled out the heavy artillery. A Disneyland backdrop and lots of pictures with the Disney gang." When Bruce Morton covered Dukakis riding in a tank, the story was the image. "In the trade of politics, it's called a visual," said Morton. "The idea is pictures are symbols that tell the voter important things about the candidate. If your candidate is seen in the polls as weak on defense, put him in a tank."

And when Bush showed up at a military base to observe the destruction of a missile under an arms control treaty, ABC's Brit Hume began his report by telling his viewers that they were watching a media event. "Now, here was a photo opportunity, the vice president watching a Pershing missile burn off its fuel." He went on to describe how the event was staged for television.

Standing in front of an open field, Hume reported, "The Army had even gone so far as to bulldoze acres of trees to make sure the vice president and the news media had a clear view."

So familiar is the turn to theater criticism that it is difficult to recall the transformation it represents. Even as they conveyed the first presidential campaign "made for television," TV reporters in 1968 continued to reflect the print journalist tradition from which they had descended. In the marriage of theater and politics, politics remained the focus of reporting. The media events of the day—mostly rallies and press conferences—were covered as political events, not as exercises in impression management.

By 1988 television displaced politics as the focus of coverage. Like a gestalt shift, the images that once formed the background to political events—the setting and the stagecraft—now occupied the foreground. (Only 6 percent of reports in 1968 were devoted to theater criticism, compared with 52 percent in 1988.) And yet, for all their image-conscious coverage in 1988, reporters did not escape their entanglement. They showed the potent visuals even as they attempted to avoid the manipulation by "deconstructing" the imagery and revealing its artifice.

To be sure, theater criticism was not the only kind of political reporting on network newscasts in 1988. Some notable "fact correction" pieces offered admirable exceptions. For example, after each presidential debate, ABC's Jim Wooten compared the candidates' claims with the facts. Not content with the canned images of the politicians, Wooten used television images to document discrepancies between the candidates' rhetoric and their records.

Most coverage simply exposed the contrivances of image-making. But alerting the viewer to the construction of television images proved no substitute for fact correction. A superficial "balance" replaced objectivity as the measure of fairness, a balance consisting of equal time for media events, equal time for commercials. But this created a false symmetry, leaving both the press and the public hostage to the play of perceptions the campaigns dispensed.

Even the most critical versions of image-conscious coverage could fail to puncture the pictures they showed. When Bush visited a flag factory in hopes of making patriotism a campaign issue, ABC's Hume reported that Bush was wrapping himself in the flag. "This campaign strives to match its pictures with its points. Today and for much of the past week, the pictures have been of George Bush with the American flag. If the point wasn't to make an issue of patriotism, then the question arises, what was it?" Yet only three days later, in an ABC report on independent voters in New Jersey, the media event that Hume reported with derision was transformed into an innocent visual of Bush. The criticism forgotten, the image played on.

Another striking contrast between the coverage of the 1968 and 1988 campaigns is the increased coverage of political commercials. Although political ads played a prominent role in the 1968 campaign, the networks rarely showed excerpts on the news. During the entire 1968 general election campaign, the evening news programs broadcast only two excerpts from candidates' commercials. By 1988 the number had jumped to 125. In 1968 the only time a negative ad was mentioned on the evening news was when CBS's Walter Cronkite and NBC's Chet Huntley reported that a Nixon campaign ad—showing a smiling Hubert Humphrey superimposed on scenes of war and riot—was withdrawn after the Democrats cried foul. Neither network showed the ad itself.

The networks might argue that in 1988 political ads loomed larger in the campaign, and so required more coverage. But as with their focus on media events, reporters ran the risk of becoming conduits of the television images the campaigns dispensed. Even with a critical narrative, showing commercials on the news gives free time to paid media. And most of the time the narrative was not critical. The networks rarely bothered to correct the distortions or misstatements that the ads contained. Of the 125 excerpts shown on the evening news in 1988, the reporter addressed the veracity of the commercials' claims less than 8 percent of the time. The networks became, in effect, electronic billboards for the candidates, showing political commercials not only as breaking news but as stand-ins for the candidates, and file footage aired interchangeably with news footage of the candidates.

The few cases where reporters corrected the facts illustrate how the networks might have covered political commercials. ABC's Richard Threlkeld ran excerpts from a Bush ad attacking Dukakis's defense stand by freezing the frame and correcting each mistaken or distorted claim. He also pointed out the exaggeration in a Dukakis ad attacking Bush's record on Social Security. CBS's Leslie Stahl corrected a deceptive statistic in Bush's revolving-door furlough ad, noting: "Part of the ad is false. . . . Two hundred sixty-eight murderers did not escape. . . . [T]he truth is only four first-degree murderers escaped while on parole."

Stahl concluded her report by observing, "Dukakis left the Bush attack ads unanswered for six weeks. Today campaign aides are engaged in a round of finger-pointing at who is to blame." But the networks also let the Bush furlough commercial run without challenge or correction. Before and even after her report, CBS ran excerpts of the ad without correction. In all, network newscasts ran excerpts from the revolving-door furlough ad ten times throughout the campaign, only once correcting the deceptive statistic.

It might be argued that it is up to the candidate to reply to his opponent's charges, not the press. But the networks' frequent use of political ads on the evening news created a strong disincentive for a candidate to challenge his opponent's ads. As Dukakis found, to attack a television ad as unfair or untrue is to invite the networks to run it again. In the final weeks before the election, the Dukakis campaign accused the Republicans of lying about his record on defense, and of using racist tactics in ads featuring Willie Horton, a black convict who raped and killed while on furlough from a Massachusetts prison. In reporting Dukakis's complaint, all three networks ran excerpts of the ads in question, including the highly charged pictures of Horton and the revolving door of convicts. Dukakis's response thus gave Bush's potent visuals another free run on the evening news.

The networks might reply that the ads are news and thus need to be shown, as long as they generate controversy in the campaign. But this rationale leaves them open to manipulation. Oddly enough, the networks were alive to this danger when confronted with the question of whether to air the videos the campaigns produced for their conventions. "I am not into tone poems," Lane Venardos, the executive producer in charge of convention coverage at CBS, told *The New York Times*. "We are not in the business of being propaganda arms of the political parties." But they seemed blind to the same danger during the campaign itself.

So successful was the Bush campaign at getting free time for its ads on the evening news that, after the campaign, commercial advertisers adopted a similar strategy. In 1989 a pharmaceutical company used unauthorized footage of Presidents Bush and Gorbachev to advertise a cold medication. "In the new year," the slogan ran, "may the only cold war in the world be the one being fought by us." Although two of the three networks refused to carry the commercial, dozens of network and local television news programs showed excerpts of the ad, generating millions of dollars of free airtime.

"I realized I started a trend," said Bush media consultant Roger Ailes in *The New York Times*. "Now guys are out there trying to produce commercials for the evening news." When Humphrey and Nixon hired Madison Avenue experts to help in their campaigns, some worried that, in the television age, presidents would be sold like products. Little did they imagine that, twenty years later, products would be sold like presidents.

Along with the attention to commercials and stagecraft in 1988 came an unprecedented focus on the stage managers themselves, the "media gurus," "handlers," and "spin-control artists." Only three reports featured media advisers in 1968, compared with twenty-six in 1988. And the numbers tell only part of the story.

The stance reporters have taken toward media advisers has changed dramatically over the past twenty years. In *The Selling of the President* (1969), Joe McGinniss exposed the growing role of media advisers with a sense of disillusion and outrage. By 1988 television reporters covered image-makers with deference, even admiration. In place of independent fact correction, reporters sought out media advisers as authorities in their own right to analyze the effectiveness and even defend the truthfulness of campaign commercials. They became "media gurus" not only for the candidates but for the networks as well.

For example, in an exchange with CBS anchor Dan Rather on Bush's debate performance, Stahl lavished admiration on the techniques of Bush's media advisers:

STAHL: "They told him not to look into the camera. [She gestures toward the camera as she speaks.] You know when you look directly into a camera you are cold, apparently they have determined."

RATHER [laughing]: "Bad news for anchormen I'd say."

STAHL: "We have a lot to learn from this. Michael Dukakis kept talking right into the camera. [Stahl talks directly into her own camera to demonstrate.] And according to the Bush people that makes you look programmed, Dan [Stahl laughs]. And they're very adept at these television symbols and television imagery. And according to our poll it worked."

RATHER: "Do you believe it?"

STAHL: "Yes I think I do, actually."

So hypersensitive were the networks to television image-making in 1988 that minor mishaps—gaffes, slips of the tongue, even faulty microphones—became big news. Politicians were hardly without mishaps in 1968, but these did not count as news. Only once in 1968 did a network even take note of a minor incident unrelated to the content of the campaign. In 1988 some twenty-nine reports highlighted trivial slips.

The emphasis on "failed images" reflected a kind of guerrilla warfare between the networks and the campaigns. The more the campaigns sought to control the images that appeared on the nightly news, the more the reporters tried to beat them at their own game, magnifying a minor mishap into a central feature of the media event.

Early in the 1988 campaign, for example, George Bush delivered a speech to a sympathetic audience of the American Legion, attacking his opponent's defense policies. In a slip, he declared that September 7, rather than December 7, was the anniversary of Pearl Harbor. Murmurs and chuckles from the audience alerted him to his error, and he quickly corrected himself.

The audience was forgiving, but the networks were not. All three network anchors highlighted the slip on the evening news. Dan Rather introduced CBS's report on Bush by declaring solemnly, "Bush's talk to audiences in Louisville was overshadowed by a strange happening." On NBC Tom Brokaw reported, "He departed from his prepared script and left his listeners mystified." Peter Jennings introduced ABC's report by mentioning Bush's attack on Dukakis, adding, "What's more likely to be remembered about today's speech is a slip of the tongue."

Some of the slips the networks highlighted in 1988 were not even verbal gaffes or misstatements, but simply failures on the part of candidates to cater to the cameras. In a report on the travails of the Dukakis campaign, Sam Donaldson seized on Dukakis's failure to play to ABC's television camera as evidence of his campaign's ineffectiveness. Showing Dukakis playing a trumpet with a local marching band, Donaldson chided, "He played the trumpet with his back to the camera." As Dukakis played "Happy Days Are Here Again," Donaldson's voice was heard from off-camera calling, "We're over here, governor."

One way of understanding the turn to image-conscious coverage in 1988 is to see how television news came to partake of the postwar modernist sensibility, particularly the pop art movement of the 1960s. Characteristic of this outlook is a self-conscious attention to art as performance, a focus on the process of image-making rather than on the ideas the images represent.

During the 1960s, when photography and television became potent forces for documentation and entertainment, they also became powerful influences on the work of artists. Photographers began to photograph the television set as part of the social landscape. Newspapers, photographs, and commercial products became part of the collage work of painters such as Robert Rauschenberg. Artists began to explore self-consciously their role in the image-making process.

For example, Lee Friedlander published a book of photography, *Self Portrait*, in which the artist's shadow or reflection was included in every frame. As critic Rod Slemmons notes, "By indicating the photographer is also a performer whose hand is impossible to hide, Friedlander set a precedent for disrupting the normal rules of photography." These "postmodernist" movements in art and photography foreshadowed the form television news would take by the late 1980s.

Andy Warhol once remarked, "The artificial fascinates me." In 1988 network reporters and producers, beguiled by the artifice of the modern presidential campaign, might well have said the same. Reporters alternated between reporting campaign images as if they were facts and exposing their contrived nature. Like Warhol, whose personality was always a presence in his work, reporters became part of the campaign theater they covered—as producers, as performers, and as critics. Like Warhol's reproductions of Campbell's soup cans, the networks' use of candidates' commercials directed our attention from the content and toward the packaging.

The assumption that the creation of appearances is the essence of political reality pervaded not only the reporting but the candidates' self-understanding and conduct with the press. When Dan Quayle sought to escape his image as a highly managed candidate, he resolved publicly to become his own handler, his own "spin doctor." "The so-called handlers story, part of it's true," he confessed to network reporters. "But there will be no more handlers stories, because I'm the handler and I'll do the spinning." Surrounded by a group of reporters on his campaign plane, Quayle announced, "I'm Doctor Spin, and I want you all to report that."

It may seem a strange way for a politician to talk, but not so strange in a media-conscious environment in which authenticity means being master of your own artificiality. Dukakis too sought to reverse his political fortunes by seeking to be master of his own image. This attempt was best captured in a commercial shown on network news in which Dukakis stood beside a television set and snapped off a Bush commercial attacking his stand on defense.

"I'm fed up with it," Dukakis declared. "Never seen anything like it in twenty-five years of public life. George Bush's negative television ads, distorting my record, full of lies, and he knows it." The commercial itself shows an image of an image—a Bush television commercial showing (and ridiculing) the media event where Dukakis rode in a tank. In his commercial, Dukakis complains that Bush's commercial showing the tank ride misstates Dukakis's position on defense.

As it appeared in excerpts on the evening news, Dukakis's commercial displayed a quintessentially modernist image of artifice upon artifice upon artifice: television news covering a Dukakis commercial containing a Bush commercial containing a Dukakis media event. In a political world governed by images of images, it seemed almost natural that the authority of the candidate be depicted by his ability to turn off the television set.

In the 1950s Edward R. Murrow noted that broadcast news was "an incompatible combination of show business, advertising, and news." Still, in its first decades television news continued to reflect a sharp distinction between the news and entertainment divisions of the networks. But by the 1980s network news operations came to be seen as profit centers for the large corporations that owned them, run by people drawn less from journalism than from advertising and entertainment backgrounds. Commercialization led to further emphasis on entertainment values, which heightened the need for dramatic visuals, fast pacing, quick cutting, and short sound bites. Given new technological means to achieve these effects—portable video cameras, satellite hookups, and sophisticated video-editing equipment—the networks were not only disposed but equipped to capture the staged media events of the campaigns.

The search for dramatic visuals and the premium placed on showmanship in the 1980s led to a new complicity between the White House image-makers and the networks. As Susan Zirinsky, a top CBS producer, acknowledged in Martin Schram's *The Great American Video Game,* "In a funny way, the [Reagan White House] advance men and I have the same thing at heart—we want the piece to look as good as [it] possibly can." In 1968 such complicity in stagecraft was scorned. Sanford Socolow, senior producer of the "CBS Evening News with Walter Cronkite," recently observed, "If someone caught you doing that in 1968 you would have been fired."

In a moment of reflection in 1988, CBS's political correspondents expressed their frustration with image-driven campaigns. "It may seem frivolous, even silly at times," said Schieffer. "But setting up pictures that drive home a message has become the No. 1 priority of the modern-day campaign. The problem, of course, is while it is often entertaining, it is seldom enlightening."

Rather shared his colleague's discomfort. But what troubled him about modern campaigns is equally troubling about television's campaign coverage. "With all this emphasis on the image," he asked, "what happens to the issues? What happens to the substance?"

POINTS TO PONDER

1. What is the difference between media reporters covering the issues of a campaign and covering the "theatrics" of a campaign?
2. If your opponent runs a misleading and deceptive political ad attacking you, is it better to ignore it or to attack the ad as misleading?
3. What impact has the shrinking size of sound bites had on the coverage of politics?

46

"DIPLOMACY IN A TELEVISION AGE: THE DANGERS OF TELEDEMOCRACY"
David R. Gergen

The conduct of foreign affairs has been profoundly affected by the emergence of television as an independent force. New technologies allow "real time" coverage of events throughout the globe. David Gergen, adviser to Presidents Nixon, Ford, Reagan, and Clinton, argues in this excerpt from Simon Serfaty's The Media and Foreign Policy *that U.S. officials have too often shaped their policies to fit the needs of television coverage in a misguided attempt to influence public opinion.*

After pointing out the advantages and liabilities of television as a medium, Gergen argues that Americans are woefully uninformed about international affairs. Thus foreign policy decisions should be made on the basis of U.S. national interests rather than with an eye toward public opinion. But just as important, officials should carefully weigh their explanations of foreign policy actions so that the public receives a coherent description rather than a constantly changing story based on inadequate information.

Since the early 1970s, it has been axiomatic that television constitutes an independent force in international affairs. President Richard Nixon carefully choreographed his visit to China for prime-time viewing back home. President Jimmy Carter's administration engaged in "verbal ping-pong" with Tehran as the two sent messages back and forth through the channels of television; and President Reagan converted "photo ops" into a science in his foreign trips. And even President Bush, though lower-keyed, chose Malta as the site for his first Soviet summit, searching for the perfect visual effect.

The Television Revolution

Recognizing the camera's power, foreign leaders, diplomats and terrorists have all followed suit, tailoring their messages to television audiences in America and elsewhere. Egypt's Anwar Sadat was one of the first foreign leaders to hire

American communication experts; the Sandinistas are only among the most recent. And who will soon forget the Chinese students in Tiananmen Square carrying aloft their Goddess of Liberty or the young men and women dancing atop the Berlin Wall, sending a euphoric message to television viewers across the world?

The stunning events of 1989 and 1990 have made the world understand how positive a force television can be in human affairs. Time and again, evidence has surfaced that televised pictures from the West were a catalyst for people in communist countries of the East to press for change and that, in turn, repressed people used the medium to build public support in the West. Were it not for modern communication technologies—from television to the fax machine—modern revolutions might never have occurred. The past two years have been the most triumphant in television's short history.

Yet there is reason to ask whether in the land that invented the cathode ray tube, the United States, public officials have learned that there are also limits to television and the role that it should play in a democracy. Too often in recent years, U.S. officials have substituted the power of television for the power of their own reasoning, believing that successful policies must first and foremost please the Great God of Public Opinion. This emphasis on teledemocracy marks a serious departure in American diplomacy. For most of U.S. history, diplomats have been guided by their own judgments and only later have worried about public reaction. Indeed, in the first twenty years after World War II, American diplomacy was conducted with the rather certain expectation that public opinion would support it. Daniel Yankelovich has found that whenever a President like Eisenhower spoke to the nation on television, half his audience would automatically grant him the benefit of the doubt on any foreign issue simply because of who he was and what his office represented. Congress also was a ready partner.

It is well understood that Vietnam shattered the postwar foreign policy consensus, leading Congress to become more obtrusive and causing the executive branch to become much more concerned with public support. It is less appreciated that changes were also taking place in television technology which brought the world more fully into American living rooms. During the 1970s, for example, television introduced the portable videotape camera (or minicam), which allowed editing shortcuts. Soon after, satellites were sent aloft and earth stations were built in most nations. By the end of the decade, American television was prepared to broadcast instantaneously from almost everywhere in the world. The "global village" was upon us.

Increasingly during the 1980s, government officials have shaped their policies with an eye toward generating positive and timely television coverage and securing public approval. What too often counts is how well the policy will "play," how the pictures will look, whether the right signals are being sent, and whether the public will be impressed by the swiftness of the government's response—not whether the policy promotes America's long-term interests.

Given the number of hours that Americans spend in front of their television sets and the degree to which they depend on it for information, such preoccupation with the power of the camera is understandable. The camera is an extraordinarily powerful instrument. No other technology in history has so influenced a culture. Nonetheless, there is no need for leading officials to be mesmerized or intimidated by television and public opinion.

Realities of Television

Before the world turned upside down in 1989, the charge most often hurled against the networks was that they regularly neglected international affairs in favor of domestic news, soft features and personalities. In fact, as Michael Mosettig, a former NBC producer now a writer for Public Television's "MacNeil'-Lehrer Newshour," pointed out in the late 1980s, "The foreign news content of the evening programs has doubled and trebled since 1976. . . . Ten years ago U.S. network coverage consisted largely of canned film features; now it runs like a wire service, with morning and evening cycles of updated news and pictures." A study by James F. Larson of evening news broadcasts over the period of a decade (1972–81) found that on average the networks devoted ten of their twenty-two minutes—40 percent—to coverage of foreign affairs. Only the most serious American newspapers come anywhere close to that proportion of foreign news; most smaller papers give less than 10 percent of their "news hole" to foreign affairs.

Moreover, the Larson study does not take account of the foreign affairs coverage by the networks, PBS, and CNN during non-evening hours. "Nightline," for example, was born during the Tehran hostage crisis and continues to emphasize international issues such as apartheid. The morning news shows not only carry reports from overseas, but sometimes move their entire operations to countries such as China and South Korea. CNN has not only built a far-flung system of correspondents, but is broadcasting by satellite to elite audiences in many other countries. The problem, therefore, is not indifference to foreign news.

In fact, the problem with television inheres in the medium itself. By its very nature, television is an instrument of simplicity in a world of complexity. In a report of 80 seconds—150 words at most—a television reporter cannot provide context or background. No matter how many stories it devotes to international affairs, a thirty-minute news broadcast must essentially be a headline service. It cannot be educational, nor does it even attempt to be. A former network president and veteran of the industry was dismissive when I once asked him whether his network had a duty to enlighten. "We have a duty to tell people the news—period," was his response. As many old-timers in television admit, they see their task as asking each day two essential questions about the news: Is the world still safe today? Is my family still safe today? If everything is alright, they feel perfectly justified providing entertainment.

Another limitation is that television cannot and does not provide continuity in its coverage of international affairs. As a medium that depends on drama, it is drawn to conflict and crisis. It shuns the quiet periods in which most people live. For instance, in 1982, when El Salvador held a critical election, television crews descended on the country, turning it into a center of world attention. American senators and congressmen inundated the region. Within forty-eight hours of the election, however, the cameras had left to cover the Falklands War. It was as if the lights went out over El Salvador, and the country's subsequent struggle to preserve democracy disappeared from sight. Out of sight, it also passed out of mind for American viewers. Television loves sagas in which someone wins and someone loses. It abhors long, tedious, complex stories and will usually ignore them if possible.

It is also obvious that television has terrible blind spots. In his study, James Larson found that the major networks rarely cover Latin America, sub-Saharan Africa, South Asia or Australia. Canada was also lucky if it made the news. Instead, stories were heavily centered on Europe, the Soviet Union and the Middle East. The most egregious mistake made by television in the past concerned Cambodia. A study by William Adams found that during the height of the worst massacre in modern times, the networks' evening news coverage of Cambodia averaged only ten minutes a year. The carnage was virtually ignored until it was far too late to arouse world attention. Television was also slow to recognize the extent of famine in Africa. American television was eager to dramatize ethnic conflicts in Azerbaijan and Armenia, two hotspots in the Soviet Union; should similar trouble develop in Yugoslavia, it is doubtful they will attract one tenth the coverage.

To be fair, networks are often handicapped by government restrictions on movement and coverage. For example, the Soviet invasion of Afghanistan would have caused much more of a sensation if Western television had had early access to the fighting. Many African nations are reluctant to grant visas to journalists, and the Soviet Union until recently has been highly restrictive. Restrictions on television coverage have also spread to industrialized nations such as South Africa, Israel, and Britain. The pattern is alarming because it appears to work to the short-term political advantage of the censoring nation. Should it take hold, television's "window on the world" will be even cloudier than it already is.

Room for Improvement

There was a time when observers thought that the development of new technologies would make television more thorough and complete in its coverage of the world, but the most recent breakthroughs—mini-cams and satellites—have actually been a setback to the quality of coverage. Because it is now possible to fly a crew to the scene of a crisis and instantaneously send back information, television is even more addicted to "parachute journalism" than before. "Technology has ruined the life of the foreign correspondent," NBC's Richard Valeriani has said, underscoring the point that correspondents now seem to spend more time jetsetting than concentrating on a small handful of countries. Moreover, reporting in one time zone while feeding stories to New York on another can make for grueling eighteen-hour days, hardly a lifestyle conducive to reflect reporting as Valeriani and others have admitted.

The cost of maintaining a foreign news operation has skyrocketed as the dollar has declined in value overseas. Some news organizations have found that maintaining a correspondent in Tokyo requires more than $200,000 in supplemental expenditures to meet that city's high costs of living. Cutbacks in foreign staffs have already occurred in several organizations. Between 1985 and 1989, for instance, *Time* magazine's masthead showed a cut from thirty-six to twenty-six in the number of overseas correspondents. The number of journalists sent scrambling overseas increased sharply in 1989–90, but whether that same commitment to international coverage will remain after the world calms down is highly uncertain.

Television clearly serves many excellent purposes. Yet it is a mistake to expect too much of the medium. In particular, policy makers cannot assume that television alone will ever create a public informed and enlightened about international affairs. Television can awaken people's interests, but it does not yet have the capacity to educate them.

Realities of Public Opinion

Just as it is important for policy makers to accept television's limitations, it is equally important to understand and accept at least three hard truths about public opinion:

First, even though their exposure to foreign affairs has increased, Americans in general have an abysmal understanding of the world. A number of surveys over the years have shown a startling lack of knowledge among the mass public. In 1981, for example, a *Washington Post*–ABC national survey asked the question, "One of these two nations, the United States or the Soviet Union, is a member of what is known as the NATO alliance. Do you happen to know which country that is, or are you not sure?" Through random guessing—say, by flipping a coin—50 percent should have given the correct response. Only 47 percent actually answered the question correctly. In the same survey, the public was asked which two countries were involved in the SALT talks: only 37 percent knew the answer. Another poll during that period asked for the location of El Salvador; 25 percent knew the answer. Barry Sussman of the *Post* concluded: "Whether they realize it or not, people are intentionally turning away from public affairs. It is not a lack of brains that is involved here. The little poll quizzes do not measure intelligence; they measure the storage of bits of information. A person need not be bright to avoid telling an interviewer, as one did, that El Salvador 'is in Louisiana, near Baton Rouge.'"

Second, Americans show little appetite for increasing their understanding of the world. At the elite or opinion-maker level, there is a keen interest in gobbling up new information about the world, most recently about Japan. *The Economist*, for example, has experienced its most rapid sales growth in the United States and circulation here now outpaces that in the United Kingdom. But consider a recent experience of the three major American news magazines, *Time, Newsweek,* and *U.S. News & World Report.* These three magazines all featured on their cover the 1985 summit meeting in Geneva between President Reagan and General Secretary Gorbachev, a splashy event that attracted saturation coverage by television. Ordinarily, magazines featuring events that have received widespread television attention score well on the newsstands. Yet, for all three magazines, the Geneva cover was that year's worst-selling cover. Other covers on foreign affairs, unless they concern crises of Americans in trouble, share a similar fate. It is hardly surprising, therefore, that only a modest number of magazine covers are devoted to foreign affairs. Recent events in Eastern Europe provided further evidence that the public is not easily drawn into major international events: ratings for national news programs actually went down during the period when communism was collapsing. Polls suggested that the public felt too confused to watch closely.

Third, there is no reason to believe that public opinion will grow more informed. In early 1989, *National Geographic* published the results of a disappointing survey by the Gallup organization, showing that Americans know less basic geography than the citizens of Sweden, West Germany, Japan, France and Canada, and considerably less than they knew forty years ago. More distressing, eighteen- to twenty-four-year-old Americans knew less than their counterparts in any nine countries; America was, in fact, the only country where young adults knew less about geography than did adults aged fifty-five and over. There is, as Gilbert M. Grosvenor, president of the National Geographic Society, has reported, a shocking lack of geographic knowledge throughout this country. And several surveys have demonstrated that familiarity with foreign languages is also low.

These findings do not support the view that Americans are dumber than other people. It has been aptly said that while one should not overestimate the amount of information Americans have, one also should not underestimate their intelligence. On many occasions, Americans have demonstrated sound common sense. Recent polls, for example, show that while approval ratings for Gorbachev have shot upward in the United States, the public still urges caution in trusting the Soviets and in extending financial help. Clearly, the American public has not forgotten the lessons behind the failures of détente. Moreover, despite the fears expressed by some about conflict escalation, Americans supported recent government efforts in the Persian Gulf, correctly sensing that they were in the national interest.

Americans have also demonstrated that, if a strong case can be made, they are open to persuasion. The Carter administration, for example, was able to turn public opinion around on the Panama Canal treaty. The larger point, however, is that Americans do not pay close attention to foreign affairs, even if they are frequently exposed to them. As Walter Lippmann noted in the early 1920s, most citizens spend their time thinking about their jobs, their families, their neighbors and communities. They cannot and should not be expected to keep up with every twist and turn in a fast-changing world. That is the job of their elected representatives.

Lessons for Foreign and National Security Policy Making

From these realities one can draw certain obvious lessons about the formulation of foreign policy. Most important, policy decisions ought to be made with an eye first and foremost toward what is sound and in the national interest, not toward what is temporarily popular in the opinion polls or toward what will gain a quick, favorable notice on television. A government cannot make sound decisions about, for example, the use of military force based on a referendum or some theory of participatory democracy. The public simply does not know enough about the world to be able to render sound judgments on issues such as the Strategic Defense Initiative, the START negotiations, or the ABM treaty. Rather, it is entitled to expect its elected and appointed officials to act on these issues and then to have the chance to throw them out of office if they fail. Were foreign policy to be dictated solely by public opinion, several sound decisions would never have been taken. It is highly likely that the United States would long ago have canceled its foreign aid program, for instance, and it is very unlikely that we would have instituted a peacetime draft before World War II.

By the same token, it is a serious mistake for executive branch officials to make policy hastily in order to meet news broadcast deadlines. Policy makers should respect the power of television and learn how to utilize it in conducting policy. They should not be cowed by it. In retrospect, several key members of the Carter administration thought they were wrong to respond within hours to the Soviet invasion of Afghanistan, a decision based in part on a perceived need to make the evening news. A better U.S. policy would have resulted from larger deliberations inside the U.S. government. Similarly, some members of the Reagan administration believed it was a mistake to rush out with a full-scale condemnation of the Soviet shootdown of Korean Airlines flight 007. Some of the information that the administration had in hand at the time later turned out to be wrong. In retrospect, it would have been more effective to build an air-tight presentation over a period of days so that the credibility of the strong case against the Soviets could not be undermined. Officials sometimes argue that the American public demands fast answers from its government, especially in a television age. There is no evidence to support this view. On the contrary, the public seems to care more about results and consequences than about one-night headlines.

To sustain a policy, the executive branch must also have a clear rationale for what it is doing *before* it acts. It is not necessary to have public approval in advance, but if public support is needed after the fact, the government must have a persuasive case that will stand up over time. The Reagan administration blundered, for example, in failing to develop a clear rationale for sending marines to Lebanon. When there was no obvious mission that could be explained to the country, support for the exercise crumbled, and the marines eventually had to be withdrawn. Similarly, it is now clear that the administration's efforts to bolster the Contras were badly handicapped by the lack of a clear rationale for the policy. In this case, the public became confused because the administration kept shifting its argument.

Once it has adopted a policy, there is also a clear need for an administration to conduct an open dialogue with the press on its purposes and thinking. Obviously, in order to carry out a policy, an administration will need to build and maintain public support. Past administrations have demonstrated that such support can be sustained. For instance, the Reagan administration demonstrated a remarkable effectiveness in convincing the European public to accept the deployment of missiles on their soil.

There is, however, another equally compelling reason for such a dialogue: in a representative system, a government that assumes the responsibility to make decisions must also accept a high degree of accountability for its actions. We do not permit the Supreme Court to issue fiats when making major decisions. It is expected to issue carefully written opinions explaining its reasoning. Similarly, the executive branch has a clear-cut responsibility to explain its policies and thinking, to answer questions, and to be *accountable*. The American media have a legitimate and important role in insisting on those explanations and in pressing for a clear public accounting.

* * * *

POINTS TO PONDER
1. According to Gergen, what are the biases of television as a medium?
2. What impact has television had on the conduct of U.S. foreign affairs?
3. What does Gergen recommend for the way presidents conduct foreign and national security policy making?

47

"THEY'VE GOT YOUR NUMBER"
Charles Kenney

The importance of public opinion polls in political campaigns and even in government is well established. Certainly public opinion ought to be weighed heavily in a democracy, and there are hundreds of polling firms that conduct opinion polls from the local to the national levels. But how much confidence can we have in the accuracy of these modern-day oracles? To answer this question journalist Charles Kenney of the Boston Globe *presents a brief history of public opinion polling, highlighting a few famous blunders to illustrate the dangers of poor techniques.*

In this 1987 article, Kenney emphasizes that the reliability of the poll is crucially dependent upon the randomness of the sample of people surveyed. The size of the sample and the nature of the questions asked also affect the amount of confidence we can have in the results. To be informed citizens we should all understand enough to know which polls we can have confidence in and which polls we should dismiss as incompetent or biased.

America's first great polling fiasco came not during the 1948 presidential campaign, when so many pollsters predicted that Thomas E. Dewey would beat Harry S. Truman, but during Franklin Delano Roosevelt's 1936 campaign for reelection. In those days, a New York magazine called *Literary Digest* ran the oldest and most highly publicized survey on presidential campaigns. It had picked the winner of presidential races from 1920 through 1932. In 1936, the *Digest* wanted to conduct the broadest possible survey, so its editors, in a rather spectacular blunder, settled upon two lists: a compilation of names from telephone directories and a list of people who had registered automobiles.

Months before the election, the *Digest* mailed out 10 million mock ballots to people whose names appeared on the two lists. By late October the *Digest* received 2,376,523 completed ballots. On the basis of that information, the *Digest* predicted that Alfred M. Landon would defeat Roosevelt in a landslide, that the president would receive a mere 41 percent of the vote. (Naturally, Democrats challenged the *Digest*'s findings, none more vigorously than a group of Massachusetts Roosevelt supporters who offered to bet the *Digest*'s editors $100,000 that FDR would win. The editors declined the wager.)

As it turned out, of course, Roosevelt won in a landslide, taking 63 percent of the popular vote and winning every state except Maine and Vermont. So spectacularly wrong was the *Literary Digest* poll that it brought down upon itself the swift and fierce wrath of polling skeptics (and partisan Democrats). Only days after the election, Sen. Kenneth D. McKellar, a Tennessee Democrat, proposed a congressional investigation into the *Digest* poll and suggested that the federal government strictly regulate all straw polls. Nonbelievers in the infant quasi-science of polling wondered, along with believers: How could the *Digest* poll have been *so* wrong?

Henry E. Brady, an associate professor of political science at the University of Chicago and an expert on polling, says the *Digest*'s flaw was as obvious as it was fatal. "In the midst of the Depression," says Brady, "only the rich had telephones and automobiles." As a result, he says, the *Digest* wound up with a sample in which there were too many wealthy people and Republicans and not enough poor people and Democrats.

Thus did *Literary Digest* commit polling's mortal sin: It did not base its survey on a random sample of the electorate. Random sampling is the *only* way to conduct an accurate poll because only a purely random sample guarantees that every voter in the population has an equal chance of being questioned.

Since the *Digest* catastrophe delighted polling skeptics 51 years ago, the survey-research business has changed radically. What was then a fledgling business has grown into a massive industry. Where once only a few national pollsters struggled to find buyers for their numbers, today hundreds of polling companies provide tens of thousands of surveys to a seemingly insatiable clientele that includes national, regional, and even local newspapers, and radio and television stations as well as politicians running for every imaginable office. For numbers and analyses that are sometimes insightful, sometimes meaningless, the purchasers of polls pay anywhere from $5,000 to more than $50,000. An average telephone survey—a good one—costs about $20,000.

By far, the greatest number of surveys conducted in the United States these days are not political but market research—on every conceivable type of product from liquid laundry detergents to teen-age movie idols. Our focus here, however, is on political-survey research, where, as the business has grown—particularly during the past 10 to 15 years—the quality of polls has improved. Pre-1970s methods could be maddeningly slow, clumsy, and imprecise. Results published weeks or more after a survey was conducted were as stale as last month's news. Today, largely through the use of computers and telephones, polls are strikingly fast and often as fresh as today's bread. And because today's survey methods are more sophisticated, polls are more reliable than ever before.

Polling is not a science, but it is constructed on a foundation of sound, widely accepted scientific principles. Some of the best pollsters, well grounded in mathematics and probability theory, are also artful analyzers of raw data (the worst pollsters are ignorant of methods *and* politics). The work of the best people can be precisely executed methods that lead to brilliantly inspired insight. Other pollsters, entrepreneurs who have gotten in on the boom times to make a buck, produce polls that are quick and dirty, overnight wonders by schlock operators with shaky methodology.

Polls from the fascinating to the ridiculous, the perplexing to the unfathomable, will be on display during the next 14 months, leading up to the 1988 presidential election, a campaign during which Americans will be inundated with polls as never before. But as you face all those numbers, graphs, and charts, there's no need to throw up your hands and give in to the avalanche. Understanding polls is easier when you know where they come from; why they work (or don't work); how they were conducted; who uses them (and for what); who conducts them; and what distinguishes a good poll from a bad one.

And if you think it odd that this relatively young industry has so captured the American imagination, consider that our hunger for information about ourselves—and even more so for glimpses of what lies ahead—is as old as civilization.

"There is a constant need in society for prediction, forecasting: for what academics call the 'reduction of uncertainty.' People want to know what's going to be around the corner in life," says Gary Orren, an associate professor at Harvard's John F. Kennedy School of Government.

"Almost every society has an important place for oracles, soothsayers, prophets. You'd be hard-pressed to find any group that doesn't have someone who serves that role of prediction and forecasting. Pollsters are the 20th century's version of soothsayers."

Polls and Possums

Early pollsters were a favorite target for tart-tongued commentators who saw the new business as a fraud. In 1939, a Louisiana newspaper called *The American Progress* reported on a trip by some of George Gallup's interviewers to New Orleans: "Three months ago a half-dozen postgraduate 'Social Science Workers' from Princeton University, augmented by seven or eight East Side New Yorkers who had never in their lives seen a possum, tasted a sweet potato, or chewed a plug of tobacco, arrived in New Orleans to conduct a so-called survey of public opinion.

"After taking a few sightseeing trips, getting some fancy grub at the famous restaurants in New Orleans, looking at some swamps, and sending picture postcards back home, they then wrote some mystic figures in their little black books and hurried back to their boss, a low-ceiling guy with bifocal glasses who sits enthroned way up there in Princeton, New Jersey, like the Wizard of Oz and peers owlishly at figures all day long until he looks like a left-handed figure 4.

"And out of this hocus-pocus of numbers and dope sheets and form charts, lo and behold, if up didn't jump The Gallup Poll!"

A popular target for mockery, Dr. George Gallup Sr. was also probably the most important figure in polling history. The University of Chicago's Brady says Gallup did no less than "institutionalize political polling."

Gallup, who grew up in Iowa, began his survey work during the 1920s, while he was teaching journalism at the University of Iowa. For years he experimented with dozens of different methodologies, finally settling upon a random-probability method of interviewing voters—an approach that was the subject of his PhD dissertation in 1928. Using his then-revolutionary methods, Gallup received some national exposure in 1934 when he polled, rather accurately, as it turned out, some of that year's congressional races. The following year Gallup founded his company and began by selling the results of his surveys—in the form of a column that he wrote—to 35 newspapers.

Respect for Gallup soon increased, when, as the *Digest* poll was found to be worthless, Gallup and two other fledgling polling companies—Crossley and

Roper—all predicted a landslide for Roosevelt. That inspired some confidence in the new business, but it wasn't long before pollsters suffered a hugely discouraging setback. In the 1948 presidential election, the major survey-research organizations—with Gallup very much in the lead—stopped polling several weeks before the election, in the belief that few voters change their minds late in a campaign. Gallup and the others predicted that Dewey would win. But as Truman triumphantly showed the next morning, in the famous photo with the now-notorious headline announcing a Dewey victory, the pollsters stopped too soon to detect a massive late shift in support for Truman, Dark days followed: Gallup was widely ridiculed, and his client list shrank. A book was mailed to his company entitled *What Dr. Gallup Knows about Polls.* Its pages were blank.

Since that embarrassment of 1948, two devices have improved the speed and quality of polls: computers and telephones. Until the late 1960s, most surveys were conducted by hired interviewers, men and women who visited voters in their homes clipboards in hand, a process that usually took at least an hour per interview. While long interviews provided pollsters with more information than they could get on the phone, in-person interviewers couldn't be supervised as closely as phone callers, and the possibility of bias—as slight as a knowing glance or rolled eyes during an interview—was always there. The answers from those interviews—mounds of paper—were hand-tabulated, which could take days or even weeks. Today, interviews can be conducted in minutes over the phone, and results can be produced by computer within hours.

"The telephone is a leap forward for public opinion polls," says Geoffrey D. Garin, president of Garin-Hart Strategic Research in Washington. "Because such a large percentage of the American population lives in households equipped with phones—it's up in the 90s—you can contact people very quickly and much less expensively and with relatively little bias. Now we can do things virtually overnight. Between having telephones and computers there are campaigns where we will do the interviewing from 6 in the evening until 9:30 and complete 400 interviews. It will be key punched and processed at my office and by 12 o'clock that night, sitting in front of the results on my computer at home, I can be on the phone with the campaign manager, talking about the results and the implications for the campaign."

How Polls Work: A Layman's Guide

On the face of it, the notion that by talking with 1,500 Americans one can accurately reflect the views of 120 million voters seems preposterous. The idea, however, is rooted in time-honored principles of probability theory. The notion is simply this: If a random sampling of a universe is taken, that sampling will accurately represent the entire universe.

Edward H. Lazarus, a partner in the Washington polling firm of Information Associates, taught political science and survey methodology at Yale before going into the polling business full time. Lazarus says that "a randomly selected sample would be in every way representative of the population at large because every individual in the universe has an equal probability of being picked. If that holds true, your attitudes, demographics, geography will be represented proportionally in the sample."

Garin, of Garin-Hart Strategic Research, explains that the "reliability of a sample is almost never perfect. You can't interview a sample and be absolutely sure the results are identical to what you'd get if you interviewed everybody in the universe. There is a margin of error. If you do everything perfectly right there is still a margin of error, and the most important part of determining the margin of error is the sample size."

A mathematical formula based on probability and statistical theories places the margin of error for a sample size of 400 at plus or minus 5 percent. Garin says that means that "in 95 out of 100 cases, the difference between the results of the survey and the results of interviewing everybody in the universe would not differ by more than 5 percent in either direction."

Perhaps the most mind-boggling aspect of polling is that the size of the universe being polled is irrelevant to the accuracy of the survey. Neil Beck, a political science professor at the University of California at San Diego, takes this point a little further, into what might seem like the ionosphere of mathematics. A random sampling of 1,000 voters, says Beck, would just as accurately reflect the views of 10,000 voters as it would 20 trillion voters. In fact, he says, the theory of probability assumes the population being studied is an infinite number. Laymen don't understand it, Garin says, "but it's the truth."

Most pollsters, says Garin, don't interview fewer than 400 people because the margin of error rises exponentially as the sample size goes down. When a sample drops to 200, for example, the margin of error rises to 7 percent, a sample of 800 yields a margin of error of about 3.5 percent, while a sample of 1,500—the standard size used in polls in the United States—has a margin of error of about 2.5 percent.

Most pollsters select their sample of people to be interviewed from lists of voters or randomly selected phone numbers (random–digit dialing). The advantage of using voter lists is that the pollster is sure the people surveyed are eligible to vote, while the advantage of random dialing is that even voters with unlisted phone numbers may be reached. Both methods are considered reliable.

Modern polling is far from trouble-free, however, Orren says there are three kinds of errors pollsters make. The first, which is the least frequently made, according to Orren, is a sampling error. These aren't as egregious as the *Literary Digest* mistake in '36, but the absence of randomness still renders a survey worthless.

The second type is known as a "measurement error," which usually involves poorly worded questions. For example, some pollsters ask voters whether they rate a politician's performance as excellent, good, fair, or poor. What does a voter who says "fair" mean? asks Orren. " 'Fair' for some people means pretty good." For others it means not so good. Because of the ambiguity, "fair" shouldn't be offered as a category, says Orren.

The third type of mistake, says Orren, is a "specification error," meaning "you've got a bad theory looming behind your questions. It means you might get the right answers to the wrong questions." For example, he says, he once did a survey on busing in a Boston suburb and found that most residents favored busing as a means to achieve school integration. However, he found that many of the people polled didn't much care about the issue. Among those who did care about it—enough to vote for or against a politician based on his position on busing—opposition to busing was overwhelming. Pollsters often make the mistake, says Orren, of conducting polls based on the belief that "everyone cares about everything and that it has the same political consequences for everyone."

The Making of a Poll

Most of the best and most reputable pollsters follow similar methods in conducting their surveys for clients who are running for public office, using five essential steps:

1. Draft a questionnaire. All pollsters ask voters interviewed for standard demographic data such as age, income, race, party identification, and so on. And most also ask about a politician's performance and whether voters like the politician. Once the questionnaire is drafted, the pollster submits it to the politician for approval. Each question adds time on the phone during the interview process—and so to the cost—so Washington pollster Ed Lazarus says that in formulating a question, he asks himself: "What would we or could we do differently if we knew the answer to this question?" If the answer is that very little or nothing would be done differently, he doesn't ask the question.

2. Generate a sample. Samples can be drawn in dozens, if not hundreds or thousands, of ways. Some pollsters select their samples from voting lists, others use telephone books. Like many pollsters, Lazarus buys his samples. He pays for a computer-generated list of randomly selected phone numbers—minus most business phones—in the state he's polling. This method is more likely than some others to produce a random sample because it reaches people with unlisted phone numbers. In a statewide race, particularly in a large state, most pollsters do at least 800 interviews. This size sample—which is not dramatically more accurate than one with 400 interviews—permits a pollster to break out subgroups—women, blacks, or residents of a particular media market, for example. If the sample is much smaller than 800, it will probably include too few members of subgroups for a reliable analysis. If Lazarus wants 800 completed interviews, he begins with a list of about 5,000 numbers. Many numbers aren't

attached to working phones, some business numbers slip through, some people refuse to talk, others (in the case of random dialing) aren't registered to vote, and still others aren't at home to answer the phone. That makes call-backs crucial. One of the most important features of any good survey is that interviewers always try to call back a voter who is not home on the first try. Says Harrison Hickman, "We want to make sure every person has an equal opportunity to be selected, and you're not doing that if you're only calling each person one time."

3. Conduct the interviews. Rare is the pollster these days who has interviews conducted in person. Hiring someone to visit a voter costs about twice as much as a phone interview. Some survey companies have phone banks in their offices and hire and train a cadre of callers. Others, like Lazarus, contract their calls out to a telephone-interviewing service. Lazarus uses a company in suburban Philadelphia to which he ships the phone numbers and the questionnaires. Does it make a difference who makes the calls? A big difference, says Lazarus. "It's important that it be someone who is not going to irritate or annoy you by their voice or diction or language, someone who can establish a rapport quickly so the respondent has an investment in this process." Lazarus says it is important that the callers not know about or care about the candidates. Callers in Philadelphia aren't concerned with the outcome of a US Senate race in Nevada or California and therefore won't be biased in their interviewing. The longest phone interviews pollsters will conduct run 35 or 40 minutes, and some, like Lazarus, are uncomfortable trying to keep voters on the phone for more than 25 minutes. Surveys conducted early in a campaign take three, four, or even five nights to complete. Near the end of a heated campaign, most pollsters complete a new survey every night, between the hours of 6 and 9:30.

4. Process the results. After the interviews are completed, the questionnaires are key punched so the data can be processed by a computer. The computer provides hundreds, sometimes thousands, of pages of data, mostly in the form of cross-tabulations such as the popularity of a candidate among women, the major issue among Hispanics, or the character trait most appealing to undecided voters.

5. Analyze the results. The pollster studies the data, searching for particularly salient information. The pollster will then provide the client with answers to major questions, such as job rating and the horse race. Over the course of a few days, or sometimes weeks—particularly if it is *very* early in the campaign—the pollster than prepares a detailed, written report. The report is generally delivered when the pollster makes an oral presentation to the client, which usually lasts for several hours and consists mainly of advice—based on the survey findings—about what direction the campaign should take.

The *real* last step, of course, is getting paid. A statewide telephone survey of 800 interviews with a lengthy questionnaire runs between $20,000 and $30,000. In general, phone surveys cost in the neighborhood of $30 to $35 per interview—about $12,000 to $15,000 for a 400-sample survey; about $45,000 to $55,000 for a 1,500-sample survey.

How Polls Are Used

Newspapers, magazines, and television and radio stations use polls as news items. Candidates use them to formulate strategy. The oft-repeated cynic's cliche about polls holds that candidates read them so they can pander to the populace. But candidates who shift directions with every political zephyr don't often go far in politics—Americans generally see to it that their elected leaders have a bit more heft than that. Do unscrupulous candidates use polls for manipulative purposes? Of course, but probably far less often than doubters suggest.

The cynical notion that politicians use surveys to tailor their positions to the majority of voters' has grown rather tired through the years. A politician shifting views on major topics purely to remain in tune with the polls would quickly become transparent. That is not to say that politicians don't use polls to help them get elected—that's precisely what they do. How can a poll help? Let's say, for example, that a candidate for president finds that because of his position on oil-import quotas he has no chance at all of winning Louisiana. But he has a remote shot at taking New Jersey. That small bit of information is valuable because it tells a campaign that it should not waste its major resources—advertising dollars and the candidate's time—in Louisiana but might profitably concentrate on New Jersey.

Or let's say that a state representative is running for mayor of Boston and finds through a poll that he is quite popular throughout the city with one exception—elderly voters don't much like him. Let's say this candidate, as a state rep, had a strong record of supporting causes popular among senior citizens, but, for some reason, the poll reveals that many seniors don't see this candidate as a friend (perception and reality are often at odds in politics). That poll data is of immense value because the problem that has been detected through the survey can be corrected. The candidate can step up activity among the elderly, visiting more senior centers. And the campaign can target direct-mail and radio advertising to the elderly, focusing on the candidate's record on senior-citizens' issues.

Predictably, pollsters get rather grumpy when asked about the use of polls for what some see as manipulation. Harrison Hickman, of Hickman-Maslin Research in Washington, D.C., says polls provide information that allows his clients to be shown in the best possible light. A trace of indignation creeps into Hickman's voice when he poses what he clearly considers an absurd question: "We should be obligated to tell the *worst* side of our client's story?"

Polls are a way for candidates to listen to the voters, says Hickman. And once a candidate has begun executing the strategy—that is, attempting to communicate a specific message about himself or his views through news stories and advertising—a poll is a way to measure whether the message is getting through to voters.

Oddly enough, even though polling had been around for at least 30 years, the first candidate to have a pollster working within his campaign was John F.

Kennedy in 1960. His pollster was Louis Harris, leader of one of the oldest and most established polling companies in the nation.

The Big-Name Pollsters

While polling companies have sprouted up around the country to fill the demand of local and regional media outlets and to service candidates for lesser offices, the pollsters who handle the major campaigns could easily fit in a small jet. Most pollsters—Democrat and Republican alike—seem to agree that the best in the business are two well-established, very successful Republicans: Richard Wirthlin of Decision Making Information in Washington, whose best-known client currently occupies the White House, and Robert Teeter, president of Market Opinion Research in Detroit. Both men are considered very smart and thoughtful, and both understand not only the science of polling but political strategy.

Among the Democrats, the well-respected pollsters include Peter Hart of Garin-Hart, William Hamilton, Edward Lazarus, Harrison Hickman, and Edward Maslin, all based in Washington. Perhaps the most controversial of all American pollsters is Patrick Caddell, who gained fame as a wunderkind barely out of his teens in the 1972 McGovern presidential campaign. Some colleagues consider Caddell a brilliant strategist; others regard him as a has-been.

A number of the major pollsters come from academia, where they studied and taught political science, statistics, and survey methodology. But many other pollsters operating throughout the country have little if any formal training. Polling is an unregulated business. There is no licensing authority or professional association. Anyone with a basic knowledge of polling and a personal computer can open up shop.

Reading Polls Intelligently

At times during the next year or so it may seem that you hear or read about two or three different polls a day. The key to becoming a smart consumer of polling information is to look for a few indications that often reveal the differences between polls you can trust and polls you can't.

Perhaps the most important aspect of any poll is its author. As a general rule, you can feel safe in trusting polls conducted by the likes of Wirthlin, Teeter, or the major national newspapers or television networks.

Next, make sure the precise question asked is printed in full. Read the question carefully. Does it strike you as fair? Or does it seem, through loaded wording, to have an inherent bias that tilts the respondent toward a particular response?

Not all polls provide information about methodology, but look for how the sample was selected. If the people interviewed were selected either from voter lists or through random-digit dialing, you can feel comfortable about it.

Next, look for a sample of at least 600 interviews. If fewer than 400 people were polled, you can skip the survey. If it consists of at least 400 randomly selected people, the overall results may be fine. But if the sample is only 400, or even 600, don't trust results from subgroups. A poll with a sample of 400 would have a subsample of, say, undecided voters, that was simply too small to analyze intelligently.

Also look for a sample where voters are screened so that the results reflect the attitudes of voters who are likely to vote, particularly in primaries. Some pollsters force respondents to pass tough screens. They ask not only whether the voter plans to vote but whether he or she voted in the past few elections, if the voter can name the candidates running for certain offices, and if the voter knows the date of the election.

Finally, see when the poll was conducted. If all the interviews were done over the Labor Day weekend, when people with the opportunity are likely to be away on vacation, chances are very good that the survey overrepresents poor and working people and underrepresents the wealthy. If the interviews were done only during the day, the survey probably oversampled women and older people.

Ours is a healthy if not voracious appetite for polling information, yet there seems little doubt that our collective hunger will be sated by the heaps of polling offered for our consumption during the coming election season. Many of us will even become statistics as we are interviewed by pollsters for whom we, as randomly selected individuals, represent the attitudes, hopes, and frustrations of, say, 80,000 other Americans. That is a heavy responsibility, indeed, and if the soothsayers and oracles of our times are to operate with any intelligence, we ought to cooperate and provide honest responses to their queries.

So even if you are approached by " 'Social Science Workers' from Princeton University, augmented by seven or eight East Side New Yorkers who had never in their lives seen a possum . . . ," you might set skepticism aside momentarily, if not in honor of probability theory, then at least for civility's sake.

POINTS TO PONDER

1. Why did the *Literary Digest* presidential preference poll in 1936 fail to predict the Roosevelt landslide?
2. What does it mean to select a "random sample" of respondents, and why is this important in polling?
3. Is the ready availability of frequent polling results about public policy issues helpful or harmful to successful governance of the country?

PART IV

Public Policy

Chapter 13

DOMESTIC POLICY-MAKING

As is evident from the structure of the Constitution, the Framers intended to create a system that would inhibit any majority faction from easily capturing control of the government. The separation of powers has been admirably successful at achieving that purpose. It has created a system in which any major change in the direction of public policy can be frustrated unless there is extraordinary support for the change. There are many points of access to the government, and many points at which a change in policy can be stopped. We have a system of governance that is strongly biased in favor of the status quo. Overcoming this inertia is a difficult political task. The gridlock about which Americans have often complained is a direct result of this framework.

Previous chapters in this book have examined the governmental and non-governmental institutions that formulate public policy and the constitutional framework within which they operate. We turn now to look at the policy process and policy outcomes. Public policy can be defined as a course of action that the government will take. Official statements of these courses of action can be found in public laws, executive orders, agency regulations, and court decisions. There are some general characteristics of the political and policy process in the United States that must be understood in any consideration of the system.

Stages in the Policy Process

Despite the complexity of the policy process in the American political system, it is possible to lay out a general framework that can help us get a sense of the broad outlines of the process. The process can be categorized into five separate phases: (1) agenda setting, (2) policy development, (3) policy adoption, (4) implementation, and (5) evaluation. Although these stages often overlap and may happen simultaneously, the distinctions are often useful to make.

During the agenda-setting stage an issue comes to be seen as a problem on which the government should take action. Issues can be brought to the public agenda in a number of ways. For instance, an economic downturn can lead to a change in economic policy, as happened in the 1930s and the 1980s. Technological innovations, such as in the biological or communications fields, may lead to the need for public policy changes. Interest groups, the media, or scholars might bring long-standing issues to public consciousness and convince Americans of a need for a change in public policy.

Once an issue is recognized as a problem on which government should act, specific and concrete plans to deal with that problem must be developed. That is, the details of various approaches to solving the problem must be worked out and measured against each other. Much of the work in this policy development phase is done in universities and think tanks. But as the possibility of government action becomes more likely, the policy shops in the executive branch bureaucracies and committee staffs in Congress begin to examine the options in detail. All these actions will be reported in the media, and there will be public deliberation and political argument over the merits of the various plans. Interest groups will maneuver to influence outcomes in their favor. Politicians in and out of the government will position themselves to take advantage of possible policy changes.

The range of serious options will be narrowed down by public exploration, and at some point specific pieces of legislation or other official policy proposals will be drafted and the policy adoption process will begin. In the congressional process, various drafts will be considered in subcommittees and committees of both houses. If, after floor passage of the resulting bills, the two houses disagree on any aspect, a conference committee will be formed to iron out the differences. The president and other executive branch officials will probably be active throughout this process to influence the outcome. If the final bill is passed, it will go to the president for signing, marking official adoption of the policy. In addition to the legislative process, parallel policy development and adoption processes take place in executive branch agencies and the court system.

But passage of a law is only the beginning. The program must now be administered, either by an existing executive branch organization or a new one. In this implementation stage, money must be allocated and personnel assigned to carry out the policy. Depending on the complexity of the undertaking and on whether the program is a new departure for the government, this process can take very little time or a number of years. Many of the difficulties of actually carrying out a program cannot be foreseen when it is created, and so the program must be altered and fine-tuned in the process of implementation. Timetables for action must be established and enforcement mechanisms devised. Coordination among different agencies and levels of government may be necessary. The courts, of course, may intervene at any time if significant legal or constitutional questions arise.

Finally, the operating program will be examined in the evaluation stage. This evaluation may be done by professional policy analysts making careful measurements of the impact of the program on society. Analysts might use sophisticated techniques such as cost-benefit analysis, but the validity of the judgments will depend on the accuracy both of the data and the reporting process. Feedback may also take the form of political pressure applied either in favor of the program and possible expansion, or in opposition, forcing modification of the program.

Development of Policy Activism

The reality of fragmented power is reflected in the struggle between the president and Congress over public policy. Congress dominated domestic policy-making in the nineteenth century, but since the 1930s the presidency has become increasingly more aggressive in asserting policy-making agendas. Congress has contributed to presidential power by delegating large amounts of discretion to the president and executive branch bureaucracies. But it has also kept tight reins by dictating many of the details in the implementation of public policy.

Despite inherent biases against change, there have been surges of activism in which presidential leadership has combined with congressional support to produce major changes in the direction of public policy. The 1930s were such a period of activism—the federal government dealt with the Great Depression by creating scores of new programs and expanding governmental activity into areas previously left to private control. After the activism of the New Deal and the mobilization of the country for World War II, the 1950s were a period of relative quiet and restraint of governmental activity.

During the 1960s, however, under the leadership of Lyndon Johnson, the federal government again expanded its range of influence by creating programs in policy areas previously reserved for state or local governments or in which there was not much government activity at all. The selection by Hugh Heclo examines national policy on poverty, which was first systematically addressed in the New Deal and then transformed by the Great Society and War on Poverty programs of the 1960s. The more conservative Republican administrations of Presidents Nixon, Reagan, and Bush significantly slowed down though did not reverse the trajectory of governmental activity.

The Readings

The readings in this section will address both the process and substance of important areas of domestic policy in the United States, including specific examples of policy-making about income distribution.

The 1980s—the Reagan era—is analyzed below by Kevin Phillips who contrasts historical periods of governmental activism and redistribution with eras of affluence and the emphasis on capitalism. He documents the shift in income toward the more affluent and explains some of the political consequences of this shift. Phillips's analysis points out how seemingly incremental changes can have large effects in politics.

An incremental approach seems to characterize the U.S. attitude toward poverty, reflected in Hugh Heclo's analysis of poverty policy over the past two centuries. According to Heclo, poverty policy has always had trouble distinguishing the "deserving poor" (those who are poor through no fault of their own) from those who are poor because of indolence and unwillingness to work. Heclo concludes that the condition of poverty is inherently intractable and that any improvement will entail a long-term approach of incremental progress. There are no quick-fix solutions. In this sense, poverty is similar to many other social and economic problems facing modern industrial societies. As Heclo says in another article,

> matters such as improving race relations, protecting the environment, reviving long-term economic growth, and so on, are not so much "problems" to be "solved" as they are collective nouns for an enormous web of challenges that have to be addressed again and again, on one front after another in both government and civil society.

The implication of this observation is that we should not expect quick, neat solutions to deeply based societal problems. Just because the problems are not easily solved, however, is no excuse for us not to try.

KEY TERMS

deserving poor: those who are poor not because of laziness but because of circumstances beyond their own control

incrementalism: making policy by small changes rather than through sweeping, comprehensive, and rational approaches

public policy: a course of action to which the government is committed. It might be a legislative, judicial, or executive branch course of action.

48

"THE POLITICS OF RICH AND POOR"
Kevin Phillips

In this selection from his book, The Politics of Rich and Poor *(1990), journalist and political activist Kevin Phillips argues that the 1980s were an era of American politics in which the rich got richer. He presents a variety of data to back up his claim and argues that the 1980s were similar to earlier eras in American politics—the late nineteenth century (the Gilded Age) and the 1920s (the Roaring Twenties). These periods*

have alternated with periods when populist forces or redistribution impulses have domi-
nated American politics, such as the New Deal of the 1930s or the Great Society of the
middle 1960s. Phillips's critical tone is striking because he was one of the chief political
analysts of the 1968 Republican presidential campaign and later served as an assistant
attorney general in the Nixon administration.

The Triumph of Upper America

The 1980s were the triumph of upper America—an ostentatious celebration of wealth, the political ascendancy of the richest third of the population and a glorification of capitalism, free markets and finance. But while money, greed and luxury had become the stuff of popular culture, hardly anyone asked why such great wealth had concentrated at the top, and whether this was a result of public policy. Despite the armies of homeless sleeping on grates, political leaders—even those who professed to care about the homeless—had little to say about the Republican party's historical role, which has been not simply to revitalize U.S. capitalism but to tilt power, policy, wealth and income toward the richest portions of the population. The public understood this bias, if we can trust 1988 public opinion polls; nevertheless, the Democrats shunned the issue in the election of 1988, a reluctance their predecessors had also displayed during previous Republican booms.

That discussion is now unfolding. From Congress to the executive branch, "money politics"—be it the avarice of financiers or outright corruption of politicians—is shaping up as a prime political theme for the 1990s. Class structures may be weak in the United States, but populist sensitivities run high. Wealth in this country has always been fluid, volatile and migratory. Unlike Europe, we have needed no revolutions for its redistribution. In America the reallocation of income and assets has usually followed consumer fads, population shifts and technological innovations. But politics and political ideologies have also been important keys to the cashbox. Changing popular and governmental attitudes toward wealth have always influenced who gets what. Decade after decade illustrates the point; the Reagan era was not unique.

The 1980s were a second Gilded Age, in which many Americans made and spent money abundantly. Yet as the decade ended, too many stretch limousines, too many enormous incomes and too much high fashion foreshadowed a significant shift of mood. A new plutocracy—some critics were even using the world "oligarchy"—had created a new target for populist reaction. A small but significant minority of American liberals had begun to agitate the economy's losers—minorities, young men, female heads of households, farmers, steelworkers and others. Television audiences were losing their early-eighties fascination with the rich. And many conservatives, including President George Bush himself, were becoming defensive about great wealth, wanton money-making and greed.

No fixed caste, class, ideology or geographic section has long governed America's lively pursuit of money and success. Sectional competition has been pursued always and everywhere, and has yielded every kind of regional advantage. Relative affluence in the United States has moved West (almost from the first days of settlement), gone North (after the Civil War) or South (with the rise of the Sunbelt). The 1980s boom in the Boston-Washington megalopolis, coupled with hard times on the farm and in the Oil Patch, produced a familiar conservative economic geography—a comparative shift of wealth toward the two coasts. *And* toward income groups already well off.

This preference was nothing new. Twice before in the last hundred years, wealth also further accumulated in the hands of those *already rich*—during the late nineteenth century, then again during the 1920s. To some extent, these buildups have also served the larger purpose of stimulating capitalist growth, entrepreneurialism and technological innovation. Avarice was only one ingredient. At other times, and also for at least partly valid public policy reasons, Washington has gone in the opposite direction and redeployed upper-income assets to fatten thinner wallets, expand low-income purchasing power and rebuild the social fabric of poorer Americans. So debtors have occasionally gained as have creditors. Farmers have outmaneuvered bankers, although rarely, but regardless of the direction it's hard to overstate the importance of American politics to American wealth—and vice versa.

Candor in these matters is rare. But in the words of an iconoclastic journalist of the Reagan era, William Greider, "Concentration of wealth was the fulcrum on which the most basic political questions pivoted, a dividing line deeper than region or religion, race or sex. In the nature of things, government might choose to enhance the economic prospects for the many or to safeguard the accumulated wealth held by the few, but frequently the two purposes were in irreconcilable conflict. The continuing political struggle across this line, though unseen and rarely mentioned, was the central narrative of American political history, especially in the politics of money." Greider's thesis is generally supported by history. Since the American Revolution the distribution of American wealth has depended significantly on *who controlled the federal government, for what policies, and in behalf of which constituencies.*

From this perspective, the Reagan era reversed what late-twentieth-century Americans had become used to. The liberal style that prevailed from 1932 to 1968 had left a legacy of angry conservatives indignant over two generations of downward income redistribution. A reorientation in the opposite direction was all but inevitable in the 1980s—and there were precedents aplenty.

In the years after 1790, when Alexander Hamilton persuaded Congress to assume debts incurred by the states during the Revolution, the result was a redistribution of wealth to bondholders, many of whom had bought the low-valued debt instruments as speculation. Then in the 1870s, restoration of the gold standard squeezed out the last vestiges of Civil War inflation, providing a similar preference to creditors over debtors. And the Harding-Coolidge tax cuts of the 1920s, in which the top individual federal income tax rate fell from 73 percent to 25 percent, furnish yet another example of realignment upward. This periodic upward bias is as much a fact of U.S. history as the liberal bias with which it alternates.

Even in this most optimistic of countries, economic individualism yields to community-minded reform on a cyclical basis as the public grows indignant over the political distribution of wealth. By the mid-1920s, and especially during the New Deal, muckraking interpretations of the economic motives of conservative governance were a dime a dozen. Historian Charles Beard became famous for his *Economic Interpretation of the U.S. Constitution* and other books arguing the premise that the Founding Fathers and their descendants had served their own class interests as well as American patriotism. Populist or progressive periods have often nurtured such materialistic views, and the 1990s are likely to regard the Reagan era as a seamless web of preoccupation with wealth and moneymaking. By 1989, after all, the statistics *were* in: once again, just as in the 1790s, the 1880s and the 1920s, conservative and upper-bracket groups had been the major gainers. As a percentage of overall national income, the shift wasn't big, of course. Yet increases of two, three and four points in the share of income held by the top 1 percent of Americans—accompanied, meanwhile, by some decline in the bottom two fifths of the population—have been the stuff of major economic and political movements.

* * * *

The Critical Duality of the Reagan Years

As the Reagan years ended, the uncertain future hung like a temperature inversion over America's substantial prosperity. The economy was enjoying the century's longest peacetime recovery cycle. But economic power and riches were realigning around the world, and the two most striking economic groups of 1989 represented a stark contradiction: billionaires—and the homeless. Prophecies for the future were just as mixed.

Some pop culturists had written epitaphs for the decade right after the stock market crash of October 19, 1987. A year later, by Election Day, sentiment for new leadership, while commanding a nominal majority, had eased. Optimism was justified, in part, simply by the failure of pessimism to fulfill its prophecies. Southern California real estate prices were soaring again. Art auctions and corporate takeover bids were setting new records.

Yet, to judge by political debate and public opinion polls, the country was nervous. America's record debt levels were becoming an issue in Congress as well as in the bond markets. People felt that an era would end on that January day when the seventy-seven-year-old Reagan climbed into Air Force One for his last official flight home to California. The next president was going to be different. George Bush's postelection comments had made that clear. And possibly he would not be so lucky.

What loyalists hoped for was more of the same. The Republicans were on a roll. In their eyes, Reagan's eight-year presidency had sparked the creation of nineteen million new jobs, an exploding technology and unprecedented prosperity, and had rekindled national pride. So many Americans had been making so much money that the term "millionaire" became meaningless: in Manhattan, where midtown parking could cost fifty dollars a day, "millionaire" had come to mean only persons with yearly *incomes* over one million dollars (a level usually bespeaking assets in the $5 million to $10 million range). A Georgia marketing expert, Thomas J. Stanley, counted almost one hundred thousand "decamillionaires"—people worth over *$10 million*. Back in 1960 there hadn't been that many plain-vanilla *millionaires*.

Meanwhile Reagan's critics described another country. In their eyes the eighties were a last national fling with credit-card economics, a gaudy orgy of unprecedented domestic and international indebtedness, luxury imports, nouveau riche consumption and upper-bracket tax reduction, all indulged in with the greatest recklessness while beggars filled the streets and the average family's real disposable income declined toward a dimming future. For the first time in seventy years America had even become a net international debtor. Back in 1986 this dual vision had prompted California Democratic congressman Tony Coelho, who had been chosen to reply to one of the president's Saturday radio speeches, to recall that "Charles Dickens once began a story by writing 'It was the best of times, it was the worst of times.' The same could be said of today." For the next two years, it *was* said—in many ways.

The surprise was that the 1988 presidential election—or at least the Dukakis campaign—did so little with the powerful opposition themes so many others had raised. Dukakis was too caught up in Massachusetts' own affluence and high civic culture to promote populist economics—at least until late October, when flagging polls left him no choice. Most Republican strategists were relieved by the Democrats' failure, although a few had private doubts about having to manage the debt-ridden economy for four more years.

Back in January and February 1988, though, as the Reagan era was beginning its final year, and as the Democratic and Republican presidential nomination races were moving into their Iowa and New Hampshire killing grounds, most of the men who wanted to lead America toward the approaching millennium had begun to address these economic jitters. Jesse Jackson decried a nation "merging, purging and submerging" its workers. Missouri Democratic congressman Richard Gephardt, picturing a United States in decline, characterized the decade as "eight grey years." Robert Dole, Republican leader of the U.S. Senate, rejected his party's 1984 theme of "Morning Again in America." More accurately, he said, "it's High Noon." Even Bush, who boasted of the late 1980s economy and was careful not to attack the administration in which he served, promised to "create a more reliable prosperity."

Many Americans on the lower half of the economic ladder had been losing ground. And even the affluent, enjoying their champagne and raspberries, wondered how real the good times were. For the 20 to 30 percent of citizenry in circumstances prosperous enough to grump at but pay for $7 movie tickets or to disregard restaurant prices outrunning the cost-of-living index, the eighties had been good years. Yet troubling undercurrents had begun to make it all look shaky. Perhaps the economic music *was* about to stop; maybe the eighties *were* a decade of high living on borrowed money for which the bills were about to become due. In April, as the Democratic presidential nomination campaign moved toward its climactic showdown between Michael Dukakis and Jesse Jackson in the Wisconsin and New York Democratic primaries, the ABC News/Money magazine poll found that only 38 percent of the public rated the U.S. economy "excellent" or "pretty good"; 62 percent chose to describe it as "not so good" or "poor." That number would not change much until more upbeat attitudes took over in late summer; through August nearly 60 percent of Americans remained skeptical.

What the public was choosing to read in early 1988 mirrored this new mood. The appearance of books like Tom Wolfe's *The Bonfire of the Vanities* and Lewis Lapham's *Money and Class in America* suggested growing doubts about the country's obsession with money. So did Texas economics professor Ravi Batra's gloomy tome warning of a depression several years hence because of the overconcentration of wealth. And Yale historian Paul Kennedy's *Decline and Fall of the Great Powers* stayed on the 1988 best-seller lists because of popular apprehension about America's own decline, not because of some belated national curiosity about the imperial ebb of Hapsburg Spain, maritime Holland or Edwardian Britain.

Yet as 1988 unfolded, luxury purchases flourished as if the crash had never taken place. Unemployment reached 5.3 percent, the lowest level in a decade and a half. Inflation was down by two thirds from Carter administration highs. And throughout the year the unbroken economic recovery dating back to January 1983 kept setting records—sixty-seven straight months by mid-summer, seventy-two by December. Records keepers also saluted the unprecedented 62 percent of Americans gainfully employed, despite doubts about how many mothers were taking jobs to salvage family purchasing power. Manufacturing rose with resurging exports. The sales of books predicting hard times began to fade. Ronald Reagan, on tour in the Middle West, boasted to election-year audiences that the Rust Belt was becoming the Boom Belt.

Behind the façade of favorable monthly data, however, deeper worries about debt had also become fashionable. Years of debate had turned the enormity of the federal budget deficit into a cliché. Yet the headlines of 1987–88 had begun to announce a related problem, the *international* consequences of ongoing American borrowing: not just the budget and trade deficits, but the meaning of the United States' extraordinary transformation from the world's largest creditor nation to the world's largest debtor. Conservative insistence that it really didn't matter rang increasingly hollow as U.S. international indebtedness passed $269 billion at the end of 1986, reached $368 billion at the end of 1987, and was projected to exceed a trillion dollars by 1992. One New York investment banker, Daniel Schwartz, managing director of Ulmer Brothers, had even taken unintended issue with the president of the United States over the future of the Rust Belt. He told *Fortune* magazine that Japanese purchases might turn it into the Sushi Belt.

Vivid grass-roots trends fleshed out the official statistics: *Wealth within the United States had been changing hands, regions, vocations, economic sectors and income strata with a vengeance.* Magazines ran endless surveys of the new mega-fortunes, and of the lesser but soaring compensation packages of investment bankers and corporate chief executives. The clumsiest television producer could film the pain in boarded-up Iowa farm towns, empty Ohio steel mills and city parks full of homeless drifters—or show the BMW-thronged streets of Connecticut suburbia, retooling export plants and West Coast port cities flush with the profits of unloading and transshipping Japanese cars and Korean color televisions. Few observers doubted the rich were getting richer, while the poor were fulfilling their half of the cliché.

When Dickens wrote his novels, in economically divided mid-nineteenth-century Britain, huge fortunes were being piled up by the country's new railroad, machinery and textile magnates even as their ever more numerous wage laborers—refugees, many of them, from declining British agriculture—overflowed the squalid slums of London, Manchester and Glasgow. When Alexis de Tocqueville, the French observer of the United States, visited England in 1835, he was so struck by the same duality that confronted the creator of Oliver Twist and Ebenezer Scrooge that he prepared a "Memoir on Pauperism" for delivery to the Royal Society of Cherbourg. One sixth of Britain was on the dole versus less than 5 percent of the population in much poorer Spain and Portugal. Why? Well, for one reason, because the more highly developed the society, the more things there are to want—and to "need." Welfare, he thought, might be another cause.

A third factor suggests itself to the modern observer. Nations sometimes find themselves caught up in great currents of international economic change, and the late twentieth century's enormous upheaval in finance, commerce and technology—in which old-line manufacturing and humdrum shop and office vocations yielded to high-skill service industries—ranks in scope both with the Industrial Revolution that Dickens chronicled and with the earlier Renaissance and the rising capitalism that accompanied it. Much as in those eras, the forces of the late twentieth century have required double-entry bookkeeping: new wealth in profusion for the bright, the bold, the educated and the politically favored; economic carnage among the less fortunate. In short, the United States of the 1980s.

* * * *

The Seamless Web of 1980s Capitalist Revival

Stresses of the sort that produced the gains and losses of the Reagan era had been anticipated years earlier in economist Joseph Schumpeter's description of modern capitalism as creative destruction—progress and pain at work together. The Reagan years were one of America's "capitalist blowouts," the vivid display of what Schumpeter was talking about. In the United States, transitions of this magnitude have usually coincided with new national attitudes toward wealth and poverty. Evolving policies that seem distinct are really linked. So are specific changes in the national mood. In each such transition, whether in the late nineteenth century, the 1920s or the 1980s, slowly but surely, and without real precision as to which came first, the country has witnessed, *ensemble*, Horatio Alger cultural renewal, tax reduction, entrepreneurialism, enormously popular books by the likes of Henry Ford or Lee Iacocca, stepped-up mergers and corporate restructuring, extraordinary technological innovation, disinflation, suffering in the agricultural and extractive sectors, strong financial markets, philosophic laissez-faire, economic deregulation, doubts about the role of government, and a slow further concentration of wealth and income among the already affluent. The scope of these events has been impressive—and so has their repetition, although the two heydays of the twentieth century have involved increasingly more paper manipulation and less of the raw vigor typical of late-nineteenth-century railroad and factory expansion.

The exaggerations of cyclical theorists notwithstanding, these policy shifts and mood swings *do* seem to have recurred at forty- to fifty-year intervals. There has even been a somewhat predictable sequence of outcomes: economic benefits have come first, as enterprise-oriented policies unleash latent capitalist energies; then the dislocations have followed, including speculative excesses and even market crashes. After ten to fifteen years of heyday psychology, *some* major economic or market contraction occurs.

The United States, under Republican political leadership, had arguably passed through three such commercial epochs—the Gilded Age (cresting from 1880 or so to the mid-1890s), the 1920s and the Reagan era. [There are] many economic and cultural parallels, from depressed commodity markets and Wall Street binges to the repetitious ethos of free enterprise unleashed. The similarities aren't all-encompassing, to be sure, but they *are* revealing—even in the way go-getter eras have always been followed by swings back to a more populist, community-minded or government-activist period. Does disinflation and prosperity bring tax cuts or vice versa? Like the chicken and egg conundrum, the question may have no answer. But it also may not really matter.

These three Republican heydays began among three roughly similar moods and circumstances. The common denominators are important. One was the great desire to curb the successive inflations following the Civil War, World War I, and then Vietnam and the emergence of the OPEC petroleum cartels.

Inflation usually prods property owners and creditors to mobilize. A second factor has been a concomitant public demand for stability, for "normalcy" (as Warren Harding so pithily misphrased it in 1920) and for a return of traditional economic and cultural behavior. Traditional values, of course, are conservative, even though conservative economic policy, as Schumpeter saw, would have radical effects. A third common theme is public fatigue with overexpanded government promoted by either wartime or inflationary challenges. Disenchantment with government and renewed attention to individual enterprise have gone together. Nor should we omit the periodic, almost inbred desire of Americans to build things, to create new tastes and open new frontiers.

In all three periods of capitalist expansion, ideas were also a vital force—from the Social Darwinism of the 1870s to the supply-side theories a century later. The proponents of these ideologies have always been more deeply committed to their causes than liberal opponents have made them out to be. They were *believers* convinced of the importance of the economic forces they sought to deploy. In that sense, the supply-side stalwarts of 1981 were not unlike the Jesuits of an earlier time or Hawaii-bound nineteenth-century Congregationalist missionaries. Conviction suffused their effort, making investment, free markets and entrepreneurialism a popular cause, not just a dry fiscal rationale. This periodic evangelism has been a boon to American capitalism. In each of the three great U.S. capitalist eras, although most shallowly in the commercial 1920s, genuine philosophic and cultural conviction expanded, elevated and prolonged the wave of capitalist expansion. That it ultimately encouraged excess is another part of the story, and we shall get to it before long.

The resemblance between the policy framework of the 1980s, the Coolidge era and the Gilded Age was not a coincidence. Striking similarities existed in fiscal, monetary, deregulatory and reduced-government approaches—and led to similar inequalities of wealth and income distribution. The new economics of the 1980s had gained momentum, to be sure, because of a *preexisting*, broader national conservative trend and coalition, reinforced in the late 1970s by a larger wave of inflation and popular frustration with big government. Yet it was absolutely critical that reemergent capitalism also enjoyed something more: a missionary spirit—and dedicated missionaries.

POINTS TO PONDER

1. According to Phillips, what key factor determines the distribution of wealth in the United States?
2. According to Phillips, what are the benefits and negative aspects of the eras of capitalist expansion?
3. If you follow the logic of Phillips's analysis, what type of politics is likely to characterize the 1990s?

49

"ALMS WITHOUT END?"

Hugh Heclo

Poverty has been a public policy problem in Western societies for the past six hundred years. There were poor people before that, but their problems were not considered a concern of government. In this 1992 article, political scientist Hugh Heclo of George Mason University traces the development of poverty policy in the United States. Federal government programs began to deal seriously with the problems of the poor in the 1930s during the Great Depression. In the 1960s Lyndon Johnson's War on Poverty created a number of programs and put significant fiscal resources behind fighting poverty. Although many of these programs accomplished much good, the age-old problem of distinguishing the "deserving poor" from those who were merely too lazy to work remained a fixture of public policy. Heclo concludes that dealing with unemployment and welfare is a costly and slow process and that short-run, dramatic fixes are impossible.

For anyone seeking to reform the welfare system, the history should be sobering. For at least six hundred years reformers in Western societies have been trying to rationalize public assistance so as to help the truly needy while denying a free ride to work-shy scroungers. And always the latest new idea to distinguish the deserving from the undeserving has failed to live up to expectations. Some critics claim the prevailing welfare system is too punitive, hurting people who are poor through no fault of their own. Others respond that welfare is too permissive, creating dependency among those it seeks to help. The cycle of reform, argument, and counterargument seems to repeat itself from one generation to the next.

Until roughly the fifteenth century, "welfare" was scarcely considered a social problem as we understand the term today. Idealized views of Christian poverty and the religious duty to give alms coexisted with fear of rebellious paupers and distrust of troublesome beggars. In either case, almsgiving and other charitable acts were routine customs justified mainly by the good they did for the giver, not the recipient or society at large.

By the 1400s traditional religious charity was increasingly being supplemented by civil authorities' efforts to cope with the surges of pauperism and wandering beggars brought about by urban growth and economic changes in the countryside. As the Reformation accelerated the seculiarization of poor relief, the now familiar arguments began to be heard. Reformers criticized individual almsgiving as an encouragement to begging and ineffective in dealing with the needs of the poor. The fundamental question, they recognized, was how to keep the genuinely needy from starving (or rioting) without breeding a class of paupers who chose to live off public charity. Civil authorities evolved a variety of techniques to distinguish the "true pauper" from the "unworthy beggar," and these became known collectively as the old poor law.

Early America

Early settlers to America brought with them this bundle of traditions, laws, and social regulations. In general, each township or county (parish in the South) was legally responsible for organizing relief for any destitute inhabitant who did not have kin to care for him or her. Rough classifications were applied such that the aged or infirm without relatives might be offered alms or a place in an almshouse, orphaned children apprenticed out to farmers or artisans, and the able-bodied set to work or threatened with punishment. As a typical saying of the time had it, "work for those that will labor, punishment for those that will not, and bread for those who cannot."

In practice, provisions varied greatly and distinctions between deserving and undeserving poor were never clear-cut. Four techniques were typically combined and in widespread use at the end of the eighteenth century: (1) Settlement laws emphasized the local basis of relief policy, as poor persons were shunted from one township to the next in an often cumbersome legal process of trying to find the home jurisdiction with responsibility for support. (2) Auctions were held by local officials to find the lowest bidder who would contract to support one or more poor persons for a given period of time. (3) Almshouses, or poor houses, could often be found in the larger cities, usually with the sick, elderly, insane, orphaned, and otherwise homeless indigents jumbled together. (4) Finally, "outdoor relief" (so-named for being given outside an institutional setting) was commonly given by locally chosen overseers of the poor. Such relief usually took the form of winter fuel, clothing, food, and small amounts of cash.

After 1800

As the pace of social and economic change accelerated after 1800, reformers argued with good reason that the traditional poor law was hopelessly out of date. By midnineteenth century numerous efforts had been made to replace the old customs with a new, more deliberately and systematically organized poor law that was claimed to be both more humane and more efficient. Specialized institutions such as asylums, penitentiaries, orphanages, and reform schools proliferated. But the centerpiece of social reform was the poorhouse, which eventually became a well-known presence in nearly every county in the country. Poorhouse advocates pointed to the cruelty of the auctioning system, the ineffectiveness and costs of resettlement, and above all to the growing welfare rolls that were said to be created by the indiscriminate giving of relief. As the Report of the Massachusetts Committee on the Pauper Laws put it in 1821, all of the "evils" of the current poor law system could be traced to the same root: "the difficulty of discriminating between the able poor and the impotent poor [i.e., incapable of work] and of apportioning the degree of public provision to the degree of actual impotency." Advocates claimed that properly run poorhouses would not only deter the unworthy and shiftless poor. They would rehabilitate people through good work habits and prohibition of alcohol, educate pauper children, and save money by having inmates perform useful work. Poorhouses (or poor farms) spread.

As it turned out, poorhouses usually failed to live up to reformers' expectations. Administration of poorhouses did not attract particularly competent people and desensitized those who entered the work with good intentions. Expectations of productive work from impoverished, wretched people proved unrealistic. Above all, hopes for humane treatment and appropriate rehabilitating services were flatly contradicted by the pervasive desire to hold down costs and avoid attracting people who should support themselves. Poorhouse keepers who did not minimize costs could expect to run afoul of locally elected overseers of the poor as well as taxpayers, who were generally billed separately for the "poor rate" (i.e., earmarked taxes for public poor relief).

"Scientific Charity"

Although they failed in their original more positive purposes, poorhouses continued throughout the nineteenth century and into this century as custodial institutions deterring potential paupers. Outdoor relief also expanded as industrialization, immigration, and sharper, nationwide swings in the business cycle strained local relief budgets. By 1870, New York State, with a population of 4.4 million, had 64,000 residents in poorhouses and 106,000 on outdoor relief. By then a new round of reforms was beginning, as socially concerned middle-class men and women took up the cause of "scientific charity." Mobilized across the country in Charity Organization Societies, the reformers sought to systematically apply scientific principles learned through the giving of relief. In this view, public outdoor relief should be replaced by private charity, which would be given by persons whose personal knowledge of cases would tailor the aid to avoid doing moral harm to the recipients. All public aid should be given in institutions (poorhouses, asylums, etc.) where proper care, moral discipline, and education could be assured. As one of the founders of the movement, Josephine Shaw Lowell, put it in 1883: "To cure paupers and make them self-supporting, however costly the process, must always be economical as compared with a smaller but constantly increasing and continual outlay for their maintenance."

The scientific charity movement achieved only modest and temporary success. Of the forty American cities with populations over 100,000, about one-quarter had abolished outdoor relief by 1899. For one thing, many poor resented the often condescending visits by middle-class charity workers, who were trying to be both case investigators and morally uplifting friends. Then too, urban political machines, merchants, and overseers of the poor resisted efforts to abolish outdoor relief and the benefits they derived from its distribution. Above all, periodic economic crashes simply overwhelmed Charity Organization Societies' efforts to deal with the floods of needy people.

Mothers' Pensions

The next major attempt to change assistance under the poor law occurred early this century with Mothers' Pensions. Such pensions were begun in 1910 on the initiative of a few reformist juvenile court judges in the Midwest. In these pre-Social Security days, mothers who lost the family's male bread-winner typically faced two financial alternatives if they did not have relatives to support them. Either they and/or their children had to go to work or else they had to throw themselves on poor law relief and possibly see their children sent to an orphanage. The aim of Mothers' Pensions was to provide state funds to localities that could be used to help mainly widowed mothers stay in the home and have their children in school rather than the work force. The cause was taken up by federations of women's clubs across the country and a few key reformers in married women's magazines. Campaigners for Mothers' Pensions spoke of "an honorable salary to remove the stigma of pauperism . . . allowing mothers to build a good home life, the highest product of civilization . . . providing the State the best possible type of citizen."

Against the opposition of private charity organizations, which repeated their familiar argument that such use of public money for outdoor relief was morally corrupting, women's groups had succeeded in enacting Mothers' Pensions in forty states by 1920. In practice, Mothers' Pensions were quite restrictive. Most states and localities were reluctant to support deserted or divorced women, and by 1931, only three states allowed such pensions to go to unmarried mothers. As the New York State Commission on Relief for Widowed Mothers put it, "to pension desertion or illegitimacy would, undoubtedly, have the effect of putting a premium on these crimes against society." Widows themselves had to demonstrate they were personally worthy, which is to say living soberly, in a clean home, without male partners and without work outside the home. They had to do so both in applying for aid and in monthly "proper-home" visits by many of the same charity workers who had originally opposed Mothers' Pensions.

Even so, state funding was never adequate to cover all those eligible or to allow recipients more than the barest physical necessities without at least some part-time work. The discretionary nature of the program also produced huge local variations in the presence and level of Mothers' Pensions. By 1931, forty-six thousand families with one-quarter million children were receiving pensions. Of these, 80 percent were widows, 3 percent were black, and only 55 recipients in the entire nation were unmarried mothers.

The 1935 Social Security Act

With no political fanfare, a process of transformation began with the 1935 Social Security Act. In that year, the Federal Children's Bureau in effect slipped
Mothers' Pensions into an obscure portion of the Social Security bill. This
section provided federal matching grants for state welfare assistance to two
other categories of needy persons deemed deserving: the aged and blind.
With Mothers' Pensions renamed Aid to Dependent Children (ADC), children of what were assumed to be mainly widows took their place alongside
impoverished aged and blind persons as one of the three categories of non-
ablebodied people presumed deserving of federally supported cash relief.

Immediately there began a sustained skirmishing between liberal national
officials hostile to the racist and paternalistic administration of welfare in many
jurisdictions, on the one hand, and local forces together with their representatives in Congress, on the other. The latter were intent on keeping control of a
system that still carried many echoes of the poor law while taking advantage
of the new federal funds. In the 1935 act liberal New Dealers managed to win
elimination of local residency requirements and a maximum five-year limit on
state residency requirements for these welfare programs, thus all but abolishing
the settlement provisions of the centuries-old poor law. They also obtained a
provision in the law requiring operation of federally supported welfare programs in all state subdivisions, thereby reducing the patchy coverage that had
bedeviled Mothers' Pensions. This did much to raise the number of children
aided under Mothers' Pensions/ADC from three hundred thousand in 1935
to seven hundred thousand in 1939. But in all other important respects—such
as eligibility conditions and benefit levels—fiscal conservatives and southern
Democrats in Congress succeeded in keeping administrative control of federally supported welfare localized.

Thus the New Deal created federal aid for the three categories of deserving
poor on "welfare" and a Social Security system that eventually would raise
more people, mainly the elderly, above the poverty line than all means-tested
"welfare" programs combined. Beyond this, the Depression years saw little effort to change the prevailing welfare system, much less engage in social engineering to educate and train poor people for self-support. First, emergency
cash relief (the dole) for the unemployed and then work relief (so-called
make-work projects under the WPA and other federal agencies) were used to
provide temporary help and tide over employable people in the 1930s. But
Franklin Roosevelt in traditional fashion warned that to dole out relief was
"to administer a narcotic—a subtle destroyer of the human spirit," and the
president declared that the federal government "must and shall quit this business of relief." As work relief programs faded away with the onset of World
War II's full employment, all responsibility for general relief assistance for those
poor persons who were presumably unemployable was left where it had always
been, with state and local governments. Supporting more than four million

families annually between 1936 and 1940, state-run general assistance programs aided more Americans than any other social program, federal or state.

Covering More and More People

In 1939, liberalizations in Social Security began the process of covering an ever-greater percentage of widows under the survivors' benefits of the nation's social insurance program. The result was that after the end of World War II, ADC caseloads increasingly became composed of divorced, deserted, and unmarried mothers' children. National welfare officials kept adding to the federal rules and regulations of ADC in an effort to bring about more equal treatment. Conservative politicians and local officials responded with "suitable home" and other requirements that typically served to withhold benefits from illegitimate children and nonwhites in general. White southern leaders in particular worried about the effect of federal ADC benefits on the supply of cheap black labor. As Georgia Gov. Eugene Talmadge put it: "The Federal [Social Security] Board in Washington is going to make them add on nearly every Negro of a certain age in the country to this pauper's list. What will become of yᵣ ur farm labor—your washwomen, your cooks, your plowhands?"

In 1950, officials in Washington succeeded in adding a caretaker grant for mothers to ADC benefits, something that had been present in Mothers' Pensions but had been dropped out as an oversight in hurriedly drafting the 1935 act. Thus, mothers were formally added to the federal "welfare" rolls, and the program's name was changed to the now-familiar AFDC (Aid to Families with Dependent Children). At the same time, Congress added an amendment to the welfare program requiring local welfare agencies to notify law enforcement officers whenever aid was granted to children whose father had deserted the family. Aware or not of this provision in national law, many state and local welfare officers made "midnight raids" to catch fathers or other employable males visiting overnight with mothers on welfare.

Criticism of AFDC

As the incidence of broken families increased in the postwar years, criticisms of the AFDC welfare system rose apace. In point of fact the societal changes under way far overweighed anything that might be attributed to federal welfare policy. The number of ADC/AFDC recipients rose from 701,000 in 1945 to 3.1 million in 1960. But the number of mothers and children in female-headed families climbed from 3.4 million in 1940 to approximately 6 million in 1960. With the numbers on welfare rising, states redoubled their efforts to cut welfare dependency. In 1960, for example, Louisiana used its suitable home rules to cut off aid to families in which the mother had given birth to another child since receiving AFDC benefits. In 1961 the city of Newburgh, New York, added to a furious public debate by adopting policies that, among other things, cut benefits to unwed mothers who had another child, limited welfare for able-bodied persons to three months, and required forced labor from able-bodied adult males.

The 1960s

The 1960s were a watershed in the struggle over welfare policy. But what happened is more complex than any current references to the "failure of Great Society programs." It was as if a number of previously disparate forces came crashing together at the same intersection of time. Today we are still living with the repercussions. The 3.1 million AFDC recipients of 1960 rose to 4.3 million in 1965, 6.1 million by 1969, and topped out in the late Nixon administration (1972–74) at about 10.8 million. From then until 1990 caseloads held generally steady, fluctuating between 10.1 and 10.9 million.

One thing that happened in the 1960s was a dawning realization that what had evolved—largely inadvertently—as the federal government's centerpiece "welfare" policy was a system of income support for unmarried, working-age mothers outside the workforce. Each of the major and growing criticisms of AFDC was directed at program features that had simply continued, as if by inertial force, the logic of Mothers' Pensions. Thus, AFDC was said to encourage family dissolution, since benefits were lost if a father or any other employable male was around the home. But that provision existed because mothers were supposed to maintain a suitable home after the loss of the father. Thus too, AFDC was said to discourage work and self-support by taking away a dollar of AFDC benefit for every dollar earned. True enough, but that provision simply reflected the original idea that mothers were supposed to devote themselves to making a home and raising their children, not toiling outside the home all day in Dickensian circumstances.

Gradually modifications began to be made to try to take account of the mismatch between early twentieth-century assumptions and later twentieth-century social realities. In the name of discouraging family breakup, AFDC amendments in 1961 gave states the option of granting benefits to two-parent families with unemployed fathers. Half the states refused the option. (It would later be made mandatory on states in the 1988 Family Support Act.) In 1962 the Public Welfare Amendments Act provided funds for intensive social services that advocates claimed would reverse the trend toward cash handouts by rehabilitating those on welfare and preventing others from falling into welfare dependency. But almost none of this traditional social work had anything to do with providing job training and employment services for working-aged women.

In 1967 Congress enacted welfare amendments imposing the first modest work- and job-training requirements on recipients. This Work Incentive program (WIN) allowed AFDC recipients to add the first $30 per month from work to their welfare check as well as keep one-third of earnings above that

$30. What became known as "workfare" provisions of the law allowed states to drop from AFDC rolls those parents and children over sixteen who declined without good cause to participate in work or training programs. But welfare officials interpreted "good cause" loosely, and as the provisions were implemented only unemployed AFDC fathers, school dropouts over sixteen, and a few mothers of school-age children with access to free day care ever had to register for work. Moreover, funds and administrative capacities were wholly inadequate for any serious job-training or day-care services to help the usually poorly educated mothers enter the work force. The tiny fraction of AFDC recipients in the WIN program who got training and jobs (about fifty-two thousand persons in 1972 after four years of operation) did little more than enter the insecure ranks of the working poor. What the work incentive amendments mainly did was to serve notice that with the growing tendency of nonwelfare mothers to enter the work force, expectations for welfare mothers—though not their realistic job prospects—were changing as well. What was once seen as the "honorable" Mothers' Pension and then as aid to "deserving" dependent children had now become a popularly despised image of "welfare mothers."

The Great Society

Meanwhile, another force crashing into the 1960s was long pent-up demands for social reform. On a variety of policy fronts these demands crystalized with the Kennedy administration and gained almost irresistible impulse after Kennedy's assassination and President Johnson's exploitation of his overwhelming 1964 election victory. This time, unlike the last major period of liberal reform in the New Deal, ambitious goals of social engineering took center place in the presidential agenda. In one sense this impulse reaffirmed a long-standing American desire to attack poverty through prevention and rehabilitation. In another sense, the Great Society programs were a wholly unique venture in using the national government to address poverty problems that had always been cast off into state and local welfare offices.

Neither Great Society programs as a whole nor the War on Poverty in particular advocated permissive, income-maintenance approaches for the poor. Apart from Medicare and other programs for the elderly, the emphasis was on creating economic opportunities and enhancing individuals' capacities to take advantage of those opportunities. None of the programs—from Head Start, education grants, Job Corps, and child nutrition to community action agencies, Foster Grandparents, rural development, and Model Cities projects— aimed merely at providing income support to poor people. In this sense the Great Society's war on poverty stood four-square with traditional norms of advancing individual opportunity and self-help, or what new thinking in the 1990s would term "empowerment."

Putting this aim into practice was another thing. In the first place, using education, job training, and other services to change people's lives proved a slow and uncertain process. When quick fixes were not forthcoming many politicians, group advocates, and policy experts lost patience with the programs.

In the second place, implementing the new programs was far more difficult in a sheer administrative sense than anyone had foreseen. In one area after another (urban planning, community economic development, job training, and so on) Washington policymakers embarked on activities where there were few strong administrative capacities to do the work in a knowledgeable, effective way. Moreover, as a price of passage in Congress, new domestic legislation invariably required accommodations to congressmen's alliances with local power centers interested in claiming a share of the new federal programs. Thus the Model Cities program, the only Great Society effort to launch a concerted attack on poverty in urban ghettos, was quickly broadened by Congress to include most congressional districts. In this and other ways the net result was to erect barriers to priority setting and effective management into the very structure of new social programs. Then too, the unforeseen consequences of America's foreign entanglement in anticommunist crusades came home to domestic policy. Vietnam contaminated domestic social programs identified with Johnson and presidential unpopularity grew. Perhaps the most powerful force to come crashing onto the scene in the 1960s was the growing turmoil over civil rights and race relations. Never before had welfare policies been developed in a context that openly confronted and legitimized demands for racial equality. In fact for almost two hundred years concerns about the poor hardly even made a pretense of considering conditions of racial inequality. In the 1960s all that changed. America's poverty agenda became inseparably and no doubt permanently bound up with the debate on race relations.

Burnout of the Great Society

The political results of trying to deal simultaneously with the problems of poverty and racial injustice were profoundly disruptive. Great Society programs originally justified in terms of individual advancement soon were perceived, and in part became, means of group advancement for blacks. Before any Great Society programs were fully in place (much less had time to adversely affect the ghetto poor as would be claimed after the Los Angeles riots of 1992), the Watts riot of August 1965 had begun the process of alienating white support from antipoverty efforts.

Not only did the potential for white backlash grow within and without the Democratic Party, along the way making AFDC welfare mothers even more unpopular. Perhaps equally important, heightened racial sensitivities also made it extremely difficult to even talk about traditional concerns in welfare policy without opening oneself to charges of racism. In the public conversation about welfare and fighting poverty, problems of illegitimacy, family stability, and work expectations became virtually forbidden territory. Hence the racist abuses of the past in welfare programs came to haunt any present thinking about antipoverty policy.

History needs to be recalled honestly. Antipoverty efforts of the 1960s did not lose public support because they contradicted basic American values. They lost support because politicians taught the people to expect quick fixes, because they were often ineffectively administered, because they became part of a racial imbroglio, and because their chief political sponsor lied to the people in fighting a fruitless foreign war.

In the midst of this political quagmire, AFDC moved toward an income-maintenance approach by default, not design. This occurred in several ways.

Increasingly confident of their professional stature, economists played a newly prominent role in the public debate on welfare policy in the 1960s. In 1964 the president's economists for the first time defined an officially measured poverty line. Once this was done, much thinking about poverty policy became dominated by what could be measured. This facilitated evaluations of policy and proposals by considering how far they managed to close the rather arbitrary income gap of those below the poverty line. Effectiveness in poverty policy could be seen in terms of how many people, after government transfer payments, had their incomes brought up to the poverty line. This orientation was reflected in the failed plans of the Nixon and Carter administrations to reform welfare with something resembling an income guarantee for closing the poverty income gap.

Advocates of a more liberal income-maintenance approach had greater success in the courts than they did in Congress during the 1960s and 1970s. In these years a complex series of decisions struck down many state eligibility restrictions, such as residency requirements and suitable home rules. The net effect was to move cash welfare assistance somewhat (but by no means all the way) in the direction of a solely need-based entitlement.

The drift toward welfare entitlements based purely on low income certainly did not proceed unopposed. Under the leadership of Russell Long (D-Louisiana), the Senate Finance Committee produced a steady stream of counterproposals to roll back the work of welfare rights advocacy groups in the courts. In 1972 the Talmadge amendment tightened work requirements for AFDC parents with children over six years (the 1967 WIN requirements applied to parents with children over sixteen), and in 1973–74 the first significant federal measures to enforce support payments from absent fathers were passed by Congress. Around the same time, California Gov. Ronald Reagan battled in the courts to maintain his more traditional, work-oriented welfare reform program in that state.

The Antigovernment '80s

These, however, were only skirmishes. In the 1980s, with a growing antigovernment mood and the arrival of the Reagan administration in Washington, a sustained attack on permissive "Great Society" approaches was under way. AFDC bills attached to budget legislation did not produce large savings, nor were they intended to. But they did reverse much of the previous court-sanctioned momentum toward needs-based income entitlements. Many state eligibility requirements overturned by the courts were statutorily re-introduced by Congress. The "work incentive" exclusion of earned income from calculations of claimants' available income was dropped, removing some four hundred thousand cases of mainly working poor persons from the AFDC rolls. Support obligations for men living with the family as spouses and "lodgers" were reinstated. But, perhaps as a sign of changing social mores, there was no congressional interest in reviving the old custom in some states (overturned by the Supreme Court in 1968) of treating any sexual partner as a substitute parent disqualifying the children in the family from AFDC payments.

The 1980s also witnessed a reassertion of the pre-1960s tradition of state variation in welfare assistance. The Nixon and Carter welfare reform proposals, as well as most court decisions in the 1960s and 1970s, carried a presumption favoring greater national uniformity in AFDC benefits and administration. In those years it was conservatives who argued in favor of giving states more discretionary control over the programs. With the advent of the Reagan administration the stances were reversed, and in 1981 it was Democrats who fought conservatives' efforts to impose mandatory federal work and other requirements on state-administered welfare programs. The result was a victory for the Democrats that allowed increased state experimentation in combining AFDC with work, training, and employment services.

These state experiences and a growing body of social science research studies of their results produced what some saw as a new consensus in the fairly small circle of politicians and poverty experts who paid serious attention to welfare policy. As one of the leaders in this network, Sen. Daniel Patrick Moynihan (D-New York), put it, "Conservatives have persuaded liberals that there is nothing wrong with obligating able-bodied adults to work. Liberals have persuaded conservatives that most adults want to work and need some help to do so." As usual, the theme throughout the debate on welfare reform in the 1980s was prevention, rehabilitation, and work, as well as criticism of the current system for its indiscriminate cash handouts. In the words of the final Family Support Act of 1988, public welfare recipients would be "encouraged, assisted, and required to fulfill their responsibilities to support their children by preparing for, accepting, and retaining such employment as they are capable of performing." Provisions were made for education and job training for AFDC recipients who needed it to work. Medical and child-care services would be continued for a year after a recipient left the welfare rolls and entered the work force. Republicans insisted on mandatory federal standards requiring states to achieve given levels of participation in work and training programs for employable AFDC clients. The final compromise, passed by congressional Democratic leaders and the Reagan White House over the heads of more liberal Democratic congressmen, required states to have one-fifth of employable recipients in work or training programs by fiscal 1995. How states do that is largely their business.

The Demise of the 1988 Consensus

Translated into practice and the play of partisan politics at both state and national levels, it turned out there was less to the policy consensus of 1988 than met the eye. That the Family Support Act had to be implemented in the midst of a sustained economic downturn certainly did not help. The result, together with the years of cuts in federal spending to aid states and cities, was a powerful squeeze on state budgets. Thus, new state spending to match federal funds for the act's various activities was often hard to obtain.

Budget pains were only part of the story. The Family Support Act had been crafted within a fairly self-contained fraternity of policymakers specializing in the subject. The mundane work of carrying through the various education, training, and employment programs aroused scarcely any political or public interest. Meanwhile, outside this circle, the "welfare problem" proved an irresistible target to other politicians in the early 1990s, especially at a time when many Americans were feeling their own economic hardship. Soon in statehouses and in Congress new "tough love" proposals for straightening out the welfare mess could be heard. These included cutting back the level of AFDC benefits, strengthening mandatory work requirements, and limiting the period of welfare receipt, tying welfare benefits to stay-in-school rules for teen parents and cutting adult parents' welfare benefits should their children fail to attend school, paying monetary bonuses to encourage marriage, and cutting benefits for additional children born while the mother was on welfare. Many of these, of course, have a familiar ring to anyone familiar with the history of welfare policy.

Holding hearings to find out what had gone awry with the intended direction and spirit of the Family Support Act, Senator Moynihan concluded, "I'm afraid all this originates with David Duke. He started talking about the 'threat' of people on welfare, and it struck a nerve." Meanwhile, the research findings on welfare reform programs continued to pile up, telling people what they did not want to hear: namely, that overcoming the employment and other problems of people on welfare for long periods is a costly and slow process that yields only modest results in terms of increased earnings and welfare savings.

Those familiar with America's welfare legacy will find little of this surprising. Serious reforms are often costly, slow, undramatic, and modest in effect. More alluring in the political arena are promises that are cheap, splashy, and short term, for politicians generally derive political rewards for proposing, not implementing changes in the welfare system. Looking from the long perspective of the poor law and welfare policy, one can also understand that there has always been a combination of positive and punitive impulses and measures, of insisting that poor people behave in certain ways and of trying to change the conditions that inhibit their ability to behave in those ways. Everyone wishes the "welfare" problem would be solved and simply go away. But it won't. That is the other lesson of history.

POINTS TO PONDER

1. How has U.S. society's idea of the "deserving poor" changed over the years?
2. What impact did the passage of the Social Security Act in 1935 have on poverty in America?
3. Why were the 1960s a watershed in U.S. poverty policy?

Chapter 14

FOREIGN AND NATIONAL
SECURITY POLICY

The authority to commit the nation to war is of vital concern in any polity. It is a decision of such magnitude that the Framers decided not to put it within the control of one person or branch of government. Just as the Framers divided the legislative power and the power of the purse between the president and Congress, they also decided to divide the power of the sword. This constitutional division has had profound consequences for our system of governance. The division of the national security powers has resulted in a shifting balance between the two branches, but has also assured a recurrent struggle over the right to direct U.S. foreign policy.

Constitutional Origins of the Power of the Sword

The prerogative to take a nation to war was long the province of kings, with their ability to raise armies and initiate conflict solely on their own judgment. The Framers decided that in a republic the power to take the nation to war was too dangerous to give to one branch, and the temptation of the executive to abuse the war power was too great. So they split the power over foreign affairs between the two branches.

To ensure that the power to commit the country to war could not be made by one person, an early draft of the Constitution stated that Congress would have the power to "make war." But since Congress would not always be in session and the nation might have to respond to sudden attacks, the wording was changed to "declare" war, so that the president could act quickly in a military emergency. But there was no doubt that the Framers intended to give the final decision to Congress. In addition, the bulk of the explicit grants of foreign policy powers in the Constitution were given to Congress. Besides the power to declare war, Congress was given the power to provide for an army and navy, to make rules for the regulation of the armed forces, and to grant letters of marque and reprisal. In addition, the Senate had to give its consent to treaties and the appointment of ambassadors. More broadly, Congress had the power to pass laws and appropriate all money, both of which are essential to foreign and national security policy.

Constitutionally, the president can appoint ambassadors and receive foreign envoys, which implies the right to recognize foreign nations and to negotiate treaties. The president also is commander in chief of the armed forces. But the power of the commander in chief, according to Alexander Hamilton in *Federalist* No. 69, was to be strictly limited:

> It would amount to nothing more than the supreme command and direction of the military and naval forces, as the first general and admiral of the Confederacy; while that of the British king extends to the *declaring* of war and to the *raising* and *regulating* of fleets and armies—all of which, by the Constitution under consideration, would appertain to the legislature.

This passage is particularly noteworthy because Hamilton was one of the leading Framers who favored a strong executive.

The Struggle Between the President and Congress

Despite this clear intention on the part of the Framers, the exigencies of international relations, precedents set by strong presidents, and the technologies of the twentieth century have combined to make the president the dominant decision maker with respect to committing the nation to war. Presidential power has increased with the world wars of the twentieth century. After World War II and the rise of the Soviet Union as the major military rival of the United States, presidential power rose along with the centralization of executive branch control in the presidency. President Truman decided to go to war in Korea without consulting Congress, and Congress delegated to President Johnson broad authority to conduct the war in Vietnam according to his own judgment.

The war in Vietnam was a turning point in relations between the president and Congress with respect to national security policy-making. The bipartisan consensus that had existed since 1941, first on opposition to the Axis powers and then on the nature of the cold war with the Soviet Union, was undermined by the war in Vietnam. As public support for the war declined in the United States, congressional opposition to Johnson's policies increased. Political opposition grew to such proportions that Johnson decided not to run for reelection in 1968. President Nixon came to office with promises of a secret plan to end the war, but his conditions for "peace with honor" extended the war and entailed the secret bombing and invasion of Cambodia.

Opposition to the continuation of the war, along with Watergate and President Nixon's other assertions of presidential prerogative, led to the reaction in Congress that culminated in the president's resignation. During the mid-1970s Congress reacted to what was perceived to be the "imperial presidency" of the Johnson and Nixon administrations. Congress became much more willing to assert itself in foreign policy-making, both in terms of overall policy direction and in the details of defense management.

The most important attempt by Congress to limit presidential foreign policy powers was the War Powers Resolution, passed over President Nixon's veto in 1973. The resolution requires that the president consult with Congress before introducing armed forces into situations where hostilities are imminent. It also requires that presidents report any commitment of troops to Congress, and, if no approval is forthcoming, withdraw the troops within 60 days (with the possible extension of 30 more days).

Presidents, however, have asserted that the strictures of the War Powers Resolution unconstitutionally infringe upon the president's powers as commander in chief. Thus the resolution, though it has been a factor in arguments about foreign intervention, has not had a major inhibiting effect on presidential actions, nor has it given Congress much say in military confrontations. Presidents have most often acted unilaterally in foreign military interventions and have informed Congress at the last minute. Congress has not had the will to force the issue by insisting that the War Powers procedures be followed.

President Bush's conduct of the Persian Gulf War was symptomatic of the congressional role in taking the country to war. President Bush ordered the deployment of 200,000 U.S. soldiers to the Gulf shortly after the invasion and occupation of Kuwait by Saddam Hussein, the leader of Iraq. Congress was informed of the action and generally supported the President. But when the president decided to double the size of the deployment, Congress was not consulted, and many in Congress expressed reservations about the wisdom of war with Iraq. President Bush argued that he did not need congressional approval to go to war with Iraq, though in January 1991 he asked for and received a congressional resolution approving his actions.

Unlike the preceding two U.S. wars, neither of which was declared by Congress, the Persian Gulf War was won quickly and overwhelmingly by the United States, and President Bush won historically high public approval ratings. It was a clear contrast with the Korean and Vietnam wars, which dragged on for years and resulted in thousands of U.S. casualties. In part because of the unpopularity of those wars, Presidents Truman and Johnson decided not to run for reelection. President Bush was defeated in his run for reelection, but definitely not because of the war.

Other Sources of Influence

Public opinion has always played an important role in U.S. foreign policy, and has often been split between isolationist and internationalist camps. This division in public opinion was largely overcome after the Japanese attack on Pearl Harbor on December 7, 1941. The nation was united in its support of President Roosevelt's leadership in World War II.

This unusual consensus was extended with the development of the cold war between the United States and the Soviet Union. But the consensus fell apart as the war in Vietnam dragged on without success and with increasing American casualties. The legacy of the war was a public split between those who felt the United States had to take a hard line toward the Soviet Union and those who favored more accommodating policies.

The U.S. victory in the Gulf War turned an ambivalent public toward broad support for President Bush and his conduct of the conflict. But the breakup of the Soviet Union in the late 1980s and the Persian Gulf victory did not lead to a new world order as President Bush had hoped. The role that the United States would play as the only remaining superpower was uncertain.

The lack of consensus on U.S. foreign policy since the 1970s has led to a more open foreign policy process. Despite the failure of the War Powers Resolution to significantly curb presidential initiatives in war making, Congress has become much more active in foreign policy issues. It has been willing to assert itself in most areas other than making war, such as arms control, diplomacy, international trade, and foreign aid. Along with increased congressional involvement has come a greater openness in the foreign policy process with new interest groups forming to try to influence foreign policy, from ideological to ethnic to trade groups. Thus the foreign policy process has become more open and politicized in the post–Vietnam War years. Foreign policy expertise has expanded, with think tanks in Washington housing scholars and former officials who participate in the debates over national security policy.

The traditional concerns of foreign and national security policy have been U.S. military strength and commitments. The underlying economic basis for American power has always been the ability of the nation's economy to support an active presence internationally and the military might to enforce its will. U.S. economic strength has been unsurpassed in the post–World War II era, but as its economic dominance has been challenged by Japan and Germany, there has been an increasing appreciation of the role of economic power in the nation's long-term national security interests. This realization has been accompanied by a new appreciation of the interdependence of modern economies in the global arena in which goods, services, talent, capital, and information flow quickly across international borders.

The Readings

The two readings in this section present surveys of U.S. national security policy-making since World War II. One concentrates on the balance between the president and Congress in directing U.S. foreign policy and on the broader dynamics of the policy-making system. The Ambrose article focuses more on the substance of policy and the different contributions that the post-war presidents have made to the U.S posture in the world.

Thomas Mann lays out the consequences of the Vietnam War for U.S. national security policy-making. In addition to the breakdown in consensus, Mann provides some examples of a Congress much more willing to assert itself in foreign policy-making. Congress passed a series of laws meant to reassert the constitutional powers that it felt had been usurped by the president. These included laws requiring that Congress be notified of covert actions and executive agreements made by the president. Oversight of executive branch actions increased considerably, and the amount of reporting by the executive to Congress was increased.

The selection by Stephen Ambrose lays out the fluctuations of presidential and congressional control of foreign policy since World War II. He analyzes failures and successes of the United States in the world arena and concludes that success is related to the degree to which the president has involved the Congress and the broader public in the deliberation over national security policy.

KEY TERMS

cold war: conflict and occasional confrontation between the United States and the Soviet Union after World War II, termed "cold" because it did not result in large-scale military battles. It ended with a peaceful revolution between 1989 and 1991 in which the U.S.S.R. returned to its Russian core.

power of the sword: constitutional authority to commit the United States to military battle and war

realism in U.S. foreign policy: the idea that only vital U.S. interests should be the object of foreign policy (rather than idealistic or humanitarian goals) and that effective military force is the only way to assure U.S. interests

50

"MAKING FOREIGN POLICY: PRESIDENT AND CONGRESS"
Thomas E. Mann

The trauma of Vietnam shattered the post–World War II consensus about foreign policy in the United States. Liberals and conservatives disagreed over the use of military power, and Democrats in Congress often disagreed with Republicans in the White House over the direction of U.S. foreign policy. In this selection from his edited book A Question of Balance *(1990), political scientist Thomas Mann of the Brookings Institution analyzes the causes and consequences of these changes.*

Mann finds the roots of the problem in an overly broad interpretation of the president's constitutional role in foreign policy along with a more divisive approach to the international role of the United States. These conflicts have led to a more open and politicized policy-making process. Mann argues for a moderation of the stridency of the debate and a more appropriate balance between the constitutional powers of the two branches.

Congress began to assert itself as an active and consequential player in the making of American foreign policy in the late 1960s, as public doubts about the wisdom of U.S. involvement in Vietnam increased. It soon became commonplace to speak of foreign policy by Congress. After bitter confrontations and dramatic reversals of policies espoused by Presidents Nixon and Ford, however, many observers began to question whether Congress could play both an active and a constructive role in foreign policy-making. Careful chroniclers noted that before the 1970s ended "much of the bloom had left the congressional rose," and that the pendulum had begun to swing back—at least partly—to the White House.

Yet the pace of congressional involvement actually accelerated during the presidency of Ronald Reagan, which featured pitched battles between the executive and legislative branches on such issues as aid to the contras, arms control, war powers, trade, and congressional "micromangement" of the conduct of foreign policy. This renewed congressional activism has spawned its own critics, who argue that congressional in foreign policy has upset the balance between executive and legislative power intended by the Constitution's Framers and has weakened this country's ability to defend its interests around the globe. Indeed, the opposition to the new role of Congress has recently gathered strength, buoyed by the publication of books bemoaning the constraints on the modern presidency and excoriating the excesses of the contemporary House and Senate and by the portrayal of Congress in the popular press as corrupt and irresponsible.

It is not a coincidence that this spirited debate about the constitutional authority and institutional competence of the president and Congress in the realm of foreign policy is occurring in the midst of an extraordinary period of divided government. The normal tensions that arise in the U.S. system of separate institutions sharing power have been exacerbated by the contemporary pattern of split-party control of the two branches. Republicans have become the party of the White House, Democrats the party of Congress. Under these circumstances, substantive differences and partisan rivalries are routinely escalated into institutional warfare, and members of the executive and legislative branches have an even greater interest in protecting and expanding their institutional prerogatives.

This is not to say that divided government is the sole or even primary source of interbranch conflict on foreign policy. The seeds of today's tensions were planted over 200 years ago in a Constitution that compelled a partnership between the executive and legislative branches. That partnership was built upon the distinctive competencies of each branch: for the presidency, "decision, activity, secrecy, and dispatch"; for Congress, democracy, deliberation, and the development of consensus. But when substantive differences between the president and Congress over the ends and means of foreign policy are sharp, each has the incentive to use its powers under the Constitution to press its views upon the other, even at the cost of violating the principles underlying that partnership.

Executive-legislative conflict on foreign policy escalates when policy disagreement is pronounced and when the constraints, both formal and informal, on institutional assertiveness are weakened. These are precisely the conditions that have shaped foreign policy making in recent years. The bipartisan consensus that allowed presidents to control American foreign policy from Pearl Harbor to the early stages of the Vietnam War gave way to ideological polarization on the substance of policy and an erosion of trust among policymakers in Washington. Substantive differences on policy, both within and between the branches, became the rule rather than the exception. And those different views about the proper course of American foreign policy, rather than being stifled in a deferential, closed, policymaking system, were fully vented in a transformed environment featuring many more pressure groups with foreign policy agendas, a vastly expanded and more ideological foreign policy establishment, an aggressive and suspicious press, and an assertive, decentralized, resource-rich Congress.

In many respects this recent politicization of foreign policy is closer to the norm in American history than the "golden era" of bipartisanship. The scope and character of congressional involvement is unusual, but the level of conflict is not. But the world and America's role in it have changed fundamentally since the days when presidents' foreign policy aspirations were routinely constrained by domestic political pressures, so it is important to identify the consequences of this renewed tension. On the one hand, conflict between the president and Congress over the objectives and methods of American foreign policy is not ineluctably harmful to the national interest nor even injurious to the president's program. Second-guessing by Congress can keep presidents from pursuing ill-conceived policies. Initiatives from Capitol Hill can also prompt presidents to consider new policies or new ways of thinking about old ones. Aggressive "bad cop" behavior by Congress can actually strengthen the bargaining position of "good cop" presidents in dealing with other countries. Open debate in Congress can help build the public support needed to sustain foreign policies over the long term and to adjust those policies to better serve the interests and values of the American people.

Yet with conflict often comes stalemate, irresolution, or inaction. From the executive's perspective, the president's ability to formulate and conduct foreign policy—to respond to military threats to the national security, to fashion arms control negotiating positions, to authorize covert action in support of American interests, or to engage in diplomacy with friends and foes—is compromised by Congress's determination to play an active role at each stage of the process. The costs flow from two types of congressional behavior. On some occasions, Congress makes a collective decision to explicitly reject a presidential policy. These are the dramatic encounters between the branches that capture the most public attention. Much more frequently, what frustrates the executive is the ability of an individual member or committee to impede or redirect American foreign policy. An administration necessarily consumed with diplomatic relations along Pennsylvania Avenue may find itself drained of creative energies and overly tentative in its diplomacy around the world.

There are clearly both costs and benefits from a Congress determined to assert itself in foreign policy and from the executive-legislative conflict that follows. As one scholar has argued, "Americans want two things that often prove incompatible in practice: *democratic government* (involving ongoing competition among a range of U.S. interests and perspectives) and *effective foreign policy* (which requires settling on specific goals and pursuing them consistently)." The question is whether current arrangements for making American foreign policy provide an acceptable balance between competing values and interests. Strong partisans of the executive branch, who nod approvingly when Oliver North and his compatriots state flatly that "the president makes foreign policy," see the problem as not one of achieving balance but rather of unshackling the president from unconstitutional restrictions imposed by Congress. Similarly, balance is not a concern of those who take the primary lesson of the Iran-contra affair to be that the president's virtually unlimited discretion to pursue his foreign policy objectives must be reduced or preferably eliminated by statute and constant vigilance. . . .

Constitutional Arguments

While it is commonplace for combatants in struggles between the branches to lay claim to the moral authority of the Framers, it is also largely fruitless. In its specific grants of authority in foreign policy, the Constitution favors Congress, the first branch of government. In addition to its exclusive authority to make laws and to tax and spend for the common defense and the general welfare, Congress was given the power to declare war, to raise and support armies, to provide and maintain a navy, to make rules for the government and regulation of the armed services, to grant letters of marque and reprisal, to define offenses against the law of nations, to advise and consent on treaties and ambassadorial appointments, and to regulate foreign commerce. The president, by contrast, was specifically authorized only to receive foreign envoys, to negotiate treaties and appoint ambassadors, and to serve as commander in chief of the armed forces.

But if Congress was given a more generous grant of specific authorities in foreign and military affairs, the executive was nonetheless expected to play a central role. The architecture of the Constitution and the debates surrounding the Constitutional Convention and ratification period show "that the Founders intended to create two vigorous, active and combative branches with significant overlapping roles in foreign policy." They produced, in the famous phrase of Edward Corwin, "an invitation to struggle for the privilege of directing American foreign policy."

The ambiguities, omissions, and overlapping grants of authority in the constitutional blueprint do not mean that the struggle is unbounded. Congress neither makes treaties nor appoints ambassadors. It leaves to the president the management of diplomatic relations with other countries and the conduct of authorized military operations. Presidents, on the other hand, ordinarily acknowledge the constitutional imperatives that they may spend no funds without congressional appropriations, conclude no treaty without Senate consent, and declare or wage no full-scale war without congressional authorization. These are largely settled questions. Moreover, it is generally accepted that neither branch may use its powers to trample on the exclusive constitutional authority of the other. For example, Congress is constitutionally bound to appropriate necessary funds to pay for an embassy in a country the president has recognized, although it feels no reticence about reversing presidents' decisions to close consular offices.

But many important foreign policy matters fall in Justice Robert H. Jackson's famous twilight zone, in which the president and Congress have concurrent authority or the distribution of authority is uncertain. Many of the controversies that have arisen in this twilight zone—the deployment of military forces, the use of executive agreements, the regulation of covert action, claims of executive privilege, and congressional control of foreign policy through the power of the purse—are expressed in constitutional terms but must be resolved or at least accommodated in the political arena. Since the primary interpreters of the foreign policy powers of the president and Congress are not the courts but the two branches themselves, it is perfectly natural for each to make its strongest case, to test the limits of what the other is willing to tolerate. The form of their partnership, the balance of institutional interests and prerogatives, is subject to constant competition and negotiation.

Through much of American history, beginning with George Washington, presidents pushed the limits of their constitutional authority and found Congress largely acquiescent. Washington established the precedent that the president plays an active and assertive role in foreign policy and military affairs, and subsequent occupants of the White House followed suit. Managing the day-to-day relations with foreign nations, reaching agreements with other governments without resort to a formal treaty (and, therefore, the advice and consent of the Senate), and deploying military forces without explicit authorization by Congress became the normal wont of presidents, as Congress implicitly acknowledged the comparative advantage of the executive to act quickly, informally, knowledgeably, and secretly.

It would be a mistake, however, to infer from these developments that strong and assertive presidents based their leadership in foreign and military affairs on claims of constitutional primacy or that Congress acknowledged its own position of powerlessness. After unilaterally declaring neutrality for the United States in the war between England and France, Washington provided a full explanation to Congress when it reconvened later in the year and conceded that he had no power to keep Congress from charting a different course in the war. After sending naval forces to the Mediterranean to fight the Barbary pirates, Jefferson sought congressional sanction; he also invoked John Locke's doctrine of emergency prerogative (the law of self-preservation), not constitutional authority, to justify his unilateral foreign policy actions that went beyond congressional authorization. Much the same can be said of the emergency policies of Lincoln and Franklin Roosevelt. Both presidents acknowledged that the extraordinary powers they claimed for the presidency were temporary, subject to ratification by Congress, and based not on a routine presidential right under the Constitution but rather on the doctrine of emergency prerogative.

Although Congress was often content through tacit concurrence or explicit delegation to let the president take the initiative in foreign policy, it reserved the right to object, which it did in a sporadic but telling fashion throughout the nineteenth and twentieth centuries. Congress has had few doubts about the breadth of its own powers [as historian Arthur Schlesinger, Jr., noted]:

> Congress has insisted that, whatever the president may do on his own initiative when Congress is silent, he may not act contrary to the wishes of Congress when they are expressed by law in the exercise of the legislature's broad powers over war and commerce with foreign nations and its power to spend for the common defense and general welfare.

Against this broadly accepted understanding of constitutional design and development, there has emerged in recent years an argument that presidents have inherent powers under the Constitution that guarantee them the primary role in conducting the foreign policy of the United States. This position is presented most explicitly and coherently in the minority report of the congressional committees that investigated the Iran-contra affair, where it undergirds the assertion that however unwise some of his actions may have been, President Reagan exercised constitutionally protected powers.

The case for inherent presidential powers in foreign policy is based on a string of arguments. Powers are separated between the branches according to underlying principles of institutional competence; the need for energy in the executive led the Framers to place the deployment and use of force, together with negotiations, intelligence gathering, and diplomatic communications, at the center of the president's foreign policy powers. The general grant of executive power to the president (which for Alexander Hamilton included all foreign affairs powers not expressly provided to the Congress), combined with his role as the "sole organ of the nation in its external relations, and its sole representative with foreign nations" (declared by John Marshall while a member of the House of Representatives), provides a basis for presidential prerogatives well beyond the powers enumerated in Article II. Early constitutional history affirmed the executive's broad foreign policy authority: presidents engaged in secret diplomacy and intelligence activities, established military and diplomatic policy with other countries, and deployed military forces without congressional approval. Finally, the president's inherent powers in foreign policy were explicitly recognized by the courts, most importantly in *U.S.* v. *Curtiss-Wright*, which referred to "the very delicate, plenary and exclusive power of the President as the sole organ of the federal government in the field of international relations."

The Iran-contra minority report concludes that the Constitution gives the president power to act on his own in foreign affairs—as the "sole organ" of the government in negotiation, intelligence sharing, and other forms of communication with the rest of the world—and to protect the lives and interests of American citizens abroad. While neither the president nor Congress can accomplish very much over the long term by trying to go it alone, "neither branch can be permitted to usurp functions that belong to the other."

Some of these arguments are consistent with the constitutional framework I identified at the outset. Surely the Framers recognized that the legislative and executive branches had distinctive institutional strengths and weaknesses and sought to separate and combine powers to maximize their comparative advantage. They also intended the president to be more than a clerk or agent of Congress, and events throughout U.S. history underscore the value of a strong presidency, particularly in foreign and military affairs. It is also generally accepted, as I argued above, that neither branch may use its powers to deprive the other of its exclusive constitutional authority.

But the signers of the Iran-contra minority report go well beyond these sensible formulations to embrace a constitutional construction that enlarges the president's domain of exclusive authority well beyond what is expressly provided in the Constitution. There is no compelling reason to believe that Hamilton is a more reliable witness to the founding than James Madison, who vigorously contested Hamilton's expansive reading of presidential power. And it seems most unlikely that this view will ever be anything but a minority dissent or that Congress or the Supreme Court will ever accept such an executive-centered interpretation of the Constitution. The fact remains that many of the most important questions of foreign policy fall in the twilight zone of concurrent authority or uncertainty. The case for a redistribution of authority and responsibility for foreign policy between the president and Congress must perforce rest on other than constitutional grounds.

The Two Presidencies

The constitutional argument that the president has the primary authority and responsibility for the conduct of American foreign policy fits well with the empirical observation that the president invariably has his way on major issues of foreign affairs. Over two decades ago Aaron Wildavsky argued that foreign and domestic policy are shaped in very different political processes.

> The United States has one President, but it has two presidencies; one presidency is for domestic affairs and the other is concerned with defense and foreign policy. Since World War II, Presidents have had much greater success in controlling the nation's defense and foreign policies than in dominating its domestic policies.

Wildavsky portrayed foreign policy-making as largely insulated from the pluralistic pressures that characterize the domestic policy process. Instead of the normal battle of interest groups, parties, and bureaucracies, foreign policy-making was seen as an apolitical, technical realm of presidential problem solving. Presidents dominated foreign policy because the new international role taken on by the United States after World War II made foreign policy extremely important to them and attracted a substantial share of their resources, foreign policy was largely outside the realm of partisan conflict, and presidents' competitors in the foreign policy arena were weak.

The intervening years have not been kind to the two-presidencies thesis; Wildavsky is the first to admit that it has limited utility in an age of political dissensus. There is little evidence to suggest that recent presidents have succeeded in pressing the view that "politics stops at the water's edge." As a description of and explanation for the president's comparative advantage in foreign and defense policy during the 1950s, and as a conceptual tool for differentiating the Truman and Eisenhower years from the periods before and after, however, the concept of the two presidencies continues to serve a useful purpose. What was distinctive about foreign policy-making in the post–World War II era was the success of presidents in attracting support from the opposition party in Congress, starting with the Truman administration's alliance with Republican Senator Arthur Vandenberg, chairman of the Foreign Relations Committee, and continuing through northern Democrats' favorable treatment of Eisenhower's internationalist policies.

However, the key to this anomaly is not presidential deference, but policy agreement. The conversion of Vandenberg from midwestern isolationism to an internationalist position that embraced the Marshall Plan, the Greece-Turkey aid program, and NATO was based on a genuine change in his view of the U.S. role in the world under the threat of Soviet expansionism. It also involved a partnership between the legislative and executive branches that went well beyond deference to presidential wishes and required intensive political bargaining to achieve victory on Capitol Hill. (Vandenberg's leadership in forging a bipartisan foreign policy did not prevent his Republican colleagues from bitterly criticizing the Truman administration on other foreign policy issues, including "the loss of China.") This new conservative internationalism initiated by Truman and Vandenberg provided the basis for cooperation on foreign policy between President Eisenhower and the Democratic Congress. Eisenhower won the strong support of northern Democrats largely because he espoused foreign policies with which they agreed.

Presidents since Eisenhower have not enjoyed a clear foreign policy advantage in dealing with Congress, at least as measured by levels of support on domestic and foreign policy roll call votes. The difference has been the withdrawal of support from members of the opposition party: no president since Eisenhower has consistently won a majority of the opposition party on foreign policy votes. This is the result of fundamental disagreement along ideological and partisan lines about the proper policy course. The consequences of the loss of opposition party support for the president are especially pronounced under divided government. Republican presidents Nixon, Ford, Reagan, and now Bush have all been forced to seek majorities in a Democratic House or Senate where there was no longer a presumption of bipartisanship in foreign policy.

Public Opinion and Foreign Policy

There is little doubt that changes in public opinion about foreign policy were the root cause of the weakening of the president's leadership position and of the chronic conflict between the executive and legislative branches that began in the late 1960s. Moreover, public opinion continues to be a prime determinant of the level of cooperation or conflict between the president and Congress. An administration that sails against the tide of public opinion invites a more active congressional role; a president who succeeds in bringing foreign policy and public opinion into closer conformance—either by adjusting his policy or by reshaping public opinion—will be more successful in diffusing opposition on Capitol Hill.

The bipartisan foreign policy consensus that prevailed for almost two decades after World War II was sustained by a leadership stratum that shared an internationalist and interventionist view of the U.S. role in world affairs, an attentive and educated group of citizens who followed and supported this leadership, and a poorly informed and largely inert mass public that tolerated official policy as long as it appeared to be working. The new elite consensus, which reflected the special challenges and opportunities posed by the postwar world, signaled the demise of both left-wing and right-wing isolationism among American leaders. This left the largely isolationist public without any stimulus to oppose presidential initiatives in foreign policy, except for real-world events that called into question the efficacy of those initiatives.

William Schneider has provided a persuasive account of how this followership model of American foreign policy making broke down after 1964.

Growing disenchantment with the Vietnam War led to an ideological polarization over foreign policy within the attentive public, while broader societal forces stimulated antiestablishment sentiments at both the mass and elite levels. Liberal internationalists harbored a deep suspicion of the use of military force as an instrument of foreign policy. They looked to a new world order based on global interdependence, and stressed détente with the Soviets, economic and humanitarian aid, and multilateralism in world politics. Conservative internationalists viewed the world primarily in East-West terms: they continued to believe that military power and the containment of communism should be the cornerstone of U.S. foreign policy. These ideological divisions on foreign policy became institutionalized within the party system as insurgent forces within both political parties successfully challenged their establishments. The parties became more internally consistent across economic, social, and foreign policy issues, reinforcing differences that had arisen out of the Vietnam experience, and the bipartisan consensus was shattered. The polarization of foreign policy opinion also coincided with changes taking place in Congress, where junior Democrats, sympathetic to the ideology of liberal internationalism, sought to wrest power from their more conservative senior colleagues.

The traumatic events of the 1960s and 1970s, made all the more vivid by their coverage on television, also had an effect on the general public. Mass opinion became less passive and more distrustful, prone to swing left or right unpredictably in response to current fears and concerns. The larger public did not internalize the ideological views of the more attentive citizenry; it remained essentially pragmatic and hoped to achieve both goals sought by the contending elites: peace and strength. As the relative salience of these two concerns has shifted over time in response to events and debates at the elite level, so has the substance of public opinion—and in turn the dominant ideological position in Congress on foreign policy issues.

Broad currents in mass opinion shape the context of presidential-congressional relations on foreign policy. Between 1964 and 1974 the primary concern of the public was peace, which provided political sustenance to the liberals. After 1975, concerns about Soviet global adventurism and American military weakness gave support to conservative forces advocating increased defense spending and a tougher foreign policy posture. The Soviet invasion of Afghanistan was the coup de grace. These shifting public sentiments did not go unnoticed or unheeded by the Carter administration in its last two years or by Congress in the first year of the Reagan presidency. Yet by 1982 public support for increased defense spending had collapsed as strong anti-Soviet feelings gave way (or gave rise) to a renewed fear of war and a consequent desire for arms control. The nuclear freeze movement embodied these public fears and had no small part in the unprecedented and influential role Congress came to play on arms control issues in the 1980s. Finally, in the wake of the dramatic moves of Gorbachev and Reagan to improve U.S.-Soviet relations and reduce the perception of a Soviet threat, by the end of the 1980s the public came to view national security increasingly in economic as well as military terms, underscoring to politicians of both parties the potential appeal of economic nationalism.

While the relative salience of peace and strength has shifted back and forth over the past fifteen years, the public has remained deeply skeptical of substantial and extended American involvement abroad and suspicious of foreign policy leaders. These attitudes provide fertile ground for critics of administration policy seeking to mobilize opposition. Presidents have a difficult time building and maintaining public support for their foreign policies because the public hears dissenting voices and is inclined to listen to them. The polarization of opinion among political activists and the rise of antiestablishment feeling in the mass public "have weakened the political preconditions that enable any president to exercise independent foreign policy leadership."

The New Foreign Policy-making Process

The changes in mass and elite opinion contributed to a transformation of the foreign policy-making process. The old foreign policy establishment of relatively homogeneous, pragmatic, and mostly bipartisan East Coast diplomatic and financial figures was replaced by a much larger, more diverse, and often ideological elite of foreign policy professionals. Dozens of research organizations and thousands of specialists joined the conversation on American foreign policy, providing ideas and information to politicians engaged in policy wars within and between the branches.

At the same time, the number of interest groups with a foreign policy agenda soared. Some of the growth was due to the globalization of the American economy. Some reflected the heightened political involvement of traditional interests (ethnic constituencies, businesses, farmers) drawn to the more open and decentralized policy process. But much of the increase came from groups concerned more with championing values than with protecting interests. On issues ranging from Vietnam to Central America, from détente to the nuclear freeze, liberal and conservative groups sought to advance their goals in Washington by bringing public pressure to bear on policymakers.

The media also became an important player in this altered process. The new-style pressure groups adopted lobbying strategies modeled on political campaigns, with major emphasis on the mobilization of public support or opposition through the mass media. Foreign policy specialists discovered that the best way to influence policymakers in an open process is through public argument (on op-ed pages and television and radio shows), not private advice. Ambitious politicians found television irresistible as a means for identifying with popular foreign policy sentiments. But the media are more than a passive vehicle through which the many players in the foreign policy process communicate with one another. A skeptical and aggressive press amplifies the policy differences that exist among elites and sharpens the criticisms that are leveled against those with responsibility for conducting foreign policy. At the same time, television, which has created a vast, inadvertent audience for news about foreign affairs, reinforces and intensifies the public's opposition to America's involvement around the world and its cynicism about its leaders' motives in promoting such policies.

The most noticeable, and perhaps significant, changes in the policy process occurred within Congress. It is by now a familiar story that the 1970s witnessed the most sweeping reforms in the history of Congress. Stimulated by the twin concerns of strengthening the legislative branch vis-à-vis the executive and breaking down the old congressional power structure, Congress moved dramatically to transform the way business was conducted on Capitol Hill. Power was taken from senior, often elderly, committee chairmen and shifted both down to aggressive junior subcommittee chairmen and rank-and-file committee members and up to the full party caucus. Committee meetings were opened to the public, roll call votes were permitted on key floor amendments, and House (and eventually Senate) sessions were televised. The staff capabilities of Congress were greatly expanded—in members' offices, committees and subcommittees, and support agencies like the Congressional Budget Office, the General Accounting Office, the Congressional Research Service, and the Office of Technology Assessment. And finally, new statutes were enacted to restrict the president's discretion over war powers, impoundments, arms sales, covert action, and human rights violations. Congress became more decentralized and democratized, stronger in its policymaking capabilities, and assertive in its dealings with the executive branch.

These changes coincided with a rapid turnover in the membership of both House and Senate, so that by the end of the 1970s Congress was dominated by members whose formative political experiences were Vietnam and Watergate. The new members were active and entrepreneurial at home and in Washington, adept at generating favorable publicity for themselves, and determined to advance their substantive interests, which more often than not were in conflict with those of the president. Unlike their elders, they were unwilling to wait for the seniority system to empower them, and they were less inclined to heed the call of presidential leadership. They had both the incentives and the resources to challenge the president on foreign policy, whatever his party, and they did so with obvious energy and relish.

The executive branch was not immune to the changes that swept through the foreign policy-making process in the wake of the collapse of the postwar bipartisan consensus. The general trend toward the centralization and politicization of executive power in the White House staff has been especially pronounced in the foreign policy arena. In most recent administrations the National Security Council staff has eclipsed the State Department, and the antipathy of the president's political advisers toward the foreign service and other parts of the bureaucracy has been exacerbated. The growth in the White House staff and its aggrandizement of executive power have put a premium on loyalty to the president. Helping the president achieve his foreign policy agenda, often over the opposition of Congress and experienced hands in the bureaucracy, takes precedence over dispassionate determination of what those foreign policies should be. The White House has assumed day-to-day management of foreign policy, and in extreme cases, such as the Iran–contra affair, "the White House staff is asked to carry out a major operational mission that the departments (State, Defense, CIA) are thought to be too clumsy, rule-bound—or astute—to attempt." As both products and shapers of the new politicized foreign policy environment, recent presidents (Carter and Reagan in particular) have often fanned the ideological fires rather than dampened them. And a more vigilant press and active Congress have provided ample outlets for executive branch officials who dissent from the president's views and hope to force a change in policy through embarrassing leaks.

In sum, the more open and ideological foreign policy-making process now encompasses the public, political parties, elections, media, experts, interest groups, Congress, *and* the executive branch. Conflict between the president and Congress must be seen as a consequence of a broader set of developments affecting America's place in the world and domestic political interests and processes. It is no wonder that the president today occupies a less than dominant position in American foreign policy. In terms of the concept of the two presidencies, foreign policy now attracts a substantial share of the resources of Congress and other interested parties as well as of the president, it is very much within the realm of partisan conflict, and the president's competitors in the foreign policy arena are strong.

But to conclude that the president no longer dominates foreign policy is not to deny that he retains substantial advantages or continues to enjoy a high degree of success in putting his personal imprint on policy. In some areas of foreign policy, to be sure, the configuration of political forces and the allocation of policy instruments between the branches limit the president's authority. For example, decisions about military installations and selected weapons procurement are made largely in the manner of domestic distributive policies, with constituency benefits and pork barrel politics leaving a distinctive mark on the ultimate policies. Similarly, the intensity of feelings among ethnic interest groups and the unquestioned authority of Congress to appropriate funds for military assistance powerfully constrain the president's ability to restructure foreign aid programs. But presidents have impressive resources—from unilateral actions to public appeals—with which to overcome obstacles and transform public debate. It has long been recognized that presidents enjoy extraordinary powers in times of crisis, based on their constitutional role as commander in chief and in response to the expectations of elites and the mass public. Presidential initiatives in response to a perceived national security threat can overcome statutory and political inhibitions and negate congressional influence. The relative weakening of America's global stature and the incentives of a plebiscitary presidency to find popular solace in foreign policy crises may be responsible for a growing trend toward executive initiative in foreign policy.

Thus, while a transformed foreign policy-making process certainly requires a change in strategy and tactics, it hardly renders the president powerless. The degree of success a president enjoys and the character of executive-legislative relations depend on several factors: the nature of the policy in question (the type of action required, the level of substantive disagreement, the amount of pressure from interest groups and public opinion, and the policy instruments available to each branch), the political division between the branches (unified or divided government), and the approaches to governance adopted by the president and Congress.

POINTS TO PONDER

1. Does the Constitution tilt the balance in foreign policy-making toward the president or Congress?
2. How did the war in Vietnam shatter the consensus over U.S. foreign policy?
3. How have the politics of foreign policy-making changed over the past four decades?

51

"THE PRESIDENCY
AND FOREIGN POLICY"
Stephen E. Ambrose

The foundation for U.S. foreign policy in the second half of the twentieth century was laid by President Roosevelt in leading the United States to victory in World War II and by President Truman in establishing the outline of the cold war. In this survey of U.S. foreign policy since 1941, from the journal Foreign Affairs *(1991/92), historian Stephen Ambrose of the University of New Orleans examines the highlights of each presidential administration with a critical eye. In his analysis he argues that realism provides a more solid and lasting base for U.S. foreign policy than does the American penchant for idealism. Ambrose observes that the president rather than Congress has come to dominate U.S. foreign policy as America's role in the world has increased. But he also emphasizes that presidential policies formulated in secret are much less likely to have staying power than are those developed through deliberation by both Congress and the public.*

In the half-century between 1941 and 1991 the ten men who have served as president of the United States have scored some stupendous successes in their role as unquestioned world leader, but they have also suffered some spectacular failures. The greatest successes—the turning back of Nazism, fascism and communism in Europe and of Japanese militarism in Asia—are of such an order of magnitude that they must be described as America's unique gift to the world. That the presidents and their nation did not achieve these triumphs for freedom on their own is obvious, but it is equally obvious that the triumphs could not have been achieved without their leadership and determination. The president's contribution to the end of another "ism"—colonialism—has been of lesser importance, though still a positive one, as also their contribution to the advent of peaceful relations between Egypt and Israel, not to mention the continuing existence of Israel.

The failures, however, have been spectacular. They include the unwillingness or inability to prevent communist takeovers in China, Southeast Asia or Cuba, or to create peaceful conditions, much less prosperity, in the Middle East, Africa and Central America. Although some progress has been made in the past few years, American presidents have failed to realize the hopes of the founders of the United Nations for a genuine collective security or an end to the arms race. And they have been unable or unwilling to slow, much less stop, the international arms trade.

The two giants among the presidents since 1941 came at the beginning of that period. Franklin D. Roosevelt committed a reluctant United States to the leading international role and, more specifically, to unalterable opposition to Nazism, fascism and Japanese militarism. Harry S. Truman committed a reluctant United States to the reconstruction of Europe, to the building of democracy in Germany and Japan, to support for Israel, to NATO and the containment of communism. Four decades later the commitments made by Roosevelt and Truman in the 1940s remain the bedrock of American foreign policy. Their successors have been successful as implementors of established policy, not as creators of new policy.

* * * *

The great successes in U.S. foreign policy tend to come in those areas in which there is a consensus and thus a continuity in policy. (This is not an iron-clad rule; consensus on isolationism, neutrality and disarmament in the 1920s and 1930s was surely wrong.) Failures tend to come in those areas in which there is not a consensus and thus confusion and inconsistency in policy. The most obvious example of a U.S. policy failure is Southeast Asia. In 1954 Eisenhower refused to intervene in Vietnam to stop communism; in 1964 President Lyndon B. Johnson entered a major war in Vietnam to stop communism, eventually sending 550,000 troops there; in 1973 President Nixon pulled the last American troops out of Vietnam, and two years later the Vietnamese communists won a total victory. By 1976, Vietnam, described by presidents through the 1960s as vital to U.S. national interest, was inconsequential to American policymakers and forgotten as a policy priority by the American people.

Beyond the absence of consensus about the importance of countries other than those of Western Europe and Japan to U.S. national interest, there are additional important causes for the rapid shifts in American foreign policy. An obvious one has been the absence of continuity in the top leadership positions. In the past fifty years there have been ten presidents, five of them Democrats, five Republicans. They were all markedly different men, in personalities, agendas, experience and political support. Only two (Eisenhower and Reagan) served more than five years; all, including Roosevelt and Truman, had major internal inconsistencies in their policies; each tried to set his own course and put his own stamp on policy; small wonder that the United States lurched first this way, then that (except in Western Europe and Japan).

The swings in the location of control of foreign policy from the White House to Congress contributed to the inconsistencies. The structural cause of these swings is constitutional. The president's most important asset in asserting control of foreign policy is Section 2, Article II, of the Constitution: "The president shall be commander in chief of the army and navy of the United States." The Constitution, however, also gives Congress power to shape foreign policy: Section 8, Article I, "The Congress shall have power to . . . declare war . . . raise and support armies . . . and maintain a navy"; Section 9, Article I, "No money shall be drawn from the treasury, but in consequence of appropriations made by law"; and Section 2, Article II, which gives the president the power to "make treaties," but only "provided two-thirds of the senators present concur." These simple declarative sentences invite a constant struggle between the executive and the legislative branches for control of foreign policy.

On the eve of Pearl Harbor Congress was in charge of foreign policy, as it had been since the Senate rejected the Versailles Treaty in 1919. President Roosevelt had a clear policy—to get the United States involved in the European war as a major participant on the side of Britain and the Soviet Union and to block further Japanese expansion in Asia—but Congress would not appropriate the monies necessary to raise and maintain armed forces capable of carrying it out, or declare war on the Axis powers.

War came anyway. After Pearl Harbor Roosevelt took command and controlled foreign policy as commander in chief almost without reference to Congress. His two most important policies, the demand for unconditional surrender by the Axis and the Yalta accords with the Soviets, were his decisions alone.

Truman operated differently, though for obvious reasons. The war was over, and thus the power of the president was necessarily diminished. He did not have the political mandate Roosevelt enjoyed, and the Republicans controlled Congress in the critical years 1947–49. Truman needed congressional approval for his great innovations, including creating America's first peacetime alliance—

NATO—and an aid package to Europe, the Marshall Plan. Whereas there had been no significant national discussion about unconditional surrender or the Yalta accords, Truman led a lengthy debate over NATO and the Marshall Plan. He eventually managed to create a consensus for the policies. His third great innovation, the Truman Doctrine, was announced during a speech to Congress on March 12, 1947. The Truman Doctrine committed the United States to contain communism anywhere in the world by aiding countries that requested help against Soviet expansionism. His speech persuaded a majority in Congress to support military aid to Greece and Turkey, but that support came only after a prolonged national debate brilliantly conducted by his administration.

Truman, however, implemented his doctrine in Korea without consulting Congress. This decision turned out to be a mistake. Because of the way Truman entered the Korean War and because of the way he conducted it—twice changing U.S. policy 180 degrees, from stopping aggression to liberating North Korea and then back to stopping aggression, in each case without involving Congress in any way—he lost both popular and congressional support. Two years after he intervened in Korea, Truman's approval rating in the Gallup Poll dropped to 23 percent, the lowest in the history of the poll (Johnson slipped to 28 percent in the fall of 1968, Nixon to 25 percent in the summer of 1974).

Eisenhower brought back presidential primacy in foreign policy. The threat posed by the Soviet Union, the development of nuclear weapons and long-range bombers to carry them (and by the late 1950s intercontinental missiles), combined with the Pearl Harbor legacy of fear of surprise attack, made Congress content—even eager—to leave foreign policy decisions to the president. Eisenhower informed, rather than consulted with, congressional leaders about his major decisions: to accept a ceasefire in Korea without liberating North Korea, to stay out of Vietnam in 1954, to use the CIA to support coups in Iran in 1953 and in Guatemala in 1954, not to go to war with China over the off-shore islands (Quemoy and Matsu), not to support the Hungarian rebels in 1956 or the British/French/Israeli cabal in Suez in 1956, to force Israel to pull out of the Sinai Peninsula in 1957, to extend aid to Tito in Yugoslavia and to hold down the cost of defense. In every case, except Vietnam in 1954, a majority of Republicans and perhaps of Congress as a whole wanted Eisenhower to adopt different policies. But thanks to his immense prestige and congressional fears he got his way.

In his less than three years in office President John F. Kennedy ran foreign policy almost without reference to Congress, most notably in the Bay of Pigs fiasco in 1961 and the Cuban missile crisis in 1962, but also in dealing with the problems of Berlin and Vietnam. Kennedy did not have Eisenhower's prestige or his political mandate, but he was the nation's leader at a time when Congress was most willing to support the president in foreign policy because the Cold War was at its hottest and American hubris at its highest.

In 1964, in the Gulf of Tonkin resolution, Congress gave President Johnson even broader powers in Southeast Asia than it had given Eisenhower in the Middle East, another reflection of the congressional attitude that "the president knows best." But although Johnson managed to get a near-unanimous vote for the resolution, he did so in the middle of a presidential election campaign and rushed it through Congress without any meaningful debate. Many congressmen later claimed they had been tricked into voting for the measure because Johnson painted the incident in the Gulf of Tonkin almost as if it were Pearl Harbor revisited. In other words the sense of permanent crisis that prevailed in the worst years of the Cold War allowed Truman, Eisenhower, Kennedy and Johnson to act almost as unilaterally as Roosevelt had during World War II by drawing on their constitutionally given strength as commander in chief.

The agony of Vietnam caused the pendulum to swing back. Congress used its power of the purse to limit President Nixon's ability to carry out policies he thought necessary and eventually forced him to agree to a ceasefire that left the United States far short of the goals he had set. It blocked his détente initiative by refusing most-favored-nation status to the Soviets. In the 1973 War Powers Resolution Congress attempted to take control of foreign policy out of the president's hands by limiting his military option through legislation—unthinkable in previous administrations—and it rejected President Ford's pleas to support South Vietnam in its final crisis.

Perhaps exhausted by its major effort in the Nixon/Ford years, certainly relieved that the Vietnam War was over, Congress retreated from its active role during the Carter presidency. It was not involved in Carter's major triumph, the Camp David accords, except to provide the money that made the agreement possible, and it played virtually no part in the major crises of 1980—Nicaragua and the Sandinistas, Iran and the Hostages, Afghanistan and the Soviet invasion.

Nor did Congress play as active a role in the eight years of Reagan's presidency as it had in the Nixon/Ford years, certainly not in his interventions in Grenada (1983) and Lebanon (1983–84), his air strike against Libya (1986) or his attempt to swap arms for hostages in Iran. Reagan simply ignored the one attempt by Congress to control policy—the Boland amendment forbidding aid to the contras in Nicaragua. (Although in that case Congress was able to use its powers of the purse to limit somewhat his intervention.) In general Congress followed the shifting winds of Reagan's policies. When Reagan was hostile to the Soviet Union, Congress appropriated massive funds to support his military buildup (in large part because of the Soviet buildup of the 1970s). When Reagan turned to détente, Congress went along.

To date President Bush has been able to set and carry out his own foreign policy, although like Truman before the Korean "police action" he has been careful to involve Congress in the debate over the use of force. In the gulf crisis of 1990–91 he persuaded Congress to vote for the functional equivalent of a declaration of war.

One of the president's assets in the struggle over control of foreign policy is his ability to act, to shoot first and answer questions later. This power was greatly strengthened during the Cold War as the United States built and maintained permanent standing armed forces. The congressional attempt to diminish this asset through the War Powers Resolution has had at best minimal effect.

One congressional asset in the struggle for foreign policy control is the power to investigate, but this can be asserted only after the fact—as in the extended hearings into the bombing of Pearl Harbor, the agreement reached at Yalta, Truman's dismissal of General Douglas MacArthur, U.S. involvement in Vietnam (the prolonged Foreign Relations Committee hearings), possible wrong-doings within the CIA (the Church committee hearings) and the Iran-contra arms deals. Such hearings can embarrass the president and sometimes, as with Vietnam or the CIA, have an impact on policy.

Still, congressional hearings are at best a cumbersome way to make foreign policy, partly because they typically come after the fact, partly because partisanship is seldom more clearly in evidence than in a congressional hearing, and increasingly because of a divided government. Eisenhower was the only Republican president who had a majority in both the Senate and the House. This situation lasted for only two years, and during that time the Republicans in the Senate tried to pass an amendment to the Constitution (the so-called Bricker amendment) designed to limit the president's power to enter into executive agreements with foreign nations (read Yalta).

* * * *

One obvious cause of the relative failures in foreign policy has been the shift in the world economy and America's position in it. When Roosevelt, Truman and Eisenhower led the United States, it was an exporter of oil, steel, automobiles and other commodities. America was the world's creditor and enjoyed a highly favorable balance of trade.

By 1965 this situation was rapidly changing; by 1975 the United States was a major importer of oil; by 1985 the country had an unfavorable balance of trade and had become a debtor nation. Europe had recovered and then some; Japan was booming beyond the wildest expectations; the remainder of noncommunist Asia was not far behind. America was richer than ever, but its relative position in the world economy had been sharply reduced. This hampered the presidents in their attempts to be the world leader. For example, in 1956 Eisenhower was able to force the British and French out of Suez and Israel out of Sinai by threatening an oil boycott and other economic sanctions. But in 1973 Nixon could not persuade the Europeans to help him implement his policy of rearming Israel during the Yom Kippur War, and in 1981 Reagan was unable to persuade the Europeans to join in an economic boycott of Poland and Russia when the Soviet Union forced the Polish government to impose martial law in order to crush the Solidarity movement.

The military balance also shifted dramatically between 1941 and 1991. In 1941 the United States had a minuscule armed force, which was the major reason Roosevelt had so little influence on world events from the Munich crisis of 1938 through the German invasion of the Soviet Union in mid-1941. By 1945 the American armed forces were vastly superior to those of the rest of the world combined. After World War II the United States made possible the rearming of Western Europe, stopped communist aggression in Korea and had a virtual monopoly on nuclear weapons. In 1962 Kennedy used America's overwhelming superiority to force Nikita Khrushchev to back down in the Cuban missile crisis.

But the Cuban experience, plus the continuing expansion of the American arsenal instituted by Kennedy, caused Khrushchev to start his own crash program of building nuclear weapons and missiles. Kennedy had aimed to stockpile enough weapons and missiles to give the United States clear-cut nuclear superiority, but in 1968 Secretary of Defense Robert McNamara announced that the Soviets had caught up with [the] United States in terms of nuclear weapons. McNamara argued, however, that this was not undesirable, since the behavior of both states was now constrained by mutual assured destruction (MAD).

In conventional forces, meanwhile, the United States cut back its number of ships, planes and tanks, while the Soviets expanded theirs. The number of men and women in the U.S. armed services also decreased after Nixon introduced the all-volunteer force. The U.S. military, which had boasted in 1960 it could fight two-and-a-half major wars at once, by 1980 had become a pitiful helpless giant, capable of destroying the world in a nuclear spasm but incapable of fighting even one-half a war with much hope of success.

The power to destroy is not the power to control. Power is the man on the spot with the gun in his hand, and increasingly the United States was incapable of putting him there. This too hampered American presidents in their attempts to exert world leadership and led to inconsistencies in their policies. Simultaneously two ideas came to dominate presidential thinking and behavior. First, the world was bipolar and contained two superpowers—the United States and the Soviet Union. Excluding the superpowers, no other nation mattered very much (the British attended the first two summit meetings, at Yalta and Potsdam, as equal partners; Eisenhower took care to involve the British and French at the Geneva and Paris summits; but since 1960 summits have been limited to the United States and the Soviet Union).

Second, American hubris and the astonishing growth of the White House staff combined to reinforce the so-called Imperial Presidency, so that just as the relative importance of the president was decreasing, the presidents' views of themselves and what they could accomplish was increasing. The public agreed, which led to great expectations with each new president after Eisenhower, only to be followed by disillusion as the presidents failed to achieve their goals.

In 1960 Kennedy had set out to create a first-strike capability. By 1968 Soviet nuclear weapons deployment and advances in weaponry led to the concept of MAD. In 1970 Nixon said that he would be satisfied with strategic sufficiency, which apparently meant nuclear parity with the Soviets. In 1972 Nixon signed the Strategic Arms Limitation Treaty (SALT), an agreement with the Soviets that conceded superiority in some categories of missiles.

These fundamental policy shifts after 1960 were matched by shifts in each president's posture. Kennedy came into office full of bellicose rhetoric. He wanted to go on the offensive worldwide, ready to "pay any price, bear any burden," to ensure the triumph of freedom everywhere. He sponsored an invasion of Cuba—and then backed down at the critical moment. He took a strong stance on Berlin—and then backed down when Khrushchev built the Wall. He escalated the war in Vietnam—and then allowed the CIA to participate in a plot to overthrow the South Vietnamese president, Ngo Dinh Diem. He faced down Khrushchev in the Cuban missile crisis—and then entered into an agreement in which he promised that the United States would never invade Cuba, a promise he had no authority to make and that, had he presented it to the Senate in the form of a treaty, would never have been ratified.

* * * *

The gap between Johnson's rhetoric and promises on the one hand and his performance on the other was even greater. Johnson said he would not send American boys to Asia to do the fighting that Asian boys ought to be doing themselves, but he then ended up sending 550,000 American soldiers. Johnson said he sought no wider war, even as he widened the war. He said he would never play politics with peace and then called a bombing halt one week before the 1968 election. He said he would see to it that there was no reward for aggression and then offered to negotiate the removal of American troops while the communists held large portions of South Vietnamese territory.

Nixon extracted the United States from Vietnam, opened the door to China, promoted détente with the Soviet Union and negotiated the first Cold War arms control agreement. In each case what he did represented a retreat, for America and for Nixon, who had stridently advocated opposite policies for two decades. When he withdrew U.S. troops from Vietnam, Nixon claimed to have achieved peace with honor. From the perspective of the South Vietnamese, what he had achieved was surrender with humiliation. What he had accomplished was to get America out of Vietnam without setting off a right-wing revolt within the United States and to give the Saigon government a chance to stand on its own two feet—not much of a chance, to be sure, but still a chance. That was an accomplishment Nixon could have pointed to with pride but, Nixon being Nixon, he had to grossly exaggerate and claim peace with honor. Saigon fell because of the incompetence and corruption of its own government. It was not Nixon's fault, but he must shoulder some of the blame for failing to make that government reform itself.

If Nixon was the man most responsible for opening the door to China in 1972, he was also one of the key men who had been most responsible for keeping it closed for the preceding 23 years. When he changed his mind, he sprang his new policy on the nation as a surprise. There had been no national debate on the subject, and thus no constituency had emerged behind it. The door, therefore, did not open very wide. Nixon was not able to solve the problem of Taiwan or establish diplomatic relations or trade agreements with China, much less enter into an alliance with that country.

Détente with the Soviets, for all its promise, was also substantially flawed by Nixon's penchant for secrecy. He negotiated in secret, especially using back-channels to cut out the State Department. Rather than consult with the Senate, he tried to go over its head or around it. He thus left his policy vulnerable to ambitious senators, led by Henry Jackson (D–Wash.), who used their power to scuttle such critical aspects of détente as most-favored-nation status for the Soviets. Détente had no staying power—recall that President Ford banned the use of the word détente in the White House—and at least part of the reason was Nixon's love of surprise and secrecy.

Carter also was unable to set a course and hold to it. In sharp contrast to the realpolitik of the Nixon/Ford administrations, the chief characteristic of the Carter administration was its idealism. In his inaugural address in 1976 Carter said he wanted to eliminate nuclear weapons and to stop arms sales abroad. He made a firm commitment to human rights, calling them "the soul of our foreign policy." But the nuclear arsenal grew during the Carter years at the same pace as in the Nixon/Ford years. Arms sales abroad actually increased. Carter's emphasis on human rights badly damaged America's relationship with many of its oldest allies. It caused resentment in the Soviet Union and contributed to Carter's failure to reach arms control agreements and to the downfall of America's most important ally in the Middle East, the shah of Iran.

Human rights had been good politics for Carter as a candidate. The issue pleased both right-wingers, who could and did use it to criticize the Soviet Union, and left-wingers, who could and did use it to criticize Chile, Brazil, South Africa and others for their human rights abuses. But the issue made for terrible policy. It was directed against America's allies, who were vulnerable to Carter's pressures, rather than its enemies, who were basically immune. It made little sense to weaken such allies as South Korea, Argentina, South Africa, Brazil, Taiwan, Nicaragua, Iran and others because of objections to their human rights record while continuing to advance credits, sell grain and ship advanced technology to the Soviet Union, which had one of the worst human rights records in the world and was clearly no friend of the United States.

The Carter human rights policy represented American hubris at its most extreme, willfully ignoring the reality of America's power and ability to dictate developments abroad. It makes no sense to commit to a policy that one has no power to enforce. This applies to Roosevelt's policy toward Poland as enunciated in the Yalta accords of 1945, to the Republican promise of liberation for Eastern Europe as enunciated by Secretary of State John Foster Dulles in 1952, to the policy of paying any price to ensure the survival of freedom around the world as enunciated by Kennedy in 1961, and to Carter's human rights policy.

Further, Carter's preaching to the Soviet Union on its human rights obligations contradicted U.S. attempts to improve relations with the Kremlin. The president tried to assure the Soviet leaders that a new day had dawned in Washington, but as he pulled back from America's advanced positions around the world, for example by ordering the removal of nuclear weapons from Korea without demanding some balancing arms reduction by the Soviets, the Soviets responded by moving forward. They continued their arms buildup and became involved both in the Horn of Africa and Angola.

The climax came in December 1979 when the Soviets invaded Afghanistan. Carter's reaction was extreme, as was the triggering Soviet action. He placed an embargo on grain sales to the Soviets and on high technology goods. He withdrew SALT II, drawn up by Nixon and endorsed by Ford, from the Senate ratification process. He sharply increased defense spending and announced that restrictions on CIA activities would be lifted. These were serious steps that reversed long-standing policies, not to mention his own stated goals. When Carter left office, relations with the Soviet Union were much worse than they had been when he was inaugurated. Each side had more bombs and missiles, less trade and trust. Carter in 1980 was the antithesis of Carter in 1977. By 1980 the word most often used to describe his foreign policy was "waffle." It was a stinging indictment.

Nonetheless Carter did manage some solid foreign policy successes. Most notably, the president was instrumental in negotiating the Camp David accords in 1979, the first peace treaty between Israel and an Arab state, Egypt. Another notable success was the Panama Canal treaty in 1978, returning full sovereignty over the canal zone to Panama. The treaty had been denounced by presidential candidate Reagan, endorsed by Ford and former Secretary of State Henry Kissinger. Carter put the full weight of the presidency into the debate; the treaty narrowly passed. He also established full diplomatic relations with China. But he failed completely to achieve his stated goals of ending the Cold War, improving human rights, stopping the arms race or eliminating nuclear weapons.

With regard to the event that led to Carter's defeat in the 1980 election, the Iranian Revolution and the taking of American hostages by the revolutionaries, he moved from blunder to blunder. He praised the shah far beyond any justified level (on the eve of the revolution he called Iran an island of stability in a turbulent sea). He failed to support the shah when the revolution began. He failed to open lines of communication with the revolutionaries.

He recognized a government in Iran that could not govern. He decided to allow the shah into the United States despite clear warnings about the repercussions. He had a highly emotional and grossly exaggerated response to the taking of the hostages, insisting absurdly that he was spending every waking moment on the hostage problem. He delayed and then botched the use of a military rescue option.

Reagan was also inconsistent. He came into office as the most belligerent president since Kennedy, denouncing the "evil empire," and ended up as Mikhail Gorbachev's friend and virtual ally. He entered office aiming for a first-strike capability and ended up signing the first arms reduction agreement of the Cold War. He promised never to pay ransom for hostages, then secretly sold weapons to the Iranian government in return for the release of hostages (a policy that never resulted in the release of hostages and completely undermined the U.S. boycott of arms sales to Tehran). Reagan did preside over a major increase in America's armed forces, but more often than not he was frustrated in his attempt to use the military option, as in Nicaragua. In Lebanon he was hamstrung by contradictions in his policies. He sent the marines to Beirut with no clear mission, putting them in a provocative position with orders not to shoot. In Richard Neustadt's telling judgment, he succeeded in "combining ignorance with insistence."

Still, Reagan had some impressive firsts. His administration coincided with a number of arms reduction agreements, and it managed eight years without a major war (but with a popular invasion of Grenada and an even more popular military strike against Libya). According to his admirers, Reagan's arms buildup was responsible for the retreat of communism from central and eastern Europe. They argue that the Soviet effort to keep up with the Americans bankrupted the communists. This may be true, although critics argue that communism collapsed because it is a rotten system and that it lasted as long as it did only because of the perceived threat against the Warsaw Pact nations by the Reagan buildup. Back in 1953 Eisenhower had said that the proper policy for the West was to keep up its defenses, not to threaten and to wait for communism to self-destruct. That was a restatement of the Truman Doctrine, and it worked, thanks to its support by all of Truman's successors.

In any case, with regard to Reagan's policies, it was the contradictions that stood out. He launched the most expensive weapons development program in history, the Strategic Defense Initiative, even as he sought arms reduction. In 1986 at the conclusion of the Reykjavik Summit with Gorbachev, Secretary of State George Shultz reported that the two leaders had agreed on the elimination of all nuclear weapons and the missile systems to deliver them, and that this process of disarmament was to be completed in ten years. It seemed too good to be true, and it was. Shultz went on to say that these agreements in principle had been abandoned because Reagan refused to accept Gorbachev's demand that the United States stop its SDI program. In the Iran-contra affair, the administration violated the law and tried to cover it up, to the point that

Reagan might have been impeached had the Democrats not felt that one threatened impeachment a century is enough. His administration survived, but revelations in the Iran-contra hearings seriously crippled his ability to conduct foreign policy. When he left office, Reagan was popular with the public as a person, but his policies were in danger of becoming an object of ridicule.

To date President Bush's policies have been, except toward China, popular and successful. America's relative power position in the world has continued to decline, and congressional attempts to cut back on the powers of the Imperial Presidency through investigations and revelations from Watergate through Iran-contra have proved embarrassing for the White House. Yet in his first major crisis Bush was able to mobilize public opinion within his country and around the world, leading a serious debate, fully involving Congress and consulting constantly with other leaders. In the process he demonstrated beyond all doubt that the American president is still the most important person in the world. No other world leader could have put together the coalition that fought the Gulf War. Bush also demonstrated that no other nation could project so much power so far from home as the United States. A year later, in August 1991, Bush's condemnation of the coup leaders in the Soviet Union as criminals, his support for Gorbachev and Boris Yeltsin, brought him praise and thanks from Soviet leaders, who said that his policy was of fundamental importance to the democratic elements in Moscow.

* * * *

This brief survey of a half-century of presidential foreign policy demonstrates some basic truths: realism is more effective than idealism; a strong military is essential to implementing an activist foreign policy; Congress is less likely to sustain an activist policy than the president; the struggle between Congress and the president over foreign policy will continue so long as the Constitution lasts; and consistency in foreign policy is difficult to achieve but immensely powerful when it happens.

But the great lesson is that secrecy and surprise are the enemies of democracy; open and prolonged debate are the great power of democracy. The policies that have failed have tended to be those adopted by presidents without meaningful debate—Roosevelt's Yalta policy toward Poland, Kennedy's intervention in the Bay of Pigs, Johnson's intervention in Vietnam, Nixon's détente and China policies, Carter's human rights policy, Reagan's Iran-contra policy, among others. The policies that have succeeded have been adopted by Congress and the people after meaningful debate—Roosevelt's commitment to total victory, the Truman Doctrine, the Marshall Plan and NATO, Carter's Panama treaty, and the Camp David accords, arms control (where the debate has been too long and too strident, but where a consensus is building), Bush's policy of using all-out force to turn back naked, unprovoked aggression. Of course there are exceptions (unconditional surrender in World War II, Nixon's China opening and others), but when the president involves Congress and the people in the creation of new policy it is most likely to work and have staying power.

For the historian looking back over a half century what stands out is the strengthening of the president's power to conduct foreign policy. When one contrasts how hampered Roosevelt was before World War II by a Congress determined to impose its policy—neutrality and disarmament—with the adoption by all presidents since Roosevelt of his policy of collective security and military preparedness, the adjective that comes to mind to characterize that strengthening is "enormous." Obviously, in such a diverse country with such volatile politics over such a long period of time, it has not been a straight line of growth. In this connection it is ironic that the most innovative of the Cold War presidents, Nixon, was the one most frustrated by congressional interference. Nevertheless in general over the past half century, the Oval Office is where foreign policy for better or worse has been made. Except for the administrations of Theodore Roosevelt and Woodrow Wilson, that had not been the case in the first four decades of the twentieth century and seldom in the nineteenth century. Since Pearl Harbor the best way to describe the situation is that as America's role as world leader increased, so has the power of the president.

POINTS TO PONDER

1. According to Ambrose, how has the domination of U.S. foreign policy shifted between the president and Congress?
2. What impact has the changing strength of the U.S. economy had on U.S. military presence around the world?
3. According to Ambrose, what are the consequences of secrecy in foreign policy and the unwillingness of presidents to engage in public debate over the ends of U.S. foreign policy?

Chapter 15

❧

CIVIL RIGHTS AND LIBERTIES

Civil rights and liberties are central to any system of governance based on the premise that individuals are the reason for the existence of governments. First, any concept of fundamental justice necessarily entails the right of individuals to conduct themselves as they see fit without undue government interference (civil liberties) within the broad strictures of the rights of others and important community interests. But second, any sort of democracy or government responsive to the people would be impossible without the civil rights, such as freedom of speech and assembly, to engage in a dialogue about public matters. This section takes up the enduring issues of civil rights and liberties in the United States and traces their development from their constitutional origins to current controversies.

Constitutional Origins of Civil Rights and Liberties

The Americans who advocated separation from Great Britain in 1776 proclaimed in the Declaration of Independence that all persons held "certain unalienable rights," including "life, liberty, and the pursuit of happiness." A decade later, after the Revolutionary War, the Framers of the Constitution were very concerned with individual rights and liberties, and had some hesitation about enumerating basic rights for fear that the government might feel free to ignore any that were not specifically listed. But those favoring an explicit list of rights were persuasive, and one of the greatest obstacles to ratification of the Constitution was the lack of a specific list of rights and liberties. Those favoring ratification promised that the deficiency would be remedied immediately after ratification, and the Bill of Rights was added as the first ten amendments to the Constitution.

The Bill of Rights prohibited the national government from abridging many of the basic rights of citizens, though the specific meaning of the phrases *free speech, fair trial, due process,* or *unreasonable search* had yet to be worked out in practice. The working out of much of the specific content of the rights guaranteed in the first ten amendments has come through decisions of the Supreme Court. And much of that specification has come through decisions that have applied the Bill of Rights to the states.

The Bill of Rights initially applied only to the national government, because the First Amendment provides that "Congress shall pass no law respecting . . . ." State governments were not specified, perhaps because the Framers feared the power of the new national government and wanted to make sure that it did not infringe on the rights that many of the states guaranteed their citizens. In the judgment of some, however, the state governments ought not to have the power to violate rights guaranteed in the Constitution, but in order for the constitutional restrictions to apply to states as well as the national government, the Supreme Court had to make a series of decisions applying the Bill of Rights to the states.

Application of the Bill of Rights to the States

The vehicle for the application of the Bill of Rights to state governments came through the Fourteenth Amendment, passed after the Civil War to ensure equal rights of citizenship to the newly freed slaves. The Fourteenth Amendment provided that "No state shall . . . deprive any person of life, liberty, or property, without due process of law; nor deny to any person within its jurisdiction the equal protection of the laws." The question then arises, what specifically constitutes "due process of law" or the "equal protection of the laws"? Until the 1930s, the Supreme Court's interpretation of the due process clause was to protect businesses from any regulation by the states that was deemed to deprive them of property without due process of law.

But as times changed and membership on the Court changed, the Fourteenth Amendment was used increasingly to protect individual rights and liberties from abridgment by the states. Those rights fundamental enough to be protected were defined and gradually expanded from the 1920s to the 1950s. But under the leadership of Chief Justice Earl Warren (1953–1969), the Supreme Court led a "revolution" in individual liberties and due process. During the Warren years almost all the protections of the Bill of Rights were incorporated into the Fourteenth Amendment and applied to the states. These rights include those basic to citizenship and democratic government, such as freedom of speech and assembly and freedom of the press. Democratic government would be impossible without these guarantees to citizens of the rights to dissent from governmental policy and to organize peaceful opposition to the government. The civil liberties of freedom of religion and conscience were also incorporated in various ways.

There is a range of civil liberties that includes the rights of those whom the government suspects of crimes to be assured fair treatment and due process of law before the government deprives them of liberty or property. These rights are embedded in the Fourth, Fifth, and Sixth Amendments, which require the government to provide those accused of crime a fair and public trial with the assistance of counsel. These amendments also prohibit unreasonable searches and seizures, double jeopardy, and compulsory self-incrimination. The application of these rights to the states has profoundly affected criminal justice systems throughout the nation.

Civil Rights and Affirmative Action

Perhaps the most contentious and far-reaching question of civil rights of people in the United States involves the status of African Americans. After all, the Civil War was fought over the issue of slavery. The struggle for full inclusion of black Americans in the civil and economic life of the nation has continued over the centuries and is still a major issue of public policy.

The initial constitutional recognition of the rights of African Americans was established in the three "Civil War Amendments." The Thirteenth Amendment prohibits slavery; the Fourteenth prohibits the states from violating due process rights and equal protection of the laws; and the Fifteenth assures African Americans of the right to vote. Despite these formal constitutional declarations, the rights of African Americans continued to be violated by the state and federal governments as well as by private individuals and businesses. As the civil rights movement gathered momentum in the 1940s and 1950s, conditions improved, particularly with the landmark 1954 Supreme Court case *Brown v. Board of Education* and the follow-up cases. The Court declared that separate facilities for education were inherently unequal, and a series of further decisions along with laws ended the official segregation of the races in the United States.

But the declaration of formal rights, from the Civil War Amendments to the Civil Rights Acts of the twentieth century, did not end discrimination or achieve economic justice for African Americans. The vestiges of racism and discrimination continue to plague the American polity. In the 1970s the quest to overcome the legacy of racism included the idea of "affirmative action." Affirmative action is an attempt to go beyond the minimum of nondiscrimination to try to achieve equality in the economy, especially in hiring, firing, and promotion decisions and in access to educational opportunities.

Affirmative action has also been applied to the struggle of women to overcome discrimination and eliminate centuries of enforced inequality. It was not until the passage of the Nineteenth Amendment in 1920 that women even became full citizens in achieving the right to vote. But just as with the rights of black Americans, the formal recognition of equality is only the first step in a long journey toward full equality in U.S. society.

To remedy the injustice of racism and discrimination, affirmative action policies have been adopted, and one of the key questions is what actions are justified under the concept of affirmative action. Not much controversy exists over the original requirements that employers take special care to ensure that job notices reach qualified minority candidates or to ensure that minority employees be given opportunities to prepare for and apply for promotions. But when these and similar efforts do not result in any differences in hiring or promotion outcomes or in composition of the work force, advocates of affirmative action argue that there has to be some numerical goal or quota to ensure that subtle discrimination does not overcome the affirmative action requirements.

The Readings

The readings in this section take up some of the most contentious issues in our system of governance. These issues touch on Americans' feelings of personal security, especially those that deal with the rights of the accused and with the limits of police actions. Other issues involve personal attitudes and public policies concerning racism and sexism. The issues may be disturbing, but society cannot escape them.

The first selection, by D. Grier Stephenson, Jr., surveys the rights that are guaranteed in the Bill of Rights and shows how crucial the formal specification of these rights was to the ratification of the Constitution. Stephenson then looks at how the definition of these rights has developed over the ensuing two centuries. Perhaps his most important point is that the preservation of the rights of citizens cannot be left to judges but must be the constant concern of all Americans. Only vigilance on the part of citizens can guarantee continuation of the freedoms that we enjoy.

The next two selections deal with the problem of affirmative action. Herbert Hill argues that affirmative action is crucial to achieve justice for blacks as a group who still suffer from the legacy of racism. In contrast, African-American economist Thomas Sowell argues that there is a big difference between equal opportunity for all and an approach to affirmative action that tries to guarantee equality of outcomes by enforcing numerical goals or quotas.

Those who denounce quotas, like Thomas Sowell, argue that individual qualifications are all that should matter and that giving members of a particular group any special advantage can amount to reverse discrimination. That is, better-qualified whites (or men) may be passed over in order to promote (or admit to a professional school) a less-qualified minority person or woman. Thus an injustice could be done to one person in order to make up for past injustices to other persons (blacks or women). Sowell and other opponents of affirmative action argue that two wrongs do not make a right. Affirmative action may also harm its intended beneficiaries by perpetuating the perception that any promotion received is based not on superior qualification but on adherence to affirmative action policy.

Part of the argument against affirmative action rests on the premise that the instruments used to measure qualifications (for example, written exams) are in fact accurate means of determining capability, whether for a job or admission to a school. Advocates for affirmative action argue that tests can distinguish gross differences, such as in basic job skills or educational achievement. When measuring differences among those who are all highly qualified, however, the distinctions are less meaningful. Thus the choice of a black person or a woman over a white male who scored slightly better in a test is not necessarily a preference for someone who is clearly less qualified, unless you believe that the tests are perfect, which they seldom are. This, of course, is little comfort to those who feel they are being treated unjustly.

There are parallels between racism and sexism; each practice denies to individuals equal treatment based solely on their race or gender. Those who backed the Equal Rights Amendment (ERA) argued that laws against discrimination on the basis of gender were not sufficient to guarantee women full rights as citizens. Even though both houses of Congress passed the ERA, it failed to gain support from the three-fourths of the states necessary to amend the Constitution. Jane Mansbridge in the final selection explains the political and rhetorical dynamics of the debate over ratification of the ERA.

Regardless of the specifics of affirmative action policies, the United States has to live with its legacy of racism and the terrible human toll it has taken on African Americans. Our society also must live with the effects of discrimination against women in our public and private lives. To remedy these injustices, actions must be taken, whether affirmative action or other measures, to continue the struggle for full equality for all citizens of the United States.

KEY TERMS

affirmative action: the attempt to assure through rules and laws that minorities and women have an equal opportunity to enjoy civil rights and liberties as well as economic rights

antifederalists: those who argued against ratification of the Constitution because it created too strong a central government

Bill of Rights: the first ten amendments to the Constitution specifying rights of all Americans that cannot be violated by the government

civil liberty: individual freedom to act as one sees fit within the law and to be free from undue governmental interference. Civil liberties include the right to own property, freedom of religion, the right to a fair trial, and the right to privacy.

civil rights: those rights of citizenship that are necessary for individuals to participate in the political process, including freedom of speech, freedom of assembly, and the right to vote

Fourteenth Amendment: one of the Civil War Amendments, it prohibited the states from depriving persons of life, liberty, or property without due process of law or denying persons the equal protection of the laws. Most of the rights and liberties of the Bill of Rights have been applied to state governments through this amendment

52

"IS THE BILL OF RIGHTS IN DANGER?"
D. Grier Stephenson, Jr.

In tracing the development of the Bill of Rights, in his article from USA Today Magazine (1991) D. Grier Stephenson, Jr., professor of government at Franklin and Marshall College, points out that the antifederalists, those who opposed ratification of the Constitution, were responsible for the Bill of Rights. Under attack from the antifederalists, the federalists realized that in order to gain enough support for ratification they had to promise to amend the Constitution immediately after it was ratified to include an enumeration of rights. This list became the Bill of Rights and the first ten amendments to the Constitution.

The Ninth Amendment makes it clear that the specification of the included rights did not create rights but merely recognized rights that already were possessed by individuals. In addition, the listing did not imply that those were the only rights possessed by citizens. Stephenson goes on to show how the practical application of those rights evolved over the past two centuries and argues that all citizens bear some responsibility to ensure that our basic rights endure and are not eroded by current exigencies accompanied by good intentions.

Just over 200 years ago, Thomas Jefferson was in France on a diplomatic mission. When he received a copy of the proposed U.S. Constitution from his friend James Madison, he let him know as fast as the slow sailing-ship mails of the day allowed that the new plan of government suffered one major defect— it lacked a bill of rights. This, Jefferson argued, "is what the people are entitled to against every government on earth. . . ." Two centuries later, events in Europe have transformed Jefferson's words into a rallying cry. Old tyrannies have tumbled head over heels into the rudiments of constitutionalism. The idea of a bill of rights seems contagious. Yet, despite its embrace abroad, is the American Bill of Rights in danger at home? Answering this question requires an examination of two preliminary ones: What is the Bill of Rights and why do we have it?

At the Constitutional Convention in 1787, John Dickinson of Delaware advised the delegates to let experience be their guide; theory might mislead them, he cautioned. Adopted in 1791 as the first 10 amendments to the Constitution, the Bill of Rights reflects the Founding Fathers' experience with, and understanding of, the dimensions of personal freedom. The First Amendment protects free expression—in speech, press, assembly, petition, and religion. The Second Amendment safeguards liberty against national tyranny by affirming the self-defense of the states. Members of local militia—

citizens primarily, soldiers occasionally—retained a right to bear arms. The ban in the Third Amendment on forcibly quartering troops in houses suggests the emphasis the framers placed on the integrity and sanctity of the home. Other provisions—the Fourth, Fifth, Sixth, Seventh, and Eighth Amendments—guard freedom by setting forth standards government must follow in administering the law, especially the criminal law. In addition, one clause in the Fifth Amendment forbids the taking of private property for public use without just compensation, and so limits the power of eminent domain. Along with taxation and conscription, this is one of the most comprehensive powers any government can possess. The Ninth Amendment mentions no specific rights, but reflects the dominant political thought of the 18th century. In the English tradition and in the spirit of the Declaration of Independence, a bill of rights did not itself confer rights, but merely recognized existing ones. The Ninth Amendment makes sure that the listing of some rights does not imply that others necessarily have been abandoned. If the Ninth offered reassurances to the people, the Tenth was designed to reassure the states that they or the people retained those powers not delegated to the national government. Today, the Tenth is mainly symbolic of the integral place of the states in the Federal system.

The protections found in the first 10 amendments do not exhaust the meaning Americans commonly give to the Bill of Rights. At the outset, it applied only to the national government, not to the states. Except for the few restrictions in the original text of the Constitution which explicitly limited state power, states were restrained only by their individual constitutions, not by the Federal Bill of Rights. So, Pennsylvania or any other state could shut down a newspaper or deny religious freedom without violating the First Amendment.

The first step in closing this gap came with the ratification of the Fourteenth Amendment in 1868. Section one contained majestic, but undefined, checks on the states that begged for interpretation: "*No State* shall make or enforce any law which shall abridge the privileges or immunities of citizens of the United States; nor shall any State deprive any person of life, liberty, or property, without due process of law; nor deny to any person within its jurisdiction the equal protection of the laws" (emphasis added). Acting for the most part in a series of cases after 1920, the Supreme Court has construed the Fourteenth Amendment to include almost every provision of the Bill of Rights. This was the second step in closing the gap. State and local governments became bound by the same restrictions that had applied all along to the national government. The consequences of this process scarcely can be exaggerated since so much government policy is that of state and local governments.

The Fourteenth Amendment also reinvigorated the debate over whether the Constitution protects rights not spelled out in the words of the document. As early as the 1790s, justices on the Supreme Court speculated that there were rights no government could infringe upon, even if they were not protected expressly by the Constitution. What are those other rights? Constitutionally protected liberty long has been viewed as open-ended. While including most of the liberties enshrined in the Bill of Rights, the Fourteenth Amendment does not stop there. The Supreme Court has said that other rights—those deemed fundamental—are protected.

Thus, in 1923, the Court struck down a Nebraska law banning the teaching of foreign languages to children below the ninth grade. In 1965, it set aside a Connecticut law that criminalized the use of birth control devices. In a 1973 decision that remains at the center of controversy, the Court invalidated the abortion laws of almost all the states. The reasoning was that laws forbidding abortions under all but the most extreme circumstances infringed on the fundamental right of the woman to decide whether to carry a pregnancy to full term. In cases such as these, the justices "discover" rights implied by the basic idea of liberty—even though the Constitution's words say nothing about learning a foreign language, preventing a pregnancy, or aborting a fetus.

In these situations, the question is not whether the framers of the Bill of Rights or the Fourteenth Amendment anticipated and therefore intended that their handiwork should apply to foreign language instruction, birth control pills, and terminated pregnancies. If that were the question, the answer to the question whether those subjects implicated the Constitution in a meaningful way almost always would be no. There is no requirement of omniscience to be a delegate to a constitutional convention or a member of Congress or a state legislature. Rather, in each of these instances, government had restricted personal liberty. Is the liberty at issue sufficiently important to be ranked as "fundamental"? If so, the Court requires that government adduce compelling justification for the infringement, a standard nearly impossible to meet. If the liberty is not fundamental, government only need have a reason—judges use the term "rational basis"—for the restriction. However, the important question remains: What makes a liberty fundamental? The answer is a function of the values of five justices of the Supreme Court.

This transformation leads to the second question: Why does the Constitution contain a Bill of Rights? The framers were united in their belief that government should rest on the authority of the people. That had been the premise of the American revolution. They were nearly as united in the belief that government should not be *too* responsive to the people. That had been the problem with other experiments in democratic government. Tyranny by the majority often had replaced tyranny by the few.

Diffusion of Power

The framers preferred a different plan. They rejected the term "democratic" to describe their creation. Instead, they called it republican, or free, government. The system of checks and balances among the executive, legislative, and judicial branches plus a division of political authority between the national and state governments made sense because power thereby was diffused and dispersed. A majority of the people would have a difficult time seizing control of all parts of the political system and running roughshod over the rights of the minority. At least among those white males admitted to the political community in 1787, liberty would be secure because no group could easily become strong enough to deny liberty to others. Freedom would be assured through "political grid-lock."

For some, this diffusion of power was sufficient. For constructive critics like Thomas Jefferson, however, the Constitution did not go far enough. Inherent in the idea of a written constitution are constraints on what government may do. In a government based on the consent of the governed, limits on authority mean limits on the majority. A declaration of rights would enrich the Constitution's design. A bill of rights would help political minorities get an untroubled night's sleep.

Opponents of the proposed constitution, called Antifederalists, quickly seized on this defect. Ostensibly, they worried about the threat to individual liberty posed by the new government. Of greater concern were threats to the prerogatives of state governments. The standard response from supporters of the Constitution, called the Federalists, was that a bill of rights was unnecessary. If the national government was to be one of delegated powers, they reasoned, why bar the exercise of powers not delegated? Moreover, adding a bill of rights might be dangerous. Anything not expressly mentioned could be presumed to be omitted purposely by the framers.

The Federalist explanation backfired. As it left the hands of the framers, the Constitution contained several specific prohibitions on the power of the national government. Without a bill of rights, Antifederalists could make the valid point that all unspecified rights now stood in danger. The potential elasticity of the "necessary and proper" clause of Article One only strengthened their case. Moreover, existing bills of rights in state constitutions would be of little help because the new Constitution made it clear that national laws would pre-empt state laws and constitutions. The Federalists therefore promised a bill of rights to achieve ratification, and thus took the wind out of the Antifederalists' sails by removing the main cause around which popular opposition to the Constitution could gather. If it wasn't for the Constitution's sharpest critics, we might never have gotten the Bill of Rights.

The Federalists made good on their word. As one of the first orders of business in the new Congress, Madison introduced a series of amendments in the House of Representatives on May 26, 1789. House members added others. Seventeen proposed alterations then were sent to the Senate, which began debate on Sept. 2. Senators made editorial changes, fused some amendments, and forwarded a revised package of 12 amendments to the House on Sept. 19. By Sept. 25, both houses had approved the same list of 12. Of this number, the states ratified 10. Not ratified were two unrelated amendments—one dealing with the apportionment of the House and the other delaying any increase in Congressional salaries until after the next election. As the 11th state to act, Virginia's ratification on Dec. 15, 1791, made the Bill of Rights officially part of the Constitution. (Among the last to approve the Bill of Rights, Virginia had been first to adopt a declaration of rights in 1776, three weeks before the signing of the Declaration of Independence.) The remaining three states—Connecticut, Georgia, and Massachusetts—did not ratify until the 150th anniversary of the Bill of Rights in 1941.

Yet, the Antifederalists obtained little of what they wanted. States' rights weighed more heavily than their concern for personal rights. Instead of "substantial amendments," complained South Carolina's Pierce Butler, here were a few milk-and-water amendments . . . such as liberty of conscience, a free press, and one or two general things already well secured." Georgia's Congressman James Jackson agreed, saying the amendments were not worth a "pinch of snuff."

The idea of a bill of rights was not original with the Antifederalists. Following the example of several English statutes, the Continental Congress had adopted a Declaration of Rights in 1774, and state constitutions since 1776 contained their own declaration of rights. The American contribution after 1791 lay in making liberty a juridical concept, devising a way to enforce constitutional guarantees. So, it became significant that the Supreme Court soon assumed the role of guardian of the Constitution. Through the development of judicial review—the authority of courts to set aside laws which in their view violate the Constitution—judges came to be protectors and even shapers of constitutional values. Without judicial protection, the words of the Bill of Rights might have remained little more than moral exhortations. Experience has taught that exhortation often may not be enough. In place of trust in the people, the Bill of Rights stands for mistrust. These amendments rest on the premise that the majority is likely to be neither correct nor tolerant all of the time.

Yet, is the Bill of Rights secure today? Ironically, the answer is that it is secure only if each generation of Americans believes its liberties are in danger. Consider, for example, the problems of interpretation, faithfulness, and reliance.

The Constitution ordinarily speaks in generalities, not particulars. It is a document of enumeration, not of definition. The First Amendment protects freedom of speech, among other values, but does not define the "speech" that is protected. Thus, one should not be surprised to find a cottage industry among scholars, judges, lawyers, and journalists grinding out competing interpretations.

Reasonable minds differ, for instance, over whether sexually explicit pictures and language merit constitutional protection. While the Supreme Court never has said that the First Amendment protects the sexually obscene, the definition of obscenity is so narrow that all but the hardest of hardcore pornography now is protected constitutionally. Some say that far too much explicit material is therefore available, contributing to abuse of women and children and to a general moral decay.

In similar fashion, people disagree over the constitutional protection to be accorded verbal attacks on other races and religions. Should a person be allowed to preach messages of hate? At a state university, which is founded on the utility of the free exchange of ideas, should students, faculty, and staff be disciplined for uttering remarks judged to be offensive to others? Moreover, recall the furor in 1989 and 1990 after the Supreme Court declared that the states and Congress were powerless to punish those who burn the American flag as a form of symbolic expression. For many, such speech contributes nothing either to the betterment of society or the advancement of knowledge. If such speech is worthless, no harm can be done by its suppression. Others reply that, if such words or acts are beyond constitutional protection, the net of criminality is bound to be cast too wide. Moreover, even if most could agree on a clear standard, it is risky to exempt speech from the First Amendment's protective shield. If one person's message is not safe, is anyone's? From this perspective, self-interest dictates tolerance of the thoughts and depictions we hate.

Which Liberties Should Be Protected?

Accordingly, one should expect debate when the Bill of Rights is applied to concrete situations. This debate is healthy because people learn about the purposes of liberty when they disagree over what those liberties should encompass. However, debate alone does not mean that the liberties in the Bill of Rights are beyond danger. Sometimes, the Bill of Rights has meant the least when its protections have been needed the most. Faithfulness to the document is essential to prevent its words from becoming empty promises.

The current war on drugs may test our faithfulness. Polls taken in the summer of 1989 indicate a willingness of a majority of the American people to give up some of their constitutional rights. They may get the chance. In war, there are few rules.

Consider the Fourth Amendment, for example: "The right of the people to be secure in their persons, houses, papers, and effects, against unreasonable searches and seizures, shall not be violated, and no Warrants shall issue, but upon probable cause, supported by Oath or Affirmation, and particularly describing the place to be searched, and the persons or things to be seized." For a long time, American courts construed the Fourth Amendment to mean that a person could not be detained or searched by the police without some evidence that he or she was violating the law. This is the standard of probable cause. Even when the police acted without a warrant—that is, without the prior approval of a judicial officer—a search would be deemed a violation of the Fourth Amendment unless the officer later could demonstrate to a judge's satisfaction that sufficient cause existed to justify the search or arrest. Judges have disagreed over how much "cause" is sufficient, but, until recently, all agreed that at least some particularized suspicion was necessary—that is, evidence which pointed to a single person as a possible lawbreaker.

In *Camara v. Municipal Court* (1967), the Supreme Court made an apparently harmless exception to this rule in a case involving building inspections. It held for the first time that inspection of a building for fire or safety hazards required a warrant. At a glance, the decision seemed to be an expansion of constitutional protections because now the Fourth Amendment applied to administrative searches, not just to those by police. However, the Court then added that the warrant did not need to be particularized. An official could conduct an inspection without showing evidence in advance that *this* house or *this* factory might be unsafe. All that was needed was a general showing that certain kinds of structures tended to have certain kinds of defects. No particularized suspicion was necessary because the purpose of the inspection was not to discover criminal violations, but to protect the public's health and safety.

Here was born the doctrine of special need. Where the government conducts a search for reasons other than punishing violators, the Fourth Amendment does not apply with its usual rigor. Instead, the Constitution is satisfied as long as officials act "reasonably"—a fuzzy standard that allows any behavior appropriate for the situation at hand.

This is the theory that allows searches of all persons in certain areas of airports. Officials conduct searches of passengers and their belongings not because they think they are lawbreakers, but because they want to prevent planes and passengers from being blown out of the sky.

When applied to drug testing, the results of this judicially crafted exception to the Fourth Amendment are plain. In 1989, the Supreme Court upheld the constitutionality of two different programs. *Skinner v. Railway Labor Executives Association* involved a policy of the Federal Railroad Administration requiring urinalysis of all crew members of a train involved in an accident, even when there was no evidence that any member of the crew had been using illegal drugs. *Treasury Employees v. Von Raab* contested a rule of the Customs Service mandating urinalysis for all employees seeking transfer to certain sensitive positions. No particularized suspicion was needed. In both situations, the Court found the testing compatible with the Fourth Amendment because the government's objective was something other than law enforcement—public safety in the railroad case and public confidence in a drug-free workforce in the customs case. Similar reasoning led the Court a year later, in *Michigan Department of State Police v. Sitz*, to approve brief stops by police of all motorists at sobriety checkpoints, even when they had no grounds to believe that any particular driver was intoxicated.

It remains to be seen whether the Court will extend this thinking to other testing situations. Nonetheless, the fact remains that the Court has upheld these policies. In each, the objective is laudable. Who can be in favor of buildings that are firetraps, airplanes that carry bombs, train engineers who use drugs, customs agents who are junkies, or drivers who are drunk? Would the same reasoning, however, excuse random searches of persons on the street in an effort to reduce the number of illegal handguns in circulation? If so, what is left of the Fourth Amendment? Does it hold out protection for a dimension of privacy Americans no longer prize?

These exceptions to the Fourth Amendment lead to a third consideration—reliance on the attitude of "leave it to the judges." When we expect judges to be the exclusive guardians of the Bill of Rights, our confidence may be misplaced. To say that courts are important protectors of liberties is not to say that they should be, or even can be, the only safeguard. In the first place, what courts say the Bill of Rights means sooner or later reflects the dominant opinion in the nation. It is unreasonable to expect an institution staffed by persons not exempt from the actuarial tables to hold out for very long against tides of change.

In the second place, undue reliance on the courts excuses the rest of us from taking responsibility for the preservation of our own liberties. Through expressions of citizenship ranging from the vote to government service, people have much to say about the scope of freedoms they enjoy. Actions and attitudes of school boards, city councils, legislatures, and administrative agencies help to determine the real freedoms of all Americans. Indeed, for most citizens, the police officer on the corner is the first interpreter of the Bill of Rights. Since so few arguable violations of liberty ever are actually adjudicated in court, the practical meaning of the Bill of Rights, by necessity, is a shared responsibility.

The current controversy over abortion is a good example. One may or may not agree with the Supreme Court in *Roe v. Wade* (1973) that the Constitution protects a woman's right to terminate her pregnancy in most instances. Still, from 1973 until 1989, the right to abortion was almost exclusively a judicially protected right. Then, in 1989, five members of the Supreme Court, in *Webster v. Reproductive Health Services,* cut back on *Roe,* making it clear that states could impose new restrictions on abortion. Now, restraints on abortion largely are matters for state legislators, not judges, to decide.

A cry of protest has gone up from pro-choice forces, lamenting the demise of a woman's freedom. They say the Constitution means less after the 1989 decision. However, what has happened? Long dependent on the courts, the pro-choice side has become more active politically, seeking support from the public at large. There has yet to be a stampede of states to impose significant restrictions on abortion. While the struggle is far from over, the practical meaning of a right to abortion will not be a question decided solely by the courts.

Yes, the Bill of Rights may be in danger. Its enemies, yesterday as well as today, are misguided intentions, insensitivity, and indifference. Designed to help democracy protect itself, the document ultimately needs the support of those—the majority—who endure its restraints. Without support among the people, its provisions rest on a weak foundation. As with religion, the risk in the democratic experiment is that the form may outlive the substance of the faith.

POINTS TO PONDER

1. How can civil rights and liberties be undermined by good intentions?
2. How did the Bill of Rights come to be applied to the states in addition to the federal government?
3. What is one argument against including a list of specific rights in the Constitution?

53

"RACE, AFFIRMATIVE ACTION AND THE CONSTITUTION"

Herbert Hill

Long after the major breakthroughs in civil rights in the twentieth century that outlawed the segregation of blacks from whites, the legacies of slavery still plague the United States. The major attempt to overcome the legacies of racism in the 1980s and 1990s is affirmative action, which calls public officials to go beyond mere nondiscrimination to ensure that African Americans have all the economic opportunities in the workplace that whites have always had. These efforts have taken different forms, one of which is the statistical comparison of black employees with the percentage of blacks in the population or pool of job applicants. In the Rosenberg/Humphrey Lecture at the City College of New York (1988), Herbert Hill, professor of Afro-American Studies at the University of Wisconsin, traces the development of affirmative action policies and argues that establishing numerical goals is the only way to avoid mere symbolism or tokenism in trying to achieve racial equality.

. . . 1988 begins the third century of the United States Constitution and having survived the ritual celebration of the 1987 bicentennial, it is appropriate that we take a fresh critical look at that document and its legacy. As we examine the historical circumstances in which the Constitution emerged, we must acknowledge the continuing centrality of race in the evolution of the Constitution and of this nation.

Under the original Constitution, a system of slavery based on race existed for many generations, a system that legally defined black people as property and declared them to be less than human. Under its authority an extensive web of racist statutes and judicial decisions emerged over a long period. The Naturalization Law of 1790 explicitly limited citizenship to "white persons," the Fugitive Slave Acts of 1793 and 1850, made a travesty of law and dehumanized the nation, and the Dred Scott Decision of 1857, where chief Justice

Taney declared that blacks were not people but "articles of merchandise," are but a few of the legal monuments grounded on the assumption that this was meant to be a white man's country and that all others had no rights in the law.

With the ratification of the 13th, 14th, and 15th Amendments in 1865, 1868 and 1870 respectively and the adoption of the Civil Rights Acts of 1866, 1870 and 1875, a profoundly different set of values was asserted. This new body of law affirmed that justice and equal treatment were not for white persons exclusively, and that black people, now citizens of the nation, also were entitled to "the equal protection of the laws."

The Civil Rights Amendments and the three related Acts proclaim a very different concept of the social order than that implicit in the "three-fifths" clause contained in Section 2 of Article I of the Constitution. A concept that required the reconstruction of American society so that it could be free of slavery, free of a racism that was to have such terrible long-term consequences for the entire society.

The struggle to realize the great potential of the Reconstruction amendments to the Constitution, the struggle to create a just, decent and compassionate society free of racist oppression, is a continuing struggle that has taken many different forms in each era since the Reconstruction Period and one that continues today. In our own time the old conflict between those interests intent on perpetuating racist patterns rooted in the past, and the forces that struggle for a society free of a racism and its legacy continues in the raging battle for and against affirmative action.

During the late 1950's and early 1960's, as a result of direct confrontation with the system of state imposed segregation, together with the emergence of a new body of constitutional law on race, a hope was born that the legacy of centuries of slavery and racism would finally come to an end. But that hope was not yet to be realized. The high moral indignation of the 1960's was evidently but a passing spasm which was quickly forgotten.

A major manifestation of the sharp turning away from the goals of justice and equality is to be found in the shrill and paranoid attacks against affirmative action. The effort to eliminate the present effects of past discrimination, to correct the wrongs of many generations was barely underway when it came under powerful attack. And now, even the very modest gains made by racial minorities through affirmative action are being erased, as powerful institutions try to turn the clock of history back to the dark and dismal days of a separate and unequal status for black Americans.

Judging by the vast outcry, it might be assumed that the remedy of affirmative action to eliminate racist and sexist patterns has become as widespread and destructive as discrimination itself. And once again, the defenders of the racial *status quo* have succeeded in confusing the remedy with the original evil. The term "reverse discrimination" for example, has become another code word for resisting the elimination of prevailing patterns of discrimination.

The historic dissent of Justice John Marshall Harlan in the 1883 decision of the Supreme Court in the Civil Rights Cases defines the constitutional principle requiring the obligation of the government to remove all the "badges and incidents" of slavery. Although initially rejected, the rationale of Harlan's position was of course vindicated in later Supreme Court decisions, as in *Brown* v. *Board of Education* in 1954 and *Jones* v. *Mayer* in 1968, among others.

The adoption by Congress of the Civil Rights Act of 1964 further confirmed this constitutional perception of the equal protection clause of the 14th Amendment and reinforced the legal principle that for every right there is a remedy. I believe that what Justice Harlan called the "badges and incidents" of slavery include every manifestation of racial discrimination, not against black people alone, but also against other people of color who were engulfed by the heritage of racism that developed out of slavery.

In this respect, I believe that an interpretation of the law consistent with the meaning of the 13th and 14th Amendments to the Constitution holds that affirmative action programs carry forth the contemporary legal obligation to eradicate the consequences of slavery and racism. In order to do that, it is necessary to confront the present effects of past discrimination and the most effective remedy to achieve that goal is affirmative action. Mr. Justice Blackmun in his opinion in *Bakke* wrote, ". . . in order to get beyond racism, we must first take account of race. There is no other way."

By now it should be very clear, that the opposition to affirmative action is based on perceived group interest rather than on abstract philosophical differences about "quotas," "reverse discrimination," "preferential treatment" and the other catch-phrases commonly raised in public debate. After all the pious rhetoric equating affirmative action with "reverse discrimination" is stripped away, it is evident that the opposition to affirmative action is in fact the effort to perpetuate the privileged position of white males in American society.

In his dissent in *Bakke*, Justice Thurgood Marshall wrote, "The experience of Negroes in America has been different in kind, not just in degree, from that of other ethnic groups. It is not merely the history of slavery alone but also that a whole people were marked as inferior by the law. And that mark has endured. The dream of America as the great melting pot has not been realized for the Negro; because of his skin color he never even made it into the pot."

I propose to examine some important aspects of the historical process so aptly described by Mr. Justice Marshall. A major recomposition of the labor force occurred in the decades after the Civil War. By the end of the 19th century the American working class was an immigrant working class and European immigrants held power and exercised great influence within organized labor. For example, in 1900, Irish immigrants or their descendants held the presidencies of over fifty of the 110 national unions in the American Federation of Labor. Many of the other unions were also led by immigrants or their sons, with Germans following the Irish in number and prominence, while the president of the AFL was a Jewish immigrant. Records of labor organizations confirm the dominant role of immigrants and their descendants in many individual unions and city and state labor bodies throughout the country at the turn of the century and for decades later.

For the immigrant worker loyalty was to the ethnic collective, and it was understood that advancement of the individual was dependent upon communal advancement. Participation in organized labor was a significant part of that process and many of the dramatic labor conflicts of the 19th and 20th centuries were in fact ethnic group struggles. For blacks, both before and after emancipation, the historical experience was completely different. For them, systematic racial oppression was the basic and inescapable characteristic of the society, north and south, and it was the decisive fact of their lives. The problems of the white immigrant did not compare with the oppression of racism, an oppression that was of a different magnitude, of a different order.

Initially isolated from the social and economic mainstream, white immigrants rapidly came to understand that race and ethnic identity was decisive in providing access to employment and in the eventual establishment of stable communities. For white immigrant workers assimilation was achieved through group mobility and collective ethnic advancement that was directly linked to the work place. The occupational frame of reference was decisive.

Wages, and the status derived from steady work could only be obtained by entering the permanent labor force and labor unions were most important in providing access to the job market for many groups of immigrant workers. In contrast to the white ethnics, generations of black workers were systematically barred from employment in the primary sectors of the labor market, thereby denied the economic base that made possible the celebrated achievements and social mobility of white immigrant communities.

An examination of briefs *amicus curiae* filed in the Supreme Court cases involving affirmative action reveal the active role these two historically unrelated groups, white ethnics and labor unions have played in the repeated attacks against affirmative action. With some few exceptions, this has been the pattern from *De Funis* in 1974 and *Bakke* in 1978 to the most recent cases. Given the context in which this issue evolved, the historical sources of the opposition to affirmative action are not surprising.

The nineteenth-century European migrations to the United States took place during the long age of blatant white supremacy, legal and extralegal, formal and informal, and as the patterns of segregation and discrimination emerged north and south, the doors of opportunity were opened to white immigrants but closed to blacks and other non-whites. European immigrants and their descendants explain their success as a result of their devotion to the work ethic, and ignore a variety of other factors such as the systematic exclusion of non-Caucasians from competition for employment. As white immigrants moved up in the social order, black workers and those of other non-white races could fill only the least desirable places in a marginal secondary labor market, the only places open to them.

The elimination of traditional patterns of discrimination required by the Civil Rights Act of 1964 adversely affected the expectations of whites, since it compelled competition with black workers and other minority group members where none previously existed. White worker expectations had become the norm and any alteration of the norm was considered "reverse discrimination." When racial practices that have historically placed blacks at a disadvantage are removed to eliminate the present effects of past discrimination, whites believe that preferential treatment is given to blacks. But it is *the removal of the preferential treatment traditionally enjoyed by white workers at the expense of blacks as a class* that is at issue in the affirmative action controversy.

In many different occupations, including a variety of jobs in the public sector such as in police and fire departments, white workers were able to begin their climb on the seniority ladder precisely because non-whites were systematically excluded from the competition for jobs. Various union seniority systems were established at a time when racial minorities were banned from employment and union membership. Obviously blacks as a group, not just as individuals, constituted a class of victims who could not develop seniority status. A seniority system launched under these conditions inevitably becomes the institutionalized mechanism whereby whites as a group are granted racial privileges.

After long delay and much conflict, a new comprehensive body of law is emerging that has a significant potential and gives hope to women and racial minorities in the labor force.

On March 25, 1987, in *Johnson* v. *Transportation Agency*, the Supreme Court issued its fifth affirmative action ruling within an eleven month period. In *Johnson*, the Court upheld a voluntary affirmative action plan for hiring and promoting women and minorities adopted by the Transportation Agency of Santa Clara County, California. *Johnson* firmly supports the conclusion that affirmative action is a valid remedy to eliminate discrimination in public sector employment.

In *United States* v. *Paradise*, the Court upheld a lower court's decision requiring the Alabama Department of Public Safety to promote one black state trooper for each white promoted until either 25 percent of the job category was black or until an acceptable alternative promotion plan was put into place.

Wygant v. *Jackson Board of Education*, in which the Court struck down a provision in a collective bargaining agreement which provided that, in the event of teacher layoffs, the percentage of minority personnel laid off would be no greater than the percentage of minority personnel employed by the Jackson, Michigan school system at the time of the layoffs. However, a majority of the Court agreed that voluntary affirmative action plans by public employers are constitutional in some instances.

Local 28 of the Sheet Metal Workers International Association v. *EEOC*, in which the Court upheld a lower court's order requiring a New York construction union to adopt an affirmative action plan, including a special fund to recruit and train minority workers and a 29 percent minority membership goal. This decision was the culmination of almost forty years of struggle in state and federal courts to end the racist practices of the AFL-CIO affiliate. Other cases involving unions in the building trades have a similar history and after years of litigation are still pending in Federal courts. (See for example, *Commonwealth of Pennsylvania and Williams* v. *Operating Engineers, Local 542*, 347 F. Supp. 268, E.D.PA. 1979.)

Local No. 93, International Association of Firefighters v. *City of Cleveland*, in which the
Court upheld a consent decree which contained promotion goals for minorities
and other affirmative action provisions in settlement of a job discrimination suit by
minority firefighters.

The adverse decision in *Wygant* notwithstanding, these decisions of the
Supreme Court in conjunction with the Court's 1979 decision in *Steelworkers*
v. *Weber* make it very clear that the principle of affirmative action applied in
several different contexts is well established in the law and recognized as an effective and valid remedy to eliminate traditional discriminatory employment
practices. But the opponents of affirmative action continue their attacks. Powerful forces, through a well-orchestrated propaganda campaign, based upon
misrepresentation and the manipulation of racial fears among whites continue
their efforts to perpetuate discriminatory practices. In this, they have been
aided and abetted again and again by the Reagan Administration, the most reactionary administration on civil rights in the 20th century.

In reviewing the attacks upon affirmative action, it is necessary to note the
disingenuous argument of those who state that they are not against affirmative
action, but only against "quotas." Affirmative action without numbers,
whether in the form of quotas, goals, or timetables, is meaningless; there must
be some benchmark, some tangible measure of change. Statistical evidence to
measure performance is essential. Not to use numbers is to revert to the era of
symbolic gesture or, at best, "tokenism."

White ethnic groups and many labor unions frequently argue that affirmative action programs will penalize innocent whites who are not responsible for
past discriminatory practices. This argument turns on the notion of individual
rights and sounds very moral and highminded. But it ignores social reality. It
ignores the fact that white workers benefitted from the systematic exclusion of
blacks in many trades and industries. As has been repeatedly demonstrated in
lawsuits, non-whites and women have been denied jobs, training and advancement not as individuals but as a class, no matter what their personal
merit and qualification. Wherever discriminatory employment patterns exist,
hiring and promotion without affirmative action perpetuate the old injustice.

Before the emergence of affirmative action remedies, the legal prohibitions
against job discrimination were for the most part declarations of abstract
morality that rarely resulted in any change. Pronouncements of public policy
such as state and municipal fair employment practice laws were mainly symbolic, and the patterns of job discrimination remained intact. Because affirmative action programs go beyond individual relief to attack long-established
patterns of discrimination and, if vigorously enforced by government agencies
over a sustained period can become a major instrument for social change, they
have come under powerful and repeated attack.

As long as Title VII litigation was concerned largely with procedural and
conceptual issues, only limited attention was given to the consequences of
remedies. However, once affirmative action was widely applied and the focus

of litigation shifted to the adoption of affirmative action plans, entrenched interests were threatened. And as the gains of the 1960's are eroded, the nation becomes even more mean-spirited and self-deceiving.

Racism in the history of the United States has not been an aberration. It has been systematized and structured into the functioning of the society's most important institutions. In the present as in the past, it is widely accepted as a basis for promoting the interests of whites. For many generations the assumptions of white supremacy were codified in the law, imposed by custom and often enforced by violence. While the forms have changed, the legacy of white supremacy is expressed in the continuing patterns of racial discrimination, and for the vast majority of black and other non-white people, race and racism remain the decisive factors in their lives.

The current conflict over affirmative action is not simply an argument about abstract rights or ethnic bigotry. In the final analysis it is an argument between those who insist upon the substance of a long-postponed break with the traditions of American racism, and those groups that insist upon maintaining the valuable privileges and benefits they now enjoy as a consequence of that dismal history.

POINTS TO PONDER

1. What is the difference between affirmative action and nondiscrimination?
2. According to Hill, why are numerical goals necessary?
3. What is meant by "reverse discrimination"?

54

"FROM EQUAL OPPORTUNITY TO 'AFFIRMATIVE ACTION'"

Thomas Sowell

In this selection from his 1984 book Civil Rights: Rhetoric or Reality?, *African-American economist Thomas Sowell of the Hoover Institute at Stanford University takes issue with the advocates of affirmative action. He argues that the original goal of the civil rights struggle in the twentieth century was "equal opportunity" for all persons, regardless of race, sex, age, or other social categories. The requirement was that people be judged* without *regard to group membership. But, he argues, this initial ideal has been perverted by transforming the original goal into the requirement of affirmative action with specific statistical quotas by which to measure progress. Sowell argues that these affirmative action requirements distort the intentions of the Civil Rights Act of 1964 and that many factors besides discrimination can explain the differential performance of different ethnic groups in U.S. society.*

The very meaning of the phrase "civil rights" has changed greatly since the *Brown* decision in 1954, or since the Civil Rights Act of 1964. Initially, civil rights meant, quite simply, that all individuals should be treated the same under the law, regardless of their race, religion, sex or other such social categories. For blacks, especially, this would have represented a dramatic improvement in those states where law and public policy mandated racially separate institutions and highly discriminatory treatment.

Many Americans who supported the initial thrust of civil rights, as represented by the *Brown* v. *Board of Education* decision and the Civil Rights Act of 1964, later felt betrayed as the original concept of equal individual *opportunity* evolved toward the concept of equal group *results*. The idea that statistical differences in results were weighty presumptive evidence of discriminatory processes was not initially an explicit part of civil rights law. But neither was it merely an inexplicable perversion, as many critics seem to think, for it followed logically from the civil rights *vision*.

If the causes of intergroup differences can be dichotomized into discrimination and innate ability, then non-racists and non-sexists must expect equal results from nondiscrimination. Conversely, the persistence of highly disparate results must indicate that discrimination continues to be pervasive among recalcitrant employers, culturally biased tests, hypocritical educational institutions, etc. The early leaders and supporters of the civil rights movement did not advocate such corollaries, and many explicitly repudiated them, especially during the congressional debates that preceded passage of the Civil Rights Act of 1964. But the corollaries were implicit in the vision—and in the long run that proved to be more decisive than the positions taken by the original leaders in the cause of civil rights. In the face of crying injustices, many Americans accepted a vision that promised to further a noble cause, without quibbling over its assumptions or verbal formulations. But visions have a momentum of their own, and those who accept their assumptions have entailed their corollaries, however surprised they may be when these corollaries emerge historically.

From Rights to Quotas

"Equal opportunity" laws and policies require that individuals be judged on their qualifications as individuals, *without regard* to race, sex, age, etc. "Affirmative action" requires that they be judged *with regard* to such group membership, receiving preferential or compensatory treatment in some cases to achieve a more proportional "representation" in various institutions and occupations.

The conflict between equal opportunity and affirmative action developed almost imperceptibly at first, though it later became a heated issue, repeatedly debated by the time the Civil Rights Act of 1964 was being considered by Congress. The term "affirmative action" was first used in a racial discrimination context in President John F. Kennedy's Executive Order No. 10,925 in 1961. But, as initially presented, affirmative action referred to various activities, such as monitoring subordinate decision makers to ensure the fairness of their hiring and promotion decisions, and spreading information about employment or other opportunities so as to encourage previously excluded groups to apply—after which the actual selection could be made *without regard* to group membership. Thus, it was both meaningful and consistent for President Kennedy's Executive Order to say that federal contractors should "take affirmative action to ensure that the applicants are employed, and that employees are treated during employment, without regard to their race, creed, color, or national origin."

Tendencies toward shifting the emphasis from equality of prospective opportunity toward statistical parity of retrospective results were already observed, at both state and federal levels, by the time that the Civil Rights Act of 1964 was under consideration in Congress. Senator Hubert Humphrey, while guiding this bill through the Senate, assured his colleagues that it "does not require an employer to achieve any kind of racial balance in his work force by giving preferential treatment to any individual or group." He pointed out that subsection 703(j) under Title VII of the Civil Rights Act "is added to state this point expressly." That subsection declared that nothing in Title VII required an employer "to grant preferential treatment to any individual or group on account of any imbalance which may exist" with respect to the numbers of employees in such groups "in comparison with the total number or percentage of persons of such race, color, religion, sex, or national origin in any community, State, section or other area."

Virtually all the issues involved in the later controversies over affirmative action, in the specifically numerical sense, were raised in the legislative debates preceding passage of the Civil Rights Act. Under subsection 706(g) of that Act, an employer was held liable only for his own "intentional" discrimination, not for societal patterns reflected in his work force. According to Senator Humphrey, the "express requirement of intent is designed to make it wholly clear that inadvertent or accidental discriminations will not violate the Title or result in the entry of court orders." Vague claims of differential institutional policy impact—"institutional racism"—were not to be countenanced. For example, tests with differential impact on different groups were considered by Humphrey to be "legal unless used for the purpose of discrimination." There was no burden of proof placed upon employers to "validate" such tests.

In general there was to be no burden of proof on employers; rather the Equal Employment Opportunity Commission (EEOC) created by the Act "must prove by a preponderance" that an adverse decision was based on race (or, presumably, other forbidden categories), according to Senator Joseph Clark, another leading advocate of the Civil Rights Act. Senator Clark also declared that the Civil Rights Act "will not require an employer to change existing seniority lists," even though such lists might have differential impact on blacks as the last hired and first fired. Still another supporter, Senator Harrison Williams, declared that an employer with an all-white work force could continue to hire "only the best qualified persons even if they were all white."

In short, Congress declared itself in favor of equal opportunity and opposed to affirmative action. So has the American public. Opinion polls show a majority of blacks opposed to preferential treatment, as is an even larger majority of women. Federal administrative agencies and the courts led the change from the prospective concept of individual equal opportunity to the retrospective concept of parity of group "representation" (or "correction" of "imbalances").

The key development in this process was the creation of the Office of Federal Contract Compliance in the U.S. Department of Labor by President Lyndon Johnson's Executive Order No. 11,246 in 1965. In May 1968, this office issued guidelines containing the fateful expression "goals and timetables" and "representation." But as yet these were still not quotas, for 1968 guidelines spoke of "goals and timetables for the prompt achievement of full and equal employment opportunity." By 1970, however, new guidelines referred to "results-oriented procedures," which hinted more strongly at what was to come. In December 1971, the decisive guidelines were issued, which made it clear that "goals and timetables" were meant to "increase materially the utilization of minorities and women," with "under-utilization" being spelled out as "having fewer minorities or women in a particular job classification than would reasonably be expected by their availability . . ." Employers were required to confess to "deficiencies in the utilization" of minorities and women whenever this statistical parity could not be found in all job classifications, as a first step toward correcting this situation. The burden of proof—and remedy —was on the employer. "Affirmative action" was now decisively transformed into a numerical concept, whether called "goals" or "quotas."

Though lacking in either legislative authorization or public support for numerical group preferences, administrative agencies of government were able to enforce such policies with the support of the federal courts in general and the U.S. Supreme Court in particular. In the landmark *Weber* case the Supreme Court simply rejected "a literal interpretation" of the words of the Civil Rights Act. Instead, it sought the "spirit" of the Act, its "primary concern" with the economic problems of blacks. According to Justice William Brennan, writing the majority opinion, these words do not bar "temporary, voluntary, affirmative action measures undertaken to eliminate manifest racial imbalance in traditionally segregated job categories." This performance received the sarcastic tribute of Justice Rehnquist that it was "a *tour de force* reminiscent not of jurists such as Hale, Holmes, and Hughes but of escape artists such as

Houdini." Rehnquist's dissent inundated the Supreme Court with the legislative history of the Act, and Congress' repeated and emphatic rejection of the whole approach of correcting imbalances or compensating for the past. The spirit of the Act was as contrary to the decision as was the letter.

Equality of Rights and Results

Those who carry the civil rights vision to its ultimate conclusion see no great difference between promoting equality of opportunity and equality of results. If there are not equal results among groups presumed to have equal genetic potential, then some inequality of opportunity must have intervened somewhere, and the question of precisely where is less important than the remedy of restoring the less fortunate to their just position. The fatal flaw in this kind of thinking is that there are many reasons, besides genes and discrimination, why groups differ in their economic performances and rewards. Groups differ by large amounts demographically, culturally, and geographically—and all of these differences have profound effects on incomes and occupations.

Age differences are quite large. Blacks are a decade younger than the Japanese. Jews are a quarter of a century older than Puerto Ricans. Polish Americans are twice as old as American Indians. These represent major differences in quantity of work experience, in an economy where income differences between age brackets are even greater than black–white income differences. Even if the various racial and ethnic groups were identical in every other respect, their age differences alone would prevent their being equally represented in occupations requiring experience or higher education. Their very different age distributions likewise prevent their being equally represented in colleges, jails, homes for the elderly, the armed forces, sports and numerous other institutions and activities that tend to have more people from one age bracket than from another.

Cultural differences add to the age differences. . . . [H]alf of all Mexican American wives were married in their teens, while only 10 percent of Japanese American wives married that young. Such very different patterns imply not only different values but also very different future opportunities. Those who marry and begin having children earlier face more restricted options for future education and less geographic mobility for seeking their best career opportunities. Even among those young people who go on to colleges and universities, their opportunities to prepare themselves for the better paid professions are severely limited by their previous educational choices and performances, as well as by their selections of fields of study in the colleges and universities. All of these things vary enormously from one group to another.

For example, mathematics preparation and performance differ greatly from one ethnic group to another and between men and women. A study of high school students in northern California showed that four-fifths of Asian youngsters were enrolled in the sequence of mathematics courses that culminate in calculus, while only one-fifth of black youngsters were enrolled in such courses. Moreover, even among those who began this sequence in geometry, the percentage that persisted all the way through to calculus was several times higher among the Asian students. Sex differences in mathematics preparation are comparably large. Among both black and white freshmen at the University of Maryland, the men had had four years of mathematics in high school more than twice as often as the women.

Mathematics is of decisive importance for many more professions than that of mathematician. Whole ranges of fields of study and work are off-limits to those without the necessary mathematical foundation. Physicists, chemists, statisticians, and engineers are only some of the more obvious occupations. In some colleges, one cannot even be an undergraduate economics major without having had calculus, and to go on to graduate school and become a professional economist requires much more mathematics, as well as statistical analysis. Even in fields where mathematics is not an absolute prerequisite, its presence or absence makes a major difference in one's ability to rise in the profession. Mathematics is becoming an important factor in the social sciences and is even beginning to invade some of the humanities. To be mathematically illiterate is to carry an increasing burden into an increasing number of occupations. Even the ability to pass a civil service examination for modest clerical jobs is helped or hindered by one's facility in mathematics.

It is hardly surprising that test scores reflect these group differences in mathematics preparation. Nationwide results on the Scholastic Aptitude Test (SAT) for college applicants show Asians and whites consistently scoring higher on the quantitative test than Hispanics or blacks, and men scoring higher than women. Nor are these differences merely the result of socioeconomic "disadvantage" caused by "society." Black, Mexican American, and American Indian youngsters from families with incomes of $50,000 and up score lower than Asians from families whose incomes are just $6,000 and under. Moreover, Asians as a group score higher than whites as a group on the quantitative portion of the SAT and the Japanese in Japan specialize in mathematics, science and engineering to a far greater extent than do American students in the United States. Cultural differences are real, and cannot be talked away by using pejorative terms such as "stereotypes" or "racism."

The racial, ethnic, and sex differences in mathematics that begin in high school (or earlier) continue on through to the Ph.D. level, affecting career choices and economic rewards. Hispanic Ph.D.'s outnumber Asian Ph.D.'s in the United States by three-to-one in history, but the Asians outnumber the Hispanics by ten-to-one in chemistry. More than half of all Asian Ph.D.'s are in mathematics, science or engineering, and more than half the Asians who teach college teach in those fields. By contrast, more than half of all black doctorates are in the field of education, a notoriously undemanding and less remunerative field. So are half the doctorates received by American Indians, not one of whom received a Ph.D. in either mathematics or physics in 1980. Female Ph.D.'s are in quantitatively-based fields only half as frequently as male Ph.D.'s.

Important as mathematics is in itself, it is also a symptom of broader and deeper disparities in educational choices and performances in general. Those groups with smaller quantities of education tend also to have lower qualities of education, and these disparities follow them all the way through their educational careers and into the job market. The children of lower income racial and ethnic groups typically score lower on tests all through school and attend lower quality colleges when they go to college at all, as well as majoring in the easier courses in fields with the least economic promise. How much of this is due to the home environment and how much to the deficiencies of the public schools in their neighborhoods is a large question that cannot be answered here. But what is clear is that what is called the "same" education, measured in years of schooling, is not even remotely the same in reality.

The civil rights vision relies heavily on statistical "disparities" in income and employment between members of different groups to support its sweeping claims of rampant discrimination. The U.S. Civil Rights Commission, for example, considers itself to be "controlling for those factors" when it examines people of the same age with the same number of years of schooling—resolutely ignoring the substance of that schooling.

Age and education do not begin to exhaust the differences between groups. They are simply more readily quantifiable than some other differences. The geographic distributions of groups also vary greatly, with Mexican Americans being concentrated in the southwest, Puerto Ricans in the northeast, half of blacks in the south, and most Asians in California and Hawaii. Differences in income between the states are also larger than black-white income differences, so that these distributional differences affect national income differences. A number of past studies, for example, have shown black and Puerto Rican incomes to be very similar nationally, but blacks generally earn higher incomes than Puerto Ricans in New York and other places where Puerto Ricans are concentrated. Their incomes nationally have shown up in these studies as similar, because there are very few Puerto Ricans living in low-income southern states.

One of the most important causes of differences in income and employment is the way people work—some diligently, carefully, persistently, cooperatively, and without requiring much supervision or warnings about absenteeism, tardiness, or drinking, and others requiring much such concern over such matters. Not only are such things inherently difficult to quantify; any suggestion that such differences even exist is sure to bring forth a storm of condemnation. In short, the civil rights vision has been hermetically sealed off from any such evidence. Both historical and contemporary observations on intergroup differences in work habits, discipline, reliability, sobriety, cleanliness, or cooperative attitude—anywhere in the world—are automatically dismissed as evidence only of the bias or bigotry of the observers. "Stereotypes" is the magic word that makes thinking about such things unnecessary. Yet despite this closed circle of reasoning that surrounds the civil rights vision, there is some evidence that cannot be disposed of in that way.

Self-employed farmers, for example, do not depend for their rewards on the biases of employers or the stereotypes of observers. Yet self-employed farmers of different ethnicity have fared very differently on the same land, even in earlier pre-mechanization times, when the principal input was the farmer's own labor. German farmers, for example, had more prosperous farms than other farmers in colonial America—and were more prosperous than Irish farmers in eighteenth-century Ireland, as well as more prosperous than Brazilian farmers in Brazil, Mexican farmers in Mexico, Russian farmers in Russia, and Chilean farmers in Chile. We may ignore the forbidden testimony from all these countries as to how hard the German farmers worked, how frugally they lived, or how sober they were. Still, the results speak for themselves.

That Jews earn far higher incomes than Hispanics in the United States might be taken as evidence that anti-Hispanic bias is stronger than anti-Semitism—if one followed the logic of the civil rights vision. But this explanation is considerably weakened by the greater prosperity of Jews than Hispanics *in Hispanic countries* throughout Latin America. Again, even if one dismisses out of hand all the observers who see great differences in the way these two groups work, study, or save, major tangible differences in economic performance remain that cannot be explained in terms of the civil rights vision.

One of the commonly used indices of intergroup economic differences is family income. Yet families are of different sizes from group to group, reflecting differences in the incidence of broken homes. Female headed households are several times more common among blacks than among whites, and in both groups these are the lowest income families. Moreover, the proportion of people working differs greatly from group to group. More than three-fifths of all Japanese American families have multiple income earners while only about a third of Puerto Rican families do. Nor is this a purely socioeconomic phenomenon, as distinguished from a cultural phenomenon. Blacks have similar incomes to Puerto Ricans, but the proportion of black families with a woman working is nearly three times that among Puerto Ricans.

None of this disproves the existence of discrimination, nor is that its purpose. What is at issue is whether statistical differences mean discrimination, or whether there are innumerable demographic, cultural, and geographic differences that make this crucial automatic inference highly questionable.

POINTS TO PONDER

1. How have the original goals of the civil rights revolution been distorted over the years, according to Sowell?
2. In Sowell's view, why is affirmative action harmful to the interests of African Americans?
3. According to Sowell, what other factors might account for what appears to be racial discrimination?

55

"WHY WE LOST THE ERA"
Jane J. Mansbridge

Despite passage by both houses of Congress, ratification by 35 states, and general support in public opinion, the Equal Rights Amendment to the Constitution failed to be ratified by the required three-fourths of the states (38). According to political scientist Jane Mansbridge of Northwestern University in her book, Why We Lost the Era *(1986), both the proponents and the opponents of the measure had a stake in believing the passage of the amendment would produce more changes in the short run than was actually likely. How this ironic outcome came about is the focus of her analysis in this selection.*

1. Equality of rights under the law shall not be denied or abridged by the United States or by any State on account of sex.
2. The Congress shall have the power to enforce, by appropriate legislation, the provisions of this article.
3. This amendment shall take effect two years after the date of ratification.

—Complete text of the Equal Rights Amendment

In March 1972 the Equal Rights Amendment to the United States Constitution—the ERA—passed the Senate of the United States with a vote of 84 to 8, seventeen votes more than the two-thirds required for constitutional amendments. In the ensuing ten years—from 1972 to 1982—a majority of Americans consistently told interviewers that they favored this amendment to the Constitution. Yet on June 30, 1982, the deadline for ratifying the amendment passed with only thirty-five of the required thirty-eight states having ratified.

How did this happen?

This book will argue that if the ERA had been ratified, the Supreme Court would have been unlikely to use it to bring about major changes in the relations between American men and women, at least in the foreseeable future. Nor did the American public want any significant change in gender roles, whether at work, at home, or in society at large. The groups that fought for the ERA and the groups that fought against it, however, had a stake in believing that the ERA *would* produce these kinds of changes. With both the proponents and the opponents exaggerating the likely effects of the ERA, legislators in wavering states became convinced that the ERA might, in fact, produce important substantive changes—and the necessary votes were lost. Considering the large number of legislative votes required to amend the Constitution, the puzzle is not why the ERA died but why it came so close to passing.

Contrary to widespread belief, public support for the ERA did not increase in the course of the ten-year struggle. In key wavering states where the ERA was most debated, public support actually declined. Much of the support for the Amendment was superficial, because it was based on a support for abstract rights, not for real changes. Many nominal supporters took strong antifeminist positions on other issues, and their support evaporated when the ERA became linked in their minds to feminist positions they rejected.

The irony in all this is that the ERA would have had much less substantive effect than either proponents or opponents claimed. Because the ERA applied only to the government and not to private businesses and corporations, it would have had no noticeable effect, at least in the short run, on the gap between men's and women's wages. Furthermore, during the 1970s, the Supreme Court began to use the Fourteenth Amendment to the Constitution to declare unconstitutional almost all the laws and practices that Congress had intended to make unconstitutional when it passed the ERA in 1972. The exceptions were laws and practices that most Americans approved. Thus, by the late 1970s it was hard to show that the ERA would have made any of the substantive changes that most Americans favored.

While the ERA would have had few immediate, tangible effects, I nonetheless believe that its defeat was a major setback for equality between men and women. Its direct effects would have been slight, but its indirect effects on both judges and legislators would probably have led in the long run to interpretations of existing laws and enactment of new laws that would have benefited women. The lack of immediate benefits did, however, deeply influence the course of the public debate. Because ERA activists had little of an immediate, practical nature to lose if the ERA was defeated, they had little reason to describe it in a way that would make it acceptable to middle-of-the-road legislators. As a consequence, the most influential leaders in the pro-ERA organizations and many of the activists in those organizations chose to interpret the ERA as delivering radical results.

Most proponents contended, for example, that the ERA would require the military to send women draftees into combat on the same basis as men. ERA proponents adopted this position even though it reduced their chances of achieving the short-run goal of passing the ERA and despite the fact that the Court was not likely to interpret the ERA as having this effect. They did so in part because their ideology called for full equality with men, not for equality with exceptions. In a somewhat similar manner, certain feminist lawyers argued in state courts that state ERAs required states to fund medically necessary abortions if they were funding all medically necessary services for men. Such arguments also reduced the chances that legislators in the key unratified states would vote for the federal ERA.

The struggle reveals how impossible it is, even in the most favorable circumstances, to dispense with "ideology" in favor of practical political reasoning when the actors in the drama give their energies voluntarily, without pay or other material incentives. Volunteers always have mixed motives, but most are trying to do good and promote justice. As a result, most would rather lose fighting for a cause they believe in than win fighting for a cause they feel is morally compromised.

Because the ERA offered its supporters no tangible benefits, activists worked hard for it only if they believed strongly in equality for women. They had no reason to "betray" that principle by compromise for compromise offered no concrete benefits, either to them personally or to women generally. ERA opponents took relatively extreme positions for similar reasons. But their "radicalism" cost them less, because they had only to disrupt an emerging consensus, not to produce one.

Refusing to compromise is, of course, often better than winning. It is not the focus on principle rather than practice that should give the reader of this story pause. It is the difficulty both sides had assimilating information about the struggle in which they were engaged. This institutionalized deafness meant that neither the activists nor the general public could make even an informed guess about what passage of the ERA would accomplish. As a result, there was no serious national debate about whether the Amendment was the best way of accomplishing what the proponents sought or whether it really threatened the values that opponents sought to defend. Nor did the proponents, who ran the gamut from feminist lawyers to grass-roots activists, ever engage one another in a wide-ranging discussion of strategy.

The only possible way to have persuaded three more state legislatures to ratify the ERA would have been to insist—correctly—that it would do relatively little in the short run, and to insist equally strongly—and correctly—on the importance of placing the principle in the Constitution to guide the Supreme Court in its long-run evolution of constitutional law. In addition, the pro-ERA movement would have had to develop an ongoing, district-based political network capable of turning generalized public sympathy for reforms that benefit women into political pressure on specific legislators in the marginal unratified states. But even this strategy might not have worked. Comparatively few state legislators were open to persuasion on this issue, and the troops for district-based organizing were often hard to mobilize—or keep mobilized.

The movement away from principle and the increasing focus on substantive effects was probably an inevitable result of the ten-year struggle for the ERA. Inevitable or not, the shift did occur. In the near future, therefore, the only way to convince legislators that the ERA would not have undesirable substantive effects would be to add explicit amendments limiting its application to the military, abortion, and so on. No principled feminist, including myself, favors an ERA that includes such "crippling" amendments. In the present political climate, therefore, the future of the ERA looks even dimmer than its past.

The death of the ERA was, of course, also related to broader changes in American political attitudes. Two of these changes were especially relevant: growing legislative skepticism about the consequences of giving the U.S.

Supreme Court authority to review legislation, and the growing organizational power of the new Right.

Suspicion of the Supreme Court, and of the role of lawyers and judges generally, certainly played a significant role in the ERA's demise. For its advocates, the ERA was a device for allowing the Supreme Court to impose the principle of equality between the sexes on recalcitrant state legislators. For legislators, that was precisely the problem. They did not want their actions reviewed, much less reversed, by federal judges whom they did not even appoint. There was a larger problem as well. The ERA embodied a principle, which was supposed to apply, without exception, to specific pieces of legislation. But most people—including most legislators—do not derive their preferences from principles. Instead, they derive their principles from their preferences, endorsing principles they associate with outcomes they like. Because the justices of the Supreme Court of the United States put somewhat more weight than ordinary citizens do on the principles they have evolved from the Constitution, they often find themselves taking controversial or even unpopular stands. As a result, much of the public has come to view the Court as "out of control." Although the Court's unpopular decisions have not yet reduced its power, they took their toll on the ERA. If the primary cause of the ERA's defeat was the fear that it would lead to major changes in the roles of men and women, a major subsidiary cause was legislative backlash against "progressive" Court decisions, starting with the 1954 school desegregation decision. Many state legislators were unwilling to give the Court "new words to play with," rightly fearing that this could eventually have all sorts of unforeseeable consequences they might not like and would not be able to reverse.

The same sense of impotence in the face of national changes that fueled the reaction against the Court also fed the conservative backlash against feminism and the growth of the "new" Right. For many conservative Americans, the personal became political for the first time when questions of family, children, sexual behavior, and women's roles became subjects of political debate. Leaders of the "old" Radical Right, who had traditionally focused on national defense and the Communist menace, became aware of the organizing potential of these "women's" issues only slowly. Once assimilated, however, the "new" issues turned out to have two great organizational virtues. First, they provided a link with fundamentalist churches. The evangelizing culture and the stable geographic base of the fundamentalist churches made them powerful actors in state legislatures once they ventured into the political process. Second, "women's issues" not only gave a focus to the reaction against the changes in child rearing, sexual behavior, divorce, and the use of drugs that had taken place in the 1960s and 1970s, they also mobilized a group, traditional homemakers, that had lost status over the two previous decades and was feeling the psychological effects of the loss. The new women's issues, combined with improvements in computer technology that reduced the cost of processing large numbers of names, made it feasible for the first time to contact by direct mail and thus bring into concerted political activities many who had previously been concerned only with a single issue or not been involved in politics at all.

State legislators were predisposed to oppose a constitutional amendment that gave the federal government power in one of the few areas that was still primarily in the province of the states, namely, family law. The entry of new conservative activists into the political process enhanced this "natural" resistance. As fundamentalist women became more prominent in the opposition, the ERA came to be seen as an issue that pitted women against women and, moreover, women of the Right against women of the Left. Once the ERA lost its aura of benefiting all women and became a partisan issue, it lost its chance of gaining the supermajority required for a constitutional amendment.

There are two lessons to be learned from the story told here. The first is a lesson about the politics of promoting "the common good." We have known for a long time of the extraordinary inequities built into the way different groups can influence legislators in a pluralist democratic system. We have also known that because it is harder to organize for the general interest than for particular interests, the general interest will—all other things being equal—count less in the political process than most people want it to. The story of the ERA struggle reveals a third, less widely recognized, obstacle to promoting the common good. Organizing on behalf of the general interest usually requires volunteers, and mobilizing volunteers often requires an exaggerated, black or white vision of events to justify spending time and money on the cause. Ironically, the greatest cost in organizing for the public interest may be the distortion, in the course of organizing, of that interest itself.

A second, practical lesson follows from the first. While organizations that depend on volunteers to promote the common good seem to have an inherent tendency toward ideological purity and polarized perceptions, they can develop institutions that help correct these tendencies, ranging from small-group techniques through formal systems of representation. Although ongoing organizations are susceptible to the temptations of speaking only to themselves, they are also our main repositories of past experience and our main mechanism for avoiding the endless repetition of past errors. Effectively promoting the common good thus requires that we keep such organizations strong and consistently funded, while at the same time trying to ensure internal dialogue on substantive issues.

POINTS TO PONDER

1. What were the main arguments for and against the ERA?
2. What role did ideology play in the political battle over the ERA?
3. What are the implications of the political battle over the ERA for organizing for causes concerning the general good rather than particular interests?

CONCLUSION:
ALTERNATIVE FUTURES

In this final section of the book we move away from focusing on the immediate pressures and institutions of governance to peer into the future. In order for any government to endure, a nation has to prepare for the future, and that preparation is often in conflict with the concerns of the present. In our personal lives present sacrifices must be made in order to invest our resources (money and time) so that our future capacity will be expanded. The same kind of investment is necessary on a national scale, whether it involves preparing for the defense of the country or investing in the education of its citizens.

But just as it is difficult for individuals to sacrifice present consumption for future capacity, it is also difficult for societies to make sacrifices in the present. It is perhaps the defining characteristic of true political leadership to prepare the polity for the future by convincing citizens that it is worth sacrificing present consumption for the collective future well-being of the society. In a democracy this is particularly difficult, for all of the pressures favor present consumption. The focus of powerful interest groups is the well-being of their members, and the most powerful interests naturally favor the status quo. The tendency of representatives in a republic is often to win the next election by responding to the short-run perspectives of their constituents.

Thus we all yearn for the political visionary who can convince us that shared sacrifice for the future will be fairly distributed and that our common sacrifices will result in a richer nation for our children. But wise, visionary leadership is in short supply, and we are skeptical of making sacrifices that are not absolutely certain to pay off in the end.

The Readings

The selections in this section each attempt to step back and view the present in broad, historical perspective in order to draw the needed vision to lead us into the next century. They look for patterns of the past that will continue or emerging trends that will transform the world. The end of the cold war is useful as a point of perspective from which to view the future.

The selections present three different visions of the future of the world and the place of the United States in it. The scenarios are not mutually exclusive, but they focus on different aspects of the past, present, and future. Each seeks to alert us to the changes in the world and point us in the right direction to deal with the vast changes that may be dawning.

The first selection is by political scientist Samuel Huntington who argues that the major fault lines among human societies are changing. Wars of the past were fought first among monarchs, then among nations, then among differing ideologies. But the major conflicts and potential wars of the future will be fought among different civilizations. Huntington defines a civilization as having such common elements as history, language, customs, and, most important, religion. He argues that, while the West is at the peak of its influence, the rest of the world is increasing in relative economic and military power. Leaders in non-Western countries no longer see Western institutions as the way to prosperity but are returning to their own cultural roots, as evidenced in fundamentalist movements around the world. Huntington argues that the West can ignore these developments only at its own peril.

Peter F. Drucker has been one of the most highly visible and visionary management experts in an age of large-scale organizations. Drucker has always had his fingers on the pulse of our organizational society, and in his selection he argues that the world is passing through a transitionary stage to what will become the "knowledge society." He compares the present transformation to the rise of trade in the thirteenth century, the dispersion of movable type in the fifteenth century, and the rise of capitalism in the eighteenth century.

The challenges of this new era in human history will be to recognize the inevitability of the knowledge revolution and to prepare our society for it. This adaptation necessarily includes the creation of economic arrangements that will include the "service workers"—those who will not have the education to participate in the knowledge revolution. Also imperative is the inclusion of the Third World in the modern economy of the developed world. If we do not respond to these challenges, civil conflict or war is likely.

The final selection by historian Jack Goldstone brings the focus back to the United States and the ability of our system of governance to face up to the economic and political challenges of the twenty-first century. Goldstone argues that the indicators of the declining international influence of the United States are in part symptoms of internal imbalances. The most obvious imbalance is the difference between our national expenditures and our willingness to tax ourselves to pay our bills. In the 1980s and 1990s, the United States has run many annual deficits of over $200 billion, and our national debt has increased from about $1 trillion in 1980 to $4 trillion in the 1990s. It will surpass $5 trillion by the turn of the century.

Goldstone argues that the solution to our problem is simple to state. We need greater investment in the economy and in the public sector to raise future productivity, and we need to raise revenues to cover our national expenditures (that is, we need to balance our budget). But the solution is as difficult to achieve as it is easy to state, because it entails reducing consumption in the present. In order to make current sacrifices for future gains we need "ennobling leaders" who can convince us that the sacrifice is necessary and that the costs will be distributed equitably.

These three visions of the future share warnings about the future of humankind, and each holds out hope that we can create the vision to prepare for the next century. The political science perspective of Huntington is pessimistic with respect to the deep historical and cultural roots of the differing world views of the civilizations he describes. Drucker's focus on technology and the changes that may be possible through new breakthroughs produces the most optimistic view of the future of humankind. Goldstone lays out a relatively clear path for improvement for the United States, but is not optimistic about the political will to take that path. Despite the strain of pessimism that runs through these three selections, the authors all agree that the real solution to human problems of the twenty-first century is visionary political leadership.

KEY TERMS

civilization: the broadest level of group cultural identity short of that which distinguishes humans from other species. Its members possess a common language, history, religion, customs, institutions, and self-identity.

deficit: the difference between what the national government spends each year and the revenues (taxes) it raises. The difference must be made up by borrowing money—that is, by selling bonds.

nation: a group of people who share a territory, a common language, religion, race, customs and traditions. It may coincide with a state.

national debt: the cumulation of annual deficits that have not yet been paid off. The national debt of the United States is about $4 trillion.

state: a political community having a government, specific territory, and sovereignty

the West: the civilization that developed the Judeo-Christian religious tradition and gave birth to the idea of liberal democracy, geographically located in Europe and North America

56

"THE CLASH OF CIVILIZATIONS?"
Samuel P. Huntington

Wars of the past were fought first between monarchs, then nations, then ideologies. But with the end of the cold war and its ideological struggle, world politics has entered a new phase, according to Harvard political scientist Samuel Huntington in this article from Foreign Affairs *(1993). The fault lines of the new world will be among civilizations, distinguished by common elements of language, history, customs, and particularly religion. Of the seven or eight civilizations of the world, the most likely conflict will be between "the West and the rest." Huntington argues that in the long run the West is going to have to make efforts to understand the basic religious and philosophical concepts underlying other civilizations and find elements of commonality in order to achieve co-existence in peace.*

The Next Pattern of Conflict

World politics is entering a new phase, and intellectuals have not hesitated to proliferate visions of what it will be—the end of history, the return of traditional rivalries between nation states, and the decline of the nation state from the conflicting pulls of tribalism and globalism, among others. Each of these visions catches aspects of the emerging reality. Yet they all miss a crucial, indeed a central, aspect of what global politics is likely to be in the coming years.

It is my hypothesis that the fundamental source of conflict in this new world will not be primarily ideological or primarily economic. The great divisions among humankind and the dominating source of conflict will be cultural. Nation states will remain the most powerful actors in world affairs, but the principal conflicts of global politics will occur between nations and groups of different civilizations. The clash of civilizations will dominate global politics. The fault lines between civilizations will be the battle lines of the future.

Conflict between civilizations will be the latest phase in the evolution of conflict in the modern world. For a century and a half after the emergence of the modern international system with the Peace of Westphalia, the conflicts of the Western world were largely among princes—emperors, absolute monarchs and constitutional monarchs attempting to expand their bureaucracies, their armies, their mercantilist economic strength and, most important, the territory they ruled. In the process they created nation states, and beginning with the French Revolution the principal lines of conflict were between nations rather than princes. In 1793, as R. R. Palmer put it, "The wars of kings were over; the wars of peoples had begun." This nineteenth-century pattern lasted until the end of World War I. Then, as a result of the Russian Revolution and the reaction against it, the conflict of nations yielded to the conflict of ideologies, first among communism, fascism-Nazism and liberal democracy, and then between communism and liberal democracy. During the Cold War, this latter conflict became embodied in the struggle between the two superpowers, neither of which was a nation state in the classical European sense and each of which defined its identity in terms of its ideology.

These conflicts between princes, nation states and ideologies were primarily conflicts within Western civilization, "Western civil wars," as William Lind has labeled them. This was as true of the Cold War as it was of the world wars and the earlier wars of the seventeenth, eighteenth and nineteenth centuries. With the end of the Cold War, international politics moves out of its Western phase, and its centerpiece becomes the interaction between the West and non-Western civilizations and among non-Western civilizations. In the politics of civilizations, the peoples and governments of non-Western civilizations no longer remain the objects of history as targets of Western colonialism but join the West as movers and shapers of history.

The Nature of Civilizations

During the Cold War the world was divided into the First, Second and Third Worlds. Those divisions are no longer relevant. It is far more meaningful now to group countries not in terms of their political or economic systems or in terms of their level of economic development but rather in terms of their culture and civilization.

What do we mean when we talk of a civilization? A civilization is a cultural entity. Villages, regions, ethnic groups, nationalities, religious groups, all have distinct cultures at different levels of cultural heterogeneity. The culture of a village in southern Italy may be different from that of a village in northern Italy, but both will share in a common Italian culture that distinguishes them from German villages. European communities, in turn, will share cultural features that distinguish them from Arab or Chinese communities. Arabs, Chinese and Westerners, however, are not part of any broader cultural entity. They constitute civilizations. A civilization is thus the highest cultural grouping of people and the broadest level of cultural identity people have short of that which distinguishes humans from other species. It is defined both by common objective elements, such as language, history, religion, customs, institutions, and by the subjective self-identification of people. People have levels of identity: a resident of Rome may define himself with varying degrees of intensity as a Roman, an Italian, a Catholic, a Christian, a European, a Westerner. The civilization to which he belongs is the broadest level of identification with which he intensely identifies. People can and do redefine their identities and, as a result, the composition and boundaries of civilizations change.

Civilizations may involve a large number of people, as with China ("a civilization pretending to be a state," as Lucian Pye put it), or a very small number of people, such as the Anglophobe Caribbean. A civilization may include several nation states, as is the case with Western, Latin American and Arab civilizations, or only one, as is the case with Japanese civilization. Civilizations obviously blend and overlap, and may include subcivilizations. Western civilization has two major variants, European and North American, and Islam has its Arab, Turkic and Malay subdivisions. Civilizations are nonetheless meaningful entities, and while the lines between them are seldom sharp, they are real. Civilizations are dynamic; they rise and fall; they divide and merge. And, as any student of history knows, civilizations disappear and are buried in the sands of time.

Westerners tend to think of nation states as the principal actors in global affairs. They have been that, however, for only a few centuries. The broader reaches of human history have been the history of civilizations. In *A Study of History*, Arnold Toynbee identified 21 major civilizations; only six of them exist in the contemporary world.

Why Civilizations Will Clash

Civilization identity will be increasingly important in the future, and the world will be shaped in large measure by the interactions among seven or eight major civilizations. These include Western, Confucian, Japanese, Islamic, Hindu, Slavic-Orthodox, Latin American and possibly African civilization. The most important conflicts of the future will occur along the cultural fault lines separating these civilizations from one another.

Why will this be the case?

First, differences among civilizations are not only real; they are basic. Civilizations are differentiated from each other by history, language, culture, tradition and, most important, religion. The people of different civilizations have different views on the relations between God and man, the individual and the group, the citizen and the state, parents and children, husband and wife, as well as differing views of the relative importance of rights and responsibilities, liberty and authority, equality and hierarchy. These differences are the product of centuries. They will not soon disappear. They are far more fundamental than differences among political ideologies and political regimes. Differences do not necessarily mean conflict, and conflict does not necessarily mean violence. Over the centuries, however, differences among civilizations have generated the most prolonged and the most violent conflicts.

Second, the world is becoming a smaller place. The interactions between peoples of different civilizations are increasing; these increasing interactions intensify civilization consciousness and awareness of differences between civilizations and commonalities within civilizations. North African immigration to France generates hostility among Frenchmen and at the same time increased receptivity to immigration by "good" European Catholic Poles. Americans react far more negatively to Japanese investment than to larger investments from Canada and European countries. Similarly, as Donald Horowitz has pointed out, "An Ibo may be . . . an Owerri Ibo or an Onitsha Ibo in what was the Eastern region of Nigeria. In Lagos, he is simply an Ibo. In London, he is a Nigerian. In New York, he is an African." The interactions among peoples of different civilizations enhance the civilization-consciousness of people that, in turn, invigorates differences and animosities stretching or thought to stretch back deep into history.

Third, the processes of economic modernization and social change throughout the world are separating people from longstanding local identities. They also weaken the nation state as a source of identity. In much of the world religion has moved in to fill this gap, often in the form of movements that are labeled "fundamentalist." Such movements are found in Western Christianity, Judaism, Buddhism and Hinduism, as well as in Islam. In most countries and most religions the people active in fundamentalist movements are young, college-educated, middle-class technicians, professionals and business persons. The "unsecularization of the world," George Weigel has remarked, "is one of the dominant social facts of life in the late twentieth century." The revival of religion, "la revanche de Dieu," as Gilles Kepel labeled it, provides a basis for identity and commitment that transcends national boundaries and unites civilizations.

Fourth, the growth of civilization-consciousness is enhanced by the dual role of the West. On the one hand, the West is at a peak of power. At the same time, however, and perhaps as a result, a return to the roots phenomenon is occurring among non-Western civilizations. Increasingly one hears references to trends toward a turning inward and "Asianization" in Japan, the end of the Nehru legacy and the "Hinduization" of India, the failure of Western ideas of socialism and nationalism and hence "re-Islamization" of the Middle East, and now a debate over Westernization versus Russianization in Boris Yeltsin's country. A West at the peak of its power confronts non-Wests that increasingly have the desire, the will and the resources to shape the world in non-Western ways.

In the past, the elites of non-Western societies were usually the people who were most involved with the West, had been educated at Oxford, the Sorbonne or Sandhurst, and had absorbed Western attitudes and values. At the same time, the populace in non-Western countries often remained deeply imbued with the indigenous culture. Now, however, these relationships are being reversed. A de-Westernization and indigenization of elites is occurring in many non-Western countries at the same time that Western, usually American, cultures, styles and habits become more popular among the mass of the people.

Fifth, cultural characteristics and differences are less mutable and hence less easily compromised and resolved than political and economic ones. In the former Soviet Union, communists can become democrats, the rich can become poor and the poor rich, but Russians cannot become Estonians and

Azeris cannot become Armenians. In class and ideological conflicts, the key question was "Which side are you on?" and people could and did choose sides and change sides. In conflicts between civilizations, the question is "What are you?" That is a given that cannot be changed. And as we know, from Bosnia to the Caucasus to the Sudan, the wrong answer to that question can mean a bullet in the head. Even more than ethnicity, religion discriminates sharply and exclusively among people. A person can be half-French and half-Arab and simultaneously even a citizen of two countries. It is more difficult to be half-Catholic and half-Muslim.

Finally, economic regionalism is increasing. The proportions of total trade that were intraregional rose between 1980 and 1989 from 51 percent to 59 percent in Europe, 33 percent to 37 percent in East Asia, and 32 percent to 36 percent in North America. The importance of regional economic blocs is likely to continue to increase in the future. On the one hand, successful economic regionalism will reinforce civilization-consciousness. On the other hand, economic regionalism may succeed only when it is rooted in a common civilization. The European Community rests on the shared foundation of European culture and Western Christianity. The success of the North American Free Trade Area depends on the convergence now underway of Mexican, Canadian and American cultures. Japan, in contrast, faces difficulties in creating a comparable economic entity in East Asia because Japan is a society and civilization unique to itself. However strong the trade and investment links Japan may develop with other East Asian countries, its cultural differences with those countries inhibit and perhaps preclude its promoting regional economic integration like that in Europe and North America.

Common culture, in contrast, is clearly facilitating the rapid expansion of the economic relations between the People's Republic of China and Hong Kong, Taiwan, Singapore and the overseas Chinese communities in other Asian countries. With the Cold War over, cultural commonalities increasingly overcome ideological differences, and mainland China and Taiwan move closer together. If cultural commonality is a prerequisite for economic integration, the principal East Asian economic bloc of the future is likely to be centered on China. This bloc is, in fact, already coming into existence. As Murray Weidenbaum has observed,

> Despite the current Japanese dominance of the region, the Chinese-based economy of Asia is rapidly emerging as a new epicenter for industry, commerce and finance. This strategic area contains substantial amounts of technology and manufacturing capability (Taiwan), outstanding entrepreneurial, marketing and services acumen (Hong Kong), a fine communications network (Singapore), a tremendous pool of financial capital (all three), and very large endowments of land, resources and labor (mainland China). . . . From Guangzhou to Singapore, from Kuala Lumpur to Manila, this influential network—often based on extensions of the traditional clans—has been described as the backbone of the East Asian economy.

Culture and religion also form the basis of the Economic Cooperation Organization, which brings together ten non-Arab Muslim countries: Iran, Pakistan, Turkey, Azerbaijan, Kazakhstan, Kyrgyzstan, Turkmenistan, Tadjikistan, Uzbekistan and Afghanistan. One impetus to the revival and expansion of this organization, founded originally in the 1960s by Turkey, Pakistan and Iran, is the realization by the leaders of several of these countries that they had no chance of admission to the European Community. Similarly, Caricom, the Central American Common Market and Mercosur rest on common cultural foundations. Efforts to build a broader Caribbean-Central American economic entity bridging the Anglo-Latin divide, however, have to date failed.

As people define their identity in ethnic and religious terms, they are likely to see an "us" versus "them" relation existing between themselves and people of different ethnicity or religion. The end of ideologically defined states in Eastern Europe and the former Soviet Union permits traditional ethnic identities and animosities to come to the fore. Differences in culture and religion create differences over policy issues, ranging from human rights to immigration to trade and commerce to the environment. Geographical propinquity gives rise to conflicting territorial claims from Bosnia to Mindanao. Most important, the efforts of the West to promote its values of democracy and liberalism as universal values, to maintain its military predominance and to advance its economic interests engender countering responses from other civilizations. Decreasingly able to mobilize support and form coalitions on the basis of ideology, governments and groups will increasingly attempt to mobilize support by appealing to common religion and civilization identity.

The clash of civilizations thus occurs at two levels. At the micro-level, adjacent groups along the fault lines between civilizations struggle, often violently, over the control of territory and each other. At the macro-level, states from different civilizations compete for relative military and economic power, struggle over the control of international institutions and third parties, and competitively promote their particular political and religious groups.

* * * *

The West versus the Rest

The West is now at an extraordinary peak of power in relation to other civilizations. Its superpower opponent has disappeared from the map. Military conflict among Western states is unthinkable, and Western military power is unrivaled. Apart from Japan, the West faces no economic challenge. It dominates international political and security institutions and with Japan international economic institutions. Global political and security issues are effectively settled by a directorate of the United States, Britain and France, world economic issues by a directorate of the United States, Germany and Japan, all of which maintain extraordinarily close relations with each other to the exclusion of lesser and largely non-Western countries. Decisions made at the U.N. Security Council or in the International Monetary Fund that reflect the interests of the West are presented to the world as reflecting the desires of the world community. The very phrase "the world community" has become the euphemistic collective noun (replacing "the Free World") to give global legitimacy to actions reflecting the interests of the United States and other Western powers. Through the IMF and other international economic institutions, the West promotes its economic interests and imposes on other nations the economic policies it thinks appropriate. In any poll of non-Western peoples, the IMF undoubtedly would win the support of finance ministers and a few others, but get an overwhelmingly unfavorable rating from just about everyone else, who would agree with Georgy Arbatov's characterization of IMF officials as "neo-Bolsheviks who love expropriating other people's money, imposing undemocratic and alien rules of economic and political conduct and stifling economic freedom."

Western domination of the U.N. Security Council and its decisions, tempered only by occasional abstention by China, produced U.N. legitimation of the West's use of force to drive Iraq out of Kuwait and its elimination of Iraq's sophisticated weapons and capacity to produce such weapons. It also produced the quite unprecedented action by the United States, Britain and France in getting the Security Council to demand that Libya hand over the Pan Am 103 bombing suspects and then to impose sanctions when Libya refused. After defeating the largest Arab army, the West did not hesitate to throw its weight around in the Arab world. The West in effect is using international institutions, military power and economic resources to run the world in ways that will maintain Western predominance, protect Western interests and promote Western political and economic values.

That at least is the way in which non-Westerners see the new world, and there is a significant element of truth in their view. Differences in power and struggles for military, economic and institutional power are thus one source of conflict between the West and other civilizations. Differences in culture, that is basic values and beliefs, are a second source of conflict. V. S. Naipaul has argued that Western civilization is the "universal civilization" that "fits all men." At a superficial level much of Western culture has indeed permeated the rest of the world. At a more basic level, however, Western concepts differ fundamentally from those prevalent in other civilizations. Western ideas of individualism, liberalism, constitutionalism, human rights, equality, liberty, the rule of law, democracy, free markets, the separation of church and state, often have little resonance in Islamic, Confucian, Japanese, Hindu, Buddhist or Orthodox cultures. Western efforts to propagate such ideas produce instead a reaction against "human rights imperialism" and a reaffirmation of indigenous values, as can be seen in the support for religious fundamentalism by the younger generation in non-Western cultures. The very notion that there could be a "universal civilization" is a Western idea, directly at odds with the particularism of most Asian societies and their emphasis on what distinguishes one people from another. Indeed, the author of a review of 100 comparative studies of values in different societies concluded that "the values that are most important in the West are least important worldwide." In the political realm, of course, these differences are most manifest in the efforts of the United States and other Western powers to induce other peoples to adopt Western ideas concerning democracy and human rights. Modern democratic government originated in the West. When it has developed in non-Western societies it has usually been the product of Western colonialism or imposition.

The central axis of world politics in the future is likely to be, in Kishore Mahbubani's phrase, the conflict between "the West and the Rest" and the responses of non-Western civilizations to Western power and values. Those responses generally take one or a combination of three forms. At one extreme, non-Western states can, like Burma and North Korea, attempt to pursue a course of isolation, to insulate their societies from penetration or "corruption" by the West, and, in effect, to opt out of participation in the Western-dominated global community. The costs of this course, however, are high, and few states have pursued it exclusively. A second alternative, the equivalent of "band-wagoning" in international relations theory, is to attempt to join the West and accept its values and institutions. The third alternative is to attempt to "balance" the West by developing economic and military power and cooperating with other non-Western societies against the West, while preserving indigenous values and institutions; in short, to modernize but not to Westernize.

* * * *

Implications for the West

This article does not argue that civilization identities will replace all other identities, that nation states will disappear, that each civilization will become a single coherent political entity, that groups within a civilization will not conflict with and even fight each other. This paper does set forth the hypotheses that differences between civilizations are real and important; civilization-consciousness is increasing; conflict between civilizations will supplant ideological and other forms of conflict as the dominant global form of conflict; international relations, historically a game played out within Western civilization, will increasingly be de-Westernized and become a game in which non-Western civilizations are actors and not simply objects; successful political, security and economic international institutions are more likely to develop within civilizations than across civilizations; conflicts between groups in different civilizations will be more frequent, more sustained and more violent than conflicts between groups in the same civilization; violent conflicts between groups in different civilizations are the most likely and most dangerous source of escalation that could lead to global wars; the paramount axis of world politics will be the relations between "the West and the Rest"; the elites in some torn non-Western countries will try to make their countries part of the West, but in most cases face major obstacles to accomplishing this; a central focus of conflict for the immediate future will be between the West and several Islamic-Confucian states.

This is not to advocate the desirability of conflicts between civilizations. It is to set forth descriptive hypotheses as to what the future may be like. If these are plausible hypotheses, however, it is necessary to consider their implications for Western policy. These implications should be divided between short-term advantage and long-term accommodation. In the short term it is clearly in the interest of the West to promote greater cooperation and unity within its own civilization, particularly between its European and North American components; to incorporate into the West societies in Eastern Europe and Latin America whose cultures are close to those of the West; to promote and maintain cooperative relations with Russia and Japan; to prevent escalation of local inter-civilization conflicts into major inter-civilization wars; to limit the expansion of the military strength of Confucian and Islamic states; to moderate the reduction of Western military capabilities and maintain military superiority in East and Southwest Asia; to exploit differences and conflicts among Confucian and Islamic states; to support in other civilizations groups sympathetic to Western values and interests; to strengthen international institutions that reflect and legitimate Western interests and values and to promote the involvement of non-Western states in those institutions.

In the longer term other measures would be called for. Western civilization is both Western and modern. Non-Western civilizations have attempted to become modern without becoming Western. To date only Japan has fully succeeded in this quest. Non-Western civilizations will continue to attempt to acquire the wealth, technology, skills, machines and weapons that are part of being modern. They will also attempt to reconcile this modernity with their traditional culture and values. Their economic and military strength relative to the West will increase. Hence the West will increasingly have to accommodate these non-Western modern civilizations whose power approaches that of the West but whose values and interests differ significantly from those of the West. This will require the West to maintain the economic and military power necessary to protect its interests in relation to these civilizations. It will also, however, require the West to develop a more profound understanding of the basic religious and philosophical assumptions underlying other civilizations and the ways in which people in those civilizations see their interests. It will require an effort to identify elements of commonality between Western and other civilizations. For the relevant future, there will be no universal civilization, but instead a world of different civilizations, each of which will have to learn to coexist with the others.

POINTS TO PONDER

1. What are the major factors that distinguish one civilization from another?
2. According to Huntington, why will these differences lead to conflict?
3. What is the best hope for preventing these conflicts from becoming violent?

57

"THE POST-CAPITALIST WORLD"
Peter F. Drucker

The major previous transformations of the Western world occurred in the thirteenth century with the rise of the city and trade; in the fifteenth century with the impact of movable type and the Protestant Reformation; and in the eighteenth century with the rise of capitalism and the industrial revolution. According to management guru Peter Drucker in this article from The Public Interest *(1992), the world is presently undergoing one of these sharp transformations. After the age of capitalism, the world of the nation-state is being transformed into the "knowledge society."*

Power in this new world will be controlled by those who create and control information. The challenges in this new era will include assuring dignity to the service workers who will not be part of the knowledge elite and helping the developing nations modernize so that they can join the knowledge revolution. Drucker's vision differs from Huntington's in that he sees the determining factors being the new technology of information rather than the ancient roots of language, custom, and religion that define civilizations.

Every few hundred years in Western history there occurs a sharp transformation. Within a few short decades, society—its world view, its basic values, its social and political structure, its arts, its key institutions—rearranges itself. Fifty years later there is a new world. And the people born then cannot even imagine the world in which their grandparents lived and into which their own parents were born. We are currently living through such a transformation.

One such transformation occurred in the thirteenth century, when the Western world suddenly, almost overnight, became centered on the new city. There was the emergence of the city guilds as the new dominant social class; the revival of long-distance trade; the appearance of the Gothic, that eminently urban new architecture; the new painting of the Sienese; the shift to Aristotle from theology as the foundation of new wisdom, the new urban universities replacing the monasteries in their rural isolation, as the centers of culture; the new urban religious orders, the Dominicans and Franciscans, the carriers of religion, of learning, of spirituality; and within a few decades, the shift from Latin to the vernacular, with Dante creating a European literature.

Two hundred years later, the next transformation took place. It happened in the sixty years between Gutenberg's invention of printing with movable type and with it the printed book in 1455, and Luther's Protestant Reformation in 1517. These were the years of the blossoming of the Renaissance (peaking between 1470 and 1500 in Florence and Venice); of the rediscovery of Antiquity; of the discovery of America; of the first standing army (the Spanish Infantry) since the Roman Legions; of the reinvention of the study of anatomy and with it of scientific inquiry in general; and of the widespread adoption of Arabic numerals in the West, providing a new ease of computation. And again, no one living in 1520 could easily have imagined the world in which his grandparents had lived and into which his parents had been born.

The next transformation began in 1776—the year of the American Revolution, of Watt's perfected steam engine, and of Adam Smith's *Wealth of Nations*. It came to a conclusion forty years later, at Waterloo—forty years during which all modern "isms" were born. During these years capitalism, communism, and the Industrial Revolution emerged. These forty years produced, in effect, a new European civilization. Again, no one living in 1820 could easily imagine the world in which his grandparents had lived and into which his parents had been born. One had to read novels to learn about that world.

A New Era

Our time, 200 years later, is again such a period of transformation. Only this time it is not confined to Western society and Western history. Indeed, one of the fundamental changes is that there is no longer a "Western" history or a "Western" civilization. There is only world history and world civilization—the creation, to be sure, of Western history and Western civilization. Whether this transformation began with the emergence of the first non-Western country, Japan, as a great economic power (that is, around 1960) or with the first computer (that is, with information becoming central) is debatable. My own candidate would be the American G.I. Bill of Rights after World War II, which gave every returning American soldier the money to attend a university—something that would have made absolutely no sense only thirty years earlier at the end of World War I. The G.I. Bill of Rights, and the enthusiastic response to it on the part of America's veterans, signaled the shift to the knowledge society. We are still in the middle of this transformation—indeed, if history is any guide, it will not be completed until 2010 or 2020. But already it has changed the political, economic, social, and moral landscape of the world. No one born in 1990 will easily imagine the world in which his grandparents (i.e., my generation) grew up, or the world into which his own parents were born.

The first successful attempt to understand the transformation that began in 1455 and turned the Middle Ages and Renaissance into the Modern World was not even attempted until fifty years later, with the *Commentaries* of Copernicus (written between 1510 and 1514), Machiavelli's *The Prince* (written in 1513), Michaelangelo's synthesis and transcendence of all Renaissance art in the ceiling of the Sistine Chapel (painted between 1510 and 1512), and the reestablishment of the Catholic Church in the Tridentine Council of the 1530s. Similarly, the next transformation—the one that occurred 200 years ago, ushered in by the American Revolution—was first understood and analyzed sixty years afterward, in Alexis de Tocqueville's *Democracy in America*, written between 1835 and 1840.

We are today far enough advanced into the new post-capitalist society—because the post-industrial society is really that—to review and revise the social, economic, and political history of the age of capitalism and of the nation-state. To foresee what the post-capitalist world itself will look like is, however, still very risky. What new questions will arise and where the big new issues will lie, we can, I believe, already discover with a high degree of probability. We can also, in many areas, describe what will not work. But "answers" are in most cases still hidden in the future. The one thing we can be sure of is that the world that will emerge from the present rearrangement of values, of beliefs, of social and economic structures, of political concepts and systems, of world views, will be different from anything anyone today imagines. But in some areas—and especially in society and its structure—basic shifts have already happened. That the new society will be both a non-socialist and a post-capitalist society is practically certain. And it is certain also that its primary resource will be knowledge and that, therefore, it will have to be a society of organizations. In politics we have already shifted from the 400 years of the sovereign nation-state to a pluralism in which the nation-state will be one rather than the unit of political integration. It will be a component—although still a key component—in what I call the "post-capitalist polity," a system in which transnational, regional, nation-state and local, indeed tribal, structures compete and coexist.

These things have already occurred. They can therefore be described.

Only twenty years ago "everybody" knew that a post-capitalist society would be of a Marxist complexion. Now we all know that a socialist society is the one thing the next society is not going to be. But most of us also know—or at least sense—that the developed countries are moving away from anything that could be called "capitalism." The market will surely remain the effective integrator of economic activity. But as a society the developed countries have already moved into post-capitalism with new "classes" and a new central "resource."

Capitalist society, as it peaked in the nineteenth century, was dominated by two social classes: the "capitalists," who owned and controlled the means of production, and the "workers." The "workers" eventually became the "affluent" middle class as a result of what has been called the "productivity revolution"—the revolution that began at the very time of Marx's death in 1883, and reached its climax in every developed country shortly after World War II.

Around 1950, the industrial worker—no longer a "proletarian" but still "labor"—seemed to dominate politics and society in every developed country. But then, with the onset of the "management revolution," blue-collar workers in manufacturing industry rapidly began to decline both in numbers and even more in power and status. By the year 2000 there will be no developed country in which traditional workers making and moving goods account for more than one-sixth or one-eighth of the work force.

The capitalist probably reached his peak even earlier—by the turn of the century, and surely no later than World War I. At least no one since has been able to match in power and visibility the likes of Morgan, Rockefeller, Carnegie, and Ford in the United States; of Siemens, Thyssen, Rathenau, and Krupp in Germany; of Mond, Cunard, Lever, Vickers, and Armstrong in England; of de Wendel and Schneider in France; or of the families that owned the great *zaibatsu* of Japan—Mitsubishi, Mitsui, and Sumitomo. By the time of World War II they had all been replaced by "professional managers." There are still a great many very rich people around, of course, and they are still prominent in the newspapers' society pages. But they have become "celebrities." Economically they have almost ceased to matter. The head of a corporation who retires with $50 million, or even double that amount, is an economic non-entity.

Today it is the well-established pension funds that increasingly control the supply and allocation in developed countries. In the U.S. in 1991 these funds owned half the capital of the country's largest businesses and held almost as much of these companies' fixed debts. The beneficiary owners of the pension funds are, of course, the nation's employees. If "socialism" is defined as ownership of the means of production by the employees, then the U.S. has become the most "socialist" country around—while still being the most "capitalist" one as well. And the pension funds are run by a new breed of "capitalists"—the faceless and anonymous employees who run the pension funds as investment analysts and portfolio managers.

But equally important: The real and controlling "resource" and the absolutely decisive "factor of production" today is neither capital, nor land, nor labor. It is knowledge. And instead of "capitalists" and "proletarians," the relevant "classes" of the post-capitalist society are "knowledge workers" and "service workers."

The Shift to the Knowledge Society

The move to the post-capitalist society began shortly after World War II. But only with the collapse of Marxism as an ideology and of communism as a system did it become clear that we have already moved into a new and different society.

The moral, political, and economic bancruptcy of Marxism, and the collapse of the communist regimes, were not "The End of History." Even the staunchest believers in the free market surely hesitate to trumpet its triumph as the Second Coming. But 1989 and 1990 did indeed signify the end of one kind of history. They brought to a close 250 years that were dominated by a secular religion—what I have called "belief in salvation by society." Its first prophet was Jean-Jacques Rousseau. The Marxist utopia was its ultimate distillation and apotheosis.

But the same forces that destroyed Marxism as an ideology and communism as a social system are also rapidly making capitalism as a social order obsolescent. For 250 years, from the second half of the eighteenth century on, capitalism was the dominant social ideology. Both are rapidly being superseded by a new and very different society and way of thinking about the world.

Whatever this new society will be, it will not be a socialist one. It surely —to say it again—will use the free market as the one proven mechanism of economic integration. It surely will not be an "anti-capitalist society." It will not even be a "non-capitalist society"; the institutions of capitalism will survive, though some (e.g., banks) may play quite different roles. But the new society—and it is already here—is a "post-capitalist" society. Its center of gravity, its structure, its social and economic dynamics, its social classes, and its social problems are different from those that characterized the last 250 years, dominated them, informed them, and defined the issues around which political parties, social groups, social value systems, and personal and political commitments crystallized.

The basic economic resource is knowledge. The wealth-creating activities will be neither the allocation of capital to productive uses nor "labor"—the two poles of nineteenth- and twentieth-century economic theories whether classical, Marxist, Keynesian, or neo-classical. They will center around "productivity" and "innovation," both applications of knowledge to work. The representative social groups of the knowledge society will be neither the "capitalist" nor the "worker," the two groups which characterized society since the Industrial Revolution 250 years ago. The ruling group will be knowledge workers, knowledge executives, knowledge professionals, and knowledge entrepreneurs who have the insight to allocate knowledge to productive use, the way the "capitalists" knew how to allocate capital to productive use. Practically all of them will be employed, either originally or eventually, in organizations. Yet unlike traditional employees, these knowledge workers own their knowledge, the new "means of production," and can take it with them wherever they go. The economic challenge of the post-capitalist society will therefore be the productivity of knowledge work and the knowledge worker.

But there will also be a second representative group—I call them "service workers"—who will lack the necessary education to be knowledge workers. And in every country, even the most highly advanced ones, they will constitute a majority. The social challenge of the post-capitalist society will thus be to ensure the dignity of service work and the service worker.

The post-capitalist society will also be divided by a new dichotomy of values and of aesthetic perceptions. It will not be the "Two Cultures"—the humanist, literary culture and the scientific culture of which the English novelist, scientist, and government administrator C.P. Snow wrote—though that split is real enough. It will be a dichotomy between "literati" and "managers," the former being concerned with words and ideas, the latter with people and work. To transcend this dichotomy in a new synthesis will be a central philosophical and educational challenge for the post-capitalist society.

Outflanking the Nation-State?

The late 1980s and early 1990s also marked the end of another era, another "kind of history." If the fall of the Berlin Wall in 1989 was the climactic event that symbolized the fall of Marxism and communism, the formation of a transnational coalition opposing Iraq's invasion of Kuwait was the climactic event that marked the end of the 400 years of history in which the sovereign nation-state was the main—and often the only—actor on the political stage. Future historians will surely rank January 1991 among the "big dates." There is no precedent for such transnational action, no earlier occasion where nations, without a single dissenter of consequence (and almost without dissent altogether), put the common interest of the world community in putting down terrorism ahead of their own national sentiments and, in many cases, ahead even of their own national interests. There is no precedent for the all-but-universal realization that terrorism is not a matter of "politics" to be left to individual national governments, but rather a threat that requires non-national, transnational action.

In the 400 years since the French lawyer-politician Jean Bodin invented it (in his 1576 book *Six Livres de la Republique*), the nation-state had become the sole organ of political power, internally and externally. And since the French Revolution it had also become the carrier of the secular religion, the belief in "salvation by society." Totalitarianism—communist as well as Nazi—was the ultimate distillation and apotheosis of the doctrine of the sovereign nation-state as the one and only organ of power.

Political theory and constitutional law still know only the sovereign state. And in the last one hundred years it has steadily become more powerful and more dominant. It has mutated into the "mega-state." It is also the one political structure we so far understand, are familiar with, and know how to build out of prefabricated and standardized parts—an executive, a legislature, courts, a diplomatic service, a national army, and so on. Every one of the 200-odd new countries that have been carved out of the former colonial empires has been set up as a sovereign nation-state. And this is what every one of the various parts of the last of the colonial empires, the Soviet empire, aspires to become.

Yet since the end of World War II the sovereign nation-state has steadily been losing its position as the one organ of power. It is fast becoming instead one among many such organs. Internally, developed countries are fast becoming pluralist societies of organizations. Externally, some governmental functions are becoming transnational, others regional (i.e., the European Economic Community), others are being tribalized.

The nation-state is not going to "wither away." It may remain the most powerful political organ around for a long time to come. But it will no longer be the indispensable one, and will increasingly share power with other organs, other institutions, other policymakers. We are moving fast toward the "post-capitalist" polity. And the division of power, the division of tasks, the division of responsibilities and accountabilities between the various levels of this post-capitalist polity are still to be defined: What is to remain the domain of the nation-state? What is to be carried out within the state by autonomous institutions? What is to be "supernational"? What is to be "transnational"? What is to be "separate and local"? Resolving these questions will be the central political agenda for decades to come. In its specifics, the outcome is quite unpredictable. But whatever it will be, the political order fifty years hence will look different from the political order of the last centuries, when the actors differed in size, wealth, constitutional arrangements, and political creed but were uniform as nation-states, each sovereign within its territory, and each defined by its territory.

The last of what might be called the "pre-modern" philosophers, Gottfried Leibnitz (1646–1716), spent much of his life in a futile attempt to restore the unity of Christendom. His motivation was not the fear of religious wars between Catholics and Protestants or between Protestant sects—that danger was already past when Leibnitz was born. But he feared that without a common belief in a supernatural God, secular religions would emerge. And a secular religion, he was convinced, would—almost by definition—have to be a tyranny and suppress the freedom of the individual.

A century later Jean-Jacques Rousseau proved Leibnitz right by asserting that society could and should control the individual human being. It could and should create a "New Adam." It could and should create universal human perfection. But it also could and should subordinate the individual to the impersonal, super-personal "general will" (*volonté générale*)—what Marxists later came to call the "objective laws of history." Since then salvation by society has been the dominant creed of Western Man. And however much it pretends to be "anti-religious," it is a religious belief. The means are, of course, non-spiritual: banning liquor; killing all Jews; universal psychotherapy; abolition of private property. The goal, however, is religious: to establish the Kingdom of God on earth by creating the "New Man."

And for more than one hundred years the most powerful, the most pervasive and near-universal of these secular creeds, with their promise of salvation through society, was, of course, Marxism. Indeed it was the religious promise of Marxism—far more than its convoluted ideology and its increasingly unrealistic economic theory—that constituted its tremendous appeal, especially to intellectuals.

Communism collapsed as a system. It collapsed economically. Its material promises proved hollow. Instead of creating wealth it created misery. Instead of creating economic equality it created a nomenklatura of functionaries enjoying greater economic privileges than the world had ever seen. But as a creed, Marxism collapsed because it did not create the "New Man." Instead it brought out and strengthened all the worst in the "Old Adam": corruption, greed, and lust for power; envy and mutual distrust; petty tyranny and secretiveness; lying, stealing, and denunciation; and, above all, cynicism. Communism, the system, had its heroes. But Marxism, the creed, never had any saints.

The human being may well be beyond redemption. The Latin poet may have been right: Basic human nature always returns through the back door no matter how many times the pitchfork tosses it out the front door. Maybe the cynics are right who assert that there is no virtue, no goodness, no selflessness, only self-interest and hypocrisy (though there are enough witnesses to the contrary, as I remind myself in my darkest hours).

But surely the collapse of Marxism as a creed signifies the end of the belief in salvation by society. What will emerge we cannot know—we can only hope and pray. Perhaps nothing beyond stoic resignation? Perhaps a rebirth of traditional religion addressing itself to the needs and challenges of the person in the knowledge society? The explosive growth of what I call "pastoral" Christian churches in America—Protestant, Catholic, non-denominational— might be a portent. But so might be the resurgence of fundamentalist Islam. For the young people in the Moslem countries who now so fervently embrace Islamic fundamentalism would, forty years ago, have been equally zealous Marxists. Or will there be new religions? In any event, redemption, self-renewal, spiritual growth, conversion, goodness, and virtue—the "New Man," to use the traditional term—will be seen as existential, i.e., as applying to a person with an inner nature and commitment and experience, rather than as raw material for a social goal and political ideology. In that sense, too, we are seeing the end of one kind of history.

What about the Third World?

The Third World houses two-thirds of the world's population; and by the time the present period of transition comes to an end—around 2015 or 2020—the Third World will house three-quarters of the world's population. I consider it highly probable that within the next decade or two there will be new and startling "economic miracles" in which poor, backward countries transform themselves virtually overnight into highly developed, fast-growing economic powers. It is even possible that there will be far more such transformations than there have been in the last forty years, that is, since we first began to talk about "economic development." There is the vast potential of the coastal, urbanized areas of Mainland China—from Tsienstin in the North to Canton in the South. All the economic elements for rapid growth are present there: a huge domestic market; a highly educated population with tremendous respect for learning; an old entrepreneurial tradition; close ties to the "overseas Chinese" in Singapore, Hong Kong, and Taiwan, with access to their capital, trading networks, and knowledge workers. All this might be released in an explosion of entrepreneurial growth if only Beijing's political and economic tyranny could be removed, and removed peacefully. There is India, with enormous untapped potential. There is Latin America, and especially Latin America's larger countries, which offer an adequate domestic market—Mexico may already be in the "takeoff" stage. Brazil might surprise everybody by the speed of its turnaround once it has mustered the political courage to follow Mexico's recent example and abandon the suicidal policies into which it plunged itself fifteen years ago. And no one could possibly foretell what surprises the former communist countries of Eastern Europe might produce.

But the developed countries also have a tremendous stake in the Third World. Unless there is rapid development there—both economic and social—the developed countries will be inundated by Third-World immigrants, far beyond their economic, social, or cultural capacity to absorb, assimilate, and integrate. But the forces that are creating a post-capitalist society and a post-capitalist polity originate in the developed world; indeed, they are the product and results of its development. The answers to the challenges of a post-capitalist society and a post-capitalist polity will not be found in the Third World. If anything has been totally disproven it is the promises of the Third World leaders of the 1950s and 1960s—Nehru in India, Mao in China, Castro in Cuba, Tito in Yugoslavia, the apostles of Negritude in Africa and such neo-Marxists as Che Guevara—that the Third World would find new and different answers. The Third World has not delivered on the promises made in its name. The challenges, opportunities, and problems of post-capitalist society and the post-capitalist polity can only be dealt with where they originated. And that is in the developed world.

Society, Polity, Knowledge

I am often asked whether I am an optimist or a pessimist. For any survivor of this century to be an optimist would be fatuous. And we do know that we are nowhere near the end of the turbulence, the transformations, the sudden upsets that have made this century one of the meanest, cruelest, bloodiest in human history. Anyone who deludes himself that we are anywhere near the "End of History" is in for very unpleasant surprises—the kind of surprises that afflicted President Bush when he first bet on the survival of the Russian Empire under Mr. Gorbachev, and then on the success of Mr. Yeltsin's "Commonwealth of Independent States."

But surely this is a time to make the future. Nothing "post" is permanent or even long-lived. Ours is a transition period. And what the future society will look like, let alone whether it will indeed be the "knowledge society" some of us dare to hope for, depends on how the developed countries—their intellectual leaders, their business leaders, their political leaders, but above all, each of us in his own life and sphere—respond to the challenges of this transition period, the post-capitalist period.

POINTS TO PONDER

1. How do the visions of Drucker and Huntington differ?
2. If the main economic cleavage in the age of socialism and capitalism was between capitalists and workers, what will be the main cleavage in the post-industrial society that Drucker foresees?
3. According to Drucker, what stake will the developed world have in the economic status of Third World countries?

58

"THE DECLINE OF THE UNITED STATES: A COMPARATIVE PERSPECTIVE"

Jack A. Goldstone

In this final selection, Jack Goldstone, a historian at the University of California at Davis, draws parallels between the United States at the end of the twentieth century and France toward the end of the eighteenth century, before the French Revolution. He draws attention to disparities in income, eroding support for public institutions, and large national debts financed by foreign borrowing.

In this excerpt from his book Revolution and Rebellion in the Modern World *(1991), Goldstone argues that the solution to fiscal and demographic imbalances in the United States is to cut consumption and increase investment in order to increase future productivity. Although this solution may be simple to state, it is an extremely difficult political problem that will require "ennobling leadership."*

The success of the West lies in a combination of two factors, both of which emerged in complex and gradual fashion: personal freedom based on toleration, broad civic participation, and protection of individual rights; and capitalist economic organization. Without personal freedom and toleration providing scope for economic and social innovation, even private property-based economies—as in Qing China, the Ottoman Empire, and Bourbon Spain—remained rigid and stagnant rather than dynamic. Without capitalism, economic organization remains inefficient and unable to cope with changing demands. It is the *combination* of liberal freedoms and capitalism that is essential for success. . . .

State breakdown is not likely to produce freedom, and . . . seeking to implement state control of ideological orthodoxy rather than tolerance of individual conscience and freedom in the wake of a state crisis is liable to stifle, not accelerate, economic progress. The policies adopted by many nations that seek to emulate Western success—revolution followed by state control of culture and the economy—are thus dead wrong, and their failure is to be expected. Adoption of the opposite policies—political reform to broaden participation and secure individual rights, toleration of cultural pluralism, and a dominant economic role for capitalist organization—holds much greater promise.

The Decline of the United States

It is ironic that precisely when the above ideas are gaining wide acceptance, the leading exemplar of these ideas—the United States—is troubled by intimations of decline. . . .

The United States' ills have sometimes been traced, using an oversimplified version of Paul Kennedy's (1987) model of state competition, to excessive international military commitments, or "imperial overstretch." But this simple idea provides an incorrect diagnosis, even of the past. The notion that imperial overstretch—a nation taking on commitments that exceeded its resources—was responsible for the decline and fall of early modern states is profoundly mistaken. Overstretch may apply to the campaigns of particular commanders, such as Napoleon's Russian campaign, but it is not the reason for the crises that overturned long-established early modern monarchies and imperial states. . . . The English, Ottoman, and Ming Chinese states broke down in the seventeenth century, and the French state in the late eighteenth century, because of fiscal crises, elite factionalism, and rising mass mobilization potential. But in each case, within a few decades after the crisis, these states enormously expanded their power and international influence. Cromwell's navy wrested the seas from the Dutch, where the early Stuarts had failed; the Ottomans again threatened Vienna in 1689 and soundly defeated Peter the Great in Russia in 1711; the Qing Empire soon exceeded that of the Ming in territory and population; and Napoleon's empire far exceeded the Bourbons' wildest dreams. If the Stuarts, Ottomans, Ming, and Bourbons had overstretched their nations' capacities, how is it possible that their successors quickly reasserted or even extended their international reach?

Selfish Elites and National Decay

The answer is that these regimes fell because they had used their nation's resources poorly. Inefficient tax systems failed to capture a growing share of national wealth. We have noted that English gentry in the seventeenth century reduced their own assessments, privileged French nobility and bourgeois elites were exempt from the *taille*, Ottoman magnates converted their lands to *vakifs* or sought *malikânes*, and Chinese officials sheltered the land of dependents and associates. These persistent efforts by elites to resist or evade taxation, despite being massively undertaxed, led to excessive state debts and reduced the state's ability to respond to domestic demands and foreign threats. Straitened state finances also restricted pay to officials, leading to corruption and rapid turnover in bureaucratic posts.

In short, a key difficulty faced by regimes in decline was *selfish elites*. Nations that were the richest countries in their day suffered fiscal crises because elites preferred to protect their private wealth, even at the expense of a deterioration of state finances, public services, and long-term international strength. By "selfish elites" I do not mean, of course, simply elites' aspirations to maintain disproportionate shares of wealth and power. That ambition is a universal constant. What I wish to emphasize is that in some eras in history, elites have identified their interests with the national state and the public weal, and they have been willing to tax themselves heavily to expand the influence and resources of their nation and its government. At other times, particularly times of elite insecurity owing to inflation and to rising social mobility and competition within their ranks, elites have turned into competing factions, driven by self-enrichment at the expense of their rivals and opponents, even when that meant starving the national state of resources needed for public improvements and international competitiveness.[5]

In addition, declining regimes were beset by factionalism within the elites that paralyzed decision making. Struggles for prestige and authority took precedence over a united approach to resolving fiscal and social problems. Among English gentry in Parliament, within the French Estates General and the National Assembly, among Ottoman officials, and within the ranks of Chinese scholars, partisanship prevailed over consensus—with disastrous results.

It is quite astonishing the degree to which the United States today is, in respect of its state finances and its elites' attitudes, following the path that led early modern states to crises. As in the past, inability to sustain international influence is merely symptomatic of deeper internal decay.

For example, lack of consensus among U.S. elites has virtually immobilized efforts to deal with a persistent federal budget deficit, and has hamstrung state action in many foreign policy theaters and in much domestic policy planning. The only consensus that has prevailed in the last decade is precisely that which

5. The fall of the Roman Empire in the West, while the empire continued to flourish for several more centuries in the East as the Byzantine Empire, may have been due to similar causes. Downey observes that "the structure of the [Roman] government differed significantly in the East and West. In the West, the land-owning aristocrats . . . contribut[ed] much less than they should to the cost of the army and the government. The Eastern Empire, in contrast, . . . received in taxes a higher proportion of the national income than the Western government could enjoy."

history tells us is the most disastrous, namely, the consensus that private consumption should take precedence over all public expenses, and that raising taxes to realistic levels to meet state obligations should be fiercely resisted. Hence the U.S. government has been running a growing debt, sustained only by foreign borrowing.

The result has been just what the history of earlier states who have been denied adequate taxation and relied on debt would lead us to expect: private individuals among the elite have become enormously richer, while basic public services that support the economy as a whole—primary and secondary education, airports, trains, roads, and bridges—are neglected, overburdened, and deteriorating. Moreover, public officials have become ruinously underpaid compared to their counterparts in the private sector. The chief executive of a $3-billion-per-year automobile company may earn $20 million annually, whereas in public service, the secretary of defense, chief executive of a $300 billion per year operation, is paid less than $100,000 annually.[6] Lower-level public managers suffer in proportion. The 1984–1985 Commission on Executive, Legislative, and Judicial Salaries reported that from 1969 to 1985, while the real income of corporate executives rose 68 percent, the real income of top federal officials *declined* by 40 percent. Thus, public officials have succumbed to subtle (and sometimes not-so-subtle) forms of corruption, using their government offices as launching pads to more lucrative private-sector jobs. One-third of recent presidential appointees to top government jobs have stayed for one and a half years or less; their *average* length of service is two years. Professionalism, experience in office, and commitment to public service can not long survive such conditions.

It has become popular of late to lament the lack of ethics in public life. But how does one judge the ethics of a society that expects its public officials to pursue careers that pay only 5–10 percent of what their responsibilities and talents would merit elsewhere? I have seen modern Westerners chuckle at stories about the Chinese bureaucracy, which paid its officials ludicrously low official salaries, expecting them to make their living from private donations received in return for favorable use of their influence in office. But did the United States in the 1980s treat its top bureaucrats any differently?

The United States thus enters the 1990s with several evident problems: factional divisions among elites that undercut policy consensus, widespread resistance to realistic taxes, an overreliance on debt, and a polarization of private incomes while public services—and public servants—are grossly underfunded and losing their ability to support the economy. The key element in this decay is not, as it is sometimes portrayed, a decay of American manufacturing ability or of American foreign power, or a threat of imminent economic catastrophe; instead it is a steady erosion of public institutions and public services. This

---

6. As of 1987, after a substantial raise in federal pay that took effect in January of that year, U.S. cabinet secretaries received an annual salary of $99,500.

decay threatens to undermine the social and infrastructural foundations that supported American economic growth in the first three-quarters of this century. If unchecked, it is certain that the long-term results, which are now only slightly apparent but will accumulate rapidly in the coming decades, will be a relative decline in the living standards, freedom of decision, and international position of the United States as compared with other industrialized nations. How did this impasse develop?

Part of the answer is again demographic: the impact of the U.S. "baby boom." The cohort of individuals born from 1950 to the early 1960s was exceptionally large. Economists have argued extensively over the economic impact of this cohort. However, two points are sufficient to clarify recent developments. First, the growth in the labor force halted the growth in real wages, making it sensible for corporations to substitute labor for capital, and thus to defer investment. Second, the slow growth of investment, and hence of capital per worker, has stalled productivity. This means, very simply, declining international competitiveness, and declining rates of per-capita economic growth. At the same time, the overall expansion in the size of the economy with the maturing of the baby boomers greatly increased the economic opportunities for the few who did make it to the top. Thus a successful minority shows remarkable incomes, while most baby boomers find it difficult to match, much less surpass, the living standards of their parents. The economic "pinch" on the large baby-boom cohort as it entered the marketplace and struggled for promotions has led to greater competition within that cohort. Other things being equal, therefore, it is understandable that members of this cohort devote more attention to their own upward mobility as individuals and less to the support of investments and taxation for public goods, such as education and infrastructure, that will aid future generations but slightly reduce their own immediate level of consumption. America in the wake of the baby boom, therefore, has seen in milder form much the same syndrome that was seen in early modern economies under pressures of rapid population growth: polarization of incomes, stagnant real wages, reluctance to pay taxes, and greater struggles for personal advancement.

Since 1960 demands have grown for federal government action in a wide variety of fields—support of education, research, and medical care; protection of the environment; enforcement of safety in the workplace, in pharmaceuticals, in cosmetics and food additives, and in consumer goods; intervention against the distribution and use of narcotics; provision of a "safety net" for the poor; support for troubled family farmers; aid to state and local governments; provision and regulation of national transportation, including highway construction, airport management, and subsidies for rail and mass transit; provision of greatly expanded postal services; provision of national statistics, weather forecasting, library and information services; and provision of various guarantees and subsidies for private loans, pensions, mortgages, and savings institutions. All of these services, which are to provide for a population that has grown by 39 percent from 1960 to 1987, are *in addition* to the burdens of providing social security for a rapidly growing older population and providing national defense and foreign aid to protect and further the United States' international security in an increasingly complex world. In short, the *real demands* on the federal government have enormously increased. Yet the percentage of GNP collected by the federal government has *not* risen, but has *fallen* very slightly, from 1960 to 1987.[7] We thus find a familiar pattern—despite increasing demands on the state, taxation receives a declining share of national wealth. The result is the federal deficit and a public infrastructure increasingly unable to meet national needs.

Such trends and attitudes may be a short-term "blip" in American politics, with the post-baby-boom generation having different values. Unfortunately, to the extent that the current political majority—self-focused, and demanding state services but resisting taxation—supports state policies that accumulate an enormous debt burden, the next generation, regardless of its values, will face massive problems in reconciling state resources with state commitments. Aside from accumulated government debt, the neglect of problems in the water, fuel, and transportation infrastructure, in the accumulation of radioactive toxins from U.S. weapons programs, and in the U.S. banking system and other systems of state-guaranteed liability for private loans and pensions, has left a legacy of currently unfunded government commitments running into the hundreds of billions of dollars.

Furthermore, once serious undertaxation and decay of public services and infrastructure has begun, a strong momentum sets in. As urban centers become unsafe, wealthier elites move to more isolated—even privately guarded—residential communities. As schools deteriorate, the middle and upper classes send their children to private schools. As public hospitals decay, the wealthier seek treatment from private facilities. As roadways decline, there is talk of building private toll roads. All these trends—each entailing the substitution of private for formerly public services—create a situation in which those who are economically better off feel compelled to resist taxation, so that they can afford to live in more exclusive communities and send their children to private schools; moreover, they then become even more intolerant of taxes, since they no longer consume the public services that such taxation provides. Their heightened resistance to taxation then leads to further underfunding and deterioration of public services, which reinforce the trend of private substitution in an accelerating cycle. The long-term result of a loss of faith in the public sector, a greater polarization and fragmentation of society, and a loss of a sense of shared community. Once begun, a trend toward glorification of private consumption and denigration of the public sector thus gathers institutional mo-

---

[7]. The percent of GNP collected by the federal government has been remarkably constant, despite the increase in federal responsibilities. This percentage was 19.0 percent in 1960, 18.99 percent in 1970, 18.93 percent in 1980, and 18.87 percent in 1987. The data in this paragraph are from U.S. Bureau of the Census.

mentum that can long outlast the value orientation that initiated the trend. For these reasons, the accumulation of government debt and the decay of public services is extremely difficult to reverse.

Early modern regimes, based on narrow imperial or monarchical authority, on traditional status systems with a limited ability to absorb new elites, and on a relatively inflexible agrarian economy, had only limited ability to cope with elite conflict and fiscal strains. Worse yet, early modern governments and their elites generally did not understand what was happening to their societies, and blamed each other for the ills brought by rising population and diminishing economic returns.

The United States has greater flexibility, and a greater number of options. Where in early modern states it took state breakdown and reconstruction to change traditional tax systems, to overhaul elite recruitment and status systems, and to restore the balance of population and productivity, the United States can accomplish such goals through elections, legislation, and innovation. Moreover, the problems of the United States are far milder. The United States is faced not with the threat of state breakdown but merely with the loss of relative international economic standing and political influence. Still, it must be noted that today's problems are not widely understood.

Demographic Overhang and the Coming Decline

One clear sign of America's lack of understanding of the coming crisis is the nature of the debate over the federal deficit and budgeting for social security. The problem is often posed as an accounting issue—should the United States run a deficit? How many dollars, or bonds, does the U.S. need to save to ensure that social security claimants in the twenty-first century will receive their checks? Yet these questions overlook an obvious fact: the ability to pay off deficits and provide a secure retirement for the baby boomers depends primarily on future U.S. production. No matter how many dollars are "saved," *they will be useless to holders of government bonds or to those receiving social security checks unless the economy is producing enough goods and services for recipients to make desired purchases.*

If the funds placed in the hands of retirees are chasing too small a supply of goods and services, then social security disbursements will bring ruinous inflation rather than comfortable retirement. The deficit and social security questions are therefore not a matter of "saving," but one of *productivity*; a sound standard of living in the next century depends not on how many dollars will then be stashed in various accounts, but on how many goods and services the economy will then be *producing* for purchase.

We can examine more precisely America's needs in the way of productivity growth. In 1989, the U.S. labor force comprised 119 million individuals, who supported a retired population of 27.6 million. Thus the ratio of workers to retirees was 4.3:1. Thirty years from now, in 2020, when the baby-boom generation has retired, the ratio of workers to retirees is expected to be only 2.7:1. In order merely to maintain today's standard of living, then, each worker in 2020 will have to produce 59 percent *more* output to provide for both personal needs and those of the additional retirees. The change in the age structure thus creates a demographic overhang in the next thirty years, such that a 59 percent increase in per capita productivity is required merely to stand still. This works out to a required annual increase in productivity of 1.6 percent. Any smaller increase will lead to an inevitable decline in living standards.[8]

From 1973 to 1988, U.S. productivity (real GNP per worker) rose by only 0.86 percent per year, or only *half* the rate needed to offset the demographic overhang.[9] Moreover, from 1990 to 2020 the United States will have greater burdens: payment of interest on the existing debt, rescue of the savings and loan industry, repair of current infrastructure, and cleanup of toxic wastes will entail spending hundreds of billions of dollars. Yet these expenditures will not raise productivity or living standards one iota—they are necessary simply to arrest drastic decline. To offset the demographic overhang, the United States will have to double the current rate of growth in productivity; that will require public investment to provide a skilled labor force and improved transportation, health care, and resource management. Improving productivity will also require massive private investment to equip the labor force with the latest capital and technology. The dilemma is therefore stark and simple: money must be found for government to make the expenditures needed to arrest drastic decline. Money must also be found for both the government and private industry to make productivity-raising investments.

At present, too few resources are going to such expenditures and investments; thus productivity growth is too small by half to offset the impact of the coming demographic overhang. American living standards are therefore set to decline over the next three decades.

Reversing this trend will require a very different set of commitments than those found among today's political elites.

What the U.S. Requires: Ennobling Leadership

Why we have not already resolved these problems is simply understood: we have preferred the short-term benefits of policies that favor our consumption over the long-term policies that maintain a stable and developing economy over time. The history of societies that have followed this course is plain to

8. Data are from U.S. Department of Labor, U.S. Department of Health and Human Services, International Labor Office, and U.S. Bureau of the Census. Retired population in 2020 is based on the projection of population aged sixty-five and over in U.S. Bureau of the Census.

9. Productivity gains have varied considerably in this period: .5 percent per annum from 1973 to 1979, then 1.1 percent to 1988. However, the latter period included rapid but short-lived gains during the initial recovery from the 1981–1982 recession. In 1987, productivity increase was .8 percent, about the average for the period since 1973 as a whole.

see—decay, decline, and internal turmoil or external defeat. The parallels between U.S. fiscal policy in the 1980s and French fiscal policy in the 1770s are startling. Both countries had economies easily strong enough to close their state budget deficits, with only slight increases in taxation. But both countries lacked the necessary political will to do so. Elites and popular groups, the former enjoying extraordinary riches owing to economic expansion that they considered their due, the latter under pressure owing to declining productivity, combined to resist further taxation. Each state resorted to borrowing, both international and domestic.

Forced to pay higher rates of interest than its neighbors, each state prided itself on the strength of its currency. At the same time, its higher interest rates discouraged productive investment and encouraged financial speculation. Faced with higher real interest rates, these countries invested less in new industrial capacity, and their productivity failed to keep pace with their competitors. Instead, investors turned to the high yields available on government bonds and more speculative investments. Financiers thus grew richer through lending to the state, while workers in traditional industries faced ever greater difficulties. In each case, the largest and wealthiest country in its area and era—France in eighteenth-century Europe, the United States in the twentieth-century world—lost ground to foreign economic competitors. France was shortly overtaken economically, despite its military strength, first by England and Belgium and later by Germany. The United States is now in danger of being overtaken economically by Japan and by the leading economies of Western Europe. In France by the 1780s, chronic borrowing reached a point at which the government was forced to borrow merely to pay the interest on its debt, a situation the United States will reach in the early 1990s given present trends. State fiscal weakness and income polarization led to elite factionalism and popular unrest in France; similar trends have led to elite factionalism in the United States, and may lead again to riots to complement the current gang warfare in U.S. inner cities.

To restore U.S. strength, a simple prescription is required: adequate taxation instead of debt to finance government, and improved funding of public services and officials; emphasis on investment and research to raise productivity over consumption; and consensus on domestic and foreign policy goals, so that sacrifices can be uniformly sought and efforts consistently directed. Unfortunately, that simple prescription is extremely difficult to fill. What is needed is leadership that is both effective *and* ennobling.

"Effective" leadership brings a variety of individuals and groups together to focus on a common cause. In this sense, Ronald Reagan was an extraordinarily effective leader. However, the causes that were the focus of his leadership in the period 1982–1988—achieving higher personal consumption and stronger national defense through replacement of taxation by state debt—did not require any sacrifice; instead they brought immediate satisfaction. The lowering of income taxes and the borrowing to increase spending on defense were policies aimed at emotional needs, namely, fears stemming from the inflation and the Iranian hostage crisis of 1978–1981. Reagan's policies were not aimed at the long-term needs of American society: increasing productivity and bringing personal, corporate, and government expenditures more in line with incomes, to allow a surplus for investment and future growth. Thus for example, borrowing money to pay defense engineers and military servicemen created jobs, including jobs for those restaurant, clerical, and other domestic service industries that served the communities with military facilities. But this job expansion did nothing to promote more efficient production of manufactures, services, or capital goods for the international marketplace.

"Ennobling" leadership brings a variety of individuals and groups together to focus on a common cause that does *not* immediately satisfy current desires. Instead, such leadership asks individuals and groups to make immediate sacrifices, and to tolerate immediate discomfort, by refocusing their interest on long-term gains. The policies needed to provide long-term gains for the U.S. economy, and long-term effectiveness of the United States in world leadership, are often pointed out. The United States must increase its investment and reduce its dependence on foreign borrowing. However, since investment equals total output plus borrowing minus consumption, simple arithmetic tells us we cannot get from here (low investment and high foreign borrowing) to there (high investment and low foreign borrowing) without *reducing* consumption, at least until our total output increases enough to reduce our borrowing requirement. The difficulty we have had in adopting such policies is not that the right measures are hard to find, but rather that the reduction in consumption cannot be implemented without effective and *ennobling* leadership to gain its acceptance. Unless the American public is convinced that some sacrifice of immediate consumption is necessary to prevent an inevitable economic and political decline of the nation, the necessary steps to restore U.S. strength cannot be taken.

To demand sacrifice is extremely difficult for any leader. It is rendered easier by war or by depression. It is for this reason that great leaders more easily emerge in such catastrophes—catastrophe predisposes people to be more open to ennobling leadership. The specter of being left behind in international competition is rarely sufficient, for in the short term this threat creates emotional needs that are satisfied by aggressive trade policies and protectionism. This provides a path for effective leadership that is not ennobling and does little for long-term prosperity: restrictive trade policies that maintain a market for today's products are of no use if tomorrow's economy does not produce goods that are widely sought, such as video recorders or memory chips.

The prospects for the future economic and political standing of the United States thus depend greatly on the emergence of leaders who can truly lead, rather than merely satisfy, public opinion. Given the difficulties faced by the baby-boom generation, a reduction in consumption will be difficult to achieve. The great challenge of American political leadership in the 1990s is therefore to persuade Americans, whether or not they experience a devastating recession, to make the sacrifices needed to raise investment and the level of public goods.

The study of early modern history suggests that the current U.S. course will lead to heightened factional conflict and economic weakness. But it also suggests that such decline is not inevitable. Early modern monarchies and empires declined because they lacked the flexibility to respond to changing balances of population and resources. The United States has the flexibility to respond; the question is whether it has the will.

POINTS TO PONDER

1. According to Goldstone, why is the United States in decline?
2. What are the parallels between France in the 1770s and the United States in the 1990s?
3. What is necessary in order to overcome the problems Goldstone describes?
4. Who among the three writers about the future—Huntington, Drucker, and Goldstone—is most optimistic? Most pessimistic? Give reasons for your answers.

Credits

658

JOHN P. ROCHE From "The Founding Fathers: A Reform Caucus in Action" from the AMERICAN POLITICAL SCIENCE REVIEW, Vol. LV, December 1961. Reprinted by permission of the American Political Science Association.

FRANCIS E. ROURKE "Bureaucracy in the American Constitutional Order" from POLITICAL SCIENCE QUARTERLY 102 (Summer 1987):217–232. Reprinted with permission of Political Science Quarterly.

ROBERT H. SALISBURY From "The Paradox of Interest Groups in Washington—More Groups, Less Clout" in THE NEW AMERICAN POLITICAL SYSTEM 2/e, edited by Anthony King, 1990. Reprinted with the permission of The American Enterprise Institute for Public Policy Research, Washington, D.C.

ARTHUR M. SCHLESINGER, JR. FROM "After the Imperial Presidency" and "The Short Happy Life of American Political Parties" in THE CYCLES OF AMERICAN HISTORY by Arthur M. Schlesinger, Jr. Copyright © 1986 by Arthur M. Schlesinger, Jr. Reprinted by permission of Houghton Mifflin Company. All rights reserved.

HEDRICK SMITH "Old-Breed Lobbying, New-Breed Lobbying" from THE POWER GAME: HOW WASHINGTON WORKS. Copyright © 1988 by Hedrick Smith. Reprinted by permission of Random House, Inc.

THOMAS SOWELL From "From Equal Opportunity to 'Affirmative Action' " in CIVIL RIGHTS: RHETORIC OR REALITY by Thomas Sowell. Copyright © 1984 by Thomas Sowell. Reprinted by permission of William Morrow and Company, Inc.

D. GRIER STEPHENSON, JR. "Is The Bill of Rights in Danger?" from USA TODAY Magazine, May 1991. Copyright 1991 by the Society for the Advancement of Education. Reprinted by permission.

JAMES L. SUNDQUIST "American Federalism: Evolution, Status, and Prospects" from No. 6 BROOKINGS DISCUSSION PAPERS IN GOVERNMENTAL STUDIES, May, 1986. Reprinted by permission of the Brookings Institution and the author .

JAMES L. SUNDQUIST From "Needed: A Political Theory for the New Era of Coalition Government in the United States" in POLITICAL SCIENCE QUARTERLY 103 (Winter 1988–89):613–635. Reprinted by permission of the Academy of Political Science, New York.

DENNIS F. THOMPSON From "Mediated Corruption: The Case of the Keating Five" in AMERICAN POLITICAL SCIENCE REVIEW, Vol. 87:2, June 1993. Reprinted by permission of the American Political Science Association.

LAURENCE H. TRIBE "The Myth of the Strict Constructionist: Our Incomplete Constitution" from GOD SAVE THIS HONORABLE COURT by Laurence H. Tribe. Copyright © 1985 by Laurence H. Tribe. Reprinted by permission of Random House, Inc.

JAMES Q. WILSON "The Changing FBI—The Road to Abscam" from THE PUBLIC INTEREST, No. 59 (Spring 1980) pp. 3–14. Copyright © 1980 by National Affairs, Inc. Reprinted by permission of The Public Interest and the author.

JAMES Q. WILSON From BUREAUCRACY: WHAT GOVERNMENT AGENCIES DO AND WHY THEY DO IT by James Q. Wilson. Copyright © 1989 by Basic Books, Inc. Reprinted by permission of Basic Books, a division of HarperCollins Publishers, Inc.

Excerpts throughout the text from ALEXANDER HAMILTON, JAMES MADISON AND JOHN JAY: The Federalist Or, The New Constitution, edited by Christopher Bigsby, 1992. First published in Everyman's Library 1911. We are not using editor's footnotes or introductory material, only public domain material.

"The Constitution as an Economic Document" from AN ECONOMIC INTERPRETATION OF THE CONSTITUTION OF THE UNITED STATES by Charles A. Beard 1941. First published in 1913.

Report of the Congressional Committees Investigating the IRAN-CONTRA AFFAIR—U.S. Government Printing.

"Speaking in a Judicial Voice" by Ruth Bader Ginsburg from MADISON LECTURE AT THE NEW YORK UNIVERSITY SCHOOL OF LAW, March 9, 1993.